The Art of Editing

This memorable picture of Apollo 11 on the moon shows Commander Neil A. Armstrong at the flag's staff (left) with Astronaut Edwin E. Aldrin, Jr., lunar module pilot, deploying the flag of the United States on the surface of the moon. [*Courtesy National Aeronautics and Space Administration.*]

The Art of Editing

Floyd K. Baskette
University of Colorado

Jack Z. Sissors
Medill School of Journalism, Northwestern University

The Macmillan Company   *New York*
Collier-Macmillan Limited   *London*

The Macmillan Company
866 Third Avenue, New York, New York 10022

Collier-Macmillan Canada, Ltd., Toronto, Ontario

Library of Congress catalog card number: 72–126516

First Printing

Foreword

The very title of *The Art of Editing* constitutes a comprehensive grasp of what goes on around copydesks, small and big alike.

Copyediting indeed is an art. Principles contained here, buttressed by countless examples of "do do" and "don't do," will be helpful alike to the frightened cub and to the deadline-scarred pro. This is because the authors are pros and educators.

Their work is not directed exclusively to newspaper men and women but, instead, to present and future craftsmen in all media who practice the art. Thus there are chapters on broadcast news editing, newspaper magazine editing and picture editing. Then, for the Sizzling Seventies, the book touches on computer editing.

No text on editing can be an ironclad compendium workable on all newspapers in all situations. Local ground rules always will prevail.

But *The Art of Editing* does provide goal posts applicable on all newspapers and in all situations. It will fill a longstanding need on desks and in classes.

> HOWARD B. TAYLOR
> Editorial Consultant
> Copley Newspapers
> La Jolla, California

Preface

A handbook can describe the mechanics of editing, but few books or even a set of books can tell a copyeditor how to edit fast and accurately. Editing demands judgment, imagination, dedication and some creativity—all qualities derived from experience rather than from principles and formulas. In fact, most formulas for writing or editing are shunned in the newsroom.

To help beginners recognize some of the many kinds of errors that get into print or are "nailed on the rim" before they appear in print, the authors have relied on scores of examples recited in critiques compiled by editors for their staffs. In many instances, the editors' comments are as priceless as the examples themselves. The teacher may find these examples more realistic and more stimulating than contrived ones as laboratory exercises.

Because credit cannot be given for all the examples as they appear throughout the text, the authors gratefully acknowledge these sources: Chicago *Tribune, English 1;* Cleveland *Press, Tips and Slips;* Indiana *Daily Student, Us Last Week;* Flint (Mich.) *Journal, Journalisms;* Hackensack (N.J.) *Record, Second Look;* Louisville (Ky.) *Times, Better Late Than Never;* Minneapolis *Star, Stars and Gripes;* Wilmington (Del.) *News-Journal, Hits and Misses;* Richmond (Va.) *Times-Dispatch, T-D Topics;* Winston-Salem (N.C.) *Journal and Sentinel, Pats and Paddles;* Chattanooga (Tenn.) *Times, Sum of the Times;* Indianapolis *News, "How We're Doin'";* and New London (Conn.) *Day, Cares That Infest the Day.*

Other sources from which examples have been used are Carl Byoir & Associates, Inc., *Ripples in the Copy Stream;* U.P.I.

Reporter; AP *Log;* APME *News;* ASNE *Bulletin;* the International Council of Industrial Editors *Reporting; Editor & Publisher; The Quill; Publishers' Auxiliary;* the Baltimore *Evening Sun Blue Book;* and numerous stylebooks.

The authors are indebted to their colleagues, students and professional workers who read chapters and gave many helpful suggestions. Special gratitude should be given to the Denver *Post* (on picture and magazine editing), the Boulder (Colo.) *Daily Camera* and the Denver bureau of the Associated Press (on wire editing) and to radio station KBOL in Boulder and television station KLZ-TV in Denver (on broadcast news editing). Other credits are given within the text.

As the title suggests, editing is an art, but editing itself needs the skills of many—writer, photographer, artist, printer and engineer—to fulfill its purpose. These, and others, all have a hand in shaping the message for the media.

Practices and terms may vary from one newsroom to another. The use of the computer in some phases of editing is likely to create even more differences. Basically, however, editing is the same art no matter where or by whom it is practiced. To all who will accept the challenge of careful editing, this volume is dedicated.

Boulder, Colorado   F. K. B.
Evanston, Illinois   J. Z. S.

Contents

1

The Copyeditor as Editor

Every editor edits. That is, he decides what shall and what shall not go into his publication on the basis of what he conceives to be the publication's mission and philosophy.

Of the various subeditors who help the editor carry out his job, one is the copyeditor, the man or woman who makes raw copy palatable for the reader.

Although each editor works at different levels, all have to edit. Adolph Ochs of the New York *Times* insisted that copyreading is editing. "A good copyreader," he said in a talk at the Pulitzer School of Journalism in 1925, "is truly and in the full meaning an editor. The most useful man on the newspaper is one who can edit."[1]

One may describe the duties of the editor, but no one can analyze how an editor works, anymore than one can describe how a poet composes a poem. Norman Podhoretz, editor of *Commentary* magazine, came close to defining one obligation of the editor—"to improve an essentially well-written piece or to turn a clumsily written one into, at the very least, a readable and literate article, and, at the very most, a beautifully shaped and effective essay which remains true to the author's intention, which realizes that intention more fully than he himself was able to do. He cares about the English language; he cares about clarity of thought and of grace of expression; he cares about the traditions of discourse and of argument."[2]

---

[1] Adolph Ochs, as quoted by Stanley Walker in *City Editor* (New York: Stokes, 1934), p. 90.

[2] Norman Podhoretz, "In Defense of Editing," *Harper's*, p. 143, (October 1965).

The term *copyeditor* is more apt than the traditional word *copyreader* because it connotes the essential job of editing copy. It suggests the art of correcting, refining and polishing a piece of copy. Editing, as crossword-puzzle fans know, means redacting, or bringing back, getting together, collecting, arranging, reducing, composing, framing, translating, selecting or adapting for publication. A redactor, therefore, is an editor. One aspect of redacting is copyediting, the British equivalent of subediting.

Automation is giving the newspaper more copy from more sources than ever before, thereby demanding greater selectivity and keener judgments on the desks. Automation provides instant retrieval of background material, thereby providing the desks with another means to assure accuracy and completeness of the report. The new tools—light pencils and light erasers instead of copy pencils and art gums—make editing faster, enabling an editor or copyeditor to edit copy on a screen as fast as the copy is being written. The effect is that more editors are becoming involved in the editing process.

Even the new methods will not radically change the contents and presentation. As pointed out by Nathaniel M. Gerstenzang of the New York *Times*, new methods may change red ink to black on newspaper balance sheets, but they won't assure publishers of the best and fullest use of the most valuable commodity—the news column. "The assurance," Gerstenzang said, "can be given, in the last analysis, only by human brains—specifically by competent copyeditors."[3]

The copyeditor has talents that cannot be replaced by computers. One of these talents is the ability to edit copy; another is the ability to compose headlines. The first is as important as the second, if not more so, because editing demands many intangibles—judgment, scholarliness, background, memory, aggressiveness, motivation, imagination, curiosity, discretion, cynicism, skepticism and even some genius.

More than anyone else on the staff, the deskman is a prime communicator. Acting as a conscience for the reader, he strives to make each story clear, meaningful, orderly and straightforward. He judges not whether news executives can understand the story and its significance but whether the reader can understand it and feel its impact. The copyeditor then tries to coax the reader into the story with a compelling headline. Thus, both as an editor and as a creative writer, he communes with the reader.

Describing a publisher's editor in the Trade Winds column in the *Saturday Review* (February 10, 1968, p. 12), Herbert R. Mayes gave some attributes that apply equally well to the copydesk expert: "An editor, like a gardener with a green thumb, has a knack. There is no specific training involved. There is no college to offer a doctorate in editing, because editing is an em-

---

[3] Nathaniel M. Gerstenzang, "The Newspaper's Biggest Personnel Problem," *Columbia Journalism Review,* 4:40 (Winter 1966).

pirical art. There is nothing scientific about it. There are no statistics, except after the fact, that can be relied on. Editing is intuitive. Experience confirms intuition but does nothing to develop it. Intuition is for what is the right writing for a given audience, of course, but no less for what makes the members of any audience laugh and cry, love and hate, be decent or vulgar, vengeful or sympathetic, greedy or generous, brave or cowardly."

If copyediting involved no more than comma chasing and label writing, the paper might as well have no copydesk and permit the reporters to write their own headlines. This would mean, in most cases, that the copy would get no editing because many reporters habitually misspell some words, have trouble distinguishing between *like* and *as* and all too often compose their story at such speed that what they intend to say isn't always what appears in the copy. An excellent staff without a copydesk conceivably might produce a fair newspaper. A mediocre staff with a competent copydesk can produce an acceptable newspaper. But an excellent staff, backed by an excellent desk, guarantees an excellent paper. Such is the testament of a former executive, L. R. Blanchard of the Gannett Newspapers, who added, "No man is qualified to be his own copyeditor. No matter what his reputation, his writing will benefit from another's look."[4] And another—this from Stan Amisov of *Newsday*— "There are many elements that go into the making of a fine newspaper, but one of the least heralded and most important is an outstanding copydesk. It can make a good newspaper better. It can make a better newspaper the best."[5] The copyeditor is a trustee with obligations extending to the men and women in the news as well as to the reader and his newspaper.

The copyeditor has been called the midwife to the story, the reporter's best critic. He is like the unsung craftsmen in a dramatic production whose skills put the quality into the material that draws the applause for the stars. Rudolph Burke of the Atlanta *Journal*, in a letter to *Editor & Publisher* (July 8, 1967, p. 7) has said that the byline lures the enthusiastic beginner, but every managing editor knows there is often a great deal of difference between what the reporter writes and what the reader reads after the story has gone through the hands of anonymous editors.

A few reporters grouse because the copyeditors "butcher all their good stuff." But most writers respect their collaborator on the desk, the ever-alert copyeditor who gives the copy a final look before it goes to the composing room and then to the reader. It was the small author who ever resented the touch of the editorial pencil upon his precious effusions, said Edward Bok in *The Americanization of Edward Bok*.[6]

[4] L. R. Blanchard, *Editor & Publisher*, p. 44, (August 9, 1964).
[5] Stan Amisov, *Editor & Publisher*, p. 66, (February 6, 1965).
[6] Edward Bok, *The Americanization of Edward Bok* (New York: Scribner, 1922), p. 382.

Almost all critics lead lonesome lives, but at least they have the respect of those they have taught. One of the most demanding of all editors was Harold Ross of the *New Yorker*, of whom Ogden Nash wrote in a letter quoted in James Thurber's *The Years With Ross*, "He was an almost impossible man to work for—rude, ungracious and perpetually dissatisfied with what he read; and I admire him more than anyone I have met in professional life."[7]

The copyeditor is a diamond cutter who refines and polishes, removes the flaws and shapes the stone into a gem. His main tool is his pencil, which he uses as surely and as confidently as the stonecutter does his tools. He searches for the ills in copy and meticulously scans the product for flaws and inaccuracy, ever searching for the maximum power of words. He knows when to prune the useless, the redundant, the unnecessary qualifiers. He gets movement in the piece by substituting active verbs for inactive ones, specifics for generalities. He obtains color by changing faraway words to close-up words. He keeps sentences short enough so that readers can grasp one idea at a time and still not suffer primer prose. He strives for pacing. If the sentence clothes several ideas majestically and in good order, he has the good sense to let the writer have his way. He realizes he is not the storyteller. His talent is in what he can do with another's copy to make it sparkle.

Lest this description suggest that the copyeditor is like a bored teacher correcting English themes, consider that the copydesk is one of the exciting places in the newsroom. On the desk tumbles all the copy of the day—the major battles, the moon landings, robberies, the cure for cancer, the election of a president, the Kentucky Derby winner, the rescue of a lost child. The desk is the heart that throbs with all the news from near and far, waiting for someone to shape it, size it, display it and send it to the reader.

"Because copyediting is an art," said J. Edward Murray of the Arizona *Republic*, "the most important ingredient, after training and talent, is strong motivation. The copyeditor must care. Not only should he know his job. He must love it. Every story. Every edition. Every day. No art yields to less than maximum effort. The copyeditor must be motivated by a fierce professional pride in the high quality of editing."[8] No one can tell a copyeditor how to edit—he has to experience it for himself.

Although Mr. Murray's statement is eloquent and inspiring, it is not entirely realistic. Surely there are some stories the deskman does not love to handle. The authors remember Oswald, the ace city hall reporter who had been on his beat so long he knew the executives as well as the office girls by their first names. No fact escaped him and he dutifully recorded it all, not in separate

---

[7] James Thurber, *The Years with Ross* (Boston: Little, 1957), p. 123.
[8] J. Edward Murray, "Editing Artists: The Men Around the Rim," *The Quill*, p. 12 (March 1964).

items, but in one rambling tome. He was thorough; his opposition considered him tough competition. When the offices at city hall closed, Oswald retired to the pressroom, where he banged out his copy on a typewriter with a chewed-up ribbon. Later, he bustled into the city room, puff-puffing his pipe. He flipped his opus on the desk of the city editor and took a chair in the corner of the city room. Eventually the city editor picked up the piece, glanced over the first two pages, and penciled in a byline. Then, gently holding his nose, he flipped the copy to the chief of the copydesk. That was the signal for the copyeditors to visit the men's room.

The handling of Oswald's copy meant cutting and pasting, trying to make sense of long and involved sentences, removing parts to be used as side bars or separate items, adding rows of figures to make sure the sums were correct, eliminating the inconsequential "posh" and trying to hold the copy to some reasonable length.

Oswald stayed around the city room long enough to clarify facts that could be misunderstood. When the headline finally emerged and the copy went up the tube to the composing room, Oswald relit his pipe, put on his coat and left.

Doubtless he had his coterie of admirers, some of whom might have considered proposing him for a Pulitzer Prize. He covered his beat competently, but as a writer he couldn't have passed the seventh grade. He got his bylines, but the stories as they appeared belonged as much to the unsung copyeditors as they did to the reporter. Few would have loved every minute they spent slaving over his copy.

There are Oswalds on practically all big newspapers. They even include some big-name foreign correspondents who not only tend to be windy but who massacre the language and find syntax a mystery. Readers may regard such Oswalds as great reporters and fine writers, not knowing that the copyeditors in their home offices helped to make their reputations.

A newspaper without a circle of geniuses around the copydesk would have been unthinkable to the sage of American journalism, Carl Lindstrom, formerly of the Hartford *Times*. He regarded the desk as the backbone of the paper. "The copydesk," he once observed, "is the abiding place of curiosity, discretion, cynicism, sympathy—all those human instincts personified in men who give your paper its flavor; newshounds all, with noses in the air for the scent of human interest and for libel. I salute the copydesk, the sacrificial altar of the sacred cow."[9]

Ask youngsters fresh out of a journalism school what they are looking for in their professional lives. The thoughtful ones will reply, "I want a job that offers an opportunity for growth. I want a chance to continue to expand my education. I want a place where I can, by my own incentive, advance to the higher ech-

[9] Carl Lindstrom, as quoted in *Journalism Quarterly*, **42:4**:638 (Autumn 1965).

elons of responsibility." Mention the copydesk and they are likely to repeat the stereotypes of the desk as the haven for tired, worn-out newsmen who spend their days marking paragraphs and hurriedly composing commonplace headlines so they can get back to their crossword puzzles. The great and the near-great are those of the editors, the reporters, the columnists, the news commentators. Whoever heard of a hero of the copydesk?

Yet, no place on a publication offers a greater opportunity for growth, a chance to continue an education, an incentive to reach the higher places of responsibility. The deskman, even a mediocre one, must of necessity accumulate a warehouse full of facts, facts he has gleaned from the thousands of stories he is compelled to read and edit or from the references he has had to consult to verify information.

Think of him as a superdetective, one who incessantly searches the story for clues that could transform a mediocre piece into an epic. Let him study ocean charts and maps and astronomical formulas, as did Carr Van Anda of the New York *Times*, to find the missing links in the routine story. Think of him as a lawyer conducting a cross-examination. Let him study Harold Ross, who, as noted previously, made life miserable for writers on the *New Yorker* but who never let a piece escape him unless the meaning was crystal clear. Thurber, again in *The Years with Ross* (page 257), recalled a typical opinion sheet penned by Ross. "It isn't a typical party you're talking about here—doesn't include the kind of mild parties you've enumerated in preceding paragraph, but a party typical of this particular circle, the Spencer-Thurber circle. Also, suggest that these people here be pegged as suburban, as I have marked, or some such, for later in the piece, much later, it turns out that they live in places with stairs, which means houses, not apartments. You start a story like this off with a suburban plant and a reader assumes you're talking about metropolitan apartment house life, and is unfairly surprised when he comes to a passage about someone going upstairs."

In another passage (page 267), Thurber described an English journalist who said the biography of Ross should be called *The Century of the Comma Man*. "He picked out a sentence in a *New Yorker* casual: 'After dinner, the men went into the living room,' and wanted to know why I, or the editors, had put in the comma. I could explain that one all right. I wrote back that this particular comma was Ross's way of giving the men time to push back their chairs and stand up."

The greatness of both Ross and Van Anda was that they were mentally curious, a trait that should occupy all copyeditors. Few copyeditors today would correct an Einstein formula, as Van Anda did, but—if they are willing—they can probe, question, authenticate and exercise their powers of deduction.

If a copyeditor is blessed by a good copydesk chief, he will learn. Day by day he will improve. If in college he worked under a wise and experienced professor on the staff, rather than under a graduate assistant who regarded a copydesk lab as a chore, he will likely love editing. Girls, who seem to have a special knack for grammar and literature, get the impression the copydesk is a man's domain. But this tradition is dying, and some of the best copyeditors to grace a newspaper or magazine copydesk in the future will be women. Already, on some metropolitan papers, women with editing skill have risen to important positions, in charge of copyediting and layout of sections that run to many pages.

Whether copyeditors, as a class or a craft group, are a vanishing breed is debatable. Some editors think they are. A typical comment might be: A few very good ones exist here and there, but as individuals and not as part of a great fraternity that was with us thirty or forty years ago. Newspapers are poorer because of this, and I suspect that those who survive are lonesome. They were "swifts" and could handle large piles of copy with an unerring eye for big and little errors, misspelled words, factual faults.

If, in fact, good copyeditors are hard to come by, publishers may start paying more attention to the experts on the desk. A copyeditor with a good education and the opportunity to advance his knowledge will benefit the newspaper more than a reporter will. Let management recommend a deskman as a Nieman Fellow, or give him an opportunity to attend the American Press Institute at Columbia University, or give him a leave of absence to ground himself at the London School of Economics, or give him a chance to trade jobs for a year with a copyeditor in another part of the country or invite him to sit in on office conferences where policy and philosophy are discussed.

Editors might keep trainees or interns on the copydesk at least long enough to find out whether the trainee will make a good deskman. By rotating good reporters on the desk, editors might find that both the desk and the reporters will profit.

A reporter who had been on general assignment and a beat for nearly fifteen years broke his leg and was assigned to the desk until the leg healed. After a month, he had recovered enough to go back on his beat. "I think I'd like to stay on the desk," he said. "I've had more fun than I ever did on the streets, and I've learned a lot more."

Because copyeditors have some knowledge of typography and have skill in using space, they have an advantage over reporters in advancing to executive positions. In a survey by Nathaniel M. Gerstenzang (mentioned previously), the following question was asked of editors: "If you were to fill the job of your top assistant, would you choose your best-qualified reporter or your best-qualified deskman?" The ratio was 10:1 in favor of the deskman. For telegraph editor, the ratio was 21:0 in favor of the deskman, and for cable editor, 18:0. For city editor, the reporter was preferred by a ratio of 2:1.

The emphasis in this book is on copydesk work. But editing is not the sole province of rim-men and slotmen. Only about 25 per cent of wire service workers are reporters and writers. The others are rewritemen, copyeditors, filers and those who perform mechanical tasks. Many broadcast newsrooms have editing experts. Some editing is required in all phases of all the mass media, including advertising.

2

The Copyeditor and the Reader

The copyeditor can perceive copy as pieces of paper that come from machines and flow along an assembly line to the press. In this role the copyeditor is a mere copy fixer or assembly-line worker. On the other hand, he can view copy as messages destined for readers and thus can concern himself not only with copy but audiences as well.

The Nature of Audiences

Much of the editing in the past was based on guesswork and myths about readers. But readership studies and the continuing appraisal of the American newspaper audience generally have indicated that many old notions about readership are untrue of today's readers and certainly will be untrue of tomorrow's readers.

Research has shown that the old ideas about readership in relation to the sex of the reader and to position in the paper or on the page should not be regarded as strictly as they once were. Men and women tend to read much the same thing, although there are obvious statistical differences. The left-hand page is as well read as the right-hand page. Small items at the bottoms of pages may attract as much attention as big displays at the tops of pages. Frequently, the best-read stories are not those displayed prominently on page 1.

Differences in reading are determined more by age, education and economic status than by sex or race. Of course, more women than men read the women's pages and more men than women read the sports pages, but readership research suggests that the quality of stories, rather than their placement, is what attracts and holds the audience.

Most readership research is intended to test hypotheses that editors have about the nature of news and audience behavior. In the opinion of Dr. Chilton R. Bush, former head of the Department of Communication at Stanford University, research itself does not create; editors create. They may use some results of readership surveys to help take the guesswork out of editing. They may determine from a survey what readers read on a certain day. But a survey cannot tell editors what readers will read because newspapers change every day and the reading of news content also changes from day to day and from paper to paper. The selection of timely, interesting news articles is still very much the editor's art.

Summaries of readership surveys can be found in the News Research Bulletins published by the American Newspaper Publishers Association (ANPA) and in a series of booklets titled *News Research for Better Newspapers*, compiled and edited by Dr. Bush and published by the ANPA Foundation. Most of the statements on readership in this section have been extracted from the booklets with the permission of Dr. Bush.[1]

One of the earliest and most comprehensive readership studies was *The Continuing Study of Newspaper Reading*, conducted by the Advertising Foundation, which surveyed readers of 138 newspapers between 1939 and 1950. The summary was published in 1951. A similar study of the readership of western dailies was conducted by Dr. Bush for the Hometown Daily Newspapers of the West.

Both studies concentrated on what readers read. Both demonstrated that most readers read their newspaper intensively, page by page. They expose themselves to everything in their paper to make sure they are not missing anything of interest. Women look at pages directed mainly to men and men look at pages directed mainly to women.

What readers read must be appraised continually because audiences as well as news definitions constantly change. We can predict that the audience for news will become increasingly younger and better-educated. The U.S. Bureau of the Census (*Current Population Reports*, 1968) has estimated that 34.2 per cent of the population in 1975 will be in the range of 14 to 34 years (27.5 per cent in 1960) and 39.8 per cent will be 35 years and older (42.8 per cent in 1960). The bureau projects that the median age of the total population in 1985 will be 25.6 years if there should be a high level of births or 29.5 years if there should be a low level of births A median age of 25.6 years means that half the population will be above 25.6 years and half below 25.6 years. For nonwhite persons, the median age in 1985 could range from 19 to 25 years.

Educational attainment is also increasing. As time goes on, the older, less-educated people in the population are replaced by

[1] Volume I—April 1966; Volume II—Feb. 1967; Volume III—Feb. 1968; Volume IV —Feb. 1969. Citations will be to volume and page.

The Art of Editing

younger people with more education. The census bureau in *Projections of Educational Attainment* (1968) estimated that 15.2 per cent of the males and 9.3 per cent of the females aged 25 years and older will have four or more years of college by 1975. The average (median) number of years completed in school is expected to reach 12.4 or 12.5 years in 1975.

Newspapers will have to offer more stories than they have in the past to get more variety of content and thus satisfy diverse tastes. This does not mean, necessarily, that readers will read more items or will spend more time reading newspapers. But what they read may be more satisfying to them. The majority of adult readers now spend an average of forty minutes with each weekday paper, whereas less than one fourth of teenage readers spend that much time reading weekday papers (Bush, I:16, 17 and 18).

Carl J. Nelson Research, Inc., has found that of 90 general news stories offered in the average metropolitan newspaper, a man will read 17 (19 per cent) and a woman 13 (14 per cent) *Survey of the Month*, No. 23 (October 13, 1967). Teenagers read about one eighth of the major content. The Minneapolis *Star and Tribune* uses 20 per cent as a yardstick of reader performance. Apart from page 1, any given item of news content has a 1:5 chance of being read by the typical adult reader (Bush, I:143).

Assuming an average reading rate of 250 words a minute, the majority of adult readers will read a maximum of 10,000 words a weekday in newspapers. Nelson has found that readers will consume about the same proportion of stories regardless of the total. The Newsprint Information Committee showed that the kinds of things that people want and get out of the paper are much the same regardless of how much time they spend reading it: "The readers who spend a lot of time and the readers who spend less time do not differ significantly with regard to preferences for local versus national and international news or for news versus features" (Bush, I:10, 11 and 12).

The early fears that radio and television would diminish newspaper reading have proved unfounded. In fact, exposure to events by the broadcast media tends to increase readers' interest in those events.

Reader interest in local and nonlocal news is about the same, although more women than men prefer local news. Frequently the highest interest scores are for individual national and international news items. In his surveys, Nelson noted a better reading of wire stories than of local items *Survey of the Month*, No. 23 (October 13, 1967).

As the reader grows older he uses a newspaper less for entertainment and more for information and serious viewpoints on public affairs. Interest in comics and sports declines, and the reading of public affairs news and editorials increases (Bush, I:45).

In a sampling of Omaha (Neb.) *World-Herald* readers, women showed more interest than men in music, drama, art, medicine, religion and education. Men showed more interest than did women in science and business. However, women showed more interest in business than in some other topics. More men read the comics regularly than did women. Women who read the women's pages regularly outnumbered men who read sports pages regularly. Women who read the sports pages regularly outnumbered men who read the women's pages regularly. Women showed a slightly higher interest in pictures than did men (Bush, II:47).

In Minneapolis, the reading interests of men tended to focus on news of politics and government, taxes, business and sports. They showed greater interest than did women in editorials and in opinion columns. Women were more likely to read articles that dealt with human interest themes, with health and family care and with children; they read the obituary columns, vital statistics, food and fashion material, church and school news, the social columns, tips on home decorating and flower gardens and recipes. Both men and women readers showed interest in accident stories and crime news (Bush, I:143).

A survey in Denver, Colorado, indicated that boys are interested primarily in front page stories, comics, radio and television listings, movies and entertainment and sports. Girl readers listed front page news, comics, movies and entertainment, radio and television listings and personal advice columns (Bush, III:76).

Both men and women who are interested in sports have definite preferences as to the kinds of sports stories they read. This was borne out in 1969 in the APME Sports Readership Survey conducted by the Associated Press Managing Editors' Association Sports Committee with the professional guidance of the Nelson Research firm. Among the findings are the following:

Most sports page readers preferred separate game stories to roundup stories They preferred stories emphasizing background and explanatory material to straight, detailed game accounts. Most readers, particularly women readers, liked to read personal stories about sports stars. Rather than being bored by tabulated details such as box scores, football summaries, league standings and racing entries and results, readers said they wanted these statistics.

Both men and women readers interested in sports said they turned to page 1 first, but nearly one third of the men readers turned first to the sports pages. A slightly higher percentage of women readers turned to the sports pages first rather than to the women's pages.

Both men and women revealed that their greatest interest was in professional football, followed by college football and then professional baseball. Women readers showed as much interest in horse racing as did men and showed more interest than did men in skiing and tennis. Interest in golf and bowling was approximately the same for both sexes.

Both groups reported they wanted more human interest and behind-the-scenes stories and more photographs, especially sequence photos.

Evidently readers want to get the news as fast as they can because shorter items suffer less loss of readers than do longer ones. However, this may be because of story content and style rather than length. Stories of five paragraphs or longer and written in inverted pyramid structure tend to lose more readers than stories of the same length in feature form.

In an early study, Dr. Wilbur Schramm of Stanford University noted that a story in conventional style showed a readership drop-off of 11.33 per cent in the first five paragraphs, 3.46 per cent in the second five, 1.74 per cent in the third five and .54 per cent in the fourth five paragraphs (Bush, I:76–80).

A readership survey in Eugene, Oregon, demonstrated that a feature story pattern will get greater readership than a story written in conventional style, provided the feature story also has a feature headline. Dr. Galen R. Rarick at the University of Oregon had two feature stories with conventional heads in half the press run of the *Register-Guard* and two feature stories with feature heads in the other half of the press run. Dr. Rarick found that the readership of one story increased from 30.4 per cent (regular head) to 40 per cent (feature head) and that for the second story readership increased from 27.5 to 55.4 per cent (Bush, III:15).

In *Survey of the Month*, No. 23 (October 13, 1967), Nelson found that more than one half of the readers who began reading two of five stories with five or more parts completed them. Each part consisted of four paragraphs. In other samplings, Nelson Research found a relatively high story completion rate by both men and women readers and a lower completion rate by teenagers. With regard to news stories, 41 per cent of the men readers started the stories and 78 per cent of these men completed the stories. For women readers, 32 per cent started the stories and 76 per cent of these completed the stories. For boys, 14 per cent started the stories and 68 per cent of these completed the stories. Likewise, 14 per cent of the girls started the stories and 70 per cent of them completed the stories. Girls and boys rated higher than men and women in thorough reading of the television logs (Bush, III:9–14).

On longer stories that continue from one page to another, the loss of readership occurs both on the initial page before the jump and on the jumped portion. The variables are length of story, the position on the page of the jumped portion, the size and kind of headline on the jumped portion and whether art is carried over to the jump page. Some papers place all jump stories from page 1 on the back page or on the back page of the first section.

The Minneapolis *Star and Tribune* noted that about half of the readers who start a page-1 story that jumps follow the story to the jump page. One of the Nelson Research surveys showed that the majority of readers who turned to the jump portion completed the story regardless of the story length. The Nelson Research surveys indicate a range of total loss of readers on jump stories of from 6 to 82 per cent (Bush, III:9).

Two thirds of the readers start reading on page 1 then go through the paper, page by page. The rest turn first to some particular item, feature or section, then return to the beginning. Dr. Bush suggested that this reading pattern leads to other questions for further research, such as the function of indexes, the utility (or nonutility) of news digests, the decision to "anchor" or "float" certain features and the utility of departmentalization (Bush, I:10).

Researchers have yet to find out why readers do some of the things they do. One executive suggested, "We don't know enough about that lightning-fast process in the reader's mind that causes him to read an item at the top of column two on page 47— but reject, or skip, adjacent news items in columns one and three" (Bush, I:149).

Perhaps one answer can be found in the hypothesis formulated in 1949 by Dr. Wilbur Schramm that a reader selects news in expectation of a reward. Said Schramm, "Leaving out chance, conflicting mental sets, and the qualities of presentation which call attention to one item over others or make one item easier to read than others, we can hypothesize that a person chooses the items which he thinks are likely to give him the greatest reward. . . . In general there seems to be greater expectation of reward when there appears to be greater possibility of the reader identifying himself with the news" (Bush, II:13–18).

The effort to help the reader identify himself with the news is a first principle in good editing. Even if editors could know precisely what readers read or might want to read, there is no likelihood that editors would limit news content to "best-read" types. If they did, they would get a paper described by Sidney S. Goldish, one-time research director of the Minneapolis *Star and Tribune*, as "the most flamboyant, sensational and frivolous newspaper ever published—because the best-read stories, day in and day out, are usually those heavily vested with violence, sex, controversy and so-called human interest qualities." It was Goldish's opinion that the editor will continue to use his own professional judgment of what is important, consequential and significant in the day's news (Bush, I:147).

Readability Measurements

Readership measures the extent to which an item is read. Readability measures the ease with which an item can be read, or, more accurately, it tries to measure some of the things that make reading difficult.

A readability measure is no formula for writing, nor was it ever intended to be. Rather, it is a tool that may be used in rewriting or editing to improve the writing or to check the writing style from various departments within a newspaper or from the wire service news report.

Most readability formulas are based on concepts long familiar to newspaper editors. Short sentences generally are easier to read than long ones and short words generally are more likely to be comprehended than long ones.

Two of the better-known formulas developed by readability experts use sentence and word lengths. The Flesch formula, devised by Dr. Rudolph Flesch, uses 100-word samples to measure average sentence length and number of syllables in the sample. The formula multiplies the average number of words in the sentences by 1.015 and the total syllable count by .846. The two factors are added, then subtracted from 206.835 to arrive at a readability score.[2]

Robert Gunning uses a similar procedure to determine the *fog index*. He adds the average sentence length in words and the number of words of three syllables or more (omitting capitalized words; combinations of short, easy words like *butterfly;* and verb forms made into three syllables by adding –ed, –es, or –ing). The sum is multiplied by .4 to get the fog index.[3]

Suppose the sample contains an average of 16 words to the sentence and a total of 150 syllables. By the Flesch formula the sample would have a readability score of 64, which Flesch rates as standard or fitting the style of *Reader's Digest*. In the same sample and assuming the hard words at 10 per cent, the fog index on the Gunning scale would be 10, or at the reading level of high school sophomores and fitting *Time* magazine style.

Two wire services thought enough of both formulas to get an evaluation of their news reports. Gunning conducted the evaluation for United Press and Dr. Flesch did two measurements for the Associated Press.

Neither Flesch nor Gunning tests content or word familiarity. All they suggest is that if passages from a story or the whole story average more than 20 words to the sentence and the number of hard words in a sample of 100 words exceeds 10 per cent, a majority of newspaper readers will find the passages difficult to understand.

Nor would the formula designers recommend that copyeditors pare all long sentences to twenty words or less and all long words to words of one and two syllables. Long sentences, if they are graceful and meaningful, should be kept intact. Mixed with

---

[2] Rudolph Flesch, *The Art of Readable Writing* (New York: Harper, 1949).
[3] Robert Gunning, *The Technique of Clear Writing* (New York: McGraw-Hill, 1952).

shorter sentences, they give variety to style. A long word may still be a plain word.

An editorial executive of the New York *Times* preferred to measure density of ideas in sentences rather than sentence length itself and came up with a pattern of "one idea, one sentence." A special issue of the newsroom publication *Winners & Sinners* No. 79 (February 4, 1955) was devoted to this pattern, with reports of reading tests on two versions of the same articles. One tested the comprehension of the articles as they were written originally. Another tested the articles when rewritten to lower the density of ideas in the sentences. The "one idea, one sentence" dictum is not taken literally even at the *Times*, but the editors insist, "Generally it speeds reading if there is only one idea to a sentence."

The number of unfamiliar words in passages has also been found to be an element in readability. Edgar Dale and Jeanne S. Chall at Ohio State University, prepared a list of 3,000 words known to 80 per cent of fourth graders. The word-load factor in the Dale-Chall formula consists of a count of words outside the list. Only 4 per cent of the words on the Dale-Chall list are words of three or more syllables.[4]

The editing of stories to reduce the number of words outside the word-familiarity list would be time consuming and probably impractical because the lists would have to be revised periodically to take out words that no longer are familiar and to add new words that have become part of everyday language—even to fourth graders.

Most readability formulas use a few fundamental elements but neglect context or story structure. Thus a passage in gibberish could rate as highly readable on the Flesch, Gunning and Dale-Chall scales. This was demonstrated by Dr. Wilson L. Taylor at the University of Illinois' Institute of Communications Research. Dr. Taylor developed the *cloze* procedure (from "close" or "closure" in Gestalt psychology) to test context. In this procedure he omitted certain words—usually every fifth word—and asked respondents to fill in the missing words, then graded them on the number of correct words they could fill in. Of passages from eight writers, the Taylor method ranked samples of Gertrude Stein's semi-intelligible prose as next to the most difficult. The most difficult was a passage from James Joyce. Both the Dale-Chall and the Flesch scales rated the Stein passage as the easiest to read and the Joyce passage in a tie for fourth with a passage from Erskine Caldwell (Bush I:92, 93). To test for human interest, Flesch measures personal words and sentences. Sentences that mention persons and have them saying and doing things increase readability.

[4] Edgar Dale and Jeanne S. Chall, *Readability: An Appraisal of Research and Application* (Columbus: Ohio State University Press, 1958).

The cloze procedure suggests that unfamiliar words may be used and understood if they are placed in a context where the reader can learn the words' meanings.

Few copyeditors will apply any of the readability formulas described because, as one author said, editing is an art, not a science. Still, the beginning copyeditor might profit from testing story passages by formula to help him see where and how the structure can be tightened or broken up into more easily digestible bits.

Common-sense editing applies many of the elements used in testing readability. The skilled copyeditor knows when to break a long sentence into two and when to substitute a simple word for a hard one. Unconsciously, he poses this question when he edits copy: Is the story as clear and simple as it can be made?

In 1966 a group of well-educated young people gave editors some reasons some news stories are unreadable, unclear and unbelievable. The main reasons can be summarized as follows:

The Gallagher Readership Survey

Poor organization of the story
Wordiness
Vagueness
Lack of explanation
Use of unfamiliar terms
Too much quotation and too
  many fragmentary quotes

Sources unclear or questionable
Too many statistics
Unfamiliar locations
Too many side plots
Subject matter uninteresting

The responses were given in a study titled The Gallagher Readership Survey, named for Wes Gallagher, then general manager of the Associated Press. The survey was financed by the AP, was planned jointly by representatives of the AP and the Associated Press Managing Editors and had the professional services of Carl J. Nelson Research, Inc.

The 425 interviewees were between the ages of 21 and 30 and all had attended college. They were asked to evaluate six wire dispatches on three subjects. Three of the stories were straight news types; the others had been given a different treatment. Because the survey did not compare "like" things, its validity may be questioned. The answers, however, suggest some things that make news stories difficult to read and understand.

In the first group was a straight news story, bearing a Tokyo dateline, about the activities of the Red Guard in China. It was paired with an interpretive piece with a New York dateline. The stories included the following:

TOKYO, Aug. 25 (AP)—A mob of teen-aged Red Guards today broke into Peking's Sacred Heart Academy, a Roman Catholic school run by French nuns, and hoisted a red flag over it.

Japanese correspondents in the Communist Chinese capital reported they also put a bust of Mao Tze-tung in the school and plastered its walls with signs reading "get out, foreign devils," and "chase out the running dogs of imperialism."

The Red Guards and adults backing them blocked the school doors and made it impossible to hold classes.

The Sacred Heart Academy, almost 100 years old, has not been under the jurisdiction of the Chinese Communist government.

The teen-agers continued to surge through the streets howling for reforms which ranged from renaming Peking "The East Is Red" (Tung Fang Hung) to the abolition of Chinese checkers and Western chess.

The Catholic school, said to be one of the few remaining still run by foreigners, is attended by children of foreign residents in Peking.

Diplomats' Protests Unheeded

The Tokyo newspaper Yomiuri said students, their parents and foreign diplomats who tried to protest against the demonstration by the youths were helpless.

The Japan Broadcasting Corp. Peking correspondent said the youthful Red Guards, who seemed to be directing their wrath at Westerners, posted notices on the walls of the Catholic school which read: "Christianity is akin to imperialism."

Reports said the militant teen-agers ordered persons hiring domestic servants to pay their salaries and send them home within five days. They also ordered the upper classes and overseas Chinese to leave the cities within three days and work on the farms.

NEW YORK, Aug. 25 (AP)—"Dare to organize the masses," said a Chinese Communist party directive issued several weeks ago. Now the "masses" are organized and in full cry, and those who dared are becoming the masters of what begins to look like a Fascist China.

Indoctrinated teen-agers, glorying in a license for mass cruelty, are potent weapons in the hands of a dictator. Today they roam the streets of Chinese cities, inflicting outlandish humiliations on random victims who have suddenly become "enemies of the people."

Evidently the stage is being set for a climactic act of the purge the party calls "the great proletarian cultural revolution," and evidently some men in high—perhaps very high—places are about to fall. Those who have "the masses" in their hands also have the nation—at least for now. They will be tough. Ominously, the theoretical journal Red Flag announced this week:

Mobs Attack Opposition

"Any person, no matter how high his position, how old his standing and how great his fame, as long as he fails to do things according to Mao Tze-tung's thinking . . . should have his erroneous views boycotted and a determined struggle should be waged against him until he is dismissed from his official posts."

The impression left by the spectacle going on in Red China is that within a short time Peking will make known to the world the more important results of the purge. Whatever opposition existed to the current line of policy is being remorselessly crushed under the mass attack of the mobs of youngsters.

What is relatively certain already is that China has a military dictator masquerading as a proletarian. Defense Minister Lin Piao, a marshal when the army had ranks, is the emerging boss, and the "great proletarian cultural revolution" seems designed to establish the line of succession after the ailing Mao Tze-tung.

Two stories from Washington dealt with Medicare. One was a general lead on the start of Medicare; the second was a question and answer piece explaining the program. The stories began as follows:

WASHINGTON, July 1 (AP)—Here are answers to some of the questions most frequently asked about the medicare* system, starting today for all 19 million Americans 65 and older:

Q. If the hospital I choose is overcrowded, does medicare guarantee me a bed?

A. No. Medicare just helps pay the bill.

Q. If I have to go back into the hospital two or more times, do I pay the $40 "deductible" each time?

A. No. You pay just the first $40 of hospital charges in each "spell of illness."

Q. What's a "spell of illness?"

A. To medicare it's a period of time, not an ailment. It starts the day you enter a hospital. It ends 60 days after your discharge from the hospital (or from a nursing home—after next Jan. 1, medicare will provide posthospital convalescent care in nursing homes for those needing it.)

A Different Sickness?

Q. Suppose I go back to the hospital for a different sickness?

A. To medicare it doesn't matter. It's all one "spell of illness" if the new admission comes within 60 days of the last discharge.

Q. What if I'm sent back later than 60 days from the discharge?

A. Then it's a new "spell of illness," with a new $40 charge and a whole new set of benefits—full coverage by medicare for the first 60 days of hospitalization, then all but $10 a day for the next 30 days.

Q. Do I have to go back to the same hospital?

A. No. Your benefits follow you from hospital to hospital and from city to city.

WASHINGTON, July 1 (AP)—The massive medicare program providing hospital insurance for all 19 million of the nation's senior citizens went into effect today, hailed by President Johnson as "a blessing for older Americans."

Swinging into operation with the program was an optional doctor-bill insurance plan for which 17.3 million elected to pay $3 a month.

The two programs were brought into being at 12:01 A.M. in one of the biggest operations in medical history.

Doctors and patients reserved any prognosis, but the President pronounced it a success in advance. He called it "a test of our willingness to work together."

By Public Health Service count, 6,714 institutions—or 91 per cent of all the country's 7,374 general hospitals with roughly 93 per cent of the beds—opened their doors for the insured care of any American aged 65 or over.

Nonparticipants in South

The nonparticipating hospitals were mainly in the South. Most were barred from medicare payments by their failure to comply with the no-racial-discrimination provisions of the Civil Rights Act.

* Lower case "m" in Medicare is AP style.

To make extra sure that no one dies for want of access to a participating hospital, the Government ruled last night that federal hospitals—veterans', military and others—may be used for critically ill medicare patients in emergencies.

Previously it had been announced that any other nonparticipating hospital could be used—private or public, with medicare picking up the bill—if a bed in a participating hospital could not be found to avert the threat of death "or serious impairment of the health."

The third group matched a wrap-up story on a day's activity in the war in Vietnam with a vignette on the activity of one small American unit in Vietnam.† Parts of these stories follow:

SAIGON, Aug. 5 (AP)—One of the largest U.S. ground forces ever massed in Viet Nam swept the central highlands today seeking North Vietnamese regulars holed up in jungles or pulling back toward Cambodia.

As elements of the 10,000-man U.S. force maneuvered in helicopters, eight-engine B52s from Guam swept in and hammered the North Vietnamese positions in the Chu Phong Mountains four miles from Cambodia's border.

The purpose of the action in the air and on the ground was to keep the North Vietnamese off balance and to prevent a possible enemy monsoon drive. Somewhere in the hills and jungles, the Americans believe, are three North Vietnamese regiments, although they think some enemy troops may have retreated into Cambodia.

Buffer Zone Bombed

The B52s came over in two waves, hitting targets 2½ miles apart in the plateau country 235 miles north of Saigon. Earlier in the day, other sky giants from Guam bombed suspected enemy targets in the demilitarized zone. It was the fourth raid by the B52s on the buffer zone between North and South Viet Nam since Saturday.

Peking radio said the North Vietnamese government protested the Superfortress raids on the zone Thursday and Friday to the International Control Commission of India, Canada and Poland, set up by the Geneva Convention in 1954 to police the truce. The Geneva Convention ended the fighting between the French and Communists and divided Viet Nam.

There were no reports of new air raids against North Viet Nam. But Peking radio asserted without confirmation that two U.S. planes were shot down in raids near the port of Haiphong.

The U.S. Command disclosed that in raids Thursday, U.S. warplanes attacked regional military headquarters 24 miles northeast of Haiphong. Pilots reported destroying four large buildings and damaging seven others with their bombs and rockets.

IA DRANG VALLEY, Viet Nam, Aug. 5 (AP)—As the rain swept in upon their piece of scraggly jungle, and the shouting North Vietnamese voices got closer, the five men hidden there made a whispered pact.

"We won't surrender, right?" said Sgt. Willie Glaspie from Magnolia, N.C.

Sgt. Francisco Pablo from Guam answered: "When they come, we fight to the finish."

† Spelling of Viet Nam has since been changed to Vietnam.

A Vietnamese interpreter nodded in agreement. The two other Americans, both of U.S. 1st Air Cavalry, and both wounded, muttered assent.

Cut Off From Reinforcements

It seemed only a matter of time. The five thought they were the only survivors of a platoon from "A" Company, 2nd Battalion, 7th Regiment. The platoon had leaped from helicopters into a tiny landing zone in the northern Ia Drang Valley Tuesday, was cut off from reinforcements because of bad weather, and was systematically cut to pieces.

But there were other survivors.

One was Sgt. Leroy Shockey from Philadelphia, a squad leader lying in agony 50 feet away in a clearing. Shockey was searched six times by looting North Vietnamese troops, and had his rifle, ammunition, billfold and money taken. He thought his breathing had given him away, but the North Vietnamese did not harm him.

Shockey remembers how at noon Tuesday his platoon leader, a young U.S. lieutenant, was killed in the premature blast of his own grenade.

The platoon's sergeant was bleeding from wounds suffered in the first, furious minutes of the battle that engulfed them as they leaped from helicopters.

"You'll Have to Take Over"

"Sgt. Shockey," the wounded sergeant called out. "I'm dying, the commander's dead. You'll have to take over the platoon."

Then the platoon sergeant lurched to his feet. As more bullets struck him he cried out, "My God, what's going to happen to my wife and children?"

Shockey himself was soon wounded. Surrounded by dug-in enemy machine guns and automatic weapons, Shockey and his men were sitting ducks.

RED GUARD STORIES. About one fourth of the men and more than one third of the women readers said that the straight story on the Red Guards in China was partly unclear or not understandable at all. The main reasons given were that the story lacked organization. It jumped around with too many side stories to the point where the aim of the main story was lost. Many said the story was so wordy it confused them.

Nearly one half of the men readers and one third of the women readers felt the story used vague words or phrases that were not clearly defined and that the style of writing was so long and involved that the story was difficult to understand. "Too many things going on," some said. "It's all mixed up." Some commented that the writer did not complete one idea before going to the next. Nearly half the readers thought the story was too long. Nearly half said they would not have read the story at all. Most said that the subject was interesting but that because of the repetition in the body of the story, it would not be necessary to read all the story to get the message.

About one half of the readers thought the story untrue, probably because of the extensive quotes used in the story from Red Chinese sources.

Men readers preferred the straight story to the analysis. The opposite was true for women readers. Both groups, however, would have been more likely to read the straight account because it was more interesting, contained more specifics, had more action and contained less "editorializing."

A review of readers' comments suggests some tips for editing. A copyeditor can understand why a story on China may carry a dateline of New York or Tokyo rather than Peking. That some readers are puzzled by this convention is shown in these comments: "Story started in New York, ended in China"; "Didn't quite get why we are relying on Japanese correspondents"; "Didn't get the connection between Red Guard and Tokyo."

When explanations are missing the story is bound to be confusing and unclear. The point is well illustrated in the first story used in the survey. The story's lead read, "TOKYO, Aug. 25 (AP) —A mob of teen-aged Red Guards today broke into Peking's Sacred Heart Academy, a Roman Catholic school run by French nuns, and hoisted a red flag over it." Who and what are the Red Guards? The story failed to explain until the fifteenth paragraph. Then it told the readers the Red Guards were mostly recent high school graduates who were on the loose because they couldn't enter colleges until the colleges were reorganized on a revolutionary basis.

Commented some readers: "Object of the story not clear"; "Could not figure out what the central part of the story was."

The analysis attempted more documentation than the first story but became snagged in numerous fragmentary quotes and in vague attributions for the quotations. The readers protested, "Too many quotations"; "Quotes can be out of context, especially with no credited sources"; "Confusing statements in quotation marks"; "Made quotes and then questioned them."

In general the reasons given for too-long stories were the same for both stories—that the material was repetitious and that both stories could have been condensed to a more readable, informative item. Many said that editing out the side plots in the first story would have made it a better and shorter story.

MEDICARE STORIES. The two stories on Medicare fared better than the stories on the Red Guards. This was especially true of the question and answer story, which was rated clear by 90 per cent of the readers. The straight story, readers said, used too many statistics and jumped around from one subject to another without fully explaining any one portion.

Cluttering by numbers is illustrated in one portion of the straight story, which reported that 17.3 million elected to pay $3 a month for optional doctor bill insurance, that the program started exactly at 12:01 a.m. and that 6,714 institutions—or 91 per cent of all the country's 7,347 general hospitals which have roughly 93 per cent of the beds—opened their doors for the insured care of all Americans aged 65 and over.

Reader comments included: "Too many statistics"; "Too involved in numbers"; "Just skimmed over the figures."

Seven of the nineteen paragraphs in the straight story were direct quotes or contained partial quotes. Two paragraphs of quotes were attributed to an unnamed source—"one Public Health Service official." Readers responded with "Facts and quotations not connected"; "Too many quotations of political speech"; "Am not interested in what the President had to say."

The question and answer story avoided most of the statistics and all the quotes, which may help to explain its preference by readers.

Readers placed high credence in both stories, especially the question and answer story (88 per cent said they thought the story completely true), possibly because the short, quick answers to specific questions looked more believable.

Those who thought the Medicare stories were too long said it was a vital subject but not one that persons of their age needed to go into in depth—that it would be many years before the subject would concern them directly. This would confirm the Schramm theory of reader identification with the news.

VIETNAM WAR STORIES. Reader responses to the Vietnam War stories showed that a story told in specific, individualized terms appeals to both men and women more than a story dealing with the subject in a broad, impersonal manner. The impact of the individualized story was even greater with women than with men. Although most readers said the wrap-up story gave more information than the vignette, the majority said they were more likely to read the vignette than the straight story.

Only one third of the women readers would have read all the straight story, whereas two thirds said they would have read all the vignette. More than 10 per cent of both sexes said they would have read none of either story. One third of the men and more than one half of the women readers said they did not read accounts of day-to-day action of the war.

The wrap-up story shows the problem of presenting a fresh approach to a continuing story. One day's report on a skirmish or bombing reads much like that of the previous day. Another problem is pinpointing for the reader where the action is taking place. Names of villages and rivers are meaningless unless the reader has a map. Typical comments: "Am tired of reading about Vietnam."; "It's the same thing over again."; "I just scan this type of article."; "Not familiar with locations cited."; "Need a map to follow the locations."

The general story used figures almost to the point of absurdity: "In attacking other targets in the north Thursday, pilots reported they destroyed or damaged 38 storage buildings, 59 barges, nine bridges and 20 trucks. U.S. pilots in the south said they destroyed or damaged 607 enemy huts, 21 bunkers and 20 sampans."

Readers put little faith in either story. Only about half the respondents felt either story was true. They expressed the belief that they were not getting all the facts about the war, that you couldn't believe the war stories: "Story vague, biased and false." Some said they would not have read the vignette because they did not feel it was a news story.

UNFAMILIAR TERMS. The readers cited nearly 100 terms with which they were unfamiliar in the three pairs of stories. Among the terms mentioned most frequently were

Bourgeoisie	Prognosis
Mao Tze-tung	Poo-poohed
Ideological	Compliance
Imperialism	Jubilant
Red Guard	Utilization review
Tientsin	Posthospital
Exploiting classes	Convalescent
Reactionary	Vietnamese names
Christianity too akin to imperialism	Ia Drang Valley
Reactionary academic authorities	Battalion
Militant	Regiment
Red Flag	

The survey also asked the readers to define ten World War II terms as follows:

	Men (%)	Women (%)
Dunkirk		
City in New England	10	16
Place of British retreat in World War II	85	80
English nobleman	2	1
Don't know	3	3
Blitz		
Fast-moving aerial and tank attack	95	89
Bad thunderstorm	1	3
German professor	2	5
Don't know	2	3
Gestapo		
Italian general	3	2
German Secret Police force	94	96
River in Italy	2	1
Don't know	1	1
Snafu		
Chinese politician	3	17
Town in India	9	14
Fouled-up situation	80	66
Don't know	4	7
Munich		
A dishonorable appeasement	61	49
Brand of beer	11	10
German politician	22	34
Don't know	6	7

Stuka

Town in Austria	19	21
German divebomber in World War II	70	54
Russian diplomat	8	14
Don't know	3	11

Blackout

Turning out all lights in war time	96	96
Musical show	3	4
Restricted area	1	—
Don't know	—	—

GI

Vietnamese general	—	1
U.S. industrial firm	1	—
Government Issue / American soldier	98	99
Don't know	1	—

Gobbledy-gook

A fast eater	5	1
Confused statement	86	90
Korean turkey	6	7
Don't know	3	2

Concentration camp

Gathering place for intellectuals	1	—
Camp for boy scouts	1	—
Prison for political prisoners	98	99
Don't know	—	1

The report concluded: "The answer given to these questions indicate that if World War II terms are used in news dispatches a sizeable number of young, well-educated adults would miss the connotation. If this group, who have had above average education, fail to understand these terms, we would anticipate a larger number of less well-educated young people would fail to interpret them correctly."

3

Tools and Rules

**The Copyeditor
and Policy**

The primary function of every newspaper is to present the news. What a paper selects to present and the way it presents it reveal the paper's tone and character. The overall policy set by an owner, publisher or editor determines whether the product is to be sensational or moderate, aggressive or restrained.

Selection and emphasis, then, are key elements in the whole process of editing, and the copyeditor's role in this is only slightly less than that of the various news executives.

In one sense, all copy has been edited before it reaches the copyeditor's hands. In selecting and arranging facts for a story, the reporter exercises an editing function. All wire copy goes through the editing process before it is delivered to the agency's clients. And when copy reaches the copydesk it has been selected and evaluated by a city editor, a wire editor, a news editor or a similar news executive. The desired length of the story may be noted on the copy, such as .25 (one fourth of a column) or "trim." The story's emphasis or importance is indicated by the headline order and whether or not the story is intended for the front page.

When the copyeditor receives the copy, he performs the final act of editing before the story gets into the paper. After he has gone through the story to find out what it is all about, he then turns to editing. He studies the story structure, the reporter's choice of words, the details, the unanswered questions—if any— and the story movement. He may mentally take the place of the readers. He asks himself, "Who will read this?" "How much of it will they read?" "Will they understand the story?" "Will the story bore them with too many details or leave them guessing because of too few details?"

He edits the copy as well as he can, writes the best headline he can compose and submits his efforts to the desk chief. If the story and headline pass the desk chief, the story will appear in the paper, at least for one edition, depending on the demands of other stories awaiting to be told.

The edited copy still has to pass other check points after it leaves the desk. The story is committed to type and one set of proofs goes to a proofreader. The proofreader compares the typescript with the galley proof but may question a point overlooked by the copyeditor. Another set of proofs goes to a news executive, who checks the editing and the headline.

Even with all the care taken to produce a readable story, the story still may wind up on the dead bank. This would happen, say, if the story appealed to a limited group in the paper's circulation area covered in one edition but would not appeal to readers in other areas covered in succeeding editions.

This is the real art of editing, from the top executive to those who actually process the copy. The processing requires certain tools and rules, which will be explained now.

By tradition, the copydesk (Figure 3–1) is a large desk shaped like a horseshoe. Inside the ring is the slot, and around the outside edge is the rim. The executive who occupies the slot is, obviously, the slotman.

The Slot and the Rim

Even on newspapers that have long since abandoned the horseshoe copydesk, the old terms survive. The desk chief is still referred to, on some publications, as the slotman. "Nailed on the rim" means that an error has been caught by a copyeditor.

Copy can be edited anywhere—on a typewriter desk, on one of the more sophisticated specialized desks or at a computer. On the smaller daily the copyeditor may be simultaneously the wire editor, city editor, deskman, reporter, proofreader and even editorial writer. He may operate from a typewriter desk, compose headlines on a typewriter and keep a mental account of copy flow. He prepares no makeup dummy. Instead, he goes to the composing room to direct makeup of page 1 and some of the inside pages. For him, editing is a secondary task.

On larger publications, editing is a specialty. The desk chief controls all the copy, doling out stories to the copyeditors, accepting or rejecting the edited version and headline, keeping a schedule of the copy and relaying the copy to the composing room. It may be a universal copydesk that processes copy from all departments—wire, syndicated material, local, sports, business, women's pages, Sunday edition. Or it may be a universal desk arranged in compartments, with each section handling only special types of copy. Or each department may have its own copydesk.

Whatever the system, someone has to determine what is acceptable for publication and how to accommodate the copy into the space available, how to keep the copy flowing and how to co-

Figure 3-1. The copydesk. This H-shaped copydesk serves both The *Courier-Journal* and The Louisville *Times* in Louisville, Kentucky. Each desk module in the H formation has a typewriter table connected at a right angle, and each table has a telephone as well as controls and earplugs for three color television sets placed above each end of the arrangement. This seating pattern provides working space for more than twenty copyeditors. In the foreground is the Kentucky and Indiana crew, and in the background are the foreign and national editors with their copyeditors. The center arm of the H is occupied by the news editor, assistant news editor, managing editor and assistant managing editor. The city editing crew is slightly off to one side of the big desk. [*Photo courtesy of The Courier-Journal and The Louisville Times.*]

ordinate the copydesk with other departments such as makeup and art.

The copydesk occupies a vital link between the news and mechanical departments. This relationship can be seen in the flow of copy. A story moves from a typewriter or a teletype machine to an editor (city, wire, sports, society, business, Sunday), from the editor to the copydesk where the copy is processed, then to the composing room where the copy is set into type, to the proofreaders who correct typographical errors on the galley proofs, to the ring machine (a linotype) where incorrect lines are reset, to the makeup department where type and pictures are assembled into a page form, to the stereotypers where mats impressed from the forms are molded into plates, to the presses and finally to the mailing or delivery room.

The executive who presides over the copydesk has many functions, one of the most important of which is to keep copy moving. Any delays on his desk throw the mechanical department off schedule and break the rhythm of newspaper production.

The desk chief gets performance on the desk by knowing which of his copyeditors can handle copy rapidly, which ones can perform under pressure and not panic. He knows the interests and specialties of each of his workers, whether they are experts on astronautics, Southeast Asian affairs or whatever. He trains the younger deskmen so that they, too, can produce as efficiently as the veterans.

A slotman can glance at a story and tell immediately whether the copy has been well-edited and whether the headline is accurate and clear. He, too, is a talented headline writer. Not only does he pass judgment on all headlines produced on the desk, but frequently he must revise a major headline or produce a new one.

Whether or not makeup is part of his job, he has to know the elements of page display and be able to make quick changes in makeup when the occasion arises.

He is the desk's arbiter on style, punctuation and grammar.

He anticipates the needs of future editions, such as the Sunday paper, and moves along plug copy or advance stories.

To perform his many tasks, he must know the nature of the day's news, the plans of the various departments for handling the news and the paper's overall news policies.

The man on the rim has the authority and responsibility to question every piece of copy put before him. He may challenge facts, words, grammar, organization and style. He may add to or subtract from the copy. The changes he makes are the final ones before the story gets into type. The headline he puts over a story determines, to a large extent, whether the reader will be induced to read the story.

To him, editing is a state of mind, not a mechanical job. So strong is the urge to edit that the copyeditor automatically keeps a copy pencil poised near whatever he is reading. He catches errors in advertisements, editorials and special departmental items whether or not his desk has edited copy for those sections. Reading critically is one of the acquired traits of a copyeditor.

When the deskman receives a piece of copy, he first notes the instructions supplied by the desk chief or some other editor. The information at the top of the copy may include the source, the slugline or identification, the head size, the page and edition, the set (column width and type size), the release time, the extent of the trim, whether the copy goes with art and sometimes certain indicators as to how the copy is to be handled. "R.C. Must" might mean that the editor wants this particular story used with few changes. BOM (business office must) copy is less sacred because it usually concerns a promotional item.

The copyeditor's skill tells him how to make copy more readable and more comprehensible. Judgment tells him what to leave in and what to take out. The beginner is likely to be too timid in editing. He checks for errors but hesitates to use his pencil as a screw to tighten the story. If he must shorten the story, he is more likely to delete whole paragraphs than to excise within sentences. Few stories are so tightly written that they can defy the editing pencil. Even if the editing conserves no more than one or two words in each line of copy, the accumulated space saving during the day can amount to more than a galley of type. A copyeditor who can reduce a story by the equivalent of one paragraph without robbing the story of a necessary detail or one touch of color earns his pay on the desk.

If he must take out large chunks from the story, he should alert the slotman. It is possible that an editor in another department already has marked in, or dummied, the unedited story on a page. If the story has been cut in half on the copydesk, the page plan (dummy) will have to be corrected.

After he has edited the copy and written a headline, the deskman takes a final appraisal. The mental inventory goes something like this:

Does the edited version read smoothly?

Are the instructions for the composing room clear and complete?

Does the headline accurately reflect the story?

Does the slug appear on both the story and the headline copy?

Have I indicated at the top of the copy the length of the edited story?

Have I put my initials on the copy so the desk chief will know who edited the story?

After submitting the copy to the slotman, some copyeditors perform a final act. They jot down the story slug and head size. This allows the copyeditor to keep track of his own production. It also protects him should he be accused of committing an error in a story he did not edit.

The slugline consists of one or two words and is used to match the headline and story after both have been set into type. The following is an example: Hotel blaze—#2. The "#2" indicates the headline size.

Given the conditions under which a copyeditor must work, it is a miracle that any story can be thoroughly and intelligently edited. Few people in a newspaper office have more persons crowding their elbows than the men and women on the copydesk. Yet the copyeditor must learn to tune out his deskmates, to shut out the din of the typewriters and the teletypes, to ignore the parade that constantly passes the desk. He knows he has to check words, verify facts and names, polish the copy and write an acceptable headline within a matter of minutes. He has no time to brood or to reflect or even to change his mind. Either he beats the clock or he gets off the desk.

He is a lonely man in a busy corner of a crowded room. He is allowed few possessions in his little nook—a few copy pencils, a paste pot, an eraser, a tear-rule or shears, a stack of half-sheet copy paper. If he is fortunate enough to have a desk drawer, he can store the headline schedule and stylebook (when available), a pocket dictionary, a thesaurus, a map, an almanac and perhaps some clippings.

If copy were his only concern, he could be reasonably happy and secure and have satisfaction in his performance. But there is the desk chief, who has his own pressures and irritations, his own whims and idiosyncrasies, his own feelings about how the copy should be edited and what the headline should say. Much of the effort on the desk, therefore, is spent in personality accommodation. The desk chief has to find the right devices to prod, wheedle, coax or praise his deskmen. They, in turn, study the slotman to determine what pleases or displeases him. A competent, confident, compassionate slotman can make the desk a pleasant world. He can make it an efficient one, too, provided he has men opposite him who are willing to learn.

One of the most efficient slotmen ever employed by the Hearst newspapers never spoke to the men on the rim. He penciled short notes with instructions and criticisms. He was a cold, hard taskmaster who knew his business, and as such he was respected. But he was a machine who thought of the rim-men as machines. Today there are very few like him. Most slotmen think of the deskmen as persons, as stated above, and seek to get the person's best from each of them.

In its critique, *Hits & Misses* (February 1966), the Wilmington (Del.) *News* offered this advice to copyeditors from its compiler, Charles T. Alexander, Jr.:

Copyediting is a sport, despite what many unsporting souls might call it. H&M—referred to variously as the copyeditor's best friend and worst enemy—offers some guidance in the form of a "mixed sportaphor":

1. Be relaxed, but don't be lax. You can handle a story only as quickly as you can comprehend it. Don't press; remove all other considerations from your mind and concentrate on that story to the exclusion of all else.

2. Keep your head down. Small talk is essential on a copydesk in slack times to relieve tension; it is a menace in times of heavy copy flow since it distracts others from their work for no good purpose. Remarks addressed to the slot concerning a particular story are not disruptive; remarks addressed to the assemblage are.

3. Do a few laps every hour. In times of heavy copy flow, you need a moment's relaxation periodically. Get up and get a drink of water, go to the rest room, or just walk around a minute before tackling another story. But don't take too long; you're needed as soon as you get the kinks out.

4. Always follow through. If an editing change is intricate, make the change, then copyread your own handiwork. A rereading will turn up those extra or missing words that a hasty pencil missed as you were unscrambling the mess.

5. Don't switch mounts in mid-race. Every time you see a name in a story ask yourself two questions: Is this the first reference or has the person been fully identified before? Is this the same name that was used in previous references? It is not uncommon for "Trevor Jones" to become "Trevor" in the course of a story or for "John Jones, president of the Andrews Corp.," to become "Andrews."

---

6. Don't break stride. Reporters may bring over additional material or it may come from the wire desk. Be sure that the alteration reads in smoothly and does not conflict with other material that remains in the story. If you are in the midst of an involved change when such material arrives, complete the procedure at hand and then make the change. Others will rave and rail at your methodical handling, but you won't have to answer embarrassing questions later.

7. Compete in one event at a time. Don't try to handle two or more stories at once.

8. Be confident. You may not be proud of the job you do in reading every story or in every headline you come up with; but you can come up with something reasonably acceptable, no matter how great the pressure, and confidence will go a long way toward making it a better "something" than if you spend your time feeling sorry for yourself because you have been subjected to this pressure. The fact that you got the copy under such conditions reflects confidence on the part of the slot that you will do an acceptable job with it.

9. Don't look back. You'll blow one occasionally, no matter how good you are. Take a minute or two to figure out why you blew it and if there is something you can do to guard against a recurrence, but don't brood about it. It's your average that counts. If your performance is generally good, you can stand a few losses—even the heartbreakers.

Symbolic Communication

The copyeditor uses symbols to communicate with the composing room or with perforators (Figure 3–2a, b, c). Marks used

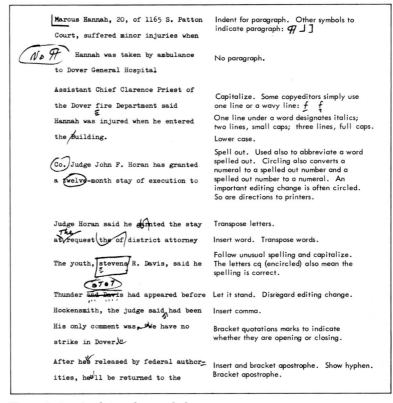

Figure 3–2a. Applying the symbols.

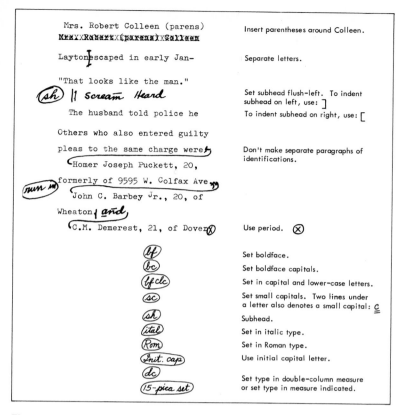

Mrs. Robert Colleen (parens)	Insert parentheses around Colleen.
~~Mrs. Robert (parens) Colleen~~	
Layton escaped in early Jan-	Separate letters.
"That looks like the man."	
(sh) || Scream Heard	Set subhead flush-left. To indent subhead on left, use:]
The husband told police he	To indent subhead on right, use: [
Others who also entered guilty	
pleas to the same charge were;	Don't make separate paragraphs of identifications.
Homer Joseph Puckett, 20,	
(run in) formerly of 9595 W. Colfax Ave.	
John C. Barbey Jr., 20, of	
Wheaton, and,	
C.M. Demerest, 21, of Dover⊗	Use period. ⊗
(bf)	Set boldface.
(bc)	Set boldface capitals.
(bf clc)	Set in capital and lower-case letters.
(sc)	Set small capitals. Two lines under a letter also denotes a small capital: c
(sh)	Subhead.
(ital)	Set in italic type.
(Rom)	Set in Roman type.
(Init. cap)	Use initial capital letter.
(dc)	Set type in double-column measure
(15-pica set)	or set type in measure indicated.

Figure 3–2b. Applying the symbols, continued.

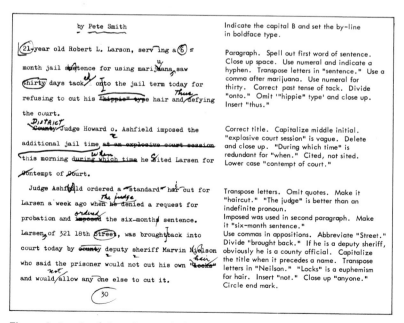

by Pete Smith	Indicate the capital B and set the by-line in boldface type.
(21) year old Robert L. Larson, serv ing a (6) =	Paragraph. Spell out first word of sentence. Close up space. Use numeral and indicate a hyphen. Transpose letters in "sentence." Use a comma after marijuana. Use numeral for thirty. Correct past tense of tack. Divide "onto." Omit '"hippie" type' and close up. Insert "thus."
month jail sentence for using marijuana, saw	
thirty days tack, onto the jail term today for	
refusing to cut his "hippie" type hair and defying	
the court.	
District County Judge Howard o. Ashfield imposed the	Correct title. Capitalize middle initial. "explosive court session" is vague. Delete and close up. "During which time" is redundant for "when." Cited, not sited. Lower case "contempt of court."
additional jail time, at an explosive court session	
this morning during which time he cited Larsen for	
contempt of Court.	
Judge Ashfield ordered a "standard" hair cut for	Transpose letters. Omit quotes. Make it "haircut." "The judge" is better than an indefinite pronoun. Imposed was used in second paragraph. Make it "six-month sentence." Use commas in appositions. Abbreviate "Street." Divide "brought back." If he is a deputy sheriff, obviously he is a county official. Capitalize the title when it precedes a name. Transpose letters in "Neilson." "Locks" is a euphemism for hair. Insert "not." Close up "anyone." Circle end mark.
Larsen a week ago when The judge denied a request for	
probation and ordered the six-months sentence.	
Larsen, of 321 18th Street, was brought back into	
court today by county deputy sheriff Marvin Nielson	
who said the prisoner would not cut his own hair "locks"	
and would not allow any one else to cut it.	
(30)	

Figure 3–2c. Applying the symbols, continued.

on copy should indicate to the composing room precisely what the copydesk wants. Some general pointers follow:

1. Copy should be marked in bold, black strokes. If words or phrases are crossed out, the remainder should be closed up with connecting lines. If a paragraph is deleted, the copyeditor uses a connecting line to guide the compositor. Even excessively edited copy will pose no problem in the composing room if the editing marks are neat and distinct. If the reporter strikes over a letter, the copyeditor prints the correct letter over the strike-over. If the copyeditor wants the eighth paragraph of a story moved to the third paragraph, he clips and pastes. He does not use arrows. The compositor or the perforator must have copy in proper sequence. Marks used above typewritten lines are easier to follow than marks below the line or in margins.

2. On all copy except Teletypesetter (TTS), editing marks are placed within the copy itself. On TTS copy, the copy is treated as a galley proof, and marks are placed in the margins.

3. Wire services number each item sent on the circuit. This is the book number. It is especially important in TTS copy because of tape handling. If a TTS story has a new lead, the deskman must preserve the book numbers of both the original and the alteration.

4. Slugs are all-important. They indicate the route of the copy. On the first page of story copy, the following generally is included: the slug of the story (Fire), the department (City), the zone, the edition (One Star), the writer and, if appropriate, his source or the rewriteman (Smith—Gallagher). The end of the first page ends with the notation MORE. Each succeeding page bears the story slug and page number. On a story handled in takes (each section on separate sheets), the notation is more complete: First Add Fire . . . City . . . One Star. And the copy is left open by writing MORE at the bottom of each take until the final one. It is slugged as follows: Fourth and last add Fire . . . City . . . One Star. It ends with an endmark. A story marked 30's Music Bureau Smith 40 3 Wagon indicates that the story must be used that day, that it has a 30-point head, that the first two words of the head are Music Bureau, that the writer is Smith, that the story is forty type lines long and that the story is accompanied by a three-column picture slugged "wagon."

As soon as the deskman has edited the final take, he writes the headline. If he has a story and carbon, he edits the original, sends it to the composing room and writes the head from the carbon. Or, near an edition deadline, he may edit the first take, slug it HTK (head to come), edit the remaining takes, then write the headline. He may make notes while editing the first take to refresh his memory for the headline. He usually notes the take number. An "Add 2" is the third take, not the second. A *take* is a portion of a story, usually no more than one-half sheet of copy paper.

5. The endmark (30, #, // or 2) is important and must be included. Without one of these marks the type could end up on the hold bank in the composing room awaiting additions.

6. If additional material on a story comes in after the story has left the desk, the deskman uses a proof, called a fix (or mark or marker), to show where new material is to go. He marks the galley CX (or Makeup) to show that the proof is to go directly to the forms, bypassing the copy-cutter and the ring machines. A new lead forces the editor to show the lines of the old story that are to be deleted in favor of the new lead and the remaining part of the story that is to be picked up, designated by the notation "pick up." If it is to be an insertion within the story, the deskman again calls for the marker and shows on the galley proof where the insertion is to go by using the guide TR for insert A. A second insert within the same story would be marked TR for insert B. TR is a direction to the printer to turn a rule in the galley of type so he will know where the insertion is to be placed. TS, or turn slug, means the same thing.

7. In communicating with the composing room, the deskman leaves nothing to chance. If a story has an accompanying picture, the notation on the copy...w/2-col. cut...alerts the makeup man to match picture and story. If a *precede* tops a story, the copyeditor uses slugs to guide the makeup man. A *follow* story must show unmistakably what story it is to follow. Material, such as *side bars*, may be inserted anywhere within the body of a story and is frequently called a *floater*. The deskman may indicate that the copy is to be set boldface, indented and ruled top and bottom. The slug of the story into which the floater is to be inserted is retained. The deskman communicates daily with the composing room, yet he may never have the opportunity to go there. If the symbols the deskman uses are adequate, all goes well.

Matters of Style

Style rules have one virtue. They help to assure consistency throughout the paper. Style is arbitrary, varying from paper to paper, but without some guidelines, usage would be entirely at the whims of the compositor or the tape puncher.

Some newspapers stubbornly cling to a peculiar style—usually spelling—even though they are in a minority. The Fort Collins *Coloradoan*, for instance, will not recognize *Coloradan* even though it is the common spelling throughout the state. The Chicago *Tribune* insists on the shortened form for some words and abbreviations: altho, tho, thru, av.

Usage does not always employ logic. Once *Viet Nam* and *Vietnamese* were used. Eventually the wire services changed to *Vietnam*.

Although good reasons can be given for excessive compounding, hyphens certainly would help readers comprehend some words more quickly: transatlantic (trans-Atlantic), bobsledding

[*Courtesy of the Baltimore Evening Sun.*]

(bob-sledding), weightlifting (weight-lifting), followup (follow-up), antiaircraft (anti-aircraft).

Similarly, some newspaper-preferred spellings may be more recognizable in longer forms: employee, busses, kidnapped (all approved in dictionaries).

Style is the user's preference. The leading arbiter for the majority of daily newspapers is the joint newswire stylebook issued by Associated Press and United Press International. Trouble ensues when a newspaper tries to use both the newswire stylebook and its own style. For example, a paper decrees that numerals be used exclusively, even starting a sentence. A local story starts as follows: "2 boys were arrested. . . ." Next to this is a wire story: "Two boys were arrested. . . ." Surely many readers will wonder whether the paper's right hand knows what its left hand is doing.

Rules governing style are given in Appendix I. Comments on style are in Chapter 4.

4

Style Notes

Shakespeare knew the value of a name. In *Othello* he had Iago say, "But he that filches from me my good name / Robs me of that which not enriches him / And makes me poor indeed." A name misspelled is a person misidentified. Of all the errors a newspaper is capable of making, the most serious is a misspelled or a misused name. In radio and television it is the mispronounced name.

One of the important functions of the copyeditor is to make sure that all names in the copy are double-checked. The proper form is the form the person uses. He may be Alex rather than Alexander, Jim rather than James, Will rather than William. He may or may not have a middle initial, with or without a period (Harry S Truman). Anyone resents an attempt at cleverness where his name is concerned. Such "cuteness" should be felled on sight:

> Orange County will have a lemon as district attorney. Jack Lemon was elected to the job yesterday.

> Of the five patrolmen on the staff, two are crooks.

> The last name was Crook.

A title generally precedes a name unless it is a long title. It is Harley F. Taylor, principal of Philip C. Showell School, rather than Philip C. Showell School Principal Harley F. Taylor.

Nor should the story make the reader guess at the identification. Here is an example:

Identifications

Albert A. Ballew took issue with Mayor Locher today for announcing in advance that the post of administrative assistant in the Safety Department will be filled by a Negro.

The president of the Collinwood Improvement Council commended the mayor for creating the post, but added. . . .

Now then, who is the president of the Collinwood Improvement Council? Will readers assume it is Ballew? The solution is so simple: "Ballew, president of the Collinwood Improvement Council, commended the mayor. . . ."

A married woman or a widow, if addressed as *Mrs.*, is referred to by her husband's Christian name, not by hers. It is Mrs. John Smith. If he dies, it is still Mrs. John Smith. If they are divorced, it is Mrs. Helen Smith. If a woman has become well known by her maiden name and wishes to be known by that name professionally after she is married, that is her privilege. But it is incorrect to make her half maiden and half married. It is Mrs. Richard Harris Jr., not Mrs. Dorothy Harris Jr. Her husband may be Jr., but she is not.

A maiden name can cause trouble: "He married the former Constance Coleman in 1931." This is incorrect; Constance Coleman was Constance Coleman when he married her. He married Constance Coleman. His wife is the former Constance Coleman.

Mrs. and *Miss* are used with all adult female names because they are needed to denote marital status. Use *Miss* with high school students and older.

Woman is used as a general descriptive possessive—woman's rights. *Women's* is used as a specific—women's club (but Woman's Christian Temperance Union). It is women fliers, Young Women's Christian Association, women workers, but woman suffrage. It is never the Smith woman.

Jewess and *Negress* may be offensive. A Jew can be a man or a woman; so can a Negro.

Foreign names are tricky. In Spanish-speaking countries, individuals usually have two last names, the father's and the mother's—Adolfo Lopez Mateos. On second reference, Lopez Mateos should be used. In headlines, Lopez Mateos is preferred, but Lopez will do.

A Chinese family name is usually given first, and the second part of the hyphenated name is given in lower case—Chiang Kai-shek, Lee Su-kun. On second reference, use Chiang, not Kai-shek.

In Arab names, *al* generally is hyphenated—al-Sabah, al-Azhar. Some Arabs drop the article—Mamoun Kuzbari, not al-Kuzbari. Compound names should be left intact—Abdullah, Abdel, Abdur. Pasha and Bey titles have been abolished. Royal titles are used with first names—Emir Faisel, Sheik Abdullah. *Haj* is used with the first name in both first and subsequent references—Haj Amin al-Hussein, Haj Amin.

The *U* in Burmese names means uncle, our equivalent of *Mr.* *Thakin* means master. *Daw* means Mrs. or Miss. Many Burmese have only one name—U Thant. If a Burmese has two names, both should be used—U Tin Maung, Tin Maung.

Some Koreans put the family name first—Kim Il-sung. The second reference should be Kim, not Il-sung, the given name.

Many Indonesians have only one name—Sukarno, not Achmed Sukarno.

Swedish surnames usually end in *–son*, and Danish names usually end in *–sen.*

Put nicknames in parentheses, not in quotes. Thereafter in the story the nickname needs no punctuation.

Trade Names

Few editors have escaped letters that begin something like this: "Dear Sir: The attached clipping from your paper of July 14th contains a mention of our product and we very much appreciate this unsolicited publicity. However, the name of our product was used with a lower-case "c." As you know. . . ."

Makers of trade-name products want to protect their rights under the Lanham Trademark Act of 1947 and insist that in any reference to the product name the manufacturer's spelling and capitalization be used. This is to protect the trade name from becoming generic, such as aspirin, cellophane, escalator, milk of magnesia, zipper, linoleum, thermos, and shredded wheat.

Much of the confusion and protest can be eliminated simply by using a generic term rather than the specific trade name—petroleum jelly for Vaseline, freezer for Deepfreeze, fiber glass for Fiberglass, tranquilizer for Miltown, expanded polystyrene for Styrofoam.

Where the product is trade-named and there is no substitute, the trade name should be used, especially if it is pertinent to the story. The withholding of such information on the ground of free publicity is niggardly.

Institutions should be labeled correctly—Bell Telephone System, not Bell Telephone Company; Lloyd's, not Lloyd's of London; D'Oyly Carte; J.C. Penney Co. (Penneys in ads, Penney's in other usages); American Geographical Society; National Geographic Society.

Simple Arithmetic?

Time magazine in its letters column admitted it slipped on mathematics. A reader complained as follows: "As mathematicians, *Time* et al. couldn't pass a seventh-grade arithmetic test. 'Over the past ten years M.I.T.'s gain: 365%. Thus $1,000 invested in M.I.T. shares ten years ago would be worth $3,650 today.' You get zero on that one. My twelve-year-old says to tell you it's $4,650. In the same sentence you state that if same amount had been in savings bank over same interim at $3\frac{1}{4}\%$, it would grow to $1,417. Honest, boys, it wouldn't. The twelve-year-old volunteers that $1,000 at $3\frac{1}{2}\%$ compounded quarterly for ten years would hit $1,417. Maybe that's what you meant." The editor's reply: "*Time,* zero; twelve-year-old, 100%."

Chided for failing to catch a simple arithmetical error, a student copyeditor explained, "I never was any good at figures. That's why I chose journalism over mathematics." But copyeditors do have to know some arithmetic. For instance, they should know the difference between percentages and percentage points: "Jones pointed out that the retail markup for most other brands is approximately 33 per cent, whereas the markup on Brand J is 50 per cent, or 17 per cent higher." No. It is 51.5 per cent higher. Divide 17 by 33.

"Dover's metropolitan population jumped from 16,000 ten years ago to more than 23,000 last year, an increase of better than 70 per cent." Wrong again. It's a little less than 44 per cent.

A story reported a prediction that 39 per cent of the South's college-age youth would be enrolled in southern colleges and universities by 1970, as compared with the present 29 per cent. The head read **10 pct. enrollment boost/goal in southern colleges.** Actually, the increase would be about 35 per cent.

Percentages can be misleading. A statement that a company's profit is up 50 per cent may mean little. A profit of $1,500 this year compared with $1,000 last year is an increase of 50 per cent but is still a small profit. A struggling young college that boasts a 100 per cent increase in enrollment is still small even if the number of students increased from 100 to 200.

Is the figure misleading or inaccurate? The story said, "A total of $6,274 was raised at each of the four downtown stations." This adds up to $25,096. What was meant was that "A total of $6,274 was raised at four stations." A not-so-sharp deskman let this one get by: "Almost 500,000 slaves were shipped in this interstate trade. When one considers the average price of $800, the trade accounted for almost $20 million."

Are terms representing figures vague? In inheritance stories, it is better to name the amount and let the reader decide whether the amount is a "fortune." One of the wire service editors noted, "Fifteen thousand might be a fortune to a bootblack, but $200,-000 would not be a fortune to a Rockefeller."

For some reason, many stories contain gambling odds, chances and probabilities. When a princess gave birth to a son, reporters quickly snatched on to the odds on his name. Anthony was 1:2, George was even money and Albert was 3:1. One headline played up the third in the betting. The name chosen was David, an 18:1 shot. All of this shows the foolishness of newsmen who play into the hands of gamblers. If odds must be included in the story, they should be accurate. The story said that because weather records showed that in the last eighty-six years it had rained only nineteen times on May 27, the odds were 8:1 against rain for the big relay event. The odds mean nothing to readers except to those who like to point out that in the story just mentioned the odds actually were $3\frac{1}{2}$:1.

"Dr. Frank Rubovits said the children came from a single egg. He said the chance of this occurring 'probably is about 3 million to 1.'" He meant the odds against this occurring. The chance of this occurring is 1 in 3 million.

"The Tarapur plant will be the world's second largest atomic generator of electricity. The largest will be the 500-ton megawatt plant at Hinkley Point in Britain." A 500-ton megawatt plant makes no sense. What the writer meant was a 500-megawatt plant.

Some readers may rely on the idiom and insist that "five times as much as" means the same as "five times higher than" or "five times more than." If so, five times as much as $50 is $250 and five times higher than $50 is still $250. Others contend that the second should be $300. If earnings this year are 3½ times as large as last year's, they are actually 2½ times larger than last year's.

Insist on this style: 40,000 to 50,000 miles, not 40 to 50,000 miles; $3 million to $5 million, not $3 to $5 million.

"The committee recommended that a bid of $26,386.60 be accepted. After recommending the higher bid, the committee also had to recommend that an additional $326.60 be appropriated for the fire truck, since only $26,000 was included in the budget." The sum is still $60 short of the bid.

Equivalents should be included in stories that contain large sums. Most readers cannot visualize $20 billion, but they can understand it if there is an indication as to how much the amount would mean to each individual.

Unless the stories contain the common equivalent for measurements, the deskman has the job of supplying the equivalents so the reader can understand the story. Some of these conversions are listed in Appendix I. Here are others:

G, G force, is gravitational pull equal to about 32 feet per second per second in acceleration. Thus a flier (plane, rocket) subjected to a force of 5 G's is accelerating at five times the force of gravity at the earth's surface, or roughly at a rate of 160 feet per second per second.

Mach numbers refer to the speed of a body (aircraft, missile) in relation to the speed of sound. Mach 2 would be twice the speed of sound. A rule of thumb for speed of sound is 750 miles an hour at sea level and 660 miles an hour at 30,000 feet.

Thrust is the measure of a driving force, or power, expressed in pounds. Jet engine and rocket powers are expressed in pounds. Thrust in pounds times speed in miles an hour divided by 375 converts thrust to horsepower.

Nothing is duller or more unreadable than a numbers story. If figures are the important part of the story, they should be related to something—or at least presented as comparisons.

Two of the most common mathematical errors in news copy are the use of millions for billions and vice versa and a construction such as "Five were injured . . ." with only four persons listed.

Financial News   A news release from a bank included the following: "The book value of each share outstanding will approximate $21.87 on Dec. 31, and if the current yield of 4.27 per cent continues to bear the same relationship to the market price it should rise to $32 or $33, according to . . ." The desk changed the ambiguous *it* to *the book value.* Actually, the release intended *it* to refer to the market price, which shows what can happen when the desk-man changes copy without knowing what he's doing.

Another story quoted an oil company official as saying that "the refinery would mean $7,000,000 in additional real estate taxes." It should have been obvious that this was a wholly un-realistic figure, but for good measure there was an ad in the same paper that placed the total tax figure at around $200,000 and said, "The initial installation will add about $7,000,000 a year to the economy of the state, not including taxes."

A story and headline said the interest on the state debt ac-counted for 21 per cent of the state government's spending. An accompanying graph showed, however, that the figure was for debt service, which includes both interest and amortization.

All who edit copy for financial pages should have at least some elementary knowledge of business terms. If they can't distin-guish between a balance sheet and a profit and loss statement, between earnings and gross operating income, and between a net profit and net cash income, they have some homework to do.

This was brought home by a syndicated financial columnist who cautioned business news desks against using misleading headlines such as **Stocks plummet—Dow Jones average off 12 points.** It may be a loss, the columnist noted, but hardly a calam-ity. Dow Jones may indicate that the market is up, whereas it is actually sinking. Freak gains by a few of the thirty stocks in the Dow may have pushed up that particular indicator. Nor does a slight market drop call for a headline such as **Investors lose millions in market value of stocks.** They lost nothing of the sort. On that day, countless investors the nation over had substantial paper profits on their stocks. If they sold, they were gainers on the buying price in real terms; if they held, they had neither gains nor losses.

The Dow Jones Industrial Average is one of several indexes used to gauge the stock market. Each uses its own statistical technique to show market changes. The Dow Jones bases its index on thirty stocks. It is an index-number change, not a per-centage change.

Reports of dividends should use the designation given by the firm (regular, special, extra, increases, interim) and show what was paid previously if there is no specified designation such as regular or quarterly.

The story should say if there is a special, or extra, dividend paid with the regular dividend and include the amount of pre-vious added payments. When the usual dividend is passed, or reduced, some firms issue an explanatory statement, the gist of which should be included in the story.

Newswire stylebooks recommend that news of corporate activities and business and financial news should be stripped of technical terms. There should be some explanation of the firm's business (plastics, rubber, electronics) if there is no indication of the nature of the business in the firm's name. The location of the firm should be carried.

Savings and loan firms object to being called banks. Some commercial banks likewise object when savings and loan firms are called banks. There need be no confusion if the institution is identified by its proper name. In subsequent references the words *firm* or *institution* are used. Some newspapers permit *S&L Firm* in tight headlines. Actually a *firm* is a partnership or unincorporated group. It should not be used for an incorporated company. *Concern* is a better word for the latter.

Jargon has no place in the business story. "Near-term question marks in the national economy—either of which could put a damper on the business expansion—are residential housing and foreign trade, the Northern Trust company said in its December issue of *Business Comments*." Are near-term question marks economy question marks? If so, can they put a damper on anything? Isn't all housing residential?

Major producers scrambled today to adjust steel prices to newly emerging industry-wide patterns. . . . The welter of price changes was in marked contrast with the old time industry practice of posting across-the-board hikes.

This approach apparently breathed its last in April, 1962, when it ran into a Kennedy administration buzzsaw, and a general price boost initiated then by United States Steel corporation, the industry giant, collapsed under White House fire.

Readers of financial pages read for information. False color is not needed to retain these readers. The following story should have been butchered on the desk:

Stock of the Communications Satellite Corporation went into an assigned orbit yesterday on three major stock exchanges, rocketing to an apogee of $46 a share and a perigee of $42 and closing at $42.37, unchanged.

It was the first day of listed trading on the exchanges. The stock previously was traded over-the-counter.

The countdown on the first transaction on the New York stock exchange was delayed 12 minutes by an initial jam of buy and sell orders. . . .

Death Stories

Persons die of heart *illness,* not "failure"; after a *long* illness, not an "extended" illness; *unexpectedly,* not "suddenly"; *outright,* not "instantly"; *following* or *after* an operation, not "as a result of" an operation; *apparently of a heart attack,* not of an "apparent heart attack."

The age of the person who died is important to the reader. The deskman should check the age given with the year of birth. Generally, the person's profession or occupation, the extent of the illness and the cause of the death are recorded, but without details. The length of the story is dictated by the fame of the person. Winston Churchill's obit ran eighteen pages in the New York *Times*.

A person *leaves* an estate; he is *survived* by his family. Usage varies as to whether he is survived by his wife or his widow. He is survived by his children if they are children and by sons and daughters if they are adults.

If the family requests that the story include the statement that donations may be made to such-and-such organization, the statement should be used. Whether such a statement should contain the phrase "in lieu of flowers" is a matter of policy. Some papers, in deference to florists, do not carry the phrase.

A straightforward account of a death is better than one told euphemistically. The plain terms are *died,* not "passed away" or "succumbed"; *body,* not "remains" or "corpse"; *coffin,* not "casket"; *funeral* or *services,* not "obsequies"; *burial,* not "interment," unless interred in a tomb above the ground. Flowery expressions such as "two of whom reside in St. Louis" and "became associated with the blank company shortly after college" show no more respect for the dead than do the plain expressions "live in St. Louis" or "went to work for the blank company."

Few stories in a newspaper are more addicted to formula writing than the obituary. There isn't much the desk can do about the conventional style except to contrast it with those that take a fresh approach. Here is a lead from an Associated Press story:

New York—If you are a movie fan, you will remember Mary Boland as the fluttery matron, the foolishly fond mother, the ladylike scatterbrain.
The character actress who died yesterday at the age of 80 was none of these in real life.

The deskman should be on guard for the correct spelling of all names used in the death story and for slips such as "cemetary" for *cemetery* and "creamation" for *cremation.* Errors are inexcusable:

A post mortem failed to disclose the cause of death because the girl's body was too badly decomposed.

Thousands followed the cortege. The thousands must have been *in,* not "following," the cortege (the funeral procession). Even after death, a medal won by a serviceman is awarded to him. It may be presented to his widow, but it is not awarded to his widow.

If the service is held at a funeral establishment, the name of the funeral establishment should be included for the convenience of mourners. It is not a "funeral home." A funeral service is held *at* a place, not *from* it. A mass is *offered;* a funeral service is *held.*

The passage should leave no doubt for whom the service was held. This one did leave doubt: "Services for 7-year-old Michael L———, son of a Genoa Intermediate School District official who was struck and killed by a car Monday in Bay City, will be held. . . ."

People are *people,* not "assaults" or "traffic deaths" or "fatals" or "dead on arrivals":

A youth stabbed at a downtown intersection and a woman pedestrian run down by a car were among assaults on six persons reported to police during the night.

Hugo woman / among nine / traffic deaths

Dead on arrival at Hurley after the crash was Oscar W——, who was decapitated.

The events in a person's life that should be included in his obituary pose a problem for the desk. One story recited the death of a former school administrator who died at the age of 87. It said he had been the first principal of blank high school and had served in that capacity for seventeen years. Then the story recalled that he resigned two months before he was found guilty of taking $150 from the school yearbook fund and was fined $500. Should an account of a minor crime committed a quarter of a century ago be included in the obituary? To those who knew the former principal intimately the old theft was not news. Those who didn't know him so intimately could hardly care about the single flaw in an otherwise distinguished career.

Medical news

Reporters and copyeditors have no business playing doctor. If a child is injured in an accident, the seriousness of the injury should be determined by medical authorities. To say that a person who was not even admitted to the hospital was "seriously injured" is editorializing.

Hospitals may report that a patient is in a "guarded condition," but the term has no meaning for the reader and should be spiked. The same goes for "he is resting comfortably."

No one can sustain a "fractured leg." He may sustain a *fracture of the leg* or a *leg fracture* or, better still, simply a *broken leg.* Injuries are *suffered,* not *received.*

A story described a murder suspect as "a diabetic of the worst type who must have 15 units of insulin daily." The quotes were attributed to the FBI. An editor commented, "In my book, that is a mild diabetic, unless the story means that the suspect is a diabetic who requires 15 units of regular insulin before each meal.

A wire service should not rely on the FBI for diagnosis of diabetes and the severity of the case."

Another story said that Charles De Gaulle peered myopically through his thick-lensed spectacles. An ophthalmologist objected, in a letter to *Time* (March 20, 1966): "As is the case with the vast majority of people who have undergone cataract surgery, he now peers hyperopically through his thick-lensed spectacles."

The name of the doctor can be used in a medical news story under these circumstances:

1. If he is the attending physician to a prominent person, such as a governor, the President or the Pope.

2. If he is the officially designated spokesman for his medical society.

3. If his medical society has furnished his name as one from whom authoritative information may be obtained in his specialty and he has consented to the use of his name.

4. If he is an official, such as a state epidemiologist, the doctor is treated the same as any other individual in the news.

Doctor and *scientist* are vague words to many readers. *Doctor* may be a medical doctor, a dentist, a veterinarian, an osteopath, a minister or a professor. The story would be clearer if it named the doctor's specialty or the scientist's specific activity, whether biology, physics, electronics or astronautics.

Medical doctors diagnose the illness, not the patient. The proper term to use in determining the remedy or in forecasting the probable course and termination of a disease is *prognosis*.

Mothers are *delivered;* babies are *born*.

A person dies *of* a disease, not *from* a disease.

Everyone has a temperature. *Fever* describes above-normal temperature.

Everyone has a heart condition. It is news only if someone's heart is in bad condition.

"The wife of the governor underwent major surgery and physicians reported she apparently had been cured of a malignant tumor." It is unlikely that any doctor said she was *cured* of a malignant tumor. They avoid that word with malignant growths.

"A team of five surgeons performed a hysterectomy, appendectomy and complete abdominal exploration." Why the unnecessary details? It would have been enough to say, "Five surgeons performed the abdominal operation."

Unless they are essential to the story, trade names of narcotics or poisons should be avoided. If a person dies of an overdose of sleeping pills, the story should not specify the number of pills taken.

Also, use *Caesarean section* or *Caesarean operation*.

Usually, no sane person has his leg broken or his pockets picked. Use the passive tense: "His leg was broken"; "His pockets were picked."

Use the expression *physicians and dentists,* not *doctors and dentists.* The second suggests that dentists are not doctors.

A doctor who specializes in anesthesia is an anesthesiologist, not an anesthetist.

A person may wear a sling on his right arm. He doesn't wear his right arm in a sling.

"He suffered a severed tendon in his right Achilles heel last winter." It was the Achilles tendon in his right heel or his right Achilles' tendon.

"A jaundice epidemic also was spreading in Gaya, Indian health officials said. The second disease claimed 30 lives." Jaundice is not a disease but a sign of the existence of one or another of a great many diseases.

Technical terms should be translated:

Term	Translation	Term	Translation
Abrasions	Scrapes	Suturing	Sewing
Contusions	Bruises	Hemorrhaging	Bleeding
Lacerations	Cuts	Obese	Fat
Fracture	Break	Respire	Breathe

Weather

An editor said, "Ever since the National Weather Service started naming hurricanes after females, reporters can't resist the temptation to be cute." He then cited the lead, "Hilda—never a lady and now no longer a hurricane—spent the weekend in Louisiana, leaving behind death, destruction and misery." That, the editor said, is giddy treatment for a disaster causing thirty-five deaths and millions in property damage.

Another editor noted that a story referred to "the turbulent eye of the giant storm." He remonstrated that the eye of the hurricane is the dead-calm center.

A story predicted that a hurricane was headed for Farmington and was expected to cause millions of dollars in damages. So the Farmington merchants boarded their windows, the tourists canceled their reservations—and the hurricane went around Farmington. This is the trouble when a deskman lets a reporter expand a prediction into a warning.

The headline **Freeze tonight expected / to make driving hazardous** was based on this lead: "Freezing temperatures forecast for tonight may lead to a continuation of hazardous driving conditions as a result of last night's snow and freezing rain." The story made no mention of anyone's saying there would still be dampness on the ground when freezing temperatures arrived. There wasn't and driving was unimpeded.

A lead said, "One word, 'miserable,' was the U.S. weatherman's description today of the first day of spring." The head was

---

Snow predicted / it's spring, miserable. It was the weatherman's prediction, not his description. The sun stayed out all day, the clouds stayed away, and readers of the paper must have wondered where this U.S. weatherman was located.

Temperatures can become *higher* or *lower,* not "cooler" or "warmer."

On flood stories, the copy should tell where the flood water came from and where it will run off. The expression *flash flood* is either a special term for a rush of water let down a weir to permit passage of a boat or a sudden destructive rush of water down a narrow gully or over a sloping surface in desert regions, caused by heavy rains in the mountains or foothills. It is often used loosely for any sudden gush of water.

Weather stories, more than most others, have an affinity for the cliché, the fuzzy image, overwriting, mixed metaphors, contrived similes and sundry other absurdities.

"A Houdini snow did some tricks yesterday that left most of the state shivering from a spine-tingling storm." Houdini gained fame as an escape artist, not as an ordinary magician. Did the snow escape, or was it just a tricky snow? After the lead, the twenty-two-inch story never mentioned the angle again. *Spine-tingling* means full of suspense or uncertainty or even terror. Sports writers are fond of using it to describe a close game, called a heart stopper by more ecstatic writers, often in conjunction with a gutsy performance. If a cliché must be used, a very cold storm is *spine-chilling,* not "spine-tingling."

"Old Man Winter yesterday stretched his icy fingers and dumped a blanket of snow on the state." How would reporters ever write about the weather without Old Man Winter, Jack Frost, Icy Fingers and Old Sol? Why do rain and snow never *fall?* They are always "dumped."

"At least two persons were killed in yesterday's snowstorm, marked at times by blizzard-like gales of wind." By Weather Service standards, this is an exaggeration and a contradiction. By any standard, it is a redundancy. A blizzard is one thing. Gales are something else. Gales of wind? What else, unless maybe it was gales of laughter from discerning readers.

An editor's moral: Good colorful writing is to be encouraged. But a simply written story with no gimmicks is better than circus writing that goes awry. To quote a champion image-maker, Shakespeare, in *Sonnet 94,* "Lilies that fester smell far worse than weeds." The writer who plants the festering lilies is only a little more guilty than the copyeditor who lets them grow. They have a way of reproducing.

Blizzards are hard to define because wind and temperatures may vary. The safe way is to avoid calling a snowstorm a *blizzard* unless the Weather Service describes it as such. Generally, a blizzard occurs when there are winds of 35 m.p.h. or more that whip falling snow or snow already on the ground and when the temperatures are 20 degrees above zero Fahrenheit, or lower.

A severe blizzard has winds that are 45 m.p.h. or more, temperatures 10 degrees above zero or lower and great density of snow either falling or whipped from the ground.

The Weather Service insists that ice storms are not sleet. Sleet is frozen raindrops. The service uses the terms *ice storm, freezing rain* and *freezing drizzle* to warn the public when a coating of ice is expected on the ground.

A cyclone is a storm with heavy rain and winds rotating about a moving center of low atmospheric pressure.

A *hurricane* has winds above 75 m.p.h.

A typhoon is a violent cyclonic storm or hurricane occurring in the China Seas and adjacent regions, chiefly from July to October.

Wind Table

Light	up to 7 m.p.h.	Strong	25 to 38 m.p.h.
Gentle	8 to 12 m.p.h.	Gale	39 to 54 m.p.h.
Moderate	13 to 18 m.p.h.	Whole gale	55 to 75 m.p.h.
Fresh	19 to 24 m.p h.		

The word *chinook* should not be used unless so designated by the Weather Service.

Temperatures are measured by various scales. Zero degree centigrade is freezing, and 100 degrees centigrade is boiling. On the Fahrenheit scale, 32 degrees is freezing, and 212 degrees (at sea level) is boiling. On the Kelvin scale, 273 degrees is freezing, and 373 degrees is boiling. To convert degrees centigrade to Fahrenheit, multiply the centigrade measurement by nine fifths and add 32. To convert degrees Fahrenheit to centigrade, multiply the Fahrenheit measurement by five ninths and subtract 32. Thus, 10 degrees centigrade is 50 degrees Fahrenheit. To convert degrees Kelvin to centigrade degrees, subtract 273 from the Kelvin reading.

Weather Clichés

Fog rolled (crept or crawled) in	Mercury dropped
Jupiter Pluvius	(dipped, zoomed, plummeted)
Fog-shrouded city	Rain failed to dampen
Winds aloft	Hurricane howled
Biting (bitter) cold	Storm-tossed
Hail-splattered	

Disaster

Conjecturing about possible damage to settlements from forest fires is as needless as conjectures on weather damage. The story should concentrate on the definite loss. Stories of forest fires should give the specific area burned, the area threatened and the type of timber.

Most stories of earthquakes attempt to describe the magnitude of the tremor. One measurement is the Richter scale, which shows relative magnitude. It starts with magnitude 1 and progresses in units with each unit ten times stronger than the previous one. Thus, magnitude 3 is ten times stronger than magnitude 2, which, in turn, is ten times stronger than magnitude 1. On this scale the strongest earthquakes recorded were the South American earthquake of 1906 and the Japanese earthquake of 1933, both at a magnitude of 8.9. Intensity generally refers to the duration or to the damage caused by the shock.

In train and plane crashes the story should include train or flight number, the place of departure, the destination and times of departure and expected arrival. "Passenger train" is adequate. "Crack passenger train" is a cliché. Airplanes may collide on the ground or in the air (not "midair"). Let investigators *search* the wreckage, not "comb" or "sift" it.

In fire stories, the sad truth is that in nine of ten cases where somebody is "led to safety," they're not. Except for an occasional small child, they simply have the common sense to beat it without waiting for a fireman to "lead them to safety."

In both fire and flood stories the residents of the area are rarely taken from their homes or asked to leave. Instead, they're always told to "evacuate" or they're "evacuated." What's wrong with *vacate?*

Eliminate terms such as *three-alarm fire* and *second-degree burns.*

"An estimated $40,000 worth of damage was done Jan. 29. . . ." Damage isn't worth anything. Quite the contrary.

"The full tragedy of Hurricane Betsy unfolded today as the death toll rose past 50 and damages soared into many millions." *Damage* was the correct word here. You collect *damages* in court.

Disaster Clichés

Rampaging rivers	Tinder-dry forest
Weary firefighters	Raging brush fire
Fiery holocaust	Traffic fatals or triple fatals
Flames licked (leaped, swept)	(police station jargon)
Searing heat	

Labor Disputes

Stories of labor controversies should give the reasons for the dispute, how long the strike has been in progress and the claims by both the union and the company.

Deskmen should be on guard against wrong or loaded terms. Examples: In a closed shop the employer may hire only men already members of the union. In a union shop, the employer may select his employes but the workers are required to join the union within a specified time after starting work. A conciliator in a labor dispute merely recommends terms of a settlement. The decision of an arbiter or a mediator is binding. There is a tendency in labor stories to refer to management proposals as "offers" and to labor proposals as "demands." The correct word should be used for the correct connotation.

Strikebreaker and *scab* have no place in the report if used to describe men who act as individuals in accepting positions vacated by strikers. The expression "honored the picket line" frequently appears in the report even though a more accurate expression is "refused (or declined) to cross a picket line."

Union leader is usually preferred to *labor leader*. A longshoreman is a waterfront leader. A stevedore usually is considered an employe.

On estimates of wages or production lost, the story should have authoritative sources, not street-corner guesses. An individual, however voluble, does not speak for the majority unless he has been authorized to do so. Statements by workers or by minor officials should be played down until they are documented.

If a worker gets a 10-cent-an-hour increase effective immediately, an additional 10 cents a year hence and another 10 cents the third year, he does not receive a 30-cent-an-hour increase. His increase at the time of settlement is still 10 cents an hour. "The company has been on strike for the last 25 days." No. The employes are on strike. The company has been struck.

Criminal court terms should not be applied to labor findings unless the dispute has been taken to a criminal court. The National Labor Relations Board is not a court, and its findings or recommendations should not be expressed in criminal court terminology. In most settlements, neither side is "found guilty" or "fined." A finding or a determination may be made or a penalty may be assessed.

Religion

Jewish congregations should be identified in news stories as Orthodox, Conservative or Reform, and the terminology of the congregation concerned should be followed in naming the place of worship as a temple or a synagogue. When grouping, the generic term is "Jewish houses of worship."

To help readers, the deskman should insert "branch of Judaism" or whatever other phrase might be necessary to convey the proper meaning.

Most Orthodox congregations use *synagogue*. Reform groups use *temple* and Conservative congregations use one word or the other, but *synagogue* is preferred. It is never *church,* which applies to Christian bodies.

Sect has a derogatory connotation. Generally it means a church group espousing Christianity without the traditional liturgical forms. *Religion* is an all-inclusive word for Judaism, Moslemism, Christianity, and so on. *Faith* generally is associated with Protestants. *Denomination* should be used only when referring to the church bodies within the Protestant community.

Religious labels can be misleading. *Jews* and *Judaism* are general terms. *Israelis* refer to nationals of the state of Israel and *Jews* to those who profess Judaism. The state of Israel is not the center of or the spokesman for Judaism. Some Jews are Zionists; some are not.

Not all denominations use *Church* in the organization's title. It is the First Baptist Church but the American Baptist Convention. It is the Church of Jesus Christ of Latter-day Saints (not Mormon Church); its units are Missions, Stakes and Wards. It is the Episcopal Church, not the Episcopalian Church. Its members are Episcopalians, but the adjective is *Episcopal:* Episcopal clergymen.

Mass may be *offered* or *celebrated.* High mass is *sung;* low mass is *said.* The rosary is *recited* or *said.* If mass is sung, the "high" should be omitted. The deskman can avoid confusion by letting the statement read something like this: "The mass (or rosary) will be at 7 p.m." An official presides at solemn high mass. Requiem mass is not necessarily high, but it usually is. It is *offered,* never "celebrated" or "sung." The Benediction of the Blessed Sacrament is neither "held" nor "given"; services close with it.

The order of the commandments varies depending on the version of the Bible used. Confusion can be spared if the commandment number is omitted. Also to be deleted are references to the burning of a church mortgage unless there actually is a burning ceremony. It is an elegant but ridiculous way of saying the mortgage has been paid off.

The usual style in identifying ministers is *the Rev.,* followed by his full name on first reference and *the Rev. Mr.* on second reference. If he holds a doctorate, the style is *the Rev. Dr.,* or simply *Dr.* on subsequent references. *Reverend* should not be used standing alone, nor should plural forms be used, such as the Revs. John Jones and Richard Smith. Churches of Christ do not use the term *reverend* in reference to ministers. They are called *brothers.*

Rabbis take *Rabbi* throughout.

Catholic priests who are members of orders take the initials of their order after their surnames: S.J., S.S., etc. Priests who are rectors, heads of religious houses or presidents of institutions and provinces of religious orders take *Very Rev.* and are addressed as *Father.* Priests who have doctorates in divinity or philosophy are identified as *the Rev. Dr.* and are addressed either as "Dr." or "Father."

The Church of Christ is not the same as the United Church of Christ. It is Seventh-day Adventists, but Seventh Day Baptists. When used as an adjective, Bahai is spelled Ba-hai.

The words *Catholic* and *parochial* are not synonymous. There are parochial schools other than Catholic schools. The writer should not assume that a person is a Roman Catholic simply because he is a priest or a bishop. Other religions also have priests and bishops.

Not all old churches merit the designation of *shrine.* Some are just old churches. *Shrine* denotes some special distinction, historic or ecclesiastical. Usually, shrines are structures or places that have religious connections or that are hallowed by their associations with events or persons of historic significance, such as Mt. Vernon.

Use *nun* when appropriate for women in religious orders. The word *sister* is confusing except with the person's name (Sister Mary Edward).

Ships and Boats

Belay using nautical terms unless they're used properly. "Capt. Albert S. Kelly, the 75-year-old pilot who manned the Delta Queen's tiller yesterday. . . ." What he manned was her *helm* or her *wheel*. Few vessels except sailboats are guided with a tiller.

A story referred to a 27-foot ship. Nothing as small as 27 feet is a *ship*. *Ship* refers to big seagoing vessels such as tankers, freighters and ocean liners. Sailors insist that if it can be hoisted onto another craft it is a boat and that if it is too large for that it is a ship. Specific terms such a *cabin cruiser, sloop, schooner, barge* and *dredge* are appropriate.

"A rescue fleet ranging from primitive bayou pirogues to helicopters prowled through the night." That should send the copyeditor to a dictionary so he can explain to readers that a pirogue is a canoe or a dugout.

"The youths got to the pier just before the gangplank was lowered." When a ship sails, the gangplank is *raised.*

Commercial ships are measured by volume, the measurement of all inclosed space on the ship being expressed in units of 100 cubic feet to the ton. Fuller description gives passenger capacity, length, age, and so on. Naval vessels are expressed in tonnage, the weight in long tons of a ship and all its contents (called displacement). A long ton is 2,240 pounds. All this is "Greek" to many readers. Deskmen should translate into terms recognized by readers, who can visualize length, age and firing power more readily than tonnage: "The 615-foot Bradley, longer than two football fields, end to end. . . ."

A knot is a measure of speed, not distance (nautical miles an hour). A nautical mile is about $1\frac{1}{7}$ land miles. "Knots per hour" is redundant.

Some readers may understand when the story says, "The limestone carrier was en route home in ballast." All will understand if the story says simply that the ship was en route home empty.

Sports

Some of the best writing in American newspapers appears in the sports pages. So does some of the worst.

Many of the weaknesses could be minimized if sports copy were submitted to a universal desk for editing or if the sports copydesk were permitted to edit for all readers—the women, the teenagers and those with only a lukewarm interest in sports, as well as the sports experts. Too often, the sports copydesk not only permits the abuses of sports copy but magnifies the excesses.

Sports pages should be, and are, the liveliest in the paper. They have action photos, a melange of spectator and participant sports and an array of personalities. Sports writers have more latitude than do other reporters. The good ones are among the best in the business; the undisciplined ones are among the worst.

Attractive pages and free expression mean little if the sports section is unintelligible to half the paper's readers. Too often, the editing reflects the attitude that if the reader doesn't understand the lingo he should seek elsewhere in the paper for his information and entertainment.

The potential for readers of the sports section is greater than ever because of the growing number of participants in golf, bowling, fishing, boating and tennis. The spectator sports, especially automobile racing, football, golf, basketball, baseball and hockey, attract great audiences, thanks to the vast number of television viewers. Thus the sports pages, if edited intelligently, can become the most appealing section in the paper. But first, writers and deskmen must improve their manners.

A report of a contest or struggle should appeal to readers if it is composed in straightforward, clear English. The style can be vigorous without being forced, honest without being awesome. Sports fans do not need the fillips to keep their interest whetted. Those who are only mildly interested won't become sports page regulars if the stories are not understandable.

Know the Game One of the elementary rules in sports writing is to tell the reader the name of the game. Yet many stories talk about the Cubs and Pirates but never say specifically that the contest is a baseball game. Some writers assume that if the story refers to the contest as a "dribble derby" all sports page readers must understand that the story concerns a basketball game.

The story may contain references to parts of the game yet never mention the specific game. Here is an example:

Three Teams Tied in Sliceroo

Three teams tied for low at 59 in the sweepstakes division as the 11th annual Sliceroo got under way Thursday at Lakewood Country Club.

Deadlocked at 59 were the teams of. . . .

In the driving contest, it was. . . .

In the putting and chipping contest,. . . .

A best ball is set for Friday and a low net for Saturday, final day of the Sliceroo. A $5,000 hole-in-one competition on the 124-yard 11th hole is set for both final days.

Golfers will understand this story. But nongolfers, even many who enjoy watching golf matches on television, should be told outright that the story concerns a golf tournament. The added information would not offend the golfers. It might encourage a nongolfer to read on.

Some stories fail to state categorically who played whom. Again, the writer assumes that if he names the opponents' managers, all hard-core sports readers will recognize the contestants. Perhaps so, but the general reader might like to know, too. The legend under a two-column cut read, "They can't believe their eyes. Coach Andy S---, left, and Manager May S---, right, showed disbelief and disgruntlement as the Braves belt Pitcher Don C--- for five runs in the eighth inning of their exhibition baseball game Wednesday at Clearwater, Fla. The Braves won, 10–2." Now, whom did the Braves play?

Not all readers understand the technical terms used to describe a sports contest. It might be necessary to explain that a seeded team gets a favored placement in the first round, and that if Smith beats Jones 2–1 in match play it means that golfer Smith is two holes ahead of golfer Jones with only one hole left to play and is, therefore, the winner. The name of the sport should be used in reference to the various cups. The Davis Cup is an international trophy for men tennis players. The Heisman Trophy is an award presented annually to the most outstanding college football player in the nation. America's Cup refers to yachting, and Americas Cup to golfing. Technically, it is *All-America,* not "All-American."

Answering more questions is one way to win more readers for the sports department. The key questions frequently overlooked are how and why. Why did the coach decide to punt on fourth down instead of trying to make one foot for a first down? How does a tournament get the funds to award $200,000 in prizes?

"The shadow of tragedy drew a black edge around a golden day at Sportsman's Park yesterday, bringing home the danger of horse racing with an impact that cut through the $68,950 Illinois Derby like a spotlight in darkness." So, what happened?

Unanswered Questions

The best training for a copyeditor for the sports desk is a stint on the news copydesk. But before he goes on the sports desk he should become familiar with the intricacies of all sports so he can catch the technical errors in sports copy. Here are examples:

"Center fielder Tony Cafar, whose fine relay after chasing the ball 'a country mile,' held Ripley to a triple." Unless Tony also made a throw of "a country mile," another player, the shortstop or second baseman, made the relay throw after taking a good throw from Tony.

When a writer covering a basketball game refers to a "foul shot," his reference should be nailed on the sports desk rim. The fouled player gets a free throw from the free-throw line, not the foul line or the charity lane.

The deskman also has to be alert for some of the wild flights of imagination used by sports writers. "The Tar Heels hurdled their last major obstacle on the way to an unbeaten season but still had a long row to hoe." Is this a track meet or a county fair?

The following passage is a sure way to discourage sports page readers:

Kanicki's troubles in yesterday's 27–6 victory over the Dallas Cowboys before 72,062, largest crowd ever to see the Texans, was the reason Gain was in the trenches to receive a shattering kick with 6:24 left in the game.

This example suggests another tendency in sports copy—turning the story into a numbers game. Box scores, league

---

standings and records have a place in the sports story, but generally they should have a subordinate rather than a dominant role. It is questionable whether gambling odds or the role of gamblers should be used in either the story or the headline. Such intrusion often comes in races with their extra-special payoffs.

Abbreviated Sports

The addiction for abbreviation is strong in both sports copy and headlines. **Broncos get first AFL win over NFL** announces a headline. It means that Denver's professional football team scored the first victory of an American Football League team over a National Football League team.

The seventh paragraph of a story referred to the NPSA. The reader, if he was interested, had to reread the lead to know that the initials stand for National Professional Soccer League.

A headline referred to the Nats, yet nowhere in the story was it explained that this is a term for the Washington Senators in professional baseball's American League.

"Color" in Sports

An editor told his colleagues, "There is nothing more exciting than a good contest. There is nothing duller than reading about it the next day." Yet many spectators who watch a Saturday contest can't wait to read about it the next morning. What were the coaches' and players' reactions to the game? What was the turning point? How long was the pass that won the game? What's the reporter's comment on the crowd's behavior?

This should argue that if there is an audience for the report of a contest, the story needs no special flourishes. Loaded terms such as "wily mentor," "genial bossman," "vaunted running game," "dazzling run" and "astute field general" add little or nothing to the report. Adjectives lend false color. The Associated Press reported a "vise-tight race," "the red-hot Cardinals" and the "torrid 13–4 pace" as if these modifiers were needed to lure readers.

If all deskmen were permitted to aim their pencils at copy submitted by the prima donnas of the sports world there would be no sentence structures like the following ones: "Benny (Kid) Paret showed 'very slight improvement' in his battle for life today while his embittered manager branded the New York State Athletic Commission's report absolving Referee Ruby Goldstein of blame for the boxer's condition as a whitewash."

"Maris, who has been bothered by a sore rib this spring, played eight innings yesterday, collected two singles and drove in a run." He didn't collect them; he hit them.

"Ortiz threw his first bomb in the second round when he nailed Laguna with a left and right to the jaw." How can you nail something with a bomb?

"Left-hander Norman, who started on the mound for Chicago, recovered from a shaky start and pitched six-hit ball for eight innings before a walk and a botched-up double play caused Manager Bob Kennedy to protect a 4 to 1 lead, as a result of a three-run homer by Ernie Banks in the seventh." The sentence is hard to understand because it is overstuffed and because the facts are not told in chronological order. Revised: "Left-hander Norman started on the mound for Chicago. He recovered from a shaky start and pitched six-hit ball for eight innings. Then a walk and a missed double play caused Manager Bob Kennedy to bring in a new pitcher. Chicago was leading, 4 to 1, as a result of a three-run homer by Ernie Banks in the seventh."

Here is how to tell a story upside down: "Waldrop's 17-yard explosion for his eighth touchdown of the season punctuated a 65-yard march from Army's reception of the kickoff by a courageous Falcon team which had gone ahead for the second time in the game, 10 to 7, in the ninth minute of the final period."

An overstuffed sentence of any sort will be just as damaging, and harder to repair, than compound sentence leads. Note this one: "The heaviest betting non-holiday Monday crowd in the Balmoral Jockey club's eight years at Washington Park poured $1,066,919 into the machines yesterday on a nine-race program headed by the $7,500 Harvey purse, a six-furlong dash which drew six starters and was won by Mighty Fennec, piloted by Bill Hartack." Revised: "Horse-race fans put $1,066,919 into the Washington Park machines yesterday on a nine-race program. It was the heaviest betting non-holiday Monday crowd in the Balmoral Jockey club's eight years at the park. The $7,500 Harvey purse for the six-furlong race drew six starters. It was won by Mighty Fennec, ridden by Bill Hartack."

"'Statistics don't tell the story,' he explained, looking many straight in the eye." If he looked more than one person straight in the eyes while he said that, he must have been a long time between words.

It takes some editing to convert sports writers into Homers and Hemingways. At least, though, the deskman can try to help writers improve their ways of telling a story.

Synonym Sickness

He can excise clichés such as "pay dirt," "turned the tables," "hammered (or slammed) a homerun," "Big Eight hardwoods," "circuit clout," "gridder," "hoopster," "thin clads," "tanksters," "sweet revenge," "rocky road," "free loads" (foul shots), "droughts" (losing streaks), "standing-room-only crowds," "put a cap on the basket," "as the seconds ticked off the clock," "unblemished record," "paced the team," "outclassed but game," "roared from behind," "sea of mud," "vaunted defense," "coveted trophy" and "last-ditch effort."

He can insist on the correct word. Boxers may have *altercations* (verbal) with their managers. They have *fights* with other boxers.

He can tone down exaggerated expressions like "mighty atom of the ring," "destiny's distance man" or "Northwestern comes off a tremendous effort Monday" (Northwestern tried hard). He can cut out redundancy in phrases like "with 30,000 spectators looking on."

He can resist the temptation to use synonyms for the verbs *wins, beats* and *defeats*: annihilates, atomizes, batters, belts, bests, blanks, blasts, boots home, clips, clobbers, cops, crushes, downs, drops, dumps, edges, ekes out, gallops over, gangs up on, gouges, gets past, H-bombs, halts, humiliates, impales, laces, lashes, lassoes, licks, murders, outslugs, outscraps, orbits, overcomes, paces, pastes, pins, racks up, rallies, rolls over, romps over, routs, scores, sets back, shades, shaves, sinks, slows, snares, spanks, squeaks by, squeezes by, stampedes, stomps, stops, subdues, surges, sweeps, tops, topples, triggers, trips, trounces, tumbles, turns back, vanquishes, wallops, whips, whomps and wrecks.

He will let the ball be *hit,* not always banged, bashed, belted, blooped, bombed, boomed, bumped, chopped, clunked, clouted, conked, cracked, dribbled, drilled, dropped, driven, hacked, knifed, lashed, lined, plastered, plunked, poked, popped, pumped, punched, pummeled, pushed, rapped, ripped, rocked, slapped, sliced, slugged, smashed, spilled, spanked, stubbed, swatted, tagged, tapped, tipped, topped, trickled, whipped, whistled, whomped and whooped.

He will let a ball be *thrown* and only occasionally tossed, twirled, fired and hurled.

He will let a ball be *kicked,* occasionally punted and never toed or booted.

He will resist the shopworn puns: Birds (Eagles, Orioles, Cardinals) soar or claw; Lions (Tigers, Bears, Cubs) roar, claw or lick; Braves (Tribesmen, Indians) scalp or tomahawk; Mustangs (Colts, Broncos) buck, gallop, throw or kick.

He will insist on neutrality in all sports copy, avoiding "home policy" slanting.

He will not make verbs out of nouns: "AP—Chicago manager Eddie Stanky nonchalanted the White Sox strike-breaker, saying, 'My food's going to taste the same....'"

He will not string modifiers endlessly: "UPI—The Pistons won 29 and lost 40 under the guidance of the then only 24 years old DuBusschere."

He will never be guilty of writing sports heads such as:

**Astros defeat Houston 1–0 /
on Wynn's home run in 6th**

McNally hurting
Oilers end set / for surgery Monday

First win over Oilers since 1962
Houston's win earns AFL lead

**Wilson pitches good, runs poorly
in 4–1 Tiger victory**

**Lack of scoring hurts Owosso / in winless
basketball season**

The Art of Editing

One of the brighter changes in newspapers has been the transformation of the society pages, with their emphasis on club and cupid items, to the women's section or the family section, with a broader-based appeal. The philosophy of the new approach has been well expressed by two editors:

> Pages of the Women's Section are edited not for the ladies who write the stories, not for the ladies who are the source of the stories and not for the gruff voice of the advertising department. They're edited for the people who buy the paper.

> Women's pages were formerly edited for the few. Now the pages appeal to the woman as mother and working girl and as an intelligent human being involved in the total society.

Such sections still carry engagement announcements and wedding stories, but their added fare is foods, fashions, finance, health, education, books and other cultural affairs. They are edited for active women in all ranks, not solely for those in the top rank of society. They also are edited for the increasing number of men readers.

The better editors regard readers of the women's section as alert individuals who are concerned with problems such as prostitution, racism, civil disorders, women's prisons, alcoholism among housewives and educational reforms. Such editors strive to make their pages informative as well as entertaining.

Improvements are likely to continue. Some executives argue that newspapers should not segregate women, that material of special interest to the family should be scattered throughout the paper. Some maintain that club and social news should be held to a minimum because of low reader appeal. Others argue that the preoccupation with foods, fashions and furnishings squeezes out important items of women's activity. A quarter of a page devoted to a picture of a cherry pie might be trimmed a bit to accommodate a good story.

Some papers now handle engagements, weddings and births as court of record items. And a few charge for engagement and wedding stories and pictures unless the event is obviously news, such as the wedding of the President's daughter.

In many daily newspapers, especially the medium-sized and smaller ones, reports of engagements and weddings will perish slowly, if they will die at all. Still, some conventions may change —such as giving the bridegroom a break for a change. This point was delightfully argued by Paul Brookshire in his column in the South Dade *New Leader,* Homestead, Fla., and reprinted in *The Quill* (October 1967). Here are some excerpts:

> In these days when the world is quaking in its boots and news of great significance is daily swept into newspaper trash cans for lack of space, it is sickening to read paragraph after paragraph about some little girl changing HER name to HIS.

The groom? He apparently wasn't dressed at all . . . if he was even there. But Mother and Mother-in-Law? Yes. They were fashion plates in beige ensembles and matching accessories or something.

I ask you. Is it a wedding or a fashion show?

If it is a fashion show, why isn't it held in a hotel ballroom and why isn't the groom given a tiny bit of credit for the showing up with his clothes on?

The blackout of the bridegroom in wedding accounts is an unpardonable sin. If the groom is mentioned at all he is afforded as much space as an atheist gets on the church page.

And pictures. Did you ever see a photograph of a bridegroom? Maybe in the Post Office but not in the newspaper.

I'm going on record right now in favor of wedding announcements being run as legal notices—payable in advance by the father of the bride.

Better still, if the bride insists on giving a minute, detailed description of every inch of clothing she happens to have on her person, I suggest she take out a paid display advertisement.

In this manner, trade names may be used and shops that sold the girl all her glorious gear could get equal space on the same page.

Newspapers would reap untold profits from this arrangement and readers might be able to get some world news for a change instead of bouffant skirts highlighted with tiers of lace and aqua frocks with aqua tipped orchids and maize silk linen ensembles with . . . whatever you wear with maize silk linen ensembles.

Even though many newspapers have refined the society section, some retain a static style, especially on engagement and wedding stories. Wedding story leads usually read like these:

First Methodist Church in Littleton was the setting for the double-ring wedding rites of blank and blank.

Miss Blank has become the bride of Blank, it was announced by her parents, etc.

After a wedding trip to Las Vegas, Nevada, Mr. and Mrs. Blank will live in. . . .

All Saints Roman Catholic Church was the setting for the single-ring rites. . . .

Newspapers continue to use the following:

Stock words and phrases—holy matrimony, high noon, benedicts, exchanged nuptial vows.

Descriptive adjectives—attractive, pretty, beautiful, charming, lovely.

Non sequiturs—"Given in marriage by her parents, the bride wore a white silk organza gown with a sabrina neckline and short sleeves." "Wearing a gown of white lace cotton over taffeta with empire waistline, square neckline and short sleeves, the bride was given in marriage by her father."

Confusing collectives—"The couple is on a trip to northern Wisconsin and will live at blank Fairmount ave., Whitefish Bay, when they return." Generally, a collective noun takes a singular verb when the noun indicates a group acting as a unit and a plural verb when it means individuals performing individual actions: "The Board of Park Commissioners gave its blessings. . . ." "The platoon fought its way up the hill. . . ." "Their headquarters is in the Bennett building. . . ." "The crew have returned to their homes." Therefore, make it couple *are,* not *is.*

Details—gown and flower descriptions and social affiliations that reflect status.

Euphemistic headlines—**Betrothal told, Holy vows exchanged, Wedding ceremonies solemnized.**

Copyeditors who handle news and features for the women's section will not allow writers to single out women's achievements by sex, such as housewife and woman doctor. They will delete phrases like "is affiliated with," "refreshments will be served," "featured speaker," "special guests," "noon luncheon," "dinner meeting." They will refuse to let a person "host (or hostess) a party," "gavel a meeting" or "chair a committee."

They will not let reporters go out of their way to use *female, feminine* and *ladies* in all manner of sentences where the word *women* would be proper and more appropriate.

They will catch slips such as "Mrs. Richard Roe, nee Jane Doe." *Nee* means "born" and people are born only with their surnames. The first (not Christian) name is given later.

They will remain on guard for awkward sentences:

Do you keep track of your weight and lose the first five or ten pounds too much?

Seniors realize the importance of proper dress more than younger students, but after a while they catch on.

All copy for this section, as well as for the other sections of the paper, should be edited for its news value. This should apply to the syndicated features as well as to the locally produced copy. The headlines should reflect as much care and thought as do those on page 1.

The deskman should not allow any story aimed at younger readers to contain anything that patronizes these readers. Even terms like *teen, teenager* and *youth* can be avoided, or at least can be held to a minimum. The deskman should make sure that both copy and headline talk up, not down, to these readers.

5

Writing and Editing

Making the news available is only half the job. News has to be presented so well that readers will be compelled to read it. To be read, the news must be readable.

Precision in Writing

Journalism has always attracted good writers. The best on today's newspapers compare favorably with the star reporters of the past. The level of writing probably is higher today than it has ever been. Even so, the best writers still face the handicap of writing under pressure. They are still bound by the strait jacket of structured news style.

The mechanics of newspaper publishing have had something to do with the traditional style of news presentation. Advertising has had first priority in the page forms, with the remaining space accommodating editorial matter. Too often, makeup has controlled the length of the story, not the content of the story itself. Trimming has been from the bottom, thus forcing the inverted pyramid form, the "hugger-mugger" lead and details in descending importance.

Now that it is possible through computers to store both ads and editorial material until final makeup or to rearrange the makeup pattern, editorial material can have priority. Indiscriminate trims and plugs with inane fillers are no longer necessary. No story need be robbed of important and interesting details that may appear near the bottom of the story.

Stories need not be longer but they should give more serious treatment to a wider range of topics. Some executives see an increasing application of the narrative, magazine style to the newspaper story. There may be no news peg at all, but rather a wealth of new and interesting information that will make it news nevertheless.

Some of these concepts already have been tried successfully. Some news events heavily covered by television have been presented in the narrative rather than in the traditional news style. On the assumption that readers will remember a good narrative far longer than the cold, routine summary story, UPI put out two leads on a Notre Dame-Southern California football game. The regular lead went as follows:

SOUTH BEND, Ind., Oct. 23 (UPI)—Fullback Larry Conjar tied a modern Notre Dame record with four touchdowns today to lead the aroused Fighting Irish to a 28–7 victory over Southern California.

The Trojans were the only team to defeat Notre Dame last year. They did it on a touchdown with 93 seconds left in the last game of the season. The Irish fans didn't let their team forget that loss today, spurring them constantly with shouts of "Remember!"

The alternative lead read as follows:

SOUTH BEND, Ind., Oct. 23 (UPI)—It was fourth down on Southern California's two-yard line when that chant first went up—"Remember! . . . Remember!"

It rolled across packed Notre Dame stadium and rose to the glowering rain clouds overhead. And the Irish remembered, with a vengeance.

With "Remember" in his ears, Fullback Larry Conjar grabbed the ball from Quarterback Bill Zloch and dived over the Trojan goal line for the first of a personal parade of four Irish touchdowns and the start of a stunning 28–7 Notre Dame rout over unbeaten and fourth-ranked Southern California.

In justification of the second treatment, UPI said, "The challenge was to produce a story that would not only serve the standard purposes for the uninformed but that would also be of interest, and have something extra to offer, to the many who had seen every move on TV." [*U.P.I. Reporter* (October 28, 1965)]

An alternative to the more orthodox lead would be the following:

WASHINGTON (UPI)—It was this kind of an opening day game— Lyndon Johnson went home after five innings.

He didn't miss much because as a contest, the Washington Senators-New York Yankees clash that inaugurated this year's baseball season with pomp and pageantry was over even before then.

It ended for all practical purposes when Bill Robinson. . . .

Another example used the narrative approach:

MADRID (UPI)—"You will write about me and my photo will be published on every front page," boasted 16-year-old Mariano Garcia two years ago. "I will be a great bull fighter one day."

This was his dream and the theme he returned to time and again during our 200-mile drive from Saragossa to Madrid.

It was on Feb. 23, 1964, in the outskirts of Saragossa that Mariano had asked me for a ride.

"I want to go to Madrid and start a career as a bull fighter," the boy said in the accents of his native Mancha.

Mariano's was a classic story of Spain: The eager youth deserting the misery of his sun-baked village with its white-washed walls for the danger and glory of the bull ring.

When he learned that I was a newsman, Mariano pulled a pencil stub and sort of calling card out of his pocket. The card bore an amateurish sketch of the Virgin Mary and Jesus. Across it he scrawled his name in bold letters.

"The Virgin and the Christ are my protectors," he said.

Then he talked with wide-eyed dreaminess of how the bull paws the ground with his left forefoot when excited, of his sudden charges, of the secrets of the matador's capework and of the "pata, rabo y orejas"—the hoofs, tail and ears of the bull—the highest honors the fickle Spanish crowd can pay a matador.

For two years, Mariano tried to get a start on the road to fame and fortune. It came not in Madrid, but at San Martin de Lavega.

The bull he met Thursday was six years old, fat, limping, and the sharp tips of his horns had been clipped. But the old bull could be dangerous. He had survived the ring once and remembered well how the matador evaded his charges and the hooking of his horns.

Mariano made three or four passes with his cape. But the bull was old and the boy was young and the fickle crowd was bored.

"Just a meletilla," some shouted, "just a beginner."

Another matador stepped in to divert the bull. But the animal had his eyes fixed on Mariano. Suddenly, he charged the boy and knocked him down.

Then the old bull drove his blunted left horn into Mariano's skull.

It was a quick kill, as the good matador's sword should be quick.

Mariano Garcia's mother and father carried his body in a blood-stained sheet to the local cemetery. And today I wrote the story Mariano promised I would write.

This type of storytelling has the quality once described by Earl J. Johnson of UPI: "to hold the reader's interest and stimulate some imagination to see, feel and understand the news."

Another journalistic tradition that might well be challenged is the business of keeping the reporter out of sight in his story. The tradition arose as part of news objectivity and is generally held to be sacred. However, some critics of reporting argue that the source should tell his story to a reporter, not to the journal, that the reporter should talk to the source in first person. Then, say the critics, we will get intimate, personal accounts, not dull, anonymous reports.

Keep It Objective

Whatever the style of presentation, the report must be objective. This principle should be fundamental to students as well as to professional newsmen. An interpretative story may expound the "how," the "why" or relative information. It should not offer value judgments. "Herman was a mean man" is a subjective, evaluative statement. A factual statement would be "He dumped his trash on his neighbor's yard, slapped his wife."

An alert copyeditor should force the reporter to stick to factual statements, not opinionated ones.

Whatever pattern the story takes, the basic elements of style, grammar and usage must be observed. No formula and no computer can turn slum writing into a prose masterpiece.

Make It Readable

Imprecision with words, unclear sentences, involved leads, redundancies and repetition, improper and fragmentary quotations, lack of important details and all the other evils of poor writing will continue to challenge the copyeditor. Newspapers cannot afford to justify the all-too-common impression that journalistic writing is "sloppy" writing or that copyreading is often "sloppy reading."

A writing committee of the Associated Press summed up readability in the second *AP Writing Handbook* (1959):

> Our first duty is to tell what has happened in language the average reader can grasp at first reading. Every lead—and every subsequent paragraph—should be clear, incisive and interesting, so that he will be impelled to continue. We must not delay him with wordiness, confuse him with imperfect sentence structure or discourage him with dull, technical phraseology. We must give him the drama and color that come from judicious selection of detail and a relaxed, conversational technique. We must not overfeed him by forcing who-what-why-when-where into a single sentence.

The copyeditor's job is to tighten the loose-jointed, the wordy and the repetitious. He turns zigzag sentences into straight-line ones, the sleeper-jump into the close-coupled, the roundabout into the straightforward. Like this:[1]

Loose-jointed	*Tight*
The police officer accompanied the two men to Utah last week inasmuch as it was felt that young Melvin could be of use in helping to locate or identify the killer.	The policeman accompanied them to Utah last week, hoping young Melvin could locate the killer.

Wordy	*Tight*
Police said the victim was identified as. . . .	Police said the victim was. . . .

Repetitious	*Tight*
Former Gov. Goodwin J. Knight and his wife arrived Wednesday with no plans except for a little golf and a lot of relaxation. "I haven't any plans," Knight told a news conference. "I want to take a rest for about a month and play some golf."	Former Gov. Goodwin J. Knight and his wife arrived Wednesday with no plans, he said, except to rest for about a month and play some golf.

[1] Examples from the *AP Writing Handbook* (1959).

Needless Detail

Superior Judge Edward R. Brand imposed the sentence after denying a plea to place Patterson on probation on condition that he seek psychiatric treatment.

Tight

Superior Court denied probation. Patterson had offered to seek psychiatric treatment. [The judge didn't comment significantly; his name was unnecessary. The prison term imposed was stated in an earlier paragraph.]

Zigzag

An inventor of a top secret device has won the right to sue the government for compensation behind closed doors.

Straight Line

The inventor of a top secret device, suing the government for compensation, has won the right to trial behind closed doors.

Sleeper-jump

Arizona voters, prompted by a torrid senatorial race and warm sunny weather, turned out in heavy force today.

Close-coupled

Arizona voters turned out in heavy force today, prompted by warm, sunny weather and a torrid senatorial race.

Roundabout

One pilot parachuted to safety but the other fought for control of his plane before also bailing out after the jet fighters collided.

Straightforward

After the jet fighters collided, one pilot quickly parachuted to safety. The other fought to control his plane before bailing out.

Other Examples

Original

A transfer of $80,000 to $90,000 to operational grants from construction grants for special education programs by the Genesee Intermediate School District will enable the intermediate district to make up for a portion of a 9 per cent cut in state aid for special education.

The Intermediate Board of Education voted Monday to transfer extra monies, expected to be left at the end of the fiscal year in June, and from its plan for reimbursement of operations of special education programs in the local districts.

Edited

Money will be transferred from one fund to another to make up part of a 9 per cent cut in state aid to school districts for special education.

This was decided Monday by the Genesee Intermediate Board of Education, which will use $80,000 to $90,000 in construction money expected to be left at the end of the fiscal year next month.

Establishment of the Blanc Community Foundation to allow bequests and donations to be made directly to a community foundation for the benefit of residents of the community has been announced by the Citizens Commercial & Savings Bank, which is the trustee of the foundation's assets.

A foundation has been set up to accept bequests and donations to be channeled directly to community agencies.

A proposal to turn the County General Hospital over to Suncrest Hospital, the county's medical care facility for the aged, and to build a new general hospital on county land near Suncrest was announced Wednesday by the governing boards of the two hospitals.

A new building for County General Hospital is being proposed. The present plant would be used for medical care for the aged.

The Minneapolis *Star* in its July 20, 1970, issue of *Stars and Gripes* commented, "With our space situation becoming more critical each day, we need tight writing and tighter editing." The compiler then gave an example of tight editing that saved five lines of type in a news article of 39 lines in its original form and suggested, "This type of space saving can result in more articles being published, not to mention an easier job for the reader."

Original	*Edited*
The Ramsey County Board skated deftly over some *pretty* thin political ice Monday when it was asked to *make a decision on* where to *locate* two proposed hockey arenas *for the county.*	The Ramsey County Board skated deftly over thin political ice Monday when it was asked to decide where to put two proposed hockey arenas.
The *State Legislature in 1969* inextricably mixed the arenas with politics when it *decided to authorize* the construction of eight arenas in the county, one *to be located* in each of the county's eight state senatorial districts.	The 1969 State Legislature inextricably mixed the arenas with politics when it authorized the construction of eight arenas in the county, one in each of the county's eight state senatorial districts.
The county board was *given authority* to issue $3 million in bonds to *erect* the arenas and *purchase* a golf course.	The county board was authorized to issue $3 million in bonds to build the arenas and buy a golf course.
It was later decided that $2 million would go *to the* ice arenas and that the *sites for the buildings* would be determined by a citizens' recreational facilities commission.	It was decided later that $2 million would go for ice arenas and that the building sites would be determined by a citizens' recreational facilities commission.
Earlier this year, the board decided that eight arenas were not needed *now* and *it* authorized *the issuance of* $750,000 in bonds *that would* pay for three arenas, one *to be located* in rural Ramsey County and two in St. Paul.	Earlier this year, the board decided that eight arenas were not needed and authorized the $750,000 in bonds to pay for three arenas, one in rural Ramsey County and two in St. Paul.

Following is a routine story as it appeared in a small daily:

Three escapees from the Roubideau Honor Camp near Delta were captured this morning about 8:30 one mile north of Delta by Cedaredge Marshall Ed Marah and Delta Police Department Patrolman Robert Tafoya, ending approximately 32 hours of freedom for Lawrence Jaramillo, 21, Robert Murphy, 20, and a 17-year-old youth.

One of the men was evidently on Highway 50 when he was picked up and the other two escapees were found on a nearby side road, according to the Colorado State Patrol dispatcher at the Montrose office. The unarmed men offered no resistance to the officers.

The law enforcement officers may have been patrolling the highway when the escapees were spotted, the CSP dispatcher said.

The search for the inmates who apparently walked away from the low-security camp seven miles west of Delta between 12:30 and 2:30 a.m. Tuesday was made by about 25 law enforcement officers including Honor Camp personnel.

The edited version is in Figure 5–1.

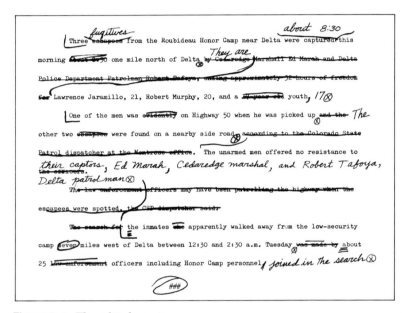

Figure 5–1. The edited version.

Following is the rationale for the edited version:

The lead contains too many ideas. *Fugitives* is easily recognized; *escapees* is contrived. If the lead is confined to the capture, the identities of the fugitives would normally follow. The original lead contained 51 words. The edited version has two sentences of 19 and 9 words.

The second paragraph of the original version contains too many ideas. The attribution doesn't seem important.

The third paragraph of the edited version identifies the captors and corrects the spelling of *marshal*. The third paragraph of the original story is indefinite and therefore adds nothing to the story.

The fourth paragraph contains two distinct ideas and should not be combined. "Law enforcement officers" is a euphemistic way of saying *policemen, patrolmen* or simply *officers*. *Personnel* obviously is too broad.

Apply a readability test to the original. Five sentences average 28 words. The number of words of three syllables or more (not counting capitalized words or combinations of short easy words) is 12, or 8 per cent. The total of the average number of words a sentence and the percentage of difficult words is 36. Multiplication of this figure by .4 (an index used by Robert Gunning, an authority on readability measurement mentioned previously) produces a fog index of 14.4, far above Gunning's danger line.

The edited version reduces the original by 44 words but has eight sentences instead of five, for an average of 12 words a sentence. The number of words of three syllables or more has been reduced to four, or approximately 4 per cent, resulting in a fog index of 6.4. This would be rated as extremely easy reading.

Obviously no copyeditor edits by a readability "yardstick." But "tight" editing produces the same results. The copyeditor's job is to help the reader understand the story. If the story has human interest it will invite readers, provided the idea density isn't too great, the vocabulary is in fairly common terms and the sentence structure reflects that of a writer reasonably well versed in syntax.

Desk Responsibility

A reporter should choose his words as carefully as he selects facts for story presentation. If he doesn't, the deskman has to step in to assure precision in both fact and language. An error in print is the responsibility of the deskman because he is the last line of defense against error.

A copyeditor's too-heavy pencil cannot be condoned, but he should be meticulous in choice of words that convey the correct meaning. For example, he should insert "close-up" words for vague words: "The city retains its old-world character (atmosphere)." "He had one thing (characteristic) in common with others." "She is the ambitious type" (She is ambitious). "A mixture of a cloudy nature" (A cloudy mixture).

How To Obtain Economy with Words

Allan Nevins characterized Robert Leckie, author of *The Wars of America,* as "a writer who knows how to get as much into one paragraph as most authors manage in a page." [*Saturday Review* (March 2, 1968), p. 25.] Compression is one of the cardinal virtues in all writing. Many news writers have the knack. Those who don't must be aided by the deskman.

The copyeditor looks for needless repetition. Why let the reporter say in four successive paragraphs that the subject made his statement in a news conference? If the fact is established once, that should suffice. If the story quotes a speaker in the second paragraph as saying, "We will make no more compromises with the unions," it is unnecessary to use the same quote seven paragraphs later.

Compression means short cuts to ideas. "It is always a baffling thing" becomes "It always baffles," thus saving some words and changing a weak verb into a strong one. "The field is 50 feet in length" becomes "The field is 50 feet long." "He is said to be resentful" becomes "He is said to resent." "Can be beneficial" becomes "Can benefit."

Long words are replaced by short ones to quicken the pace—*big* for *enormous, lives* for *resides, find* for *discover*. Long phrases are reduced—"applying its stamp of approval" (*approving*), "the fact that Smith had not succeeded" (*Smith's failure*), "throughout the world" (*abroad*), "work in the fields" (*fieldwork*), "every single one of" (*all*), "a great deal of" (*lots*).

Complex forms become simple ones—"commuted by automobile" (*drives his car*). Double-talk is eliminated—"plans *for the future*," "re-elect *to a second term*," "*advance* predictions," "*pre-selected* targets," "*sometime* in mid-August." Compression eliminates the superfluous—"pledged *to secrecy* not to disclose," "was electrocuted *accidentally*," "wrote a *formal* letter of resignation" (*resigned*), "read from a *prepared* statement," "go into details" (*elaborate*).

It removes word definitions—"The heavy-duty tires pulverize the dirt into a fine powder" (*The heavy-duty tires pulverize the dirt*).

The deskman can save space by removing all circumlocutions. Such pruning saves the readers' time, too. Deskmen can add to this list:

A bolt of lightning (lightning)
A great number of times (often, frequently)
A greater number of (more)
A little less than (almost)
A small number of (few)
A large number of (many)
A period of several weeks (several weeks)
A sufficient number of (enough)
Absolute guarantee (guarantee)
Accidentally stumbled (stumbled)
Acres of land (acres)
Add an additional (add)
Added fillip (fillip)
Advance planning (planning)
Advance reservations (reservations)
All of a sudden (suddenly)
Already existing (existing)
Angry mob (mob)
Any one of the two (either)
Apartheid segregation (either, but not both)
Arrived here (arrived)
As a general rule (usually)
As in the case of (like)
Assessed a fine (fined)
At a later date (later)
At that time (then)

At the present time (now)
At which time (when)
At regular intervals of time (regularly)
At some future date (sometime, later)
At the hour of noon (at noon)
At 12 noon (at noon)
At 12 midnight (at midnight)
At the conclusion of (after)
At a meeting held here (at a meeting here)
At the corner of 16th and Elm (at 16th and Elm)
At the rear of (behind)
Auction sale (auction)

Baby boy was born (boy was born)
Bald-headed (bald)
Basic fundamentals (fundamentals)
Bitter quarrel (quarrel)
Bouquet of flowers (bouquet)
Brought to a sudden halt (halted)
Brown-colored cloth (brown cloth)

Called attention to the fact (reminded)
Came to a stop (stopped)

Canary bird (canary)
Cannot be possible (cannot be)
Climb up (climb)
Collie dog (Collie)
Combine into one (combine)
Commute back and forth
  (commute)
Complete monopoly (monopoly)
Completely decapitated
  (decapitated)
Completely destroyed (destroyed)
Completely filled (filled)
Completely surrounded
  (surrounded)
Consensus of opinion (consensus)
Continue on (continue)
Controversial disputes (disputes)
Cost the sum of $5 (cost $5)
Current trend (trend)

Dead body (body)
Despite the fact that (although)
Detailed information (details)
Different kinds (kinds)
Disclosed for the first time
  (disclosed)
Draw to a close (end)
Due to the fact that (because,
  since)
During the time that (then,
  while, as)
During the winter months
  (during the winter)
Dwindled down (dwindled)

Easter Sunday (Easter)
Empty cavity (cavity)
End result (result)
Ended his talk (concluded)
Entered a bid of (bid)
Entire monopoly (monopoly)
Entirely destroyed (destroyed)
Equally as (equally)
Established precedent (precedent)
Estimated at about (estimated at)
Estimated roughly at
  (estimated at)
Exact replica (replica)
Exchanged wedding vows
  (married)

Fellow classmates (classmates)
Few in number (few)
Filled to capacity (filled)
Final climax (climax)
Finally ended (ended)
First began (began)
First priority (priority)
First prototype (prototype)
Fishing trawler (trawler)

Flaming inferno (inferno)
Floor carpeting (carpeting)
For a period of 10 days (for
  10 days)
For a short space of time (for
  a short time)
For the purpose of advancing
  (to advance)
Free gift (gift)
Free pass (pass)
Fused back together (fused)
Future plans (plans)

General conclusion (conclusion)
General public (public)
Gemini twins (Gemini)
Golden wedding anniversary
  (golden wedding)
Guest speaker (speaker)

Heat up (heat)
Hidden pitfall (pitfall)
Hostile antagonist (antagonist)
Hot water heater (water heater)
Huge throng (throng)
Human being (human)

If that were the case (if so)
Important essentials (essentials)
Incumbent governor (governor)
In addition to (and, besides, also)
In back of (behind)
In case of (if, concerning)
In excess of (more)
In order to balance (to balance)
In respect to (about, on)
In the absence of (without)
In the near future (soon)
In the not too distant future
  (eventually)
In the event that (if)
In the immediate vicinity of (near)
In the neighborhood of (about)
In view of the fact that
  (considering)
Informed those attending the
  meeting (said)
Introduced a new (introduced)
Introduced for the first time
  (introduced)
Invited guests (guests)
Is going to (will)
Is a resident of Dover (lived
  in Dover)
Is in the process of making
  application (is applying)
Is of the opinion that (believes)
Is opposed to (opposes)

Jewish rabbi (rabbi)

Kept an eye on (watched)
Kept steady company (kept company)
Kept under surveillance (watched)
Killed outright (killed)

Large-sized man (large man)
Last of all (last)
Lift up (lift)
Long chronic illness (long illness, chronic illness)

Made an investigation of (investigated)
Made good his escape (escaped)
Major portion of (most of)
Married his wife (was married)
Matinee performance (matinee)
Meet for the selection of (meet to select)
Mental telepathy (telepathy)
Merged together (merged)
Midway between (between)

New bride (bride)
New construction (construction)
New innovation (innovation)
New record (record)
New recruit (recruit)
None at all (none)
Noon luncheon (luncheon)
Not any one of the two (neither)
Null and void (void)

Off of (off)
Official business (business)
Officiated at the ceremony (officiated)
Old adage (adage)
Old cliché (cliché)
Old pioneer (pioneer)
Old traditions of the past (traditions)
On a stretch of road (on a road)
On account of (because)
On behalf of (for)
On two different occasions (twice)
Once in a great while (seldom, rarely)
Opens its session Monday (opens Monday)

Past experience (experience)
Past history (history)
Past records (records)
Period of time (period)
Personal charm (charm)
Personal friendship (friendship)

Placed its seal of approval on (approved)
Portable walkie-talkie (walkie-talkie)
Possibly might (might)
Postponed until later (postponed)
Preprogrammed (programmed)
Prerecorded (recorded)
Present incumbent (incumbent)
Presently planned (planned)
Prior to (before)
Private business (business)
Private contractor (contractor)
Private industry (industry)
Probed into (probed)
Promoted to the rank of (promoted)
Proposed project (project)
Put in an appearance (appeared)

Qualified expert (expert)

Received his education at (attended)
Recur again (recur)
Reduce down (reduce)
Refer back (refer)
Regular weekly meeting (meeting)
Rejected a proposal (refused)
Remand back (remand)
Repeat again (repeat)
Reported to the effect that (reported)
Revise downward (lower)
Rio Grande River (Rio Grande)
Rise up (rise)
Rose to the defense of (defended)
Rough rule of thumb (rule of thumb)

Sahara Desert (Sahara)
Self-confessed (confessed)
Served as toastmaster (was toastmaster)
Short space of time (short time)
Sierra Mountains (Sierras)
Since the time when (since)
Soaked to the skin (soaked)
Specific example (example)
Split in the middle (split)
Sprung a surprise (surprised)
Started off with (started with)
Still persists (persists)
Strangled to death (strangled)
Suddenly collapsed (collapsed)
Suddenly exploded (exploded)
Summer season (summer)
Surprising upset (upset)
Sworn affidavits (affidavits)

Taken to the hospital for treatment
(taken to the hospital)
Temporary recess (recess)
Tendered his resignation
(resigned)
Therapeutic treatment
(therapy or treatment)
There is no doubt that (doubtless)
Thorough investigation
(investigation)
Threatened walkout averted
(walkout averted)
Told his listeners that (said)
Total operating costs (operating
costs)
True facts (facts)
Two twins (twins)

Underground subway (subway)
United in holy matrimony
(married)
Unsolved problem (problem)
Until and unless (unless)

Violent explosion (explosion)
Voiced objections (objected)

Well-known traditions (traditions)
Went on to say (continued,
added)
Went up in flames (burned)
When and if (if)
Widow of the late (widow)
Widow woman (widow)
With the exception of (except)

An ear for language is as important as an eye for grammar. "This doesn't sound right," the copyeditor protests when he spots fuzzy passages. Careful reading of copy and application of his copy pencil will enable the deskman to ferret out unclear expressions. Lack of clarity may be caused by nonsense, omission, wrong words, wrong order, confusing modifiers or referents, redundancy, questions, backwardness and superfluous words.

Is the Meaning Clear?

Nonsense

As explained by one engineer to Mrs. Reed, one of the reasons for the high cost of repairing the streets is that the space between the concrete and the ground presents problems of pumping liquid concrete between.
We can only hope that Mrs. Reed understands.

Gangs of white rowdies roamed the area last night attacking cars bearing Negroes with baseball bats, bricks and stones.
Who had the bats?

The public launching ramps at Gordon Park are clogged full of the drifting debris and completely block off their possible use by early season trailer boaters.
The writer should try to parse that sentence.

A very nearly nude picture of actress Jayne Mansfield was flashed on the floor of the South Carolina Senate during discussion of a bill to ban obscene literature.
Why were they flashing her picture on the floor?

Three counties, Meigs, Pike and Vinton, get more than 85 per cent from the state. Morgan gets 90.3 per cent.
Eh?

Most of them are high school graduates averaging about 20 years old.
Just how long do they stay in high school?

Many of the 800 executives and clerical people will be transferred and some probably will be eliminated.
That's rough on people.

Omission Dodson told police he had awakened and found his wife missing.
He didn't wake up and find her missing. He woke and found that his wife was missing.

Robert Lowell, Pulitzer Prize-winning American poet who refused a White House invitation to express his disapproval of American policies in Vietnam, has been nominated. . . .
The writer meant to say Lowell refused the invitation because of his disapproval.

Wrong Words The new hospital has spot lighting to give plenty of illumination to a late reader while letting his bed-neighbor go to sleep.
What he means is next-bed neighbor.

The zoo is planning a program to propagate extinct animals.

Two of the nation's top automotive executives have criticized federal regulations as a way to improve highway safety.

The writer meant they would retard progress in automotive safety.

Wrong Word Order She was shot and killed through the throat.

An insufficient water supply problem for fire-fighting at Fitch Senior High school will be discussed next Thursday.
Try this: "The problem of insufficient water supply for fire-fighting at Fitch. . ."

White segregationists waving Confederate flags and Negro integrationists marched past each other yesterday.
Or did white segregationists waving flags march past Negro integrationists yesterday?

Joseph H. Hughes Jr. of Los Angeles wrote to many of his late son's, Coast Guard Ensign Joseph H. Hughes III, friends.
Translation: "wrote to many friends of his late son. . . ."

The students are mostly Negro.
Are we saying they are half and half? Mulatto? Spell it out: "Most of the students are Negroes."

The robbery weapon was an old children's cap pistol.
Young children grow up to be old children, naturally.

Confusing Antecedent Fenton has been in trouble—jumping out a Detention Home window, trying to escape from County Jail, shot at by police in a stolen car, stealing, sleeping in basements and hallways.
We will not comment on the construction of the sentence, but simply suggest we should get those policemen out of that stolen car.

The accidental ruling by the coroner last month removed the possibility of suicide in Miss McDonald's death.
The coroner did not make an accidental ruling. He made an accidental-death ruling.

The Art of Editing

The most intriguing new product of the year could be the atomic golf ball turned out by Goodrich, which can be found in the weeds by a small Geiger counter.

He caught one farm pond lunker on a plastic worm that weighed 6 pounds, 9 ounces.
Some worm.

Donald Vann, 22, was fined $25 yesterday on two charges after being accused of hitting a waitress during an argument with a crutch.
Who won the argument, Donald or the crutch?

His head shaved and drugged with sleeping pills, the youngster was dropped off on a residential street.
Does this mean the victim's head was shaved with sleeping pills?

Coach John Janosek will introduce his staff and team in an informal program to be followed by a short scrimmage.

A man is being held on charges of making obscene telephone calls to women which police say were filthy.

Miss Adele Hudlin agreed to give the dog a home, even though she already had two of her own.
Does she have two homes or two dogs?

The shooting took place in the predawn hours at a heavily traveled intersection during daylight hours.
Once is enough.

Redundancy

Longevity of life was a trademark in the Lanigan clan.
The Malutich family lives on the Ellwood City-New Castle Road, between Ellwood City and New Castle.
That's telling the reader the obvious.

The first question to ask in this re-examination of the platitudes of public relations is this: "Is public relations a necessary function in the administration of today's large-scale enterprises or is it a bureaucratic appendage of the kind that inevitably develops in institutions of size and flourishes in time of prosperity?" The answer to this question is a clear-cut "yes."
Now if we only had a clear-cut question to go with the clear-cut answer. "Will you have lemon or milk in your tea?" "I'll give you a clear-cut answer: 'yes.'"

Such Big Questions

The big question was: "Who dropped the dime in the phone slot and tipped off the Fifth District vice squad to come raiding at 5909 Kinsman Rd. last night?"
Such a big question, we doubt if it was ever asked.

Transferring to a vacant three-bedroom home they own in another part of the city were Mr. and Mrs. John J. Grindstone.

Backward Sentences

Gisele MacKenzie came disguised as a French lady painter.
She paints ladies?

Superfluous Words

The permit will permit the establishment to remain open.

Exactness in Writing

The copyeditor, no less than the reporter, constantly seeks to improve his knowledge of language. A dictionary may not be his best guide because some dictionaries are permissive and frequently try to define one term with another as if the two words were synonymous. Greater precision in usage can be found in works such as Bergen and Cornelia Evans, *The Dictionary of Contemporary American Usage* (New York: Random House, Inc., 1957); Theodore Bernstein, *The Careful Writer* (New York: Atheneum Publishers, 1965); Roy Copperud, *A Dictionary of Usage and Style* (New York: Hawthorn Books, Inc., 1964); Wilson Follett, *Modern American Usage: A Guide* (London: Longmans, 1966); Marjorie Skillin and Robert Gay, *Words into Type*, rev. ed. (New York: Appleton-Century-Crofts, 1964); H. W. Fowler, *A Dictionary of Modern English Usage,* 2nd ed. (New York: Oxford University Press, 1965); and William Morris and Mary Morris, *Dictionary of Word and Phrase Origins* (New York: Harper & Row, Publishers, Vol. I, 1962, Vol. II, 1967). When the aspiring copyeditor has become familiar with books such as these, he can take his first step in editing.

The desk chief of the Denver *Post* devised a system to help his copyeditors overcome word problems. During the day he kept notes of errors that got by the men on the desk or raised questions on the desk. At night he transcribed his notes and placed the transcriptions alphabetically on loose-leaf sheets in the copydesk "bible." The book went through many revisions and additions. The system is recommended for every copydesk.

Most editors insist that the low level of writing cannot be permitted to go its own untutored way, beneath the reach of corrections. Examples of good and bad writing cited by editors in their own critiques constantly remind both writers and copyeditors of the need to substitute good writing habits for bad ones.

Know the Idiom

Careless use of the idiom (the grammatical structure peculiar to our language) occurs frequently in the news report. Usually the fault lies in the prepositions or conjunctions.

Three times as many Americans were killed than [as] in any similar period.

Casualties are twice as many who fell in the Revolutionary War [twice as many as those].

It remains uncertain as to when the deadline for the first payment will be made. [Omit *as to*.]

She had always been able to get through the performance on [of] this taxing role.

It succeeded because of the tolerant policy by [of] the school.

The plan requests an immediate study on [of] the feasibility of a high school complex.

The economist accused him with [of] failing to make a decision. [You charge somebody with blundering but you accuse him of it.]

Among the major concessions was the right for [of] the independent union.

He said the guns are against the law except under [in] certain specified situations. [But, under conditions or circumstances.]

Steps have been taken to substitute the metal scraper blades with [for] nylon blades.

Dressen is no different than [from] other experts. [*Different* may be followed by *than* when introducing a clause: "The patient is no different than he was yesterday."]

Five men were pelted by [with] stones.

The reason for the new name is because the college's mission has been changed [is that the college's mission has been changed].

He said he would not call on [for] assistance from police except as a last resort. [Call the police or call on the police for assistance.]

The council said that if open military force by Russia against Czechoslovakia is allowed to take place [to be exerted] without opposition, the "usefulness of the United Nations will be terminated." [Events, not force, take place.]

Costs have continued to rise but the brand still proudly refuses to knuckle down [under] the increasing economic pressure. [*Knuckle down* means to work energetically or apply oneself seriously. To *knuckle under* is to yield or give in.]

The students barricaded themselves inside the building in protest of [against] the University's policy. [Protests are directed to someone but against something.]

As a rule, boys stop growing between 18 to [and] 20 years of age.

Several speakers paid credit [tribute] to former Gov. Stratton. [You pay tribute to but give credit.]

The proposals forbid lawyers, police and prosecutors from uttering [to utter] anything that might prejudice a future trial. [You forbid a person to do something but you prevent him from doing it.]

She presented the mayor a bouquet of roses. [She gave the mayor a bouquet; she presented the mayor with a bouquet.]

He was shot by [with] a .22 caliber bullet. [He was shot by a companion with a pistol. He was run over by an automobile.]

One question asked in official circles was the possibility that Tshombe had financed his well-paid mercenary force . . . by printing extra money. [A possibility can be in question but it cannot be a question. Revised: "Officials wondered if Tshombe had financed. . . ."]

Gerunds, but not past participles, require the possessive:

"His letter stemmed from the company notifying county officials" ("from the company's notifying").

Little Words

Little words can cause as much trouble as big ones. When a reporter can't decide which of two points is the more worthy of attention, he resorts to journalese by writing both into the lead, connecting them with *as.* "The school tax referendum was approved last night by a margin of nearly 18,000 votes as a strong campaign by anti-busing groups to defeat the increase failed."

Other examples include the following:

Due to—Incorrectly used at the beginning of a sentence or as a preposition. It must always modify a noun: His absence was due to illness. It should not be used in the sense of "because of."

Feel—Save the word *feel* for touching and feeling things and stop using it as a synonym for *think* or *believe.*

In, into—If you're in the lake and feel like jumping, you jump in the lake. If you're in a boat on the lake and feel like jumping overboard, you jump into the lake.

Kin—Relatives collectively, not as individuals.

Kudos—"The kudos in design . . . go to the creators of goods and services." *Kudos* is a singular noun and is generally considered humorous or colloquial.

Last, latest, past—Last few days, in the past, his latest book.

Less, fewer—*Less* with amount; *fewer* with numbers. "Less sugar, fewer miles." *Fewer* means not so many. *Less* means not so much in quantity and not so very good in quality.

Like, as—Reporters shouldn't use *like* as a conjunction as the Winston cigarette commercial does. Use *as,* a conjunction, to introduce a noun or pronoun of comparison; use *like,* a preposition, to introduce a clause or phrase of comparison. "You should heed his advice, as most of us do, like good boys and girls." "If you are like me you will do as I do." "Smells like a rose." "Looks as you would like to look."

None—Often takes the singular verb, as do the following: *each, each one, everybody, everyone, nobody.* But if the distributive expression is followed by a plural noun, *none* should take a plural verb. "None of the volcanoes in Chile are active." When the meaning is "not one" it is better to use *not one* than *none* with a singular verb.

Only—Almost invariably this word is misplaced, thus altering the meaning of the sentence. Notice the changes in meaning by placing *only* in the following: "I hit him in the eye yesterday."

Prone—If a man is lying prone on the beach, nobody can step on his stomach. *Prone* means lying face down. *Supine* means lying face up.

Via—It means "by way of," not "by means of."

Would, could, should—A judge was quoted as saying a boy would remain in an institution until his eighteenth birthday.

Actually, the judge sentenced the boy to an indefinite term and said he could remain there until his eighteenth birthday. To the boy's mother, there was a big difference. In reporting a speech concerning the problem of tobacco advertising as a hazard to children, the paper quoted the speaker as saying the broadcaster should make corrective moves on his own. In a follow-up story, the paper quoted him as saying the broadcaster would take corrective steps. One little word is involved here, but its connotation looms large to broadcasters.

A veteran editor wrote that words may be aimed in the general direction of the target or at the bull's-eye. "What we want are bull's-eye words," he said.

Greater Precision with Words

Absenteeism—"While pupil absenteeism in Cleveland public schools was not unusual, the survey showed that in some areas far more teachers than usual were out." Sometimes the word we use is technically correct but it gives the wrong connotation. By usage, the word *absenteeism* has come to mean deliberate, unnecessary absence. The word *absences* would have been better.

Adopted, passed—Resolutions are adopted or approved; bills are passed. In legislative jargon, *passed* also can mean passed by for the day or for that meeting.

Aggravate, irritate—The first means to make worse. The second means to incite or provoke.

And, but—**State treasurer is Democrat but also servant of people,** the headline said. The implication here is that the official is a servant of the people despite the fact that he's a Democrat.

After, following—The first means next in time. The second means next in order.

Allude, refer—The first suggests without naming the thing specifically. The second names specifically.

Alternative, choice—The first refers to two. The second refers to more than two.

Amateur, novice—An *amateur* is a nonprofessional. A *novice* is a beginner.

Anesthesia—"Creighton had not even received anesthesia." The patient does not receive anesthesia. *Anesthesia* is the condition produced by an anesthetic.

Automated, mechanized—There is a tendency to write of things as automated where the thing is merely mechanized. *Automation* refers to the automatic control of machines.

Avenge, revenge—*Avenge* for another. *Revenge* for self.

Bale, bail—A farmer's hay is baled; water is bailed out of a boat; a prisoner is released on bail. (*Bond* is cash or property given as a security for an appearance or for some performance.)

Belabor, labor—When one needlessly or tiresomely presses a point of argument or explanation he is laboring it. To *belabor* is to beat, hit or whip, primarily in the physical sense. A second

---

Writing and Editing

meaning of *belabor* is to beat with words, perhaps repetitiously and perhaps even with considerable emphasis, but still by no means beating anyone with words.

Before, prior to—"Police said Trumbull's car went through a stop sign prior to the accident and that the investigation is continuing." *Before* is a thoroughly acceptable word.

Biannual, biennial—The first means twice a year. The second means every two years. The copyeditor could help the reader by substituting "every six months" for *biannual* and "every other year" for *biennial.*

Bills, legislation—"The President announced he will send Congress legislation aimed at liberalizing trade with Eastern Europe." *Legislation* is the laws enacted by a legislative power. The President, of course, is not such a power. What he sends to Congress is proposed legislation or bills.

Callus, callous—The first is the noun. The second is the adjective. Similarly: mucus, mucous; phosphorus, phosphorous.

Canvas, canvass—The first is a cloth. The second means to solicit.

Celebrant, celebrator—A *celebrant* presides over a religious rite. A *celebrator* celebrates.

Center around—Something can be centered in, centered at or centered on, but it cannot be centered around.

Chafe, chaff—*Chafe* means to irritate. The heating appliance is a chafing dish. *Chaff* means to ridicule good-naturedly. It also means husks or rubbish.

Coiffeur, coiffure—"It seems that a few females in this city want to be able to change coiffeurs, depending on the occasion, the same way women in general change clothes." No. What they want to change is their *coiffures.* A good coiffeur is too hard to find. A *coiffeur* is a hair-dresser. A *coiffure* is the style of hair dress.

Collision—"Cars driven by Robert F. Clagett and Mrs. Lois Trant were damaged yesterday when they collided on Denison Ave. Stonington police reported that Mrs. Trant stopped her car before making a turn into Isham St. and it was hit in the rear by the other vehicle." Two objects can *collide* only when both are in motion and going—usually but not always—in opposite directions. It is not a *collision* when one car is standing still.

Combine—"Maid o' Silk combined the spirit of old America in a modern dress for this year's holiday offering." When you combine you must put together at least two things. What Maid o' Silk did was to embody the spirit of old America in a modern dress—or convey it, or wrap it, or achieve it.

Compared to, compared with—The first uses specific similarities or differences: "He *compared* Johnson with Wilson." The second notes general or metaphysical resemblance: "You might *compare* him to a weasel."

Comprise, compose—*Comprise* is not synonymous with *compose*, but actually almost its opposite. "The secretaries of State,

The Art of Editing

Defense, Interior and other departments compose the cabinet." That is, they constitute it. "The cabinet comprises the secretaries of the State, Defense, Interior and other departments." That is, it includes, embraces, contains them.

Concert, recital—two or more performers give a *concert*. One performer gives a *recital*.

Conclude—Arguments *conclude*. Speeches close or end.

Conscious, aware—We are *conscious* of what we feel, and *aware* of what we know.

Continuous, continual—If it rains steadily every day for a week it rains *continuously*. If it rains only part of every day for a week it rains *continually* or intermittently.

Cords, chords—The first refers to a string or small rope, an anatomical structure such as a spinal cord or vocal *cord*. Or it may be ribbed fabric or a unit of volume of wood. A *chord* is a string of a musical instrument or a combination of tones.

Couturier, couturiere—The first is a male. The second is a female.

Dedication—"The dedication that Rev. Mr. Davis had for his mission was instilled early by his mother." *Dedication* means act or rite of dedication to a sacred use. What Mrs. Davis may have done was instill a sense of dedication in her young son's mind.

Deign—"How this case will eventually be decided we do not deign to say." *Deign* means to condescend, not dare or care.

Derelict—"'Lake Erie is so big,' Frank Kelly kept saying to his companion in their derelict 16-foot boat which had no power, no lights, no food." For a boat to be *derelict*, it has to be abandoned.

Details—"United States military spokesmen gave little details about the raids on the north." If you give little *details* you give much detail, but if you give few details you give little detail.

Disrobe—A haughty way of saying undress, unless done by royalty, priests and judges.

Enormity—Applies preferably to abnormal wickedness, but is often misused to mean enormousness.

Epitaph, epithet—The first is an inscription on a tombstone. *Epithet* is a descriptive adjective applied to someone—"old curmudgeon."

Escapees, escapers—The dictionary recognizes both. Why not settle for *fugitives*?

Farther, further—The distinction is between extension of space and expansion of thought.

Flaunt, flout—The first means to wave or flutter showily. The second means to mock or treat with contempt. "The students *flouted* the authority of the school board."

Flounder, founder—Horses *flounder*—struggle, thrash about—in the mud. Ships *founder* or sink. Of course, horses can founder when they become disabled from overeating.

Fluoride, fluorine—Stories have referred to water being fluoridated by the use of *fluoride*. The element is *fluorine* and the medium through which it is introduced into the water is one of a number of fluorides. Say, simply, "a fluoride is used."

Fulsome—Fulsome praise is insincere praise, not copious. It means offensively excessive, insincere.

For example—"By eliminating the uncertainty of erratic weather the growers were able to develop stronger plants and better flowers. Jones' orchid seedlings, for example, are shipped to such distant points as Australia, Hawaii and South America." The distance to which they are shipped may be related to their strength and quality, but it isn't an *example* of that unless set forth in those terms, something like this: "Jones' orchid seedlings, for example, have successfully survived shipments and transplantings to points as distant as Australia."

Fortunate, fortuitous—The first means coming by good luck. The second means happening by chance.

Gantlet, gauntlet—You run a *gantlet*, a form of punishment. You put on a *gauntlet* or glove.

Gendarme—This is not the proper title for a Paris police officer. A city policeman is an *agent de police; gendarme* is reserved for the small-town officer.

Gibe, jibe—The first is to jeer, taunt or flout. The second means to shift sails, alter a course or, colloquially, to be in harmony.

Gorilla, guerrilla—The first is an ape. The second is a soldier or raider.

Grant, subsidy—A *grant* is money given to public companies. A *subsidy* is help to a private enterprise.

Grizzly, grisly—"Miss Karmel begins her work in a valley of shadows that deepen and darken as she heaps one grizzly happening upon the next." One *grizzly* heaped upon the next produces only two angry bears. The word the writer wants is *grisly*.

Half-mast, half-staff—Masts are on ships. Flagstaffs are on buildings or on the ground.

Hardy, hearty—A story of four visiting policemen from Africa said they expressed appreciation for their hardy welcome. If that's what they said, they meant *hearty*.

Haul, hale—The first means to drag. The second means to take (haled into court).

Historic, historical—*Historic* means famous in history; *historical* pertains to history, such as historic sites and historical novels. *Historic* is an overworked adjective used to describe an event that may or may not find a place in history.

Honor, celebrate—"The dinner was in honor of Brown's 50 years in the business." The dinner honored Brown, not his years in business. Use *celebrated* or *observed*.

Hopeful, hopefully—Incorrect for "it is hoped" or "I hope." Literally, "in a hopeful manner."

Impassable, impassible—The first is that which cannot be passed. The second is that which can't suffer or be made to show signs of emotion.

Imply, infer—The speaker does the *implying,* and the listener the *inferring.*

In charge of—The person is in charge of the thing rather than vice versa.

Loath, loathe—The first means unwilling. The second means to hate.

Masterly, masterful—The first means skillful. The second means domineering.

Measles—A child has measles, not the measles. So, too, with mumps. Treat both as singular: "*Measles* is a virus disease."

Meticulous—"Attending physicians attribute the fact that she is still alive to the meticulous and devoted nursing she receives from her mother." As used here, *meticulous* is intended to mean careful, painstaking, watchful, vigilant, etc. It doesn't mean any of those things. On the contrary, it means being overcareful, finical or fussy about trivialities. In fact, a meticulous person really is a fuss-budget.

Negotiate—"He could not negotiate the hill in front of the hospital." You *negotiate* a loan or a treaty; you climb a hill.

Numbered—"Numbered among the pioneers of the industry is George Blandish." Can't tell the pioneers without a number?

Oral, verbal—All language is *verbal*—"of words." But only *oral* language is spoken.

Peaceable, peaceful—The first is restricted to persons. The second is restricted to periods and countries.

People, persons—*Person* is the human being. *People* are the body of persons—"American people." There is no rule saying a large number can't be referred to as *people*—"61 million people."

Plunge—"A dramatic cold front zipped through the city at 9 a.m. today plunging the thermometer 17 degrees in 25 minutes." Plunge the mercury or the temperature, but not the poor thermometer.

Podium, lectern—The first is a footstool or platform. The second is what speakers thump.

Populous, populated, populace—"Miss O'Brien's home is in a populated area in the center of town." Use *populous. Populace* means the common people of a community.

Predict—"Present and anticipated demand for goods indicates that last year should be another record-breaking year, officials of the firm predicted." You don't *predict* that something "already is."

Presently—This means after a little time or shortly. It does not mean at the present time. Try *currently* or *now.*

Prophecy, prophesy—The first is a noun. The second is a verb.

Quell, quench—Uprisings, disorders, riots and the like are quelled. A fire—because water is the chief agency for putting it out—is *quenched,* doused, extinguished.

Raise, rear, raze—You raise animals and rear children. *Raze* means to destroy.

Ravage, ravish—The first means to damage or devastate. Armies may *ravage* a town. *Ravish* has several meanings—to fill with joy, to carry off by force, to rape. A ravishing blonde is enchanting.

Realtor—This is a registered trade name. It should be capitalized and used only to designate members of the National Association of Real Estate Boards.

Retire, resign, replace—*Replace* for *retire* is a cold, curt and cruel word with which to publicly acknowledge years of faithful and interested service. Subtle differences in words can be important. To say that someone has quit a job when he resigned to accept another job suggests that he left in a huff.

Roughshod, slipshod—"Mrs. Lawless told the *News* that traffic runs slipshod over her property." She meant *roughshod,* didn't she? *Slipshod* means slovenly.

Sewage, sewerage—*Sewage* is human waste, sometimes called municipal or sanitary waste. *Sewerage* is the system to carry away sewage. They are sewerage (not sewage) plants. Industrial waste is the waste matter from factories. Some cities have storm sewers to carry away rain water and sanitary sewers for sewage.

Scheduled—"The meeting is scheduled next Saturday." When referring to an event in the future, the word *scheduled* must have a preposition after it, usually *for*.

Smith, smithy—*Smith* is the blacksmith. *Smithy* is the blacksmith shop.

Stanch, staunch—The first is a verb. The second is an adjective.

Sustenance, subsistence—"The two survived despite little besides melted snow for subsistence." No wonder they almost starved. The word is *sustenance*.

Tall, high—Properly, a building, tree or man is *tall*. A plane, bird or cloud is *high*.

That, which—Use *that* in a dependent clause: "This is the house that Jack built." In an independent clause, *which* is correct: "Jack's house, which has been in the same family for nearly a century, has been sold."

Total—May be either singular or plural as idiom dictates. When the word is itself the subject, treat it as singular when it has a definite article and as plural when it has an indefinite article. "The total of boxes found looted was eight." "A total of eight boxes were found looted." "A total of 239 Negroes have been jailed in Selma."

6

Slips in Writing

The deskman uses his copy pencil as a scalpel rather than as a cleaver when he goes to work on a piece of copy. First he examines the patient to detect the ailments. Then he tries to effect a cure.

The writer may try to include the answers to the basic questions of who, what, where, when, why and how. The copyeditor supplies one additional question: "So what?" He searches every story for its significance, tries to weave this element into the story, if it is not already there, then emphasizes it again in the headline.

One mark of an experienced copyeditor is his awareness of the peculiar mistakes that particular writers are likely to make. Copy from at least two sources requires special attention. One is transcribed telephone copy. No matter what the copy says, the copyeditor knows that Isaiah could not have written, "They shall beat their swords into plush chairs," or that the orchestra did not play On Dante (andante). Another is the publicity handout. Too many of these are written from the viewpoint of the institution, not the newspaper reader. Such releases may please company officials but they bore city editors and are a menace to copyeditors who have to try to make them readable and interesting. Two examples will suffice:

The first third of a release by Hawaiian Pineapple Co., Ltd. reads as follows:

The pineapple plant, producer of the fruit long a favorite on American menus, may soon become a major source of a proteolytic (protein-digesting) enzyme with important industrial and medical uses, the Hawaiian Pineapple Co. announced Thursday.

Henry A. White, Hapco president, announced at the annual meeting of Dole stockholders that the company has started pilot plant production in Honolulu of bromelain, an enzyme recovered from the stumps of pineapple plants.

Proteolytic enzymes are presently used primarily in the brewing, food and leather industries. Limited quantities of Dole bromelain are being sold to breweries, where the enzyme "digests" protein particles which would otherwise cause beer to become cloudy when chilled.

Plans are being made to expand production for other uses as quickly as possible.

Independent medical research on the properties of bromelain indicates that it may be useful medically.

"It is necessary to emphasize, however, that a great deal of independent research must yet be carried out to explore more fully the medical potentialities of bromelain," Mr. White declared.

"Initially, the bulk of our enzyme production will be for industrial uses, and our projections are based on its use as an industrial product."

In many respects, he said, bromelain shows promise of being a by-product ideally suited to Hapco's operations. It lends itself to large-scale agricultural and factory production, and ultimately to attractive pricing for customers.

Rewriting, not editing, is demanded here if the story is to mean anything to the reader. A feature treatment will make the story entertaining as well as informative. A feature lead automatically inspires a good head:

The Hawaiian Pineapple Co. has come up with a substance that can:
Keep your beer from turning cloudy when you chill it.
Tenderize a tough old steak.
Help you make cheese easier.
The substance is called bromelain. It is recovered from the stumps of pineapple plants.

URBANA, Ill., Jan. 8 (Special)—A week-long newswriting course for new employe prospects with no previous newspaper editorial experience will be held Jan. 30 to Feb. 3 here at the University of Illinois college of journalism and communications.

Sponsored by the Illinois Press association and the university, the course is designed to meet the personnel shortage by providing prospective employes with the training that I.P.A. members find to be expedient.

Commented *English I* (January 1967) after the Chicago *Tribune* had run the release without changes, "The story is a model of how to conceal news and discourage reading. Its principal fault is that it was written from the viewpoint of the school, not the newspaper reader. The news is that the shortage of editorial help of some of the newspapers in Illinois is so severe that wholly untrained recruits are being sought. The publishers have turned to the school for help but are unwilling to spare more than a week for training their prospective employes. You can figure all this out after a second reading of what appears to be a journalism school handout. *Week-long* adds nothing to the dates given in the lead sentence and its significance is not clear at first. *New employe prospects* doesn't mean much of anything until you have been told whose new employe prospects they are."

Press agentry frequently is characterized by floss. The following is from *English I* (February 1963):

Flossy

The United Motor Coach company has been authorized to take out loans totaling $225,000 in conjunction with a new garage and general office building it will construct in Des Plaines.

Cost of the facility is estimated at $321,000. It is estimated that the new building will save the company $25,000 a year through consolidation of bus storage and other operation economies.

The Illinois Commerce commission approved the real estate and chattel mortgage loans which the company will get from the Harris Trust and Savings bank.

Edited

The United Motor Coach company has been authorized to borrow $225,000 for a new garage and general office building in Des Plaines.

The building will cost about $321,000 and is expected to save the company $25,000 in bus storage and other operation economies.

The Illinois Commerce commission approved the real estate and chattel mortgage loans the company will get from the Harris Trust and Savings bank.

Read the advice of an editor to his copydesk:

Your job is to edit, not just read. You know you must guard against libel and against errors of fact, grammar and style. But your biggest job is to make the copy read better, to pep up tired writing.

Double-check every sentence in every story to see if it can be made shorter, more vigorous, more colorful. Be sure each sentence has no unnecessary words, each story no unnecessary sentences. This does not mean each sentence and graf must be short. It does mean every word must count.

Watch for repetition. Watch for clichés. Watch for trivia.

Do the verbs shift from one tense to another? Dig into the copy and recast the sentences if they need it. If you think the whole story misses the point and needs rewriting, tell the slotman. If you make a major change in a story, the head of the department from which the copy came should be notified.

Do not be afraid to make the changes that will make the story better.

Taking it for granted that the star writer always has his facts straight is a dangerous attitude. So is the belief that wire copy is sacred. If the deskman says, "I don't get this but the writer ought to know what he is talking about," the chances are that the reader won't get it either. And, again, the sole purpose of editing is to help the reader.

What right has the deskman to change a writer's copy? He has every right because that's his job. He is paid to catch the slips that the writer, working under pressure, is bound to make. As stated previously, the slip that gets into the paper is the fault of the copydesk, not the reporter.

Slips in Writing

Often it is the tedious error that gets by unless the deskman takes the trouble to double-check. Here are examples:

1. Double-check all dates. Your source material may say Wednesday, March 6. A check will show March 6 is Tuesday. Then recheck and don't guess which date is correct.

2. Check and recheck names. Publicity agents guess too often. Is the spelling of the name consistent throughout the story? Does it match the name in the cutline of the accompanying picture?

3. Make sure in using figures that your totals check with the details of figures you have in the story.

4. Double-check the sources. A map, for instance, is not necessarily the authority for place name spelling. Is the source pinpointed? Are the "river experts" really experts or are they several barge captains or fishermen?

Newspapers strive first for accuracy and reliability. Their second goal is to be crisp and interesting. The copyeditor has a hand in both.

Honing the Lead

Editors are leery of formulas for writing, but on one principle they are nearly unanimous: The lead of the story must be short. How short? A Hearst editor demanded short leads and finally got a one-word one. The Chicago *Tribune* applauded this three-word lead: "Money and race." Probably a better one: "Are nudes prudes?"

Some newspapers have set twenty words as the maximum. "If you can tell the story in fewer words, feel free to do so," they say. Ralph McGill, former editor of the Atlanta *Constitution,* liked what he called a flawless lead in the Bible: "There was a man in the land of Uz, whose name was Job."

The copyeditor's eye brightens when he reads leads that rank with these classics:

Only in Russia could Peter and the Wolf die on the same night [Stalin's death].

They're burying a generation today. (Texas school explosion.)

The moon still shines on the moonshine stills in the hills of Pennsylvania.

Fifty thousand Irishmen—by birth, by adoption and by profession—marched up Fifth Avenue today.

Most lead problems arise when the reporter tries to see how much he can pack into the lead. Rather, he should try to see how much he can leave out of the lead:

The Thumb Area Economic Opportunity Commission, Inc., has 13 projects with an	Thirteen projects are under way or are be-

estimated cost of about $250,000 either in operation or in various stages of planning, Robert Benko, commission director, reported to the County Community Action Committee Tuesday. [38 words]

ing planned in the Thumb's war on poverty. [15 words]

Put a reporter on a copydesk for six months writing headlines and he will soon learn how to write an effective lead. He will be on his way when he begins to think of the lead in terms of an appropriate headline.

A good lead contains qualities other than brevity. It must inform and summarize. It must be straightforward; it cannot back into the action. It sets the mood, the pace and the flavor of the story. It accomplishes what the term implies: It guides, directs, points to and induces. If it is a suspended-interest lead, it must be so tantalizing and intriguing that the reader cannot help but continue.

The problems in achieving a good lead are many. The deskman will be especially alert for the following.

In his effort to get the maximum punch in his lead, the overzealous reporter may "needle" the opening. That is, he lets the lead overreach the story. The lead ignores some facts contained in the story. It stretches and therefore distorts. It is the type of lead that says, "All hell broke loose in city hall last night." Then the final sentence says, "When the dispute subsided the councilmen shook hands and the mayor adjourned the session."

Leads that Mislead

"No matter how appealingly you wrap up the lead, it is no good if it gives a wrong impression or tells a lie," Joseph G. Herzberg told readers of *Late City Edition* (New York: Holt, Rinehart and Winston, Inc., 1947, pp. 141, 143). And again, "It is a plain fact that to some papers, the simple truth of the story is never enough. They dress it up and pump it up and they don't merely present it to the reader, they all but cram it down his throat."

The "souped-up" lead invites a sensational headline. If the deskman lets the overextended lead stand, then tries to top the lead with a calm headline, he is likely to have the headline tossed back with the suggestion he put more punch into it. Some deskmen have been known to "doctor" the lead to justify a sensational headline.

Akin to the sensationalized lead is the opinion lead. This type of lead offers a judgment rather than fact. Often it fails to distinguish between mere puffery and news: "Construction features described as newer in concept than space travel will be part of the easy to operate and easy to shop in Almart store soon to open on the Kirkwood Highway."

Delayed-news leads back into the news, are detailed when they should be tight, are indirect when they should be direct or are inactive when they should be active.[1]

Delayed-News Leads

[1] Examples from *Writing for the AP*, 1959.

Delaying the News	*Telling the News*
Dean David E. Snodgrass of the University of California's Hastings College of Law says the American Bar Association's long-time ban on news photographs in courtrooms is archaic and unrealistic.	The rule against news photographs in courtrooms is archaic and unrealistic, says a law school dean.

Indirect	*Direct*
An Atlanta businessman who joined two anti-Negro, anti-Jewish groups and turned over information to the FBI, today associated a man on trial for dynamiting the Jewish temple with race-hating John Kasper.	A man on trial for dynamiting the Jewish temple was linked today with race-hating John Kasper by an FBI undercover agent.

Inactive	*Active, Tight*
A top-ranking rocket AFD space weapons expert coupled a disclosure of his resignation from the Air Force today with a blast at the senior scientists upon whom the services rely for technological advice.	A top-level Air Force space weapons expert blasted civilian scientists today and said he has resigned.

Soft	*Hard*
A thunderstorm struck southwest Iowa early today causing loss of life and vast property damage. More than 13 inches of rain fell in a few hours. [Dramatic details were buried deep in the story.]	Nine persons were drowned, homes and buildings were washed away, bridges were ripped out and crops were flattened by a thunderstorm in southwest Iowa today. Thirteen inches of rain fell in a few hours. Hundreds of families were evacuated.

Cluttered Leads   Lead cluttering occurs when the writer tries to pack too many ideas into the opening statement. A compound sentence in the lead is questionable because one point has to be put ahead of the other. It is better to facilitate an understanding of both ideas instead of blurring them. One trick is to make two short sentences of one long one:

LONDON, June 2—Ten years ago today, a 27-year-old princess was crowned Queen Elizabeth II, and Britain, in an outpouring of emotional fervor unmatched since, hailed her coronation as the beginning of a new Elizabethan era of splendor and achievement.	LONDON, June 2—Ten years ago today, a 27-year-old princess was crowned Queen Elizabeth II. Britain, in an outpouring of emotional fervor unmatched since, hailed her coronation as the beginning of a new Elizabethan era of splendor and achievement.

The lead should be pruned of minor details that could come later in the story if they are needed:

Donald E. Brodie, son of William Brodie, for more than three decades a member of the display ad-	Donald E. Brodie, son of Mr. and Mrs. William Brodie, 106 W. 41st St., was graduated from Jefferson

vertising department of the News, and Mrs. Brodie, 106 W. 41st St., was graduated from Jefferson Medical College last week.

Medical College last week. For more than three decades, William Brodie was a member of the display advertising department of the News.

The lead need not be long to be cluttered:

First National is one of four American banks, and the American Express company, which issues travelers checks throughout the nation.

First National, three other American banks, and the American Express company issue travelers checks throughout the nation.

The deskman can tidy up cluttered writing in three ways. He can break up complicated sentences into one-idea sentences. He can rearrange the word order to form a more logical pattern. He can remove wasted words:

Cluttered	*Uncluttered*
Ray S---, mayor of Streator, La Salle county, who was inducted into office for the second term Monday night, was arrested yesterday by Federal Bureau of Investigation agents after he accepted a cash kickback on a sewer contract in the bar of the Water Tower Inn, 800 North Michigan Ave.	F.B.I. agents arrested Ray S---, newly elected mayor of Streator, La Salle county, yesterday. The mayor was charged with accepting a cash kickback on a sewer contract. The kickback was accepted in a bar of the Water Tower Inn, 800 North Michigan Ave. S--- was inducted into office for his second term Monday night.
Mrs. Buckley began collecting dolls 20 years ago and stuffed them into closets and under beds until she had amassed so many that three big truckloads were needed to convey the lot to new quarters in Webster Ave.	Mrs. Buckley began collecting dolls 20 years ago. She stuffed them into closets and under beds. She found she had three truckloads of them when she moved to new quarters on Webster Ave.
Grand Duchess Charlotte and her party flew to Washington from Philadelphia, where they arrived yesterday from London, in a Marine helicopter.	Grand Duchess Charlotte and her party, who arrived in Philadelphia yesterday from London, flew to Washington today in a Marine Corps helicopter.
Dr. Szilard was credited by his fellow scientists, with the late Dr. Enrico Fermi, of being co-fathers of the atom bomb.	Dr. Szilard and the late Dr. Enrico Fermi were credited by their fellow scientists with being co-fathers of the atom bomb.
Data-processing instructors who have been teaching high school students have found them quicker to learn than the average class of adults.	Instructors have found high school students learn data processing more quickly than adults.
The state department issued a statement reaffirming United States support for the plans and policies aimed at integrating Ka-	The state department reaffirmed United States support of the plan to hold Katanga within the Congo as proposed by U Thant, United

tanga into the Congo central government enunciated by U Thant, United Nations secretary general and Congolese Premier Cyrille Adoula.

Nations secretary general, and Congolese Premier Cyrille Adoula.

Cliché Leads

Quick action by two alert policemen was credited with saving the life of. . . .

Police and volunteers staged a massive manhunt today for a man who. . . .

Say-Nothing Leads

If a say-nothing lead causes the deskman to ask, "So what else is new?" the chances are the readers will have the same reaction.

DETROIT—Somber was the word for the memorial services to American dead of the War of 1812 Sunday.

Home, public, and traffic safety were discussed today at a Safety Leadership Conference in the Hotel Du Pont.

William J. Miller Jr. today gave the Lions Club traffic engineer's statistics which add up to the fact that "highway problems are still a very important consideration for each of us."

It's doubtful that many readers got beyond the last deadly lead. But anybody who read sixteen inches of type, with no news to the inch, eventually found out—two paragraphs from the bottom of the story—that U.S. 13 may become a controlled access highway throughout the state. That's the news. It should have been in the lead. The point of the story is what Miller said, not that he spoke to the Lions Club or repeated a lot of statistics.

Fire so hot it burned the mud guards off and melted a small section of an aluminum trailer body damaged the trailer. . . .

This is almost like writing, "Fire so hot that it burned the roof and walls and destroyed all the furnishings damaged the house of John Doe. . . ."

Illogical Leads

Frequently, illogical leads occur when the writer presents the idea backwards or uses a non sequitur.

State police attributed an auto collision and the alertness of witnesses to the rapid apprehension of Benjamin Petrucci. . . .

Either the apprehension was attributed to the collision and the alert witnesses or the collision and the witnesses were credited with the apprehension.

Hoping to encourage transient parking at its facilities, the city parking authority yesterday voted to increase rates at two lots.

Charging more for parking hardly seems the way to encourage more of it.

Three small brothers died last night in a fire that burned out two rooms of their home while their father was at work and their mother was visiting a neighbor.

Note how much clearer the revision is: "Left unattended, three small brothers perished in a fire last night that destroyed two rooms of their home. Their father was at work and their mother was visiting a neighbor."

Too much delay in identifying the central character presents problems:

Other Lead Problems

An executive of the So-and-So League said today that . . .

A 15-year-old boy confessed . . .

A 19-year-old girl was injured . . .

A 73-year-old woman is alive . . .

A 55-year-old man ran berserk . . .

Such construction cannot help but bore the reader and is maddening to the copyeditor who is instructed to trim the story to one paragraph.

Another problem is overlong identification, sometimes even preceding the name:

Former Assistant Secretary of State for Latin American Affairs Lincoln Gordon said today . . .

At 7 p.m. yesterday 60 persons fled a three-story apartment building at 2523 E. 38th St. when a carelessly discarded cigaret sent smoke billowing through the building. [King-sized?]

Too Many Statistics

Louis Ezzo, 29, of Plainville, a school bus driver, was charged by state police with speeding and violation of a statute limiting school bus speeds to 40 miles an hour at 3:30 p.m. yesterday on I-95 Groton.

Cain Adams, 26, of 41144 Outer Eden Drive, today killed his brother, Abel Adams, 25, same address, after an argument which their mother, Eve Adams, 42, formerly hostess at the Garden of Eden Nudist Colony, said began at a barbecue. [From the *Bulletin of the American Society of Newspaper Editors*, (April 1, 1952) p. 4.]

A 14-year-old boy fired three shots into a third-floor apartment at 91 Monmouth St. yesterday to climax an argument with a 39-year-old mother who had defended her 9-year-old daughter against an attack by the boy.

Mimi La Belle, Blanktown exotic dancer, was arrested on a charge of indecent exposure last night, according to Officers George Smith and Henry Brown.

Overattribution

An Associated Press reference book comments, "Don't be afraid to begin a story by naming the source. It is awkward sometimes, but also sometimes is the best and most direct way to put the story in proper perspective and balance when the source must be established clearly in the reader's mind if he is properly to understand the story." An example:

All Delawareans over 45 should be vaccinated now against Asian flu.

The attribution should have been in the lead since this is opinion, the consensus of a number of health officials.

Second-Day Lead on a First-Day Story Every veteran deskman knows that frequently a wire story's first lead is better than its second, third or fourth. A lead telling the reader an airliner crashed today, killing fifty passengers, is better than a later lead saying an investigation is under way to determine the cause of an airline crash that killed fifty passengers. If the first lead tells the story adequately, why replace it with a second, and often weaker, lead?

First lead—"Nearly 800 prisoners at the Maryland House of Correction rioted and held four guards as hostages before they were subdued by state police today."

Second lead—"About half of the 800 rioting prisoners at the Maryland House of Correction were forced back into their cells tonight, less than three hours after they went on a destructive rampage."

First lead—"HOLYOKE, Mass.—At least six persons—four of them children—perished early today when a fire, reportedly set by an arsonist, swept a five-story tenement."

Second lead (with second-day angle)—"HOLYOKE, Mass.—The body of a little boy about two years old, was recovered today, raising the death toll in a tenement house fire to seven."

Third lead (back on the beam)—"HOLYOKE, Mass.—Seven persons—five of them children—perished when a general alarm midnight blaze, believed set, destroyed a five-story tenement."

Newspapers should be edited for their own readers, not for opposition newspapers or for radio and television stations. A new development may be the latest, but it is not necessarily the most important.

Adjectives Are Suspect

Effective adjectives strengthen nouns if they are informative rather than descriptive: "7-foot 1-inch Wilt Chamberlain" rather than "towering Wilt Chamberlain."

Many adjectives are redundant, "loaded," incorrect or misplaced.

Redundant—armed gunmen, chilly 30 degrees below zero, exact replica, foreign imports.

Editorial adjectives—blistering reply, cocky labor leader, so-called liberal, strong words.

Incorrect adjectives—"Whirring or grinding television cameras": Television cameras are electronic devices and do not whir or grind. "A Pole with an unpronounceable name": Every name is pronounceable by somebody. "An unnamed man": Every man has a name; the adjective should be *unidentified*.

Improperly placed adjectives—"Unfair labor practices strike": The practices, not the strike, are unfair. "The treacherous 26-mile Arkansas down-river race": The river, not the race, is treacherous. "The criminally insane building of Delaware State Hospital." "Juvenile Judge George Brown." "So their names have been removed from the barred from running for office for five years list": How's that again? "For area as well as migratory game bird hunters nationwide, the U.S. Fish and Wildlife Service has announced a most welcome change in migratory bird hunting regulations for the coming season": The reference is to hunters of migratory birds, obviously.

A reminder from a wire service sums up the adjective problem: "A statuesque Roman beauty" appeared as a witness in a trial. Ted Williams was said to be engaged to "a beauteous girl model." Dayton picked up "an attractive blonde." A New York girl arrested for possessing narcotics lived in "a lavish apartment" in the West Fifties. An actress killed herself in her "luxurious apartment." Most of these terms aren't really descriptive. How big is "statuesque," how pretty is "beauteous," what specific qualities make a woman "attractive" (and to whom?) and what is a "lavish" apartment? The arrested girl's abode turned out (the next day) to be an apartment of 2½ small rooms.

Searching for the right word takes time. Editors urge deskmen to omit an adjective rather than to rely on a shoddy term.

The more melodramatic the story the less the need for melodramatic rhetoric. Example:

INDIANAPOLIS—Across from a makeshift morgue of ice, somber experts scratched among piles of broken concrete tonight, seeking the cause of a gas explosion which killed 64.

David Staten, 14, whose parents and grandmother were killed by the explosion, died tonight in a hospital.

A flaming geyser of death erupted in the state fairgrounds Coliseum last night only minutes before the scheduled final curtain of a gay Halloween "Holiday on Ice" show watched by more than 4,000.

The blast spewed bodies, debris, and blood-splashed mink coats onto the rink and carved a gaping hole in the Coliseum's choice box seats. Hospital counts showed 385 injured.

The bodies were stretched on impromptu slabs on the rink today as a towering crane gingerly picked at the rubble, unearthing what officials hoped would be a key to the tragedy.

A copyeditor's pencil would make the lead read: "Investigators scratched in piles of broken concrete tonight, seeking the cause of a gas explosion that killed 64 persons." The pencil would poise over "flaming geyser of death," "spewed bodies," "gaping hole," "choice box seats," "impromptu slabs" and "towering crane."

Clichés

A good writer uses a fresh and appropriate figure of speech to enhance his story. The copyeditor should distinguish between the fresh and the stale. This isn't always easy because some words and phrases are used repeatedly in the news report.

The Associated Press ran nearly 400,000 words of its copy through a computer to determine which of the tired words and phrases were used most frequently. The result: hailed, backlash, in the wake of, informed, violence flared, kickoff, death and destruction, riot-torn, tinder dry, racially troubled, voters marched to the polls, jam-packed, grinding crash, confrontation, oil-rich nation, no immediate comment, cautious (or guarded) optimism, limped into port.

Deskmen can add to the list of tired expressions:

Acid test	Experts
Aide (health aide)	Fashioned
Alert policeman	Fiery or bosomy actress
Area girl	Fiery holocaust
Average height, reader, voter	Fingered (pointed out)
Banquet (never a dinner)	Fire broke out, swept
Based (Dover-based)	Fire of undetermined origin
Bitter dispute	First and foremost
Blistering accusation	Flawed
Bloody riots	Freak accident
Blueprint (for plan)	Fuzz (for police)
Bold bandits	Gap (credibility, generation, etc.)
Bombshell announcement	Giant teamsters union
Briefing	Go into a huddle
Brutal murder or slaying	Guidelines
Cardinal sin	Hammer out
Caught the eye of	Hard core
Charisma	Heated exchange
Charming lady	Highlighted
Circles (informed circles)	High-powered cars
Combed (for searched)	Hike
Controversial issue	Hosted
Coveted trophy	Hurled
Crack troops, train, liner	Identity crisis
Crippling amendment	Implementing
Critical times	In nothing flat
Crushing burdens	–ize (finalize, formalize, dieselize, weaponize)
Cutback	Jaundiced eye
Daring daylight holdup	Junket
Deficit-ridden	Keeled over
Devastating flood, fire	Know-how
Devout Catholic, Moslem	Led to safety
Do your own thing	Local girl
Down under (Australia)	Lonely lovers lane
Dumped	Long-smouldering
–ees (trainees, escapees)	

Luxurious apartment, love nest
Made off with
Middle-aged woman
Miraculous escape, cure
Moderate smoker
Momentous occasion
Nitty-gritty
Normalcy
Overwhelming majority
Pad (for room)
Paddy wagon
Particular
Passing motorist
Phased in, phased out (started or
    stopped; hired or fired)
Plush hotel, apartment
Police were summoned
Powerful House Rules Committee
Pressure (as a verb)
Pretty blonde, housewife
Probe
Rampaging flood
Reportedly, reputedly
Restless dragon (China)
Senior citizen
Simplistic
Snuffed out
Socialite
Staged a riot or protest
Standing ovation

Steaming jungle
Stems from
Stinging rebuke
Stomped
Structuring
Sweeping changes
Swing into high gear
Task force
Teeny-boppers
Tell it like it is
Tense or uneasy calm
Thorough or all-out investigation
Top priority
Tragic accident
Triggered
Two-way street
Ugly tempered mob
Unveiled
Value judgment
Vast expanse
Veep
Verbalize
Vicious tornado
Violence erupted
Violent explosion
Well-known citizen, lawyer
Whirlwind tour, junket
Wreathed in smiles
Yardstick
Young boys or girls

Jargon

A university press release announcing a significant engineering meeting on the campus reported that one of the major papers would be on "The aerodynamic heating of blunt, axisymmetric, re-entry bodies with laminar boundary layer at zero and at large angles of yaw in supersonic and hypersonic air streams." To the consumer of news, that title is "Greek," or, as Maury Maverick would have termed it, *gobbledygook*. Translated, the topic suggested, "How hot does a space ship get when it swings back into the air around the earth?"

Doctors, lawyers, educators, engineers, government officials, scientists, sociologists, economists and others have their professional jargon or shoptalk peculiar to the profession. Sometimes this jargon is used to impress the uninitiated; sometimes it is a cover-up.

Here is how Daniel Melcher, president of the R. R. Bowker Company, translated three examples of gobbledygook (*The Library Journal,* September 1, 1964):

A mnemonic code of three, four or five characters was assigned to each primary source.
"Producers and distributors names are abbreviated."

Sources were provided with an effort-saving structured response form.
"Questionnaires were sent to producers and distributors."

The Art of Editing

The editorial work is paralleled by a machine processing effort that translates the worksheets into decks of punched cards.

"The entries are typed on cards which are then punched for ease of sorting."

A judge's ruling on a case involving an actress contained this sentence: "Such vanity doubtless is due to the adulation which the public showers on the denizens of the entertainment world in a profusion wholly disproportionate to the intrinsic contribution which they make to the scheme of things." That's pretentious verbosity. So, too, is this from an educator:

The educator will hold a practicum for disadvantaged children who are under-achieving in reading.

"Slow learners who can't read."

Translation is needed when a story on education contains "professional terms" such as *paraprofessionals, academically talented, disadvantaged* (culturally deprived, impoverished students), *ghetto* (inner-city or center-city) *schools* and *ungraded* and *nongraded classrooms.*

Some examples of overwriting indulged in by government workers are contained in Lawrence R. Klein's study for the U.S. Department of Labor (Mimeographed report, "High Symmetry," 1965):

Diffusibility of knowledge through the environment in which the families are to move is essential if the full expression of their potentiality is to become explicit in action. Facts pertaining to experience of every sort that the family is in the course of digesting give the context and full flavor of consciousness to their experience.

"Full knowledge of the family and its history by all concerned is necessary if its move to a new community is to be successful."

The fact that detail provided by the Bureau of the Census by years indicates that in the period April 1953 to April 1954, the rate of household formation had dropped below the level of annual increase projected as a medium estimate has led many to accept the latter as the most probable projection of new households to be expected over the next five years.

"Census data for April 1953 to April 1954 show that the rate of household formation was below the projected annual increase. This has led many to accept the medium estimate as the most probable five-year projection."

The new federal investigational use regulations announced Jan. 7 require that the distribution of this drug be in accordance with an acceptable plan of investigation set forth by these rules; authorization under a public health service license, or under an approved new drug application of the FDA.

The writer might have escaped the log jam if he had started the sentence, "The new federal regulations for the testing of drugs. . . ."

In a special study of state wire reporting, the Associated Press found that unintelligible jargon appeared in legislature stories ("resolves," "engrossment," "tucked in committee"), in alphabet soup references to agencies and organizations (SGA, the UCA, CRS, LTA and MMA), in Weather Service forecasts and in market reports. AP then noted, "Neither weather reports nor markets are sacrosanct to editorial pencils."

The deskman can help the reader by substituting laymen's words for technical terms and by killing on sight words like *implement* and the *–ize* words.

Following are translations of some technical terms that frequently appear in the news report:

Term	*Translation*
Motivated or motivationed	Moved
Objective	Aim or object
Mentality	Mind
Percentage	Part
Ideology	Faith
Assignment	Task or job
Astronomical	Big

Nice-nelly expressions used as a cover-up are euphemisms:

Term	*Translation*
Audio-visual aids	Classroom movies
Container	Can
Continental breakfast	Juice, roll and coffee
Dialogue, conversation	Talk, discussion
Planned parenthood	Birth control
Revised upward	Raised
Social disease	Syphilis
Underachiever	Loafer
Withdrawal	Retreat

Alden S. Wood, director of communications for New England Life and author of a column, "The Typochondriac," for *Reporting,* applied his editing judgment in the November 1967 issue to a piece written by a "visual communications specialist":

If time permits, visuals can be tested for effectivity prior to publication.

Effectivity is a drossy nonword hoked-up to impress people who may not have heard of *effectiveness.* Why *prior to* instead of *before*?

Even a sampling of 25 people can be most helpful in determining if a visual communicates your message.

Whether is more exact than *if.*

The roll of the visual element should be to provide a penetration of complex concepts, and on certain glorious occasions to represent the concepts directly.

Roll is illiterate for *role.*

Pictures can even span linguistic barriers.

Barriers are surmounted; rivers, etc., are spanned.

We might begin by discussing criterial attributes. . . . These are the attributes that have the potential to act as discriminada for sorting and resorting the objects in the perceptual world.

Criterial is another unnecessary neologism. What's wrong with *criteria* . . . period? *Discriminada* we find in no available source book. *Resorting* should be *re-sorting.*

Break each visual down . . . and our visual aids will be worth much more than "10,000 words." Its up to you how the puzzle fits together.

We'll allow our sweating v.c.s. his misuse of *visual,* an adjective, as a noun, but that *Its* should be *It's.* As far as "10,000 words" go, if they're words like these, we *will* take a picture.

Slang

Many editors will agree with this advice from the Associated Press: "Use of slang should be a rarity in the news report." Some editors might even dream that use of slang can be reduced in sports stories, in the signed columns, in comic strips and in ad messages.

Slang in direct quotations helps reveal the speaker's personality. The reader expects the gangster to use terms of the underworld. He does not expect the reporter to resort to slang such as "The Brinton household is a go-go preparing . . . for guests."

Some slang words should be avoided because they are offensive ("cops" for *policemen,* "gobs" for *sailors,* "wops" for *Italians*): others are avoided because they reveal a writer's carelessness ("got clobbered" for *defeated soundly*).

A few examples from a wire service show how a copyeditor can overcome the slang:

"The Supreme Court ruled today that a lower court goofed." What's wrong with the proper word *erred*?

A Los Angeles story spoke of a couple getting "a few belts in one of the local bars." What's wrong with *drinks* if that's what they got?

A Washington reporter wrote that "well-heeled admirers of the senator have shelled out $7,000." We suppose that *well-heeled* means wealthy and that *shelled out* means contributed.

There is no law against good slang in the correct place. However, in the following sentence the slang is not especially good and it gives a facetious tone to a serious problem:

The result is a major flap among mothers of youngsters who will be 5 years old in October.

Headlinese words are bad enough in headlines; they are even more atrocious when they appear in the report: "enforcing the ban," "curb the growing shortage," "hike wage rates," "in the slaying area."

Mock Ruralisms

Following in some advice from Leon Stolz of the Chicago *Tribune* in *English I* (June 1968): "If you hold your quota to one mock ruralism a century, your readers will not feel deprived." Expressions such as "seeing as how" or "allowed as how" are supposed to give a folksy touch. They don't. They merely make the writer sound stupid.

Foreign Words

When the deskman comes across foreign expressions in the news report he should be sure of the spelling, the use and the translation. Unless it is a commonly known expression, the deskman provides the translation if the reporter has not done so. Fowler's *Dictionary of Modern English Usage* (New York: Oxford University Press, 1965) says, "Those who use words or phrases belonging to languages with which they have little or no acquaintance do so at their peril." The headline writer who tried to add a flavor of French with "C'est La Killy" needed advice on proper usage of French articles. The number in Latin words can cause trouble. For instance, *data* is plural and *datum* is singular. But *datum* is rarely used and *data* can be either singular (as a synonym for information) or plural (as a synonym for facts). *Trivia* is always plural; *bona fides* is always singular. *Media, criteria, insignia* and *phenomena* are plural.

A foreign expression has its place in the report if it supplies a real need or flavor or has no precise native substitute (*blasé, chic, simpatico*).

Copyeditors frequently are confronted with problems of translation, not as a rule directly from a foreign language but from a foreign correspondent's translation. Translations made abroad are often hurried; many are the work of men and women more at home in a foreign language than in English, commented *English I* (October 1967). The translations may be accurate but not idiomatic. Following are examples cited in *English I:*

An AP dispatch telling of a factory explosion in Germany said, "Most of the victims were buried when the roof of a large factory hall came down following the explosion. . . . The blast . . . damaged five other halls. . . ." What is a factory hall? The copyeditor would have saved readers a puzzled moment if he had altered the dispatch to read, "Most of the victims were buried when the factory roof fell on them. The blast . . . damaged five other sections of the plant."

VATICAN CITY (AP)—The Vatican newspaper *l'Osservatore Romano,* commenting on the tragic soccer riot in Lima, Peru, said Monday that partisan zeal in sports must avoid "excesses that debase human conditions."

The Vatican daily carried a story from Lima on the Argentina-Peru soccer match incident in which hundreds were killed. A brief editorial comment printed at the end of the story expressed sorrow over the deaths.

"We do not refer to sports as a loyal and direct competition of wholesome energies," *l'Osservatore* said.

"Excesses that debase human conditions" is not idiomatic English. Humanity or the human condition may be what the Italian had in mind. We do *not* refer to sports as a loyal and direct competition of wholesome energies. The story as sent says the opposite of what was apparently meant.

The UPI Berlin bureau sent out a story quoting Chancellor Erhard: "We are ready also with the Soviet Union and the east European states to achieve good relations and an understanding that would make it possible for us to live together peacefully— as we have overcome a tragic past with our western neighbors." The words are English but the word order is Germanic. The translation in idiomatic English would have been as follows: "Just as we have overcome the tragic past in our relations with our western neighbors, so we are ready for an understanding with the Soviet Union and the east European states to establish good relations and enable us to live together peacefully."

Discretion must be used when the copyeditor undertakes revision of the translation. "We should not invite an international crisis by substituting a mistranslation for an unidiomatic one," cautioned an editor. Usually, the copyeditor, having called the matter to the attention of the head of the desk, can and should make the necessary repairs.

Abusage

Alden Wood observed in his column "Typochondriac," in *Reporting* (March 1968), "Errors in spelling are unforgivable. Errors in basic grammar are only slightly less damning. Editors and writers, by virtue of their titles, must be the experts in these and all areas of writing. If they do not perform as professionals, they will not be respected as such."

No one can say what the most common grammatical errors in news writing are, but near the top must be the misuse of the relative pronoun and punctuation. Punctuation is discussed in Appendix I.

Relative Pronoun

Leon Stolz of the Chicago *Tribune* advised reporters and deskmen, "If you have trouble deciding whether the relative pronoun should be who or whom, you can usually find the right answer by remembering that who is nominative, like the personal pronouns he, she and they. Whom is objective, like him, her and them. Turn the clause into an independent sentence and substitute a personal pronoun for the relative pronoun" [in *English I* (January 1968)].

Applying the Stolz formula:

After his decision to cancel the trip, he sent most of the officials who he had invited to attend.

He invited *they* to attend?

The repeal gives property owners absolute freedom in deciding who they will rent or sell to.

They will rent to *they*?

Miss Barbara Warren, who he met while they were medical students at Passavant hospital. . . .

He met *she*?

In his last eight games, covering 13⅔ innings, the skinny Texan, who teammates call "Twiggy," has held opponent scoreless.

They call *he* Twiggy?

Mayor Daley will select the Democratic nominee to run against Dirksen, whom many feel is invincible as a candidate.

Many feel *him* is invincible?

The paper said two residents of the housing project were known to have seen a young man whom they said looked like the description of the sniper.

They said *him* looked like the description of the sniper?

Bachmann, who police quoted as saying he was inspired by Dr. Martin Luther King's assassination to shoot Dutschke, was recovering from wounds he received in a gun battle with police.

Police quoted *he* as saying?

He called on his listeners, whom he said "represented the mainstream of the Democratic and Liberal parties, "to reject" such a negative course, productive of nothing."

He said *them* represent?

The American was Leonard Levison, whom an air line official said was believed to be a merchant marine officer.

An air line official said *him* was believed to be a merchant marine officer?

Whomever you are and whatever your interests are, you would be entranced. . . .

You are *him*?

Good usage insists that similar ideas or elements in a sentence be phrased in a similar structural or grammatical form. You would say, "I like gardening, fishing and hunting," not "I like gardening, fishing and to hunt." In the following, the word *requiring* makes a nonparallel construction: "Instead of requiring expensive cobalt drill bits, disposable brass pins are used."

Comparisons should compare similar things. Here is a sentence that compares an apple (the increase) with a pumpkin (the sales): "Consolidated sales of Cottontex Corp. for the first six months of this year were $490,000,000, an increase of $27,000,-000 compared with the first half of last year." Use "an increase of $27,000,000 over the previous year's first half." "The soldier was ragged, unshaven, yet walked with a proud step." Make it read, "The soldier was ragged and unshaven, yet walked with a proud step."

Omission of *and* produces a nonparallel construction: "He worked on newspapers in Washington, New Jersey, New York, and on the Paris *Herald Tribune*." Use "He worked on newspapers in Washington, New Jersey and New York, and on. . . ."

But *and* should not be used superfluously: "He was identified as John Delanor Smith, three times convicted on narcotic charges and who reportedly serves as an enforcer for Mafia drug bosses on the east coast."

A non sequitur is an error in logic; the phrase means "it does not follow":

A guard at the Allied Kid Co., he died at 7:10 a.m., about five minutes after one of the youths implicated in the attack was taken into custody.

Guards die at 7:10 a.m., workers at 8:10 and executives at 9:10.

Worn on a chain with swivel and button, this model retails at $39.95.

How much if I just carry it loose in my pocket?

The man who directs the Blank organization is a big, hearty six-footer who looks far younger than his 59 years. But even in 1933 he was no stranger to the business.

Because, even then, he was six feet tall?

"Because breath is so vital to life," Burmeister explained, "the field of inhalation therapy and the development of breathing equipment has become increasingly important in medical science today."

It may be true that these things are increasingly important, but not because breath is vital to life. Breath was just as important to life 3,000 years ago as it is today.

Designed by the Caloric appliance people, this dispenser can be built into the wall or mounted on the surface.

Because the Caloric appliance people designed it?

Parallelism

Non Sequiturs

Slips in Writing

105

Stored in an air-conditioned room in lower Manhattan, the tapes contain information on the reading habits of one million Americans.

The nature of the information on those tapes is not in any way related to the place of their storage, or the condition of the air there. An easy way to edit this sentence is to start with the subject: "The tapes, stored in an air-conditioned room in lower Manhattan, contain information. . . ."

Deferred Subject

Planned by Jones, Blake and Droza, Detroit architects, the new school has 18 classrooms in addition to such standard facilities as cafeteria and library.

This implies that it's a natural thing to expect a school planned by that particular firm to have 18 classrooms, etc.

Acclaimed as a collector's item, the new Early American decanter will make its appearance in stores in time for the holiday gift season.

Aside from the odd deferment of subject, how could any collector acclaim this new decanter before it even hit the market?

Completed three years ago, the plant is 301 feet by 339 feet and is a one-story structure containing. . . .

A plant of exactly that size could have been completed fifty years ago, or yesterday.

Unmarried, Jones is survived by his mother, Mrs. . . .

This says Jones is unmarried. He is not. He's dead. He was not married.

Born in Glens Falls, N.Y., Horton received his early art training at Hillsdale college in Michigan.

This makes it sound as though Hillsdale is the obvious and logical college for a Glens Falls native.

Watch for Danglers

The dangling participle is one of the most common errors committed by beginning writers and by all who write in a hurry. The writer knows what he means but he doesn't say exactly what he means, thus forcing the reader to rearrange the sentence so he can grasp its meaning. Examples:

If convicted of the assault and battery charge, a judge may impose any sentence he sees fit on the defendants.

"If convicted" applies to the defendants, not to the judge.

Utilizing two pipelines, 112 tons of carbon dioxide was pumped into the . . .

By mixing chemicals with the gas, the flame will change colors.

"Mixing chemicals with the gas causes the flame to change colors."

Besides being cut on the left cheek and bloodied in the nose, Zeck's purse was attached for $825.

Already hospitalized a month, doctors estimate it will be three or four months before he is out again.

An E-shaped building, the fire started in the southwest wing.

A "natural" fertilizer, he predicted that it would solve many problems.

After blowing out the candles atop his birthday cake in three puffs, a movie camera flashed old fight films on the screen near the bar.

The fluoroscopic system makes moving pictures and tape recordings of the mouth and throat while speaking, chewing and swallowing.

Short and readable, I finished it off in about 45 minutes.

Marines stationed atop the observation towers can watch the surrounding terrain for Viet Cong activity. Once spotted, marines are dispatched to chase the enemy.

Once spotted, marines probably had chicken pox or measles, or just spilled soup.

A man of many surprises, Johnson's announcement was his most stunning move.

Doctors told him he would eventually lose his sight after a chemical tank exploded in his face while serving in the European theater of World War II.

Married to an American girl, his food favorites still are Indian.

Munching idly on a salted cashew one day, a thought suddenly occurred to me.

Although spotted around MIG airbases in North Vietnam, yesterday's report was the first that the choppers were being used in combat.

Knowing that Peck was her favorite actor, he was invited to visit the girl in the hospital when he made a trip to Boston.

"Known to be her favorite actor, Peck was invited. . . ."

False Passive

CINCINNATI (AP)—UCLA quarterback Gary Beban was presented Wednesday night a $1,000 scholarship-athletic award, the first such grant to be given by Mrs. A. B. "Dolly" Cohen, Cincinnati philanthropist. Beban, Heisman Trophy winner, will use the award for graduate study. It was presented at a banquet.

What was presented to whom? It was not Quarterback Beban who was presented. Instead, a $1,000 athletic scholarship was presented to Quarterback Beban.

Mixed Metaphors

Legislative Hall here was swarming with lobbyists as the second session of the 121st General Assembly got under way yesterday.

With lawmakers treading water while awaiting Gov. Elbert N. Carvel's State and budget messages, due tomorrow, lobbyists had a field day.

In two paragraphs the story pictured Legislative Hall as a beehive, a swimming pool and an athletic field.

Breaking domestic ties with gold would make the nation's gold stock a real barometer of international fever for gold.

Do you shove that barometer under your tongue or what?

The TVCCA's board of trustees revealed last night that its own administrative funds are exhausted, thus adding fuel to the concern and consternation expressed by public and private agencies.

One way to repair that "mixaphor"—although not recommended—would have been to say, "adding fuel to the already blazing c. and c., etc."

They hope to unravel a sticky turn of events that was further complicated recently.

Did you ever try to unravel glue, molasses, maple syrup or other similar strings or yarns?

A former Texas rancher sank his spurs into one of the fondest dreams of Wilmington business and political leaders yesterday, then calmly stood and waited for the explosion.

Auerbach embarks on new milestone

One usually embarks on a water-borne vessel. How would you like to try embarking on a milestone?

A wire story lead from New York contained the phrase "a fire-drenched battleground." Copyeditors began wondering if the next flood story would refer to "water-scorched" lowlands.

Waldor plans to use the gathering to set the wheels in motion to launch himself as a mayoralty candidate.

A launching on wheels; the Navy might be able to use that.

Tense

A dispute arose when a wire service story included this sentence: "Nehru said he would go before the U.N. tomorrow to seek a vote on Hungarian intervention." *Would* go or *will* go? Either is correct. The tendency is to use the future rather than the past tense.

State Health officials disclosed yesterday they were [are?] investigating a "mild epidemic" of a disease similar to the encephalitis outbreak in Houston, Tex.

Mrs. Geraldine Roberts, president, said her group was [is?] seeking more members and was [is?] planning a school to train household help.

When a statement is credited directly to a source, the tense used follows the time element meant. When the credit is implied, the indirect verb form is used.

A physician told the American College of Surgeons that smoking was a deliberate "form of suicide."

Did he say it *was* or it *is*?

He said lung cancer was the most frequent of all cancers and the survival rate was about 1 in 19 patients.

Does not the word *was* imply that the statement is no longer factual? Lung cancer was the most frequent, but today it is not?

In parallel constructions, the tenses generally agree: "The Baltimore Colts are threatened with the loss of their ace quarterback Johnny Unitas just when they have taken [not "took"] sole possession of first place in the Western Division." "A doctor recently discovered the nail in a bronchial tube and recommended [not "had recommended"] surgery."

For situations that may change between the time the story was written and the time the paper is published, the wire services frequently use the past perfect: "The strike by 60,000 longshoremen was expected to last. . . ."

Although it is sometimes used, there is no justification for the pseudo present tense: "Hollywood launches a new whodunit series next fall. . . ."

As for the battle over past tense versus present tense, many editors will insist that the legitimate use of the present tense gives life to the sentence and makes the story more compelling.

Colored Versus Colorful

Copyeditors will agree that a key word in their profession is *accuracy*. This means accuracy of impression as well as of fact. It means accuracy of writing so that reader judgment or conclusion is based on facts, not on a response to something inherent in words themselves.

The writer who selects words to appeal to the bias, prejudice or emotionalism of readers is dangerous because he preys on readers who won't stop to realize they are being victimized by words.

The copyeditor can easily recognize these word manipulators. They use "fat" for *big*, "crafty" for *clever*, "mob" for *group*, "turncoats" for *defectors*, "new-fangled" for *new*, "rehash" for *summation*.

Or they may use words deliberately to elicit a favorable reaction. They say "patriot" for *nationalist*, "advanced" for *modern*, "peace-loving" for *conciliatory*, "freethinker" for *atheist*, "strong man" for *absolute ruler*, "progressive" for *liberal*.

The copyeditor cannot change the prejudices of readers, but at least he can do his part to keep labels and colored metaphors from appearing in the publication. He can edit out the inferential statements and retain the observational. The vocabulary is rich enough so that he can replace neutral terms for favorable or unfavorable ones. He should know the tricks of semantics and not allow his readers to become pawns of the spellbinders.

Loaded Political Terms

Loaded political terms creep in under the guise of colorful descriptive writing. A story describes one presidential candidate as being backed by *well-heeled* groups. Among the top presidential candidates, are there any who are poorly backed? To say a white candidate has been "defeated" whereas a Negro has been "beaten" can be discriminatory, if not inflammatory. In a political race there is a victory and a defeat. There is no "upset."

Politicians seldom "refute" anything. They *dispute* many things. That is their business. Describing public figures as "outspoken" has a favorable connotation and is editorializing.

"The world today 'is enduring a rather peaceful kind of war, as wars go, or a warlike peace,' U.S. Rep. Harris B. McDowell Jr. said in a partisan political speech last night." If McDowell was speaking at a political rally, one could safely infer it was a political speech. If it was a political speech, no doubt it was partisan.

Negro ghettos? The anatomy of a *ghetto,* if there is one, is at least as much economic as racial. Whites, too, are in *ghettos,* thousands of them, low-paid.

A report from Dallas said that the woman who hit a prominent politician snarled back when he questioned her. "Snarled back" has editorial overtones and is an inaccurate description.

Excerpts from a staff memo written by Sam Blackman of the Associated Press should help alert copyeditors to some of the pitfalls in election coverage:

Preciseness is the key to accurate, hard-hitting, colorful and factual election coverage. The haste of campaign coverage is no excuse for the careless phrase, the wrong verb or the trite adjective or adverb used in the mistaken belief that it adds impact.

A survey of past ills prompted this memorandum: Most arguments arise over what a candidate said. Did he actually make the statement or just imply it? The best way to report his views is to use exact quotes. Avoid such phrases as these: A candidate *plugged for . . . made a pitch for . . . coaxed support . . .*smiled *benevolently* on the crowd . . . the candidate made an *earnest* restatement of his position . . . displayed *remarkable pulling* power . . . completed three days of *successful* campaigning . . . made a *bold* foreign policy attack on . . . *beat the drums, took pot shots, put on the gloves, locked horns.*

Editorial variations of that wonderful word *said* (warn, charge, blast, blister, indict, lambaste). What makes a candidate so omnipotent that he can *warn* us the country is going to pot unless his program is supported?

A candidate often will attack an opponent without naming him. If he does, we should say so but we should also say, with documentation, to whom the gibe apparently implies.

The very fundamentals of our democracy—the judgments that our voters exercise at the ballot box—hinge to a very large degree on the excellence of our achievements in covering campaigns and elections.

Roger Tartarian gave similar advice to UPI reporters and editors: "We have again reminded all who handle political copy to avoid labels wherever possible—and that very often it will be possible to avoid them."

7

The Copyeditor on Guard

Perils of the Superlative

Saying that something is the "first," "only," "biggest," "best" or "a record" seldom adds to a story. Usually it backfires.

When President Johnson rode in a Canadian government plane, one wire service said he was the first American president to travel aboard an airplane of a foreign government. He wasn't. President Eisenhower flew in a Royal Air Force Comet from London to Scotland in 1959 to visit Queen Elizabeth.

Another wire service characterized Gouverneur Morris as "the penman of the Constitution" and Lewis Morris as the "only New York signer of the Declaration of Independence." The man who penned the Constitution was Jacob Shallus and there were four New York signers of the Declaration of Independence.

When President Johnson ordered the American flag to be flown at half-staff in mourning for Winston Churchill, the stories said, "This is the first time such an honor has been accorded to a foreigner." This is not so. President Kennedy ordered half-staffing after the death of Dag Hammarskjold.

A California obituary identified a woman as the "first postmistress" in the nation. A Missouri story reported the closing of America's "shortest commercial railroad." Both statements were disproved.

The Associated Press described Herbert Lehman of New York as "the first person of the Jewish faith ever to hold a Senate seat." The AP had to acknowledge that it was wrong by at least six men and more than 100 years. Jewish senators who preceded Lehman were David Levy Yulee of Florida, Judah P. Benjamin of Louisiana, Benjamin F. Jonas of Louisiana, Joseph Simon of Oregon, Isidore Raynor of Maryland and Simon Guggenheim of Colorado.

When United Press International described the Flying Scotsman, a famous British locomotive, as the first steam locomotive to exceed 100 miles an hour, railroad buffs hurried to set the record straight. United States records show that on May 10, 1893, the New York Central No. 999 was timed unofficially at 112.5 m.p.h. on a one-mile stretch between Batavia and Buffalo, New York. On March 1, 1901, the Savannah, Florida and Western (later part of Atlantic Coast Line, later Seaboard Coast Line) No. 1901 was timed at 120 m.p.h. On June 12, 1905, the Pennsylvania Special traveled three miles near Elida, Ohio, in 85 seconds for an average of 127.1 m.p.h.

A story described New York's 15-cent municipal transit fare as the lowest in the nation. San Francisco's also was 15 cents. Another story said Disneyland's 306-foot painting of the Grand Canyon would be "the longest painting in the world." The Battle of Atlanta painting in Atlanta's Cyclorama Building is 400 feet long.

A story from Louisville described a conviction as the first under a new law barring interstate shipment of gambling material. Two months earlier two men had been convicted under the same law. A Billy Graham rally was described as the largest for a single meeting. But a Rosary Crusade in San Francisco had been attended by 500,000, bigger than Graham's.

The story said, without attribution, that Mary Martin had been "seen by an astonishing 100 million persons in her two performances of Peter Pan." No one knows exactly how many persons watched the performances. At best, it was an estimate based on a projection of percentages of sets in use tuned to a certain program.

The foregoing are examples of the abused statistic that invades the news report. One story said that New York City has 8 million rats. Another quoted the American Medical Association as saying that only 5 per cent of Americans dream in color. How can anyone know such exact figures? Each year highway deaths become greater—because each year there are more vehicles on streets and highways. Highway deaths on holiday weekends are higher than normal because such weekends usually are longer. "The toll has dropped so that last year there were only 81 traffic deaths here, an all-time low." Since when? 1492? 1776? 1900? "The ships were built in record time." What was the previous record?

All superlatives should be checked. If they cannot be verified, at least they can be softened: "One of the most despicable crimes in the world . . ."; "One of the hardest-working actresses in Germany. . . ."

Most historical references also should be checked. A story said that Mrs. Helga Kraft, who was born in 1893, had been a former singer on the Chautauqua circuit and had appeared with Mme. Schumann-Heink and Jenny Lind. Jenny Lind died in 1887, six years before Mrs. Kraft was born.

Beware of the Hoax

Old stories have a way of appearing on the copydesk disguised as news. The following hoaxes are likely to show up occasionally:

—The story of a 16-year-old baby sitter who adhered to a freshly painted toilet seat for hours. A doctor administered to her, tripped and knocked himself out. Both were carried off in an ambulance for repairs and both sued the man who engaged the sitter.

—A woman driver flagged by a stalled motorist who asked her for a push. Told she would have to get up to 35 miles an hour to get the stalled car started, she backed off, gunned the motor and rammed his car at 35 miles an hour.

—The sheriff who was called to a farm to investigate the theft of 2,025 pigs discovered that only 2 sows and 25 pigs were missing. The farmer who reported the loss lisped.

—A farmer armed with a shotgun went to a chicken house to rout a suspected thief. The farmer stumbled, and the gun went off, killing all his hens.

—The story, usually from some obscure hill hamlet in the east of Europe or in Asia, of an eagle carrying off a three-year-old child.

—A Sunday driver who called police to report that someone stole the steering wheel and all the foot pedals from his car. A squad car was sent to the scene but before police arrived the man called back and said, "Everything is all right. I was looking in the back seat."

—Someone reports he has found a copy, in near perfect condition, of the Jan. 4, 1800, issue of the Ulster County *Gazette*. The paper is prized not only for its age but because it contains a statement made by the U.S. Senate to President John Adams following the death of George Washington twenty-one days earlier and refers to Washington as "Father of our country." Few copies of the original exist, but there are many reproductions.

—A story from Harrisburg, Pennsylvania, told about six students permanently blinded by looking at the sun after taking LSD. It was not until after the story had received wide play and had been the subject of editorials and columns that the hoax was discovered.

—Another story, this one in the form of a bulletin on the stationery of the Health Division of the Federal Housing Administration, warned that young women were in danger of developing fat legs by wearing miniskirts and exposing their legs to extremely cold weather. The story even went into clinical detail about how fatty tissue builds up as a protection against cold weather.

—A group of young stockbrokers got credit for plotting a hoax against New York newspapers during the depression days of the 1930s. They created a fictitious football team at a fictitious college and every Saturday during the fall they phoned in the results of the fictitious football game. The hoax was uncovered near the end of the football season when the fictitious college team began appearing in the ranks of the untied and undefeated teams.

—The bricklayer story makes the rounds periodically, usually with a change in locale. The story may have been reworked from a vaudeville gag of earlier days. It is recorded by a British accent comedian as a monologue under the title of "Hoffnung at the Oxford Club." Fred Allen used it as a skit on one of his radio shows in the 1930s. In 1945 the story was retold in an anthology of humor edited by H. Allen Smith. Three versions had their setting in Korea, Barbados and Vietnam. In World War II the "bricklayer" was a sailor on the USS Saratoga requesting a five-day leave extension. Here is the Barbados version, courtesy of UPI (1957):

LONDON, June 13—The Manchester Guardian today quoted as "an example of stoicism" the following unsigned letter—ostensibly from a bricklayer in the Barbados to his contracting firm:
"Respected Sir,
"When I got to the building, I found that the hurricane had knocked some bricks off the top. So I rigged up a beam with a pulley at the top of the building and hoisted up a couple of barrels full of bricks. When I had fixed the building, there was a lot of bricks left over.
"I hoisted the barrel back up again and secured the line at the bottom, and then went up and filled the barrel with the extra bricks. Then I went to the bottom and cast off the line.
"Unfortunately, the barrel of bricks was heavier than I was, and before I knew what was happening the barrel started down, jerking me off the ground. I decided to hang on and halfway up I met the barrel coming down and received a severe blow on the shoulder.
"I then continued to the top, banging my head against the beam and getting my fingers jammed in the pulley. When the barrel hit the ground it bursted its bottom, allowing all the bricks to spill out.
"I was now heavier than the barrel and so started down again at high speed. Halfway down, I met the barrel coming up and received severe injuries to my shins. When I hit the ground I landed on the bricks, got several painful cuts from the sharp edges.
"At this point I must have lost my presence of mind, because I let go the line. The barrel then came down, giving me another heavy blow on the head and putting me in the hospital.
"I respectfully request sick leave."

Perhaps, as one editor has suggested, the original version dealt with the building of the Cheops pyramid or the Parthenon. The story seems to appeal to the new generation of reporters and copyeditors.

Some others, though not hoaxes, are impossible or misleading:
—A man received a series of summonses to pay a tax bill. The notices said he owed $0.00 in taxes and $0.00 in penalties. He was warned that his personal belongings would be attached if he didn't pay. He sent the tax office a check for $0.00 and got a receipt for that amount. Sometimes the yarn is applied to the nonpayment of a noncharge from an electric company and a threat

to cut off service unless the bill is paid—or to a tuition demand on a student studying at a college on a tax-free scholarship.

—A fake obituary may be hard to catch but not this fraud that got by the desk of a New York newspaper: "The thallus or ruling monarch of the principality of Marchantia will arrive here today on a two-day visit as part of a State Department tour."

—Newspapers have worn out the gag about the man who answered "twice a week" opposite "sex" on a census questionnaire. Others that newspapers could do without include:

Undercover investigators yesterday said they ended a suburban sex ring where housewives worked as call girls to supplement the family income.

Smith will help to direct a volunteer effort embracing several thousand housewives, who will be calling on their neighbors for contributions.

In Germany yesterday, Mrs. R--- issued a statement to the German press agency in which she denied ever having improper relations with men other than her husband while in Washington.

Misquotations The careful copyeditor would do well to keep a quotation reference at his elbow as he handles copy containing references to often-repeated quotations or attribution of such quotations.

He will stop reporters from attributing "Go west, young man" to Horace Greeley. The advice was given by John Babsone Lane Soule in 1851. Greeley used the expression in an editorial in The New York *Tribune* but amplified it: "Go west, young man, and grow up with the country."

Charles Dudley Warner, not Mark Twain, should get credit for "Everybody talks about the weather, but nobody does anything about it." Bill Nye, the humorist, originated the saying, "There are just two people entitled to refer to themselves as 'we'—one is the editor, and the other is the fellow with a tapeworm." Mark Twain later revised the statement: "Only Presidents, editors, and people with tapeworms have the right to use the editorial 'we.'"

Voltaire is wrongly credited with the quotation, "I may not agree with what you say, but I will defend to the death your right to say it." Most likely it is a paraphrase of Voltaire's "Think for yourselves, and let others enjoy the privilege to do so too." General John J. Pershing did not exclaim, "Lafayette, we are here!" It was uttered by Charles E. Stanton, chief disbursing officer of the American Expeditionary Forces.

Careless writers attribute the "gilded lily" business to Shakespeare. But what Shakespeare wrote was, "To gild refined gold, to paint the lily." Likewise, the Bible does not say that money is the root of all evil. It says, "Love of money is the root of all evil." Music doesn't have charms to soothe the savage beast. Congreve said, "Music hath charms to soothe a savage breast." And Thomas Gray did not refer to "the maddening crowd," but to "the madding crowd."

Up to the time of his death, a South African dentist, Dr. Philip Blaiberg, had survived with an implanted heart. In an account of Dr. Blaiberg's death, a UPI reporter wrote that Dr. Blaiberg's last act was to scribble a quote from the Persian poet Omar Khayyám: ". . . for I shall not pass this way again." A Connecticut editor questioned the attribution, causing UPI to send out a correction. The probable author is Stephen Grellet and the usually accepted full quotation is, "I shall pass through this world but once. If, therefore, there be any kindness I can show or any good thing I can do, let me do it now. Let me not defer or neglect it, for I shall not pass this way again."

A sports column tribute concluded, "In the words of the late Grantland Rice: 'When the great scorer comes to write beside your name, / It's not whether you won or lost but how you played the game.'" What Rice really said was, "When the One Great Scorer comes to write against your name— / He marks—not that you won or lost—but how you played the game." Reporters should never quote poetry from memory. When poetry shows up in a piece of copy, the copyeditor should assume it's wrong and look it up.

The cutlines began, "Like Topsy, Baptist Hospital and Bowman Gray School of Medicine apparently just grew." The literary allusion is to Topsy's reply to Miss Ophelia's question, "Do you know who made you?" in *Uncle Tom's Cabin:* "'Nobody, as I knows on,' said the child with a short laugh . . . 'I 'spect I growed. Don't think nobody made me.'" It is a fine point, but it can be presumed that those familiar enough with the book to recognize the simile would wince at Topsy's newly acquired polish.

The story quoted a structural linguist's feelings about people who object to ending sentences with prepositions: "You remember what Winston Churchill said when an aide corrected a line in one of Churchill's speeches because it ended in a preposition? Churchill told the aide: 'This is an outrage up with which I will not put.'" Churchill was misquoted. What he said (and even this may be apocryphal) was, "This is the type of arrant pedantry up with which I shall not put."

A column criticizing the overuse of the word *gourmet* said, "I am reminded of the line of poetry which told of the moth flitting its wings signifying nothing." Was it perchance not a poem but a Shakespeare play, and not a moth flitting its wings but "a tale told by an idiot, full of sound and fury, signifying nothing?"

"We've come a long way since Commodore Vanderbilt said, 'The public be damned.'" But the commodore never said it. It was William H. Vanderbilt, son of Cornelius, the so-called commodore, who made the remark.

"Robert Burns, the old Scotchman, said: 'Oh that we would see ourselves as others see us.'" Burns was a distinguished poet, hardly the "old Scotchman." Careful writers prefer *Scot* or *Scotsman* to *Scotchman,* as do the Scots themselves. The actual

---

quotation: "Oh wad some power the giftie gie us / To see oursels as others see us!"

A deskman often has to decide whether to make corrections in direct quotations. Should he correct the syntax of the speaker? If the goof is within quote marks, should it remain? Did the speaker use poor English or did the reporter write poor English?

Generally, a person quoted deserves a friendly pencil, especially if he is one who is expected to use proper English, such as a school superintendent.

Attributions   The copyeditor will save reporters from attribution log jams if he remembers this question: Is it clear who is talking? If the reporter shifts to a second speaker, the story should identify the new speaker immediately, not at the end of the quotation. The reader assumes the first speaker is still talking.

Sometimes the source cannot be named, yet his statement is newsworthy. The editor assumes readers understand this when a story contains phrases like "a spokesman," "an usually reliable source," "a government official" and "it was learned." Many editors prefer not to use quotes around either fact or opinion ascribed to an unnamed source. Some observers understandably deplore the faceless source protection. These observers say, in effect, if "a government official with a special interest in Latin American Affairs" terms a resolution "worse than useless," why can't the fearless official be named? By withholding identity, papers shamelessly do other people's bidding.

Some editors say that nonattribution denies the reader a very essential fact—often *the* essential fact—the source of the information, of the idea, of the speculation, of the proposal, of the supposition—even, sometimes, of the accusation. "Republican State Headquarters issued a statement today blasting. . . ." This is a statement of faceless political critics. Such statements should be attributed either to individuals or to official party organizations who are willing to stand behind them. There's no such organization as Republican State Headquarters.

SYNONYMS OF ATTRIBUTION.   Is the synonym for *said* apt? Do "pointed out," "offered," "admitted," "disclosed," "noted," "revealed," "indicated," "conceded," "explained" or "cited the fact that" give the quotation an editorial tone?

Do the synonyms for *said* convey a hint of doubt as to the veracity of the credited source ("according to," "said he believes")? "According to" actually refers to the content, not to the speaker: "According to the mayor's letter . . . ," not "According to the mayor. . . ."

Does the writer use gestures for words?

"We're gonna put on a show, too," grinned Wags.

"Now I can invite my friends to play on the grass," Donna beamed.

"The bill will be paid," the official smiled.

"I heard something pop in my shoulder," he winced on his way to the dressing room.

No matter how good a grinner or wincer, how bright a beamer
or how broad a smiler, you just can't grin, wince, beam or smile
a quote. If it's a quip, that should be obvious from the context.
If it isn't, saying so won't make it so. An exclamation mark may
be used after a brief expletive but it looks silly after a long sentence.

Said is a simple verb that usually is preferable to others used
in an effort to convey determination, skepticism, wit, and so on.
Most times the quoted matter can speak for itself. Many of the
best writers use *said* almost exclusively. *Said* used repeatedly
can give emphasis; it is not weakened by repetition.

Does the quoted word invite the reader to disbelieve the statement?

"Father Divine's blonde wife was at his bedside, along with
his 18 'secretaries.'" By placing quotes around secretaries, the
writer expressed an opinion, not a fact.

Do scattergun quotations bewilder the reader?

"The actress said she would wed Wilding 'at the end of the
week.'"

"The blood-covered body of a 'brilliant' 19-year-old Williams
College sophomore was found today—a rifle nearby—in a fraternity house room. Police Chief George A. Royal said it was
'apparently murder.'"

Is the source given immediately in a controversial quotation?

Where the information is disputable, the source should come
at the beginning, not appended to the statement. "The administration budget has imposed a tremendous burden on consumers, it was contended by Senator John Doe in calling for
revisions." Change it to read, "Senator John Doe called for revisions, contending that the administration budget has imposed
a tremendous burden on consumers."

Does the quotation reveal precisely what the speaker said?
"Stewart still maintains 'he called it as he saw it.'" You can't
quote someone in the third person.

Does an awkwardly split quote interrupt the speaker? "'He,'
said Jones, 'needs a wig.'"

Are the circumstances of the statement clear? Was the statement made in an interview, a report, a letter, a public speech?
Was it in English or a translation? Was it prepared or extempo-
raneous? Was it made over a network or a single station? What
network? What station?

Is the attribution overworked? In some crime or accident
stories, phrases such as "police said" or "Patrolman Jones reported" are used in almost every sentence. A blanket attribution
such as "police gave this account of the accident" would ease
the monotony for the readers.

Added is not a good synonym for *said* unless it is used for an
unimportant afterthought.

Do the persons quoted get a friendly or an unfriendly pencil on
the desk? Perhaps it was the writer rather than the speaker who

---

used poor grammar. Usually the language is corrected in direct quotes unless, as one editor commented, it is done with malice aforethought when "we want to show someone ain't no good at talking," or the speaker is expected to abuse the language or a speaker, such as the President, makes a slip of the tongue.

Tell Them, Don't Tease Them

News is regarded one way in the newspaper office and another way in the home, where, presumably, the reader reads his newspaper. In the newsroom the reporter is constantly admonished to "keep 'em short." "How much do you have on that hotel death?" the city editor asks. "Enough for about four books," answers the reporter. "Hold it to two," orders the superior, "we're short on space today."

So the reporter prunes his story to two books. The story lands on the copydesk and a copy pencil goes to work to get it even tighter.

All this, of course, is unknown to the reader who sits down to enjoy his newspaper. A headline catches his eye: **80-foot fall at hotel / ends actor's grim joke.** He begins the story: "'Watch me do a trick,' said the 26-year-old actor to his companion, and he stepped out the eighth-floor window of their downtown hotel early Sunday." Muses the reader, "I was downtown early Sunday morning. I wonder what hotel it was and what time." The story doesn't answer his questions. It did identify the victim. Also his companion. Near the end of the story was a brief description of the companion, Paul Lynde: "Lynde is a widely known actor, investigators said." "Funny I never heard of him," the reader again muses. "Wonder what he appeared in?" This was the story as sent by the Associated Press. For the morning papers the story failed to identify the hotel, did not give the time of the fall and identified Lynde only as a widely known actor. Readers of afternoon papers got some of the missing details. The hotel was the Sir Francis Drake, the time was "the wee hours Sunday morning" and Lynde was identified as a comedian who appeared in the Broadway and film versions of "Bye Bye Birdie" with Dick Van Dyke and in the movie "Under the Yum Yum Tree" as Imogene Coca's henpecked husband.

The ability to give details is the newspaper's great advantage over its competitors. Readers relate themselves to the news. The more involved they become in the events, the more avid readers they become. In short, they demand the whole story down to the last detail. If the story says, "Hastings Banda, the leader of Nyasaland, received his education in Ohio," the reader wants to know, "Where in Ohio?" "At what university?" "When?" He relates himself to the news. "I wonder if that's the same Banda I knew when I was at Ohio State in the fifties?"

A wire story on a plane crash in New York City said the 79 passengers included "two young opera singers en route to a South Carolina concert, prominent Southern businessmen, a former Virginia college beauty queen." The story as sent drew this protest from a client's managing editor: "Who the people are who die in these crashes is a point of equal or more interest than the circumstances of the crash. We all identify with them—where they are going, where they are coming from. I want to know what opera those opera singers were going to sing in." The details were in a side bar but the side bar did not go out on the single circuit.

Blankton University has received a $32,739 Rehabilitation Services Administration grant for five graduate traineeships in speech pathology-audiology.

Assoc. Prof. Ned Boulder, chairman of the school's department of speech and pathology and audiology, said the grant includes stipends of $2,400 for three master's degree level students, $2,800 for a first year doctoral student and $3,400 for a third year doctoral student.

Certainly some readers might wonder, if the copyeditor didn't, how $18,600—the difference between the grant and the total for stipends—is to be spent. Obviously there is more to the story than was contained in the brief publicity release.

A newspaper had a three-column photo and a six-inch story of the announcement that the Speakman Co. would move its general offices to new quarters. And what does the Speakman Co. do? The story didn't say.

A story related that a man had gone to court to fight for a seat in the legislature, but it did not tell which party he belonged to. Another told of a woman mugged while waiting for a bus at Delaware and Woodlawn avenues, but did not give the time of this incident, which would be of interest to every woman who rides a bus.

When handling a story about an airplane crash, the cost of the plane is an important part of the piece and should be included well up toward the beginning.

In a wire story about a fighting cop, the gist of the story was that the outcome of the bout would determine whether the policeman would try for the jackpot in the ring or give it up for his pay as a patrolman. Everything seemed to be in the story except the weight division, an important item to some boxing fans.

A story was about a drunk chimpanzee that supposedly escaped and created havoc around the countryside by trying to break into homes. But the story failed to tell who owned the chimp, what he was doing in the county, how he got anything to drink and what finally happened after a game warden arrived on the scene. These were basic questions the reporter forgot to answer. The deskman should have checked.

A paper had a three-column picture and story about consecration ceremonies at the Cherry Hill Methodist Church's new "Harlan House." The story told that Harlan House was named for "Miss Mollie" Harlan, that the Rev. Dr. Darcy Littleton took part in the ceremonies, that "Miss Mollie" is now buried in the Cherry Hill Cemetery, that Littleton is now with Goodwill Industries in Wilmington and that Dr. G. Harlan Wells spoke and the Rev. R. Jerris Cooke conducted the service. But when all this was said and the picture was examined, readers were still left to guess what Harlan House is or who Mollie Harlan was that the house should be named for her. Was she related to Dr. G. Harlan Wells?

A paper reported in detail the arrest of a minister on charges of operating a motor vehicle without a license, failure to carry a car registration card, disorderly conduct and disobeying a police officer. When three of the four charges were dismissed, the story failed to tell why. Answer: It is standard procedure to dismiss the license and registration charges when a driver has only forgotten to carry the documents with him.

A page-1 story told the fascinating details of a divorce decree upheld by the state supreme court but failed to mention the names of the parties in the case.

Another story gave an account of the senate's 78–8 approval of the President's trade bill but failed to tell who the eight opponents were and, even worse, how the senators from the paper's state voted on the measure. This was a revolutionary trade measure that had been in the news for months and was finally opposed by only eight men. Wasn't anyone who handled the story curious about their names?

A story under a March dateline said "the Bahais will celebrate New Year's eve at the Bahai center. There will be readings and music." The story continued, "New Year's Day tomorrow is known as Naw-Ruz." Couldn't the music and the refreshments be dropped and tell instead who or what are Bahais and what the heck New Year's is doing in the middle of March?

A skindiver stayed under water for thirty-one hours and spent much of his time reading a paperbacked book. No word to explain what kept the pages from disintegrating. (The paper was a glossy stock.)

A housewife won a fat prize in a magazine advertising contest. No hint what she did to win, a point made more important by the statement that the woman could neither read nor write.

Another story concerned a judge who reversed his own conviction of a union leader for breach of the peace. The reversal, said the story, was based on "new evidence" but failed to tell readers the nature of the new evidence.

A wire story from Los Angeles said that a legless man was ordered before his draft board to present documented evidence as to why he should not be registered 1-A. The story failed to tell how he lost his legs, a point that must have bothered several editors because a correction added the information that he had been without legs since birth.

The story said that the black students, 105 of the 120 Negroes enrolled at Northwestern, marched out of the building singing. It failed to mention the songs they sang, a detail that might have shed more light on their behavior.

The Art of Editing

If any part of the story is confusing, the copyeditor should supply explanations to make the story understandable. Obviously, the explanation should not be as hard to understand as the phrase itself. For instance:

Congress in 1946 waived government immunity to suits in tort (a civil wrong in which a legal action may lie) and permitted suits on tort claims against the United States.

The parenthetical explanation hardly aids most readers. If an explanation is required it should be one that really helps:

As a rule, a sovereign government may not be sued by its citizens unless the government consents. In 1946 Congress gave blanket permission to citizens to sue the United States government if they thought it was responsible for injuries to them or their property.

The principal substance which acts to ward off the threat of such clots is called an enzyme, or chemical policeman, which dwells on the inside linings of artery walls, it was explained.
It is this potent triggering agent which activates still another enzyme cop assigned by the body to dissolve a body compound called fibrin, a whitish substance which is the essential ingredient of blood clots.

"Chemical policeman" doesn't explain an enzyme to the reader. Nor do "triggering agent," "whitish substances" and "body compounds." Here is one way an enzyme could have been explained: "The principal substance that acts to ward off the threat of such clots is an enzyme, a chemical produced by the body. This enzyme is found on the lining of the arteries. It activates still another enzyme capable of dissolving fibrin, the essential ingredient of blood clots."

The story told of a boy who died, apparently of suffocation after he choked on a hot dog in his home. Police said the boy left the table after dinner and was found choking in his bathroom. His mother slapped him on the back in a vain attempt to dislodge the obstacle. Firemen took him to a hospital where he was pronounced dead. A few lines of first-aid instruction at the end of the story might have served to save other lives.

A woman who was hospitalized twice in a short time asked to be transferred from one hospital to another to be near her husband. What ailed hubby? It wasn't explained.

The Royal Navy dropped the unit *fathom* and started measuring depths in meters. The story told all about it. All, that is, except how long a fathom is.

A story contained the statement "where family income is below federal poverty levels" but neglected to tell the readers what the poverty level is by federal standards.

"There is little change in the pattern of news," an AP executive said. "The important difference is improvement in presentation, through explanation and interpretation."

"A bell captain in a midtown hotel was arrested for scalping World Series tickets." Why the reluctance to name the hotel? A directive reminded editors, "In these days, when GIs, businessmen, students, school teachers et al. are traveling throughout the world, such identification is often of interest to many readers. The part of town where a news event occurs is sometimes pertinent too in stories from the big cities that are frequented by travelers."

Here is a complete story as one newspaper printed it:

TALLAHASSEE, Aug. 8—The simmering feud between Republican Gov. Claude Kirk of Florida and his Democratic cabinet erupted into a full-scale shouting battle today, and Kirk ordered an end to weekly cabinet meetings for the first time in state history.

Cabinet members immediately declared they would go on meeting anyway.

The stormy session began with the cabinet refusing to spend $35,000 on a federal state liaison office which Kirk wants to open in Washington.

Some readers must have wondered how a Republican governor came to have a Democratic cabinet, what officials belong to the cabinet, what can be accomplished by cabinet meetings not attended by the governor and whether the weekly meeting is required by law.

The first rule in writing or editing a story is to ask yourself who are likely to read the item and what will they most want to know about the subject. Both the writer and the deskman should pare the story for word economy. They should not pare it for fact economy.

Extraneous Facts   News presents the pertinent facts. That is, every story should answer all the questions the reader expects answered. If a big story returns after having been out of the news, it should contain a short background or reminder. Readers don't carry clips to check background.

Robert J. Casey, Chicago *Daily News* reporter and author, once observed, "Too many facts can louse up a good story." If a fact isn't vital in telling the news, it should be omitted. It is an example of string saving. Stray bits have a way of bringing trouble. A buried reference to a thirty-year-old hanging "from an apple tree on Joe Smith's farm" brought a libel suit. Joe Smith was still living; the hanging wasn't on his farm. The reference added nothing to the story but taught the editor a lesson.

The following could be held to a short cutline; it is not worth five column inches of type:

Robert F. Kelly today was named chairman of this year's Democratic Jefferson-Jackson Day dinner.

The appointment was announced jointly by Democratic State Chairman John M. C––– and National Committeeman William S. P–––.

Kelly, administrative assistant for 12 years to ex-Sen. J. Allen F––– Jr. in Washington, said he will name a dinner committee, site, date, and speaker in a "few days."

The Jefferson-Jackson Day dinner, traditionally held in late April or early May, is the largest meeting of its kind held by the Democrats each year.

Kelly said he already is trying to line up a "nationally known" speaker for the occasion.

Kelly, now associated with the legal department of the D--- Co., has been a member of the dinner committee for several years. This is his first assignment as chairman of the affair.

Kelly was a vice chairman of last year's Community Fund drive and has a wide background in party and civic affairs.

He is a past president of the Delaware State Society and the Administrative Assistants and Secretaries Club in the Nation's Capital.

A school board (or board of education) is a group of individuals elected by the citizens to direct the operation of the school system. It is not a place, not an office, not a building, not the school system.

More Precision

"He studied French under E. B. DeSauze, the retired supervisor of the School Board's language department." DeSauze was supervisor of foreign languages for the public schools. The School Board has no language department.

It is the American Museum of Natural History, not Museum of Natural History in New York City, the Smithsonian Institution, not the Smithsonian Institute.

The U.S. Supreme Court did not ban prayers in school. The court banned the requirement that children pray any particular prayer, or the writing by public authorities of a required prayer. The decision had to do with public schools. It did not interfere with required prayers in church-operated schools.

Gas and *gasoline* are not synonymous. Gas is either natural or manufactured. Some explosions are caused by gas, some by gasoline. The story and headline should contain the precise term. Similarly, in stories of food poisoning, the copy should specify whether the story is referring to canned or bottled foodstuffs.

The Selective Service Board doesn't draft anyone. It merely orders men for induction. One of the Armed Forces does the drafting (or inducting).

Reporters and headline writers are fond of saying that taxes will "eat up" a will or a fortune or an estate. Taxes may deplete the check account but they can't eat up anything.

"A defective 20-millimeter cannon . . . suddenly fired and the shell killed one airman and injured another." The writer should have said *unexpectedly* rather than "suddenly," *a shell* rather than "the shell," *bullet, slug* or *projectile* rather than "shell."

Pistol is a general term for a small firearm. It can be single-loading, a revolver or an automatic. Clip-loading pistols are sometimes called automatics but they usually are semiautomatics or self-loaders. The barrel diameter of rifles and pistols is expressed in calibers (.22). A shotgun bore is expressed by its gauge (12-gauge) except for the .410.

The Copyeditor on Guard

"A 20-year-old robber was dead as the result of a gun battle in which 14 shots were fired at point blank range." "Point blank range" is an archaic expression based on the firing of cannon. Inasmuch as the expression is meaningless to today's readers, why use it?

Ethnic Groups
"It is perhaps the most cosmopolitan area in the city, stronghold of the Poles and densely populated with other ethnic groups including Czechs, Bohemians, Slovaks and some Italians." Czechs and Bohemians are one and the same people. The Czech lands include Bohemia and Moravia. Some Bohemians prefer to be called Czechs. Slovaks are a separate people, although there is a strong language affinity. There is a difference between a Slovak and a Slovenian, as any editor will soon realize should he confuse the two.

News service copy sometimes fails to explain terms common in one section of the nation but not in another. For instance, readers may deduce that *bracero* is a Mexican laborer. If the word can't be explained, it should be eliminated so as not to puzzle readers who don't know Spanish.

An executive city editor gave the copydesk trouble for its failure to catch the idiocy of an "anti-Soviet" play written in the czarist days. Even though *Soviet* refers to, technically, an organizational system within the Communist structure, it is now generally accepted as a reference to the U.S.S.R. Russia, of course, is only one of the republics in the Soviet Union but is used as the equivalent of U.S.S.R. In headlines, *Russia* or *Soviet* means Soviet Union.

Britain or *Great Britain* refers to the largest of the British Isles and consists of England, Scotland and Wales. *United Kingdom* should be used when England, Scotland, Wales and Northern Ireland are meant. A Briton is a native or subject of Britain. Despite the fact that other nationals of the United Kingdom may be annoyed when *England* is used as the equivalent of *Britain* or the *United Kingdom*, the use of *England* in the wider sense is acceptable.

Edit to the Final Stop
"Tanglewood Barn Theater ended its regular season with a bang in its production of 'Wonderful Town' Wednesday night." Last paragraph: "The show will be repeated at 8:15 p.m. through Sunday."

"His companion said Fennell dived from the boat, swam away, went under and never came up." Last paragraph: "Interment will be in Mt. Zion Cemetery." What was to be interred in lieu of the body that never came up?

"The largest single cost of the trial was jury expenses, which total $3,807." Later: "Another cost was $20,015 paid to extra guards and bailiffs."

A story concerned a robbery. Part of it went like this: "The suspect apparently hid in the store when it closed at 9 p.m. About 11 p.m. he confronted a security guard, Paul H. Hogue, 57, of

5625 Lowell Blvd., as he was turning off the lights in the budget store of the basement." Last paragraph: "According to parole officials, Hogue's parole was suspended June 6 for failure to report and he was being sought as a parole violator." A correction sufficed in this case, but a correction does no credit to the reporter or to the copyeditor.

Double Takes

Although the judge, speaking at the State Judicial Conference here, did not refer to him by name, it was clear his remarks were directed by Hilbert Schauer, director of the bureau of investigation. . . . "I personally resented the assertions attributed to Schauer in recent newspaper articles," the judge said, "and I resent them on behalf of the judiciary."

We're not suggesting you punch everyone in the nose who bothers you. . . .

Punch him in the other nose—the one that doesn't bother you.

Plans are under way for more meetings before the first one was held because of the interest shown.

Every driver would like safer and more beautiful highways, including those in the Business and Professional Women's Club.

She found the baby safe on the floor of the front seat.

The superintendent said, "We will be cleaning the street following the parade."

He arrived home to find the kitchen ablaze.

No other reason for going home?

Dry and warmer weather is expected in the area at least until last Sunday, the Weather Bureau predicted Friday.

Predicating his comment with a cowpath of contingencies, the governor said, "I haven't made up my mind firmly but, at the moment, my present inclination is not to run."

Taste

An editor of a morning newspaper said his newspaper likes to protect breakfast eaters against the incursions of unpalatable news. How then, he asked, did this sentence get to the breakfast table: "Plans to take still another sample were canceled when Hutchinson became ill and threw up." Actually, he *vomited.* Had the story said he became nauseated, anyone who is familiar with $10\frac{1}{2}$ beers—Hutchinson's load in less than $2\frac{1}{2}$ hours—would have gotten the point.

The Los Angeles *Times* and other metropolitan newspapers have adopted a screen code to control and avoid lewd advertising in entertainment copy. Marvin M. Reimer, one of the advertising executives of the *Times,* said, "It is not our intention to be either picayunish or prudish in our evaluation, but we are convinced that moral and social values have not decayed as frequently as portrayed, and we trust that together we can find a better stand-

---

ard of values in the area of good taste." Among subjects banned are bust measurements, compromising positions, double meaning, nude figures or silhouettes, nymphomania, perversion and suggestive use of narcotics, instrument or alcohol. Words avoided include cuties, girlie, lesbian, lust, nymph, party girls, play girls, scanty panties, sexpot, strippers, third sex.

The caution should apply equally to amusement promotion copy and to all other copy. Both wire services direct their editors to downplay female anatomy. Deskmen should apply heavy pencils to stories about the "ten best undressed women" and about an actress hired because of her uncommonly ample bosom.

There is no necessity to run everything turned in as news by the staff, the wire services or the syndicates. There is an obligation to print the news. There is also an obligation to edit it.

Some vulgarisms get into the report, usually when they are said by a public figure at a public gathering and in a justifiable news context. Most member papers used the following lead from London even though the AP headed the dispatch with a cautionary note: "'Gentlemen,' said Prince Philip, 'I think it is time we pulled our fingers out.'"

Is *s.o.b.* milder than the full expression? If the President of the United States refers to a syndicated columnist as an "s.o.b.," that's news. The columnist in question passed off the slur by saying the President obviously meant "sons of brotherhood." Another President used the phrase "sons of business."

When Jack Ruby shot Lee Harvey Oswald, accused of assassinating President John F. Kennedy, he is purported to have exclaimed, "I hope I killed the son of a bitch." The quote appeared in the news dispatches from Dallas. There was a day when editors would have substituted dashes or asterisks for the words. Some bannered the quote, but with initials: **Jack Ruby—"I hope I killed the s.o.b."**

Frankness used in good taste is preferable to yesterday's euphemisms, such as "social disease" for *syphilis,* "intimate relationship" for *sexual intercourse,* "assault" for *rape.* Why refer to washrooms and toilets in public buildings, such as schools, as "bathrooms?" Ever try to take a bath in one?

Negated Negatives

The House voted 63 to 94 against overriding the committee's disapproval of a bill by Rep. Charles L. Hughes to repeal the women's eight-hour law.

The reader can't be sure at first or even on the third reading whether the vote favored or opposed the eight-hour law for women. He is obliged to take the time to spell it all out. The eight-hour day for women is on the books. Hughes introduced a bill to repeal it (negative 1). The committee disapproved (negative 2) the proposal, thus sustaining the existing law. If the House had voted to override (negative 3) the committee, it would have favored repealing the law. But the House voted against (negative 4) overriding, thus upholding the law as it stands. This is what the story should have said in the first place:

The House voted 94 to 63 to keep the women's eight-hour law.

How to put five negative ideas in one sentence: "Earlier the Senate refused to override its executive committee's disapproval of a bill to eliminate the non-communist oath required for state employes." The reader would have had less trouble understanding the sentence if it had been edited to read, "The Senate agreed with its executive committee that state employes should be required, as at present, to take a non-communist oath."

"There weren't many in the Turkey Day crowd of 11,554 who could doubt that Central lacked leadership in its 13–7 victory over Northern." Revised: "Few in the crowd of 11,554 could doubt that Central was well led in its 13–7 victory over Northern."

Release Dates

The copy editor is expected to respect release dates. When he edits an advance copy, he underscores or rings the instruction "Release for Tuesday." Some embargoes are suspect. One is the story with a June 20 dateline and a June 21 release date. Another is the Sunday release, often a ploy by publicity agents to get equal play in Sunday editions of both afternoon and morning papers. A company official died on a Friday but the obituary carried a Sunday release. When the bureau checked to find the reason for the embargo, it was told, "We thought the story would get more attention in Sunday papers."

Embargoes should be reasonable and equitable to all media. Generally, premature publication or premature broadcast breaks the embargo.

A handout should not be camouflaged as an interview or as the speech itself. Both the reader and the speaker are confused if the story reports what the speaker said before he made the speech. However, releases are sometimes given on excerpts from the text to be given later by the speaker.

Technically, the breaking of a release time is a legal violation. A news agency story theoretically is the property of the agency until it is released to members or clients for publication. Also, the breaking of the embargo could be construed as a violation of common law copyright.

Trifles

A story was about a tomcat. On second reference the cat was called "she." A small point, except to the cat. In a story about a pony that had frozen, the reporter said that firemen thawed out the mare. The next paragraph reported that "the animal will be returned to Assateague when his condition has improved."

Another story referred to a black Angus bull. All Angus cattle are black. A letter to the editor contained this statement: "The

---

The Copyeditor on Guard

warden presented us with an official notice that our spaded female dog must be tagged and put under control." The word the letter writer wanted was *spayed*, meaning the ovaries were removed. Obviously, *female* was redundant.

Most newspapers on occasion carry items that would have been more appropriate for the wastebasket than for the paper. If these have to be printed, they should be trimmed. Perhaps they will be relegated to the filler role in the first edition. Examples:

A Los Altos, Calif., family returns home from a Saturday night out to find a swarm of honey bees in the house.

A frog named Ripple sets a world's record jump of 19 feet, 3⅛ inches at the annual Calaveras County Jumping Frog Jubilee.

A news service sent out a story based on a 78-page research report on coffee cooling. "Do you put the cream in right away or hold off a bit?" One newspaper that carried the trivial item appended its own recipe: "The best way is to saucer it and blow it." The wire service labeled the story "one of its biggest feature hits of the week." If true, editors must have been hard up for features that week.

8

Writing the Headline

Styles of headlines, like fashions, change constantly even though their function remains the same. Newspapers' first news display lines were short and slender, usually a single crossline giving little more than a topical label: **Latest from Europe.** By adding more lines or by varying the length of the lines, designers created the hanging indention, the inverted pyramid and the pyramid:

Headline Styles Change

```
XXXXXXXXXXXX      XXXXXXXXXXXX       XXXXX
 XXXXXXXXX        XXXXXXXXX        XXXXXXXXX
 XXXXXXXX          XXXXX         XXXXXXXXXXXX
```

Later, by indenting lines under the first line they achieved the stepped head, sometimes known as the drop head. It became one of the most popular styles of headlines and still is in use:

Heavy Rain
Shuts Down
All Beaches

The next move was to combine these elements—a stepped head, then an inverted pyramid, a crossline, then another inverted pyramid. The units under the introductory head became known as banks or decks. George Fitzpatrick, in an article in the October 1955 issue of *The Quill,* cited one he found in a western

newspaper describing a reporter's interview with General Phil
Sheridan in 1883:

FRISKY PHIL

Gazette Reporter Holds
Interesting Interview
With Hero of Win-
chester

The Great Warrior Receives the
Newspaperman with Open Arms;
He is More or Less Broken up on
the Craft Anyway

He Travels in a Special
Military Coach and Lives
On the Fat of the Land

Sheridan is Many Miles Away,
but the Champagne We Drank
with him Lingers with Us Still

*We Feel a Little Puffed
Up Over Our Success At-
tending Our Reception by
Little Phil, But Man Is
Mortal*

May He Who Watches Over the
Sparrows of the Field Never
Remove His Field Glasses from
the Diminutive Form and Great
Soul of Phil Sheridan

Throughout most of America's history newspaper headlines
have tended to depict the mood of the times as well as the tone
of the paper. **Jerked to Jesus** the Chicago *Times*, on Nov. 27,
1875, shouted in headlining the account of a hanging. Other
headlines are given in the following:

AWFUL EVENT

———

President Lincoln
Shot by an
Assassin.

———

The Deed Done at Ford's
Theatre Last Night.

———

The Act of a Desperate Rebel

**The President Still Alive at
Last Accounts.**

No Hopes Entertained of His
Recovery.

Attempted Assassination of
Secretary Seward.

Details of the Dreadful Tragedy

The New York *Times*

AMERICA IS
MISTRESS
OF AIR

**Wright's Machine Is
Perfect; Uncle
Sam Buys.**

**Overland Trip With
Passenger Succeeds**

**"We Flew Eighty Miles an Hour
Coming Back," Says
Lieutenant.**

The Denver *Post*

PEARY WIRES HE HAS NAILED STARS AND STRIPES
TO THE NORTH POLE AND IS ON HIS WAY HOME

**OFFICIAL MESSAGE
SENT ARCTIC CLUB**

**Backers Were Momen-
tarily Expecting Veteran
Explorer to Report Suc-
cessful Quest of Goal
Reached by his Rival.**

**Latter Sends His Instru-
ments and Records to the
United States for Examin-
ation and Will Prove His
Claims Before a Jury of
Scientists of Two Conti-
nents—Dispells All Doubt.**

The Denver *Post*

Writing the Headline

Big type and clamoring messages still weren't enough. According to Gene Fowler, *Timberline* (New York: Garden City Books, 1951, p. 100.) an executive told the owners of the Denver *Post*, "You've got to make this paper look different. Get some bigger headline type. Put red ink on Page 1. You've got to turn Denver's eyes to The Post every day, and away from the other papers." So the *Post* put the headlines in red to catch the readers' eyes. The message had to be gripping. According to Gene Fowler's version in *Timberline*, Harry Tammen, co-owner of the Denver *Post*, was so incensed over a lifeless banner in the *Post* that he grabbed a piece of copy paper and composed one of his own: **Jealous Gun-Gal Plugs Her Lover Low.** When the copydesk protested that the headline wouldn't fit, Tammen snapped, "Then use any old type you can find. Tear up somebody's ad if necessary." Still the desk wasn't satisfied. "It isn't good grammar," the slotman argued. But Tammen wouldn't budge. "That's the trouble with this paper," he is quoted as saying. "Too damned much grammar. Let's can the grammar and get out a live sheet."

The battle for circulation was hot. So were the headlines. Many also were colorful:

Demon of the Belfy Sent Through the Trap

Dons Planned to Skedaddle in the Night

Does It Hurt to be Born?

Bless God—They're Safe
(On rescue of seaplane crew from the Pacific.)

Conductors Robbing Little Girls of Their Half Fare Tickets

Do You Believe in God?

During and after the Spanish-American War era some newspapers used as many as sixteen decks, or headline units, to describe the story. Frequently the head was longer than the story.

With improved presses and a greater variety of type and stereotyping available, designers were able to expand the headline. Eventually the head stretched across the page and became known as the banner, streamer or ribbon. On some papers it was called, simply, the line. This headline sometimes called for the largest type available in the shop. When metal type wasn't adequate for the occasion, printers fashioned letters from wood (called furniture). A 12-liner meant that the line was 12 picas, or 144 points (two inches).

Other headline designations are as follows: A story placed above the nameplate and banner headline is called a *skyline,* with the headline also known as a skyline head. Sometimes the skyline head stands alone but carries a notation as to where the story can be found.

A headline may have several parts—the main headline and auxiliary headlines known as *decks* or *banks*. These are not to be confused with subheads or lines of type (usually in boldface) placed between some paragraphs in the story. (Figure 8–1)

A *kicker* headline is a short line of display type, usually no larger than half the point size of the main headline and placed over the main part of the headline. On some papers the kicker is termed the *eyebrow*.

The common newspaper abbreviation for headline is *hed*. HTK means "hed to kum."

A *stet* head is a standing headline such as **Today in history.**

A *reverse plate* headline is one that reverses the color values so that the letters are in white on a black background.

Streamlining the Headline

As the tone of the newspaper was moderated, so were the headlines. Banner headlines still shout the news, sometimes in red ink, but gloom and doom headlines have virtually disappeared. Understating is more likely to be found in headlines today than overstating. Extra editions have been out of date for a long time. And no longer do circulation managers hurry into the city room to demand a line that will increase the newspaper's street sales.

Between World Wars I and II the cult of simplification, known as streamlining, brought changes in the newspaper headline. Designers put more air or white space into the head by having each line flush left, with a zigzagged, or ragged, right margin. Urged by this spirit of simplification, they abolished the decorative gingerbread such as fancy boxes and reduced the number of banks or eliminated them altogether except for the deck reading out from a major head—called *readout* head. They argued that the *flush left* head was easier to read than the traditional head and that it was easier to write because the count was less demanding.

Another part of the streamlining process was the introduction of modern sans serif Gothic typefaces to challenge the traditional roman typefaces such as Century, Cheltenham, Caslon, Goudy and Garamond (described in Chapter 12). Advocates of the new design contended that the sans serif faces were less ornate than the roman ones, gave more display in the smaller sizes, contained more thin letters (thus extending the count) and afforded greater mixture of faces because of the relative uniformity of the sans serifs.

Headlines in all-capital letters gradually gave way to capital and lower case letters. In modern headline design, only the first word of the headline and proper names are capitalized.

The wider columns in modern newspaper makeup give headline writers a better chance to make meaningful statements

Movies Are Better Than Ever

| 3 Big Hits Tonight At Vista View Drive-In | Two Comedies Slated Wednesday | 'The Perils Of Pauline' |

(A) BINDER HEAD

─── *SO DOES HITCH* ───

Boyer, Ritchie 'RevampTeam'

(B) THREE-WAY BROKEN OR SPLIT BOX OR HOOD

RATH TO RECOMMEND COUNTY AID FOR CITY IN TALKS WITH BILLS

Tells Sedita He'll Ask Board Approval Of Financial Assistance for Stadium Operation

(C) DROP OR STEPPED HEAD WITH INVERTED PYRAMID DECK

Washington Intensifies Diplomatic Efforts

(D) INVERTED PYRAMID HEAD

Status of Legislation

(E) SHADED OR BEN DAY HOOD

Bare Facts

Miniskirts, New Subway Seats Don't Mix

(F) BARKER HEAD

Today In History

By Associated Press

(I) REVERSED PLATE HEAD

Rubber Workers Strike Deadline Set at Goodyear

Union Tells Firm to Expect Walkout Early on Friday If No Agreement Reached

Tieup Would Close 11 Plants

(G) FLUSH-LEFT HEAD WITH HANGING INDENTATION AND CROSSLINE DECKS

Lottery Business Is Brisk as Sale Of Tickets Opens

Sellers, Buyers Share The Excitement as 425 WNY Outlets Service Customers

(H) FLUSH-LEFT HEAD WITH FLUSH-LEFT DECK

Writers Rap TV Antics In Soccer

(J) THREE-WAY BOX OR HOOD

Inside Today...

(K) RULED OR WICKET HEAD

Figure 8–1. Sample headline styles.

because of a better count in one-column heads. The trend away from vertical makeup and toward horizontal makeup provides more multicolumn headlines on the page. Such spread heads can be told effectively in one line.

Traditionally, the headline has headed the column and hence its name. But the headline need not necessarily go over the news column (see Figures 14–4, 14–5, and 14–6, Chapter 14).

Clever headlines continue to intrigue readers. Yet some readers tend to remember only the inept, the mixed-up, or the humorous ones. Some classics come to mind readily. One was the New York *Times* headline in 1916 proclaiming Charles Evans Hughes the winner over President Woodrow Wilson. Or *Life* magazine with a full-page shot of Gov. Thomas Dewey riding a ferry across San Francisco Bay, the cutline referring to "the next president of the United States." Or the banner in one edition of the Chicago *Tribune* proclaiming Dewey the victor over President Harry Truman. Still another was the amazing banner headline **Overhead Wins Indianapolis Race** that appeared in a small daily in Colorado. The editor, a racing car buff, had messaged the Associated Press to protect his paper on the winner of the Indianapolis Memorial Day race. In confirming the request, the AP wired the editor, WILL OVERHEAD (meaning AP would send by special telegram) INDIANAPOLIS MEMORIAL DAY RACE WINNER. The editor mistook the message for the bulletin and wrote the story and headline accordingly.

Whatever its style, the purpose of the headline is to urge the reader into the story. It gives an added dimension to the news story. It must get attention, then inform or titillate the reader. It has these major functions:

Functions of the Headline

1. Attracts readers' attention to the story.
2. Summarizes or analyzes the story.
3. Depicts the mood of the story.
4. Helps readers index the contents of the page.
5. Helps set the tone of the newspaper.
6. Provides a major ingredient for page makeup.

Each newspaper has its own schedule showing headline designations and line count. Practice varies as to how headlines are designated. Here are three methods:

1. Number designation—Headlines of one or two columns are assigned a number. A 2 head, for example, might call for a one-column, two-line head in 24-point Bodoni, capitals and lower case. A 22 head would be the same as a 2 head but in two columns. Sometimes the number corresponds with the type size and style. A 24 head would be in 24 points, and a 25 would be in 24 points italic.

2. Letter designation—Here letters are used to show the type family and size. If C calls for 30-point Vogue extrabold, the head might be indicated as follows: 2C=. This means two columns, two lines of 30-point Vogue extrabold. The letter may also indicate the headline style. If D, for instance, means a one-column head in three lines of type, ½D would be one column in two lines. Or if D is a headline with a deck, then ½D would be the same head but without the deck.

3. Designation by numbers and type family—A designation such as 1-24-3 Bod. means one column, 24 points, three lines of Bodoni; 3-36-1 (or 3361) TBCI means three columns of 36-point, one line of Tempo bold condensed italic. On some papers, the first number designates the column width, the second number the number of lines and the third number the size of type (2/3/36). (See Figure 8–2.)

The smallest headline may have no size indicated. A one-line head, set in the same size as the body copy but in boldface type, might be designated as BF or LCB (lower case bold). Such headlines are used on one-paragraph items.

Following are some of the common abbreviations used in headline designations:

X for extra (VXBI means Vogue extrabold italics)
x for italics (2302 SP x means two columns, two lines of Spartan italics)
It., I. or ital. for italics
K for a kicker line or eyebrow (2302K)
H for hammer, an inverted kicker (3361H); also called barker head.
J for jump or runover head; also RO.
RO for readout, or a deck under a main multicolumn headline.
W for wicket head.
Sh for subhead.
R for roman (VXBR is Vogue extrabold roman)
Refer means lines directing the reader to a related story or picture on another page.

When a story reaches the copydesk, it bears some directions for handling, known as sluglines. The main part of the slug is the story's title, usually in one or two words (bank holdup). After the headline has been written, the story's slug is placed on the headline copy together with the headline designation.

On some newspapers the copyeditor writes the headline, then uses the first two words of the headline (plus the headline designation) to replace the original story slug. Suppose the story copy bears the slug "suspect." The deskman edits the copy and composes this headline: **Woman held / in slaying / released.** He then changes the "suspect" slug on the copy to "Woman held—1-30-3

LCB
Third Park Band Concert

14 MR
Star-Spangled Banner
Essay Contest Opens

18
Bronze Star Given
GI Killed In Viet

8
Car In Chase
Hits 3 Others

34
Freight Train
Draws Ticket
For Speeding

11
GOP Club Asks
Jury Probe Of
Walsh Case

2/2/24
Miss Grace Boardley To Do
Mission Work In Formosa

2/2/30
Fla. Crops Endangered
By Caribbean Fruit Fly

2/2/36
5,000-Mile Cruise
Begun By Manry

2/3/36
Arson Is Charged
To Man, 3 Youths
At Cambridge

Figure 8–2.
Headline
schedule.

SB (one column of Spartan bold in three lines). An advantage of this method is that a slug does not have to be placed on the head copy (Figures 8–3 and 8–4).

A third method used by some papers is to write the headline on the story copy with an indication of size and type for the head. The headline is detached in the composing room and a number is put on both the story and the head copy. The number serves as the slug to enable the printer to match the head and story after they have been set into type.

1/18 MM | Better Teaching Of Science Sought

.--⌐Improving science courses is the goal of a three-week conference in progress at the University ~~of Colorado~~.

⌐Forty science supervisors and those ~~involved in the~~ teach~~ing of~~ science in elementary and secondary schools are at the 7th Science Supervisor's Conference sponsored by the ~~ou~~ School of Education in cooperation with the National Science Supervisors Association. Financial support for the conference is from the National Science Foundation.⌐

Figure 8–3. Headline copy. The first two words of the headline will become the slugline for the copy.

Blimp 1243 | Breeze Blows Test Blimp Back to U.S.

Figure 8–4. Headline copy. Note that the slugline (Blimp) is repeated in the headline copy. The number designation is one column of 24 point Bodoni caps and lower case.

Counting the Headline

The easiest way to count a headline is by the typewriter system—one unit for all letters, figures, punctuation and space between words. If a line has a maximum of 18 units and the head shows a unit count of 15, the head will fit, unless it contains several fat letters (M and W). In that case, the writer recounts the line by a standard system: one unit for all lower case letters and numerals except f, l, i, t, and j ($\frac{1}{2}$), and m and w ($1\frac{1}{2}$); $1\frac{1}{2}$ for all capital letters except two units for cap M and W; $1\frac{1}{2}$ units for lower case m and w; $\frac{1}{2}$ unit for f, l, i, t and j; and $\frac{1}{2}$ unit for each space, for punctuation, for upper case I and for numeral 1.

The Art of Editing

Because of the variation in the widths of letters in different families of type or even within the same family, the standard system is not always correct. The letter i, for instance, is thinner than lower case t; in some faces r is thinner than d or g and a string of zeros likely will make the line too long.

Some newspapers use two count systems—the standard one and one devised by measuring with a micrometer every character in all sizes of type family. The second system would employ a count like this: 1 for spaces; ½ for tight spaces; 1 for j, i, l, t, period, comma, colon, semicolon, each quote mark, apostrophe, hyphen, parenthesis and exclamation mark; 1½ for c, e, f, r, s, I, ¢, 1, /, # and ?; 2 for a, b, d, g, h, k, n, o, p, q, u, v, x, y, z, J, S, $, 2, 3, 4, 5, 6, 7, 8, 9, 0 and dash; 2½ for w, A, B, C, D, E, F, G, H, K, L, N, O, P, Q, R, Y, U, V, X, Y and Z; 3 for m, M, and %; and 3½ for W.

The comparative count is shown in the following head in 30-point:

Here's How to Skip Car License Line
(Standard, 33; micrometer, 50)

If, by using the standard count, the writer finds this head to be within the maximum allowed, he will submit the head. If, however, the maximum indicated for a three-column head is 31 units, he will count by the micrometer system. If that count indicates that the head will fit, the compositor will set it to fit, perhaps using tight spaces. If the composing room rejects a headline because it exceeds the maximum count, the desk's only recourse is to have the head rewritten. The advantage of a micrometer system is that it makes the compositor try harder to set the head as designated.

Not all composing rooms take the trouble to reject an overlong head. Compositors set as much as they can and the head appears in the paper this way:

2nd Saline Conversi
Plant Dedicated

All headline writers are expected to keep within the maximum count allowable. It is costly and time-consuming to have heads reset. If it appears that the desired head is slightly over the maximum count, the writer may provide an optional word as a substitute for a long word. The compositor then can try to fit the head as originally written. If it won't fit, he can use the optional word.

All the trial-and-error methods of manufacturing headlines can be eliminated by an electronic system designed for use in typing headlines that will fit. A sensing bar mounted under a typewriter gives an electrical imput from the various keys to an electronic counter cabinet. A card inserted in the cabinet shows the maximum units for the type style and line length. As the headline writer types the headline, he consults the total units on the counter. If the line falls short of the total line, it will fit. If the desired line is too long, the writer merely back-spaces the typewriter to a word, retypes a replacement and again consults the counter. Whenever the line is under the maximum unit count, it will fit. Thus, no headline or cutline need ever be returned to the desk because of an inaccurate count.

Some slotmen insist that each line of the head, even in a flush left head, take nearly the full count. Others argue there is merit in a ragged right edge. In a stepped head the lines cannot vary more than two or three units or the head will not step. Unless a special effect is desired, each line should fill more than half the maximum type-line width.

Ideally, the kicker should extend no more than half the width of the main head. As its name suggests, the kicker should be terse. A simple phrase, aptly put, will suffice, and a verb is not necessary. It should not rob the main head of key words or repeat words used in the main head. It should stand on its own and not depend on the main head for its meaning. It may set the tone of the main head or supply information the writer would have used in the main head if space had been available. Sometimes it is used as a standing head: **Window of the world.**

The inverted kicker, or hammer head or block buster, carries the main idea of the story. The line underneath the hammer head supplements the hammer head. Sometimes the hammer head is a short line; more often, it fills the line.

The copyeditor does not write several heads for the same story and invite the slotman to take his pick. He submits what he considers to be the best head he can write.

Creating the Headline

Occasionally the slotman or some other executive will suggest an angle that should go into the head or call attention to an angle that should be avoided. Usually, however, the headline writer is on his own. He knows that within a matter of minutes or even seconds he must edit the copy and create a headline that will epitomize the story, that will make a statement in an easy-to-digest capsule.

By the time he has edited the copy he should have an idea brewing for the head. He begins by noting key words or phrases. These are his building blocks. With them he tries to structure a headline. The first effort in headline writing starts with an answer to the question "Who's doing what?" More than likely, the answer will provide some of the blocks for the structure: **Jets bomb ... Brothers split ... Boys convicted ... Allen vetoes. ...**

Key blocks may be a proper name or a reference to a name (Wilson, mayor, president), the setting (in Cambodia, Pueblo man), the age (baby, 100-year-old man, student), the occupation (janitor, actress, doctor) or the topic itself (accident, taxes, divorce).

With these blocks he tries to make an accurate and coherent statement. First he may try to phrase the statement in the active voice. If that fails, he uses the passive. If possible, he tries to get key words and a verb in the top line.

Take a routine accident story:

Three Atlantans were killed Friday when their car collided with a garbage truck on Hwy. 85 at Thames Road in Clayton County.

Dead were: . . .

Patrolman C. F. Thornton said the truck was driven north on Hwy. 85 by . . .

The auto pulled into the highway from Thames road and was hit by the truck, Thornton said.

The headline designation is three lines in one column that allows a maximum of nine units. In this story the lead almost writes the head. The obvious statement is "Three Atlantans killed as car and truck collide." **3 Atlantans** won't fit, so the writer settles for **3 killed.** For the second line he tries **in truck,** and for the third line **car collision.** He discards **car collision** because it is too long. **car crash** will fit. By changing the second line from **in truck** to **as truck** he gains another verb in the third line. The head now reads **3 killed / as truck, / car crash.**

Before he has written many headlines, the writer will discover several tricks. He will search the story for the action. The procedure is seldom, if ever, the headline clue. **Freshmen face curfew / under new proposal** is better than **Student affairs committee / proposes hours for freshmen.** He will look for specific nouns (*court, council, jury*) and avoid the generalized ones (*agency, board, group*). He will use abbreviated forms (*council* or *city* for "city council," *President* or *Nixon* for "President Richard M. Nixon"). He will not waste valuable headline space with words such as "Grand jury indicts." Instead, he will tell who was indicted. He will examine the lead for the words he will rephrase in the headline.

Before basing his headline on the lead, the deskman should make sure the lead is not misleading, that it delivers its promises in the body of the story. For example, the lead spoke of three servicemen who died in battle. Before the battle, they wrote letters to their families expressing the anguish they suffered while waiting to go into battle. The head dutifully reflected the lead: **Letters of dead GIs / tell battle anguish.** But the story did not bear out the lead or the head. The letters simply described the men's impatience of waiting before the fighting began. Readers who were drawn to the story by the promise of the headline were misled.

If a statement in a story is carefully qualified, the statement should not be presented as a fact in the headline.

If the lead can't suggest a good headline, the lead obviously is weak.

Take this horrible lead: "A man who has been a Mason longer than anyone in the world is getting a little tired after 106 years of an active life." Nothing specific here, only a dull, generalized statement and not likely to urge the reader to read on. The lead fetches a repetitious and equally dull head: **Oldest Mason in world is getting little tired at 106.**

Another example of a dull lead and head: "Home, public and traffic safety were discussed today at a Safety Leadership Conference in the Hotel Du Pont." Head: **Safety conference opens; national officials speak.** If any reader except a "nut" about safety ever got beyond the headline, the lead would make him put down his paper.   If a paragraph deep in the story reveals a strong headline idea, the copyeditor moves that paragraph into the lead, or near the lead, then builds his headline on the stronger statement.

Here is a typical say-nothing lead: "Miss Charlotte Elliott, epilepsy nursing consultant for the State Department of Public Health, was guest speaker Wednesday afternoon at a meeting in Jimtown of volunteers who work with the retarded in the county, some parents and nurses from the public health department." If the deskman lets this lead ride and attempts to write a head based on the lead, the result will be something like this: **Epilepsy is subject / of talk in Jimtown.**

Obviously neither the head nor the lead will inspire the reader to continue. A quotation buried in the sixth paragraph suggests a better lead idea—and a better headline: "A child with epilepsy should be treated as a normal person. He should be disciplined when he needs it and he should be allowed to pursue almost any activity he desires." By getting part of this quote into the lead, the headline writer can now make a meaningful statement in the headline: **Normal activity urged / for epileptic child.**

Many dull heads can be improved if the writer will make the extra effort. Sometimes his first idea for the head is the best; often it is not. If the slotman rejects the lifeless heads and insists on better ones, he inspires everyone on the rim to try harder. Furthermore, a good performance on news heads is likely to generate better headlines in all departments of the paper.

The job of the man on the rim is to create effective headlines for all copy that comes his way. The big story often is easier to handle than the routine one because the banner story has more action and thus more headline building blocks.

The usual death and wedding stories offer little opportunity for bright, original headlines. There are only so many ways to announce a wedding or a death in a head, and the writer dare not try to be clever in handling these topics. The standing gag on the copydesk is, "Let's put some life in these obit heads." If Jonathan Doe dies, that is all the headline can say, except to include his age: **Jonathan Doe / dies at age 65** or **Jonathan Doe / dead at 65.** If he were a former mayor, that fact would be used: **Jonathan Doe, / ex-mayor, dies.** Get the story interest in the head: **Lillian Roe, former postmaster, dies** is less newsworthy than **Lillian Roe, mother of selectman, dies.**

The headline should be as newsworthy as the story itself. The trick is to merge as many elements of the story as possible into four or five headline words. If only one element emerges in the headline, the head fails to do justice to the story. This headline is weak: **Man injured / in accident.** At least one person in a community is injured in an accident nearly every day. The word *man* is a faraway word. *Driver* is closer. "Injured in accident" can be shortened to "Injured" if the word *Driver* replaces *Man.* Now the top line can read: **Driver injured.** A second element in the story shows that he was wearing a seat belt. Marrying the two ideas produces a head like this: **Injured driver / wore seat belt.** The original head is passable but weak. The revised head gives more information and is an attention-getter.

A warning here. The few words of a headline allow little room for the writer to present several ideas clearly. It is better to have a simple, clear headline than one jumbled by too many elements.

Suppose the reader is presented with this head: **Budget block / is taken from / Rocky's drive.** What does it mean? What is the budget block? What is Rocky's drive? Who took the block away and why? The reader does not stop to formulate these questions. He passes up the story in the belief that it deals with something he doesn't understand or care about. A headline is like a cup; it will hold only so much. Too much makes a mess: **Loss of heart / recipient is / laid to lungs.**

Gimmicks Won't Work

Most readers presumably take headline words literally. Suppose the head says **Furnishings / field sports / a 'new look'.** Let's see. Field sports means football, hockey, polo, cricket. But the story is about none of these, so the reader is misled. And why the quotes around *new look?* Because, the reader may find out eventually, the new look refers not to a new style but rather to the prosperity of manufacturers and dealers. The quotation marks don't mean what they usually do. The reader is not notably helped.

Key headline words are like signposts. They attract the reader's attention and give him information. Such words, meaningfully phrased, produce effective headlines.

Note how quickly the key words (*Dutch, prince, born*) emerge in the lead of a wire story: "Crown Princess Beatrix gave birth to a son last night and Dutchmen went wild with joy at the arrival of a king-to-be in a realm where queens have reigned since 1890." One deskman used the key words this way:

Dutch treat
**A prince is born,
first in century**

Taste in Headlines

Newspapers must, of necessity, reveal man's sorrows as well as his joys, his afflictions as well as his strengths. No story or headline should mock those who have misfortunes. The newspaper belongs in the parlor where good taste is observed.

A story related that a Johannesburg motorist, whose car stalled on railroad tracks, died under the wheels of a train when he was unable to release his jammed seat belt. The victim may have been unknown to readers in an American community but death is a common tragedy and should be treated with respect, something the deskman forgot when he wrote this head: **Belted to death.**

A minor story told about a man digging his own grave, starving while lying in it for twenty-one days and dying two hours after being found. The headline writer apparently thought the situation was humorous. His head: **Down . . . and then out.**

Unless the pun is a good one, the impulse to try it should be suppressed: **Unbreakable window solves a big pane.**

Getting the News in Heads

Some stories, like announcements, offer little or no news to invite fresh headlines. Yet even if the second-day story offers nothing new, the headline cannot be a repetition of the first-day story head.

Suppose on Monday the story says that Coach Ralston will speak at the high school awards dinner. If Ralston is prominent, his name can be in the head: **Ralston to speak / at awards dinner.** On Thursday comes a follow-up story, again saying that Coach Ralston will be the awards dinner speaker. If the headline writer repeats the Monday headline the reader will wonder if he is reading today's paper. The slotman will wonder why his man on the rim won't keep up with the news in his own paper. The problem is to find a new element, even a minor one, like this: **Tickets available / for awards dinner.** So the dinner comes off on Friday, as scheduled. If the Saturday headline says **Ralston speaks / at awards dinner,** the reader learns nothing new. The action is what he said: **Ralston denounces / 'cry baby' athletes.** Or if the story lacks newsworthy quotes, another facet of the affair goes into the head: **30 athletes / get awards.**

The Title Lesson

Beginning headline writers might start with what Carl Riblet Jr., an expert in headline writing, calls the title lesson. The learner starts by listing the titles of all the books he has read. This is to demonstrate that readers can recall titles even if they have forgotten the contents. It also demonstrates the effectiveness of an apt title. A good title helps sell the product, as illustrated by those revised by alert publishers: "Old Time Legends Together with Sketches, Experimental and Ideal" (*The Scarlet Letter*), "Pencil Sketches of English Society" (*Vanity Fair*), "The Life and Adventures of a Smalltown Doctor" (*Main Street*), "Alice's Adventures Underground" (*Alice in Wonderland*).

Limiting the learner to a one-line head with a maximum of fifteen or twenty units forces him to pack action in a few words, to merge as many elements as possible from the story, to indicate the tone or mood of the story and, finally, to compose an interesting statement. Riblet gives this example:

A young man said he and a middle-aged business agent had been drinking in a saloon. They went to the older man's apartment. There they quarreled over a gambling debt. The younger man told the police he was threatened with a .30 caliber rifle. In self-defense, he picked up a bow and arrow and shot the older man in the stomach. The younger man tried to pull the arrow out but it broke and the wounded man died.

The deskman got the story with instructions to write a one-line 20-count head. He knew the paper's rule that every headline must contain a verb. He wrote: **Business agent slain.** In this instance it would seem wiser to bend the rule and get the key words in the headline: **Bow and arrow killing.** This lesson has practical value in writing the one-line head, such as the banner **Dodd censured** or **Boy for Luci!,** the kicker **Smelly problem** or **Circus magic,** the column heading **The goldkeepers,** the filler head, **Postal auction** or the magazine feature **Acrobat on skis,** or **Messy education** or **Ohio's hub city.**

Good phrasing in a headline helps the reader grasp its meaning quickly. Each line should be a unit in itself. If one line depends on another to convey an idea, the headline loses its rhythm. It may cause the reader to grope for the meaning. Note the differences in the original and the revised heads:

Phrasing the Headline

Original	Revised
Thousands join Easter parade in Philadelphia	**Thousands join Easter parade**
Men need to sleep longer study reveals	**Men require more sleep, report shows**
West Virginia reveals new plan for Negro education	**West Virginians to provide schooling for 1700 Negroes**
Stay calm Browns, you'll soon know your title foe	**Just stay calm Browns, you'll know foe soon**
Football ticket exchange to be revised next fall	**Ticket exchange for football will be revised**
Hoffa loses new bid for freedom	**Hoffa again loses bid for freedom**
Four Russian women tour Denver area	**Four women from Russia tour Denver**
Snow removal serious project in Soviet Union	**Removing snow Is task in Soviet Union**

Practices vary, but on some desks no headline writer is permitted to hang conjunctions, parts of verbs, prepositions or modifiers on the end of any line of a headline. Like many newspaper rules, this one can be waived, but only if an exceptionally better headline can be created.

Rigid rules can bring grief to copydesks. One newspaper chain has two ironclad rules: No head may contain a contraction. Every head must contain a verb. This leads to some dull and tortured heads, especially on offbeat feature stories.

The Los Angeles *Times* evidently has no policy against splitting ideas in heads. It may be argued that in the one-column headline the reader sees the headline as a unit and does not have to read each line separately as he would in a multicolumn head. Eventually experiments may be designed to test whether a reader can comprehend a split head as easily as he can one that breaks on sense. Until the results of such tests are available, the headline writer should phrase headlines by sense. The practice can't hurt him if he joins a desk that tolerates splits. A talented deskman will take no longer on a phrased headline than on a split headline.

Headline Requirements

The first requirement of a headline is that it be accurate, the second is that it be clear and the third is that it be meaningful and intriguing.

No headline should leave the copyeditor's hands until he has rechecked it against the story to make sure the head says precisely what the story says. Inaccuracies arise if the headline writer doesn't understand the story or misses some details in the story. Or he may try too hard to get punch in the head and go beyond what the story warrants. Or he may work at such speed that he misinterprets the story. Examples:

Patricia Neal well / after three strokes. The story said she wore a leg brace, heavy shoes, a patch over one eye and that she spoke poorly.

If that pooch bites / you can collect $200. The story said the animal had to have rabies and you may collect up to $200.

Didn't like her face / shoots TV announcer. The story said a man fired a gun at her but missed.

Graham backs / sterilization view. Although he backed one viewpoint, he criticized the program. A better head would have been **Graham criticizes / sterilization act.**

Unite Michigan's parochial, / public schools, Romney says. Romney did not ask for union; he flatly suggested closing parochial schools and sending their pupils to public schools.

New school / to be aired. But the story reported plans for a meeting to discuss a new private elementary school.

Private development of oil / shale resources is urged. This is false. The lead said, "A Senate committee hearing was tentatively concluded Friday with a blast by the chairman at an administration plan to permit private development of rich shale oil resources in the West."

Aaron loses sleep / in hero's role. The story was about a baseball player, Wes Covington, not his teammate, Hank Aaron.

French space / experts pass / monkey tests. It would have been more accurate to say **Monkey passes / French space / experts' test.**

Waner, prof / clash on open / housing issue. The story was devoted to what Mr. Waner said, without a word anywhere to indicate what Prof. Wade may have contributed to the discussion.

Bishop says / segregation / is justified. The lead quoted the bishop as saying that Christians are not morally justified in aiding segregation.

Schools help pay expenses / for Forsyth county's dogs. The story said the dog-tax money helps support the schools.

Renewed protests / forewarned here. *Forewarn* means to warn beforehand. Hence, people could be forewarned of the protests, but the protests cannot be forewarned.

Party vacancy speculated. The story was about the possible replacement for a chairman who had resigned. How can you speculate a vacancy?

Comedian hits President. The story merely reported a Negro comedian as saying he was surprised at the President for thinking the civil rights march on Washington was silly. This is hitting?

Civic ballet auditions / scheduled Saturday. One listens to auditions; one looks at tryouts or trials.

Youth, 19, breaks parole, / subject to whipping post. The story correctly said he had been on probation.

Nardini to ask / $60,000 hike / in salaries. The state prison commissioner said the General Assembly had cut his budget, leaving a deficit in the salary account of $60,000. He did not request a salary increase.

Agency eases policy / on birth control data. A word like *agency* is the weakest possible word for a headline. Anyway, the story did not say the agency eased its policy; it explained its policy.

Dixie Baptists lock doors to Negroes. The lead said the Southern Baptists rejected an endorsement of church integration and left the issue up to member churches.

Circus clown's daughter / dies from high wire fall. Second paragraph of the story: "The 19-year-old aerialist was reported in good condition at Paterson General Hospital with fractures of the pelvis, both wrists and collarbone."

India-China / relations / worsen. The story was datelined Jakarta and had nothing to do with India.

Teachers ask / for problems: / study Swedish. The story told of a special course arranged for teachers of French and Spanish. To remind them of the difficulties encountered by beginners, the teachers were studying neither French nor Spanish but Swedish. The teachers didn't ask for problems. A better head: **Why teachers / of French now / study Swedish.**

Chicago to see outstanding moon eclipse. *Outstanding* is the least appropriate adjective to describe an eclipse. Anyway, the story wasn't about a moon eclipse; it was about an eclipse of the sun.

Brilliant modern study / of Holy Roman emperor. That was the head over a review of a book on the Emperor Hadrian. The review showed that Hadrian was born A.D. 76 and died in 138. The Holy Roman Empire lasted from A.D. 800 to 1806.

Headlines Must Be Clear

Even accuracy in a headline is not enough. The head must not cause confusion. Perhaps headlines would make some sense if the reader had a knowledge of the story before he read the headline. But the reader reads the headline first. Then, possibly, he goes into the story. The copyeditor works in reverse. First he reads the story, then he writes the head. If the slotman rejects the headline as senseless, the deskman may grumble, "The head will make sense if you'll read the story." Unless the headline, standing alone, tells the reader precisely and clearly what the story is about, it is faulty. Examples:

Trouble dogs college aid medical bill	**Rocks in ski lift; tips over tower; 2 hurt**
Stern view of world air runs to U.S.	**Mutual cuts Clifford's hope**

One editor put it this way, "The headline-writer does a disservice both to the reporter, whose vantage point should give him a clearer perspective, and to the reader who depends on the headline for his key to the story when the writer puts obscure angles in the headline."

The headline must reflect what the story reveals totally, not what may be implied in parts of the story. Look at this example:

SALT LAKE CITY (AP)—A U.S. District Court judge ruled Friday that the federal government was liable for damages caused by negligence of a military serviceman traveling under orders by private auto, and awarded death and injury damages totaling more than $500,000.

The lead can carry the implication that it was the serviceman who was killed by his own negligence. At least, the lead was so interpreted by a headline writer, who wrote **U.S. held liable in death / of traveling serviceman.** Perhaps the headline writer did understand the story but his headline could confuse the reader. The serviceman was not killed. His car killed a private citizen. Relatives of the deceased victim, a salesman, were suing the federal government for damages caused by the negligence of the serviceman. The final paragraph of the story made this clear:

The fatal accident was June 24, 1965, near Green River, Utah. Killed was Norman Day of Price, Utah, driver of an auto involved in an accident with Williams (the serviceman). The judge held the accident was caused by Williams' negligence.

The point of the story was that the U.S. government was held liable in the death of a private citizen caused by a traveling serviceman. A more accurate headline would have said **U.S. held liable in death / caused by traveling soldier.**

Another example:

SPRINGFIELD, Ill., May 18 (AP)—Illinois public school districts get 60 per cent of their support from local property taxes, the Taxpayers' Federation said today.

State aid accounts for 24 per cent and federal aid for about 6 per cent.

The story bore this headline: **Schools get / 60% of local / property tax.**

The headline was not in accord with the story, which emphasized schools do not get 60 per cent of the local property tax. They get a proportion of the contributions of various levels of government—federal, state and local—toward the support of schools. In other words, of the amount spent on the support of schools, the local property tax contributes 60 per cent. This is far less, obviously, than 60 per cent of the total local property tax.

A headline may accurately reflect the facts in a story and still fail to tell the reader what the story means to him. Here is a fairly routine story from the Washington *Post:*

WASHINGTON—A lease is invalid if there were housing code violations on the property when it was rented, the District of Columbia Court of Appeals ruled Wednesday.

The ruling, which has the effect of law and is binding on judges in the Court of General Sessions, means that a landlord will not be able to evict a tenant for non-payment of rent if the tenant can prove housing violations were on the property when it was rented.

Previously, most judges here had ruled that a tenant must pay the rent or face eviction, regardless of the condition of the property at the time of rental.

At first glance, the key headline words are *lease, invalid, housing code violations* and *court rules.* But even juggling these to fit into a headline won't give the reader the meaning of the story. The second paragraph explains the ruling and offers a head possibility: **Code violators / face rent losses.**

The second paragraph could stand a little editing to make it read "The ruling has the effect of law and is binding on judges in the Court of General Sessions. It means that a landlord cannot evict a tenant for non-payment of rent if the tenant can prove housing violations."

Writing the Headline

Even when the teaser head is used it should convey enough to guide the reader. Here is a marginal one written by a Texas editor: **Kermit 1, 21 to 0 / But Monahans 0 to 1.** The writer was trying to say that Kermit won, 21 to 0, but that Monahans ought to have won. In another, the writer tried to be clever but failed: **Harvard wins / third race in / row vs. Yale.** The third line suggests a brawl rather than a rowing match. Actually, Harvard won three races, not merely the third.

Some Muddled Heads

Church reforms stress group worship. With so many words that can be used as either verbs or nouns, some readers will be confused. Any line running more than 25 characters or more than 50 characters in two or more lines is hard to read.

Ex-convict / fatally shot / fleeing cop. Here is the copyeditor's thought: "Ex-convict (is) fatally shot (while) fleeing cop." But the ordinary reader follows the normal order of subject, then predicate, so he reads "(An) ex-convict fatally shot (a) fleeing cop."

Eye extending
tollway into
atomic site

Rotten wood
eyed in state
fair deaths

Venereal disease talks / to eye church attitude. There has been a marked and welcome decline in the use of the verb *to eye* in headlines; the quoted head is one of the few eyed lately. Even those among us who think in headlinese must have wondered for a moment or two what in the world the author was trying to say with his "talks to eye."

Flourish floors drabness. Hint: The second word is the verb.

Trooper kills man / who had slain wife. Does this mean that the trooper killed the man who had slain his (the trooper's) wife? Or that the trooper killed a wife slayer? Or that he killed a man whose wife had been slain by someone else?

Reattached severed hand in critical period. The patient, not the hand, faces the critical period.

Coliseum head / gets pay hike. That's a journalese head that many readers won't understand. This will get twice the reader attraction: **Paul Buck's pay raised.**

5 from Mt. Pleasant win / handicapped essay prizes. What's a handicapped essay? Or was it the prizes that were handicapped?

Water falls; / calls build / to Niagara. Want to know what idea this head is trying to convey? The water pressure in Penns Grove had fallen and the water company had received many complaints.

Suit curbing shed, / fence sites loses. Sounds like a cablegram in code.

Invest $75 and get $51,000
chain bond bait held fraud

Wilson asks Rhodesia acts

Inadequate employment study urged

Luna hits but Briton
feels it wasn't easy

Youth hangs self in cell
after uncle tries to help

Ask permanent hunger plan

Heads with Double Meaning

A headline is unclear if it can imply more than one meaning, as illustrated in the last two examples of the foregoing section. Some readers may grasp the meaning intended by the writer; others won't. The ad writer for a coffee company created a double meaning in this slogan: "The reason so many people buy Red & White Coffee is that 'They Know No Better.'"

Some experts call this a two-faced expression and warn headline writers that if a line has two meanings they should start over. Place names like Virgin, Utah; Fertile, Minnesota; and Bloomer, Wisconsin, inevitably invite a two-faced headline if the town is used in the headline:

Virgin woman   **Pastor to wed**
gives birth   **Marblehead girl**
to twins

Other geographical terms:

Book in pocket   **Three Boston**
saves man shot   **waitresses shot**
in South End   **in North End**

Unusual family names of officials—Love, Fortune, Dies, Oyster—likewise invite two-faced headlines:

Oyster probes   **Picks Fortune**
unknown jam   **for Indiana**
                          revenue chief

Wallace attacks
U.S. grant

Billy Hooks   **Fink heads bridge**
patient in Durham   **charity unit**

**Winchell defies
Hoffman and Dies**

**Slaughter recreates
Constantine's Rome**

Presidents and presidential candidates have been victims of two-faced heads:

Ike to get girls' calf

**Goose given to
Eisenhower**

**LBJ giving bull
to Mexican people**

**LBJ learns of
daughter's romance
in bed**

**Robert Kennedy
stoned**

**Johnson putting rusty
on White House green**

Case and *chest* produce these headlines:

**Ord Phillips gets
two years in
cigarette case**

**Women informed
of need for new
support of chest**

**Brentwood man held
in stolen watch case**

**Chest plea issued for
mothers' milk bank**

Suit has double-meaning:

**Publisher freed
in New Orleans
mayor's suit**

**Coors drops
union suit**

Lost wife found in suit

**Solon sees backfire
in union suit**

The worst possible headline verb is *eyes:*

**Frear resting,
eyes return**

**Young breaststroker
eyes new conquests**

**Sidewalks to be eyed
in Elsmere**

More double-takes in headlines:

**Five nudes pinched
at stag show**

**Rear end crash
kills woman**

**Suspect's counsel
says: Winsett
quizzed in nude**

**Governors' seats
held key to south**

**Swine housing
to be aired**

**Flies to attend
wedding of son**

Top swine prize
to county youth

Publisher says
bar endangers
press freedom

N.J. Assembly
passes drunk
driving test
Club to serve
world culture

Relatives served
at family dinner

Proud Optimists
fathers have sons
at banquet

Man with two
broken legs saves
one from drowning

Bed aflame, jumps
from fourth floor

Colonel's wife found by
body / holding knife in
hand

Wiley tours sewage plant /
gathers ammunition for
fight / against diversion
move

Burned-out pupils
use old high school

Local option fast time
offered to skirt problem

Thieu to ask LBJ
for newer arms

No water—
so firemen improvised

Boy chasing fox
found rabid

Franklin pair
is improved
after shooting

Wife charges husband
killed her for money

Andalusia girl
improved after
drinking poison

W. Side woman
dies of burns;
mate critical

Expectant mother, 23,
is anxious for facts

Sex educator says
kindergarten's the
time

Being a parent
can be a trial

President says women
responding adequately

Wedding held
before families

New restrooms
big asset
for shoppers

Telluride women
donate pots
for airplanes

Engineers to hear
ground water talk

Illegitimacy talks

DuPont hits Talbot
on billboards

Writing the Headline

Glacier Lake still
up in the air

Handicapped
hearing set

Chef says U.S.
courts ulcers

Man who shot himself
accidentally dies

U.S. capital does well
in booming Venezuela

Stores on 4th
between Walnut and
Chestnut to dress up rears

Turnpike bonds may bar
state aid for Sound span

State hunts teeth
in swimming ban

Pentagon requests
cut by committee

Rev. Branford
funeral fixed

Even the women's pages contain two-faced headlines:

Ladies! get felt at Scriveners

Italian cookies easy to make

Fresh dates are great

O'Brien peas in squash

Male underwear
will reveal new
colorful sights

Guide, don't push child

Nurses awarded for poster art

Strong attire right for bill's death

Carries on for husband

Designer's death blow to theater

Label Heads

A headline that gives no more information than the label on a vegetable can is aptly known as a label head. Generally these are the standing heads for columns that appear day by day or week by week, like **Social Notes** or **Niwot News.** They say nothing. They defy the purpose of a display line, which is to lure the reader.

Almost as bad are the yawny, ho-hum heads that make the reader ask, "So what else is new?" The writer who grabs a generality rather than a specific for the head is more than likely to produce a say-nothing head. He prefers **Many persons killed** to **1000 persons killed.**

Notice how little information is provided in the following samples:

Financial program explained

Development plans described

Class night to be today

Pan Am jet lands safely

**Wadsworth derailment
puts 13 cars off rails**

**Rotarians hear
Korean bishop**

**Newark
Rotary told
of planning**

**Coroner seeks cause
of why driver died**

**Autopsy scheduled
for dead Akronite**

**Broyhill speaks
at big picnic**

Committee will study 2 problems

A reader reads his newspaper to get the news. If the headline tells him the obvious, he has been short-changed. Here are examples of the obvious statement:

Fall shirts / offer new / innovations

Not to be confused with those old innovations.

**Corn field selected
as place for annual
county husking bee**

**Warm house best
in cold climate**

**Turkish ship
sinks in water
near Cyprus**

**Fashion editors view fall
American designer collections**

If a story says nothing, then obviously the head cannot say something. In that case, why bother with the story at all? The reader won't. But say-nothing heads can be turned into interesting ones:

Original	*Revised*
Statistics released on test	**Here's that test, can you pass it?**
Report given on teaching experiment	**Geometry, phonics in kindergarten?**
Heart of glacier **Tunnel town inaugurated**	*Drama in Arctic* **25 imperiled by blizzard**
Kinsey Institute reports in copyrighted mag article	**Report says 1 in 10 pregnant before marriage**
State approves housing plan	**State approves another dorm**
Colonel King posts rules for drivers	**Old decal or old tag means ticket**
News-Journal lists travel forum dates	*First stop: Egypt* **Yearn to travel? it's forum time**
10¢ fare is urged for the elderly	**10¢ fare is urged for those over 65**

Neutrality in Headlines

A good headline tells the reader what the story says, not what the writer thinks the story implies. In the latter category are the imperative heads, the editorialized heads, heads that go beyond what the story says and heads that oversimplify.

A New York City newspaper splashed a 144-point headline over the story of the shooting of Medgar Evers, a civil rights advocate, in Alabama. The head: **Slay NAACP Leader!** The imperative head results when the writer starts the head with a verb: **Save eight / from fire; Buy another / school site; Arrest 50 pickets / in rubber strike; Find 2 bodies / nab suspect; Assassinate U.S. envoy.**

Gratuitous adjectives and loaded terms like *beatniks, peaceniks, thugs, cops, pinkos, yippies* and *hippies* may appear in the story but should not be used in the headline unless they can be attributed. A quote mark around a word is not an attribution.

Every word in a headline should be justified by a specific statement within the story. Some stories are deliberately contrived to fetch a headline; that is, some are written in a fashion to mislead the headline writer. Was the sergeant who led a Marine platoon into a creek, drowning six recruits, drunk? Most headlines said he was, but the story carried the qualification "under the influence of alcohol to an unknown degree." Similarly, did Gov. Adlai Stevenson call Vice-President Richard Nixon a national calamity or did Senator Joseph McCarthy actually call General George Marshall a traitor? The headlines said they did, but the quotations in both instances prove that the statements may be open to more than one interpretation.

Before writing a headline on a story quoting someone, the deskman should ask himself, "Is the quotation out of context?" Frequently, part of a quotation is used for the lead, only to be modified deeper in the story. A headline based on the unqualified statement can be a distortion.

The lead on a wire story read: "Dr. Timothy Leary, dismissed from Harvard for his experiments with hallucination drugs, told a Senate hearing Friday that use of LSD has gotten out of control, particularly among the nation's college students." The lead fetched this head: **LSD perils youth, / ex-prof tells senate.** The last two paragraphs softened the lead: "While unrestrained use of LSD by the nation's younger set has led to a crisis, Leary commented: 'This is not a crisis of peril but a crisis of challenge. There is nothing to fear from LSD. On the basis of statistics, there is more violence, more terror in a cocktail lounge of any big city on Saturday night than from 23 years of LSD.'"

Timidity has no place on a copydesk. If the story is strong, the head should be strong. Often the choice of a word can make the difference between a factual head and a slanted head. A story said an unnamed source inside the White House had protested the Soviet's policy in Berlin to the Soviet ambassador to the United States. If the headline, as one did, states **President warns / Soviet on Berlin; / calls in Dobrynin,** the reader concludes that the U.S President summoned the Soviet ambassador and issued an ultimatum regarding Berlin. The danger of this type of headline, as editor Norman Cousins pointed out in a *Saturday Review* editorial, is that it is extremely difficult to get across to others the idea that our newspapers are not an extension of government policies.

Even though the headline reports in essence what the story says, one loaded term in the headline will distort the story. If Israel, for reasons that she can justify, turns down a compromise plan offered by the United States concerning the Gaza Strip and Gulf of Aqaba problem, the head creates a negative attitude among readers when it proclaims **Israel spurns U S. compromise.**

It is hard to put qualifications in heads because of the count limitations. But if the lack of qualification distorts the head, trouble arises. A story explained that a company that was expected to bid on a project to build a fair exhibit was bowing out of the project because the exhibit's design was not structurally sound. The headline, without qualification, went too far and brought a sharp protest from the construction firm's president: **Builder quits, calls / state world's fair / exhibit 'unsound.'**

Another temptation of the headline writer is to spot a minor, sensational element in the story and use that element in the head. A story had to do with the policy of banks in honoring outdated checks. It quoted a bank president as saying, "The bank will take the checks." In intervening paragraphs several persons were quoted as having had no trouble cashing their checks. Then in the eleventh paragraph was the statement "A Claymont teacher, who refused to give her name, said she had tried to cash her check last night and it had been refused." She was the only person mentioned in the story as having had any difficulty. Yet the headline writer grabbed this element and produced a head that did not reflect the story:

State paychecks dated 1964

**Can't Cash It,
teacher says**

If a controversial story has two sides, the head should do justice to both sides. This headline reflects only part of the story: **Woodling says Piersall is getting / special privileges in Nats' camp.** A second element in the story was Piersall's strong denial. The headline should have contained that fact, too: **Woodling says Piersall is getting / special privileges; star denies it.**

This headline went beyond the story: **Quick police / action stops / park fight.** There never was a park fight to stop. There was a crowd; there might have been a fight.

Finally, the question mark can become a weapon of editorialization unless it is used only after a legitimate question, for example, **Jones has new trick up his sleeve?**

Don't Give Away the Punchline

Some feature stories are constructed so that the climax comes at the end, rather than at the beginning, of the story. Obviously, if the point of the story is revealed in the headline, the story loses its effectiveness. The following story calls for a teaser head or

The Art of Editing

even a title. The point was dramatically made in Billy Rose's column, *Pitching Horseshoes* (used with permission):

One Saturday afternoon not long ago a night watchman named Stan Mikalowsky was window-shopping with his 5-year-old daughter, Wanda, and as they passed a toy shop the child pointed excitedly to a doll nearly as big as she was.

The price tag was only $1 less than the watchman's weekly pay check, and his first impulse was to walk away, but when the youngster refused to budge he shrugged and led her into the store.

When Stan got home and unwrapped the doll, his wife was furious.

"We owe the butcher for three weeks and we're $10 short on the room rent," she said. "So you got to blow in a week's pay for a toy."

"What's the difference?" said the night watchman. "Doll or no doll, we're always behind. For once let the kid have something she wants."

One word led to many others and finally Stan put on his hat and stomped out of the house.

Mrs. Mikalowsky fed the child and put her to bed with the doll next to her and then, worried about Stan, decided to go looking for him at the corner bar and make up with him. To keep his supper warm, she left the gas stove on, and in her haste threw her apron over the back of a chair in such a way that one of the strings landed close to a burner.

Fifteen minutes later when the Mikalowskys came rushing out of the bar, their frame house was in flames and firemen had to restrain the father from rushing in to save his daughter.

"You wouldn't be any use in there," a cop told him. "Don't worry, they'll get her out."

Fireman Joe Miller, himself a father, climbed a ladder to the bedroom window, and the crowd hushed as he disappeared into the smoke. A few minutes later, coughing and blinking, he climbed down, a blanket-wrapped bundle in his arms. . . .

The local newspaper headlined its story with the line which a De Maupassant would undoubtedly have saved for the finish:

**Fireman rescues life-size doll
as child dies in flames.**

Use the Present Tense

Unless the story is about a current or future event, most news is concerned with past events. But the headline, to give the effect of immediacy, uses the present tense for past events: **British doctors vouch / for girth control bill; City has bumper crop of junk cars; Jonathan Doe / dies at age 65.**

Suppose the headline announces a future event in the present tense? The reader won't know whether the event has occurred or will occur. **Powell's / wife tells / everything** means that the wife has testified. But if the reader learns from the story that the testimony will not be given until the following day, he knows the head has misled him. The head should have read **Powell's / wife to tell / everything.** The present tense can never be used if the date is included on a past event: **Jonathan Doe / dies Wednesday.**

On future events the headline may use the future, *will be;* the infinitive, *to be;* or the present, **Traffic parley / opens Monday.**

Scheduled is a hard headline word because of its length. Convenient substitutes are *set* and *slated* and consequently are worked to death in heads over stories of future events. It happens like this: **Two speakers set.** And the reader wonders, "On eggs?"

Headline Punctuation

The full stop is never used except after abbreviations. Use single quotes instead of full quotes because the single quote takes less space and may be more appealing typographically. The comma may replace *and* and a semicolon and may even indicate a complete break: **Tumbling spacecraft tangles chute, / cosmonaut plummets to death.** Unless it is a last resort, neither the dash nor the colon should be used as a substitute for *says*. When used, the colon comes after the speaker, and the dash after what was said: **McCoy: dual role too big; Dual role too big—McCoy.**

Use Abbreviations Sparingly

Few beginning headline writers have escaped the abbreviation addiction. It occurs when the writer tries to cram too much in the head. The story said a woman under hypnosis had imagined herself as a reincarnation of an eighteenth century Bridey Murphy in Ireland. The theory was discounted by a professor of psychology at a state university. This is how a student headlined the story: **CU psych. prof. / doubts B.M. story.** A simple head such as **Professor doubts / 'Bridey' claims** would have given the reader enough information to lead him into the story.

Abbreviations clutter the headline: **Mo. village / U.S. choice / for Pan-Am.** It could have been written as **Missouri / favored as / Pan-Am site.**

An abbreviation that has more than one meaning leads to confusion, especially when the headline also is guilty of poor phrasing: **Ten girls are added to St. / Vincent Candy Striper unit** or **Ill. man asks / Pa. to join Miss. / in Mass. protest.**

Headline writers frequently overestimate the ability of readers to understand the initials used in headlines. Some are easily recognized, such as YMCA, YWCA, UN, DAR. Others aren't, such as AAUW, NAACP, ICBM. On many newspapers the style calls for abbreviations without periods in headlines.

Some contractions are acceptable in heads; others aren't. *Won't, don't* and *shouldn't* give no trouble, but *she'll, he'll, who're,* and the "s" and "d" contractions do: **Triplets 'fine' / so's mother of 22** or **Mother'd rather / switch than fight.** Try to read this aloud: **Anymore service, the town hall'll collapse.**

Grammar in Headlines

Although the headline writer must constantly compress his statements, he has no license to abuse the language. A grammatical error emblazoned in 48-point type may be worse than a half-dozen language errors buried in body type. The writer normally would say **Russian girls urged / to stop copying Paris.** But the second line was too long so the writer settled for **Russian girls urged / 'stop copying Paris'.** A comma should have been

The Art of Editing

used to introduce the quoted clause. Transposing the lines would have produced a better head. A headline read **HHH best / of 2 choices, / senator says.** He can't be the best if there are only two choices.

One of the problems on the desk is when to use and when to omit parts of the verb *to be*. Some slotmen have an aversion against the use of *to be* in all heads. Others insist that if the verb is needed to make the meaning clear, it should be used.

The examples on the left seem incomplete without the auxiliary verb:

New circulation plans part of state magazine overhaul	**New circulation plans are part of state magazine overhaul**
Dick Lee dead; newsman 80	**Dick Lee is dead; newsman was 80**
4 children die in fire while mother away	**4 children die in fire while mother is away**

Parts of the verb *to be* cannot be omitted after *says* or synonyms for *says*. Such omission leads to ambiguity. An example cited by Professor Keen Rafferty in a *Nieman Report* article (January 1952, p. 19) is the head **Physician says / President well.** "If 'president' were taken to be in the objective case," said Rafferty, "then the head would mean that the physician was a capable elocutionist." If the lines are transposed (**President well, / physician says**) the *is* is not necessary since *President* is in the nominative case and the verb is understood.

Surely there are enough limitations on the headline writer without imposing more desk restrictions. If verb parts and articles allow the head to be read smoothly, they should be permitted. Most deskmen would have to agree that the following "sound right":

It's now or never / for revenue bills

British are losing / taste for beer

A Picasso brings $532,000

Aid teachers / during strike, / NEA is urged

Husband / held, wife / is hunted

A copyeditor who can't catch spelling errors in copy has no place on the copydesk. He is a menace if he repeats the error in his headline, as some editors did in these: **Rodeo parade has / governor as marshall; Kidnap victim trys / to identify captors.**

Headlining Sports

Sports pages are concerned with contests, meaning action and drama. Headlines over contest stories should be the easiest in the paper to write. Yet, because of the jargon used by sports writers and the numerous synonyms signaling a victory of one team over another, the sports story headline has become a jumble.

A reader says to his companion, "I see where the Jayhawkers crunched the Cornhuskers." "Yeah," answers a University of Nebraska basketball fan, "how much?" "It says here 98 to 94," says the reader. If that's a crunching, what verb describes a 98 to 38 victory?

The struggle for substitutes for *wins, beats,* and *defeats* produces verbs such as *bests, downs, smears,* and *swamps.* Presumably, the reader reads a sports page to find out who wins in what races. What matter, then, if the simple word like *wins* or *defeats* is used over and over? Certainly they are better than editorialized counterparts such as *clobbers, wallops, flattens,* and *trounces.*

Correct use of the language should be regarded as highly on the sports copydesk as it is on the news copydesk. Here are two heads from a sports page: **Palmer refuses / to alibi error, Cornell takes dual.**

In the first head, the writer assumed, incorrectly, that *alibi* as a verb can take an object. In the second, the writer turned an adjective into a noun. A track meet between two schools may be a duel or it may be a dual meet, but not a dual.

Avoid Slang

A straight head that tells the reader precisely what happened in dictionary words is always better than one in which the writer resorts to slang. Slang in heads, as well as in copy, lowers the tone of the paper and consequently lowers the readers' estimation of the paper. The headline, no less than the copy, should speak to the general reader, not to newsmen and other specialists.

Here is an object lesson from a San Diego newspaper. The second edition carried a six-column head in the society section: **Kids going to pot are aided.** Under the head was a three-column cut showing a girl sitting on a bed in a holding room at Juvenile Hall. The picture also revealed a toilet stool in one corner of the room. To the relief of the embarrassed society editor, the top line in the third edition was revised to **Teen narcotic users aided.**

Don't Repeat Words

Another restriction on headline writing is that major words in the headline cannot be repeated unless done so for effect in a future head. The rule has little logic except to prevent obvious padding, such as **Campus will launch / campus chest drive** and **Wind-lashed blizzard / lashes plains states.**

If the main head contains a word like *fire*, the readout or banks could easily substitute a synonym. *Blaze* would be an acceptable one; *inferno* would not.

Repetition is sometimes used deliberately to heighten a feature: **Man leaves / nagging wife / for new nag; Thinkers failures, / professor thinks; New look? never! / old look's better; Pokey driving sends three back to pokey.**

Down with Headlinese

Faced with the problem of making a statement in a nine-unit line, the writer has to grab the shortest nouns and verbs possible. He is tempted to use overworked words such as *hits, nabs, chief* or *set* because they help to make the headline fit. Or he may reach for short words with symbolic meanings, such as *flays, slaps, grills, hop* or *probe*. Nothing is "approved"; it is "okayed" (or "ok'd") or "given nod." All are headline clichés and have no place in today's paper. Yet even the trade papers continue to use them: **Miami Herald / grills Sinatra / in libel probe.**

The headline should not falsify the story. Many of the headlinese words do, at least by implication. If the story tells about the mayor mildly rebuking the council, the headline writer lies when he used verbs like *hits, slaps, scores, raps, rips* or *flays*. An *investigation* or a *questioning* is not necessarily a "grilling"; a *dispute* is not always a "row" or a "clash." *Cops* went out with prohibition. Today's word is *police*.

Others that should be shunned are "quiz" for *question*, "hop" for *voyage*, "talks" for *conference*, "aide" for *assistant*, "chief" for *president* or *chairman*, "solon" for *legislator* or *congressman*, "probe" for *inquiry*, "nabs" for *arrests*, "meet" for *meeting*, "bests" for *defeats*, "guts" for *destroys*, "snag" for *problem*, "stirs" for *incites* and "hike" for *increase*.

Tito bares his / shift toward / Russian block. Here the headlinese *bare* muddles the head. It would have been so easy to write **Tito explains / shift toward / Russian block.**

Don't Invite Libel or Contempt

Because of the strong impression a headline may make on a reader, courts have ruled that a headline may be actionable even though the story under the head is free from libel. Here are a few examples:

Shuberts gouge $1,000 from Klein brothers

'You were right,' father tells cop who shot his son

McLane bares Old Hickory fraud charges

Doctor kills child

**'Shakedown' charges against
Judge Cook made by widow**

Gone to her drummer
A missing hotel maid being pursued by an irate parent

John R. Brinkley—quack

Claims he suspected imaginary lover

A wrong name in a headline over a crime story is a way to involve the paper in a libel action.

The headline writer, no less than the reporter, must understand that under our system a person is presumed innocent of any crime charged until he has been proved guilty by a jury. Heads that proclaim **Kidnaper caught, blackmailers exposed,** or **Spy caught** have the effect of convicting the suspects (even the innocent) before they have been tried.

If two masked gunmen hold up a liquor-store owner and escape with $1,000 in cash, the head may refer to the two as "robbers" or "gunmen." Later, if two men are arrested in connection with the robbery as suspects or are actually charged with the crime, the head cannot refer to them as "robbers" but must use a qualifier: **Police question / robbery suspects.** For the story on the arrest the headline should say **Two arrested / in robbery,** not **Two arrested / for robbery.** The first is a shortened form of "in connection with"; the second makes them guilty.

The lesson should be elementary to anyone in the publishing business, but even on the more carefully edited papers the heads are sometimes guilty of jumping to conclusions. This was illustrated in the stories concerning the assassination of President John F. Kennedy. Lee Harvey Oswald was branded the assassin even though, technically, he was merely arrested on a charge of murder. In a statement of apology, the managing editor of the New York *Times* said his paper should not have labeled Oswald an assassin.

In their worst days, newspapers encouraged headline words that defiled: **Fanged fiend, Sex maniac, Mad-dog killer.**

Even today some newspapers permit both reporter and deskman to use a label that will forever brand the victim. When a seventeen-year-old boy was convicted of rape and sentenced to twenty-five to forty years in the state penitentiary, one newspaper immediately branded him *Denver's daylight rapist.* Another paper glorified him as *The phantom rapist.* Suppose an appeal reverses the conviction? What erases the stigma put on the youth by a newspaper?

The deskman who put quotes around **Honest count** in an election story learned to his sorrow that he had committed a libel for his paper.

The following is a conviction head: **Residents glad / killer identified.**

Emphasis in the headline should be on the positive rather than the negative. If the rodeo parade fails to come off as scheduled because of rain, the head makes a positive statement: **Rain cancels / rodeo parade,** not **No rodeo parade / because of rain.** The news value is lacking in the headline that says **No one hurt / as plane crashes.** The positive statement would be **90 passengers escape injury / as plane crashes in mountain.** Here are three negating words in a headline: **Tax writers / veto lids on / oil write-off.** Better: **Tax writers / leave oil tax / as it stands.** Double negative: **President / bars ban on / Negro jobs.** Better: **President / orders jobs / for Negroes.**

The negative is illustrated in this headline from an English paper: **Only small earthquake; not many killed.**

The admonition does not apply to feature heads, where the negative helps make the feature: **No laws against drowning, but it's unhealthy; Not so gay nineties** (on weather story); **Laundry gives / no quarter until / suit is pressed.**

The question head, except on features, is suspect for two reasons: It tends to editorialize, and newspaper heads are supposed to supply answers, not ask questions. If the headline asks the reader a question, the answer, obviously, should be in the story. If the answer is buried deep in the story, the question headline should be shunned. A two-line, five-column, 48-point head asked, **Did Anastasia murder help kill barber shaves?** The lead repeated the same question, but the reader was compelled to look through a dozen paragraphs only to learn that the question referred to a frivolous remark that should have been used only to color the story.

On features, question heads have their place: **39–24–37 and that's topless?**

Put in Subheads

The copyeditor automatically inserts subheads (or column breaks) in copy that runs as much as half a column or longer. He uses a minimum of three medium words, writes the subhead in the copy, marks it *sh* or *bf,* and bases the subhead on information in the paragraph immediately under the subhead. The subhead should be meaningful and intriguing. It should contain a subject and a verb. Its purposes are to break up long areas of type and to nudge the reader into continuing the story.

Subheads should never be placed after a paragraph ending in a colon or dash. To do so disturbs the reader's train of thought. Example:

Alderman John Doe told the council:

Cites Cost of Project

"The proposed new subway system would saddle the taxpayers with costs out of all proportion to its benefits. . . ."

On some copy where the set is wider than one column, larger subheads are used, for example, two lines of 14-point type. If the subheads call for a type larger than the body type used, they should be written on a separate sheet of copy paper and should be designated to correspond with the directions in the copy, such as "subhead 1," "subhead 2," etc. This type is sometimes known as a boxcar subhead.

Writing Jump Heads

If the deskman gets a long story slugged for page 1, he assumes the story will be continued on an inside page. He therefore writes a runover or jump head. This may be a repetition of the page 1 head. If so, he indicates on the head copy that the head is to be reset or set twice for a runover On some papers the jump head is a key phrase, such as **Riot Victims.** This also would be written on the desk and turned in with the headline and story copy. Or the copy may be broken up and treated as two stories. The page 1 story would end with a notation such as "Tanks Answer Snipers. See Page 5." On page 5 is the head **Tank salvos / echo fire / of snipers,** and over the story "See Story Page 1."

Enjoy the Game

It's fun to write headlines because headline writing is a creative activity. The copyeditor has the satisfaction of knowing that his headline will be read. He would like to think that the head is intriguing enough to invite the reader to read the story. When he writes a head that capsules the story, he gets a smile from the man in the slot and, sometimes, some praise.

Somerset Maugham said you cannot write well unless you write much. Similarly, you can't write good heads until you have written many. After he has been on the desk for a while, the copyeditor begins to think in headline phrases. When he reads a story he automatically reconstructs the headline the way he would have written it. A good headline inspires him to write good ones, too.

He may dash off a head in less time than it took him to edit the copy. Then on a peewee story he may get stuck. He may write a dozen versions, read and reread the story, and then try again. As a last resort, he may ask the slotman for an angle. The longer he is on the desk the more adept he becomes at shifting gears for headline ideas. He tries not to admit that any head is impossible to write. If a synonym eludes him he searches the dictionary or a thesaurus until he finds the right one.

If he has a flair for rhyme, he applies it to a brightener: **Nudes in a pool / play it cool / as onlookers drool.**

The Art of Editing

Every story is a challenge. After the writer has refined the story it almost becomes his story. The enthusiasm he has for the story is reflected in the headline he puts over the story. He seeks to put all the drama, the pathos or the humor of the story into the headline. The clever ones, or the "heady heads," as one columnist calls them, may show up later in office critiques or in trade journals:

Council makes short work of long agenda

Hen's whopper / now a whooper

Stop the clock, / daylight time / is getting off

Lake carriers clear decks / for battle with railroads

'Dolly' says 'Golly' / after hellowful year

It's one giant leap for metkind

(Baseball's world series winner)

Tickets cricket, / legislators told

9

Handling the Wire

News and Supplemental Services

Flooding the desks of the metropolitan dailies is a torrent of news copy supplied by two major American news agencies, foreign services, the newspapers' own bureaus (both foreign and domestic), the supplemental services and the papers' staff reporters, stringers and freelancers.

Even though the news executives of these papers have more material on more topics from more world areas than ever before, they thirst for more. They still do not have adequate coverage of the range of human activities and human interests. They still seek answers to the how and why of news happenings. They still hope to help their readers see the meaning and the relationship of the many news events they report. They yearn to present a more complete and a more comprehensible news package.

Electronic machines deliver a steady stream of copy at under 100 words a minute (actually 66 words a minute on some circuits) even though equipment is devised for speeds of 2,000 words a minute or more. Teletype's Inktronic printer can deliver 1,050 words of copy a minute and has reached as high as 3,000 words a minute. The rate is expected to reach 50,000 words a minute.

If wire editors were "snowed" with copy under the slower transmission, their problem is compounded by the faster transmission. Even at the higher transmission speeds, the machines don't stop for breathers. Obviously not all the news fed into the machines by the services will be significant. Selection and tight editing are demanded as never before.

The Associated Press and United Press International cover roughly the same news events, yet there is enough difference in enterprise or in style of presentation that most metropolitan dailies feel compelled to take both services. Both agencies strive to win the "play" for their reports. Clarity and impact of the product help wire editors choose the service they use. The availability of both news services also enables wire editors to compile items from the wire services and from supplementary services, using a credit line: "From *Sun-Times* wires," "From Associated Press and the *Tribune* Press Service"—or something similar.

On the smaller dailies the editors are likely to choose the service providing the most comprehensive coverage, especially of regional news. Editors may also receive the service of foreign news agencies such as Reuters.

Both the smaller and the larger dailies have been able to expand and enrich their news presentation through use of supplemental services. The New York *Times* News Service, the Los Angeles *Times*-Washington *Post* News Service, the Chicago *Daily News-Sun-Times* Service, the Chicago *Tribune* Press Service, the Copley News Service, *Newsday* and the Dow Jones News Service are among many that make their best news enterprise available to subscribers. By syndicating their news, the publishers participating in the supplemental services are able to recoup some of the costs of their news gathering and, in fact, have been able to expand news coverage.

The services mentioned are among the more than 200 syndicates offering publishers news, features, pictures and special services. In addition to giving spot and secondary news, these services also provide sports, foods and fashions, bylined columns and features ranging from amateur photography to zoo animals. One of the supplements sends to its subscribers each day its own page 1 display of the news.

The news services are alert to editors' demands for good feature material and in-depth reports. The Associated Press, for example, used 24,000 words for "The Lingering Shadow: the Warren Report and Its Critics." More than six hours were required to transmit this story on regular equipment to members. Some newspapers received the report on automatic typesetting wire via dataspeed, cutting the transmission time to about twenty-four minutes.

Two writers spent seven months to research and write the article. The good reception it received suggests that meaningful interpretive features, however long, are welcomed by editors.

Wire Service Glossary

ADV.—Abbreviation for advance. A story intended for later use.

Agate—TTS tape intended for agate-size type. Used on items such as sports boxes and market quotations. AG is visible on the tape.

AMS, PMS—Morning newspapers, afternoon newspapers.

Budget (or BJT)—Listing of the major stories expected to be delivered by the wire service.

BUN—Abbreviation for bulletin.

Bureau code letters—Each service uses its own code letters to designate a bureau. UPI used WA for Washington, the AP uses WX.

BGNG—Abbreviation for beginning.

Circuits—Refers to wires used. The A wire is AP's main trunk news circuit. Regional news trunk systems carry letter designations such as B, G and E wires and the D wire, the nationwide business news circuit. The S wire usually refers to a state trunk circuit.

CQN—Abbreviation for correction.

CQ—Abbreviation for correct.

Cycle—Complete news report for either morning or afternoon newspapers.

Fax—Abbreviation for facsimile, a machine used to receive photos on flimsy paper.

FYI—For your information. An advisory.

Graf (also PGH)—Short for paragraph.

HFR—Hold for release. Expected release time is indicated if known.

LD—Abbreviation for lead (lede).

NL—Abbreviation for night lead.

Pickup—Used to designate where story is to be picked up after a new lead or insertion.

No Pickup—Revised story contains all material sent previously. Also, "includes previous."

Repeat—A rerun of a story for a member or client.

Roundup—An undated story involving more than one place of origin of the news. Frequently used on weather, election returns and holiday fatalities.

Sidebar—A short feature intended to accompany a main news dispatch.

Split—Term used to designate a break in a news circuit to permit the filing of other material, such as regional news.

Sub—Abbreviation for substitute.

TAB—Indicates tabular matter.

Top—New lead.

TTY—Designation used by UPI for page teleprinter circuits.

Undated—A wire story containing no dateline. Instead, the story carries the service as a byline: "By United Press International" or By the associated Press."

Visible—Visible letters punched in TTS tape. Perforations for the letters eesswyyf show up as TA 5 on the tape.

Starts and Stops

Wire editors might hope that the report they receive from news services could come completely packaged and departmentalized.

It can't happen because news is transmitted in the order of its importance and urgency. On a major, unexpected story, new developments alter the story so that it may be hours before the story can be completed for the news cycle.

The first indication of a big story is a short bulletin, followed immediately by bulletin matter add or adds. The flash is seldom used because a bulletin moves just as rapidly.

Unless the bulletin and bulletin matter arrive near an edition's deadline, the wire editor holds back the story as long as possible. Otherwise he would burden the composing room with resetting of type for corrections and would impose another burden on the deskman to rewrite headlines. When the wire editor feels that the story is complete, or nearly so, he splices all the pieces— bulletin, bulletin adds, inserts, corrections, bulletin precedes—to make one comprehensive story. Sometimes the wire service does this for him by sending a self-contained dispatch replacing all previous copy and slugged *No Pickup.*

Painstaking care must be taken in handling sectional copy for the TTS. The folio on each section must be preserved so that the proper tapes can be used.

If story corrections are needed after the copy has left the desk, the deskman sends to the composing room for a galley proof and on the proof indicates the points where insertions, kills, pickups and a new lead are to be made, as noted in Chapter 3.

The slugline is all-important on all copy handled by the desk. As noted earlier, it is the device for matching headline and story. It identifies a proof and enables the desk to recall the proof for correction instructions. It matches cutlines with pictures, and stories with accompanying pictures. It identifies precedes and sidebars with the appropriate stories. It is used in scheduling copy and in mapping a makeup dummy. On TTS copy, both the slug and the folio are the identifying elements.

Figure 9-1a shows an edited story from a wire service Tele-typesetter. The folio number, s52, indicates this was the fifty-second item on the s (state) wire. The folio number is retained so that the monitor copy can be matched with the corresponding tape. No editing can be done on the tape; it must be set in full in type.

The row of letters is the s52 visible on the tape. The symbol r18 stands for the initial of the sender and the day of the month (Figure 9–1c).

The edited monitor copy will be used as a guide to make corrections in the proof of the type set by TTS.

The slug, "Gas Line 1-24-2 Ins" is on the precede. (*Gas Line* is the slug, 1-24-2 is the head size and *Ins.* shows that the story is designated for an inside page.)

Figure 9–1b shows how s5 was edited to get both stories into one piece.

Some of the more common notations on TTS copy are as follows:

Handling the Wire

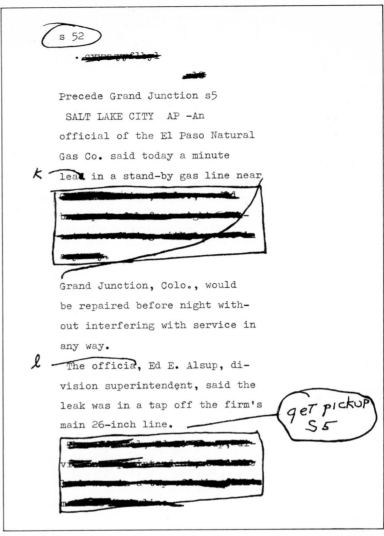

Figure 9–1a. An edited TTS precede. In this case the precede serves as a new lead (or simply lead) with directions as to where to pick up the original story. (See Figure 9–1b.)

Coal strike bjt. The coal strike story is a budget story, or one of the items on the News Digest.

ADV Pms Wednesday, Dec. 1. This is an advance story for afternoon newspapers on the date indicated. The story may be edited, then hung on a peg reserved for advances.

Elimination. This is sent as a bulletin. An example would be:

GRAND JUNCTION, Colo.—Please eliminate Standard Metrals, Inc., story s4 proposed smelter. A sub will not be sent.

Wirephoto. This indicates that a picture has been sent to go with the story. The term *Wirephoto* is followed by the sending station and a number: DX-1 (Denver, photo number one).

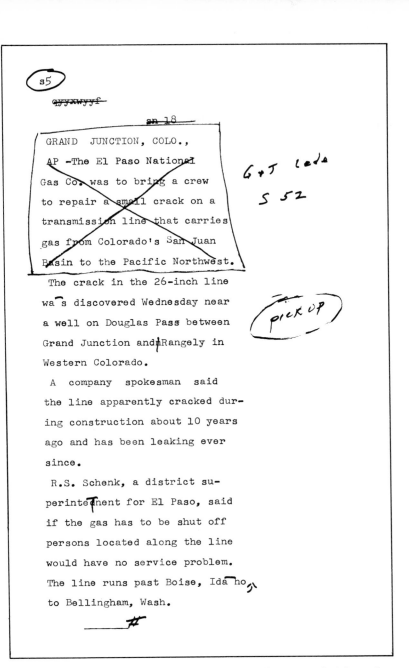

Figure 9–1b. This was the TTS story as originally received. A later development required a new lead, picking up only certain parts of the original story. If the original story (s5) had already been set in type, a proof—or marker—would be needed to show portions of the story to be deleted.

Lead. This always indicates a new lead and is always followed by a pickup unless the story closes with the notation *No Pickup.*

Release sketch biographical. This is used when a prominent person has died and a biographical sketch had been sent pre-

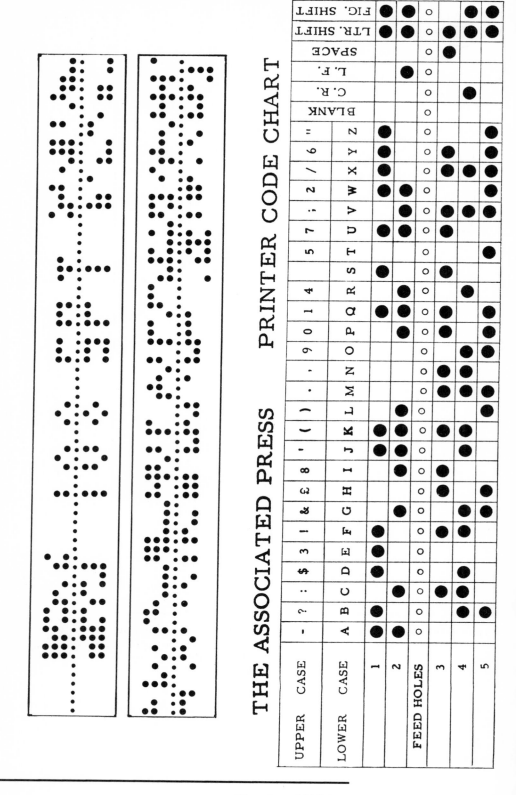

THE ASSOCIATED PRESS   PRINTER CODE CHART

viously. An identifying number always follows the word *biographical.*

The following shows the sequence, and book numbers, of the story on the death of Henry A. Wallace:

170 BULLETIN WASHINGTON (AP)—Henry Agard Wallace, former vice president, cabinet member and presidential candidate, died today at the age of 77, his son-in-law said. —Washington—Release sketch biographical 3651.

172 URGENT PRECEDE WASHINGTON DANBURY, Conn. (AP)— Former Vicè President Henry A. Wallace, 77, died today in Danbury Hospital.

A hospital spokesman said he died late this morning. He had been ill several months.

The cause of death was said to be arterial sclerosis.

176 URGENT DANBURY—add Wallace 172 Mrs. Wallace was with him when the former vice president died. . . .

182 DANBURY, Conn. Wallace 172–176 SUB 3rd graf. The spokesman said death was caused by "a respiratory arrest due to a chronic neuromuscular ailment and lateral sclerosis." Mrs. Wallace, 4th graf.

Handling TTS

The wire (or telegraph) editor of a nonmetropolitan afternoon daily newspaper arrives at his desk at 6 a.m. Already the TTS monitor machine has spewed out yards of copy delivered by the state bureau.

The first item attracting the editor's attention is a budget, or news digest, giving brief descriptions, and lengths, of the major stories to be delivered. The budget alerts the editor to the major events of the day and also helps guide him in mapping page 1 if that is part of his job.

Each item carried by the TTS printer has a folio or book number. The number also appears visibly on the perforated tape accompanying the monitor copy. The tapes are sent to the composing room where they are strung on pegs numbered to correspond with the folio numbers (peg 1 gets tapes 1, 11, 21, 31, etc.). The tapes remain on the pegs until the edited monitor copy is released by the wire editor. The monitor copy goes to an operator who manually sets the sluglines. The tape is fed into a linecasting machine. When the type has been set, it is placed in a galley, the sluglines are put on and a proof is pulled. If the monitor copy has been edited within paragraphs, the changes are set manually and handled in the manner of proof corrections.

Because editing changes in TTS copy require manual resetting of type, copyeditors feel compelled to do as little editing as possible. With computerized editing, the monitor copy can be

Figure 9–1c. Teletypesetter tape. Top shows a six-level, justified Teletypesetter tape. In the second and third groups of perforations of the top tape the number 100 and the letters SPT are visible. The second tape is a six-level, unjustified or "Idiot" tape to be fed into a computer for justification and hyphenation. The bottom is a code chart for a five-level tape in all-capital letters, showing combinations used to achieve the visible.

---

edited sharply and a new tape can be produced incorporating the editing.

If a wire editor has an Autoediting or similar device he can select the book number, then tell the machine how many paragraphs of the story he wants. The machine produces tape for the number of paragraphs requested. A computer program called ANPAT (American Newspaper Publishers Abstracting Technique) enables a computer to accept TTS tape of any wire news story and to provide abstracts or shorter stories of the original story. The computer itself can shorten the story to any instructed length by placing a numerical value on each word in the story and subsequently determining through mathematical formulas what is most important in the story.

Eventually, wire editors may look over abstracts of wire stories, then instruct the news agency to deliver the desired stories in a specified typesetting format. Following is the way James F. Darr, general manager of communications for United Press International, described the process in a talk given at a UPI editors' conference in Bermuda as reported in *Editor & Publisher* (October 11, 1969):

Teletype wires from around the world will be connected directly to a centrally located computer. There will be incoming wires carrying information from Europe, South America, Mexico, Canada, Asia and from each of our division headquarters bureaus in the United States. The wires will carry all types of news information—international news, general news, sports, business, etc.

In addition, there will be the ticker wires from the various stock exchanges.

As the stories move into the computer over the incoming wires they will be stored, probably on discs, and at the same time be printed out on conventional teleprinter machines.

The editor will scan the copy of the incoming wires and determine which of it requires editing. Instead of using a copy pencil he will turn to a keyboard-operated Cathode Ray Terminal (CRT), a TV screen equipped with a typewriter-like keyboard.

If a story requires editing the editor will call it up on his screen. He will correct the typographical errors by striking the correct character over the incorrect one. He will insert a word or a phrase or a sentence or even a paragraph by striking a key labelled "insert," and he will then just type the material as he would on a typewriter and the material will be automatically inserted in the story. He will be able to delete characters, words, paragraphs or even the whole story by simply striking a "delete" key. He finds his place in the copy displayed on the screen by moving a curser around the screen. The curser is a little bright light that can be located under any desired character or space by depressing keys on the keyboard.

After the editor is satisfied that the story is all right he will release the story by sending it back into computer storage. Now the story is ready for publication.

As the story came in on the source wire it had an item number, an identifying word keyed to the story, the date and the sending UPI bureau's call sign. Immediately following that it had an abstract, written by the person who wrote the story. The abstract will include the number of words in the story and identifying information on side-bars and other stories that will supplement the main story. It might even contain advice on where to find additional backgrounding material. The abstract will also indicate whether or not a picture is available to go with the story.

The wire editor, meanwhile, will have read the abstract wire and decided which stories he wants He will then dial the agency computer The computer will instantaneously acknowledge the call and deliver the stories requested at a minimum speed of 1,000 words a minute which amounts to about 200 11-pica lines of body type.

Without controls, such as those described in the foregoing, the entire tape has to be set in type. If the wire editor wants only four paragraphs of a ten-paragraph story, the entire tape is set automatically, then six paragraphs of type are discarded.

After the wire editor has edited the monitor copy, he writes the headline, then slugs the copy to correspond with the headline slug. He may also indicate on the copy whether the story is intended for page 1 or for an inside page. If the story is to go with art, he will also indicate that as part of the copy slug.

Unless he has developed a "feel" for TTS copy, he keeps a copy schedule on which he records the copy slug, the head size and the length of story and headline. If the space allows, say, twenty columns of wire copy, the schedule helps the wire editor fill his quota. It also guides him in selecting a variety of headline sizes.

For scheduling purposes he converts all scheduled items into column inches. Eight lines of TTS copy represent one column inch on an 11-pica column. Copy 12 inches deep corresponds roughly to 5 inches of type. Some editors multiply the copy inches by .4 to get type depth. If the wire editor uses Teletype rather than TTS, he estimates three or four lines of copy to an inch, five or more if the set exceeds 11 picas.

If pictures are to be included on the schedule, the editor records the picture slug, the width in columns and the total column inches reserved for the picture and cutline (see Chapter 10).

Picture Selection

During a lull, the wire editor scans the photo-facsimile machine and from approximately sixty pictures available selects about a dozen to use on front and inside pages. He sends the pictures to an engraving machine, which transforms the pictures into plastic or zinc plates. He sends the picture captions to the composing room for manual composition. Again, the editor uses a slugline on both picture and caption to assure that the right caption gets under the right picture.

During another lull, the wire editor looks over the offerings of a supplemental service. The copy has been received over a Teletype machine and is in all-caps. He selects the stories he desires, assumes that all the letters are in lower case and marks the letters that should be capitalized. This copy is edited, headlined and slugged before it goes to a tape-punching operator. The operator punches a nonjustified and nonhyphenated "idiot tape." This tape goes into a computer, which produces another tape, justified and hyphenated. The computer tape then goes to the typesetting machine.

On a normal day, the wire editor uses about 50 per cent of the TTS copy and about 10 per cent of the supplemental service copy available. Because of the tape handling, he avoids compiling stories. Instead, he may place related stories together in makeup or he may use printed slugs to direct readers' attention to both stories.

Before the wire editor completes his daily task, he must go through a package of news features received by mail from the paper's wire service. This material is on preprinted sheets. He clips the stories he desires, pastes them on sheets of copy paper and sends these stories, after editing, to the perforators. If the paper has a Sunday edition, the wire editor anticipates the Sunday edition needs and marks some of the features from the wire service and the supplemental service for Sunday use. If he spots a wire story that may have a local angle or a local application, he gives the story to the city desk.

Some types of copy, such as sports and markets, may be delivered over special wires. If such copy appears in a B wire circuit or a revised A wire, then the wire editor routes the copy to the appropriate editor.

Offset Service

Both wire services offer customers special copy that can be sent to the shop for paste-ups without typesetting. AP Offsetter (Figure 9–2), for instance, uses a computer that provides proper column widths that are fully justified and in a typeface that matches the newspaper's body type. The system requires no punched tape or special equipment. UPI's offset service is called Unisetter.

Offset copy comes ready for the camera room, thus enabling an offset paper to paste up copy direct from the wire. The copy can be used on any circuit and at regular circuit speeds.

Copyediting for the Computer

For years copyeditors have been using symbols and written instructions telling type compositors how to set the copy. Editing copy for computer-generated tape may call for new symbols similar to those used by computer copyeditors.

Several methods may be used in editing copy intended for the computer.

1. Traditional editing symbols are used on *hard copy* (the writer's manuscript) after which the edited copy goes to typists who prepare tape for the computer using code symbols directing the computer on type font, size, length of line and the like. For example, $ql means quad left; $t means end of take (see Figure 9–3).

The Art of Editing

ta013 zzyy ls-c339pes 10
LBJ-Labor gal 2

This would have the effect of stretching out the collective bargaining period in the rail dispute to coincide with the 80-days provided for other industries by the Taft-Hartley law which does not cover rail workers.

The trucking industry lockout that was clamped on over-the-road deliveries Saturday midnight posed a special problem for administration officials.

Mansfield said Johnson directed the Justice Department to determine the legal complications that might be involved in applying the Taft-Hartley Act's 80-day cooling-off period to the trucking shutdown.

"There is some question whether the cooling-off period can be applied in a lockout," Mansfield said.

Trucking Employers Inc., which represents 1,500 of the nation's largest trucking firms, ordered the shutdown in retaliation for what it described as a series of selective strikes by Teamsters Union drivers against member firms.

The union asserted the strikes were all minor and mostly soon over and accused Employers, Inc., of using the walkouts as a pretext to get a Taft-Hartley injunction. The ultimate aim, a union spokesman claimed, is to "win antistrike legislation from Congress."

Federal mediators called the two sides into conference in an effort to iron out their differences. Union and management were reported less than 10 cents an hour apart on a wage agreement, but still sharply divided on fringe benefits and other contract aspects. The old contract expired 10 days ago.

The trucking employers said their shutdown was 100 per cent effective but after one full business day the effects were still not clearly defined. Some industry sources said it may be days before the lack of deliveries is felt, while others predicted fairly rapid factory closings for want of supplies.

One bellwether firm, General Motors Corp., said normal production continued Monday but foresaw a slowing down of activity in some unspecified ar-

Figure 9-2. Sample of AP Offsetter copy. [*Used by permission of the Associated Press.*]

In some systems each line on each page of hard copy is numbered. Again, the copyeditor uses traditional editing symbols, then places an identifying mark at the end of each edited line. The copy is returned to typists who then retype the corrected lines.

Figure 9–3 Sample instructions to the computer and what they mean. [*Courtesy The Oklahoma Publishing Company.*]

$—instruction to follow
$t—end of take
UR—boldface (up to one paragraph)
LR—lightface (cancels UR and $z)
$z—boldface (entire take)
$b—first line bold
QC—quad center
$qr—quad right
QL—end paragraph or quad left
$dv—visual code, visual message
$g—get format statement; $g17 elevate will call out format No. 17
$it—indent take (in ens), followed by elevate
$ip—indent paragraph (in ens)
$il—indent left (in ens)
$ir—indent right (in ens)
$h—hang indent take (in ens)
$h%—cancel $h
$ih—hang one paragraph (in ens)
$cr—column width, other than one column
UR and LR—used with the hyphen in shift position will produce the agate %
jus—justify line
$1—insert leaders where $1 appears
$w—insert white space where $w appears
$db—define blank (followed by number of blank lines)
$de—define equipment (followed by punch number)
$xh—cancel hyphenation
$dh—cancel $xh (will cause the program to resume hyphenation)
$xl—cancel letterspacing
$dl—cancel $xl (resume letterspacing)
$dr—define ragged right
$xr—cancel ragged right (resume normal justification)
$d—define operator (when followed by operator number and elevate will cause the defined operator's keystrokes)
$da—define advance (gives visual ADV plus visual font and measure and sends to dump punch; $dv must also be used for the visual message other than ADV).

These corrections are fed into an Electronic Copy Reader ahead of the original copy. The computer corrects the copy and produces a hyphenated and justified tape.

2. In another system, the copyeditor uses control statements in editing hard copy. RCA's Page-1 (PAge GEneration-1) uses eighty-five statements consisting of control words and their constants (called parameters), format labels and alteration controls. If the copyeditor wants the type set in 8 points on a 10-point body he uses the control words *ps* (point size) and *bl* (body leading) along with the parameters 8 and 10 (ps,8; bl,10). Numbers also are used to identify the typeface. Thus "tf,15; ps,10" means typeface number 15 in 10-point type.

The copyeditor writes the headline and uses the control statements to indicate typeface and size. The designation "tf,10; ps,96" produces a 96-point headline in the specified typeface.

The manuscript, marked for composition instructions, goes to a typist who transcribes the manuscript onto a paper tape, which is then read into the computer for typesetting by a video compositor.

The monitor copy goes to the proofreader or the copyeditor for corrections or insertions. Again, control statements are used to make the alterations. Examples of these statements are *ea,* eliminate all material between two specified text reference points; *in,* insert the information that follows at the specified point in the text; and *aa,* alter all material between two specified text reference points with the information that follows. The changes are transcribed to tape and fed into the computer where they are merged with the original manuscript.

3. Instead of editing hard copy, the copyeditor edits monitor, or tearsheet, copy corresponding to perforated or magnetic tape. He may regard the monitor copy as proof and mark it accordingly as described in TTS handling. Or he may combine traditional editing symbols and pencil control marks on the monitor copy. If two control marks are needed, the marks must be placed under a word of three or more characters. Punctuation such as a period or an exclamation mark automatically causes the first letter of the next word to be capitalized. The same is true for extra spacing, such as the beginning of a paragraph.

Marked copy goes to the computer where the tearsheet is fed into a copy-follower and the tape from the original story into a reader. Changes may be made automatically on the copy-follower, on the computer typewriter, on the auto-edit keyboard or on all three. The original tape is converted into an edited output tape, and a printout or master is produced for proofreading.

4. The copyeditor may edit facsimile copy produced from an image of copy displayed on a television screen or he may edit directly on the display screen. After he completes the editing of the facsimile, the screen exposes a negative of the edited copy. The negative is used to make a photo-offset plate.

In editing directly on the screen the copyeditor uses a light pencil, similar to a small flashlight, to remove or alter any portions of the displayed copy (Figure 9–4). To make additions to copy he uses an input keyboard. He may call up any story he wishes to examine or, by using a secondary screen, view the clippings or notes the reporter used in writing his story. By

Figure 9–4. Editing text with a light pencil on an IBM Display Unit.

simply pushing buttons on the keyboard the editor can specify column width, page layout, type font and size. With his light pencil he can move photos or enlarge, reduce, eliminate or crop them.

He types the headline on the keyboard, then may alter it on the screen. Or he can type the headline, then instruct the computer to set the head to fit.

The editor may compile stories by calling up the stories on the screens, editing each as needed and instructing the computer to put the stories together.

Methods of Handling Vary

A spot survey of a subcommittee of the Associated Press Managing Editors shows some of the many patterns used throughout the country in handling wire reports. The following are some of these patterns:

One newspaper eliminated the universal desk and created national, foreign, local and suburban desks. The national desk consists of a national editor and two copyeditors. They are responsible for keeping up with the national news, suggesting

The Art of Editing

stories for page 1 and editing and laying out a balanced report on pages assigned to them.

The foreign desk has a foreign editor and one copyeditor. They are responsible for keeping up with foreign developments, suggesting stories for page 1 and editing and laying out a balanced foreign report on pages assigned to them.

The system provides a balanced report, forces the editors to follow the news closely and aids in departmentalization of news.

On a newspaper of 36,000 circulation the telegraph editor screens all general wire copy (except sports) and determines play. The news editor goes over the top wire stories and with the wire editor determines their play. Four copyeditors handle the special pages.

A newspaper of 48,000 circulation has no telegraph editor. The news editor selects and edits wire copy and photos and dummies all pages except women's and sports. Two copyeditors assist the news editor in editing copy and writing heads. The news editor has the responsibility of compiling wire reports.

On a paper with 85,000 circulation the telegraph editor evaluates the wire files, selects stories for inside pages, selects wire art and directs page schemes and copy to the slotman. The slotman makes preliminary selection of top stories for page 1. The final decision on play is made by the managing editor after consulting with the telegraph editor, city editor and slot editors. The telegraph editor serves as news editor of wire copy, as the city editor and as the editor of local copy. The managing editor also determines top local story play. The telegraph editor passes stories to copyeditors for review and possible combining.

The Wire Isn't Sacred

The wire services have a deserved reputation for accuracy, impartiality and speed. Generally the copy is accurate and adequately written. But the news agencies do make errors, some of them colossal ones. The source may be in error so the agency sends out a false World War I armistice story. Signals are confused and the agency sends out the wrong penalty for Bruno Richard Hauptmann, kidnaper and slayer of the Lindbergh baby. A correspondent jumps the gun and the agency sends out a premature story on the Normandy invasion of World War II. In its zeal to beat the opposition, an agency releases a story before it has been confirmed and prematurely announces the end of World War II. One wire service had a presidential candidate drinking coffee, the other had him drinking milk. The discrepancy was important to the candidate, a Mormon whose religion frowns on coffee drinking.

News agency executives readily admit they still have juvenile writing, bone-headed editing, atrocious punching and stories that don't jell.

The deskman handling a wire story has to remember that the news agency logotype does not assure a perfect story. The story may have originated from a stringer who failed to get all the facts. It may be a rewrite of a member's or client's story in which the facts were not confirmed. The story may have been delivered before it had been checked thoroughly for libel.

If wire service copy leaves pertinent questions unanswered, the wire editor should contact the nearest bureau and try to get the missing pieces. Here are two examples. The story of the bridge tragedy at Point Pleasant, W. Va., had all the details except one—the height of the bridge. Two young brothers found a paper bag containing $20,618, part of approximately $66,000 stolen from a bank. Did the bank give the boys a reward? The story didn't say.

Many errors committed by the agency are corrected before they appear in print because wire editors or managing editors feel an obligation to call the agency's attention to the errors. The cooperation of the members or clients thus enhances the performance of the agencies.

Reporters and copyeditors who use AP and UPI for writing models do so at their peril. Both agencies are notorious in use of excessive modifiers:

> The first person report of the astronauts will be Friday in the manned spacecraft center auditorium.

> Former Bowling Green, Ohio, State University basketball coach and athletic director W. Harold Anderson died Tuesday. . . .

> The group included Free Speech Movement Leader Mario Savio. . . .

> The Senate Finance Committee today approved a $4.7 billion excise tax cutting bill.

How the System Works

The "lowest," but not the least important, worker in a news wire system is the stringer. He is a local reporter hired by the service to file stories that have wider than local appeal. Such stories are sent to a bureau that processes the copy, then sends it out over the state wire. The bureau itself has its own staff to cover major governmental offices and rewrite stories supplied by member or client papers.

If stories have more than statewide interest, they are filed on a trunk line to a regional bureau. In like manner, if the stories have national interest, they are submitted to the national, or A, wire.

The heart of the newswire operation in the United States is New York, where domestic and foreign reports are collected and processed, then relayed over various wires to bureaus for distribution to members or clients. Other wires in addition to the main wire of national news significance are the B wire (which carries news of secondary importance or news of primary importance but for some regions), a sports wire, a business or D wire, a radio wire and a wire for photos.

A newspaper may receive the service of several wires or it may take only the state wire, which provides the top national, regional and state stories in addition to sports, features and markets.

In 1969 the Associated Press reorganized its communications system to concentrate editing in the hands of fewer editors and to free more of the staff for original reporting.

All copy from domestic bureaus, the New York departments and the foreign desk that is suitable for the A wire goes directly on two special news collection wires to the general desk in New York on two 150-words-a-minute printers. There the copy is examined by a quality-control editor who determines whether editing or rewriting is necessary. If so, he turns the copy over to a copyeditor or a rewriteman. When that job is completed, the quality-control supervisor takes a final look before passing the story to a filer for movement.

Another change consolidated departments such as Special Reports, Spotlights and AP Followups into the AP News Special under the supervision of an enterprise editor on the general desk. The AP Newsfeatures Sunday budget remained a separate department and retained the AP Newsfeatures slug.

The enterprise editor also supervises the assignments of special writers, such as those who handle racial stories, urban affairs, sports, science and space. The enterprise editor likewise submits copy to quality control before passing it along for filing (see Figure 9–5).

The system was put into effect to eliminate many of the corrections, inserts, and errors in punching that plagued editors along the wire and also to allow more effective analysis of the news report as a whole, thus allowing cutting of secondary stories that impinged on the movement of top stories.

Gatekeepers

The wire editor is one of many gatekeepers through which a story must pass before a reader reads the story. In a sense, the first gatekeeper is the reporter, who decides what to include and what to omit in a story. The final gatekeeper is the reader, who uses the headline to tell him whether he wants to read or to ignore the story.

Let's say a stringer for a wire service originates a story in a town in India. He submits the story to the New Delhi desk. If the story gets by this gatekeeper it is relayed to London, where it faces another gatekeeper. From London the story may travel to the New York desk, from there to a regional bureau, from there to a state bureau and from the state desk to the newspaper. The story may be killed at any of these points.

What criteria do the gatekeepers use to decide whether to relay the story or to spike it? Several judgments may come into play: the significance of the item in relation to other items of the day, the interests and prejudices of each of the gatekeepers, the volume of the day's report, the unusualness of the item because of subject matter or because of the method of telling the story.

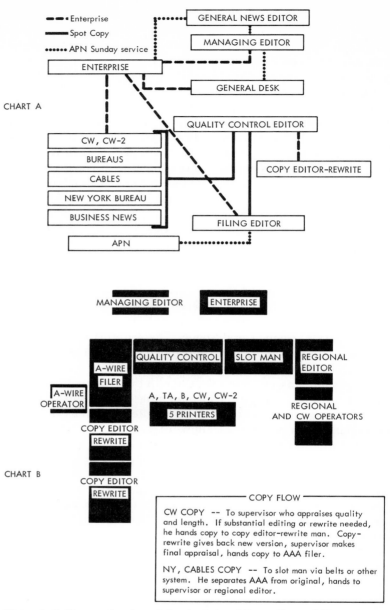

Figure 9–5. Reorganization of the Associated Press General News Organization. The original editorial structure (Chart A) was reorganized (Chart B) to improve communication. [*Used by permission of the Associated Press.*]

Agency editors all along the network try to anticipate the needs and desires of members and clients. Someone in New York has to decide whether a topic will have the same justification in Atlanta as in San Francisco. Someone in Kansas City or Dallas has to decide whether to let a story go on to Colorado or whether a story in Colorado merits more than state interest. Some types of stories are more likely to be accepted than others. What may be a catastrophe to farmers in an area of Kansas may get no mention at all on out-of-state circuits. A humorous story about a cow stuck in a well may get national coverage. Often the bizarre is more acceptable to agency editors than the more significant items.

Some areas of the globe get better news treatment than do others. The result is that too much news comes from too few places, as indicated by the relatively few datelines for the bulk of agency copy.

The temptation of the wire editor of the daily newspaper is to let the news agency do the editing for him, especially if the paper carries only one wire service and if the report is delivered by TTS. The wire editor does not have to accept the recommendation of the news service as to the top stories of the day. He can judge an item in the context of current events and play it prominently whether or not the item appears in the budget of recommended stories.

He does not have to accept the wire service judgment regarding the length and organization of a story. If a story is too long he can tighten it within sentences rather than by whacking off paragraphs at the end. He has the responsibility to edit the story for his own readers' needs and interests. He may, and some do, request coverage of items he feels the agency is neglecting. The wire editor has an opportunity to edit creatively. If more did so, they might get better agency copy.

Foreign News

Newspaper readers in America rely on the AP and the UPI for most of the information they receive about national and foreign affairs. For national news, the services have access to news developed by daily newspapers and radio and television stations in addition to their own reporters and stringers. Thus the domestic report is fairly complete and usually reliable. The same cannot be said of the foreign report.

The agencies' foreign news staffs are inadequate to cover all areas of the world. Even if these staffs were doubled, there still would be areas whose news would go unreported and there still would be gaps in news nonrelated to politics, foreign affairs and war.

Where staffs can be maintained, the correspondent faces problems such as the lack of availability of official sources, the inadequacy of translators and the bias of sources such as the country's main newspapers and wire services. The correspondent may work under the threat of dismissal if he sends out unfavorable news. He may be barred from a country. American readers cannot have adequate information about countries that ban American correspondents, thus forcing American agencies to pick up news from "listening posts" in places like Hong Kong and Tokyo or from reports from other news agencies such as Agence France-Presse.

The news services have only part of the responsibility of providing more foreign news in greater depth and variety. Part of the responsibility belongs to the agency clients, who can get more foreign news if they will demand it and then use it. A final responsibility rests with the readers, who must let it be known that they need more information and knowledge to make sound judgments about foreign news.

10

Picture Editing

Rewriting often can turn a poorly written news story into an acceptable one. Little can be done to change the subject matter of a cliché photo, such as tree plantings, ribbon cuttings, proclamation signings and the passing of checks, certificates or awards from one person to another. Yet many of these talk situations are used simply because of the tradition that "chicken dinner" stuff must be photographed.

Some events can be told better in words than in pictures. Conversely, other events are essentially graphic and need little or no text to get the message across. Originality starts with the picture. Its values are interest, composition and quality of reproduction. A small poor-quality picture is rejected because the flaws will be magnified in the enlargement. Facsimile prints may be retouched. Generally they reproduce better if they are reduced rather than enlarged.

The pictures editor faces many of the same problems as the copyeditor. If he has a good picture before him he will have the good sense to leave the photo the way the photographer intended. If he can make a good picture into a great picture by slight editing, he will do that. Only when the occasion calls for severe editing will he slash and cut and trim the photographer's work.

Regardless of the subject and the composition, many pictures can be improved by some editing. These may need no more than a slight retouching with an airbrush to sharpen the profiles or to eliminate static background. When time permits, some of the more prosaic shots can be dramatized by judicious cropping to sharpen the point of interest (Figures 10–1 and 10–2).

The Art of Editing

Even retouching and cropping may not be sufficient to achieve the maximum impact in news and feature photos. Here are some things that might be done:

1. Changing the standard sizes of photos—Some pictures editors automatically accept a standard proportion, say two columns wide and five inches deep, for the majority of pictures. Tests have indicated, however, that a picture of three or four columns will get greater reader response than a two-column picture. Even the cutline of a four-column picture gets more readership than the cutline of a two-column picture.

A good news photo, like a superb news story, deserves a smash play, big enough to bring out all the dramatic impact of the photo. It might call for a picture five columns wide and twelve to sixteen inches deep. The nearly square rectangle might be more effective in a long vertical cut or a shallow horizontal cut.

2. Changing the shapes of photos—Newspaper pictures need not adhere to the standard rectangular shapes. Advertising and magazine illustrations demonstrate the effectiveness of silhouettes or of round and oval shapes or perspective or mood shapes. Tilting can suggest more action. Some pictures can be mortised, others split and still others arranged into a montage or a collage.

3. Selecting the number of photos—The pictures editor generally has enough pictures available. His problem is to find enough good ones in the bundle to dress up the pages. Too many pictures resemble those that have been used before. Too many are used simply because they go with stories. Too many are single shots that give the readers only part of the story. Picture sequences—two or more shots of the same (or similar) scene—afford one solution. Picture sequences help give the reader a sense of continuity of action, provide a feeling of movement or contrast. They say to readers, in effect, "Here is the way it is now and here is the way it was before," or "Here's the way it looked from one vantage point and here's the way it looked from another" or "This is the way it looked from the outside and here is the way it looks from the inside."

Pictures as Copy

When the picture has been processed, someone—reporter or photographer—supplies the information for the cutline. The picture and cutline information then go to the appropriate department whose editor decides whether to use the picture and, if so, how to display it.

Before submitting a picture to the art or engraving department, the editor supplies enough information to get the correct picture in the correct place with the correct cutline. A picture,

Figures 10–1 and 10–2. Editing a picture. The original picture [ABOVE] was retouched slightly with an air brush to highlight the faces, thus preparing the lower picture for publication. [*Photographs courtesy of the Denver Post.*]

Picture Editing

like a story, generally carries an identifying slug. To assure that the picture will match the engraving, the cutline, the slugsheet and, if need be, the story, the editor uses a slugline.

A slip of paper tipped on the back of the picture normally contains information such as:

Slug or picture identification.
Size of the desired engraving.
Engraving instructions.
Department, edition and page.
Date wanted.
Date and time picture sent to engraving.
Whether the picture is with or without a story.

The picture is then routed either directly to the engravers or indirectly through the art department to the engraving department. The cutline goes to the composing room. Cutline copy contains, in addition to the cutlines, essential directions to match cutline and picture.

Some photo editors use a style like the one shown in Figure 10–3.

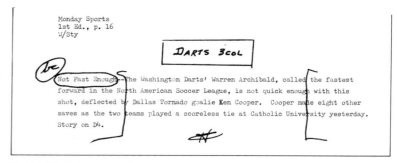

Figure 10–3. Photo cutline style.

When a picture has been edited and sent to the art department and the cutline has been written and sent to the composing room, the editor records the picture on a slugsheet. This shows the picture slug; the size of the cut; the department getting the picture; the time, date and edition; the space occupied by the cut and the cutline; and whether the picture accompanies a story.

If the picture is to go with a story, the information is carried on both the cutline and the story copy. The reason is obvious. Unless properly slugged, the story may turn up on page 3 and the photo on page 16.

Sometimes the photo may be separated from the story deliberately. A teaser picture may be used on page 1 to entice readers to read the story on another page. If a long story has two illustrations, one illustration often is used on the page where the story begins and the other on the jump page. On major events such as the death of a president, pictures may be scattered on several pages. In that event, readers are directed to these pages by a guideline such as "More pictures on pages 5, 7 and 16."

The plate returned from the engraving department contains the slug printed in crayon or grease pencil on the reverse side of the plate. The proofs accompanying the plate likewise carry the slug. Even with these precautions, the danger remains that the printed picture will carry the wrong identification.

Sometimes the plate inadvertently is made in reverse. The result can be ludicrous, particularly if the picture shows a sign, if the principals are wearing uniforms containing letters or numerals or if, as in the instance of Senator Robert Kennedy during his campaign for presidential nomination and after his assassination, pictures showed him with his hair parted on the left rather than on the right.

The person responsible for checking page proofs makes sure the correct headline is over the correct story and that the cutlines under pictures of a local politician and a jackass are not reversed.

The Enlarging, Reducing Formula

Unless the picture is to be cropped, the cut will be enlarged or reduced in proportion to the width and depth of the photograph. A simple method of determining this proportion is to draw a diagonal line from the upper-left to the lower-right corner on the back of the picture, measure the desired width of the cut along the top of the picture and make a vertical line. The point where it intersects the diagonal indicates the depth of the cut. Or, the diagonal may be drawn from the upper-right to the lower-left corner of the back of the picture. The desired width of the cut is then indicated along the bottom of the picture.

If the picture margins are uneven, the editor may place a sheet of tissue paper over the picture and draw the diagonal and connecting lines on the tissue to determine depth of the cut. Or, he may measure the picture area and use a mathematical proportion to determine cut depth. Suppose the picture is 48 picas wide and 60 picas deep and the desired width of the cut is 34 picas. Then, $48:34::60:X$. The answer is $42\frac{1}{2}$ picas (in depth).

If the editor decides to have the cut 34 picas wide and 45 picas deep, then X will be substituted for one of the picture measurements to determine the extent of the crop to produce the 34 by 45 proportion. If X is substituted for the width of the picture, then $X:34::60:45$. $45X$ equals 2040, and X equals 45.3. Subtracting 45.3 from 48 shows a crop of 2.7 picas on the width of the picture.

A slide rule, plastic disk or plastic Linkrule provided by an engraving company works out the proportion quickly and accurately.

No cropping should be attempted on a stereotype mat. If the editor desires a picture narrower than the mat, he has the mat cast, then has the cast sawed to the desired width. If the cutline

---

appears on the mat, the editor calls for a rewrite, has the cutline set, then directs the shop to saw off the cutline on the cast.

Pictures may be reduced in any proportion, but generally newspapers adhere fairly closely to standard reductions such as one fifth, one third and one half. A typical scaling (widths in inches) for 16-pica columns is:

1 column—$2\frac{1}{4}$ inches
2 columns—$4\frac{3}{4}$ inches
3 columns—$7\frac{1}{4}$ inches

4 columns—$9\frac{3}{4}$ inches
5 columns—$12\frac{5}{16}$ inches
6 columns—15 inches

Figure 10–4 shows picture cropping to achieve one-fifth, one-third and one-half reductions in 11-pica columns.

The cut usually is a bit narrower than the column or columns it is expected to occupy, especially in papers that sink the column rules. Some editors like to make pictures in outside columns flush to the outside.

PICTURE PICA SIZE	PICTURE COL. SIZE	SIZE	$\frac{1}{5}$ RED.	$\frac{1}{3}$ RED.	$\frac{1}{2}$ RED.	TYPE COL. SIZE
10.4	1 col.	$1\frac{11}{16}$ INCHES	$2\frac{1}{8}$	$2\frac{1}{2}$	$3\frac{3}{8}$	11. PICAS
21.8	2 col.	$3\frac{9}{16}$	$4\frac{1}{2}$	$5\frac{3}{8}$	$7\frac{1}{8}$	22.4
33.	3 col.	$5\frac{1}{2}$	$6\frac{7}{8}$	$8\frac{1}{4}$	11	33.8
44.4	4 col.	$7\frac{3}{8}$	$9\frac{1}{4}$	11	$14\frac{3}{4}$	45.
55.8	5 col.	$9\frac{1}{4}$	$11\frac{9}{16}$	$13\frac{7}{8}$	$18\frac{1}{2}$	56.4
67.	6 col.	$11\frac{1}{8}$	$13\frac{3}{8}$	$16\frac{3}{4}$	$22\frac{1}{4}$	67.8
78.4	7 col.	13	$16\frac{1}{4}$	$19\frac{1}{2}$	26	79.
89.8	8 col.	$14\frac{7}{8}$	$18\frac{5}{8}$	$22\frac{1}{4}$	$29\frac{3}{4}$	90.4

Figure 10–4. Reduction table for illustrations. [*Courtesy of the Denver Post.*]

Some Tips on Cropping

A photograph is a composition. The composition should help the reader grasp the picture's message clearly and immediately. If the picture is too cluttered, the reader's eyes scan the picture looking for a place to rest. But if the picture contains a strong focal point, the reader at least has a place to start. A prime job of a pictures editor, therefore, is to help the photographer take out some unnecessary details to strengthen the overall view.

It could be that some elements within the picture are stronger than the full picture. Some pictures editors try to find these interest points and patterns by moving two L-shaped pieces of cardboard over the picture. This helps to guide him in his cropping. He looks for a focal point, or chief spot of interest. If other

The Art of Editing

points of interest are present, he tries to retain them (see Figure 10–5a and 10–5b). He searches for patterns that can be strengthened by cropping. The pattern helps give the picture harmonious and balanced composition. Among these patterns are various letter shapes—L, U, S, Z, T, O and geometric patterns such as a star, a circle, a cross or a combination of these.

Because most news and feature pictures contain people, the pictures editor strives to help the photographer depict them as dramatically as possible, whether or not the finished product is pleasing to the subjects in the picture. He must decide how many persons to include in the picture, how much of a person to include and what background is essential. He may choose to crop a man's head severely but allow a woman to show off her hat or hairdo. He may crop legs or pantslegs of men but show women's hemlines, legs and feet. He lets the picture breathe by allowing some white space.

Unless the pictures editor is also an artist, he uses a blue chinagraph or grease pencil to make crop marks on the margin of the photo. Or he may place a sheet of tissue paper over the picture and make the crop marks on the tissue. Instead of using scissors to effect a silhouette, a swash cut or even a mortise, he lets the artist outline with china white and airbrush retouching. If he wants a tilted photo, he suggests that the engraver remount and retake the picture. Generally an artist is the best judge of how much retouching with an airbrush is needed (see Figure 10–6a, b).

A mortise normally should be made in a nonvital spot in the picture. For newspapers, an outside mortise, or notch, is easier and less expensive to handle than an inside mortise.

Pictures Can Lie

The pictures editor makes the same kind of editorial judgment about a picture that the city editor and the wire editor make about a local story and a wire story. Does the picture tell the whole story or only part of it? Does it distort, editorialize, mislead? Does it omit important details or include details that create an erroneous impression? In other words, is the picture loaded?

The point was raised by James Russell Wiggins, former editor of the Washington *Post*, during a lecture at the University of North Dakota (reported in *Editor & Publisher*, February 22, 1969). "The camera," he said, "can be a notorious, compulsive, unashamed and mischievous liar."

To illustrate, he said he once declined to print a photograph of President Harry Truman walking across the platform of Union Station before a backdrop formed by a row of caskets just shipped in from the Korean War. "What that camera said was that the Korean War was 'Truman's War,' just what thousands of the President's critics were saying."

He also commented on the distorted portrait of policemen during civil disorders. The pictures may have been representative

---

Picture Editing

Figure 10–5a. Footprint on the lunar soil. An example of how cropping (b) can bring out an interesting detail in a photograph (a). The close-up view was photographed with a lunar surface camera during the Apollo 11 lunar surface extravehicular activity. [*Photographs courtesy of National Aeronautics and Space Administration.*]

Figure 10–5b.

The Art of Editing

of the action but they failed to tell what really happened in perspective and why.

"The camera does not tell the truth," said Wiggins, "and because what it tells is not the whole truth, skepticism about the media rises in the minds of readers who know that policemen, whatever their undoubted faults, are not always wrong."

A picture may be striking and it may be narrative. But if it conveys a false or distorted impression it would be better left unpublished.

Picture Pages

Not all newspapers have picture pages. Some that do use a variety of patterns.

Some devote an entire page to pictures with no text (Figure 10–7). Some use part of the page for pictures, the rest for text matter. Some pages are made up with unrelated photos; some are devoted to a series or sequence of related pictures. Some use part of the page for sequence pictures, leaving the remainder for unrelated pictures or text matter. Probably the majority of papers use the back page of a section for pictures, although some use the front page of a section. More and more picture pages now appear in color.

A few pointers on picture pages follow:

1. Three or four large pictures make a more appealing picture page than eight or ten smaller ones.

2. Let one picture, the best available, dominate the page.

3. Emphasize the upper-left portion of the page either with a dominant picture or a large headline, say 72 points.

4. Crop some of the pictures severely to achieve either wide, shallow, horizontal ones or narrow, long, vertical ones. On a page made up of unrelated pictures, some should be in standard sizes (three, four or five columns) in the event the editor has to replate with new pictures.

5. In a picture series or sequence, place a big picture in the bottom-right corner of the page. It is the logical stopping point.

6. Let the page breathe. White space makes both the pictures and the text stand out. One editor figures an eight-column page as seven columns to assure adequate white space.

7. Don't align pictures with a T square. An off-alignment often provides extra white space or leaves room for a cutline.

8. If a picture page has to be made up in a hurry, pick the best picture, rough-sketch it on a dummy, slug and schedule the picture and get it to the engraver. Then go on with the other pictures. The cutlines can be written last.

9. On the completed dummy, give the printer some leeway. Indicate on which sides the cuts may be trimmed to fit the layout.

10. Vary picture page patterns. Don't make today's picture page look like last Saturday's.

11. Cutlines need not be as wide as the pictures. In fact, a narrow cutline may be easier to read than a wider one and a

Figure 10–6a. Cropping pictures to fit the story. Cropping severely to achieve vertical pictures. These pictures (Figures 10–6a and 10–6b), two in a sequence of four, were intended to depict long narrow stairs. The effectiveness of the picture shapes can be seen in the photo story (Figure 10–7). Instructions on the back of each picture carried the slug (stairs 1, stairs 2, stairs 3, stairs 4), the size (5½ by 11 inches for one and 2½ by 9½ inches for the other), the edition (City), the page (Pic Page) and the time and date each picture was sent to the engraving department.

Figure 10–6b.

UPS and DOWNS
IN LEAD, S.D.

By ROBERT W. (RED) FENWICK
Denver Post Staff Writer

This is one of Lead, S.D.'s most scenic stairways—with curving handrail, opened top and hanging foliage. Town has become tourist mecca.

There are there are probably more sociable climbers in picturesque Lead, S.D., than anywhere else in the West. Life in Lead (pronounced "Leed") is one continual round of ups and downs—up one stairway and down another.

Much depends, of course, upon where one lives with respect to his place of employment. But if he walks, the average citizen there can be fairly certain of being somewhat out of breath either when he gets to work in the morning or when he gets home at night.

Like any other good mountain city, Lead builds and maintains its streets, sidewalks and alleys. But unlike most other cities, Lead also has built and maintains a highly pictureque system of stairways to connect upper and lower streets.

In all, Lead's mountainsides are decorated with 1,126 feet of stairways (39 flights), 1,115 are built of wood, and 160 of concrete.

The longest stairway rises 272 feet from Bleeker Road to Railroad Ave. The next longest is 95 feet.

Mile-high and mile-deep Lead, now a bustling city of perhaps 6,500, was born in 1876 when gold was discovered there at the head of Gold Run Gulch. Neighboring Deadwood had ridden the gold crest a year earlier and, when Lead sprang into being, there were 25,000 wealth seekers in Deadwood Gulch.

According to the South Dakota Guide Book, Lead was the largest city in the state at one time. In March 1900, it was all but destroyed by fire. Another fire once almost burned down the upper workings of the world famous Homestake Mine there.

And during World War II, Lead almost be- came a ghost town when the federal government shut down gold production. When locations ended, the Homestake fired up and pushed its mile-deep mine shafts beneath the city in a network of more than 200 miles.

Lead once again became one of the most popular tourist attractions in South Dakota's exquisitely beautiful Black Hills.

Pictured on this page are some of Lead's many stairways, and if these pictures lead you to Lead—it will be a classic step in the right direction.

Two young residents of Lead, Jody Vorland, left, and Sandra Bauer, are going down, down, down, heading other way means puff, puff, puff.

No wonder the town's residents have to climb, steps all over the place, sidewalks seem to go up or down. These two become stairways up laborer.

narrow cutline is yet another device to allow more white space. On bottom-of-the-page pictures the cutline for the left-of-page picture might be set flush left and the cutline for the right-of-page picture flush right.

12. In sequence or series pictures, don't repeat in one cutline what was said in another.

13. If all the pictures were taken by one photographer or provided by one wire service, a single credit line on the page will suffice. Too many credits give the page a bulletin board effect.

14. In a photo-essay page, keep the cutlines as brief as possible. Usually, the pictures tell most of the story, especially if the headline has established the theme.

15. Headlines generally are more effective at the left or right of the page or under the main pictures. Sometimes the head may be overprinted on the main picture if the type does not rob the picture of important details.

Outline Guidelines

Picture texts are known by many names—cutlines, captions, underlines (or overlines), legends. A caption suggests a heading over a picture, but many editors use the term to refer to the lines under the picture. *Legend* may refer either to the text or to the heading. If a heading is used, it should be under, not over, the picture. A *leader* means the capitalized or italicized group of words, usually no more than one third to one half the line starting the cutline.

The copyeditor "sells" the reporter's story by means of a compelling headline. By the same token, the pictures editor can help control the photographic image with a cutline message. The primary purpose of the cutline message is to get the reader to respond to the photo in the manner intended by the photographer and the pictures editor.

Readers first concentrate on the focal point of the picture, then glance at the other parts. Then, presumably, most turn to the cutline to confirm what they have seen in the picture. The cutline provides the answers to questions of who, what, where, when, why and how, unless some of these are apparent in the picture.

The cutline interprets and expands upon what the picture says to the reader. It may point out the inconspicuous but significant. It may comment on the revealing or amusing parts of the picture if these are not self-evident. The cutline helps explain ambigui-

Figure 10–7. A picture story. This is an example of an exciting picture page. It describes some of the many street stairways in Lead, South Dakota, which is built on a mountainside. The stair-stepped headline in photo-type provides a mood as well as a message. Note, too, the cropping for extreme vertical pictures to emphasize the narrow stairway streets. Although pictures dominate the page, the message is not obscured. This is not a page the editor would attempt a half hour from deadline. [*Courtesy of the Denver Post.*]

ties, comments on what is not made clear in the picture and mentions what the picture fails to show if that is necessary.

The ideal cutline is direct, brief and sometimes bright. It is a concise statement, not a news story. It gets to the point immediately, avoiding the "go back to the beginning" of the background situation.

If the picture accompanies a story, the cutline doesn't duplicate the details readers can find in the story. It should, however, contain enough information to satisfy the readers who will not read the story. Ideally, the picture and the cutline will induce readers to read the story.

Even when the picture relates to the story, the cutline should not go beyond what the picture reveals. The picture itself, the cutline and the story may tell the reader essentially the same thing, thus providing several opportunities to deliver the message.

Cutlines stand out in the newspaper's sea of words and strike the reader with peculiar force. Every word should be weighed, especially for impact, emotional tone, impartiality and adherence to rules of grammar and the accepted language.

Anyone who writes or rewrites a cutline should first study the picture, then write only enough to amplify the picture. If the picture is marked for cropping, the writer makes sure the cutline confines itself to the portion of the picture the reader will see. If the cutline says a woman is waving a handkerchief, the handkerchief must be in the picture.

When the cutline has been composed, the writer should compare the message with the picture. The number of people in the picture should be checked against the number of names in the cutline. Everyone appearing prominently in the picture should be identified. If a person is so obscured in the crowd that he is not easily identifiable, that fact need not be brought to the reader's attention.

If the writer composes a cutline from a negative or engraving, he will do well to remember that the plate or negative is a reverse of the picture. The person on the left will appear on the right in the printed picture.

Writing the Cutline

1. Don't tell the obvious. If the girl in the picture is pretty or attractive, that fact will be obvious from the picture. The picture will tell whether or not a man is smiling. It may be necessary, however, to tell why he is smiling. An explanation need not go as far as it did in the following: "Two girls and a man stroll down the newly completed section of Rehoboth's boardwalk. They are (from left) Nancy Jackson, Dianne Johnson and Richard Bramble, all of West Chester." An editor remarked, "Even if some of the slower readers couldn't have figured out the sexes from the picture, the names are a dead giveaway."

2. Don't editorialize. A writer doesn't know whether someone is happy, glum or troubled. The cutline that described the judge as "weary but ready" when he arrived at court on the opening

day of the trial must have made readers wonder how the writer knew the judge was weary.

3. Use specifics rather than generalities. "A 10-pound book" is better than "a huge book." "A man, 70," is more descriptive than "an old man."

4. Because the readers know you are referring to the photograph, omit phrases such as "is pictured," "is shown" and "the picture above shows."

5. Use "from left" rather than "from left to right." The first means as much as the second and is shorter. Neither *left* nor *right* should be overworked. If one of two boys in a picture is wearing a white jersey, use that fact to identify him. If the President is in a golf cart with a professional golfer, readers shouldn't have to be told which one is the President.

6. One of the worst things you can say about a person in a photo is that he is "looking on." If that is all he is doing, he is superfluous. Perhaps something like this will help: "William McGoo, background, is campaign treasurer."

7. Don't kid the readers. They will know whether this is a "recent photo." Give the date the photo was taken. Also, let readers know where the picture was taken—but not how. Most readers don't care about all the sleet and snow the photographer had to go through to get the picture. Also, readers aren't stupid. If the cutline says three persons in a Girl Scout picture are looking over a drawing of a new camp, readers aren't fooled if the picture shows two of the girls behind the drawing; they obviously can't be looking it over.

8. The present tense enhances the immediacy of pictures. The past tense is used if the sentence contains the date or if it gives additional facts not described in the action in the picture. The cutline may use both present and past tenses, but the past time-element should not be used in the same sentence with a present-tense verb describing the action.

9. Make sure the cutline is accurate. If a commercial photographer supplies the picture and the identification, double-check the names. The paper, not the photographer, gets the blame for inaccuracies. Cutline errors occur because someone, the photographer or the reporter accompanying the photographer, failed to give the pictures desk enough, or accurate, information from which to construct a cutline. Apparently assuming that any big horn is a tuba, a cutline writer talked about a horn player with half his tuba missing. His editor was quick to reprimand, "Umpteen million high school kids, ex-bandsmen and musicians in general know better."

10. Double-check the photo with the cutline identification. The wrong person pictured as "the most-wanted fugitive" is a sure way to invite libel. It is usually safer to say *held* or *arrested* than "murder suspect."

11. Writing a cutline requires as much care and skill as writing a story or a headline. The reader should not have to puzzle

---

out the meaning of the description. Notice these jarring examples: "Fearing new outbreaks of violence, the results of Sunday's election have been withheld." "Also killed in the accident was the father of five children driving the other vehicle." "Yum! Yum! A corn dog satisfies that ravishing Fair appetite." The word, obviously, was *ravenous,* not *ravishing.* Don't hit the reader over the head with the obvious. If the photo shows a fireman dousing hot timbers after a warehouse fire and a fireman already has been mentioned in the text, it is ridiculous to add that "firemen were called" in the cutline.

12. Avoid last-line widows. The cutline should be written so that the final line is a full line, or nearly so. If the writer knows the number of characters per pica in the type used for the cutline, he can set the typewriter stops so that each typewritten line corresponds with the type line. When the lines are doubled (two 2-columns for a four-column cut), the writer should write an even number of lines. If the cutline is to be placed in the space left by a mortise, it is essential that the writer determine the maximum characters the space will accommodate. Most pictures are indented at least 1 pica on each side. A usual practice is to make a corresponding indention or more in the cutlines. Some newspapers use this count.

11-Pica Column		*14-Pica Column*
One two-column line—57 typewriter units		35 units for each column
Three-column line —1½ typewriter lines		Two-column —set 29 picas
Four-column line —2 typewriter lines		Three-column—set 44 picas
Five-column line —2½ typewriter lines		Four-column —set 59 picas

Count just under the maximum line or circle a word that could be dropped by the printer. To correct a cutline with a widow, make the correction near the end of the cutline to eliminate unnecessary resetting. In a layout of two or more pictures, running side by side, each picture should have the same number of lines beneath it, regardless of the width of the pictures.

13. Cutlines should be bright if warranted by the picture. Biting humor and sarcasm have no place in cutlines.

14. The cutline should describe the event as shown in the picture, not the event itself. Viewers will be puzzled if the cutline describes action they do not see. Sometimes, however, an explanation of what is not shown is justified. The picture shows a football player leaping high to catch a pass for a touchdown. Viewers might like to know who threw the pass.

15. Because a lapse occurs between the time a picture of an event is taken and the time a viewer sees the picture in the newspaper, care should be taken to·update the information in the cutline. The first report said that three bodies were found in the wreckage. Subsequently two more bodies were found. The cutline should contain the latest figure.

The Art of Editing

16. In local pictures, the addresses of the persons shown may be helpful. If youngsters appear in the picture they should be identified by names, ages, names of parents and addresses.

17. If the picture is exceptional, credit may be given to the photographer in the cutline, perhaps with a brief description of how he achieved his creation. On picture pages containing text matter, the photographer's credit should be displayed as prominently as the writer's.

18. Although pictures normally carry cutlines, mood or special occasion pictures sometimes appear without cutlines if the message is obvious from the picture itself. Not all who look at pictures will also read the cutlines. In fact, the drop-off is severe enough to suggest that many readers satisfy their curiosity merely by looking at the picture.

19. In writing a series of cutlines for related shots, use only one picture slug, followed by a number—moon 1, moon 2 and so on.

20. Some papers use one style for cutlines with a story and another style for cutlines on pictures without a story (called *stand-alones*). A picture with a story might call for one, two or three words in boldface caps to start the cutline. In stand-alones a small head might be placed over the cutline. Cutlines with stories usually have less detail than stand-alones.

21. The heading over the cutline should clue the reader as to the event shown in the picture. It helps him see at a glance the meaning of the picture. When possible, the heading should give the picture's locale to help the reader gauge his interest in the picture. Some studies have indicated that readers get less erroneous interpretations of the subject matter of the picture when the cutline is topped by a properly written heading.

11

Legal Limitations on the Press

The editor who lives in constant fear of a damage suit, the copyeditor who sniffs libel in every story and thereby tries to make the safe safer and the reporter who thinks it is cute to refer to an inept councilman as a simian have no place on a newspaper. The first procrastinates and vacillates, the second makes the copy vapid and the third lands the publisher in court.

Neither the reporter nor the copyeditor need be a lawyer, but both should know enough about the legal aspects of journalism to know when to consult a lawyer. Some of these trouble spots are discussed in this chapter.

The press can use its immense freedom vigorously. It is only when it abuses its freedom that it faces punishment.

We need no license to establish a press and start publishing. Nor must we submit copy to any censor before or after publication. We can criticize the government and its officials severely and have no fear that the doors to the newspaper will be padlocked. In our system, no government—federal, state, county or municipal—can be libeled. The newspaper is not a public utility. With some exceptions, it can reject or accept any story, advertisement, picture or letter it wishes.

We do not have to beg or bribe officials to get a quota of newsprint. The newspaper is not dependent on the government for government advertising (except for the possible exception of legal advertising). We do not face the threat of withdrawal of the government's privileges should we disagree with its policies.

No court can enjoin a publication. Punishment, if any, comes after publication. Long ago we rejected the notion that the greater the truth, the worse the libel. We can report, portray or comment upon anyone who becomes newsworthy. Even the President is not immune from publicity either in his public or in his private life. Criminal libel is almost nonexistent. Most libel is considered a civil wrong.

References to a half-dozen decisions will indicate the scope of the freedom the press enjoys. Our earliest cases helped to establish the principles that truth is a defense in libel, that the jury determines both the law and the fact. The court has held that there can be no previous restraint on a newspaper, even on one judged to be a nuisance. The court has affirmed that it is not libelous to comment adversely upon the government itself. The court has prohibited a discriminatory tax on the press. The court has told judges that neither an inherent nor a reasonable tendency are sufficient to justify restriction of free expression, that contempt of court is to be used only where there is a clear and present danger of interfering with the orderly administration of justice. The court has held that comment on or about public officials is privileged, even if false, provided there is no malice. The court did not license reckless disregard of the truth but accepted belief in the truth of facts stated. The privilege is now generally recognized in regard to comment on the public acts of public figures as well as of public officials.

This brief review is intended to remind editors of the unusual liberties we enjoy. It should not deter editors and publishers from maintaining a constant vigil to preserve and extend these freedoms. We still have the problems of news management at all levels of government. We still have some judges and attorneys who would dry up most news of crime until after the trial. We still have those who would like to censor what we read, hear or view. We still wrestle with the problem of what constitutes obscenity and who is to decide what is obscene. Worst of all, we have many in our society who care little about press freedom. If these people could have their way they would return to sixteenth-century England and the Court of Star Chamber where any criticism of the realm was promptly punished. What some people don't realize is that the freedom to read, to listen and to view is their right, not the special privilege of any commercial enterprise.

The Libel Hazard

Publishers and broadcasters face risks far greater than do most other professional or business executives. More than a century ago a London editor, John T. Delane of the *Times,* said, "The Press lives by disclosures." All disclosures are hazardous. If errors occur, they are public and may subject the error maker to liability.

The day is rare when any publisher or broadcaster doesn't commit errors—wrong facts, wrong names and identifications, wrong addresses, wrong dates, wrong spelling or pronunciation, wrong grammar, wrong headlines. Fortunately, only a handful of such errors are serious enough to cause or threaten a law-suit.

Few libels are deliberate. Nearly all result from erroneous reporting, misunderstanding of the law or careless editing.

Misunderstanding the Law

1. The common assumption that if a person involved in a story appears to be one who cannot prove damages as a result of the publication, it is safe enough to go ahead and use the story. Wrong, because under the law, if the article is libelous, damages are presumed. The amount is left up to the jury.

2. The common assumption that if a statement originated from an outside source, it is safe. Wrong, because a newspaper is responsible for whatever it publishes from whatever source—advertisements, letters, wire stories, syndicated material.

3. Feeling that if a person is not named, he may not sue. Wrong, because a plaintiff sometimes can be identified by means other than name.

4. The feeling that if the harmful statement concerns a group, individual members cannot sue. Wrong, because some groups are small enough (juries, team members, councilmen) so that each can be identified and therefore each may have a case.

5. Misjudging the extent of the defense of privilege to report truly and fairly a judicial proceeding.

6. Misjudging the extent of privilege in an arrest. Statements by the police as to the guilt of the prisoner or that the prisoner "has a record a mile long" are not privileged. All persons are presumed innocent until they are proved guilty.

7. The assumption that if a court case has a bizarre aspect it can be handled humorously or flippantly. *Time* magazine once used this "Dutch" lead on a story detailing the suicide of Enzo de Bonze, son-in-law of the then Prime Minister of France, Gaston Doumergue, in the presence of the minister's wife:

"Yesterday Curtis B. Dall, son-in-law of President Roosevelt, shot himself in the White House in the presence of his estranged wife and Mrs. Roosevelt. He died later in the day."

If such event were so briefly reported in the U.S. Press, neither readers nor publishers would be satisfied. Yet almost an exact parallel of that tragedy occurred in the Hotel Continental apartment of Premier Gaston Doumergue. . . .

Time's defense that the lead was purely fictitious proved to no avail.

Carelessness

1. Crime stories where there has been no arrest or charge of crime.

2. Mistaken identity. Similarity of names doesn't necessarily mean similarity of identity. Persons in trouble often give fictitious names. Identification should be qualified by phrases such as "who gave his name as. . . ," "listed by police as . . ." or "identified by a card in her purse as. . . ." In listing addresses in crime

and police court stories, some papers use the block instead of a specific number. Several families might live at the same address.

3. Stories where the defense of truth is hard to prove or cannot be accepted into evidence.

4. Clothing the damaging statement with *alleged* or *allegedly*.

5. "Needled" headlines. Qualifications are difficult in a headline because of the limited character count. The assumption is wrong that as long as the story is safe the head can take liberties. Many readers read only the headline. A cutline also may be libelous. Within the story itself, statements cannot be taken out of context to create a libel. The story must be taken in its entirety. If a story has been written as a series, all the stories must be considered together.

6. The assumption that a person with an unsavory reputation can't be libeled. Wrong. He may be a notorious drunk but that doesn't necessarily make him a thief. Further, juries may take pity on "the unfortunate" and award him nominal damages. Jurors sometimes reason peculiarly. A Fond du Lac paper said a certain man was arrested for stealing a diamond pin. It was not a pin but a brooch. The error should have been immaterial because the gist of the report was true. But the jury felt it had to find for the plaintiff because the report was not literally true. It awarded only $1.25 in damages and permitted the plaintiff to tax only $1.25 of his costs against the defendant.

7. Confession stories pose dangers until the confession has been admitted in evidence in court. In pretrial stages, it is safer to say merely that the prisoner has made a statement.

8. The assumption that any statement made by one person to another about another is privileged if the reporter can prove that the first person actually made the statement about the second. Wrong in most states. If A tells a group that B is a liar, the reporter must be prepared to prove, not that A made the statement, but that B is, in fact, a liar.

Libelous Statements

Anything in a newspaper is libelous if it is false and if it damages a person's reputation or has an adverse effect on his means of earning a living. The same applies to businesses and to institutions. An item is libelous if it is (1) communicated to others, (2) defamatory, (3) false or (4) specific.

Judge Leon R. Yankwich in *"It's Libel or Contempt if You Print It"* (see the bibliography at the end of this chapter) insists that libel is one of the hardest of all torts, or civil wrongs, to defend. The cards are stacked in favor of the plaintiff. In libel, malice is assumed. It does not have to be proved by the plaintiff except where public officials or public figures are involved. Reputation of the plaintiff is assumed, and therefore damages are assumed as a result of an assault on the plaintiff's reputation. Nor do damages have to be specified. They can be general as well as special and punitive, depending on the instructions of the judge and the whims of the jurors.

A story is defamatory if it accuses a living person of a crime or immorality or imputes a crime or immorality to him; if it states or insinuates that a person is insane or has a loathsome or contagious disease; if it tends in any way to subject the victim to public hatred, contempt or ridicule or causes others to shun him or refuse to do business with him; if it asserts a want of capacity to conduct one's business, occupation or profession.

Wrong assumptions sometimes can make a statement defamatory. In Judge Yankwich's view, a man who sets fire to a dwelling is not necessarily an arsonist. A man who kills another is not necessarily a murderer.

Some items in a newspaper are false but not necessarily defamatory. A false report that a man has died usually is not libelous. But if the person is a professional man and he can prove that because of the false statement his business has suffered to the extent of a provable amount, he may be able to collect that amount. To say of a mother that she has given birth to a daughter is not necessarily libelous. If she has been married only two months, she has a cause for legal action.

Praising a doctor for his fine work in treating certain patients may be neither false nor defamatory, but it could injure him in his profession because of his ethical code prohibiting puffery.

Libel can be avoided or at least reduced if everyone on the staff exercises responsibility in accuracy, exactness and judgment. But even when libel does occur it need not terrify the staff. Some cases are not serious enough to entice a lawyer to take the case to court. Some lawyers hesitate to get involved in libel cases, especially if they are politically ambitious and covet the newspaper's support.

A statement may cause a reader pain and anguish, but mere vituperation does not make a libel; it must be substantial. It is not enough that the statement may disturb him personally. It must damage him in the estimation of his community or of those with whom he does business.

Only the man libeled has cause for action. His relatives, even though they may have suffered because of the false and defamatory statements, have no recourse in libel. The offended person must bring his suit within the statutory period (ranging from one to six years depending on the jurisdiction). If he should die before or during the trial, there is no continuation of the case by survivors.

If he has been libeled, he may ask the publication to print a correction. This could satisfy him because it tends to set the record straight. In states having retraction laws, the plaintiff can collect only provable damages if the retraction is made on request and within a certain time limit. A correction provides evidence of lack of malice.

Some newspapers may offer to run a correction, possibly offer a nominal payment, then get a release from further liability. This procedure saves the costs and hazards of a trial.

Suppose the plaintiff insists on taking the rascal editor into court. The plaintiff must hire a lawyer and pay the filing fee. He should be advised of the defenses available to the newspaper —truth, privilege, fair comment, right of reply. Because libel concerns reputation, the plaintiff's character, good name and esteem can be put at issue. If he has a skeleton in the closet, he may hesitate to have his past revealed in court. If he is a public figure, he will have the burden of proving the material was published maliciously.

Suppose the plaintiff should win in lower court. He may get damages of hundreds of thousands of dollars—or only a few cents. If the defending publisher loses, he doubtless will appeal, even to the U.S. Supreme Court if the question involves a constitutional violation. Is the plaintiff able to pay appeal court costs if he should lose? Finally, publishers can get libel insurance at nonprohibitive costs, especially if there is a deductible clause. The protection is primarily for excessive judgments, usually of the punitive type.

Most of the larger dailies have their own lawyers to advise them on sensitive stories. Some lawyers urge, "When in doubt leave it out." But the publisher's attitude is, "This is something that should be published. How can it be published safely?" On these extrasensitive stories, where the precise wording has been dictated by an attorney, the desk should make no changes. The headline must be as carefully phrased.

Libel may involve business corporations as well as individuals. A corporation, partnership or trust or other business may be damaged if untrue statements tend to prejudice the entity in the conduct of its trade or business or deter others from dealing with it. Nonprofit organizations likewise may collect damages resulting from a publication that tends to prejudice them in the public estimation and thereby interferes with the conduct of their activities.

Criminal Libel

The gist of criminal libel is the tendency of a malicious, defamatory publication to cause a breach of the peace. Here is a typical statutory definition of criminal libel taken from the *Colorado Revised Statutes,* Chapter 40, Section 8, 1963:

A libel is a malicious defamation expressed either by printing, or by signs, or pictures or the like, tending to blacken the memory of one who is dead, or to impeach the honesty, integrity, virtue or reputation, or publish the natural defects of one who is alive, and thereby expose him or her to public hatred, contempt, or ridicule. . . . In all prosecutions for a libel the truth thereof may be given in evidence in justification, except libels tending to blacken the memory of the dead or expose the natural defects of the living.

It is prosecuted by the state upon the complaint of an individual or individuals and usually is considered a misdemeanor, with maximum punishment, say, of one year in a county jail, a fine of $300 or both.

Criminal libel differs from civil libel in these respects:

1. Criminal libel may libel the dead; civil libel cannot.

2. In criminal libel, malice must be proved by the plaintiff; in civil libel, malice is assumed, except in some circumstances.

3. Truth is not a defense in criminal libels tending to blacken the memory of the dead or expose the natural defects of the living. In civil libel, truth (or the truth published for justifiable ends) is a defense.

Libel Defenses

Criminal libel is rare because the person offended wants monetary reward and therefore would prefer to sue under civil libel. Of course, he could sue for civil libel and still instigate a complaint of criminal libel, but he rarely does. Criminal libel is used mainly as a weapon by large groups whose organization has been defamed but not the individual members. An example would be a charge filed by the Knights of Columbus against a publication that published a defamatory falsehood about that organization.

Truth

Truth is an absolute defense to libel in some states. In other states, truth must be accompanied by good motives and justifiable ends. When truth is offered in evidence, it must be substantial, not hearsay or secondary proof. Mere repetition of what someone else said is not admissible evidence of truth. The truth must be as broad and as complete as the publication upon which the charge was made. Truth offered in evidence need not mean the literal accuracy of the published charge but rather the substance or gist of the charge.

If the defending publisher relies on a document as evidence to show truth, he must be sure the document can be produced at the trial and be admitted in evidence. If he relies on a witness to give testimony as to truth, he must be assured the witness is qualified to testify. To take an extreme example, a publisher could not rely on the testimony of a doctor who is prohibited from violating doctor-patient relationships. In questionable cases of provable evidence, evidentiary matter such as notes, references and pictures should be kept in the paper's files at least during the statutory period, or time when the case can be pursued. Any republication of a story will start a new statutory period.

Privilege

Reports of official, judicial, legislative, executive or administrative proceedings—federal, state or municipal—may be published and successfully defended as qualified privilege.

The qualifications are that the report be fair and substantially accurate and complete, without comment, on matters constituting or relevant to official action or performance of such public bodies or officers.

For example, a food inspector may make an official report to a board of health describing conditions he found at a certain establishment. His information, even though false, may be reported safely as long as the newspaper observes the qualifications just mentioned. If truth is required in the newspaper account, then privilege would be worthless as a defense. What a food inspector may say about Sunday school teachers at a meeting of a service club is not privileged. It is only the official conduct of an officer, acting in his official capacity, that can be defended as privileged. If the police say something not within the scope of their duty to make public, no privilege attaches. It is not made legally safe by prefacing the report with the phrase "police say" or "police reported."

Statements of attorneys or civic organization officials usually are not privileged, nor are press releases from all government bureaus.

Not even all acts of public officials or all actions before official groups are necessarily privileged. Pretrial and grand jury proceedings, for instance, are held to determine the extent of evidence available to warrant a trial or prosecution and are frequently one-sided. The fact that a pretrial hearing was held or that the grand jury is in session and for what purpose may be reported. Results of the hearing and the returns of the grand jury, of course, may be reported.

In many states the mere filing of a complaint, petition, affidavit or other document is not privileged. Anyone can go to the court clerk and file a complaint containing false, scandalous and damaging statements about another merely upon payment of a docket fee. Proof of the fact that libelous statements are contained in the document is not a basis for privilege. The gist of the complaint, without the specifically damaging parts, may be reported, along with an answer by the defendant. Even if the defendant is not available or prepared to answer, the fact that the paper tried to give both sides evidences lack of malice.

Sealed records usually are not privileged.

Some states hold that the agenda of a city council is not privileged because it may contain complaints and criticisms that may never come before the meeting. Of course, the open meeting of the council is privileged.

Confessions usually have no legal standing until they are introduced as evidence and accepted by the court. Reporting a pretrial confession is dangerous, particularly if the defendant later is acquitted, if the court refuses to allow the confession or if the confession implicates others. The usual practice today is to state simply that the prisoner made a statement to the police or to the prosecuting attorney. Also, the fact that the police are questioning a man about a crime does not mean, necessarily, that the man is a suspect.

In detailing charges, the reporter should give specific, not generalized, accusations. Some terms used in newspaper reports, such as "black market operations," are not even statutory offenses.

Some quasi-official proceedings, such as ecclesiastical hearings or those involving labor disputes, may be reported as privileged provided the report observes the qualifications already mentioned.

Some public meetings afford no privilege in themselves, but a report of such meetings is justified when there is general public interest. Certainly the public has an interest in the discussion of taxes, public funds, health and welfare and community morals. When subjects of public interest are discussed at conventions, caucuses, community clubs, stockholders' meetings and the like, they are reported, even though the meetings are not privileged occasions. Again, even when the occasion is not strictly privileged, every attempt should be made to give both sides of the controversy.

Fair Comment and Criticism   Newspapers are free to discuss public affairs and to comment upon the conduct of public officials. This defense has three qualifications: (1) The comment is founded upon facts or what the publisher had reasonable grounds to believe are facts. (2) The comment is not made maliciously. Here, the burden of proof is on the plaintiff. (3) The comment does not involve the private life or moral character of a person except where such has a direct bearing upon his qualifications or work.

Anyone who puts himself or his work before the public is subject to public assessment of his performance, however strong the terms of censure may be. Decisions of the U.S. Supreme Court suggest that, short of malice and reckless disregard of their truths, all debates on public issues should be uninhibited, robust, and wide-open, and that it may well include vehement, caustic, and sometimes unpleasantly sharp attacks on government and public officials. The same freedom could very well apply to comments on anyone in the public eye.

This should not be construed as license. Character and public reputation are priceless possessions and are not good hunting grounds simply because a person holds public office, aspires to public office or in any manner offers himself or his talents to the public. There is a difference between assessing the fitness of a candidate or commenting upon the products of a public performer and a reckless attack on his character and reputation.

Corrections   The publication of a correction technically admits the libel and therefore negates truth as a defense. But when the defense of truth is not clearly evident, the publisher should willingly correct. The correction operates to refute the plaintiff's claim of malice. A refusal to correct may be used to show malice.

When made, the correction should be full and frank and used as conspicuously as the article complained of. The less said about out-of-court settlements, the better. No corporation should suggest to the public that it is willing to settle privately rather than fight the case in court. Every publisher should know his rights and responsibilities and not be cowed by threats.

Another possible way of indicating lack of malice is by publishing a favorable item concerning the person claiming damages or even items favorable to his relatives.

A reporter obtained her story over the phone from the judge's secretary. She took her notes in shorthand. When she transcribed her notes, she mistook DWS (driving while under suspension) for DWI (driving while intoxicated) and thus wrote falsely that a certain person had pleaded guilty to driving while intoxicated. Even if this story had been edited by another it is unlikely the copyeditor would have caught the error. The paper should have printed a correction to indicate lack of malice and to escape punitive damages should the injured person sue for libel.

But a second story was not a clear correction and this should have been corrected by a deskman. The headline read **Ex-sheriff's / patrolman / admits count.** The lead: "A man who five months ago was suspended from the Franklin County Sheriff's Patrol was arraigned in municipal court here yesterday, pleading guilty to driving for the past nine years on a suspended license." Later, the story said that the patrolman had been dropped from the force for "misuse of authority" and later qualified that statement with another to the effect the patrolman had to resign on order of the Office of Strategic Information, USAF, Ft. Ethan Allen, Vermont.

The patrolman sued for libel. The defense tried to argue that the crime of driving while the license was suspended was as serious as the crime of driving while intoxicated and therefore the newspaper should not be held accountable for a minor error. The jury disagreed and returned a judgment of $3,500 for the former patrolman.

Reply and Consent

An individual has a right to reply in a newspaper to an attack upon him made in a newspaper. Even though the reply is defamatory, it will be privileged for the individual and the newspaper, provided the defamatory matter is essential to support a contention that the original attack was false and the reply is not substantially stronger than the original.

If the disputants in a public controversy insist on arguing their cases in the newspapers—in stories, letters or advertisements—the publisher may ask the contenders to contract to assume all liabilities in the event of a suit. The device inevitably forces the arguments to be more temperate.

If an individual volunteers a comment to a newspaper in reply to a statement made against him by another, it is assumed he has consented to the publication of his comment and he would have no recourse for damages.

In all issues fraught with libel the newspaper can reduce its hazards by carefully attempting to show both sides of a controversy. If the reply can be used along with the original story, the better. By giving both sides equal prominence—in headlines or in text—the newspaper at least demonstrates a lack of malice.

Contempt of Court

The copyeditor has little if any concern with direct contempt of court—wilful disobedience in the presence of the court, such as taking photographs in the courtroom without the court's consent. The copyeditor is concerned mainly with constructive or indirect criminal contempt—accounts, headlines or cutlines that disregard the dignity and authority of the court or which tend to impede the administration of justice.

The deskman who handles a court story may find it almost impossible to verify every fact contained in the account. If the story concerns a running trial, the deskman can obtain the clippings of previous stories and at least double-check the names of the principals, the precise action and the correct legal terms.

Here are examples of reporting errors as given by one district judge to the authors: "By way of example, probation was confused with parole, the defendant was reported to have been sent to the penitentiary when such was not the case, the wrong defendant was named in one story, two cases were reported consolidated for trial which was not the case, and in another story the reporter had the action taking place in the wrong court. These are not particularly serious errors but are indicative of the inaccuracy that is common in this type of reporting."

Such errors do not reflect to the credit of a newspaper that prides itself on accurate reporting and editing of all the news it prints. Even though most errors in reporting legal proceedings are not serious enough to bring citations against the reporter or the newspaper, they have deserved the contempt expressed by many judges concerning inaccuracies in the court report. Justice Wiley B. Rutledge commented in the Pennekamp v. Florida decision (328 U.S. 331, 1946), "There is perhaps no area of news more inaccurately reported factually, on the whole, though with some notable exceptions, than legal news." And Justice William O. Douglas in the Craig v. Harney case (331 U.S. 367, 1947) said, "Inaccuracies in reporting (legal news) are commonplace."

Such comments should put the deskman on guard on all legal copy. Among the many statements that should be challenged are the following:

1. Predicting what a judge will or should do during a trial.

2. Untrue statements. A seemingly harmless statement that a decision had been arrived at by a majority of the justices of

the Supreme Court in a criminal case was held to be in contempt of court.

3. Adverse comments no matter how true. But when the case is completed, judges are subject to the same criticism as other people.

4. During the trial, any statement (beyond the actual proceedings of the trial) that reflects adversely on the hearing or is prejudicial to either side. Examples would be a rehash of the defendant's criminal record or references to a confession that has not been accepted as evidence.

Right of Privacy

As with contempt of court, the right of privacy has little importance for the copyeditor. Newspaper accounts generally concern newsworthy subjects who have forfeited their rights of privacy.

Areas where trouble might arise are feature stories of persons who are not in the news, pictures and cutlines that invade the rights of privacy of an innocent bystander, promotional and advertising material that uses a person's name for trade purposes without his consent and unwarranted publicity about relatives of one involved in criminal or moral accusations.

News and news feature accounts may concern anyone in whom the public has a legitimate interest. The duration of this interest is unknown. In one case, the court held, in effect, that there was legitimate public interest in an infant child prodigy and in a follow-up article twenty-seven years later under the heading "Where Are They Now?" When a person has served his time in the news spotlight, then disappears from the news, the newspaper generally loses interest in the person unless he reappears in the news for one reason or another. Resurrecting his past for exploitation, other than on a news basis, is more likely to be the domain of a magazine, film, or television show than of a newspaper.

The newspaper is protected even though the news value may be slight. For example, the newspaper may legitimately display the types of persons who join the Easter parade. By voluntarily appearing in a public place, a person abandons his or her privacy. Of course, if she is made the subject of ridicule, she would have grounds for libel.

Some risk is involved in printing photographs taken of people without their consent in their home or in a hospital bed. Pictures showing ways to beat the summer heat may be humorous to readers but not to the hefty lady fanning herself under a tree in her own backyard.

Plagiarism and Copyright Infringement

Plagiarism and copyright infringement are still other fringe areas concerning the copyeditor. Only the expression of news, not the news itself, can be copyrighted. Even if a newspaper does not protect itself by copyrighting the entire paper or individual stories, it still has a property right in its news and can prevent others from "lifting" the material.

It is assumed the deskman will be so thoroughly familiar with the contents of opposition papers and exchanges that he will be able to spot material that copies or paraphrases too closely the work of others.

If a wire service sends out a story based on the story of another member or client, the deskman should not delete the wire service credit to the originator of the story. Nor should he delete any credit on stories or pictures. He may, if directed, compile stories from various sources into one comprehensive story, adding the sources from which the story was compiled.

If his own paper publishes a story to be copyrighted, the deskman should insure that the notice is complete—the notice of copyright, the date, and by whom.

In editing book review copy, the deskman should have some notion of the limits of fair use of the author's quotes. The problem is relatively minor because few copyright owners would object to the publishing of extracts in a review, especially if the review were favorable. If the review has to be trimmed, the trimming probably would come in the quoted extracts.

Other Restrictions

The states as well as the federal government have regulations dealing with matters such as false reports on the condition of financial institutions, advocacy of a violent overthrow of the government and misleading advertising or promotion of stocks and securities.

Postal regulations cover a substantial range of prohibitions—libel, threatening matter, counterfeit forecasts, matter tending to aid or abet a mail fraud, photographs of money and stamps, pornography and promotion of lotteries.

A lottery is any scheme containing three elements—consideration paid, a prize or award and determination of the winner by chance. This includes all drawings for prizes and raffles and games such as bingo, bunco and keno. It is immaterial who sponsors the scheme. Pictures and advertising matter referring to lotteries and similar gift enterprises are barred from the mail.

Newspapers are not permitted to announce them or to announce results or to mention them except in states with legalized lotteries and in cases where something of news value happened as a result of the lottery. An example would be a story concerning a laborer who became wealthy overnight by having a winning ticket on the Irish Sweepstakes. This would probably be considered a legitimate human interest story rather than a promotion for horse races and lotteries.

Newspapers may use illustrations of paper money provided the illustration is in black and white, less than $\frac{3}{4}$ or more than $1\frac{1}{2}$ times the actual size and is used as nonadvertising. No individual facsimiles are permitted. In advertising, there can be no illustrations of paper money, checks or bonds, except that money may be used in numismatic advertising and savings bonds may be used in connection with Treasury Department sales campaigns. The rules apply to paper money, checks, bonds and securities.

Illustrations in black and white, but not individual facsimiles or individual photographs, are permitted for any purpose including advertising for both U.S. and foreign coins.

Color illustrations of U.S. stamps are prohibited regardless of whether they are canceled or demonetized. Color illustrations of foreign stamps are permitted provided they have official cancellation marks. Uncanceled stamps may not be shown in color.

Crime and Courts

No longer do American editors play crime by the standards of past generations. They print crime news but they no longer rely on a crime story, even a sex-triangle murder, to boost street sales. Topics such as space and ocean exploration compete with crime for the attention and interest of today's more sophisticated readers.

Crime is a part of the news record, however, and has to be carried if newspapers are to fulfill their obligations to the readers. Minor crimes, unless they have unusual angles, generally are merely listed. When it is presented in detail, the crime story should be done with the same thoroughness and sensitivity that experts give other subjects. Some observers argue that newspapers should offer more news of criminal activities—but with the constructive purpose of showing the community the origins and anatomy of crime.

The copyeditor who handles a crime story should make sure that the report contains no prejudicial statements that could deprive the defendant of a fair trial. His headline should avoid labels.

One editor admonished his staff, "We should be sensitive about assumption of guilt, not only to avoid libel but to avoid criticism and a bad impression on readers." The caution was occasioned by this lead: "With the dealer who sold a 32-caliber pistol to Mrs. Mariann C– apparently located, Shaker Heights police today were using handwriting expert Joseph Tholl to link the accused slayer of Cremer Y–, 8, to the weapon purchase." The whole tone of this lead is an assumption of guilt and the effort of police to pin the crime on somebody. It should have said the police were seeing whether Mrs. C– was linked to the gun purchase—not trying to link her.

Here is a conviction lead:

FAYETTEVILLE, N.C. (AP)—Two Negro marines are being held without bond after terrorizing a family, stealing a car, and trading shots with officers.

They were identified as etc.

They told officers after their Saturday night capture they were members of the National Abolitionist Forces, which they described as a militant Negro group.

Legal Limitations on the Press

In reference to this story, the general news editor said in part, "We do not have a formal set of guidelines for handling crime news, but this story certainly does not conform to regular AP practice. It makes us authority for that statement that the two men held had terrorized a family, stolen a car and traded shots with officers. All we should have said was that they were charged with doing all those things, and who had made the charge."

Civil Disorders

The copyeditor shares some of the responsibilities of the reporters and news executives in correcting the abuses in news of civil disorders. The abuses cited by the National Advisory Commission on Civil Disorders (Kerner Commission) in 1967 relate to three general areas: "despite instances of sensationalism, inaccuracies and distortions, newspapers, radio and television, on the whole, made a real effort to give a balanced, factual account of the 1967 disorders. . . . despite this effort, the portrayal of the violence that occurred failed to reflect accurately its scale and character. The overall effect was, we believe, an exaggeration of both mood and event. . . . ultimately most important, we believe that the media have thus far failed to report adequately on the causes and consequences of civil disorders and the underlying problems of race relations." [As given in *The Media and the Cities* (Chicago: the University of Chicago Center for Policy Study, 1968).]

For the deskman, the story of violence is checked not only for accuracy but for tone, not only for the impact the story will have on the majority of the audience—which is white—but also on the minority audience.

Terms used in the story, the headline and the cutline should be weighed carefully. A protest or a demonstration, even accompanied by violence, is not necessarily a riot. *Riot* implies conflict and destruction. It is unexpected, unpredictable and out of control. Most disorders involving minorities are expected and predictable. *Riot* is a handy headline word, not always precise but usually inflammatory. A race riot should describe a conflict between two racial groups, not the riot of one racial group alone. *Near-riot* is senseless.

The story should nail down the authority and should make certain that the spokesman is an authority. It should tell who estimated the damages in the burned-out area. The copyeditor should compare the estimate given today with the one given yesterday and compare the estimate of one authority with that of another.

When the reporter writes, "There were reports of looting in some sections," the copyeditor should ask—official reports or only rumors?

The early wire story, in all probability, lacks confirmation because it was prepared in a hurry. If possible, it should be held back until a more thorough report is forthcoming.

The Art of Editing

During the frenzy of violence, even officials are tempted to exaggerate damage estimates and to bloat the figures on the wounded and dead. The story should tell precisely how many were taken to hospitals or to the morgue, exactly how many were arrested.

The rhetoric of the groups involved needs watching. The person quoted may not be the leader but the one who is the loudest, the most sensational or the first to volunteer. The "spokesman" may represent the feelings of the mob, but his string of obscenities and his terms of degradation such as *fuzz* and *pigs* may not necessarily be the words of the whole group.

Militant has come to mean something other than one engaged in a strife. So the report invariably labels the leader as the "militant leader."

Brutality means the quality of being brutal, savage, inhuman or cruel, a term that doesn't necessarily fit the actions of a policeman confronting a group bent on violence.

Even after the copyeditor has inspected the copy for accuracy and tone he has a final chore—to make sure the story and headline are in perspective. The story should tell not only what took place but why. All stories of violence are in a context of something else—of slum misery, neglect, bias, hopelessness. The single act that triggers the explosion is seldom the cause of the reaction. Too often the story concentrates on the action and the mood of the rioters but fails to mention those who didn't riot and why.

The story of violence cannot be played down. It has a message that goes beyond the act itself. It can be told calmly, not hysterically.

Crime Publicity

Many newspapers now have their own guidelines on publicity in criminal proceedings. The Toledo *Blade* and Toledo *Times*, for example, as reported in *Editor & Publisher* (August 27, 1966), recommend that only the following information be published in stories of criminal proceedings:

The name, age and address of accused persons.

How the arrest was made and when and where.

The charges against the accused persons and the identity of the complainants.

The fact that a grand jury has returned an indictment and that a trial date has been set.

Unless special circumstances dictate otherwise, the following types of information shall not be published in cases of criminal arrests:

Any criminal record of the accused.

Any so-called "confession" the accused may have made other than the fact that he has made a statement to the police. No indication shall be made regarding the nature of the statement.

Statements by officials or others construed as detrimental or beneficial to the accused person.

Statements by lawyers either detrimental or beneficial to the accused or concerning any defense that is to be made during the trial.

Names of jurors selected for a particular trial.

Arguments made in court in the absence of the jury or any evidence excluded by the court.

Press-Bar Compacts

Several of the states have adopted compacts between the press and the bar to promote a better understanding of the constitutional guarantees of freedom of the press and the right to a fair, impartial and public trial. The guidelines are recommendations and are not binding on either profession. Like the compacts between the press and the hospitals and the medical profession, the press and bar compacts provide for liaison committees to hear grievances from either side.

The following are the main guidelines for reporting a criminal case [From Colorado Bar-Press Compact, 1969]:

1. It is appropriate to make public the following information concerning the defendant:

(a) The defendant's name, age, residence, employment, marital status and similar background information. There should be no restraint on biographical facts other than accuracy, good taste and judgment.

(b) The text of the charge, such as the complaint, information and indictment, and, where appropriate, the identity of the complaining party.

(c) The identity of the investigating and arresting agency and the length of the investigation.

(d) The circumstances immediately surrounding an arrest, including, but not limited to, the time and place of the arrest, resistance, pursuit, possession and use of weapons and a description of items seized at the time of arrest.

2. It is the duty of the law enforcement agency to solve and prevent crime. It is the duty of the press to inform, promptly and accurately. It is the duty of counsel, both defense and prosecution, to seek the truth within the confines of a fair trial. An editor, who must ultimately make the decision whether to publish or broadcast, should weigh these varying responsibilities, as well as the fact that certain types of information may create dangers of prejudice without serving a significant law enforcement or public interest function. Such dissemination may impose particular risks when it occurs after the filing of formal charges and as the time of trial approaches. It is emphasized that these

guidelines are not intended to excuse a law enforcement agency from releasing proper information to the public.

With these considerations in mind, categories of information that may jeopardize the rights of a defendant, if published, include the following:

(a) Opinions about a defendant's character, guilt or innocence.

(b) Admissions, confessions or the contents of a statement attributed to a defendant.

(c) References to the results of investigative procedures, such as fingerprints, polygraph examinations, ballistics tests or laboratory tests.

(d) Statements concerning the credibility or anticipated testimony of prospective witnesses.

(e) Opinions concerning evidence or argument in the case, whether or not it is anticipated that such evidence or argument will be used at trial.

Exceptions may be in order if the information given to the public is essential to the apprehension of a suspect, or where other public interests will be served. Stories reviewing the entire history of a criminal case, disseminated just prior to trial, should be avoided whenever possible.

3. Prior criminal charges and convictions are matters of public record and are available to the press through the police agency, court clerks and the files of the press. Law enforcement agencies should make such information available to the press after legitimate inquiry. The public disclosure of this information may be prejudicial, particularly if it occurs after the filing of formal charges and as the time of trial approaches, and should be carefully considered.

4. Photographs, still and film:

(a) Photographs of a suspect may be released by law enforcement personnel in response to a legitimate request by the press.

(b) Law enforcement and court personnel should not prevent the photographing of suspects or defendants when they are in public places outside the courtroom.

(c) The taking of photographs in a courtroom is governed by rules of the court.

(d) The possible effect on the fair trial of a defendant by the dissemination of photographs of the suspect should be considered by editors in the light of these guidelines.

5. The press is free to report what occurs in the course of the judicial proceeding itself, subject to rules of the court.

6. Nothing in these guidelines should inhibit a law enforcement agency from disclosing such information as may be necessary to enlist public assistance in apprehending fugitives from justice. Such information may include photographs, records of prior arrests and convictions and results of investigative procedures.

Correct Terminology

Newsworthy trials are covered in detail so that essential information may be conveyed to the public at a time when it will not interfere with the judicial process. Newspapers have an obligation to expose wrongful acts of public officials and to deal with crisis conditions in ways intended to restore and to maintain public order.

The deskman has to have some knowledge of legal terms and the legal process if he is to make the story and headline technically correct yet meaningful to the layman. *Arrested* is a simple verb understood by all readers. It is better than *apprehended* or *taken into custody.* It is equal to *captured.* A person who is cited, summoned or given a ticket is not arrested.

An *arraignment* is a formal proceeding where a defendant steps forward to give the court his plea of guilty or not guilty. It should not be used interchangeably with *preliminary hearing,* which is held in a magistrate's court and is a device to show probable cause that a crime has been committed and that there is a likely suspect.

Bail is the security given for the release of a prisoner. The reporter reveals his ignorance when he writes, "The woman is now in jail under $5,000 bail." She can't be in jail under bail. She can be free on bail or she can be held in lieu of bail.

A *parole* is a conditional release of a prisoner with an indeterminant or unexpired sentence. *Probation* allows a person convicted of some minor offense to go at large, under suspension of sentence during good behavior, and generally under the supervision or guardianship of a probation officer.

The word *alleged* is a trap. Used in reference to a specific person (Jones, the alleged gambler), it offers no immunity from libel. Jones may be charged with gambling or indicted for gambling. In both instances, *alleged* is redundant. The charge is an allegation or an assertion without proof but carries an indication of an ability to produce proof.

The same can be said for other qualifiers, particularly *accused.* Calling a man an "accused murderer" or an "accused abductor" in a sense convicts him of murder or abduction. If a man is first called an "accused assassin," then is freed of the charge, would he be referred to as the "exonerated assassin"? Such qualifiers are unjustified, damaging and perhaps actionable. Headline writers resort to "alleged slayer" to save space and to avoid possible action. "Slaying" is not usually listed as a statutory crime. "Shot and killed" suggests two actions; "shot to death" is better.

A jail sentence does not mean, necessarily, that a man has been jailed. He may be free on bond or free pending an appeal.

Listing the wrong name in a crime story is the surest route to libel action. Thorough verification of first, middle and last names, of addresses and of relationships is a "must" in editing the crime story.

Normally, names of suspects who are being held for questioning or investigation should not be included in the report. A person branded a suspect, then later released for lack of evidence, remains branded. There is time to list names after a formal charge has been filed. The federal government, unlike many states, first gets the evidence, then files the charges.

Names of women or children in rape cases or attempted rape cases should not be used. Nor should the story give any clue to their addresses in a way by which they can be identified. An exception is when the rape victim is murdered.

Sentences may be consecutive or concurrent. If a man is sentenced to consecutive three-year terms, he faces six years of imprisonment. If his sentences are concurrent, he faces three years. But why use these terms? The total sentence is what counts with the readers and the prisoner.

If a man has been sentenced to five years but the sentence is suspended, he gets a suspended five-year sentence, not a five-year suspended sentence.

Juries are of two kinds—investigative (grand) and trial (petit). If a grand jury finds evidence sufficient to warrant a trial, it issues a *true bill*. If sufficient evidence is lacking, the return is a *no-bill*. "Jones indicted" means as much as "the grand jury indicted Jones." To say "the grand jury failed to indict Jones" implies it shirked its duty.

A *verdict* is the finding of a jury. A judge renders decisions, judgments, rulings and opinions, but not verdicts. Although verdicts are returned in both criminal and civil actions by juries, a guilty verdict is found only in criminal actions. Judges declare, not order, mistrials. Attorneys general or similar officials give opinions, not rulings.

Corpus delicti refers to the evidence necessary to establish that a crime has been committed. It is not restricted to the body of a murder victim; it can apply as well to the charred remains of a burned house.

Nolo contendere is a legalistic way of saying that a defendant, although not admitting his guilt, will not fight a criminal prosecution. *Nolle prosequi* means the prosecutor or plaintiff will proceed no further in his action or suit. The reader will understand the translation more readily than the Latin expression.

The fifth amendment guarantees the due process of law protection for all citizens. The report should not suggest that the use of this protection is a cover-up for guilt. Phrases such as "hiding behind the fifth" should be eliminated.

The story should distinguish between an act itself and an action. Replevin, for example, is an action to recover property wrongfully taken or detained. Trouble will arise if the deskman lets the reporter translate the action too freely: "Mrs. Marsh filed the replevin action to recover furniture stolen from her home by her estranged husband." So, too, with the tort of conversion. "Wrongful conversion" may imply theft, but neither the copy nor the head should convey such implication.

Keeping track of the plaintiff and the defendant should pose no problem except in appellate proceedings where the original defendant may become the plaintiff and vice versa. The confusion is not lessened by substituting *appellee* and *appellant.* The best way is to repeat the names of the principals.

In some civil suits the main news peg is the enormous sum sought by the plaintiff. Whether the same angle should be included in the headline is questionable. In some damage claims the relief sought is far greater than the plaintiff expects to collect. The judgment actually awarded is the news and the headline.

Deskmen can "tidy up" the crime and court report by watching for the following:

Misused Terms   All narcotics are drugs but many drugs are not narcotics.

A defendant may plead guilty or not guilty to a charge or of a crime. Technically, there is no such plea as innocent. A defendant may be judged not guilty by reason of insanity. He is not innocent by reason of insanity. An acquittal means he has been found not guilty. The danger of dropping the *not* has caused some editors to insist on using *innocent* rather than *not guilty.*

All lawsuits are tried in courts. *Court litigation,* therefore, is redundant.

Statements are either written or oral (not verbal).

"Would-be robber" has no more validity than a "would-be ballplayer."

The word *bandit* is suspect because it has the flavor of heroism and tends to glorify the hoodlum.

The word *lawman* has no place in the report. It can mean too many things—a village constable, a sheriff's deputy or the sheriff himself, a prosecutor, a bailiff, a judge, an F.B.I. agent, a revenue agent and so on. *Lawman* in contemporary America is a "hillbilly" word. Its merit is that it suggests a social setting. Almost always a more precise word will be found more suitable in a newspaper.

Use *sheriff's deputies* rather than *deputy sheriffs.*

Divorces are granted or obtained. Medals are won or awarded.

"Hit-and-run," "ax-murder," "torture-murder" and the like are newspaper clichés. They should be changed to "hit by an automobile that failed to stop," "killed with an ax," "tortured and murdered."

Euphemisms   Euphemisms include "attorney" for *lawyer,* "sexually assaulted" or "sexually attacked" for *raped.* Not all jurists, who profess or are versed in the law, are judges, and certainly not all judges are jurists.

Threadbare Phrases   Following are some threadbare phrases: stern warning, brilliant defense, gin mill, shattered body, police speculated, on the lam, Portia, soberly pronounced sentence, robed justices, curfew clamped.

Example of legal jargon: "The case was continued for disposition because the attorney requested no probation report be made on the boy before adjudication."

W. J. Brier and J. B. Rollins of Montana State University in 1963 studied some Missoula, Montana, adults as to their understanding of legal terms. [Bush, *News Research for Better Newspaper*, Vol. I (1966).] Following are the terms incorrectly defined by more than half the respondents:

Accessories before the fact—those charged with helping another who committed the felony.

Extradition—surrendered the prisoner to officials of another state.

Arraigned—brought to court to answer to a criminal charge.

Bound over—held on bail for trial.

Indicted—accused or charged by a grand jury.

Civil action—pertaining to private rights of individuals and to legal proceedings against these individuals.

Extortion—oppressive or illegal obtaining of money or other things of value.

Remanded—sent the case back to a lower court for review.

Continuance—adjournment of the case until later.

Felony—a crime of a graver nature than a misdemeanor, usually an offense punishable by imprisonment or death.

Writ of habeas corpus—an order to bring the prisoner to court so the court may determine if he has been denied his legal rights.

Administratrix—administrator; always a female.

Stay order—stop the action or suspend the legal proceeding.

An information—an accusation or a charge.

Venire—those summoned to serve as jurors.

Mandamus action—a court order requiring a party to carry out a legal duty.

Demurrer—a pleading admitting the facts in a complaint or answer but contending they are legally insufficient.

Other misunderstood terms include the following:

"Released on her personal recognizance"—released on her word of honor to do a particular act.

". . . make a determination on the voluntariness of the man's confession"—decide whether his confession is voluntary.

". . . the plaintiff is . . ."—". . . the suit was filed by . . ."

Be Exact

A *robber* steals by force. A *thief* steals without resorting to force. Theft suggests stealth. A *burglar* steals by entering or breaking into a building. If a burglar is caught in the act, pulls a gun on the homeowner and makes off with the family silverware, he is a robber.

Theft and *larceny* both mean the taking of what belongs to another. *Larceny* is the more specific term and can be proved only when the thief has the stolen property on him. Pickpockets and shoplifters are thieves.

"Statutory grounds for divorce" is redundant. All grounds for divorce are statutory in the state where the divorce is granted.

Charge has many shades of meaning and is often misused. "The psychologist charged last night that Negro high school students generally do not think of the university as a friendly place." The statement was more an observation than a charge.

Members of the Supreme Court are judges or justices, but not supreme judges. The title of the U.S. Supreme Court's chief justice is Chief Justice of the United States.

Words such as *looted, robbed* and *swindled* should be used properly: "Two men were fined and given suspended sentences yesterday in Municipal Court for stealing newsracks and looting money from them." "Thieves broke into 26 automobiles parked near the plant and looted some small items." Money is not looted. That from which it is taken is looted. Nor is money robbed. A bank is robbed; the money is stolen. "A man in uniform swindled $1,579 from a war widow." No, the person is swindled, not the money.

Some papers object to saying that fines and sentences are *given,* on the ground that they are not gifts.

Some police reporters like to say a guy went berserk and barricaded himself in the house with a gun. Rarely does a man do that.

A felony is a crime of a graver nature than a misdemeanor. Generally, a felony is punishable by death or by imprisonment in a penitentiary.

Juvenile Delinquents

Some states permit the publication of news or pictures of juvenile delinquents—defined as anyone under the age of eighteen. Many officials insist that names of juvenile offenders be withheld on the theory that there is greater opportunity for rehabilitation if the youth is not stigmatized by publicity that may affect him for the rest of his life.

In some states the children's code gives exclusive jurisdiction to the juvenile court over offenders under fourteen, regardless of the acts committed, and gives concurrent jurisdiction to the district court over youngsters between sixteen and eighteen, unless the crime involved is punishable by either death or life imprisonment if committed by an adult. In murder cases involving youths fourteen and over, the district court has original jurisdiction. These states make it a misdemeanor to publish the names, pictures or identity of youths under eighteen or that of the parents, guardians, or places of residence of children involved in any crime or in dependency cases within the state's jurisdiction.

Publicity may be given under the following circumstances:

1. Public hearings—A U.S. Supreme Court decision extends to juveniles the same due process of law guarantees provided adults in criminal proceedings. The juvenile has the same rights

against self-incrimination, to representation and even to a jury trial. Even in juvenile court, the youngster has a right to a public trial if he requests it. But after the finding of the jury at a public trial, the juvenile could still be placed before a juvenile court for disposition—out of sight of the press and the public.

2. Permission of the court—If the code permits it, the judge may, at his discretion, allow publicity concerning the hearing on a juvenile. Frequently, the judge of a juvenile court allows reporters to attend juvenile court sessions but does not permit identification of the youthful offender. There may be publication of news of such cases that may serve as a warning to violators of laws for the protection of children, provided that any reference to any child involved be so disguised as to prevent identification.

3. Traffic cases—Names of persons of any age may be used in traffic cases.

Deskmen should be alert to the distinction between a juvenile and a minor, the latter being defined as anyone under the age of twenty-one.

Probate

The value of an estate contained in a will filed for probate or proving is a newsworthy item and invariably is included in the reporter's story, usually in the lead. Because the lawyer who files the will for probate is required to estimate the total value of the estate, his figure invariably is low. The exact amount will not become known until several months later when an inventory is filed.

The proportions of the bequests and to whom they are to be made are factual items. Both the story and the headline should make clear that the dollar value of the estate is only an estimate.

Bibliography on the Legal Limitations on the Press

AMERICAN BAR ASSOCIATION, *The Rights of Fair Trial and Free Press.* Chicago: American Bar Association, 1969.

AMERICAN NEWSPAPER PUBLISHERS ASSOCIATION, *Free Press and Fair Trial.* New York: American Newspaper Publishers Association, 1967.

ARTHUR, WILLIAM R., and RALPH L. CROSMAN, *The Law of Newspapers.* New York: McGraw-Hill Book Company, Inc., 1940.

ASHLEY, PAUL P., *Say It Safely,* 3rd ed. Seattle: University of Washington Press, 1966.

ASSOCIATED PRESS, *The Dangers of Libel.* New York: Associated Press, 1964.

BAKER, ROBERT K., and SANDRA J. BALL, *Mass Media and Violence,* Vol. IX. Washington, D.C.: National Commission on the Causes and Prevention of Violence, 1969.

CROSS, HAROLD L., *The People's Right to Know.* New York: Columbia University Press, 1953.

ERNST, MORRIS L., and ALAN U. SCHWARTZ, *Privacy—The Right To Be Let Alone.* New York: The Macmillan Company, 1962.

FRANKLIN, MARC A., *The Dynamics of American Law.* Mineola, N.Y.: The Foundation Press, Inc., 1968.

GILLMOR, DONALD M., and JEROME A. BARRON, *Mass Communication Law*. St. Paul, Minn.: West Publishing Company, 1969.

JAMES, HOWARD, *Children in Trouble: A National Scandal*. Boston: The Christian Science Publishing Society, 1969.

NELSON, HAROLD L., and DWIGHT L. TEETER, *Law of Mass Communications,* 5th ed. Mineola, N.Y.: The Foundation Press, Inc., 1969.

PHELPS, ROBERT H., and E. DOUGLAS HAMILTON, *Libel—Rights, Risks, Responsibilities*. New York: The Macmillan Company, 1966.

PILPEL, HARRIET F., and THEODORA S. ZAVIN, *Rights and Writers*. New York: E. P. Dutton & Co., Inc., 1960.

STEIGLEMAN, WALTER A., *The Newspaperman and the Law*. Dubuque, Iowa: William C. Brown Company, Publishers, 1950.

THAYER, FRANK, *Legal Control of the Press,* 4th ed. Mineola, N.Y.: The Foundation Press, Inc., 1962.

WESTIN, ALAN F., *Privacy and Freedom*. New York: Atheneum Publishers, 1967.

WITTENBERG, PHILIP, *Dangerous Words*. New York: Columbia University Press, 1947.

YANKWICH, LEON R., *"It's Libel or Contempt if You Print It."* Los Angeles: Parker & Company, 1950.

12

An Introduction to Type

The editor who wants his readers to read more of what has been written or wants to obtain the maximum communication from words should learn to use type effectively. If an editor does not understand type, he may order a headline in a typeface[1] that is virtually unreadable, or one that calls attention to the shape of the letters rather than to the meaning of the words. Although the words may be well written, their meaning is obscured because readers begin to notice how unusual the typeface looks. Their attention is thus distracted from the meaning of the words. It is important, therefore, to understand that type is a vehicle by which words may be printed on many copies of paper quickly. The vehicle is never a substitute for communication, only an aid to the process. Type, therefore, should be unobtrusive. One of the most important rules for using type correctly deals with its unobtrusive character. This rule holds that:

Learning How Types Differ

Any typeface that calls attention to itself rather than to the message represents a poor choice. Type calls attention to itself when it is very large (in proportion to other type on the page), when it has an unusual design or when it is set in an unusual arrangement. In such cases, type distracts the readers' attention from the message.

To use type effectively, the beginner should start by studying how typefaces differ. Thousands of typefaces exist and every year new faces are added to the list. The beginner should learn

[1] *Typeface* refers to that portion of type printed on paper. Types, like human beings, are recognized by their faces.

to dissect the characteristics of typefaces so that their differences become larger and more noticeable. Eventually, through experience, the beginner will see the differences that seemed so difficult to discern at first.

To learn how type differs, it is important to know the various classifications of differences. Types differ by size, design characteristics, style, families, widths, weights and methods of mechanical production. The following pages summarize the most significant classifications by which types are differentiated.

Classification of Typefaces by Point Sizes

Most typefaces are measured in units called *points*. A point is a unit of printer's measurement of about $\frac{1}{72}$ inch. Twelve points equal 1 pica, and 6 picas equal 1 inch. Although type could be classified by picas or inches (for example, 72-point type could be called 6-pica type or 1-inch type), it is common practice to limit classification to point-size identification.

Types come in a limited range of sizes in most print shops or newspapers, and within this range are carefully spaced intervals. For example, metal type usually is manufactured from 4 point (the smallest-sized type) to 96 point (the largest). There are some exceptions to this range, but not many in common use. The sizes of type most often available in newspapers and print shops, and considered to be standard sizes, are as follows:

6, 8, 10, 12, 14, 18, 24, 30, 36, 42, 48, 60 and 72 point

At the lower end of the range, the intervals vary by only 2 points, whereas at the upper end, the intervals vary by 12 points. The reason for this variance is that smaller sizes are used to fill a given amount of space and small variances are needed, but larger sizes are used mostly for headlines and small differences would be unnoticeable.

In some of the larger newspaper plants the smaller intervals vary by only 1 point so that the editor may be able to designate $5\frac{1}{2}$-, 6-, 7-, 8-, 9-, 10-, 11- and 12-point type if he needs it.

Occasionally, an editor may want a type size that does not exist, such as a 40-point type. In such a case he may compromise with a 36- or 42-point type, or he can take a 36-point type print and have it enlarged photostatically. Because a photostat is nothing but a picture, he must transfer the photostatic type into metal type through a process called photoengraving. Because so little time is available in the production of a newspaper, editors find it more convenient to use standard-sized type.

In Figure 12–1 are examples of the various sizes of typefaces.

Classification of Type by Families

Just as members of the same human family tend to have similar facial characteristics, so do members of a type family. A type family includes all variations of a given type having common characteristics. Some type families have many variations; others have few. Figure 12–2 shows one of the large families of typefaces.

The Art of Editing

6	abcdefghijklmnopqrstuvwxyzabcdefghijklmnopqrstuvwxyzabcdefghijklmnopqrstuvwx
7	abcdefghijklmnopqrstuvwxyzabcdefghijklmnopqrstuvwxyzabcdefghijklmnopqr
8	abcdefghijklmnopqrstuvwxyzabcdefghijklmnopqrstuvwxyzabcdefghijkl
9	abcdefghijklmnopqrstuvwxyzabcdefghijklmnopqrstuvwxyzabcdefg
10	abcdefghijklmnopqrstuvwxyzabcdefghijklmnopqrstuvwxyzabcd
11	abcdefghijklmnopqrstuvwxyzabcdefghijklmnopqrstuvwxyza
12	abcdefghijklmnopqrstuvwxyzabcdefghijklmnopqrstuvw
14	abcdefghijklmnopqrstuvwxyzabcdefghijklmnopqr
18	abcdefghijklmnopqrstuvwxyzabcdefg
24	abcdefghijklmnopqrstuvwxyz
30	abcdefghijklmnopqrstu
36	abcdefghijklmnopqr
42	abcdefghijklmno
48	abcdefghijklmn
60	abcdefghijkl
72	abcdefghij

Figure 12–1. Most frequently used type sizes. [*From A Typographic Quest, Number Three. New York: Westvaco. 1965, p. 4.*]

Oldstyle and Modern Type Classifications

Typefaces may be classified as either oldstyle or modern. Care must be taken not to be confused by these terms, however, because they do not refer to periods of time. The term *oldstyle,* for example, does not mean that this type is "old" in terms of time even though it was first created about 1470. It is still being designed today. Modern type, on the other hand, was first created around 1800 and also is being designed today. Therefore, the style elements are important and the time elements are not. Today there are many versions of both oldstyle and modern typefaces. Each designer, although keeping the main character-

---

An Introduction to Type

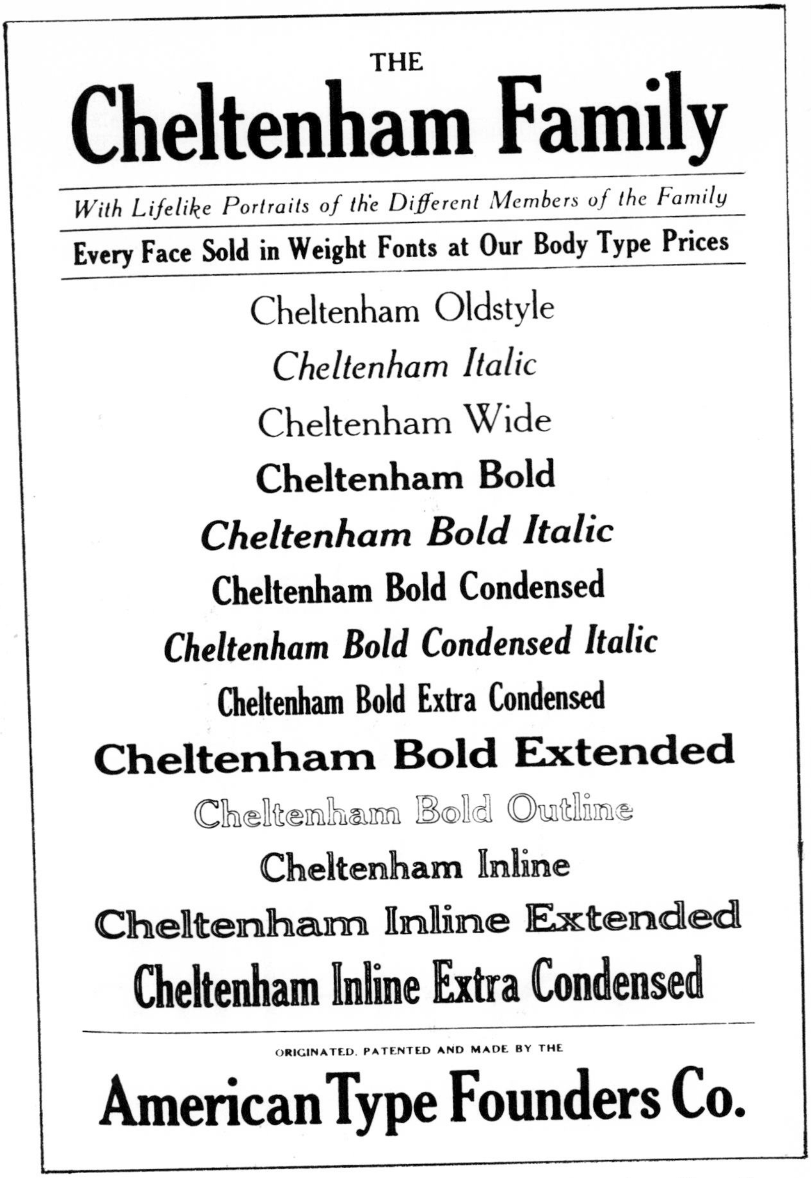

Figure 12–2. The Cheltenham family. [*Courtesy American Type Founders Co., Inc.*]

istics, creates slight differences in his typefaces to make them unique.

Oldstyle Types   Oldstyle type is considered a warm and friendly face and is often employed where large masses of type must be used, such as in books or newspapers. The following characteristics help to identify oldstyle types:

1. It has the appearance of being drawn with a broad-nibbed pen. The effect of using such a pen is the creation of variations

in the widths of most letters. Therefore letters have both thick and thin elements. But the identifying device differentiating oldstyle from modern is a gradual transition from the thin to thick elements of each letter. These gradual transitions can be created by drawing with the broad-nibbed pen. Figure 12–3 shows these transitions and how they were created.

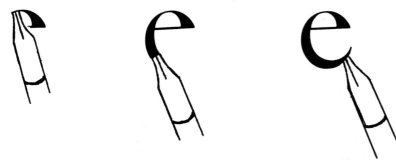

Figure 12–3. Thick and thin elements of a letter are caused by drawing with a broad-nibbed pen held at a certain angle. Type designers simply retain the thick and thin characteristics in their versions of oldstyle typefaces.

2. A serif is a horizontal line that appears at the top and bottom of most letters. Exceptions are a, c, e, g, o, t and capitals O and Q. All serifs on oldstyle types have brackets, a small curve connecting the serif to the main portion of a letter. Again the reason for such brackets is to make the transition from one element to the other gradual. Arrows point to brackets in Figure 12–4.

Figure 12–4. Various oldstyle serifs. Arrows point to brackets.

3. The weights of letters usually are distributed unevenly so they are not in the center. The thickest portion of each letter is near the bottom rather than the center. There are some exceptions to this principle but not many. The dotted lines in Figure 12–5 represent the thickest portion of the curves.

Figure 12–5. Curved letters showing uneven distribution of weights in oldstyle types.

4. Slanting serifs precede letters such as d, h, i, n, p, q and r. The slants occur at the top only. They are indicated by dotted lines in Figure 12–6.

Figure 12–6.

5. When oldstyle types are printed en masse, such as on book pages, they have a rich, mellow appearance. No single characteristic makes one letter stand out from the others. Although any one letter may have irregular contours, when printed en masse the irregularities tend to disappear. Oldstyle type, therefore, is easy to read because it is not fatiguing. Sharp, noticeable contours, such as on modern type, often bring about reader fatigue. Note the appearance of the mass of oldstyle letters in Figure 12–7.

Simplicity is a very important feature in typography, because it produces the direct appeal. It is this element of simplicity, which makes for easier reading as well as better comprehension, that the intelligent businessman seldom fails to praise, and the absence of which he seldom fails to notice and condemn. And, moreover, it is the kind of printing that is more profitable to produce from a mechanical standpoint. On the general run of work there

Figure 12–7. Sample of oldstyle type.

Modern Type

Modern type, first designed near the end of the eighteenth century, is identified by the following characteristics:

1. The thin parts of letters are very thin and there is great contrast between thick and thin elements (see Figure 12–8).

A B C

Figure 12–8. Modern type showing contrast between thick and thin elements.

2. The serifs are unbracketed (or have no curves at the bottom). Thus the thick element of the letter abruptly joins the thin serifs (see Figure 12–9).

The Art of Editing

klmn

Figure 12–9. There are no brackets on serifs of modern type.

3. The top serifs of letters such as r, n, h, i, b, d, j, k, l, m, n, q, v, u, w and x are horizontal and very thin (see Figure 12–10).

Figure 12–10. Top serifs of modern type tend to be flat.

4. The widest portion of curved letters is vertical in modern types and it is not slanted as in oldstyle (see Figure 12–11).

o p

Figure 12–11. Verticalness of wide portion of letters in modern typefaces.

5. There is an abrupt transition from the thick to thin elements in modern typefaces in contrast to the more gradual transition in oldstyle types (see Figure 12–12).

Education

Figure 12–12. Abrupt transition from thick to thin elements of letters in modern type.

6. Modern types tend to have a business-like, cold, precise connotation. They are best printed on coated papers such as enamel and usually require more space between lines than do oldstyle types. At times, modern typefaces may be fatiguing to read because of their precise appearance. Figure 12–13 shows a paragraph of modern type.

Simplicity is a very important feature in typography, because it produces the direct appeal. It is this element of simplicity, which makes for easier reading as well as better comprehension, that the intelligent businessman seldom fails to praise, and the absence of which he seldom fails to notice and condemn. And, moreover, it is the kind of printing that is more profitable to produce from a mechanical standpoint. On the gen-

Figure 12–13. A sample of modern typeface: Bodoni Light. Contrast this sample with the oldstyle type shown in Figure 12–7.

Transitional Typefaces Are Usually Called Modern

In the world of type design one may occasionally find faces having both oldstyle and modern characteristics. Sometimes these typefaces are labeled as *traditional,* but most often they are simply called modern. Transitional typefaces were created between the eras of oldstyle and modern. Because the characteristics of transitional faces tend to be a combination of both oldstyle and modern, and because there are so few faces that fall into this classification, there is no need to identify type by the term *transitional* (see Figure 12–14).

ABCDEFGHIJKLMNOPQRSTUVWXYZ
abcdefghijklmnopqrstuvwxyz

Figure 12–14. Baskerville type, a traditional face.

Classification of Type by More Definitive Style Characteristics

Roman Type

Although it helps to know the differences between oldstyle and modern typefaces, these differences are not enough to identify and/or specify type for printers. A more discriminating classification divides type into broad classifications termed roman, italic, text, sans serif, script, cursive and square serif. This method of classification has sometimes been called the *race* of a type. Thus roman types might have been created in Rome and italic types created in Italy. But it is better to think of these classifications as simply style characteristics that help in differentiating and identifying typefaces. Roman type is best identified by other characteristics. It has a vertical shape; it has serifs; it usually has combinations of thick and thin elements in each letter (called stem and hairlines, respectively) (see Figure 12–15). Some type experts consider all vertically shaped letters to be roman, even those without serifs or with no variations in the widths of letter elements (stem and hairline). This form of classification, therefore, may be confusing to the beginner because a roman type will have two purposes: one to distinguish it from sans serifs and the other to distinguish it

BCDEFGHIJKLMNOP
RSTUVWXYZ abcde

Figure 12–15. Roman typeface.

from italics. For simplicity's sake, it is best to use the classification as first described.

Italic types are characterized by their slanted letter shapes. Although italic types were originally designed to make it possible to print many letters in relatively little space, their use today is limited to citations or words that must be emphasized. They also are used in headlines and body types. Today, italic types are designed to accompany roman types, so that there is consistency in the family of design. Figure 12–16 shows a roman and an italic type of the same family.

Italic Type

ABCDEFGHIJKLMNO pqrstuvwxyz
ABCDEFGHIJKLMNO pqrstuvwxyz

Figure 12–16. Roman and italic faces of the Bodoni Bold family.

In America, printers use two terms to identify typefaces having no serifs. One is *sans serif;* the other is *Gothic.* The term *sans serif* comes from the French word *sans,* meaning "without," or *without* serifs. The other term, *Gothic,* is a misnomer. Originally Gothic type meant the churchy-looking types Americans often called "Old English." But today printers use the term *Gothic* also to refer to serifless type.

Sans Serifs (or Gothic) Types

Sans serif typefaces are made in many variations, some of whose differences are hardly discernible except to the trained eye. Figure 12–17 shows a small sample of these sans serif variations available to the editor for body type or headline purposes.

Text type is often incorrectly called Gothic because it looks like the Gothic architecture of the middle ages. But printers call it text because it appears to have a texture, like cloth, when printed in large masses. These letters were originally drawn with a broad-nibbed pen and were created to show a minimum of curves. Today the type is used for church printing or where a conservative headline is needed. Students should never have text set in all-capital letters for two reasons: (1) It was never drawn that way originally, having always utilized capital and lower case letters; (2) it is difficult to read when set all in capital letters (see Figures 12–18 and 12–19).

Text Type

Grotesque Bold

LINING GOTHIC CONDENSED NO. 3*

Lightline Gothic

LIGHTLINE TITLE GOTHIC

News Gothic

Poster

POSTER GOTHIC

RAILROAD GOTHIC

Figure 12–17. A small sample of sans serif variations.

𝕳𝕬𝕽𝕯 𝕿𝕺 𝕽𝕰𝕬𝕯

Figure 12–18. Cloister Text set in all-capital letters.

𝕰𝖆𝖘𝖎𝖊𝖗 𝖙𝖔 𝖗𝖊𝖆𝖉

Figure 12–19. Cloister Text set in capital and lower-case letters.

Script Type   Script-style letters resemble handwriting. Although the type
designers have tried to make it appear as if all the letters are
joined, small spaces can be seen between each letter. Some
script letters appear to have been written with a brush, whereas
others look as if they were drawn with a calligraphic pen. Script
type, too, should never be prepared in all-capital letters because
it is hard to read in that form (see Figures 12–20 and 12–21).

HARD TO READ

Figure 12–20. Brush script type set in all capitals.

Easier to read

Figure 12–21. Brush script set in capital and lower-case letters.

Cursive type styles are characterized by their ornateness. Although they look much like script typefaces, they are easily differentiated from script because of the amount of space between letters. Script typefaces have little space between letters. Cursives are used mostly in advertising but occasionally are used for compartmentalized headlines on the women's page (see Figure 12–22).

Cursive Types

Raleigh Cursive

ABCDEFGHIJKLMNOPQ
abcdefghijklmnopqrstuvwxyzabcdefghi 12345

Lydian Cursive

ABCDEFGHIJKLMNOPQRST
abcdefghijklmnopqrstuvwxyz 12345

Mayfair Cursive

ABCDEFGHIJKLMNOPST
abcdefghijklmnopqrstuvwxyzabcdefg 12345

Figure 12–22. Three different kinds of cursives.

Square serif type is similar to sans serif except that it has square serifs, and no brackets. Occasionally it may be called slab-serifs. There are no thick and thin elements to any parts of letters. It is a bold-looking typeface and is limited to occasional headline use. Very few newspapers use square serif types for regular headlines; it is most often used in advertising. Some varieties of square serifs are shown in Figure 12–23.

Square Serif Types

Karnak Medium

ABCDEFGHIJKLMNOPQR
abcdefghijklmnopqr 12345

Girder Heavy

ABCDEFGHIJKLMNOPTW
abcdefghijklmnopqrs 12345

Stymie Bold

ABCDEFGHIJKLMNOW
abcdefghijklmnop 12345

Figure 12–23. Three varieties of square serif types.

Type May Be Classified by Letter Widths

Most typefaces are manufactured in normal (or regular) widths. Regular widths comprise the greatest amount of reading matter. But wide and narrow type also is available. Type manufacturers have created extracondensed, condensed, expanded and extended typefaces in addition to regular. These extra widths, however, are not manufactured in all type sizes or families. Therefore, it is necessary to check with the printer to see whether he carries the width desired or whether it is manufactured (see Figure 12–24).

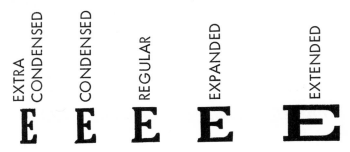

Figure 12–24. Variations in letter widths.

Type Classification by Weights

Type may be classified by the weight of the letter. Most typefaces are manufactured in lightface and boldface. Some faces are manufactured in medium, demibold heavy and ultrabold as well. The terminology here tends to be confusing. One manufacturer titles his medium-weight type demibold, whereas another calls his medium. The terms *heavy, bold* or *black* also may mean the same thing. Figure 12–25 shows common examples of type weights.

Type Differentiated by Method of Production

Type may also be differentiated on the basis of the mechanical method by which it is composed or by the manufacturer. Occasionally, a manufacturer designs a typeface that, although it uses a common family name, is different from all others. For example, Caslon is a typeface designed by many manufacturers. The Caslon manufactured by the American Type Founders may be different from that manufactured by the Ludlow Company, the Bauer Type Founders or the Merganthaler Linotype Company. If the user wants such a special typeface, he must specify which kind of Caslon he wants and identify the manufacturer. Newspaper editors usually do not require such precise choices of typefaces and therefore do not need to specify the company or method of production.

Other Ways To Differentiate Type

The following discussion concerns other facts about typefaces that should be known by persons who want to use type intelligently. These facts serve as means of further differentiating type.

A *font* is a printer's term for an assembly of letters of the alphabet purchased from the type manufacturer. The font

Bauer Beton Light

Bauer Beton Medium

Futura Demibold

Bauer Beton Bold

BERNHARD GOTHIC HEAVY

Bernhard Gothic Extra Heavy

Bauer Beton Extra Bold

Futura Ultrabold

Figure 12–25. Various weights of typefaces.

specifically refers to type of one family and one size. It includes enough capital and lower case letters to enable the printer to set sentences.

Small Capitals

Occasionally an editor may want a special-sized capital letter included in a subhead or in the text that is smaller than normal capital letters. These smaller letters are called *small capitals* and their unique characteristic, other than being small, is that they can be composed on typesetting machines without elaborate preparations. Small capitals are often used when special emphasis is needed, usually for a man's name or the titles of books. Many kinds of typefaces used for newspaper work come ready to cast small capitals with almost no special effort (see Figure 12–26).

FOURTEEN POINT WEISS ROMAN

Figure 12–26. Capitals and small capitals.

Ligatures

Ligatures are two or three letters manufactured on one piece of type. This practice started in the early days of printing and has been continued to this day, but for a different reason. In certain fonts of type, the letter "f" overhangs the letters "i," "l" or "f" and interferes with the way they print on paper. The overhang is called the *kern* of a letter (see Figure 12–27).

Figure 12–27. The kern of a letter "f" interferes with the "i."

When the kern of an "f" was forced together with the dot of an "i" or an "l" or another "f," the overhang would break. For that reason type manufacturers created ligatures, or single pieces of type on which two or three of the letter combinations were cast (see Figure 12–28).

fi ff ffi fl ffl

Figure 12–28. The five ligatures usually available in type.

When the manufacturers of high-speed line-casting machines faced this problem, they created a special letter "f" having no overhang. Nevertheless, the ligatures were still available to be used in the setting of newspaper and book reading material, and so to this day they may be used, depending on the whims of the operator. They are unnecessary except in type being set by hand. Figure 12–29 shows a word using the ligature "ff."

Effective

Figure 12–29. Use of a ligature in a word.

How To Measure Type from the Printed Page

When type is measured by laying a ruler on a letter cast in metal, there is no problem in discerning its size. Because most users of type do not have easy access to metal type, they must be able to measure type as it is printed on a type page or type specimen book. Although most such books indicate the sizes of all types shown, it is still important to know how type is measured.

A difficulty arises in measuring printed letters because it is difficult to determine where the bottom of each letter is located. Underneath each letter on a metal piece of type is a space called the *shoulder*. Shoulder space is created to allow room for the descenders of letters, such as g, p, q and y. Specifically, the problem is to estimate correctly how much space should be allowed for the shoulder when there are no descending letters in a line of printed type (see Figure 12–30).

PROFITS

Figure 12–30. This word is difficult to measure because there is no way to estimate the depth of the shoulder precisely.

To dramatize and explain this problem, Figure 12–31 shows imaginary lines by which letters are created on type. These lines are called (1) base line, on which all letters other than g, p, q and y rest; (2) cap line, to which most capital letters and tall letters rise; (3) lower-case line, where small letters align (called the "x" height of letters); and (4) descender line. Each line helps in aligning letters.

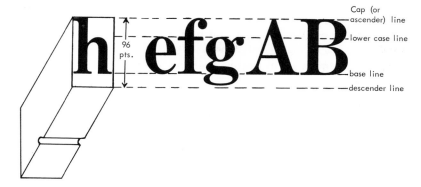

Figure 12–31. Drawing of a piece of type and imaginary lines that serve to align letters.

In measuring the letter "h" it is necessary to allow room for the shoulder underneath the letter. The ascenders rise above the lower-case line and the descenders appear below the base line. Thus, when one wants to measure type from a printed page, he must allow space for the descenders. He can accurately determine ascender space by looking for a capital letter or one with an ascender. If it were necessary to measure the point size of a line of capital letters it would be necessary to take the space normally used for descenders into consideration in order to have an accurate measurement (see Figures 12–32 and 12–33).

Figure 12–32. This word can be measured accurately by drawing a line across the ascender (the "d") and another line across the descenders ("q" and "p") and measuring the distance between the two lines.

Figure 12–33. Why type is so difficult to measure. All of these capital "E's" are 48 points in height, but each has a different size shoulder.

One of the best ways to learn how to select and use type effectively is to develop a sense of what looks right. The first step in developing this sense is to learn to differentiate typefaces easily. Once this differentiation has been learned, some simple fundamentals of type use plus artistic principles will help the beginner use discrimination in selection.

How To Select and Use Type Effectively

An Introduction to Type

For many years printers learned rules for selecting and using type. Now many of these rules have been rejected in favor of a common sense approach to what looks right in print.

For example, the old rule was never to mix oldstyle and modern typefaces. But today they may be mixed if the contrast between them is not too strong and if an unequal amount of each is used.

If a headline is set in Futura Bold (a modern typeface) and the paragraphs of an editorial are set in Caslon (an oldstyle face) the result may be pleasant. The decision to combine the two depends, however, on the knowledge that contrast in print is desirable, but it can be neither too weak nor too strong. The following principles of typography and artistic design are presented as guideposts for developing a sense of what looks right.

The Objectives of Good Typography

The foremost objective of good typography is to select legible typefaces; they are easy to read and enable a person to read faster than he could with less legible faces. Furthermore, legible faces encourage the reader to read more of what has been printed simply because they present fewer obstacles to reading.

Which typefaces are the most legible? The answer is that almost all faces manufactured exclusively for use as body type in books, magazines and newspapers are legible. But display types (18 point and larger) may or may not be legible, especially when set in long lines. In advertising, some unusual typeface may be used in a headline of one or two words. Because there may be much white space around the headline, it may not seem too illegible. But if that same typeface were to be used in a newspaper headline, it might be difficult to read. The amount of white space surrounding type affects legibility.

But the most significant difference between types that are legible and illegible has more to do with whether readers are familiar with them. Familiar typefaces, or those in most common use, tend to be read the easiest. When unusual typefaces that are ornate or grotesque are used, readers stop to look at the uniqueness of the letter shapes and this process slows reading. Figures 12–34 and 12–35 show examples of illegible and legible typefaces.

EDUCATION

Figure 12–34. Illegible, especially if set in lines, because it calls attention to its odd shape. It is an uncommon face.

Education

Figure 12–35. Legible, because it contains gentle transitions from thick to thin elements, because it does not call attention to its design, and because it is used so often that readers are familiar with it.

To achieve legibility through selection and use of typefaces, one ought to choose types most familiar to readers. If there is a need to select a typeface that readers may not find familiar, it is possible to use it if extra space surrounds it. White space has the effect of giving the reader more time to absorb the details of unusually shaped letters. If space is limited, however, it is always better to select the more common typefaces so that additional white space need not be used.

The principle of using white space to increase legibility of type accounts for the fact that type appearing in all-capital letters is read about 12 per cent slower than the same words appearing in capitals and lower case letters. There is simply more white space surrounding a line of lower case letters than a line of capitals. Another reason lower case letters are read faster than all-capitals is that it is easier to determine the shape of the word.

In addition to the general use of white space, however, legibility is also controlled by the arrangement of letters, spacing between words, spacing between lines and widths of lines. Each manner of control should be considered separately, and afterwards they should be considered in total. Here are some guidelines for each:

ARRANGEMENT OF LETTERS AND WORDS. Any style of arrangement that calls attention to itself and not the message is poor. Therefore, common arrangements are best. Flush left headlines are in common use and are interesting, yet easy to read. But if the letters should be set vertically, they would be difficult to read (see Figures 12–36 and 12–37).

All Plans Complete
For Victory Meeting

Figure 12–36. A flush-left headline. It is easy to read because it is one style often seen in newspapers.

Figure 12–37. Difficult to read. Type set like this is rarely seen. The arrangement calls attention to itself; not to the message. Also, each letter must be read separately, and then combined into words.

WORD SPACING. Narrow word spacing is always to be preferred to wide word spacing because readers do not read one
word at a time, but groups of words. Narrow word spacing
makes it possible to glance at a group of words at one time,
quickly.

LINE SPACING. The research on line spacing is indeterminate. Yet there is a feeling that lines with generous space
between them are easier to read than those tightly spaced.
Obviously, there is a point where too much space between lines
becomes unsightly. Figures 12–38 and 12–39 show examples of
various kinds of line spacing.

Heat Wave Hits Cities Near Coast

Figure 12–38. It is obvious that more spacing between lines is needed.

Heat Wave

Hits Cities

Near Coast

Figure 12–39. Words are easier to read with generous spacing between
them.

WIDTH OF LINE. Although various formulas can be used to
determine how long a line of type can become before it becomes
difficult to read, the width can also be determined in other ways.
One of the best ways is to examine a line of type as it appears in
a catalog of typefaces. Judgment based on experience can be
used to determine the point at which the typeface begins to be
difficult to read. Another consideration is that longer widths can
be used if more space is placed between the lines. The extra
white space between the lines helps the reader keep his place
and move to each succeeding line easily. Any extremes in
width, however, should be avoided. Extremely short or wide lines
are difficult to read.

READER FATIGUE. A final dimension of legibility is the
degree to which a typeface tires the reader's eyes. Unfortunately,
this is an area where there is no research and a great deal of
opinion. Common sense, however, indicates that boring typefaces (because they have no thick or thin variations in letters)
tend to be fatiguing. Therefore, all sans serif typefaces tend to

be fatiguing. Also, unusually light or very bold typefaces also tend to be tiring page after page.

A second objective of good type selection and use is to seek aesthetically pleasing typefaces. Of the thousands of existing typefaces, some are more beautiful than others. The most beautiful ones are those in prominent use. Occasionally new faces are introduced that do not find wide acceptance immediately, and these should be sought for and used despite their seeming unpopularity.

An important objective of good typography is that of selecting typefaces that harmonize with the message content. Some faces are more appropriate than others for general headlines, editorials, captions under cartoons or advertising. The connotation of typefaces, therefore, is important. Connotation of type represents the feeling that it engenders. For example, type with a very black look connotes strength, as does large type. A lightface italic, on the other hand, connotes daintiness (see Figure 12–40).

Elegance

Clearcut Initial—French Script

MODERNISM

Kabel Light

DIGNITY

Forum

UNUSUALNESS

Newfangle

Antiquity

Satanick

NATURE

Sylvan

Sincerity

Baskerville

STRENGTH

John Hancock

Distinctiveness

Civilité

CHEAPNESS

Mid-Gothic

Figure 12–40. Connotations of various typefaces. [*Courtesy of International Typographical Union.*]

WIDTH OF LETTERS. In a previous discussion, attention was directed to the variations in the shoulder space of different typefaces. Figures 12–33 showed that, although each of the letters was a 48-point typeface, there were significant and observable differences in the space underneath each letter. Now attention is called to the variations in the widths of letters. Figure 12–41 shows different 36-point typefaces. Although each is 36-point size, there are differences in widths. The only way to

Other Considerations in Selecting and Using Type

AEMNPQRSWT adegiory

Caslon Bold

AEMNPQRSWT adegiory

Stymie Bold

AEMNPQRSWT adegiory

Bodoni Bold

Figure 12–41. A comparison of various 36-point typefaces. Note variations in widths of letters.

know and appreciate these differences is to study type catalogs, where samples of different faces are printed. If the reader is aware of the differences in the widths of letters, he can choose the typeface that best meets his needs.

SELECTION OF "BODY" TYPES. Body types are used for the major part of the reading matter in newspapers. They are usually composed in sizes ranging from 7 point to 14 point. The selection of body types requires an additional consideration beyond those already mentioned: the appearance of the type in large masses. Some typographers call this appearance the "coloring" of a printed page, even though the page is printed in black print on white paper. Some types have a distinctly black appearance when they appear in large masses, whereas others have a very gray appearance. Others have what might be called a pleasant tone. Although ten different samples of body type are shown in Figures 12–42, there are obvious differences in the mass appearance of these types. One reason for the differences is the weight of the letters themselves, and the other is the amount of white space between lines. The beginner should notice that the amount of space between the lines appears to vary between samples even though standard 2-point leading has been used in each. The significance of the line space variations is that different typefaces have shoulder spaces of different sizes, which accounts for the differences in spaces between lines. It is almost impossible to know how a given typeface will appear en masse unless a sample is examined first.

Tips on Using Type

1. Italics and boldface should not be set in the same line with roman typefaces. There are two reasons: (a) There will be too much contrast in the line; (b) the compositor only has one variation of roman in his Linotype matrices. Either he can set roman and boldface or roman and italic. He cannot set all three without special time-consuming effort.

2. Type should not be set in very short or very long measures. Both are difficult to read. A rule of thumb that will help the beginner make such decisions is to use the width of $1\frac{1}{2}$ alphabet

The Art of Editing

BASKERVILLE, 12 pt.   2 pt. leaded..2.3 characters to 1 pica

Simplicity is a very important feature in typography, because it produces the direct appeal. It is this element of simplicity, which makes for easier reading as well as better comprehension, that the intelligent businessman seldom fails to praise, and the absence of which he seldom fails to notice and condemn. And, moreover, it is the

BODONI LIGHT, 12 pt.   2 pt. leaded..2.2 characters to 1 pica

Simplicity is a very important feature in typography, because it produces the direct appeal. It is this element of simplicity, which makes for easier reading as well as better comprehension, that the intelligent businessman seldom fails to praise, and the absence of which he seldom fails to notice and condemn. And, moreover, it is the

BOOKMAN, 12 pt.   2 pt. leaded..2.2 characters to 1 pica

Simplicity is a very important feature in typography, because it produces the direct appeal. It is this element of simplicity, which makes for easier reading as well as better comprehension, that the intelligent businessman seldom fails to praise, and the absence of which he seldom fails to notice and condemn. And, more-

CENTURY SCHOOLBOOK, 12 pt.   2 pt. leaded..2.1 characters to 1 pica

Simplicity is a very important feature in typography, because it produces the direct appeal. It is this element of simplicity, which makes for easier reading as well as better comprehension, that the intelligent businessman seldom fails to praise, and the absence of which he seldom fails to notice and con-

GARAMONT, 12 pt.   2 pt. leaded..2.2 characters to 1pica

Simplicity is a very important feature in typography, because it produces the direct appeal. It is this element of simplicity, which makes for easier reading as well as better comprehension, that the intelligent businessman seldom fails to praise, and the absence of which he seldom fails to notice and condemn. And,

KENNERLY, 12 pt.   2 pt. leaded..2.4 characters to 1 pica

Simplicity is a very important feature in typography, because it produces the direct appeal. It is this element of simplicity, which makes for easier reading as well as better comprehension, that the intelligent businessman seldom fails to praise, and the absence of which he seldom fails to notice and condemn. And, moreover, it is the kind of printing

SANS SERIF LIGHT, 12 pt.   2 pt. leaded..2.5 characters to 1 pica

Simplicity is a very important feature in typography, because it produces the direct appeal. It is this element of simplicity, which makes for easier reading as well as better comprehension, that the intelligent businessman seldom fails to praise, and the absence of which he seldom fails to notice and condemn. And, moreover, it is the kind of printing

STYMIE MEDIUM, 12 pt.   2 pt. leaded..2.2 characters to 1 pica

Simplicity is a very important feature in typography. It is this element of simplicity, which makes for easier reading as well as better comprehension, that the intelligent businessman seldom fails to praise, and the absence of which he seldom fails to notice and con-

TIMES NEW ROMAN, 12 pt.   2 pt. leaded..2.3 characters to 1 pica

Simplicity is a very important feature in typography, because it produces the direct appeal. It is this element of simplicity, which makes for easier reading as well as better comprehension, that the intelligent businessman seldom fails to praise, and the absence of which he seldom fails to notice and condemn. And, moreover, it

20th CENTURY MEDIUM, 12 pt.   2 pt. leaded..2.4 characters to 1 pica

Simplicity is a very important feature in typography, because it produces the direct appeal. It is this element of simplicity, which makes for easier reading as well as better comprehension, that the intelligent businessman seldom fails to praise, and the absence of which he seldom fails to notice and condemn. And, moreover, it is the

Figure 12–42. Twelve point typeface samples. Note mass appearance of variations in weights and widths of letters.

lengths as a guide. This requires that the user first either have alphabets (lower case) set to the required width or find a sample in a type book and then measure the width. Slight variations in this measured width will not matter.

3. Type rarely should be set in measures longer than 30 picas wide. Relatively few Linotypes can set longer lines. When it

becomes necessary to do so, such lines are set in two smaller sections and butted together to give the appearance of a single line. This technique may be unsightly because it will be difficult to avoid a streak of white space (called a river) appearing where the abutment takes place.

4. For headlines, too many different sizes or faces should be avoided on the same page. The best technique is to use mono-typographic harmony, meaning harmony based on the use of a single type family. But, when many different sizes or variations of the same family are used, the effect is unharmonious.

5. Agate ($5\frac{1}{2}$-point) type is used exclusively for box scores of athletic games and long lists of names (such as in a graduating class). But this type size should never be used for the main text of a story. Because of its size, it is compact and saves space, but it is always a supplement to the main body of reading matter.

6. The beginner should watch for unusual and unsightly spacing between letters of a word set in large type. This usually occurs when setting combinations of any of the following capital letters: A, L, P, T, V and W. For example, A and V have more white space between them (AV) than do N and I (NI), or other similar combinations. When any of the above letters is used in combination in large headline, the printer should be asked to cut the type in such a way as to eliminate the unsightly space. He may be willing to do so if time is available.

7. A change of pace in typefaces for headlines is attractive if it is not overdone. This means that an italic or an ultraboldface headline may be used on a page that has predominantly roman typeface headlines. When more than one such variation is used, the contrasting effect is lost.

8. Contrast is a key to beautiful typography. But the contrast should be relatively strong. When headline typefaces are used that are different, but not radically so, the mixture on a page will appear to be "a wrong font," rather than a contrasting headline.

The competent editor should know and understand how to select and use type, though the opportunity to use this knowledge may be limited, especially in smaller newspapers. Yet even within the limited number of typefaces or sizes available in any plant, there are often many alternative types that could be used. Under any circumstances, if the editor makes a poor choice of type, he may detract from the appearance of a page and make it hard to read. Therefore, he should be able to translate words into type forms to maximize communication on a page, other things being equal. It is obvious that "the other things being equal" refers to well-written and edited copy. Good type selection is no substitute for poor writing and editing, because type is the vehicle for words, not the message.

The best way to understand type is to be able to differentiate the many kinds of existing type. Unless the slight variations in letters shapes are known, one typeface may appear as good as another. Once the differences in typefaces have been learned, however, the editor can develop an aesthetic sense, or taste, of what looks attractive in print, based on some elementary artistic principles.

Developing a sense of artistic judgment in type is best done by studying type in print, no matter where it appears. For example, beautifully set type often appears in a magazine, a book or a financial report. If the editor works at developing a sensitivity for what looks good in print, he will be alert to spot such printing. Then he will make a mental note of the way type was set or why it looks so good and eventually will use this idea, by adjusting it to the newspaper environment, if it is at all possible. In this manner the editor uses type to aid communication.

How Type is Set

Type consists of letters of the alphabet (either on metal, film or acetate) that, when assembled into lines and sentences, can be used for printing purposes. The assembling of type is called *composing* or *setting* (the more common word).

Today, most type may be classified as either *hot* or *cold*. Hot type is simply type cast in metal form. The term *hot* comes from the fact that metal must be heated to about 550 degrees Fahrenheit in order to pour it into the letter-shaped molds. Cold type gets its name from the fact that no metal is used in the setting process. It is done either photographically or by simple pressure transfer processes.

Hot-Type Methods of Typesetting

The most widely used methods of setting hot type are known as Linotype, Monotype and Ludlow. Linotype, Ludlow and Monotype are trade names as well as generic product names.

LINOTYPE. Two companies manufacture automatic line-casting machines—Merganthaler Linotype Company and Intertype Company. The operating principles of both machines are identical. A line-casting machine is really three machines combined into one operation: (1) an assembling machine for gathering molds (called matrices) into lines of type; (2) a casting machine for pouring hot metal into the molds and forming the line of type; and (3) a distribution machine for distributing the matrices of each letter back into their proper storage places.

For each letter of the alphabet there are matrices stored in a metal container called a *magazine*. When the operator presses a letter key, the matrix drops into a gathering device and is kept there until a line of matrices has been assembled. When the operator presses a lever, the entire line of matrices is moved into casting position, where hot metal is forced into the crevices in the matrices, forming the line of letters (Figure 12–43).

The hot line is then pushed out to cool, while the matrices of letters are carried back to the magazine to be used for other lines of type. The line of type is typically called a *slug* or *linotype slug* (Figure 12–44).

LINE-CASTING MACHINES WITH TELETYPESETTER SYSTEM. Many newspapers have installed high-speed aux-

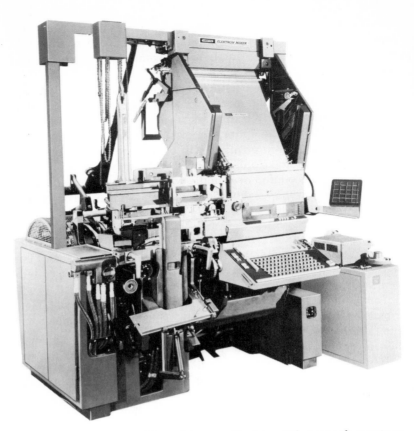

Figure 12–43. Elektron Mixer Linotype Machine. [*Photograph courtesy of the Mergenthaler Linotype Company.*]

Figure 12–44. Linotype slugs. [*Photograph courtesy of the Mergenthaler Linotype Company.*]

iliary machines in their plants to be operated in conjunction with a line-casting machine. The technique consists of two machines, which when used with a line-casting machine enables the operator to set as many as 13 to 14 lines a minute compared to the 6 or 7 lines a minute an efficient operator can set. Though the technique consists of two separate steps, it is still faster than manually set operations.

Essentially, the TTS system consists of an operator pressing keys on a perforator unit in which holes representing each letter are punched in a tape. When the tape is finished, it is placed in an operating unit attached to the side of a line-casting machine. The holes activate the keys of the line-caster and operate it at high speeds. The operation of the line-caster is the same as it would be if the machine were operated manually (see Figures 12–45 and 12–46).

Figure 12–45. Fairchild keyboard unit of a tape perforator. [*Photo courtesy of the Fairchild Graphic Equipment Company.*]

MONOTYPE. The Monotype machine also consists of two units: a tape puncher and a casting unit. But there are significant differences between the Monotype and the TTS system. The first difference is that Monotype is used primarily for setting large headlines or display type in advertisements, while tele-

Figure 12–46. Operating unit attached to a keyboard of a Comet Linotype machine. [*Photograph courtesy of Merganthaler Linotype Co.*]

typesetters are used mostly for setting body types. Relatively few newspapers have monotype equipment, although some large magazines not only have the equipment to set headlines, but body type as well.

The second difference is the manner in which each produces type. The Monotype caster produces individual letters cast from molds of each letter, while the Teletypesetter system, working in conjunction with a line-casting machine, produces single lines of type, one at a time.

The technique of setting type on the Monotype starts, however, in the same manner as that of setting type with a Teletypesetter. In both techniques, a tape is punched on a perforating keyboard, but the tape is about three inches wide compared to the TTS's one-inch-wide tape. The caster is specially made for the tape of a Monotype and will not accept any other. Because Monotype casters produce individual letters, much greater skill is required to handle them than Linotype slugs. For that reason, Monotype is used mostly for printed material where speed is not as urgent as it is in newspaper work. Newspapers rarely use Monotypes. On the other hand, books, magazines and advertising material are often set on this machine. Late-model units of a Monotype system and its type are shown in Figures 12–47, 12–48 and 12–49.

LUDLOW MACHINE. The Ludlow machine is a means of casting type from matrices that have been set by hand. The operator first assembles a line of matrices and then places them into a casting device that produces a slug. Ludlows are often used for setting large headline type because the Linotype machine will not set type larger than 36 point. Ludlow can produce type as large as 144 points. Ludlow slugs are often recognized by the fact that they have an overhang on each side of the base (see Figures 12–50 and 12–51).

Cold type generally refers to type set photographically. Many machines on the market set cold type. Some are used exclusively for body typefaces and others for headlines; some can set both. Basically, the technique of setting cold type consists of placing a negative of each letter in front of a source of light and exposing light through the negative onto light-sensitive paper. Each letter is thereby exposed in a line until an entire sentence and paragraph or more have been set. The light-sensitive paper is then developed and printed. In fact, the whole process resembles the process of taking pictures. The only difference is that in phototypesetting the letters are photographed at high speeds. Once the light-sensitive paper has been developed and printed photographically, it is ready to be converted into a metal printing plate (Figures 12–52 and 12–53).

Cold Typesetting Methods

Cold type is used primarily in newspaper operations where offset printing techniques are employed. In preparations for offset printing, columns of body type are set on photographic paper. Headlines may be set in a separate operation and later pasted at the top of appropriate columns of body type. A page is then assembled by pasting each column of photographic type in its proper position on a page until the entire page is complete. The completed page is photographed and converted into a film negative from which an offset printing plate is made.

Advertisements also may be set photographically. Because advertisements contain so many different kinds of type, they are often set in sections. All lines of a single kind of type such as Bodoni are set first. Then all lines of another kind of type are set. After each kind and size of type are set, they are cut apart and pasted into position on a sheet of paper. The advertising sheet is later pasted on a page with the necessary adjoining columns of

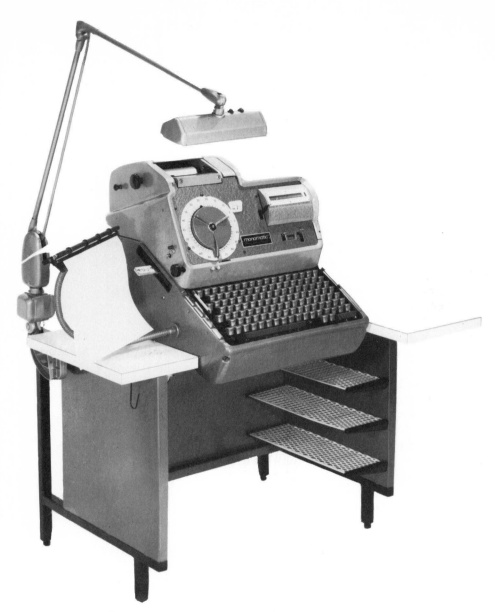

Figure 12–47. The Monotype "Monomatic II" keyboard perforator. [*Photograph courtesy of the Lanston Monotype Company.*]

body type until the entire page is complete. Then the page is ready for conversion to film and finally to offset plate form. Some cold typesetting machines are able to set the entire advertisement in one operation. Occasionally, a photoengraving can be made of these letters and they can be printed as most newspapers in this country print: by letterpress printing.

Other Means of It is worthwhile to mention that type is still set by hand.
Typesetting Letters are kept in compartments in a specially built case. The

Figure 12–48. "Monomatic II" caster. [*Photograph courtesy of Lanston Monotype Company.*]

typesetter picks up each piece of type and assembles words and sentences in a tray called a *composing stick*. When he is finished, he tightens the line (called justifying), removes it from the stick and ties the entire line so that it will not fall apart. Very large headlines are still being set this way and in some newspapers even smaller headlines and some captions are set in this manner.

COMPUTERIZED TYPESETTING. Computers have been adapted for use with both hot- and cold-typesetting machines. The computer, however, does not set type, but performs two major operations between the time words are typed on a tape-punching machine and the time that either metal or photo-

Figure 12–49. Monotype, showing that each letter is a separate piece of type. [*Photograph courtesy of the Lanston Monotype Company.*]

Figure 12–50. The Ludlow caster between two racks containing various kinds of typefaces in matrice form. [*Photograph courtesy of the Ludlow Typograph Company.*]

graphic composition is produced. The two operations are hyphenization and justification of lines.

When an operator normally sets type on a line-casting machine, he must stop at the end of each line and determine where to divide the last word, if it is too long to fit into the space allotted for the line. Or, if the operator chooses, he may decide not to hyphenate at all and place the last syllable on the next line in a complete word. This practice may take only a few seconds for

The Art of Editing

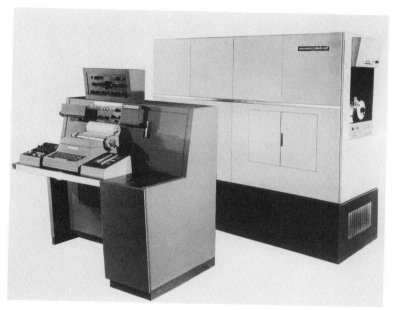

Figure 12–51. Ludlow slugs (top) cast from matrices assembled by a Ludlow composing stick (bottom). [*Photograph courtesy of the Ludlow Typograph Company.*]

Figure 12–52. Mergenthaler's Linofilm Phototypesetting machine. [*Photograph courtesy of the Mergenthaler Linotype Company.*]

each line, but multiplied by the many thousands of lines set in a single day or week, it can materially affect the volume of type set.

Justification also takes time of the operator on a line-casting machine. In this operation, space must be added or removed between the words so that letters extend to the very beginning and ends of that line. Justification makes it possible to have columns of type that align perfectly.

Computers perform both hyphenization and justification at high speeds. Therefore, the operator need not stop at the end of each line to perform either one or both tasks. He simply types the words of copy continuously and smoothly at maximum speeds. The output of a computer, then, is a punched tape that looks very much like TTS tape, in that it has holes punched in it representing letters of the alphabet set in hyphenated and justified lines. The punched tape is then fed into mechanisms that drive

Figure 12–53. Film grid for a font of type on the Linofilm machine. Light is projected through letters onto light-sensitive paper. [*Photograph courtesy of the Mergenthaler Linotype Company.*]

Figure 12–54. Transfer letters created by rubbing the top of a specially prepared letter-sheet (Trans-Artype). Letters transfer from large sheet to paper. [*Courtesy of the Artype Corporation.*]

either hot- or cold-typesetting machines, which in turn produce metal or photographic type.

TRANSFER AND PASTE-DOWN LETTERS. Occasionally an editor wants one line of type in a face the company does not own. Rather than buy this line from another typesetting company, he may buy a sheet of letters printed on acetate that can be transferred to another sheet by rubbing. The transfer sheets

Figure 12–55. A sheet containing paste-down letters called Artype. Each letter is cut from acetate sheet and is placed in position on paper. Letters hold to paper without glue. [*Courtesy of the Artype Corporation.*]

contain two or three alphabets of a given size and family of type, with some extra letters. The user simply aligns each letter over the paper on which he wants the letters to appear, rubs the back of the sheet and the letters are transferred from the acetate to the sheet.

Paste-down letters also come printed on a large sheet of paper with many letters on them. Here, however, the user cuts out each letter from the master sheet and affixes it on paper. An adhesive on the back of the letters makes them stick to paper without special effort (see Figures 12–54 and 12–55).

13

Fundamentals of Newspaper Design

When a newspaper editor arranges news, pictures and other stories on a page, he is, in effect, packaging his product. In fact, there is great similarity between editors' and manufacturers' packages. Both use the package as a convenient means of shipping contents to consumers and both use the package as a means of helping consumers use the product.

Packaging the News

An editor aids the reader when he arranges news content in an orderly and easy-to-read manner. Occasionally, news stories are so unusual or interesting that a reader will disregard poor design and suffer his way through the newspaper. But that doesn't occur every day. More often, most readers drop off after the front page until they encounter the next interesting section. An editor's goal in packaging is to help the reader read faster and read more of what has been written on all pages.

The package has another, less obvious, function than making the contents easy to read. When a manufacturer plans his label he places information about the contents in the form of a design that communicates through the appearance of the entire design as well as the words. This kind of communication may be thought of as the connotation of the design. Editors also may arrange the news so that the design resulting from his arrangement connotes something beyond the meaning of the words. Such connotations may range from a design telling the reader that a story is significant and serious to another design emphasizing a light-hearted, tongue-in-cheek approach (see Figures 13–1 and 13–2). Connotations of the newspaper's whole design may give the reader the feeling he is reading a conservative paper or one that is liberal, old-fashioned, or progressive. The editor, therefore, is concerned with the orderly arrangement of the news as well as with creating a page design with connotations that are appropriate to his philosophy of news presentation.

The term *design* may be used in three different ways in newspaper operations. *Design* may refer to the basic format of the entire newspaper. Since such a format is rarely changed, newsroom personnel are not allowed to tamper with it. It is not within the province of this book to discuss overall newspaper design, although some of the material within the next three chapters cover various aspects of it.

A second use of the term *design* refers to the structure or arrangement of news on an individual page. After a page has been made up, the arrangement represents a page design. Obviously the makeup man will try to keep each page's design consistent with the overall design of the entire newspaper.

A third use of the term is as a substitute and slightly different form of the term *makeup*. To design a page is to plan for, or conceive of, its total structure. To design a page differs from making up a page only in that there is more preplanning involved than there is in makeup.

In the following three chapters, discussion involves the latter two uses of the term.

At least two basic methods can be used to create a newspaper page design. One is a technique called makeup; the other is called the total design concept. Makeup consists of building a page, element by element, until all the space is used. Each page is sketched on a sheet of paper called a dummy by placing the most important elements at the top of the page, then placing less important stories next to or underneath the main story or picture, downward, until the space is filled. As the editor sketches the dummy, he can change the position of stories by simply erasing notations in one place and repositioning them in another place. When he has finished, the editor gives the dummy to the printer, who assembles the type for body copy, headlines and pictures (and advertisements, if any) using the dummy as a blueprint. When all the type has been assembled on a page, it is ready to be processed for the final printing of the newspaper.

A page dummy, when completed, represents a design. The concept of makeup, then, is that the sum of the parts equals a design. The term *design* means form, or structure, and the structure is not complete until the last bit of space on a page has been used. In many instances, the makeup editor has only a vague idea of how the design will eventually look. Because he is under the pressure of a deadline, he often assigns heads to stories and orders pictures without giving much thought to the final appearance of the page. Even if he has some idea of how the page should look after completing the dummy, the result may look quite different from what he planned, simply because, after placing the top stories on the page, he could not find stories of

Makeup Versus Design

[OVERLEAF—Figure 13–1 is on page 268 and Figure 13–2 is on page 269.]

Figure 13–1. Design emphasizes a significant story at top. [*Courtesy the Marion, Indiana, Chronicle-Tribune.*]

Figure 13–2. Design emphasizes a light-hearted story (upper right). [*Courtesy the Marion, Indiana, Chronicle-Tribune.*]

Legend opposes death penalty in Marion

The ghost of a Marion man dead for a century has loomed from the past in the wake of a death sentence ordered by a Grant County jury.

The long, involved — and mostly undocumented — story has been told for years in varying degrees in Marion, and has been resurrected in the past week since a Circuit Court jury convicted Charles Adams of murder and his execution was ordered for April 2.

Adams, a 24-year-old Huntington man, was charged with murder in Huntington County and the case was venued to the Grant County Court.

The jury's recommendation was unprecedented; never before had a Grant County jury sent anyone to his death — and that's the way the legend wants to keep it.

Martin Boots was one of the founders of Marion and 125 years ago he owned most of the land west of the Grant County Courthouse.

Exactly what his feelings about the death penalty were are pretty much speculation, but the legend goes like this:

Boots dedicated an acre of land at the top of what is now the Third Street hill to be used for a school.

But he supposedly tacked on the stipulation that in the event a death sentence were ever handed down, he'd take back his land — or, in the event of his death, it would revert back to his heirs.

The facts — such as they are — contradict the legend.

First, according to noted Grant County historian W. H. McGrew, Boots never dedicated the land for a school at all; in fact, the land — where Martin Boots and Horace Mann schools are now located — was set aside as the Boots family burial plot.

Boots died in 1845 and the intervening years are somewhat clouded, but eventually the graves of 26 members of the Boots family were moved to the IOOF Cemetery and the city obtained the two acres for $1 at a sheriff's auction.

Boots' will — lodged in the vast archives of the courthouse — has been studied at length by McGrew and he finds no such stipulation or indication that Boots had any idea of a

school to begin with — much less any intention of taking it back.

But regardless of w h a t Mr. Boots had in mind, there's still the "curse of White's hill" which believers say was put on the area by Boots when he and his family were tossed out to make room for the school. As a matter of record, two schools on the site have burne l down over the years.

Report Lodge may head Paris negotiating team

New York Times News Service

WASHINGTON — Usua... formed sources disclosed day that president - elect ard Nixon has asked Cabot Lodge, twice forme bassador to South Vietna serve as head of the Am negotiating team in Paris

The sources said that now American Ambassac West Germany, was eag take the job. They said Nixon is apparently delay nal action until the new tary of State has been and can be consulted appointment of a chief n tor.

The announced appoi of Lodge came only days the annual GOP governor ference where Nixon is uled to appear, presuma offer some cabinet positi members of that body.

the appointments which come this weekend are th retaries of interior, agric commerce and transporta

Nixon's apparent inten name Lodge was not con with any official in the Washington.

Congressional sources that Nixon had discusse negotiating job with Lo Key Biscayne, Fla., the end following the presi election.

Lodge, who was Nixon presidential running ma 1960, was the first foreign figure to confer with the dent - elect after the election.

Ambassador - at - La Averell Harriman, the c American negotiator whe istration, has made it p recent public remarks t has no intention of rer in the post under the N can administration.

Lodge, who is 66 year served as ambassador to Vietnam from Aug. 22 to June 23, 1964, and fron 20, 1965, to April 25, 1

In the latter period he very closely and dev warm personal relation then-Premier Nguyen Ca who, as vice president o Vietnam, has been nan supervise and control S negotiating team.

Although the Nixon st remained mum on the of selecting governors cabinet, there is consi speculation among the nors themselves.

Speculation within the has centered on Gov. W. Romney of Michigan possible Secretary of Con and Gov. John A. Vo Massachusetts as Secre Transportation. Both m known to be receptive ice in the Nixon cabine

There has also been sion of Gov. Tim M. B of Montana, who was c for re-election, as Secre either Interior or Agri Babcock was the earlies relatively small group publican governors who ed Nixon before the Go vention.

Spokesmen at the Nixon headquarters in York City have expresse whether the president will make any cabi nouncements before he east from California. B has not discouraged t the hopeful governors fr ticipation.

The Associated Press ed Lt. Gov. Robert F California has been men post in the Cabinet, pe as secretary of Health, tion and Welfare, and i ed to accept it.

(See COUNCIL on Page 2)

Urban League meeting

Quiz schoolmen on suspensions

By ED BREEN
C-T Assistant Managing Editor

A predominantly Negro audience fired a salvo of questions at a Marion school board member and two top school administrators in a meeting at the Greater Second Baptist Church Tuesday evening.

The meeting, sponsored by the Marion Urban League, was designed as a forum for questions from the Negro community about the aftermath a n d investigation of the Nov. 15 racial disturbance at Marion High School — located across 26th Street from the church.

The questions ranged from specific inquiries on suspension of 14 students after the disturbance to general questions about recruitment of Negro faculty members for the school.

But the most persistent and r e peated questions revolved around the student suspensions; how long will they remain on suspension, who will make the final decision, on what grounds were the suspensions made, will the students have an opportunity to make up the missed assignments, and how much authority is vested in the high school principal, Paul Waver.

Answering the questions were Supt. Bernard McKenzie, secondary education director Clark Folgate and school board member Dr. Joseph Casey.

Three central figures in the meeting: Waver, attendance officer Art Gross and dean of boys Virgil Kirkpatrick. All three have been the targets of charges from the disturbed Negroes.

In a letter to the school board Urban League Director Henry Curry had asked that the seven-member board appear at the meeting, but the board, in a meeting last week, declined the

invitation, citing its authority to act as a board only in official board meetings.

Curry Tuesday night explained that the meeting was held "because some of us are reluctant to go to the ivory tower" of the school administration.

"The real cause of the problem," Rev. J. D. Williams, pastor of the host church, said "is the meting out of discipline. The kids are mad. They are willing to accept punishment if it is fair and just. But in this case we have justice turned around; the kids are guilty until proven innocent."

He was referring to the suspension of the 14 Negro students within 48 hours of the Friday afternoon outbreak. All were suspended pending an investigation of their participation in the disturbance.

McKenzie told the questioners Tuesday "several of them — three or four — have returned to school."

"These students have been out of school too long," Williams said.

The mother of two boys under suspension asked if they would be allowed to make up missed classroom work.

Folgate explained that the absense is considered as "excused" they will be "given the opportunity to make up the work," but if the absense is "unexcused" they will not be allowed to get credit for the lapsed time.

Several parents and other spokesmen voiced strong objection to school policy giving Paul Weaver final authority in discipline.

"Should one man be able to suspend children from school all by himself when there has to be a witness in the courtroom on whom he had a child is paddled?" Mc-

(See SCHOOL on Page 2)

Hospital wedding

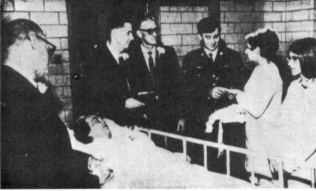

Air Force Sgt. William R. Reed, who is stationed at Grissom Air Force B a s e at Bunker Hill, Ind., places a wedding ring on the finger of his bride, the former Georgia Elaine Martin, in Thomas Memorial Hospital in South Charleston, W.Va., Tuesday. The wedding was performed in the hospital because the bride's mother, Mrs. Gerald Martin is seriously ill. The newlyweds are flanked by Sgt. Reed's father, Lester, and sister, Kathy. The bride's father, left, holds his wife's hand (AP Wirephoto)

Ambulance firm selected

By JERRY MILLER
C-T Staff Writer

A Marion man was named by city officials Tuesday night as the successful bidder for operating an ambulance service in the city next year.

James McLachlan, 27, 1709 Saxon Dr., was named by Mayor Gene Moore as the probable successful bidder on the ambulance service franchise. The mayor said members of the city board of works and the new board of county commissioners had agreed on McLachlan's selection at a meeting Monday night.

The board of works is expected to officially award the contract to McLachlan when the board meets Thursday.

McLachlan, one of four bidders for the franchise, is a native of New Zealand who came to Marion two years ago to work at Marion General Hospital. He is chief medical technologist at the hospital.

McLachlan's father is an ambulance driver in New Zealand and the Marion resident said he had been involved in ambulance work since he was 12 years old.

McLachlan said Tuesday night he had not yet obtained

Council-at-a-glance

James McLachlan of Marion was named by Mayor Gene Moore as the probable successful bidder for operating an ambulance service in Marion next year.

Marion City Council approved the appropriation of $30,000 to subsidize the 1969 operation of the private ambulance service.

The chairman of the council's traffic committee, Lawrence Zook recommended postponing any action on converting Third and Fourth streets to one-way traffic until a later date.

All nine council members were present.

his staff or equipment for the ambulance operation or determined where his headquarters would be located, but indicated he would have the service in operation by Jan. 1.

"I couldn't very well do much until I knew I was going to get the franchise," McLachlan said.

McLachlan said he would have ambulances in operation by Jan. 1, although he might not have his first-line vehicles in service until the end of January.

He added that securing fully-trained ambulance personnel to staff the operation probably would be the most difficult item in establishing the service.

The ambulance service, which will receive a $30,000 subsidy from the city with possible county participation, will utilize two four - patient ambulances and one smaller standby vehicle.

Dr. Sheppard was convicted of second-degree murder in the July, 1954, bludgeon slaying of his first wife, Marilyn, spent nearly 10 years in prison before being released on appeals through the federal courts, and was acquitted in a second trial.

city, patients will be charged an additional $1 per loaded mile for service.

Extra charges will include $3 for use of oxygen and $5 for use of a resuscitator. Long distance transport rates will be $10 plus $1 per loaded mile.

McLachlan said if the ambulance service were later placed on a county-wide basis, he probably would require one additional full-time ambulance for his operation. The possible establishment of the ambulance service on a county-wide basis is currently being discussed by city and county officials.

The city council approved Tuesday night the appropriation of $30,000 to subsidize the ambulance service. Suspending its rules, the council gave final approval to the transfer of $30,- 000 originally earmarked for a city tornado alert system.

The council also suspended its rules to pass an ordinance establishing standards for all phases of ambulance operation.

McLachlan, once he is awarded the contract by the city, would have exclusive rights to ambulance service in the city, but not in the county, where some funeral directors have indicated they will continue their service.

Marion funeral directors will drop their ambulance service Jan. 1.

Other bidders for the ambulance franchise were Marion Ambulance Service, Robert Kittle of Marion and Findley Ambulance Service, Kokomo. Marion Ambulance Service, composed of Leonard Gatten, Howard Benge and Robert Randolph, also had proposed an annual subsidy of $30,000. The other two bidders had quoted subsidies of over $100,000 a year.

In other action, Councilman Lawrence Zook, chairman of the council traffic committee, recommended the council postpone any final decision on making Third and Fourth streets one-way until plans by the Indiana Highway Department were

(See COUNCIL on Page 2)

Claims she was threatened

Sheppard's wife seeks divorce

CLEVELAND, Ohio (AP) — The blonde German divorcee who married Dr. Samuel H. Sheppard after his release from the Ohio Penitentiary has filed for divorce, charging neglect of duty and extreme cruelty.

Sheppard is the osteopath convicted and later acquitted in the much-publicized, two court battle over the death of his first wife.

In the divorce action filed Tuesday in Cuyahoga County Common Pleas Court here Jerry

E. Dempsey, the attorney for Ariane Tebbenjohanns Sheppard, charged that the woman had been threatened by her husband on several occasions.

Mrs. Sheppard asked the court for a restraining order to prevent further occurrences of the alleged incidents.

The divorce action asked that the court "enjoin the defendant from touching the person of the plaintiff or otherwise threatening or molesting her in any way."

Sheppard could not be reached for comment.

News of the divorce filing came one day after an announcement that Dr. Sheppard had resigned from the staff of Youngstown Osteopathic Hospital. Sheppard had been named in wrongful death suits asking damages totaling more than $1.2 million in the deaths of two patients on whom he had operated.

The 39-year-old Mrs. Sheppard asked for alimony and for

use of the couple's home in Bay Village, a Cleveland suburb.

The couple also had an apartment in Youngstown but maintained the home in Bay Village while Dr. Sheppard worked at the hospital.

Sheppard won his new trial on the grounds that "prejudicial news accounts" prevented him from receiving a fair trial the first time.

His second wife began corresponding with Sheppard while he was in prison and married him two days after he was released in 1964. The couple has no children. Sheppard has a son and his wife has a daughter, both by their previous marriages.

Area News

Inside Indiana

Dairyman

.AFAYETTE—Forest Foutz, ong-time Randolph county wn Swiss breeder, today was ied 1968 "Dairyman of the r" by the Indiana State ry Association.

outz and his son, John, op- e a 260-acre farm near ker. A dairyman more than quarter of a century, the r Foutz has a herd of 25 wn Swiss cows whose pro- ion averages some 30 per above the average for that ed in Indiana. Some of his eding stock has been export- to foreign countries.

outz has been active in the ry Herd Improvement As- ation and in programs re- d to animal health, disease rol and dairy product mar- ng.

outz received a plaque at annual luncheon of the ISDA Purdue University. Earlier, ers of 280 superior Indiana y herds and owners of 54 tanding herd sires received ificates from the ISDA.

ssociation directors elected three - years terms at Mon- s session were Roger Nier- , Brownstown and Charles ior, Rosedale.

Lawsuits

ROWN POINT, Ind. (AP) — nty-two suits seeking to re- er $1.5 million in poor relief ey were filed Tuesday in e Circu t Court by Deputy . Gen. Gerald S. Zore.

ne suits alleged the money misappropriated through Calumet Township trustees ce in Gary.

ne recovery of nearly $2 ion has been sought in suits since 1967. Seven suits filed year sought to recover ,000.

State Board of Accounts re- has questioned $1.9 million oor relief purchase orders in ment Township.

ormer Township Trustees old DeVault and Milton Bar- ch and 25 Gary residents, tified the operators of 21 y firms, were named in the s filed Tuesday. One of two rance companies that had ded the two trustees was ed in all 22 suits.

aromich now is serving two current one-year sentences he Indiana State Farm aft- leading guilty to two counts heft of public money. De- lt is free on bond pending ew of a 2-14 year prison ence for conspiracy to forge nterfeit poor relief orders.

nvestigation

ALPARAISO, Ind. (AP) — rge Whited, 34, of near eatfield, was held for inves- tion Tuesday in the fatal ting of his brother, Robert, as they returned from a ing trip Monday night.

obert was killed by a shot- blast in the head as he sat his wife, who was driving, he front seat of their car. brother was sitting in the seat.

ne shooting occurred about miles south of Valparaiso.

History

AFAYETTE, Ind. (AP) — story of Purdue's first 100 rs will be told next May 4 a special magazine supple- nt to be distributed through spapers of Indiana and ghboring states. About 1,250,- copies will be printed.

ne centennial celebration gazine will be called "Hail due '69." It will tell of such due accomplishments as ed- ing nine astronauts and dis- ering a new type of corn ected to increase vastly the ld supply of protein.

cholarships

HICAGO (AP) — Scholar- s were made to five moge sier boys and girls Tuesday the 47th National 4-H Con- ss.

wards of $600 scholarships e made to Patricia McKaig, Logansport; Carl Harcourt, Milroy, and Dennis Dunkel, Lagrange.

cholarships worth $500 were en in the 4-H leadership pro- m to James Findling Jr., Rt. 1, Daleville, and Cynthia chbill, 19, Auburn.

Trial set for two Peru policemen

Face brutality charges

PERU — A police brutality litigation brought by a Peru man against two city policemen is scheduled for hearing Dec. 16 in federal court in South Bend.

The charges were filed by James F. Black, of Peru, and are based on an incident which occured April 28, 1965. The defendants are Peru police officers Herb Hand and Jack Jackson.

Black is asking for $30,000 from each policemen. He alleges that both officers violated his civil rights and used undue force when they arrested him at his home for violation of a city junk car ordinance. The damage action was filed in March of 1967.

The original city court action on the violation came to trial Feb. 19, 1966, and Black was found guilty and fined $25. The conviction has since been appealed. The junk car ordinance is no longer in force in Peru.

Black was held in violation of the ordinance for having a truck parked in his driveway without a license plate.

FINAL POUR—Traffic will begin rolling over the new U.S. 35 bridge over Wildcat Creek of Greentown Saturday. Detours around the site have been in effect since last May when replacement of an iron bridge was started. Final pouring of concrete slabs was done Tuesday. The aluminum guard rails will be installed today. The only other work to be done before the bridge is opened is stoning the two approaches. The view above shows the east approach with the rails of the old iron bridge at the left. (Chronicle-Tribune Photo)

Face Down in the Succotash

BY MAUDE BURNS
Greentown, Indiana

A curse on the multiplicity of Santas! Why does every store have to have one? The children are skeptics, you know.

Lynn and her friend Gina came away from one Santa totally disgusted.

"He's got a fake beard," said Gina. "And when I told him so, he said for us to leave."

"He's not the real Santa," Lynn declared. "He is too crabby."

Not crabby, but astonished, was the Santa I interviewed for the paper where I worked a couple of years ago. I asked foolish questions of him, while the photographer from the paper adjusted lights and fiddled with meters and all those other silly-looking things photographers do.

"Okay," said the photographer suddenly. "Let us get a shot of you sitting in Santa's lap."

Santa looked at him in horror.

"See here, son," I objected, "I am a middle-aged lady. Look at this white hair and all these chins I have."

"Come on," drawled the photographer, yawning. "I got a dinner and two dances to cover tonight, yet."

So I sat down on Santa, who choked and wheezed. I licked a candy cane, smiled an asinine smile, and tried not to cry from embarrassment. The photographer took a lot of pictures.

Next day at the office, I almost did cry. A store owner called, demanding to know why the idiot broad who was doing a Santa interview at his place never showed up. Because she went off and interviewed the wrong Santa, that's why.

For city-county use

Blackford council okays joint landfill proposal

HARTFORD CITY — The Blackford County Council gave final approval Monday afternoon to an ordinance also passed by the Hartford City council for the county commissioners to purchase 16.5 acres of land upon which to operate a city-county landfill.

The agreement called for joint maintenance of the 700 foot existing entrance with additional roadway needed by the county. The present landfill and the additional ground will be operated for use by city and county residents.

A special meeting of the county council, and both Hartford City and Montpelier city councils will be held at 7:30 p.m. Dec. 18 at which time the Hartford City council will consider the transfer of funds for the city to annex the property.

In other business, the council unanimously passed all fund transfer requests. The transfers included $1,500 from the burial fund to the courthouse repair fund; $150 to other operating expenses from the election and registration fund; $150 from election and registration fund to clerical assistance; $30 for rent of rooms, from election fund; $1,000 from the hospital commitment fund to the welfare department, and $2,100 from the stone and gravel fund to the highway department.

An ordinance for an additional appropriation of $300 for office supplies in the auditor's office and $1,000 for advertising in the commissioners budget was approved by the council.

The next meeting of the county council will be Monday, Jan. 6.

Jonesboro Cub Scouts honored at pledge service

JONESBORO — Cub Scout Pack No. 221 met at Westview School with Robert Knapp, cub master, in charge. The meeting opened with the pledge to the flag. Several new members were welcomed and signed cards.

Awards were presented by Knapp to Brian Powers, three year pin; Noel Pogue, Randy Ford, Dennis McNutt, Robby Knapp, Stephen Demarcus, John Eaton, Pat Millspaugh, Martin Haughey and Mike Wickham, two year pins. One year pins went to Eddie Armes, Mike Powers, Pat McNutt, Jeff Carter, Gregg Pratt, Pat Tracy, Brian Pogue, Harold Kellogg, Richie Lewis, John Powell, Kelly Timmons, Chris Simmons, Robert Wickham, Tim Mann, Jeffrey Secrist, Brett Bishop and Dennis Cooper.

Webelos, who received achievement awards, were Dennis McNutt, artist and outdoorsman and Pat Millspaugh, naturalist.

Dennis Cooper and John Fredenberger, were awarded wolf badges. Arrow points under wolf went to Eddie Armes, one silver; Pat McNutt, two silver, one gold; Jeff Carter, one silver; Brian Pogue, one gold; Harold Kellogg, one silver. A silver arrow point under bear was presented to Pat Millspaugh. Pat Tracy and Brett Bishop received denner bars and Jeff Carter, assistant denner bar. Earl Stapleton and David Eaton, received bobcat pins. Den mothers provided refreshments and approximately 100 persons attended.

Study Club meets with Mrs. Laymon

JONESBORO—Mrs. Ted Laymon was hostess to the Childs Study Club meeting at her home on Sand Pike. Roll call responses were assigned topics. Mrs. Richard Huston, program chairman, spoke of "What Ever Happened to Neighbors?" Mrs. Oda Cragun and Mrs. James Dunn were welcomed as new members.

Mrs. Wright Tomlinson was in charge of entertainment and winners in games were Mrs. Merle Shoemaker, Mrs. Ted Laymon and Mrs. Richard Huston.

Plans for the Christmas party were discussed and Mrs. John Wade, Mrs. Max Vanderpool and Mrs. Merle Shoemaker were named as a committee in charge of arrangements. Refreshments were served to nine members.

To offer new courses in Huntington

HUNTINGTON — During the second semester several courses will be offered for the first time at Huntington County Community High School.

In the English department, a senior course in contemporary literature and a course in creative writing will be available. An advanced radio workshop class will be offered on an arranged basis for those students with their license who are interested in working in the station.

For those seniors that encounter difficulty in reading there will be a sociology "E" class similar to the civics "E" class this semester.

In the Music Department a course in music appreciation will be offered.

In the area of home economics there will be three courses that have not previously been offered. These classes will be gourmet and foreign cookery, child development and costume design and tailoring.

Smart named chamber president

HUNTINGTON — Robert B. Smart was named president of the Huntington Chamber of Commerce at a meeting of the board of directors Monday afternoon.

Smart is employed at Memcor Division of LTV Electronic Systems. Other elected were Robert Novick, vice president of industrial division; Charles Schumacker, vice president in charge of retail division, and Harold Shinebarger, treasurer. Mrs. Georgia Shape was reelected executive director.

County planners to meet today

HUNTINGTON — The regular monthly meeting of the Huntington County Plan Commission will convene at 7:30 p.m. today at the county courthouse.

The commission will consider a proposal by city plan director H. B. Crockett for revision of subdivision control regulation. The proposal calls for an amendment to a regulation that the owner of small properties could sell a portion of the land without subdividing and that the approval of sewage systems could be handled locally rather than through the state health board.

Honor Wabash soil, water conservation

The Wabash Soil and Water Conservation District was among nine Indiana districts receiving recognition Monday night at the annual banquet at Purdue University.

Dohn Wiley, Rt. 2, LaFontaine, is chairman of the Wabash district. It has been organized for 25 years.

The Huntington district received the Goodyear conservation award as winner of the state contest sponsored by the Goodyear Tire and Rubber Co.

Spencer Burris, Huntington, was named outstanding farmer cooperator in the Goodyear contest.

Thomas B. Evans, State Conservationist for the Soil Conservation Service, earlier told a general session that "in order to meet tomorrow's challenge through creative resource planning and development, Soil and Water Conservation Districts need to participate more in planning for the future with towns, cities, counties and multicounties."

"Creative resource planning and development," said Evans, "is doing everything we can in the way of planning, and then implementing these plans, to improve the quality of our total environment, not only for our generation, but for future generations as well."

Evans suggested that Soil and Water Conservation Districts in Indiana could play an important role in the future by taking the initiative in "a clean stream effort." They can do much toward "emphasizing conservation measures to keep sediment out of streams," he pointed out.

Evans urged support of the proposed Indiana Land Conservation Act, which will be submitted to the 1969 Indiana General Assembly which begins its 61-day meeting next January.

"Even though technological developments will permit us to produce ample food and fiber for immediate and short-term needs," Evans asserted, "we must never lose sight of the long-term needs."

"All of the vastly increased numbers of people in our country will need food, clothing and shelter. It is imperative, therefore, that we carefully guard our topsoil — this priceless portion of our earth that is basic to the strength and prosperity of our country."

Evans said the Soil Conservation Service, as it embraces the broadened responsibilities of resource management, "has no intention of abandoning time-honored alliances and commitments." The SCS "has every intention of strengthening the soil and water conservation program in the agricultural areas as the program envelops the entire resource community," he asserted.

Wabash Co. Hospital

Visiting hours: 2 to 4: 7 to 8 p.m.

ADMISSIONS

Edith Smallwood, Wabash.
James Garlits, Wabash.
Sandra Perkins, Wabash.
Michael Bullick, Wabash.
Karen Nichols, Converse.
Paul Harner, Wabash.
Jessie Allen, Wabash.
Phyllis Partridge, Servia.
Rex Minnick, LaFontaine.
Martha Bollinger, Wabash.
Alan Lauer, North Manchester.
Lynn Brauneller, Wabash.
Oren Murphy, Etna Green.
Kris Slater, Claypool.
Sandra Edwards, Wabash.
Berthara Dyer, Wabash.

DISMISSALS

Carla Kizer, Wabash.
Sandra Weeks, Roann.
Edna Kline, Wabash.
Josephine Bozarth, Lagro.
Linda Dill, Wabash.
Ware Wimberly, Wabash.
Thelma Teel, North Manchester.
Ruby Ribley, North Manchester.

BIRTHS

Mr. and Mrs. William Chalfin, Wabash, boy, 7:33 p.m. Dec. 3.

Purdue economist to teach farm management

ED CARSON

Ed Carson, Purdue University extension economist, will conduct two farm management schools for Grant County farmers at Fairmount High School Dec. 11 and 18.

The schools will be open to 25 Grant County farmers. Those planning to participate are to notify the county extension office in advance.

The sessions will start at 7:30 p.m. They will deal with farm organization and operation in the competitive years ahead.

To be discussed are "The Competitive Position of Indiana Farmers," "The Best Size of Business to Operate," and "Financing the Farm of the Future."

The meetings are designed to bring to Grant County farmers an analysis of current management problems coming out of the rapid changes in farming, according to Robert Sampson, Grant County agent.

Robert Henman, vocational agriculture teacher at Fairmount, is in charge of arrangements for the meetings.

The two farm management schools are the first in a series of winter extension schools scheduled for Grant County. Others will include a crop school series Feb. 3, 10 and 17 at Eastbrook School, South Campus; a series on farm management Feb. 27, March 6 and March 13 at the 4-H Park; crop yields and minimum tillage practices school March 5 at Oak Hill High School; weather in corn and soybean production March 12 at Oak Hill, and a pesticide dealer meeting Dec. 9 at the Dutch Mill, Bluffton.

Richland

MRS. ORA HIGHLEY
395-3065

YOUTH MEET

RICHLAND — The Youth Fellowship of Richland Chapel United Methodist Church met in the church Sunday evening. Kathy Gribben presented the lesson. The Rev. and Mrs. J. W. Rhine and 15 members attended.

FARM BUREAU TO MEET

RICHLAND — The Richland Township Farm Bureau will hold its regular meeting at 6:30 p.m. Dec. 9 in the Richland Chapel United Methodist Church. Dr. Henry Larzelere of the Davis Clinic will be guest speaker. A potluck supper will be served.

the correct length to fit on the page in the way he wanted them to fit. In fact, the fitting of news on a page dummy is somewhat like assembling a jigsaw puzzle, except that the result of a puzzle is predictable. Page layout may be quite unpredictable. Therefore, the page often takes shapes that are neither orderly nor attractive. Although the makeup editor may be able to emphasize the most important stories, the page design may be unattractive.

Made-up pages often are cluttered because the editor lacked control once the top stories were dummied. Sometimes, only the top half of the page is interesting, whereas the bottom half fades away. Other times makeup results in story placement where the reader may find it difficult to locate the remainder of a story continued in adjacent columns. Such problems do not occur when the entire page is planned as a total design. It would seem that the total design concept would be preferred to the technique of makeup.

Most editors, however, make up rather than design pages. But more interest is shown in preplanned pages than those built piece by piece. Designing a page represents a different approach to newspaper packaging because the designer is better able to control the final appearance of the entire page. The makeup editor can control only the placement of important stories. A designer can control not only the placement of important stories but also the appearance of the entire page, because either he has a mental picture of the page he wants or he experiments with alternative page designs by first drawing a number of rough sketches; he then selects the best design.

In the latter technique, the makeup editor gets an idea of what the entire page might look like after he has examined the stories available and attempts to visualize them in a contemporary format.

Yet page makeup also has some advantages that must be weighed against totally designed pages. Makeup is easier and achieved more quickly than designed pages. Because time is extremely important in meeting press deadlines, makeup is often preferred. Furthermore, makeup is much easier on inside pages, where the advertising department controls page design to a great extent.

Therefore the question of makeup versus design is not one that can be decided totally in favor of one or the other. The total design concept is best for pages where there are no advertisements. Makeup is best for all other pages and where little time is available. The goals of both are the same, to create pages that are easy to read in a contemporary format.

The Objectives of Newspaper Makeup and Design

Design exists primarily to facilitate readership. A newspaper is a collection of many stories, pictures, features and advertisements. When they are haphazardly placed within the newspaper or on any given page, they become a deterrent to reading because

The Art of Editing

the effect is confusing. Foremost in planning a page is the goal of making every page easy to read. Newspaper pages should be designed so that as a result of being easy to read more people will read faster than they have before and read more of what has been written.

Newspapers are in competition with dynamic media such as television and radio. But even print media such as magazines and books are much easier to read than newspapers because they are more attractively designed. Obviously, it is easier to design magazines because more time is available for the arrangement of stories. But readers are not likely to be sympathetic with the problems of newspaper makeup editors. Readers know which media are the easiest and most pleasant to read. Therefore every effort should be made to overcome any inertia readers may have when they read a newspaper page. With this general objective in mind, it is then possible to state the specific objectives as follows:

First, the editor should arrange the news in an orderly and convenient-to-read manner. When news is so arranged, the reader will be faced with a minimum of obstacles to overcome. He will know where every story starts and, if it is necessary to carry the story into another column, where the story ends. It should be easy for him to know which stories are important and which are not. It should also be easy for him to find any special news or feature of interest with a minimum of effort and confusion. Orderly arrangement is a significant criterion of good design.

Second, news should be packaged in a format whose design is consistent with the nature of contemporary design found outside the newspaper. Furniture, automobiles and the architecture of buildings all reflect contemporary design. The format of a newspaper is the frame of reference in which the news is read. Contemporary news should therefore be packaged in a contemporary format. Modern design is symbolic and tells the reader that the newspaper is attuned to the times and is perceptive of what is going on in today's world. The design should communicate nonverbal symbols such as liberalism, conservatism, strength of character or even concern for social welfare. These qualities represent the image of the newspaper. Images are only feelings, attitudes and opinions, but they are important in making the newspaper's efforts appreciated. In the field of consumer product categories, Cadillacs, for example, convey an image of high social status and affluence, whereas Volkswagens convey an image of economy and convenience. Each manufacturer plans the design of his product so that it is consistent with what he wants consumers to believe about his product.

Third, and perhaps most important, the design should be more exciting to readers than ever before. The best way for newspapers to compete with other more exciting media is to upgrade

---

the drama of design. Census data estimates show that the proportion of young persons in this country is steadily growing. If these estimates become a reality, newspapers will have to appeal more to young persons in the culture. Young persons are most appreciative of new, exciting and dramatic designs. Every effort should be made to get these persons to read newspapers more and to make it a habit.

Finally, the newspaper is a visual arts medium and is often evaluated in the same light as other visual arts. A newspaper should be attractive both as a visual arts medium and as a modern package because beauty for its own sake is one of the broader values in an affluent society. Newspaper design should reflect this value when presenting the news.

Principles of Artistic Design Applied to Newspapers

The means of achieving the objectives of design are through application of artistic principles of design. The newspaper is a graphic art form, using words, pictures, color, lines and masses subject to the same principles of artistic design as other graphic art forms. Some graphic design principles suggest underlying bases for news page designs. The principles most applicable to newspapers are known as balance, contrast, proportion and unity.

Balance: A Means of Making the Page Appear Restful

Balance means equilibrium. It means that a page should not be overwhelmingly heavy in one section or extremely light in another. The consequence of designing an unbalanced page is that readers may have a vague feeling of uneasiness because of the concentration of weight in only one or two sections of the page. Most readers do not know whether a page is balanced or unbalanced. They are not artists and do not know the principles of artistic design. Yet they often know that a certain page "feels" better to read than do other pages. The goal of good designing is to bring about a feeling of equilibrium on each page. In newspaper design, the most frequent means of bringing about imbalance is to make the page top-heavy by placing large and bold headlines at the top while using almost insignificantly light headlines at the bottom. Another cause of imbalance is the practice of placing a large, dark picture at the top without having one of similar size or weight at the bottom. As a result of imbalance, readers' eyes tend to gravitate toward the bolder sections of the page and away from the lighter portions. Assuming that every element on a page has value, an unbalanced page, theoretically, is more difficult to read than a balanced page.

Balance in newspaper design is achieved by visually weighing one element on a page with another on the opposite side of the page, using the optical center as a fulcrum. The optical center is a point where most persons think the true mathematical center is located. It is approximately a little above and to the left of the mathematical center. The practice of visually weighing one element on a page against another does not lead to precise balancing, but there is no need for that degree of precision. All that is required is a feeling of equilibrium on a page, not precise mathematical weighing.

Which elements need balancing? Any element on a page that has visual weight should be balanced. To determine which elements have visual weight one need only squint at a page and notice that much of the printed material disappears. What remains are pictures, headlines and black type rules of any kind. Although it is true that even body type has some weight, it isn't significant enough for consideration in visual weighing. The goal is to distribute prominently weighted objects pleasantly on the page.

Balance is most often done by weighing elements at the top of a page with those at the bottom, rather than doing so from side to side. The principle of balance is the same as that of balancing a heavy person on a seesaw with a light person. The heavy person must move close to the fulcrum, whereas the lighter person must move farther away on the opposite side of the fulcrum.

To implement the principle of balance, the most outstanding elements, such as bold or large headlines at the top of a page, should be weighed against similar headlines at the bottom. If the bottom of the page has no bold or large headline, the page is likely to be top-heavy. Plans should be made to include such headlines at the bottom. The same procedure should be followed in placing pictures on a page. A headline or picture at the bottom need not be as large or as bold as those at the top because it is farther away from the fulcrum. See Figure 13–3.

Page balance may be formal or informal. Formal balance is achieved by placing headlines and pictures of the same size on either side of a page. It is sometimes called symmetrical rather than formal balance because one side of the page tends to mirror the other. In that sense there is balance. But symmetrical design may be unbalanced from top to bottom. Most newspapers employ an informal balance from top to bottom. The feeling of equilibrium is there even though it is not obvious.

Contrast is the principle of using at least two or more elements **Contrast** on a page, each of which is dramatically different from the other. One may be a light headline contrasting with a bold headline. Another might be a small picture contrasting with a larger one. Because one element is different from the other, the page is made to appear lively and interesting.

Contrast, therefore, is a means of preventing artistic pieces from becoming dull. Almost all art forms are created with some contrast in them—especially musical compositions, plays and printed material. A symphony, for example, contrasts a fast and loud first movement with a soft and slow second movement. A play has a relatively quiet scene contrasting with a lively scene. A book or magazine may have most pages printed in black and white contrasting with full-colored illustrations.

In page makeup and design, contrast prevents a page from appearing too gray, a problem that occurs when there is too

ALTON EVENING TELEGRAPH

Serving Madison, Jersey, Macoupin, Greene and Calhoun Counties

Vol. 134, No. 287 © Alton Telegraph Printing Co., 1969 ALTON, ILL., FRIDAY, DECEMBER 19, 1969 30 PAGES Price 10c Est.

Burglar Blasted In Face

A would-be burglar was shot in the face after he and another man were surprised ransacking the home of a Fosterburg area woman early this afternoon.

Authorities said the two burglars fled into nearby woods after one of them had been shot in the face with a .12-gauge shotgun wielded by a man who discovered them ransacking the residence.

A manhunt by Madison County sheriff's deputies and state police was in progress later this afternoon.

The Madison County Sheriff's Office said the shooting occurred shortly before 1 p.m. at the home of Miss Sophia Prager, a teacher, who lives a mile north of Fosterburg on Rte. 1.

Authorities said her brother, Earl Prager, who lives near her home, discovered the intruders and fired the shot.

Prager told authorities he was at home eating lunch when he saw a strange car pull into the driveway of his sister's residence about one-fourth of a mile away.

Prager got his shotgun and drove to his sister's home. He walked into the residence and saw two men ransacking the place.

The burglars rushed outside with Prager in pursuit. When about 25 feet away from one of the men, Prager fired the gun, striking the man in the face.

The man was able to pick himself up, and joined the other intruder in rushing into nearby woods.

FIRST TO NOTICE—John Xipolitas, 18, who was first to notice the appearance of moisture on the glass facing covering the icon of St. Nicholas, points to two droplets. Father Elias Kalariotes, pastor of St. Nicholast Greek Orthodox Church in Tarpon Springs, Fla., says the painting has been weeping for five days. Father Elias said hundreds of people are coming to the church to view the phenomenon, which he says cannot be explained as the result of any physical process. (AP Wirephoto)

Norman Stanhope Wins Ret On Possibility He Had Amn

The Illinois Supreme Court today reversed the death penalty conviction of Norman Stanhope of Alton for the 1967 hatchet slaying of his wife and sent the case back to Madison County for a new trial.

Chief Justice Robert C. Underwood declared in a court opinion today that Stanhope may have suffered from amnesia and had not been given a proper psychiatric examination for his trial.

Stanhope, 48, was convicted Sept. 22, 1967, for the killing of his wife and sentenced to die in the electric chair on March 12, 1968, by Associate Circuit Judge I. H. Streeper, in circuit court at Edwardsville.

Stanhope was living at 1126 E. 7th Street at the time of the tragedy.

Subsequent appeals by his attorneys Malcolm Durr and John Dale Stobbs have delayed his execution at Menard State Prison.

"Perhaps the most important part of the record, the appeal stated," comes from Dr. Groves B. Smith's testimony on cross examination . . . during the prosecution's rebuttal on the last day of the trial, Sept. 22, 1967."

The appeal claimed that "at best, the witness", Dr. Smith, was "unclear and indirect in most of his answers to the extent that he was not . . . fair to the accused."

Dr. Smith, a prominent prison psychiatrist, testified that on June 16 and on Sept. 5, 1967, when he saw Stanhope, the prisoner was animated and that when he saw Stanhope again on Sept. 22, 1967, his actions and appearance were evidence of "hysterical amnesia".

This apparently is the crux of the reversal decision and is the reference used in the appeal filed by Durr.

In the appeal, Durr also referred to a colloquy regarding "hysterical amnesia" and said consider ing "Stanhope's appearance and actions at this particular time and Dr. Smith's diagnosis of "hysterical amnesia, out of to appeal able to his ow therefore and assis "Th should ha this poi determin been Stanhope continue this part Durr appeal (Continue

Arabs Set War Parley

By ELIAS ANTAR
Associated Press Writer

RABAT, Morocco (AP) — Arab leaders headed for Morocco today for their first summit meeting in two years. Their goal was a new unified war strategy against Israel.

The meeting, called by President Gamal Abdel Nasser of Egypt, is intended to lead the Arabs out of the present impasse in which they seem neither able to go forward and conquer Israel nor willing to retreat into a peace agreement which they see as a surrender.

The first session will be held Saturday.

The summit conference is the first since the Khartoum meeting of August 1967, two months after the disastrous Arab defeat. There the leaders agreed they would accept a political settlement with their adversary only on the basis of three notes—no recognition of Israel no negotiations with Israel and no peace with Israel.

Tax Reform Ba Keeps Rolling

WASHINGTON (AP) — Senate-House tax reform conferees have reached tentative agreement on a relief package that includes a boost in the personal income tax exemption from $600 to $750.

The conferees worked 16½ hours until 3 o'clock this morning and still didn't quite finish their work on the entire tax reform bill, but conference chairman Rep. Wilbur D. Mills, D-Ark., said there was no doubt action would be completed today.

It was understood the relief package decided on as the last major compromise between the widely differing House and Senate versions provided:

—An increase in the exemption to $650 starting next July. This would be coupled with a $1,100 low income allowance to help poor families and an increase in the standard deduction from the present 10 per cent with a $1,000 ceiling to 13 per cent with a $1,400 ceiling.

—A $650 personal exemption for all of 1971, with a $1,050 low-income allowance, and a standard deduction of 14 per cent and a $1,700 ceiling.

—For 1972 and thereafter, a $750 personal exemption, with a $1,000 low income allowance and a standard deduction of 15 per cent with a $2,000 ceiling.

The conferees also were reported to have agreed to accept the across-the-board 15 per cent increase in Social Security benefits of the Senate bill.

But they did not go along with the $100 minimum monthly payment for an individual which that measure also included.

President Nixon had objected to the 15 per cent boost. But the House voted for it unanimously Monday in a separate bill.

The low income allowance, which may be deducted from income in figuring taxes, will remove about 5 million poor families from the tax rolls entirely.

The conf ly the cut rates voted vor of g through an sonal exem vored by th However ed for an 1971, a fig the Socia boost, had a veto by P

Only Political, Says Elble

Staten Move Blasted

By ANDE YAKSTIS
Telegraph Staff Writer

Wood River Township Supervisor Rodger Elble today blasted as "purely political" an ultimatum from the Madison County Mental Health Board (708 Board) to either fire Jerry Staten, of Godfrey, director of the Quad Cities Mental Health Center, or face a shut down of the clinic.

Charging that Staten has poorly administered the Quad Cities Center at Granite City, the 708 Board is withholding $102,770 in tax funds from the mental health clinic until Staten quits his job, the Telegraph was told.

The move to oust Staten was angrily assailed today by Elble who accused politicians of muscling in on the mental health treatment program in an attempt to create more political patronage jobs.

Elble also criticized as a "political plum" a "sleeper" provision in the new Madison County operating budget which allots $10,000 salary for a "mental health administrator" to supervise the clinics, including Granite City and Alton.

The Wood River Township supervisor said that he has received many calls from parents of children being treated at the Granite City clinic. The parents are appealing to Elble to help keep the clinic open.

The 708's Board action to close the clinic, if Staten doesn't resign, is "tampering with the lives" of hundreds of patients at the Granite City mental health center, Elble said.

Meanwhile, the Telegraph was told today that Dr. Richard G. Murney, a psychologist affiliated with the Illinois Department of Mental Health has offered a "favorable" preliminary report of his review of the operation of the Granite City Mental Health Center.

Dr. Murney was requested by the 708 Board to begin a thorough review of the mental health center administered by Staten. Dr. Murney will submit his report to the 708 Board when the review of the center is completed.

"From everything that I have reviewed to date, the services at the Granite City center are of good quality and this reflects favorably on the administrator (Staten)," Dr. Murney told the Telegraph today.

Dr. Murney is administrator of the Madison County Subzone of Zone 7 of the State Department of Mental Health. His office is at the Alton State Hospital.

Elble accused politicians of contributing to the controversy over Staten and the clinic to create more patronage jobs.

(Continued on Page 2, Col. 1.)

L&C Park Snu Blow to Promo

By JOHN STETSON
Telegraph Staff Writer

Surprise and disappointment was registered by the Illinois Lewis & Clark Trail Commission today at the "divergent and dictatorial" decision of Illinois Conservation Director William Rutherford in turning down development of the Lewis & Clark park for state park purposes.

"This is indeed a disappointment, especially in view of the overwhelming attitude of the population to the contrary," Trail Commission Chairman Clarence Decker told the Telegraph.

Decker was responding to Rutherford's announcement this week that development of Lewis & Clark Park, which marks the confluence of the Mississippi and Missouri rivers, for state park purposes was low on the state's priority list and would, according to Rutherford, "not be done in my lifetime."

Decker has been among Lewis & Clark Commission members leading the movement to make the area a state park and was also one of 15 people in Gov. Richard Ogilvie's office Monday when the U.S. Army Corps of Engineers turned over 168 acres at the Lewis & Clark site to be included in the park area.

"The Corps of Engineers doesn't just give land away for the heck of it," Decker said. "This should be kept in mind by Director Rutherford."

Rutherford made his announcement about the Lewis & Clark park site after an erroneous news release came from Gov. Ogilvie's the $1 m plan for the next The dicated access improver for the Rutherfo Telegrap been a between Governor In real figure w what suc cost, b a propos (Continued

Execs Forming Corporation To Underwrite SIU Festival

By DOUG THOMPSON
Telegraph Staff Writer

EDWARDSVILLE — A group of businessmen in both Missouri and Illinois began work today to establish Mississippi River Festival, Inc., a non-profit corporation to underwrite the financially-troubled festival that premiered last summer at the Southern Illinois University campus here.

The SIU Board of Trustees recently voted to get out from under the festival which fell more than $150,000 into the red last year.

The businessmen's group met in St. Louis Thursday to draw up a plan for the corporation, which would foot the bill for the festival on the Edwardsville campus of SIU each year. Incorporation papers are expected to be filed in Springfield next week.

The new non-profit corporation will launch a campaign for sustaining funds throughout the metropolitan area, its backers have indicated.

A Granite City druggist, Dr. Albert Trtant, is one of the businessmen behind the new corporation. He could not be reached for comment today.

Dr. John S. Rendleman, chancellor of the Edwardsville campus of SIU, was out of his office this morning, but another spokesman for the campus said the private backing would be "heartily welcomed by the university."

The River Festival can only survive through public subscription, the spokesman said, and the university feels a legal corporation should be established to handle this.

SIU lost $150,000 in the premier festival and the cosponsoring St. Louis Symphony Society lost an additional $50,000.

Because of the losses, the SIU Board of Trustees declined to allocate any funds for the event in

(Continued on Page 2, Col. 8.)

WARMER
SATURDAY
Low 22; High 43
(Complete Weather Page B-3)

Newark's Mayor Hugh Addonizio Pleads Innocent

By JAMES MARKHAM
Associated Press Writer

NEWARK, N.J. (AP)—Mayor Hugh J. Addonizio and reputed Mafia boss Anthony "Tony Boy" Boiardo pleaded innocent today to federal charges of extortion and income tax evasion.

U.S. Dist. Court Judge James Coolahan set a period of 45 days for filing defense motions, after which a trial date will be set.

Judge Coolahan set bail for Boiardo at $50,000 and restricted his travel to New Jersey, New York City and Washington, D.C. Federal authorities have been seeking Boiardo for questioning by the federal grand jury which indicted him, the mayor and 13 other persons Wednesday.

Twelve other defendants also pleaded innocent, and the arraignment of the final defendant was set for next week because of his illness.

Addonizio, who is free in $25,000 bail on his own recognizance, was surrounded by political supporters at the court session.

On Thursday night, the board of the Greater Newark chamber of Commerce voted to ask Addonizio and other city officials indicted on the income tax and extortion charges to step aside until their cases are settled in court. A board spokesman said a formal request to that effect will be issued shortly.

The mayor has said he will not step down and has pledged the city's government will operate "efficiently and effectively" despite the indictment.

Addonizio and 11 others are charged with income tax evasion. All 15 are charged with extortion.

The indictments, alleging among other crimes the extortion of $253,000 from a contractor, were returned Wednesday by a federal grand jury probing alleged governmental corruption.

Two other federal grand juries are investigating gambling and possible links between Internal Revenue Service agents and the Mafia.

INSIDE

While 1,000 Wait for Harrison Homes . . .

HUD's Muddle Stymies Project

By ART THOMASON
Telegraph Staff Writer

Conflicting statements from the Department of Housing and Urban Development over the proposed Harrison Street public housing development have plunged the $1.7 million project into confusion, the Telegraph has learned.

The project had been tentatively approved by one agency of HUD, but apparently later did not meet the requirements of another division of the huge housing and urban development arm of the federal government.

A letter from Robert L. Tucker, assistant regional administrator for Equal Opportunity in HUD's regional offices in Chicago, indicated that the proposed Harrison Street site is not in accordance with the criteria of Title Six of the 1964 Civil Rights Act.

Tucker's letter, dated Dec. 9, 1969, conflicts with another letter from Bernard C. Mack of HUD's Housing Assistance Production Division, which indicates that on March 2, 1968 Leon D. Urbain of the HUD's production division gave tentative approval of the site. This letter was dated October 4, 1968.

The letter also states that final approval will be evident by approval of the development program, which is now pending the city council's action of a request to rezone the 10-acre site from R-2, one-family residential to R-4, multi - family residential.

Meanwhile, Mayor Paul Lenz will seek to determine whether the project will get HUD's okay, should rezoning be approved by the city council.

The mayor said he is also confused by the conflicting letters, and that HUD's position should be clarified before the city plan commission takes any action on the proposal.

Edmund Morrissey, the developer, told the Telegraph Thursday that he was surprised at the letter from HUD, indicating a disapproval of the Harrison site, after talking Monday in Chicago with HUD officials.

While the fate of Alton's latest proposed housing development for the poor is still undetermined, more than 1,000 families remain on the waiting lists of the Alton Housing Authority — pointing up a critical shortage of housing for the

(Continued on Page 2, Col. 3)

MAYOR PLEADS INNOCENT—Mayor Hugh J. Addonizio of Newark talks to newsmen before entering federal court, where he pleaded innocent to extortion and income tax evasion. The mayor a sons were indicted W federal grand jury in leged governmental c Wirephoto)

Figure 13–3. Headline and picture at the top balanced with similar elements, diagonally, at the bottom. [*Courtesy the Alton, Illinois, Alton Evening Telegraph.*]

much body copy and too many light headlines. Gray pages appear uninviting and forbidding.

Sometimes the makeup man finds that he has a similar problem on pages where he deliberately tries to balance a page at the expense of achieving contrast. His balanced page may appear too restful and dull. He can change one or two elements on that page such as a headline or picture and thereby brighten the page considerably. A bolder headline or picture, carefully placed, may provide the contrast he needs.

Indiscriminate use of contrast, however, is undesirable. If a page has too much contrast it may overpower the reader because the contrasting elements call attention to themselves and not to the page as a whole. The goal is to provide pleasant, not overpowering, contrast. To achieve this goal the makeup man will have to develop a sense of good taste.

Contrast may be achieved in four general ways: by shape, size, weight and direction. Shape contrast may consist of a story set flush on both sides in opposition to another story set flush left, ragged right. Or an outline picture may be used with a rectangular-shaped picture.

Size contrast may be shown by using a large illustration on the same page with a smaller one, or large type contrasted with smaller type.

Weight contrast may employ a picture that appears very black with a lighter picture, or a story set in bold face type contrasted with one set in lighter typefaces.

Direction contrast could show vertical shaped stories contrasted with horizontally shaped stories.

These contrast alternatives are but a few of many that are possible on any given page. An objective of designing a page, however, is to achieve pleasant, rather than harsh or extreme, contrast. Too many contrasting elements on a single page may be artistically unsound and unattractive.

Proportion

Proportion is the principle of comparative relationships. In newspaper design the length of one line may be compared with the length of another, or the shape of one story with shapes of others, or the width of a photograph with its depth. The goal of designers is to create pages in which the proportions of elements are pleasing to the eye. Certain proportions in this culture tend to look more pleasing than others. The Greeks were largely responsible for working out the proportions of many of their temples in classical dimensions. Artists and designers try to use pleasing proportions in their works because the public has come to appreciate such relationships. For example, artists rarely use a square shape in preparing their work because a square appears dull and uninteresting. More pleasing is a rectangle in which the length is greater that the width. Unequal proportions usually are more attractive than equal proportions. For that reason, newspapers, magazines and books have pages that are designed with the width being less than the depth.

In newspaper design, pleasing proportions should be considered in planning the sizes of pictures, headlines and even divisions of pages. Unfortunately the design of newspaper pages often does not reflect the principle of good proportions even though the size of paper pages does. The problem is that makeup men tend to think in terms of fitting news into columns, each of which is poorly proportioned. They can't be sure that the shape of the main story on a page is pleasantly related to other story shapes on that page. Persons using the total design concept are better able to control relationships and proportions than are makeup men.

The beginner with little or no artistic training will have to develop a sense of proportion by following certain basic principles:

1. The best proportions are unequal and thereby not obvious. Therefore, an element on a given page should not have square dimensions, whether it is a picture, story shape, box or division of a page.

2. There are many pleasing proportions that can be used, but one of the easiest and most pleasing is a 3:5 relationship. It is easy to remember and easy to use. To determine the shape of a story, for example, the makeup man needs only to decide arbitrarily one dimension (either the width or the length). Then by multiplying (or dividing) that dimension by 1.62,[1] the other dimension may be found using the 3:5 proportion.

1. PROBLEM: If one dimension of a story is 6 inches wide, how long should its depth be?
   ANSWER: Multiply 6 inches by 1.62 (6 × 1.62). This equals 9.72, or 10 inches.
2. PROBLEM: If the depth of a picture is 7 inches, how wide should it be?
   ANSWER: Divide 7 inches by 1.62 (7 ÷ 1.62). This equals 4.32, or about 4 inches.

Although the beginner can easily compute the unknown dimension to determine a 3:5 proportion, he ought not be bound by precise mathematical results. In other words, he should develop a sense of what looks well. If, in his computations, he is wrong by $\frac{1}{2}$ inch either way, the result will not affect the outcome. Most persons are not perceptive of precise mathematical proportions. But it should be obvious that a single-column story 11 picas wide and 64 picas long is not proportionately pleasing (Figure 13–4). For that reason, the page designer might divide that column into two equal-depth columns where the new dimensions would be 22.5 by 32 picas. If these dimensions were checked by the formula above, it would be found that the 32-pica

---

[1] 1.62 is a factor of a 3:5 relationship. A rectangle computed by using this factor is sometimes called a golden oblong.

dimension should really be 36.450 picas (22.5 × 1.62). But few persons will object or complain about the difference.

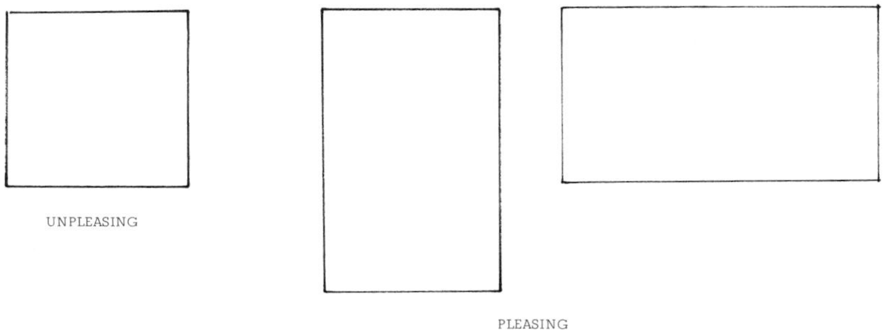

UNPLEASING

PLEASING

Figure 13–4. Unpleasing and pleasing proportions.

3. In dividing a page, some unequal proportions should be used for determining the relationship of one area to another. For convenience, a 3:5 relationship might again be used. But any proportion that is obvious should be avoided. Therefore, it would not do to divide a page in half either vertically or horizontally. The areas employed in the total design concept are those whose proportions are critical to the aesthetic appearance of the entire page. But in traditional page makeup, it is very difficult to divide a page in pleasing proportions unless the columnar approach to placement is abandoned.

In determining the relationships of parts to wholes, the goal is to avoid exaggerated proportions as well. As attempts are made to have unequal dimensions, there is the danger that they will become exaggerated. That is why the 3:5 proportion is suitable for most page design problems. When pleasing proportions are used on a page, the result may not only be interesting but attractive.

Unity

The principle of unity concerns the effect of a page design that creates a single impression rather than multiple impressions. Stories on a page that has unity appear as if each contributes a significant share to the total page design. A page that does not have unity appears as a collection of stories, each of which may be fighting for the reader's attention to the detriment of a unified page appearance.

Lack of unity often results when stories are dummied from the top of the page downward. The makeup editor is building a page piece by piece and cannot be sure how each story will contribute to the total page design until he has completed his dummy. At that point, however, he may find that he does not have enough time to shift stories around to achieve unity. The result is that readers may find it difficult to concentrate on any one part of a page because of too many centers of interest. A unified page, on the other hand, appears as if everything is in its correct position, and the page is therefore interesting.

How does one plan for a unified page? Through keeping the design of the entire page in mind at all times while working on any part of it. Each story, therefore, must be visually weighed against all other stories in terms of the probable appearance of the entire page. In page makeup, the editor may have to shift some stories around on the dummy until a satisfactory arrangement has been found. Like the other principles of artistic design, an appreciation of this one will have to be developed by makeup editors through a sensitivity to good design.

Visualizing Total Page Structure

Although the objectives of newspaper design may be clear enough, the beginner may have difficulty implementing them because he cannot vizualize the structure of a page before it has been completely dummied. Sometimes, even after a page has appeared in print, the beginner may not be able to see the design easily. To overcome this difficulty, he should resort to the process of cutting each story shape from kraft paper and pasting them on a dummy in the proper position relative to all other stories. The effect will be to wash out the words and small details, leaving only the total design sharply visible. Now he should be able to see the relationship of his dummy to his design. (see Figures 13–5, 13–6, and 13-7).

One way to create such block structures is to use black kraft paper for the heavier elements on a page and lighter-colored paper for the lighter elements. A large, dark-apppearing picture, therefore, would appear in black paper as might a large black headline. Body copy, lighter headlines and light-appearing pictures, however, would appear in light kraft paper. Then, not only the shapes but the weights of all stories will be clearly visible so that the editor can see whether his page has balance, contrast, proportion or unity.

If a page is studied in the above manner occasionally, the beginner may be able to develop a feeling for page structure that should improve his ability to create effective page designs.

How the Number of Pages in an Issue Is Determined

A preliminary step to page makeup is the decision about how many pages an issue will have. An executive may start by considering the ratio of news to advertising. In the past a popular ratio was 40 per cent news to 60 per cent advertising. Today the ratio of news to advertising may be much smaller for many newspapers (30 per cent news, 70 per cent advertising). Although the smaller percentage of news may be used, it does not necessarily mean that less news than before is appearing in the newspaper. Because volume of advertising may be greater than before, a larger amount of news may be used in a 30:70 ratio than in a 40:60 one.

Press capacity, however, is another consideration in determining the number of pages in an issue. Some presses will print only in multiples of 8. None will print an odd number of pages without wasting space. Even for those presses that will print even

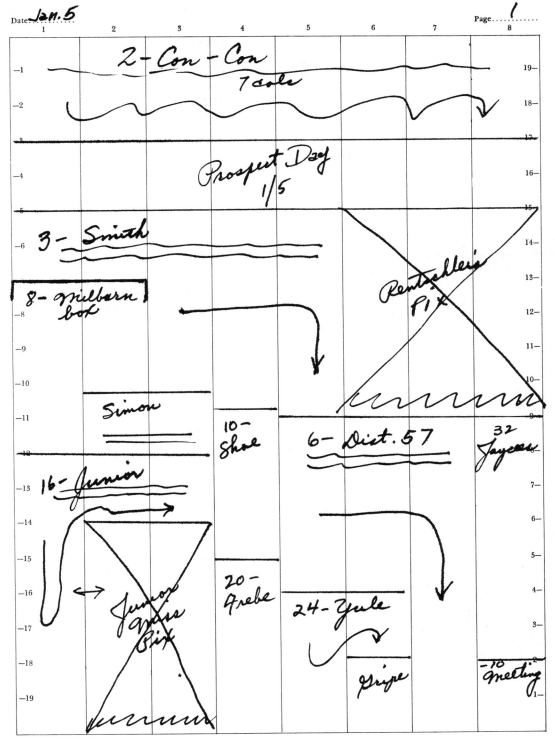

Figure 13–5. Page dummy. (See printed page on page 280).

Con-Con delegates selected for 6 major committees

By Richard Crabb

Con-Con delegates from the northwest suburbs will be nominated to six of the 12 major committees that will be the workhorses in rewriting the state's constitution tomorrow.

Con-Con President Samuel W. Witwer of Kenilworth notified the delegates by telegram on Sunday of the committees to which he would nominate them. The full convention must approve all committee appointments.

Northwest suburb delegates will be nominated for the Local Government, Education, Bill of Rights, Revenue and Finance, Judicial and Rules committees. The area will not be represented on the Legislative, Executive, Constitution Amending and Suffrage, General Government, Style and Drafting and Public Information committees.

THE NORTHWEST suburbs are double teamed on the Education Committee. Both of the delegates from the 4th District (Maine and Niles Township) will be nominated by Witwer to the education committee.

Mrs. Anne Evans of Des Plaines will be nominated as vice-chairman of the committee. Dr. Clyde Parker of Lincolnwood, the other 4th district delegate, was notified Sunday that he will be appointed to the committee. Paul E. Mathias of Bloomington will be nominated to be chairman of the committee.

Mrs. Virginia Macdonald of Arlington Heights, delegate from the 3d District, will be nominated for the Bill of Rights Committee. John G. Woods of Arlington Heights, the other 3d District delegate, had earlier been assurred by President Witwer that he would be nominated to the Committee on Local Government.

Mrs. Jeanette Mullen of Barrington, delegate from the 32nd District, was appointed to both the Committee on Revenue and Finance and the Committee on Rules and Credentials. Jeffrey R. Ladd of Crystal Lake, the other delegate from the 32d District, will be nominated to the Judicial Committee.

EXCEPT FOR Mrs. Macdonald, all delegates from the northwest suburbs are being nominated tomorrow for standing committee appointments from the list of preferences filed with the convention at the request of President Witwer.

Each was requested to list three committees in the order of preference. Woods, Parker, Mullen and Ladd are to be nominated to the committees which they listed as first choice.

Mrs. Macdonald listed the Judicial, Education and Revenue committees as her choices in that order.

"I WILL SERVE on the Bill of Rights Committee," Mrs. Macdonald told The Day shortly after receiving the Witwer telegram of notification Sunday. "I know that it will be a highly controversial committee.

"The racial issue will be but one of many important matters to be debated by this committee. The matter of capital punishment is to be decided in this committee. Search and seizure, electronic eavesdropping and the reduction of the number of persons serving on juries are just a few of the other issues that will come before the Committee on Bill of Rights.

"I would have preferred one of the three committees that I listed. It does seem strange that one of them could not have been worked out, but the Bill of Rights is one of the important committees of the convention. Certainly it will be an interesting one on which to work," said Mrs. Macdonald.

THE CONVENTION will meet at 1 p.m. Tuesday for its first meeting of the new year. The Committee on Rules and Credentials, on which Mrs. Mullen is to serve, is scheduled to meet at 10 a.m. Tuesday.

The rules committee is responsible for screening all proposals made to the Constitutional Convention to determine whether they are ones which can logically be considered by Con-Con or whether they come within the range of matters generally handled in the Illinois General Assembly.

WEATHER

Tonight: Partly cloudy, chance of snow flurries, low zero to 5 above. Tomorrow: Mostly cloudy, continued cold.

The Prospect Day

Your Home Newspaper

Telephone

255-4400

Volume 4, Number 178 — Monday, January 5, 1970 — 14 Pages — Newsstand Price 10 Cents

Senate hopefuls Smith, Rentschler to speak

By Richard Crabb

The northwest suburbs are emerging as the decisive battleground in the March 17 Republican Senate primary.

William H. Rentschler of Lake Forest, candidate for the U. S. Senate in the March 17 GOP primary, will campaign vigorously in the northwest suburbs during January, beginning with his first address in the area in Schaumburg Friday evening.

His opponent, Sen. Ralph Smith of Alton, will also be making his first campaign appearance in the northwest sub-

The meeting, sponsored by the Schaumburg Township Republican organization, is open to the public.

Rentschler will speak in Des Plaines Jan. 4 and is scheduled to appear at the Wheeling Township candidates night in Arlington Heights. On Jan. 19 Rentschler will speak to the Woman's Club in Park Ridge.

SEN. SMITH and Rentschler are the only candidates in urbs this week. He will speak at a reception in Wheeling Township at 3 p.m. Thursday afternoon at the Mount Prospect Holiday Inn.

Rentschler's first address in the area will take place Friday evening at 8:30 at the Campanelli School in Schaumburg. the race for the U. S. Senate in the March 17 Republican Primary. Smith was appointed to the Senate in September by Gov. Ogilvie after the death of the late Sen. Everett Dirksen. This is Smith's first state-wide race.

Rentschler, newspaper columnist and industrialist, ran a close race for the Senate in the Illinois GOP primary in 1960 against the winner, Samuel W. Witwer of Kenilworth, now president of the Constitutional Convention. Rentschler managed Richard Nixon's Illinois campaign in 1968.

Smith was a several-term member of the Illinois legislature and was speaker of the Illinois House of Representatives when he was appointed to the Senate.

The Rentschlers open their campaign for the U. S. Senate in the northwest suburbs! William and Mrs. Rentschler are seen talking to shoppers Saturday morning at Randhurst Shopping Center. It was their first "meet the people" effort of the campaign in the northwest suburbs. Rentschler is opposing Sen. Ralph Smith of Alton for the GOP nomination for the U. S. Senate in the March 17 Republican primary. Rentschler regards the northwest suburbs as a key battleground in his race against Smith.

Milburn Bros. gets Busse Rd. contract

The successful bidder for the 1.46 miles of concrete pavement on Busses Rd. between Golf Rd. and the Northwest tollways (I-90) is Milburn Brothers, Inc. of Mount Prospect, Illinois' Public Works Director William F. Cellini announced last week.

Milburn's bid for the contract was $1,653,817. The heavily traveled two-lane road will be torn up in stages, so that it may still be used while construction continues and the present two lanes are replaced with new concrete.

The project includes turning lanes and signalization at Dempster and Algonquin, where the village of Mount Prospect will contribute only 50 per cent of the cost from motor fuel tax funds, or a total of $74,000.

A further financial advantage to the village is the revenue it will obtain from the approximately 150,000 cubic yards of fill estimated to be needed for the project.

The dirt is to be excavated from the newly acquired West Park property near Busse and Lonnquist, where the present small retention basin will be substantially enlarged in the process.

Neighbors must be heeding Safety Council's New Year warning; For every drink wait one hour before driving. They're not home yet.

Little girl's lost shoe, may mean frostbite

Some little girl may have gotten frostbite on the way home from Sammy Skobel's Hot Dogs Plus, 34 S. Main, Mount Prospect, when she left her shoe there last Friday.

Owner, Sam Skobel, 610 William, said he found the size five, patent leather shoe about 4:30 p.m. Friday, and as of Sunday evening no one had claimed it.

On Saturday Skobel phoned a friend in Chicago who works for a radio station and a report on the lost shoe was broadcast over the air.

"It is something that very seldom happens," Skobel said, and he is anxious to have the shoe returned to its owner.

Prospect Heights beauty Illinois' Junior Miss

Marilyn Raedel, Prospect Heights' Junior Miss, became Illinois' Junior Miss Saturday at the contest at MILL Run Playhouse in Niles.

A tall, honey-blonde with an "A" average at Wheeling High School, she is the winner of a $2,000 scholarship and also the $100 prize for poise and appearance.

Marily, daughter of Mr. and Mrs. Ray Raedel, 16 N. Wildwood, Prospect Heights, is one of five children. She would like to major in business and dance at one of her three college choices--Drake, Texas Christian, or Missouri.

HER TALENT presentation was a jazz and acrobatic dance to "Aquarius." She is a National Honor society member and captain of the Wheeling High School cheerleading squad.

Marilyn enjoys snow and water skiing, skating, painting and gymnastics. She has choreographed school musicals and works as a girls' athletic teacher for a public school recreation program.

Marilyn suceeds Pamela Weir of Arlington Heights as Illinois Junior Miss.

Garnet Vaughan, 17, daughter of Mrs. Garnet Vaughan, 1215 N. Waterman, Arlington Heights, was third runner-up, and won $500.

GARNET ATTENDS Hersey High School where she participates in dramatics and the National Honor society.

The new Junior Miss of Illinois will compete with 49 other state winners in Mobile, Alabama, for the title of America's Junior Miss and a $10,000 scholarship for the winner.

The first runner-up was Debbie Stoery, Northbrook's Junior Miss. She wins a $1,000 scholarship.

Judy Clune, Chicago's Junior Miss, was second runner-up. Judy, who attends Taft High School, won $750 and the $100 talent prize.

Receiving congratulations from the 1969 Illinois Junior Miss, Pamela Wier (right) of Arlington Heights, is the new Illinois Junior Miss, Marilyn Raedel of Prospect Heights. Marilyn will compete in the America Junior Miss contest in Mobile, Ala. (Photo by LeRoy Meyers)

Mrs. Frebe is killed in crash

Mrs. Janet H. Frebe, 35, of 762 W. Dempster, Mount Prospect, was pronounced dead at Resurrection Hospital in Chicago yesterday after she was involved in a one-auto accident at 8:10 a.m. on the John F. Kennedy Expressway near Cumberland Rd. in Chicago.

Police said that Mrs. Frebe, who was employed at the Merchandise Mart in Chicago, was on her way to work, when she lost control of her car. It struck several wooden posts and a cable in the median strip of the expressway.

Police said tire marks indicate that Mrs. Frebe slammed on the brakes and the car skidded 83 feet before striking the median. However, they said they did not know what caused her to apply the brakes. They also said there were no eyewitnesses to the accident.

District 57 to negotiate on William St. property

By Maureen McNassar

Negotiations are expected to begin soon between the District 57 School Board and the Mount Prospect Park District Board on the future use and ownership of 11 acres of School District owned property on William St. in Mount Prospect.

School Board member, Jack Ronchetto, who heads the Long Range Planning Committee for the district said the School Board has authorized the committee to arrange a meeting with the park board to discuss the possibility of the park district purchasing all of or part of the south side property.

He said the property has been held by the district for several years and the chances of the district needing the property for another school are very slight.

THERE ARE currently three elementary schools on the south side and if the property were sold to the park district the School District would retain the right to buy back the property at any time that it was needed.

With this type of arrangement the School District would have the use of the funds from the sale and still be assured of additional building space if it became necessary to build an additional school.

President of the Park Board, Robert Jackson said he has been contacted by Ronchetto concerning the proposal and the board has indicated an enthusiastic interest.

WITH THE constant need for more open space in the village, purchasing of the site by the Park district would ensure the surrounding area of park facilities and protect it from being built up by developers, he said.

The Park District has worked effectively with the village on the purchase of the West Park property and with the school District on the use of the south side site for recreational development and Jackson said he believes a suitable agreement could be reached on the purchase of the 11 acre site.

Although preservation of open space is the Park District's main goal, ownership of the property would give the district the advantage of developing the property any way they want, he said.

RONCHETTO said that if the Park District did not buy the property it is not likely that the School District would sell it to be used as residential development.

The proposal for the sale of the site was brought before the School Board during December when Ronchetto reported on the Long Range Planning Committee's projection for future enrollment accompanied by several proposals for future consideration by the board.

The proposals included a suggestion that the board explore the possibility of a trade of one or two acres of Lions Park for a similar amount of property on the 11 acre site to insure ample property to allow an addition to be built on Lions Park School.

Ronchetto said he plans to contact Jackson this week to set a meeting date with the Park Board.

Postmaster thanks early mailing for relaxed Yule

Postmaster William H. Watson of the Prospect Heights Post Office said that early mailing his year enabled the post office to handle much Christmas mail before the peak of the mailing spree was reached on Dec. 16.

On Dec. 16 the post office recorded a total of 59,478 first class cancellations, double the number of pieces cancelled on the preceding day.

On an average day, he said, the post office handles about 4,000 to 5,000 pieces of mail.

WATSON SAID, "The peak for incoming mail was reached around the end of that week, and by Christmas Eve there was not a piece of Christmas mail received that morning that had not been delivered."

He said the post office is asking residents to keep the approaches to curb mailboxes clear of snow and ice.

Gripe Of The Day

Not being able to find where the Scotch tape begins. S.B.

Jaycees village survey to be released Jan. 23

Kenneth V. Scholten, 1507 Redwood Av., Mount Prospect, yesterday told The Day, that results of the comprehensive survey of the village that the Mount Prospect Jaycees took in June, 1969 will be released at a meeting Jan. 23.

Scholten, who is president of the Jaycees, said that his group intends to invite a couple of representatives from each of the community's civic groups, as well as village officials.

If interest of the general public seems great enough, said Scholten, the meeting, tentatively scheduled to be held at the Mount Prospect Community Center, may be switched to the auditorium of Prospect High School.

January was selected as the month to release the report, said Scholten, because it is "Jaycees Month" and there will be ceremonies celebrating the 50th anniversary of this national civic group.

The survey, based on a four-page questionnaire that ranged in its scope from schools to, "what's wrong with Mount Prospect and what would you like to see changed," received a 40 per cent return from the 9,000 homes canvassed door-to-door.

Meetings Tonight

School District 57, 701 W. Gregory; 8 p.m.

School District 59, Forest View Elementary School, 1901 Estates Dr., Mount Prospect; 8 p.m.

Figure 13–6. Printed page. (See dummy on page 279.) [*Courtesy the Prospect Day, Metropolitan Printing Co., Elk Grove, Illinois.*]

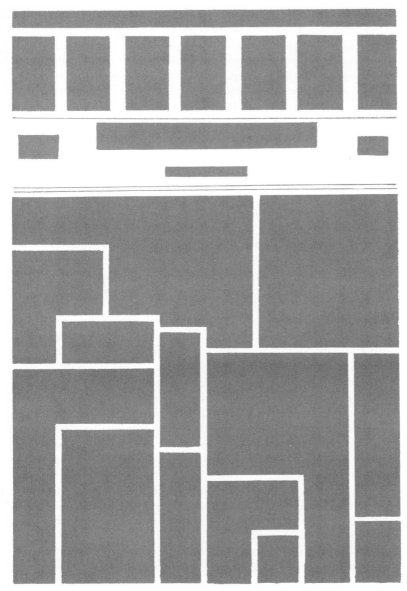

Figure 13–7. Design of the page shown in Figure 13–6.

numbers, there may be some objection by executives for printing an issue of, for example, 14 pages because a single loose sheet containing 2 pages must be inserted into a paper where three sheets are folded to print 12 pages. It is easier to increase the number of pages to 16, where four sheets of paper are folded.

When press capacity, or any other reason, requires that the volume of news or advertising be decreased, news is usually cut. Occasionally, however, an advertisement may be moved to another day in order to make the columns fit the number of pages required.

Principles of Page Makeup

Once the editor has a schedule of stories, their lengths and the page numbers that they have been temporarily assigned, he is ready to make up each page that has space remaining on it. In essence, he will position stories on each page dummy until most of the space has been filled. The remaining space is filled by the printer with leading or briefs. Some editors dummy only the most important stories and allow the printer to fill the remainder of the page. Others dummy almost the entire page. A better-looking page can be achieved if 90 per cent or more of a page has been dummied because there is better control over the entire page design than in partial-page dummying.

The Mechanics of Dummying

Page makeup consists of preparing a dummy, which serves the same purpose as a blueprint—it tells the printer where to place each story, how long it will be and how it should be shaped. A goal of the makeup editor should be to make the dummy as clear, accurate and concise as possible. Many dummies turn out to be a mass of scribbling rather than a neatly prepared blueprint that enables the printer to assemble type for a page with a minimum of confusion. The pressure of time is often blamed for hard-to-read dummies. But the consequence of poor preparation may mean that time is wasted in the composing room when the printer tries to decipher the dummy. Therefore, every effort should be taken to make the dummy neat, accurate and concise.

Some guidelines for preparing a dummy are as follows:

1. A front page dummy is started by indicating the amount of space that the nameplate will take. Some newspapers have specially prepared dummies with space already allocated for the nameplate. Where this is not available a line should be drawn across the dummy indicating that the nameplate will occupy a certain depth.

2. Because most headlines have been assigned a number or some other designation in a headline schedule, this number and the slug for the story should be written wherever the story is to be placed on the dummy.

3. When a story with a one-column headline is noted on the dummy, the headline and slug word are indicated at the top of the story and a horizontal line is drawn across the column at the end. No arrows are needed to indicate that the story is to read in a downward direction. But when a story is continued to an adjacent column, then arrows should be used to show where the story is continued. The arrows warn the printer that the story has not been completed in the column where the headline appeared. Whenever there is some doubt about where a story is continued, arrows should be used. But if they can be avoided, they should be, because they tend to clutter the dummy. When a single-column story is ended at the very bottom of the page, an endmark should be used.

4. Two-column lead paragraphs, cutlines and odd-measured stories (such as a 1½-column width) should be indicated on the

layout by drawing wavy lines the width of the type. Straight lines should not be drawn as they may be confused with finish or "30" lines.

5. Pictures or cartoons should be labeled appropriately with the slug word and an indication that it is either a picture or cartoon. Some newspapers use a large X drawn to the corners of the picture to make it clear that the space is to be used for a picture and not a story.

6. Boxes are indicated by drawing a rectangle to the dimensions required and labeling the drawing with the word *box*.

7. Jumps should be indicated by the word *jump* and the page number to which the story is to be continued.

8. If a story of two or more columns reads into a single column, then a cutoff rule will probably be used to separate the material that appears under the headline from nonrelated material. Also, an arrow should be drawn from the headline into the appropriate column where the story is to be continued. If a banner headline reads out into a deck, this too should be indicated by an arrow.

9. Any makeup arrangement that is radically different from what has been used before should be indicated with notations if there is doubt that it will be clear to the printer. Sometimes only an arrow is needed; sometimes a few words will explain the situation.

Positioning

The most important stories are assigned those places on the dummy that tend to be centers of interest. A center of interest is any position that because of its location tends to draw the reader's eyes. The upper-left-hand and upper-right-hand positions on a page are major centers of interest. The two lower corners also are centers of interest but not to the extent that the upper corners are.

Readers tend to enter a page by looking at the upper-left corner first. This is natural because most pages of books are read by starting in the upper-left corner and then proceeding in a right-hand direction until the end of the line has been reached. There is, therefore, a left to right direction in reading. Because readers start at the top of the page, both the left and right corners are major centers of interest.

Newspaper pages, however, can be arranged so that readers follow lines of directional force. A line of directional force may be a large headline, a cutoff rule, a picture or even a column of type. Such lines are simply devices that lead the reader's eyes from one part of the page to another. A banner headline, for example, is so powerful that it moves the reader from the left to the right direction until he reaches the last column. But then, instead of returning to the left as one usually does when reading lines in a book, the editor can introduce a two column readout headline at the extreme right, literally forcing the reader to remain at the right and thereby leading him downward into the column of body type. In the same manner, a single-column story with a large one-column headline can serve as a line of direc-

---

tional force urging the reader to move downward in the column.

A basic principle of positioning, therefore, is to lead the reader in an orderly manner through the strategic placement of stories. Obviously, a reader will often assert his own independence by selecting stories of interest to him regardless of the makeup editor's efforts to lead him through the page. But if stories are placed so that directions are not confusing, the reader may be encouraged to read more of the page. Perhaps, the simplest way of starting to make up a page, then, is to place the most important stories in the centers of interest first and the other stories in remaining positions until the entire page is filled.

An alternative procedure is to place the most important story in the upper right or upper left positions and then balance that story diagonally across the page at the bottom. The other two diagonally facing corners might then receive the next two stories.

Beginners should remember that the most important part of the page is the upper left rather than the upper right corner. Only when a banner headline is used does the upper right corner assume the most important position.

There are few restrictions in the positioning of pictures. Traditionally, pictures have been placed somewhere at the top of newspapers. But there is little reason for placing them there. Pictures may be placed anywhere on the page with powerful effect. *The Continuing Studies of Newspaper Readership* (cited previously) showed that readers will search for pictures no matter where they are on a page. In fact, even relatively unimportant positions such as the bottom or lower center will receive high readership. As a consequence, pictures ought to be placed on the page in positions that enhance the total design.

If it is necessary to position a picture at the top because it accompanies an important story, then attempts should be made to balance it with another picture at the bottom, diagonally. Many front pages suffer from top-heaviness because a picture is used only at the top and nothing is used to balance it at the bottom. By their nature, pictures become centers of interest and draw attention away from stories of modest weight.

Vertical and Horizontal Makeup

Another consideration in positioning is story shape. In past years, story shape has not been a major consideration of makeup editors. But within recent years, when makeup editors have sought ways of making pages more attractive, story shapes have become important. The selection of the most appropriate shapes involves a number of considerations. The first one has to do with preventing a page from becoming one-directional. If there are too many vertically shaped stories all leading the reader's eyes downward, then the page looks old-fashioned and unattractive. Newspapers circa 1850 were all vertical in shape, and vertical makeup is distinctly old-fashioned. To avoid verticalness, an attempt should be made to achieve horizontal makeup. Horizontal makeup is distinguished by the fact that stories are continued into three or more adjacent columns and the shape of such stories is horizontal. Although a story may be continued into the next adjacent column, this does not necessarily produce horizontal makeup because the shape of the story may be vertical. Another distinguishing feature of horizontal makeup is that stories are squared off at the bottom. This means that the depth of each column where the story is continued is the same (Figure 13–8). However, a page using horizontally shaped stories exclusively may be as monotonous as one where all

'Famous' on Way, Says Adams

Fabulous Beltline Development Seen

By ART THOMASON
Telegraph Staff Writer

A gigantic Christmas package was opened Wednesday at a Pride, Inc., meeting and it contained millions of dollars in future development along the Beltline Highway, including a Famous-Barr store in an enclosed mall shopping center.

Alton developer Homer Adams told the Pride board "unequivocally" that Famour-Barr will build a department store and mall containing 600,000 square feet under roof.

The announcement by Adams was the first official confirmation that Famous-Barr would build on the site located on the southeast corner of the Beltline and Seminary Road.

Famous-Barr, the parent store of the May Co., is one of the nation's largest retailers.

The May Co., is currently building one of its Venture Department discount stores on the northwest corner of Seminary and the beltline. Adams, too, developed the Venture project.

Adams said a separate development from Seminary west to Washington Avenue along the Beltline also is planned. The tract includes 14 sites designed for small businesses and not connected with the shopping center.

The shopping center will be the largest in the Alton area with enough parking for 5,000 cars, he said.

Adams also forecast that Beltline development should boost the immediate Alton area population to 100,000 by the 1970's.

The developer outlined other future development for the Beltline, some of it already under construction, including the Belscot Shopping Center, an amalgamation of the Bell Scott department stores; a Tri-City Grocery Co. store in the same shopping center complex which is under construction on the south side of the beltline near Buckmaster Lane. They were:

(1) A gigantic motor city — an elaborately designed outlay of businesses that sell anything with a motor;

(2) A 10-acre recreational center that will hopefully feature the Cinerama design, with inside recreational facilities and a large civic center;

(3) Conversion of the old brickyard at Alby Street Road into a 200-acre light industrial park, called the North Port Industrial Park;

(4) The Veterans of Foreign Wars Legion Post home, just north of the Beltline on Alby Street Road;

(5) A MacDonald's hamburger restaurant, now nearing completion near Washington Ave.;

(6) A Taco's restaurant that will feature Mexican dishes;

(7) A new Christian Science edifice near the Temple Israel, between Pierce and Levis lanes.

Adams promised that the development connected with his firm would use sophisticated landscaping techniques to protect residential areas and enhance the natural beauty.

For example, the developer pointed out that the Central Hardware Store, Bettendorfs and the Venture Store will be virtually screened from the view of residential areas behind it by using a landscaping plan that will beautify the area.

Figure 13–8. Horizontally shaped story. [*Courtesy the Alton Evening Telegraph.*]

stories are vertically shaped. The best looking pages have a mixture of shapes (Figure 13–9).

Avoiding Odd-Shaped Stories

A second consideration in makeup should be that of avoiding odd-shaped stories. In traditional makeup many stories are not squared off and take odd shapes. One such shape looks like an "inverted L" (Figure 13–10). It is caused by using a two- or three-column headline over a one-column story. The effect is like an upside-down "L." When more than one inverted L-shaped story is used on a page, they tend to destroy the simplicity of the design. Because an inverted L may be used at the upper right-hand side and another one in the upper left-hand side, the design becomes complex. Other stories and pictures must fit around these shapes and it is not an easy task. For example, the space underneath an inverted L-shaped story in the right-hand column usually requires a picture to fill the space underneath the headline. If another headline is placed underneath the upper headline, the result may be confusing (Figure 13–11). To avoid inverted L-shaped stories, the makeup editor should either use a single-column headline over a one-column story or wrap a story to the number of columns that the headline covers. A three-column headline then would have a story wrapped underneath for three columns, presumably, squared off. It is easier to design an attractive page by manipulating squared-off (or rectangularly shaped) stories than by using odd shapes such as the inverted L.

The Courier-Journal

VOL. 229, NO. 161 ******* LOUISVILLE, MONDAY MORNING, DECEMBER 8, 1969 42 PAGES 10 CENTS

For 'Outside' View

Stennis Proposes A 'Warren' Panel To Probe My Lai

By J.D. ALEXANDER
Los Angeles Times-Washington Post Service

WASHINGTON—Sen. John Stennis proposed yesterday that President Nixon appoint an impartial panel of outstanding men to determine the facts in the alleged massacre of Vietnamese civilians at My Lai, and make a special report to the President.

The Mississippi Democrat, chairman of the Senate Armed Services Committee, suggested that Mr. Nixon have ". . . people outside the government, outside the military, make a survey of the situation."

The senator said a presidential fact-finding commission could function even while the Army's court-martial of Lt. William L. Calley is pending. It would be preferable, he said, to congressional hearings which might ". . . go off in a half-dozen or a dozen different directions."

Army Impounds Company Records

The commission could conduct its inquiry without a public hearing, Stennis said, but after ". . . they are satisfied they have the facts . . . they might have an open hearing or two to bring it out and let people judge the witnesses."

Meanwhile, the Army disclosed that it has impounded daily operational records of the Americal Division company involved in the killings at My Lai, dating back to six weeks before the incident.

A spokesman said yesterday the records were being held for possible use in "an investigation." He did not elaborate on the statement, nor did he say when the documents were impounded.

Because the records of Company C, 3rd battalion, 20th Infantry, were impounded, the spokesman added, they could not be inspected by newsmen.

'No Explanation' for Delay

Stennis, appearing on the ABC television interview program, "Issues and Answers," declined to discuss specifically the allegations that U.S. Army troops killed women and children during an offensive operation in My Lai.

"I think it has been discussed too much

See STENNIS
Back page, col. 1, this section

'Old' Incidents Called Danger To Viet Policy

By HORST FAAS
and PETER ARNETT

SAIGON (AP) — "It is our Achilles heel. It could be worse for us than the Tet offensive."

That is the view of an American of many years' experience in Vietnam who notes with rising concern the shock waves that went around the world after the disclosure of the alleged killings of civilians at My Lai.

"It's a Pandora's box," another American civilian commented. "There are at least 50 incidents in the Vietnam War that could be ballooned into similar hysterical recriminations."

A third said: "What we are witnessing now is the consequence of the early years of mistaken military policy in Vietnam.

Enemy shells kills troops on Bu Dop airstrip, Page A 2.

Now these incidents are being raised out of the war environment. The results could be disastrous for our efforts here."

These three statements are from American civilian officials long close to the war scene. Senior American military men tend to shrug off My Lai as an unfortunate, inexcusable but possibly understandable consequence of a long and brutal war.

But the American civilian side in Vietnam has long argued with the military about tough tactics, particularly the "search and destroy" concept.

"If the My Lai massacres did occur they were obviously a failure in leadership and should have been investigated, publicized and punished at the time," one American said. "But there is no question in my mind that this brutal approach to civilians was encouraged by an over-all

See 'OLD' INCIDENTS
Back page, col. 1, this section

The Mudders

It was just that kind of day, yesterday. Cold, rainy, nothing going on, and, oh yes, muddy. So, four youngsters got out the old football and decided to have a go at it on a squishy playground south of Jefferson near Clay. The postgame picture at left consists of, from left, Jesse Emery, 8; Danny Moore, 12; his brother Robin, 10, and Jimmy Tindall, 13. The goatee below decorates the face of Jesse.

Staff Photos by Jon Webb

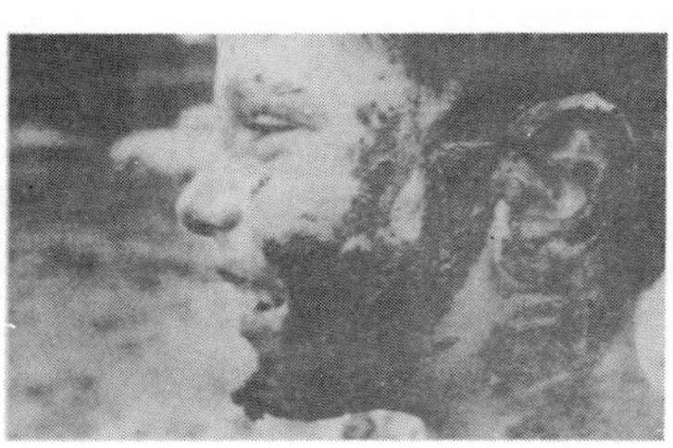

Unions Reject GE Offer, Ask a 16-Month Contract

The two unions spearheading the six-week-old nationwide strike against the General Electric Co. yesterday rejected the company's first new contract offer since the strike began.

The International Union of Electrical Workers (IUE) and the United Electrical Workers Union (UE) countered the company offer with a new proposal of their own.

The company made its new three-year offer in New York Saturday and publicly disclosed it last night.

It contained the same basic 20-cent hourly wage increase as did GE's original, pre-strike offer. But the new offer would have guaranteed at least a 3 per cent raise in both the second and third year, company spokesmen said.

End in Sight

And it contained a cost-of-living escalator that would have provided up to 2 per cent per year more, depending on the rate of inflation, they said.

The new GE offer also increased certain pension, vacation and medical benefits, the spokesmen said.

The original GE offer specified no second- or third-year raise, but would have allowed new wage talks each year. It contained no cost-of-living clause.

The new union proposal calls for a 16-month contract with a 35-cent basic hourly wage increase, with a full cost-of-living adjustment after one year.

The unions' original demand was for a 90-cent hourly raise over a 30-month contract—35 cents the first year, and 30 cents the second and 25 cents more for the final six months. It also included a full cost-of-living clause.

The company had not responded to the unions' new proposal as of late yesterday, according to Don Rock, president of Louisville's IUE Local 761 and a member of the national IUE negotiating committee.

Rock, who arrived back in Louisville from the New York negotiations last night, called GE's Saturday offer "inadequate in all departments. . . .

"There's no question that it does not meet the needs of the people. . . .

"They (GE) must realize that our employes now have an investment of six weeks (on strike). I'm certainly disappointed that the company would try to take a one-year offer that was totally inadequate and replace it with a three-year offer that is totally inadequate."

But John B. Clarke, manager of relations and utilities at Louisville's GE Appliance Park, said the new company offer means "the end of the strike could be in sight."

And John Baldwin, chief GE negotiator, said: "We're extremely disappointed by the unions' action in refusing

See 2 UNIONS
Back page, col. 2, this section

Like the Old Days

Palmer Charges to Win 2nd Straight

By RAY CRAWFORD
Miami Herald Staff Writer

MIAMI — The new Arnold Palmer is beginning to look a heck of a lot like the old Arnold Palmer.

Playing like the Palmer of the past, Arnie charged from six strokes behind yesterday to win the $125,000 Danny Thomas Golf Tournament. He did it by shooting a seven-under-par 65 for a 270 total.

You could almost hear the bugle blowing as Arnie and his Army came marching down the stretch to bury ex-Kentuckian Gay Brewer with four birdies on the last five holes. Brewer, trying to the end, saw his game slip away to a 73 and a 272 total.

Picture and Story, Page B 4.

Brewer had led all the way with three fantastic rounds of 65, 66 and 68 as movie stars mingled with the crowd at the Diplomat-Presidential Golf Course.

Palmer's 18-under-par shooting for the 72 holes over the 6,964-yard layout enabled him to become the only man to score consecutive victories this year.

As Palmer sank a 12-foot birdie putt on the 18th, Danny Thomas walked to the edge of the green to greet him.

"Arnie," Thomas said, "this was just like in the movies. You followed the script. No, you wrote the ending . . . There isn't any professional writer who could have dreamed up this finish."

Lee Trevino fired a 66 to finish third at 274 and rookies Hal Underwood and Larry Hinson shared fourth-place money at 275; each posted 69.

Palmer's rally had all the drama of the dozens which he pulled off before he passed to the shady side of the generation gap and came up with a hip ailment which threatened to end his career.

It was his second straight tournament victory, but his win in the Heritage Classic last week at Hilton Head, S.C., was routine compared to yesterday's triumph.

His victory on the Diplomat-Presidential Course, the last stop on this year's Professional Golfers Association tour, made him the only player to score consecutive victories this year.

Brewer's 35 Not Enough

Palmer played with his old flair, verve and drive in overhauling Brewer.

Arnie smiled and grimaced, he saluted his Army with his putter, a putter which had let him down for more than a year, and he responded to cries of "Go, Arnie, Go. Charge!"

The deciding holes, Palmer said, were the fifth, sixth and seventh.

"I went birdie, birdie, par and gained five strokes as Gay went par, double-bogey, bogey," Palmer said. "Along

See PALMER'S CHARGE
Back page, col. 3, this section

Blue Monday

Furnished by the U.S. Weather Bureau

LOUISVILLE area—Mostly cloudy and cold today and tonight. Partly cloudy and a little warmer tomorrow. Chance of precipitation 5 per cent today, 10 per cent tonight. High today 44, low 32.

KENTUCKY—Not much temperature change today and tomorrow. A few light rain showers northeast today. High today in the 40s to near 50, low in the upper 20s to the 30s.

INDIANA—Partly sunny today but colder in southeast, cloudy and a little colder tonight. Sunny, a little warmer tomorrow. Highs today in the 30s to low 40s, lows in the 20s.

High yesterday, 51; low, 37.
Year Ago: High, 35; low, 20.
Sun: Rises, 7:47; sets, 5:23.
Moon: Rises, 7:09 a.m.; sets, 4:27 p.m.

Weather map and details, Page A 22.

Aldermanic Chief Seeks Civic Unity

By JOHN LONG
Courier-Journal Staff Writer

The terms "East End," "West End" and "South End" are "divisive," the president of Louisville's new Board of Aldermen said yesterday, so he's asked the aldermen to quit using them.

And not only that, said Aldermanic President Carroll L. Witten, the board has ripped down the East-West barrier in its own committee system.

In announcing his appointment of the new board's standing committees yesterday, Dr. Witten said he's combined the old East and West Zoning and Public Ways committees formerly two separate bodies—to form a single committee.

The separate East and West committees "were not evidence of a united community," he said.

Such neighborhood names as "Parkland, Crescent Hill, Schnitzelburg, Germantown and Shawnee denote community pride," Dr. Witten said, in an interview, "but the other (East-West-South differentiation) is a divisive mechanism —a lumping mechanism—and any such mechanisms divide."

Consistency Sought

Under the new, combined Zoning and Public Ways Committee are four subcommittees, each with jurisdiction over three wards. Each subcommittee covers at least one ward of the eastern part of the city and at least one ward of the western part of the city.

Besides promoting city unity, Dr. Witten said he hopes the combining of the East and West committees will aid consistency in planning and zoning decisions —"to make sure there is no artificial separation of planning and zoning needs of the eastern and western sections of the community.

The new board also hopes to promote more city-county cooperation in zoning and other matters, Dr. Witten said. "Todd (Hollenbach, Jefferson County judge-elect) and I discussed this and we do hope we can work toward . . . holding

See ALDERMAN
Back page, col. 4, this section

A Growing—and Unregulated—Kentucky Business

It's Easy to Call Yourself a Private Detective

By STAN MacDONALD
Courier-Journal Staff Writer

The private detective and uniformed security guard business in Louisville is rapidly growing, according to both the Police Department and private eyes here.

"The rising crime rate is partly responsible for the growth," said Maxwell (Scoopy) Allen, head of Allen Investigating Bureau Inc.

Employe thievery from large companies and increased shoplifting from department stores has created a strong demand for private investigators and guards, he said.

But while business may be good, private police agencies are coming under increasing criticism from legal authorities in the state.

The Louisville Police Department said that in recent years it has received numerous complaints about some private agencies.

Last of a 2-Part Series

Lt. Col. Priest Fry, Louisville's chief of detectives, is critical of the "character" of some private investigators.

And William G. Mullins, attorney for the state Public Safety Department, said that "anybody can hold themselves to be private detectives" in Kentucky and they "may or may not be qualified."

Mullins, Fry, and other law enforcement authorities in the state say they favor much stiffer licensing and regulating of private police agencies.

At present, no Kentucky law applies to the agencies, said W. O. Newman, state commissioner of Public Safety.

To become a private eye or to open an agency, most towns in the state only require an annual business license which costs $10, Mullins said.

Private investigators are called upon to delve into private lives. They can employ a wide variety of eavesdropping devices from tape recorders the size of martini olives to intricate wiretapping gadgets.

Yet, an "investigator" can be hired by a private detective agency in this state even though he may have little

See PRIVATE
Back page, col. 1, this section

Figure 13–9. Mixture of vertical and horizontal shapes. [*Courtesy The Louisville, Kentucky, Courier-Journal.*]

Council of Churches Picks Woman Leader

From Our Wire Services

DETROIT, Dec. 4. — Dr. Cynthia Wedel, an Episcopalian and ardent advocate of women's rights, won overwhelmingly over a Negro clergyman Thursday to become the first woman president of the National Council of Churches.

Mrs. Wedel, of Washington, defeated the Rev. Albert B. Cleage Jr. of Detroit 387-93 in secret balloting at the NCC's triennial general assembly.

When the vote was announced, Mr. Cleage, the first Negro candidate for the presi-

Profile and Picture On Page 3

dency, went to a microphone on the assembly floor and castigated what he called the "White racist establishment of the NCC."

"This organization is anti-Christ and until young people or oppressed people take over, you'll remain anti-Christ" Mr. Cleage declared. "Time is

Continued on Page 3, Col. 8

Korean Report Raps Operation of Center By Buck Foundation

By EDWARD N. EISEN

Of The Inquirer Staff

The State Commission on Charitable Organizations made the Pearl S. Buck Foundation produce a letter Thursday from Korea's embassy highly critical of the foundation's work in that country.

The letter, by Sung Kwoo Kim, counsel and consul general at the embassy in Washington, said a 10-day inspection in August at the foundation's Sosa Opportunities Center, west of Seoul, showed unsanitary conditions, overcrowding, misuse of funds and other shortcomings.

REASONS DIVULGED

The letter was produced at a commission hearing on the foundation's appeal for a license to solicit funds in Pennsylvania. The foundation was to have presented new evidence, as demanded by Joseph J. Kelley Jr., Secretary of the Commonwealth.

Figure 13–10. Two inverted-L-shaped stories. [*Courtesy the Philadelphia Inquirer.*]

Another kind of odd shape is one in which a story is continued to adjacent columns but each column depth containing the story is a different length (Figure 13–12). Such shapes also tend to make the page look unattractive.

A major consideration in makeup is the problem of what to do with stories that must be continued into adjacent columns. Should they be jumped or wrapped into the next right-hand column? Jumps are undesirable for reasons given earlier. The best procedure is to wrap (or turn[2]) a story underneath a headline. It is very poor makeup procedure to wrap a story underneath another story because the reader may have difficulty locating the continuation. If it is necessary to wrap a story underneath another story, then a cutoff rule is used to separate the story on top from that underneath (Figure 13–13). When a story is wrapped underneath another story set in a different kind of type or a longer column width, there is less danger of confusing the reader than when it is wrapped underneath a story set in the same kind of type and same column width. Obviously, stories wrapped underneath pictures, where the cutlines are set in different kinds of type, are not apt to be confusing (Figures 13–14 and 13–15).

Wraps

[2] A *turn* is another name for a *wrap*.

Reservoir Is Rejected As School Site; Land Pledged to Developer

The City Planning Commission on Tuesday rejected suggestions to place a high school over the Belmont Reservoir because of a commitment to a group seeking to erect an office building there. Instead, the commission said, the Board of Education ought to consider using air rights over the reservoir's filter beds, just east of the reservoir.

The reservoir was one of four sites given tentative approval Monday at a meeting of the commission, the board and the Fairmount Park Commission. It was the only one involving city land.

TRADE HINTED

Two of the other sites comprise park land and the fourth a tract of "five points," Monument rd. and Conshohocken ave., owned by builder John McShain, who said he wanted to construct an apartment complex there.

The two park sites are at Edgley st. and Belmont ave. and at 53d st. and Parkside ave.

In a related development, City Council Majority Leader George X. Schwartz said he and Mayor James H. J. Tate, agreed that the city might be willing to transfer city land to the Fairmount Park Commission if the commission will surrender park land for a school site.

OFFICES PLANNED

There is ample precedent for such a transfer, he said. Schwartz, chairman of the council's finance committee, said he favored the Edgley st. and Belmont ave. site for the new school.

Charles Ingersoll, vice chair-

Tate Is Considering Ousting Mrs. Bennett From School Board

Mayor James H. J. Tate has grave doubts about whether to reappoint Mrs. Ruth Bennett to the Board of Education, he said Tuesday. Tate, reached by telephone in San Diego, Calif., where he is attending a convention, responded to searing criticism for his failure to fill three vacancies on the board from the Citizens Committee on Public Education.

The committee said it is "appalled" by Tate's failure to fill the vacant seats on the nine - member board. The mayor, the committee said, is in violation of the Home Rule Charter in leaving the seats vacant.

Tate said he is "not satisfied" with the two lists of candidates submitted to him by the educational nominating committee, which must submit from three to six names for each vacant seat. Under the charter, the mayor is required to choose from among these names.

Tate said he would reappoint board member William

Teachers Held In Drug Raid Are Suspended

Three young Philadelphia schoolteachers were suspended from their duties Tuesday following their arrests for illegal possession of narcotics.

The three were released on $1 bail each and slated for a Dec. 19 hearing at the 19th Police District, 61st and Thompson sts. after three members of the narcotics squad raided their West Philadelphia apartments Monday night and allegedly found what laboratory tests showed to be hashish and a pipe with residues of marijuana.

All three lived in an apart-

Figure 13–11. Headlines placed underneath two inverted-L stories. The effect is confusing. [*Courtesy the Phildelphia Inquirer.*]

When a story is wrapped into an adjacent column at the top of a page without a covering headline it is called a raw wrap. In many instances raw wraps are undesirable and are forbidden at all times by some newspapers. The makeup editor faced with a raw wrap should ask that a headline be written to cover the wrap and make it clear that the wrap belongs to the headline above it. But occasionally it is permissible to use a raw wrap at the top of an advertisement where there is no doubt in the reader's mind that the wrap belongs to the story on the left (Figure 13–16).

Westmoreland Assesses War

SAIGON (AP) — Gen. William C. Westmoreland, departing after four years in command of U.S. forces in Vietnam, said today American strength was greater than ever "but it is unrealistic to expect a quick and easy defeat of the Hanoi-led enemy."

"If he feels time is on his side, he can go on a long time," Westmoreland said of the enemy in a farewell news conference on the eve of his departure to become Army chief of staff in Washington.

He added that he could not predict what would happen at the peace talks in Paris, but from his view the enemy still appeared to be in search of major military victory.

"Price Can Be Raised"

Westmoreland said he felt that a classical military victory was not possible in South Vietnam in view of U.S. policy decisions not to escalate the war or to enlarge its geographic boundaries.

He added: "But the enemy can be attrited, the price can be raised. It is being raised to the point that it could be intolerable for the enemy. It may reach the point of the question of the destruction of his country, and jeopardizing the future of his country, if he continues to pay the price he is now paying and destined to pay in the future."

Westmoreland said the enemy had lost 113,000 men since the first of the year and added "he doesn't have the manpower or resources to take these losses in stride."

Sees Net Reduction

Westmoreland said that although infiltration continued at a serious pace down the Ho Chi Minh trail through Laos, the Hanoi government was not able to make up its manpower losses in the South and that since midsummer last year enemy strength had shown a net reduction.

He said Hanoi's strategy appeared to be to continue pressure against Saigon and its political structure and to seek some major victory on the battlefield.

Westmoreland departs tomorrow and will turn over the Saigon command to his deputy for the past year, Gen. Creighton Abrams Jr.

"At this time our military posture is at its height since our commitment," he said. "We are now capable of bringing major military pressure on the enemy.

"This we are doing, and the enemy is beginning to show the effect. The Vietnamese armed forces are growing stronger in size and effectiveness."

Headquarters Farewell

Earlier today, Westmoreland said goodbye with a "good luck and bless you all" to the officers and men of his headquarters.

"Please accept my very best wishes for continued success," Westmoreland told his staff,

"and my fervent hope that peace and security for the long suffering and freedom loving people of Vietnam will soon reward your efforts."

In his swing north yesterday, Westmoreland visited the headquarters of the South Vietnamese Army's 1st Military Corps in Da Nang, took a helicopter to Provisional Corps headquarters at Phu Bai 35 miles away, and visited the headquarters of the 3rd U.S. Marine Amphibious Force.

He wound up his tour with a flight to the nuclear carrier Enterprise in the Gulf of Tonkin to bid farewell to the U.S. 7th Fleet.

Figure 13-12. Odd-shaped story. [*Courtesy the Cedar Falls, Iowa, Record.*]

Town Board Announces Change in Power Rates

VEEDERSBURG, Ind. — The town board met last night with Leslie Howard, president, in charge.

Ted Byers reported the Christmas tree had been set up. Members decided to purchase additional trees for the flower tubs on the downtown streets.

Vern Rogers questioned the water line installation.

An ordinance was proposed concerning the tearing up of streets, sidewalks and alleys when digging water lines, cables

and sewage lines. Under the proposed ordinance, persons will have to contact the town board before proceeding with repairs or adjustments.

Trees that interfere with power lines and dead trees on city property are being cut. A total of 57 trees have been cut and additional trees have been trimmed.

New electricity rates were reported including a reduction for large consumers with the same rate for smaller users. The change will co-ordinate the city's rate with the public power service and with that of other towns in the area. The city also will add a penalty for delinquent bills instead of giving a discount when bills are paid by the 15th of the month.

Town board members will sponsor a Christmas dinner party, Dec. 11, at the Sterling Aid House, to entertain the town employes and their families.

Bids will be accepted for garbage truck service, including the truck and worker. These bids will be considered at a special board meeting Dec. 23.

The next regular meeting will be Dec. 16.

Figure 13-13. Wrap underneath a cutoff rule.

When there is not enough time to reset a headline to a wider column measure, another makeup procedure is to avoid having to make wraps by filling the remaining space with stories of shorter length. Or, perhaps, a longer story can be shortened by cutting off some of the longer stories and combining them with fillers.

When most of the page has been dummied, the makeup procedure is complete. Small spaces may remain because all stories did not fit precisely. The page dummy is sent to the composing

Filling Remaining Space

Conyers Offered
Replacement Tree

By RON TAYLOR

A Conyers housewife has offered a cedar she nurtured from a seedling to replace a giant artificial Christmas tree which mysteriously vanished from a Rockdale County shopping center.

Mrs. Kelly S t o c k t o n said Wednesday her tree has been fertilized "just like my flowers" and is now taller than her house.

She offered the cedar to merchants at the Rockdale Shopping Center after county residents went there Monday for tree-lighting ceremonies only to find that the 17-foot gold tree had disappeared.

It apparently had been hauled away by burglars. Merchants discovered it missing last Saturday as they prepared for Monday's celebration.

Mrs. Stockton said she nourished her mammoth tree with Vigoro after extracting it from woods when it was only 12 inches high and planting it in her front yard.

She says she has no qualms agout sacrificing her tree for the Yule season.

"IT'S BLOCKING my view from my picture window," she said, adding that she no longer has enough lights to continue her own annual Christmas decoration of the tree.

Mrs. Stockton said the tree she is offering without charge is the second cedar she has pampered to adulthood in her front yard. The merchants are weighing the offer. Another tree planted when Mrs. Stockton and her husband moved into their Flat Shoals Road home subsequently was chopped down and decorated for Christmas use in the Stocktons' living room.

Mrs. Stockston said she plans to go to the woods for another seedling after the present cedar is cut down.

Dr. Roland Reagan, president of the shopping center's merchants association, said the association would gladly accept Mrs. Stockton's gift but that he is not certain workmen will be able to get it up in time for Christmas display.

IT WAS REAGAN and several other merchants who discovered the disappearance of the big artificial tree.

It had been stored atop a store in the middle of the shopping center, but when merchants went up on the store roof Saturday they found no trace of the tree or its protective plastic covering.

Businessmen speculate burglars stole it and sold it to some other city in need of a tree.

Figure 13–14. Wrap underneath a two-column lead paragraph without a cutoff rule.

room where a printer begins to assemble type and pictures into a page form. The remaining space may be filled in two ways: (1) If the space is large enough, fillers may be used. Editors assign someone the responsibility for seeing that there are a sufficient number of fillers available each day. (2) If the space is relatively small, then it is filled by leading. Leading is first applied to the lead paragraph downward until the column is filled.

Flexibility in Makeup   In planning the makeup of large newspapers, some attention should be given to flexibility of design to accommodate late-breaking news. There are two considerations in planning for a flexible design. The first one is a mechanical consideration. Can one or two stories be replaced without too much effort? Remaking a page is a task that should be accomplished in the shortest amount of time to meet a press deadline. It may be necessary to rejustify as many as six columns of news in order to accommodate a late story. When the story to be replaced is odd-shaped, involving complex wraps, it will take more time to remake than it might if it were simply shaped. The new story may not be as long as the one it replaces, or it may be longer.

The Art of Editing

Senate approves $700 exemption on '70 wage tax

By Tom Littlewood
Sun-Times Bureau

WASHINGTON — The Senate disregarded President Nixon, its Finance Committee and the House Wednesday and voted to raise the personal income tax exemption from $600 to $700 next year and $800 in 1971.

This is the amount a taxpayer can subtract from his taxable income for himself and each dependent in the family. The amendment, by Sen. Albert Gore (D-Tenn.), carried 58 to 37.

If it survives the Senate-House conference committee and is part of the tax bill finally signed into law by the President, the exemption would redistribute some $9 billion in contemplated tax cuts. It would not affect income tax due in April.

Relief for big families

By increasing exemptions instead of cutting rates by at least 6 per cent and raising the standard deduction available for non-itemizers, the measure would give more relief to large families, especially in the middle-income group who are paying off mortgages, and less to those who make $20,000 or more.

The version reported by the Senate Finance Committee would have provided about $4.5 billion in general rate cuts. A similar rate schedule cleared the House last summer.

Mr. Nixon has warned that he might veto a tax bill that drains off too many tax dollars while inflation is still a problem.

The President wrote Senate leaders on Tuesday, saying an $800 exemption would reduce income taxes too early and by too much, about $4.8 billion. Gore disputed the short-run revenue effects of his plan.

Worried about the political risk in the easily understood exemption issue, the Republicans tried to outmaneuver Gore, but wound up more shattered and distraught than before.

First, moderates tried to put over a compromise by Sen. Charles H. Percy (R-Ill.) that would have spread smaller increases over a longer period, cushioning the inflationary impact.

But the White House and the Treasury Department refused to accept Percy's proposal of 2 $50-a-year increases until $750 was reached in 1972. Only half of the 42 voting Republicans supported Percy, and his amendment failed 72 to 23.

Scott flays administration

After Gore's amendment won, Minority Leader Hugh Scott (R-Pa.) engaged in an unusual public chastisement of the Republican administration.

He said the Treasury had "gone down to a resounding and glorious defeat" because it refused t listen to his advice and settle for the Percy compromise.

"I do hope," he told the Senate sarcastically, "that responsible officials in the Treasury of my own administration will realize we understand more about Senate strategy than they do."

North Shore salutes Crane

Representing planeloads of North Shore residents who flew to Washington Wednesday to honor their new 13th District congressman, Bernard E. Pederson (right) of Palatine presents Congressional Seal to Rep. Philip M. Crane. House minority leader Gerald Ford and the Illinois Republicans in the House later met the group at a reception. (Sun-Times Photo)

A Treasury official later said the tax cuts in Percy's proposal, combining a higher exemption and some rate reductions, were excessive over the long run.

Percy and Sen. Ralph T. Smith (R-Ill.) both
Turn to Page 26

Figure 13–15. Wrap underneath a picture. [*Courtesy Chicago Sun-Times.*]

Co-ed courses open at Y

THE WINTER session of special courses and activities begins the week of Jan. 12 at the Ravenswood YMCA. Adult co-ed courses are featured in rapid reading, scuba diving and ballroom dance.

For women only, there are courses in self-defense, dressmaking, slimnastics, swimming and "morning out."

For men only there are classes in self-defense, executive fitness and swimming.

For boys and girls, ages 3 to 5, there are gym and swim classes in the morning and early afternoon.

Other classes offered for boys or girls, ages 6 to 13, are ballet, judo and gymnastics.

All classes are open to nonmembers as well as members.

Figure 13–16. Acceptable raw wrap over an advertisement.

Therefore, planning must be geared to making the design simple and flexible enough for any contingency.

A second consideration is the effect that a major story change will have on total page design. Although it is impossible to know how a late-breaking story will be shaped, it may be possible to anticipate how various-shaped stories will affect the design. If the original design is simple, chances are that any changes can be adapted easily to the old design without destroying the original appearance.

The Total Design Concept

An alternative to makeup in the traditional manner is the total design concept, a technique in which the entire page is designed as a single entity rather than being built piece by piece until a design emerges. Because the total design is kept in mind as the page is being planned, the designer is not restricted to columnar arrangements. Traditionally, the makeup editor shaped the page design by fitting stories into columns. He could vary shapes somewhat by building vertical or horizontal stories, but the page always showed the effect of columnar planning. Totally designed pages, however, may take radically different forms. In fact, it may resemble magazine formats at times. Columns of type are not necessarily placed next to each other in a neat, traditional appearance. There may be bold and dramatic shapes that reflect contemporary design found outside of the newspaper.

To implement this concept several principles may serve as guides:

1. A general approach is to create a basic format that serves as a rough model for the entire page. One then attempts to fit the news into that model. To save time, the designer may have prepared a number of different models to serve as guides that fit the day's news (Figure 13–17). It is obvious that the nature of the news should determine the nature of the format. More spectacular formats are more appropriate for spectacular news. By having an idea book comprising many different basic formats, the designer can study the news and then find one or more that possibly, with some revision, can fit the news.

2. The nature of a basic format is a page divided into broad areas, each of which is pleasingly proportional and the sum of which adds up to an exciting design. The basis for division is the rectangle. There is no need for an odd-shaped story to appear anywhere on the page. Rectangles of different shapes, directions and weights provide the differentiation needed for an attractive total design.

3. No matter which alternative format is used as a guide, it must be simple, dramatic and contemporary. There should be no frills, no artificial devices, no clutter. Like modern architecture, there should be a great deal of open space that allows each story to breathe without severely competing for attention with a story next to it.

4. Any basic format may be changed in any way that best accommodates the news. In other words, this approach does not ask that the designer simply try to force news into a prearranged format. But the basic format, because it has been well thought out, should be kept in mind at all times while the adjustments are being made.

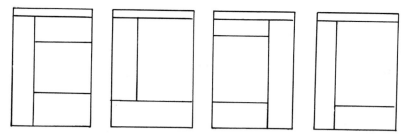

Figure 13–17. Some alternative basic formats.

5. One of the most important features of this approach is a reduction in the usual number of stories that must appear on a page. There are relatively few stories on this kind of page, and because there are so few, more white space is available between the columns, between headlines and pictures and between the lines of type. The generous use of white space, carefully placed, is essential. The white space should not appear in one part of a page when other parts appear black and crowded. It is the white space that helps make the page appear dramatic. The space between columns, for example, should never be less than 1½ picas wide and perhaps as much as 2 to 3 picas.

Because fewer stories can be used on such pages, a summary of the news is desirable. Many readers may not be inclined to search the paper for news that formerly appeared on the front page. The summary of news is a convenient way to help the reader know what is going on. Page references for additional details will enable him to read more if he wants to.

6. Another way to achieve a dramatic design is to use large stories and pictures in bold shapes that dominate the page. In addition, the use of large hairline boxes may enhance the stories and pictures inside.

7. Most of the news matter may be set to the paper's standard column widths. However, headlines may have to be written after the designer decides how a given story fits on a page. In other words, he is conscious of the total design as he decides where and how any story will appear on the page.

Although the total design concept is a way to create pages that are contemporary-appearing, there are a number of questions that invariably arise. One of the most often asked questions concerns the problem of time and cost. Will it take longer and cost more than traditional makeup procedures? The answer is that it will do both at first because the technique is new. But after a while, the makeup editor should be able to design a page in about the same amount of time that it took for the traditional makeup of the same page. It is radically new for most newspapers (Figure 13–18a, b). It will probably be used more in the preparation of offset papers where pasteup of stories is so easy. But it may be more difficult for letterpress newspapers.

Will this technique reduce the amount of news in the paper? Probably yes, because more room than before will be allotted to

Good morning, it's

THE RECORD

Make it a Record day

Today's weath

Little change in temp; se details page three.

10 cents

Cedar Falls, Iowa 50613

Paul Christensen

Robert Berg

Otis Budlong

Chamber directors

Richard Johnson

Don Lindaman

William Merner

Harold Klepfer

Ten new Cedar Falls Chamber of Commerce directors will assume duties in July.

The new directors and their firms, announced today by Chamber President Fred Kercheval, include Robert Berg, Berg's College Drug; Otis Budlong, farmer; Paul Christensen, contractor; Willis Hansen, Clay Equipment Co.; Richard Johnson, Cedar Falls Utilities; Dr. Ron King, dentist; Harold Klepfer, Harold's Men's Wear; Don Lindaman, Cedar Falls Trust and Savings; William Merner, attorney; and Marvin Ziesmer, Assistant Superintendent of Schools.

Chamber Vice President Robert Beach appointed two directors at large with board approval. They were Budlong and Hansen.

King beomes a member of the board by virtue of his position as past president of the Jaycess.

The other seven directors were elected by the membership.

During the July meeting, the new officers will be installed. The new president is Robert Beach. The new vice president is Fred Kercheval. A treasurer will be elected at the meeting to replace Robert Plagge.

Holdover board members are James Blanford, Marvin Calvert, Eugene Lehman, Dumont MacKenzie, Steve Nelson, Richard Nemmers, Thomas Sampson, Erich Teigeler and William Wood.

The July meeting will be the last for Richard Doerfer, Robert Fink, the Rev. Donald Iles, Joe McCullough, Andrew McDivitt, LeRoy Redfern, James Tucker and Allan Olsen.

Dr. King

Marvin Zeismer

Willis Hansen

PRESIDENT Nixon told reporters Thursday night that he hopes to see "some progress" in the Paris peace talks toward a solution to the Vietnam War during the next "two to three months." (UPI Telephoto)

SAFEGUARD MISSILE: 'We will win the fight on Safeguard.'

VIETNAM PEACE: 'We hope, within the next two or three months to see some progress in substantial discussions in Paris.'

FBI CONTROVERSIES: 'Mr. Hoover does enjoy my complete confidence.'

ROCKEFELLER TRIP: 'The explosive demonstrations indicate that such a trip was necessary.'

STUDENT UNREST: 'I cannot support legislative proposals which would cut off funds to any college or University in which there was a demonstration.'

Nixon: Hope to beat timetabl

WASHINGTON (AP — President Nixon voiced a hope Thursday night his administration can beat a timetable for pulling 100,000 troops from Vietnam by year's end and all ground combat troops by the close of 1970.

The timetable was proposed by Clark M. Clifford, secretary of defense at the end of the Johnson administration, in an article in Foreign Affairs Quarterly.

"I think we have started toward the withdrawal that Mr. Clifford advocated," Nixon told a nationally broadcast news conference. "I hope we can beat his timetable and not be in Vietnam as long as he suggested."

The President said, too, the target date for talks with Russia on limitation of strategic arms is sometime between July 31 and Aug. 15—perhaps in Vienna or Geneva.

The President predicted that "we will win the fight on Safeguard"—the antiballistic missile system encountering heavy going in the Senate.

SINCE RECOMMENDING it, Nixon said, he has received new intelligence information on Soviet success in testing multiple re-entry vehicles which convinces him that Safeguard is even more necessary. He said the "footprints" of this weapon that can attack many targets at once are going to fall on this country's Minuteman silos, and 80 per cent of these defensive missiles will be in danger.

The President covered assorted topics at his first news conference in two months.

On Vietnam, Nixon said the U.S. military commander there, Gen. Creighton W. Abrams, has orders "to conduct this war with a minimum of American casualties" and he believes the general is following orders.

"We have withdrawn forces," Nixon said in evident reference to his announcement of June 8 of 25,000 to be pulled out by the end of August. "We will withdraw more.

"As far as how many will be withdrawn, I would hope we would beat Mr. Clifford's timetable..."

Nixon began his comment by saying that for five years under the previous administration there was continued escalation of the war. He also said in the year during which Clifford was secretary of defense U.S. casualties reached their highest annual level.

"This is not to say that Mr. Clifford's present judgment is not to be considered," Nixon added.

OF THE PARIS peace talks Nixon reported under questioning that there is no substantial public evidence of progress in getting down to "substantive negotiations."

"We hope," he said, "within the next two or three months to see some progress in substantial discussions in Paris."

In a later question on Clifford's timetable Nixon said, "I hope we will not be in Vietnam as long as he suggested we will have to be there."

Nixon was speaking out at his first news conference in two months and his sixth since he entered the White House, He came in with a big smile to the assemblage of reporters in the East Room and encountered a question about the continuing, heating economy.

Asked if he contemplated any new moves against rising living costs and prices, Nixon said it usually takes about six months between the time of decision and their taking effect in the economic field.

HE VOICED A belief the decisions his administration has made on such things as budgeting and continuation of the surtax will begin to take effect in two or three more months.

In the political arena, Nixon got an inquiry whether he will endorse State Sen. John J. Marchi and other Republican nominees in the New York City election this fall. Marchi won a victory for the conservative wing of his party in defeating Mayor John V. Lindsay's bid for renomination in the primary Tuesday. Lindsay will run as Liberal candidate.

Nixon grinned and said he would back the winning GOP candidates but also follow a longtime practice of campaigning and taking part only in national and state elections—not local ones.

Asked about controversies involving FBI Director J. Edgar Hoover in regard to wiretapping, Nixon said, "Mr. Hoover does enjoy my complete confidence" and that there had been no discussions about his tenure in office.

On electronic surveillance, Nixon said he had checked whether it was done by the FBI on its own, or approved by the attorney general. "I found that it had always been approved by the attorney general," he said.

"It should be used very sparingly, very carefully," with regard to the rights of the individuals involved, Nixon said of wiretapping.

THE PRESIDENT said a "great deal of usefulness," will come from the trip to Latin America by Gov. Nelson A. Rockefeller of New York.

"The explosive demonstrations indicate that such a trip was necessary," the President said. He recalled his own trip to Europe in which "there were demonstrations in every city I visited—yet the trip was worthwhile."

Asked about a report by a score of GOP congressmen on campus unrest, he said "it was a very thoughtful report," and "they gave me a lot of information" which he needs to help him deal with campus unrest.

"I cannot support the legislative proposals in the House of Representatives which would cut off funds to any college or University in which there was a demonstration.

"This would be cutting off our nos spite our faces," Nixon said.

The responsibility for conta campus unrest should be on the shou of college administrators, Nixon sai

Asked about the Middle East, Nixo he sees very little improvement.

He said he trusts that four-power might develop some communic between Arabs and Israelis, and that the Soviet Union might play a

As for his Safeguard antiba missile system and its prospects i Senate, Nixon said polls indica Senators in favor and 46 against. "W win the fight on Safeguard. It will r necessary to compromise," he a although there might be some chan detail in the legislation.

He said new information on Sovie of multiple targeted re-entry vehicl convinced him that Safeguard is important.

ASKED WHAT will happen if t come surtax is not extended by Ju Nixon said Congress can pass a s resolution to take care of the situatio it acts on extension legislation.

"What is important," he said, "i the world knows that it will be exte

He said, however, he believes the had bipartisan support and "due t support, it will pass the Congress."

Asked about recent mayoral ele Nixon said the snap reaction to th Angeles victory of Mayor Sam Yort have been wrong as it was interprete white-black election.

He said he doesn't believe the majority of U.S. cities are anti-Ne anti-poor or members of hate grou

But he said Americans "are fed here by violence and lawlessness they want candidates who will t strong stand on it, that he thinks this message to political candidates.

Metro freeway plans outlined

Completed plans for a Waterloo-Cedar Falls freeway were outlined Thursday afternoon, and here Waterloo engineer Feddon Petrides presents copies of the proposed link to (from left) Mayor William McKinley, Cedar Falls, Mayor Lloyd Turner, Waterloo, and Frederick Mast, chairman of the Waterloo Urban Renewal Board. A large mock-up, prepared by the Brice, Petrides, and Associates firm, is in the background. See story on page 3. (Record Photo)

Distributors 'mum' on beer supplies

Metropolitan area beer distributors, apparently wary about starting a panicky run on their wares, are keeping mum about the availability of beer as nationwide strikes by workers at major breweries enter their third week.

One such wholesaler stated confidently his firm had seen the strikes "coming" and had managed to stockpile a quantity of bottled and canned beer, but then said, "The situation is very serious and getting more serious every day."

Most wholesale suppliers said they were showing no favorites in distributing beer to their regular customers.

"If a tavern owner came in and said he wanted to buy twice as many kegs of tap beer as he normally does, I'd have to turn him down," another wholesaler said.

"We'd end up making more enemies than friends if we started to play favorites," he said.

Keg beer has been most affected by the strikes, and one tavern owner said he knows of several bars and taverns that are selling a cheaper and less called-for brew on tap now instead of their normal premium beers.

Figure 13–18a. Pages using total design concept. [*Courtesy of the Cedar Falls, Iowa, Record.*]

od morning, it's
·· ·y, September 21, 1968

Cedar Falls, Iowa 50613

THE RECORD

Make it a Record day

Today's weather

Warmer, chance of showers, complete weather page 2.

10 cents

In the news

Around Cedar Falls...

Appraisal of right-of-way for the Highway 218 improvement program is scheduled to begin in the near future.

City councilmen will be asked Monday to approve the leasing of office space for Wallace Richmond, who has been appointed to appraise land for the project, which calls for 6-laning Hwy. 218.

The office is to be located at 114½ West 4th Street.

In other business, councilmen will hear a request from R. D. Letsch Sr., 3008 Rainbow Dr., that the city give cemetery lots to Cedar Falls servicemen who are killed in action.

Second readings will be given to a new city ordinance prohibiting the possession of beer and liquor by persons under the age of 21; a rezoning ordinance amendment for property south of the new College Square Shopping Center.

Around the World...

MEXICO CITY (AP)—About 3,000 students, some hurling rocks and firebombs, battled with 1,000 riot policemen outside a polytechnic school Friday in a new outburst of the violence harassing Mexico City as it prepares for the opening of the Olympic Games Oct. 1.

There was some gunfire and the police used tear gas in attempting to bring the crowd under control. One police truck was set on fire, and several persons were reported injured.

Hundreds of students were holed up in buildings of the Zacateco school in the northern sector of the city.

The outburst came after gunmen speeding by in two cars sprayed the College of Mexico with machine-gun bullets in the darkness before dawn Friday.

The students at the polytechnic school hurled fire bombs at the riot police trucks and at least one officer was critically injured.

Around the Nation...

WASHINGTON (AP)—Dr. John A. Wheeler of Princeton University, who helped pioneer the nuclear age, was named Friday to receive the $25,000 Enrico Fermi award.

In addition to the cash award, a gold medal and a citation will be presented to Dr. Wheeler in formal ceremonies Dec. 2 at a place yet to be selected, the Atomic Energy Commission announced.

Shortly after nuclear fission was discovered, Wheeler collaborated with another pioneer, Niels Bohr, in writing a paper on "the Mechanism of Nuclear Fission" which still is basic to understanding of the process.

ASHEVILLE, N. C. (AP)—The government says an Asheville man arrested Friday sold thousand of acres of mountain land he didn't actually own, some of it in the Great Smoky Mountains National Park.

The man is Clyde J. Leeson, 40, a real estate developer, who was indicted by a federal grand jury on 12 counts of using the mails to defraud.

Leeson is charged with selling more than 90,000 acres, three times. Of the 90,000 acres, 60,125 acres lies in the park and is owned by the U. S. Government.

Leeson, who was indicted by a federal grand jury at Stateville Tuesday, surrendered to U. S. marshal Paul eTal at Asheville Friday. He was held under $110,000 bond.

'Copter force invades DMZ to block Viet Cong thrust

SAIGON (AP) — A helicopter-borne force of 2,000 U. S. Marines has invaded the demilitarized zone between North and South Vietnam to head off an expected thrust southward on "speed trails" by the North Vietnamese army, the U. S. Command disclosed yesterday.

Elements of the 4th and 9th Marines regiment penetrated to the banks of the Ben Hai River in the tangled jungle and high ridges of the central sector of the zone to tear up the enemy's infiltration system, a Marine spokesman said.

The operation began Monday but the U. S. Command had placed an embargo on news concerning it.

Information about it was released yesterday only after an international new agency had broken the embargo, military officials said.

The Leathernecks reported killing 74 North Vietnamese regiments and seizing one prisoner in sporadic fighting during the first five days of the operation.

U. S. losses were reported as 10 Marines wounded and two dead.

The command reported that the largest kill came Sept. 17 from artillery fire on a North Vietnamese force, resulting in 25 enemy deaths.

It is the first time that an allied force has entered the central area of the once-neutral buffer zone between the Vietnams. U. S. and South Vietnamese units have made a half-dozen major probes of the zone along the eastern coastal flank in the past 16 months.

A Marine spokesman said the purpose of the operation is to disrupt a newly discovered network of enemy "speed trails." He described speed trails as cleared paths fitted with steps and hand rails at difficult spots.

This system of trails is so effective, the spokesman added, that North Vietnamese soldiers could move from the Ben Hai River to hit a Marine outpost in the Rockpile area seven miles south in about six hours.

The Marine move followed by only three days a 14-hour raid into the southern portion of the zone near the South China Sea coast by American and Vietnamese infantrymen and Marines. In that raid, also designed to throw off balance any enemy offensive across the zone, the allied units reported killing 158 North Vietnamese soldiers while suffering only four killed and 24 wounded. In that operation, the government infantrymen and U. S. Army armored units and Marines pulled back out of the zone at nightfall.

In ground action Friday, North Vietnamese troops made fresh assaults against allied outposts and an armored column securing the northwestern invasion route to Saigon, but they were thrown back with the loss of 21 men killed.

Allied casualties in three fights against an estimated 1,200 Hanoi regulars were reported as 10 killed and 36 wounded.

The battles came on the heels of reports of dogfights in the skies over North Vietnam and continued B52 saturation bombings of troop concentrations and highways just north of the demilitarized zone and near the coast at the border between the two Vietnams.

A Navy pilot, Lt. Anthony Nargi, 28, of Clifton, N. J., shot down a MIG near Vinh farther up the coast Thursday and the U. S. Command reported the loss of an F105 Thunderchief elsewhere over the North Vietnamese panhandle to ground-fire.

The MIG was the 110th shot down in the war. The United States has lost 48 planes in dogfights. The loss of the F105 was the 897th warplane lost in the North.

Hanoi's Vietnam News Agency claimed four U. S. planes were shot down over the North Thursday.

The North Vietnamese ground attacks 55 miles northwest of Saigon were centered again around Tay Ninh. The strikes were aimed at border post manned by South Vietnamese militiamen and a U. S. 25th Infantry Division field position and road-clearing detail.

About 500 North Vietnamese, using flamet throwers, mortars and antitank rockets, hit the South Vietnamese outpost late Thursday night and continued their attack into Friday morning.

The enemy destroyed 90 per cent of the militiamen's barbed wire and sandbag outpost, but the defenders held out until two companies of reinforcements moved in by helicopter.

When the fight ended at noon, the militiamen counted 30 enemy bodies—19 of them inside the fort. The government lost 9 men killed and 28 wounded.

The 25th Division soldiers accounted for 61 additional enemy slain.

Thirty-seven killed when they attacked the night perimeter of a company in the Ben Chu rubber plantation east of Tay Ninh.

The North Vietnamese pounded the American position with mortars and then charged at about 2 a.m. They were sent reeling when artillerymen lowered the muzzles of three 105mm howitzers to chest level and sprayed the outer preimeter with beehive shells, which contain thousands of tiny, arrow-shaped darts that scatter like shotgun pellets.

There had been no penetration of the perimeter when the attack broke an hour later. No Americans were killed. Five were wounded. The enemy force was estimated be a battalion of 500 men.

Twenty-four more North Vietnamese regualrs died when they tried to ambush a unit of about 60 25th Division infantrymen and a dozen armored personnel carriesr clearing Route 26 south of Tay Ninh.

Soviet satellite circles the moon

MOSCOW (AP) — The Russian probe Zond 5 has flown around the moon, carried out "its program of research in outer space" and continues its flight, the Soviet Union announced Friday.

A Tass dispatch on operations of the unmanned vehicle incidentally confirmed a news scoop by British scientists Wednesday about its lunar course.

Sir Bernard Lovell, director of Britain's Jodrell Bank Space Observatory, had disclosed, in a report denounced by the Soviet Foreign Ministry's press department at the time as "a canard," that Zond 5 passed within 1,000 miles or so of the moon that day.

Corrected Trajectory

Giving the first official Soviet word about the probe since it was launched last Sunday, Tass said it corrected its trajectory Tuesday "to study the physical characteristics of outer space in the area of the moon" and circled the moon the next day at a range as close as 1,950 kilometers 1,212 miles.

Though the news agency said the flight continues, it did not specify the location of Zond 5.

Tass reported the launching of another sputnik, Cosmos 242, with scientific equipment for "further studies of outer space." Cosmos 242 was reported circling the earth at distances ranging from about 174 to 273 miles. But Zond 5 was the Russians' big space story of the day.

Lovell has expressed belief at Jodrell Bank that the probe was returning to earth and that the Russians would try to recover it. Such a feat would be a big step toward sending a man to the moon and bringing him back. The earth-moon trip of space devices normally takes 3½ days.

In reporting the spaceship "flew around the moon," Tass did not specify whether this meant it flew past on a curving trajectory, went into continuous orbit around the moon, or made one or more orbits and then blasted off in a new direction.

The Russians ordinarily blanket aims of their space work in secrecy until objectives are accomplished.

Tass said, however: "A stable radio communication is maintained with the station and relays scientific information to the ground . . . The coordination computing center continues processing incoming information."

A spokesman of the Foreign Ministry's press department declined to say whether the denial Wednesday had been meant to cover only Lovell's statement that Zond 5 might be returning to earth, rather than that it passed near the moon.

"You have a Tass announcement," he told an inquirer. "Be guided by it."

UNITED PRESS INTERNATIONAL INC., ALL RIGHTS RESERVED

Expected to be brought home today or early tomorrow is Zong 5—the Russian moon satellite which made an historic flight around the moon. This artist's conception shows the approximate path around the moon that the satellite may have taken on its circumunar mission. (UPI Telephoto).

loth
rsage?

Not really — a specimen the giant Atmoth from Philippines, ich is part of collection ught to UNI s fall by Dr. n Downey, logy department head. Preting the moth Mrs. Margo bney, secrey of the dertme nt.- is rles Haman, istant profesof biology.

Vast development program pushed to span mid-Canada

©The New York Times

TORONTO — A group of businessmen and professors has begun a campaign to win from the Canadian public support for a vast development program stretching across mid-Canada.

The cost to the taxpayers would be at least $5 billion, which in proportion to Canada's economy would be equivalent to about $80 billion in the United States.

Reaching in a lazy curve from Labrador down to lake Superior and up to Alaska, the belt — or corridor — to be developed 200 to 500 miles wide, is described as " a treasure house of nautral resources."

Cities protected from the cold, snow and wind by clear domes would be centered around nickel, zinc, iron, asbestos, timber, power, oil and gas resources; government-built railways and highways would facilitate commercial shipments of these products.

The mid-Canada corridor, the promoters seem to suggest, would serve as a safety value for future population growth in much the way that the settlement of the American West prevented the eastern half of the U. S. from being choked by the waves of immigration between the mid-century and World War I.

According to the promoters of the program, the recent rate of population growth, if it persists, will add 100 million people to Canada's population of 20 million in the next 100 years.

The Mid-Canada development idea was put forward in 1967 by Richard H. Rohmer, a 44-year-old Toronto lawyer. He hired a prominent company of engineering consultants and managers, Acres Research and Planning, Ltd., to put statistical and verbal flesh on his skeletal idea.

Recently Rohmer and that company announced the formation of the Mid-Canada Development Corridor Foundation, Inc., to raise money for a three-part conference in 1969 to study the problems of building cities, harbors, railways, industries and roads in the proposed zone.

Between two seminar-type meetings, some of the 160 conferees wil visit northern Sweden and possibly Siberia.

Professors to Direct

Professors from three universities—, Guelph, Lakeheak, and Laurentian—will direct the foundation, along with Rohmer and Norman Simpson, president of the Acres company.

"All the equity," or ownership, in the corridor "should be Canadian," Rohmer said, although American investors would be allowed to buy bonds.

"I don't see any threat from the United States," Rohmer said, adding that Canada needed American capital, "I just think we should do something Canadian."

igure 13–18b. See caption on facing page.

white space. Because advertising revenue will not be reduced, the space will have to come from editorial materials.

A final question concerns inside pages. Can inside pages be designed with the total design concept in mind? The answer is "not very well" because the shape of inside pages is determined by the size and position of advertisements. Yet even on inside pages, it is possible to improve appearance to a great degree.

The total design concept, therefore, is only one means of radically changing the appearance of newspaper design to harmonize with the contemporary world surrounding the reader. It isn't the only way, but it is one relatively new way. The make-up editor, using traditional techniques, can achieve the same thing with more effort and time, however.

14

Details of Contemporary Makeup and Design

Almost every newspaper editorial office has a set of rules, written or unwritten, to be followed by those engaged in makeup. These rules may have been handed down from one generation to another so that over the years they may have become inflexible. Even when the rules do not have a long history, they tend to be inflexible. Young makeup editors, especially, are not expected to challenge or change them. The assumption is that because they are founded on traditional makeup practices, they must be good. Consequently, there have been few radical changes in makeup and design within the last fifty years.

Recently, however, makeup editors have been making changes, some of which appear radical when compared with traditional makeup. These editors have been evaluating all the older makeup rules and have found many to be logically indefensible. Therefore, they have substituted new and more logical makeup techniques for older ones. In some cases, they have used research to show an older makeup rule invalid.

Anyone who wants to create contemporary design ought to examine the rules of makeup to see whether they should be continued or replaced with something better. One example, perhaps, will suffice to illustrate the need for evaluation.

In its makeup manual a large metropolitan newspaper still maintains that headlines placed underneath pictures must be set in all-capital letters. The reason given is that when type is set in all caps, it forms an imaginary straight line next to the picture. If a headline is to be placed above a picture, then it should also be set in all caps so that there will be no ascenders of letters next to the picture.

**Evaluating
Makeup Rules**

The assumption underlying the rule is that lower case letters are harder to read when placed next to pictures because the ascenders or descenders form a ragged imaginary line next to the straight line of the photograph. Capital letters, on the other hand, form a straight imaginary line and are therefore easier to read.

The assumption, of course, is wrong. Research on the readability of type has shown that individuals read by recognizing the shapes of words rather than by visually sighting each letter and forming a word (Figure 14–1).[1] Only when faced with unfamiliar words might a reader sight each letter. Therefore, lines set in lower case type are really easier to read than lines set in all caps. The same research also showed that all cap lines are read about 12 per cent slower than those set in caps and lower case.[2] The rule, therefore, is invalid. Yet no one has taken the trouble to question it and even today it is still used.

Figure 14–1. Lower-case word shapes are easier to recognize and read than all-capital word shapes.

Although there is not enough research on which to base all makeup rules, some research is available. Where there is no research, rules will have to be evaluated on the basis of reason and logic. Even then, care must be taken not to confuse the needs of contemporary readers with those of the past. In a less sophisticated age, where graphic design was not considered as important as it is now, many makeup rules were appropriate. Today, such rules are not valid. The use of "30" dashes to separate the end of one story and the beginning of another is an example. Years ago it was thought to be logical to separate stories with a short line such as a 30 dash. But many such dashes on a page proved to be unsightly. Today they have been replaced with white space. Therefore, when young persons weigh makeup rules they ought to consider the age in which they live as well as each rule's potential effectiveness versus its limitations, using the standards of good makeup and design as a basis.

The following discussion suggests details that distinguish contemporary makeup from more traditional forms.

[1] Miles A. Tinker, *Legibility of Print* (Ames: Iowa State University Press, 1963), pp. 57–61.
[2] *Ibid.*

The Art of Editing

The nameplate of a newspaper (often incorrectly called the masthead) is the name usually appearing at the top of page 1. Editors sometimes want to move the nameplate to other positions on the page because they assume that everyone knows the name of the newspaper he is reading and the space occupied by the nameplate might be better used for other purposes. Once a decision has been made to move the nameplate, then a question arises: Where on the page would the nameplate be most appropriate? Editors sometimes want to move it indiscriminately, considering the significance of news the most important criterion for positioning stories. Such editors feel that the nameplate is much less significant and therefore may be moved anywhere at almost any time. At other times, the nameplate seems to be moved around on page 1 without any apparent reason.

On one hand, the logic of moving it from day to day seems reasonable. After all, most readers know the name of the newspaper without looking at the nameplate.

But on the other hand, there are a number of reasons for keeping it in the top position most of the time. In debating the reasonableness of moving it around on the front page, one must consider all the purposes a nameplate serves.

Other than for simple identification purposes, a nameplate communicates the philosophical position of the publisher. The typefaces chosen for nameplates usually are distinguished-looking and have strong connotations. The best position for communicating these connotations is at the top of the page because the top position itself communicates a feeling of authority. Any object standing foremost among other objects is judged to be more significant. When an object is buried, its importance is diminished.

But another consideration has to do with the importance of the top position in serving as an anchoring device that provides readers with a feeling of stability as they read the paper. The nameplate usually represents the starting point for examining the contents of page 1. If it is not in its traditional position, the reader may have a sense of uneasiness and a slight loss of familiarity with the paper. Whereas he knows the news may change, the nameplate position will not, and he is thereby given a page whose stability makes reading comfortable.

Furthermore, postal regulations require that a newspaper indicate that it is second-class material somewhere within the first five pages of the paper. In the past, this material might be placed in the editorial page masthead, or it might be buried in a box on page 2. But it is also placed in small type near the nameplate, perhaps within the dateline rules that appear underneath it. If the nameplate serves this purpose, then it should remain at the top.

When the nameplate is moved to a new position every day, there is little reason for even having it on page 1. Why use a

---

nameplate if it is so unimportant that it can be shifted around to whatever space happens to be open? Readers will easily recognize page 1 without a nameplate. But that isn't the purpose for using it. Assuming, therefore, that a nameplate serves other purposes, as discussed, its position should be limited to the top. Readers resent continual changes in makeup and consequently would resent continual changes in the position of the nameplate.

A final reason for keeping the nameplate at the top relates to its function in the total page design. A nameplate floated down in the page becomes a component of the page's design and thereby complicates the process of makeup and design. Left at the top, page design is concerned only with the proper display of stories.

Yet there is some logic to defend the decision to move it if the move is not radical and if it is not done often. There are times when an eight-column, horizontally arranged story might well be placed above the nameplate. This story may be of such significance that the editors want to be sure that everyone sees it. The very top position should provide such assurance. But if this practice becomes regular, the importance of the nameplate is thereby diminished (Figure 14–2).

Northwest suburbs may have to buy water from Chicago

By Bob Casey

A recently-completed engineering study for the City of Chicago predicts that increased demand for water and dwindling well supplies may force several northwest suburbs to buy their water from Chicago.

The study, titled "Report Upon Adequate Water Supply for the Chicago Metropolitan Area 1969 to 2000," says Arlington Heights, Mount Prospect, Rolling Meadows and Elk Grove Village may find themselves joining more than 90 other suburbs that will buy water from Chicago.

Seventy-one suburbs now buy water from Chicago, including Des Plaines, which also gets some water from its own wells.

The study, by the Chicago engineering firm of Alvord, Burdick and Howson, predicts steady increases in per capita water consumption over the next 30 years. Arlington Heights, the report estimates will go from 85 gallons per person each day in 1970 to 115 gallons in 2000.

Daily per capita water used will rise from 101 gallons to 122 gallons for Mount Prospect, from 129 gallons to 147 gallons for Des Plaines and from 148 gallons to 169 gallons for Elk Grove village over the next 30 years.

The study also predicts population growth that will raise total water consumption even further by the year 2000. Arlington Heights will have 80,500 population, Mount Prospect 74,200, Des Plaines 80,800 and Elk Grove Village 52,100 by that year, the study estimates.

At the same time, water levels in northwest suburban wells will be dropping, the report says. Using state water survey records, the engineering firm predicted steady declines in wells used by Arlington Heights, Mount Prospect and Elk Grove Village.

Emphasizing that its predictions are not exact, the study says that water levels in two Mount Prospect wells will drop more than 600 feet and the levels in a third will drop about 300 feet.

Predicted water levels for three of Arlington Heights wells will be from 200 to 500 feet lower than present levels in 2000 if pumping trends continue, according to the study.

Elk Grove will see the water level in two of its wells drop more than 200 feet by 2000, the study predicts.

"The prediction of the ground water level decline...cannot be considered an exact prediction of ground water levels at some future date, but, rather an indication that if conditions remain unchanged ultimately these suburbs will require a supplementary source of water to their present well supplies, the study concluded.

The engineers predict that maximum water demand will remain constant in Chicago but rise dramatically in suburbs now buying water from Chicago and in those suburbs that will start buying Chicago water.

Chicago's maximum demand will stay at 1.8 billion gallons per hour through the year 2000 but demand from present suburban water customers will go from 344 million gallons per hour to 568 million gallons per hour. Suburbs not now buying water from Chicago will have a maximum demand of 225 million gallons per hour in 2000, the report says.

The portion of Chicago-produced water being used by suburbs will rise from 14.3 per cent in 1968 to 30.6 per cent in 2000, according to the study. In 1940, Chicago used 95 per cent of the water it produced.

To accommodate the predicted suburban demand, the study recommends expenditures by Chicago of $370,432,000 for improvements to the water system.

WEATHER

Tonight: Partly cloudy, low near 17; Tomorrow: Partly cloudy.

The Prospect Day

Telephone

255-7200

Your Home Newspaper

Volume 4, Number 173   Friday, December 26, 1969   20 Pages   Newsstand Price 10 Cents

NW suburbs lead new home building parade

By Richard Crabb

The tidal wave of home building in the northwest suburbs is rolling on west and north of Arlington Heights.

When the final totals are available in a few days, they will show that in 1969 the Village of Schaumburg issued permits for single family residences than any other municipality in Illinois. Arlington Heights will be second and Schaumburg's 1969 shows that all of the top five municipalities in Illinois in the issuing of new home permits are located in the northwest suburbs. They are Schaumburg, Arlington Heights, Buffalo Grove, Hoffman Estates and Palatine.

The five villages during the first 11 months of 1969 issued more than 3000 new home permits. The new homes, exclusive of the land, cost approximately $70,000,000.

THREE OF THE ...

South Holland (south Cook County), Northbrook and Naperville.

The population of all the villages in the northwest suburbs is rising rapidly. It is now clear, the basis of growth already recorded and land available, that Des Plaines, Arlington Heights and Schaumburg are emerging as the three big municipalities of the area.

Both Des Plaines and Arlington Heights are to have 1963 that Arlington Heights has not been the Illinois leader in the building of new homes. The peak came in 1967 when 805 single family residence permits were issued in Arlington Heights. In 1968 the number was almost as great, ending with a total of 788 permits.

This year in 11 months Schaumburg issued 913 new home permits as compared to 641 for Arlington Heights, 623 for Buffalo Grove, 496 for nization, reported that family home permits in the Chicago area were down by 55 per cent as compared with a November of 1968.

THE TIGHT money situation is clouding the prospects for new records in the northwest suburbs in 1970.

Mayor Robert O. Atcher of Schaumburg told The Day this week that if money for home building were available at interest rates that prevailed a few

Figure 14–2. Story above nameplate. [*Courtesy the Prospect Day, Metropolitan Printing Co., Elk Grove, Illinois.*]

There is also some logic to support the idea that a nameplate may be moved from side to side, but always at the top of the page. One of the most unsightly makeup devices of newspapers are the ears. When the editor wishes to eliminate them, he may do so by moving the nameplate to either side of the page and moving a one- or two-column story to the top. Another reason for moving the nameplate to the side may be to make room for more news than would be possible otherwise (Figure 14–3). Perhaps the editors who are most likely to experiment with moving the nameplate are those involved with publishing college news-papers. Their decisions to move it sometimes seem to be capri-cious rather than reasoned.

There are other uses for nameplates throughout the news-paper, but these do not involve moving the front page nameplate. For example, some newspapers have identical nameplates on pages 1 and 3. The effect of this arrangement is to present a second front page to readers so that different kinds of news may be featured on each front page. While national news might be used exclusively on page 1, local news might be featured on page 3.

Finally, there are modified nameplates that may be used in various sections of the newspaper. Women's pages, sports or financial pages also might have special nameplates. In reality, however, these are standing headlines rather than nameplates, and although they are designed to resemble the front page nameplate, their function is to introduce special sections of the newspaper.

Contemporary Headline Placement

When the traditional-minded makeup editor thinks of headlines, he tends to think of large display typefaces placed at the top of stories. This treatment is logical for pages designed to be strongly vertical in appearance. But when makeup is conceived of as being horizontal through the use of rectangularly shaped stories, headlines may be set in many different ways. These ways not only serve the purpose of summarizing the news but of making the page appear modern.

When horizontally shaped stories are used on a page, the head-line may be placed in at least three places, and possibly a fourth. It may be placed at the left- or right-hand side, the center, or the bottom of the story. The last-named position is not as desir-able as the others, but all are different from the traditional top position (Figures 14–4, 14–5 and 14–6).

If the headline is placed at the side of a story, it looks best if it aligns with the top line of body type. But the headline may be set flush left or flush right, both being contemporary treatments. The best position is at the left side of stories because readers proceed from the left to the right. Occasionally, the headline may look attractive when placed at the right.

When a story is given horizontal treatment, and it is long, the headline may be embedded in the center with type on all sides.

The Skokie Life

A Lerner Newspaper serving the people of Skokie

The paper with the want ads

Vol. 24—No. 19 | Four Sections, 72 Pages | THURSDAY, JANUARY 8, 1970 | 10 Cents Per Copy | Want Ads, Section Three, Pages 6-17

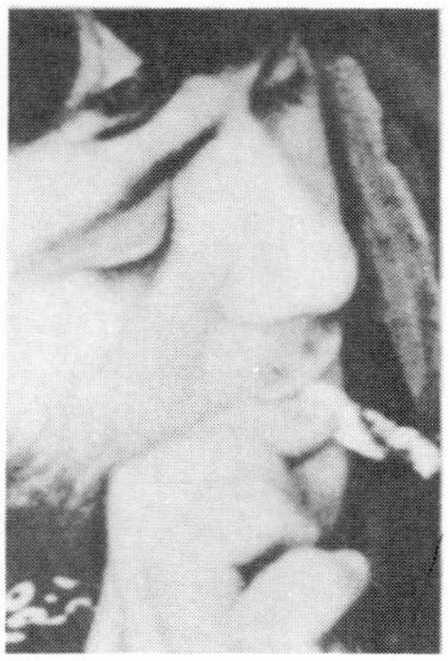

Drugs: is there an answer? See Focus on LIFE-land. Section 1-A, page one.

What's happening

CELEBRATION . . . Mr. and Mrs. Ben Wasken, 8027 Kilpatrick, Skokie, celebrated their 40th anniversary, Dec. 28, with a dinner at Pyrenees restaurant for relatives and close friends.

INSTALLATION . . . Andy Nickols of Lincolnwood is a co-chairman of the Variety Club of Illinois' installation luncheon to be held Monday, Jan. 12 at 12:30 p.m. in the Windsor room of the Pick-Congress Hotel. Henry Markbreit, 9517 Keeler, Skokie, will be installed as second assistant barker and Harry Balaban, 420 Brierhill, Deerfield, will be installed as dough guy.

ON DEAN'S LIST . . . Jean Dalicandro, daughter of Mr. and Mrs. Robert Dalicandro, 8631 Karlov, Skokie, is eligible to become a candidate for the honors program as a result of the 3.6 average earned during the Fall Quarter at Ohio State university in Columbus.

Jeanie, a Freshman in the Humanities college, is a graduate of Regina Dominican high school in Wilmette. She is listed in the 1969 Edition of Merit's Who's Who Among American High School Students, which features the top 3 per cent of the nation's graduating seniors.

VOTER REGISTRATION . . . Skokie Village Clerk William Siegel has announced that the village will conduct a voter registration drive through Jan. 20.

New residents, recently naturalized citizens, and young adults who have just turned 21 must register in order to vote in this important election year, Siegel said.

Village hall, 5127 Oakton, is open from 8:30 a.m. to 5 p.m. weekdays and from 8:30 a.m. to noon Saturdays. Call OR 3-0500 for further information.

VEEP . . . Robert Shonfeld, 6951 Knox, Lincolnwood, has been elected a vice-president of Clinton E. Frank, Inc., Advertising. Shonfeld joined the agency in 1957 as an account executive.

INSTALLATION . . . Henry Markbeit, 9517 Skokie, will be installed as second assistant chief barker of Tent 26, Variety Club of Illinois, at the installation luncheon to be held on Monday, Jan. 12, at 12:30 p.m. in the Pick-Congress hotel. Andy Nickols, 4066 Touhy, Lincolnwood, is a co-chairman for the affair.

TO SPEAK . . . Keigler E. Flake, consultant for subscription television at Zenith Radio Corp., 1900 N. Austin, Chicago, will be guest speaker Jan. 19 at the Lincolnwood Men's club.

His subject, "Subscription Television: what is it?" will include the development of STV, what it will mean to the public and action by federal authorities to control STV.

Flake, a retired U.S. Marine Corps colonel, managed Zenith's Hartford, Conn., STV experiment and was named vice-president-general manager of RKO General's WHCT-TV in 1966.

The Men's Club meeting will be held at the Kenilworth Inn, 7100 Lincoln, Lincolnwood.

2,000 residents ask tax repeal

By CHARLENE LOUIS
Lerner Newspapers Correspondent

SKOKIE—Skokie Board of Trustees was presented Monday night with some 2,000 signed cards requesting the repeal of the five per cent municipal utility tax adopted by the board last summer.

Reinforcing the citizen demand was a delegation of some 40 persons, representing both homeowners and industry.

WHILE THE people did not get what they most hoped for—an immediate board vote to repeal the tax—they did get something definite—the promise of several trustees that the board will look at the tax again, when the picture regarding monies accruing to the village from the new sales tax and state income tax is fact rather than guesstimate.

The village finance officer will probably not be able to establish a pattern from these figures until about April or May. Currently, the village has received only $64,784 as its pro-rata share of the income tax.

As confrontations go, the skirmish this night in Village hall was rather short, with the people making their presentations, and most of the trustees offering a statement in return.

PRINCIPAL spokesman for the gallery was village merchant Norman Schack. He talked about how burdensome the tax has become, and about how a group of people have banned together to ask for its review, as occurred in Morton Grove. The drive was led by Mrs. Fred Nemeroff, 8119 Kilbourn.

Schack noted that the new tax had won approval by a 4-3 vote, and suggested that perhaps some of the "ayes" might consider becoming "nays," "especially in view of the additional sales tax and state income tax monies coming to the village," he said.

However, the key point of his argument was that the utility tax monies would no longer be needed since the village won't be using some $500,000 in the budget for a capital investment this fiscal year."

SCHACK WAS obviously referring to the fact that $350,000 budgeted for new incinerator grates will not be spent in the current fiscal year. (A new method of garbage disposal is being considered).

As long as the village does not need this, let's repeal it." he said. "If you prove need, that's another thing."

The idea of "a floating $500,000 in the budget" was reputed vehemently by Trustee Edward Fleischman. A succession of business people and residents came before the podium to give their reasons for protesting this new tax.

Edwin Stone of a Skokie firm, Metal Treating and Engineering, chided that the tax imposes a great burden on the small businessman. "The amount of this tax on me will exceed what I will pay for the state income tax."

WILLIAM NIGUT, 8232 Karlov, who ran for Con-Con, charged that responsibility for the defeat of one of the Skokie library referenda could be laid on the shoulders of the four village officials who voted for the utility tax."

When it was Fleischman's turn, his remarks developed into something of a speech. He was trying to get several points across. First, that it was "wonderful" that the people come up here to express their feelings and their interest.

However, he said, "It shows that we need to amplify our reasons for needing this tax and our attitudes toward it."

THE BUDGET study, he said, pointed out that we needed more money.

"But the question was how to get it. Nobody wanted the utility tax; but we thought it was more equitable."

"We also made it part and parcel of the tax ordinance that we would have to review the tax on or before Aug. 30, 1970, because then we would know how much money these new taxes would be bringing in."

"Today, by chance," he continued, "we went over the budget income and outgo to date. We found out that as far as revenue goes, we are close to $400,000 short.

"With $350,000 unspent, if we come out with a bal-

(Continued on page 3)

NORMAN SCHACK

Brotman resigns post in District 74

By JUDITH HEYMAN
Lerner Newspapers Correspondent

LINCOLNWOOD—The Lincolnwood School Board Tuesday accepted a letter of resignation from Board Member Robert Brotman and formulated plans to appoint a successor.

The board will entertain applications from those people who have appeared before the nominating caucus or any other residents of the community.

INTERESTED persons should contact Dr. Marvin Garlich, superintendent of Dist. 74, to file an application by Thursday, Jan. 15.

Candidates will be interviewed and a selection made at the next school board meeting, Jan. 20, which will be held at 7 p.m. rather than 8 p.m., the regular scheduled hour.

The new board member will then stand for election April 11, to fulfill the remaining one year of Brotman's term.

LEGALLY, the board must fill the position by Feb. 3, 1970, or the County Superintendent of Schools can call a special election.

Brotman resigned in order to take a position in Palo Alto, Calif. He is an accountant and in the words of Board President, Shirley Garland, "has been a valuable asset to this board, and we greatly regret his leaving."

There will be three additional vacancies to be filled on April 11. The three-year terms of Mrs. Garland, Dr. Theodore Balsam and Eric Moch expire. According to nominating caucus standards (one person can serve only two successive terms) only Moch and Dr. Balsam are eligible. Mrs. Garland is completing her sixth year on the board.

NOMINATING petitions for school board membership must be filed between Feb. 25 and March 20, between 8 a.m. and 4 p.m. on any school day with Eugene Moody at the school district's administration building.

In other business the board delayed approval of a restaffing plan for Todd Hall presented by Dr. Garlich.

Since enrollment will be down, the plan called for replacing one homeroom with an art room and using the funds allotted for a section teacher to provide a full-time physical education teacher. This plan would not increase the budget.

"**THE ART ROOM** would facilitate the duties of the art teacher," according to Dr. Garlich.

He explained that dropping a section would not increase the 2nd grade-class size, which would decrease from an average of 27 or 28 pupils to about 26 per class. However, it would increase the first grade class size by about 2 pupils per room.

Board members questioned whether they should not use the decreased enrollment as an opportunity to commit themselves to smaller class size. They also wanted time to consider other possible uses for the additional space, such as a remedial reading class. A decision will be made at the next board meeting.

DR. GARLICH stated his position to a remedial reading teacher for primary grades, saying that "if the primary teacher has any expertise, it is in the field of teaching reading.

"I have never seen a successful remedial reading program for that age level, because some children will never be good readers no matter what the instruction. This kind of program simply gives the classroom teacher an excuse to evade her duties."

He added that he does believe in reading diagnosis for those grades.

Dr. Garlich defended his re-staffing program for Todd Hall stating, "We are in an enviable position in terms of enrollment. Within the next few years I also see a decrease in the enrollment at Rutledge, which may free some space there for other programs."

Employes get preview of village diabetes test project

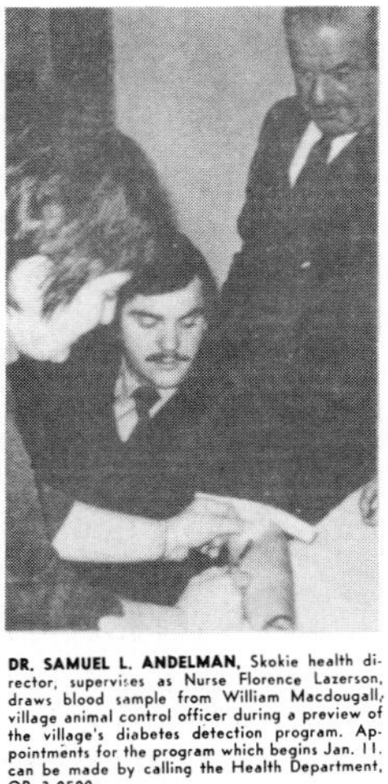

DR. SAMUEL L. ANDELMAN, Skokie health director, supervises as Nurse Florence Lazerson, draws blood sample from William Macdougall, village animal control officer during a preview of the village's diabetes detection program. Appointments for the program which begins Jan. 11. can be made by calling the Health Department, OR 3-0500.

SKOKIE—Samuel L. Andelman, health director, Skokie Health department announced that Skokie employes had a "sneak preview" of the public screening tests for diabetes detection to begin Sunday morning, Jan. 11.

Wednesday, Dec. 24, was a private day at the Skokie Health department.

Employees from Village Hall had been instructed to partake heavily of carbohydrates (sugars and starches) for the few days preceding the test and to fast from midnight the night before, with no food or water.

IN THE MORNING they drank an orange-flavored glucose solution and exactly one hour later a blood sample was drawn and sent to the laboratory to be tested for the amount of glucose in the blood.

Those who participated agreed that it was a smooth, simple procedure and were glad to find out whether or not they were suspected diabetics. The health department does not make diagnoses, what they hope to do is uncover the so-called 'hidden' diabetics.

Results of the tests are confidential and reported only to the person's private physician, with permission, if it is felt that further testing is advisable.

Dr. Matthew M. Steiner, chairman of the preventable Disease committee, and his committee, Dr. Herbert Lipschultz, chairman of the Skokie Board of Health, Dr. Melvin Chertack, Dr. Frank DiGilio, Dr. Lawrence L. Golden, Dr. John Gruhn, Bernard Kramer and Martin Lebedun, say there may be 2,500 people from 30 through 59 years of age in Skokie who unknowingly have diabetes.

If you are in this age group and live in Area 1, call Florence Hack, coordinator for the Diabetes detection program, OR 3-0500, and make an appointment.

JAN. 11, at 9 a.m. marks the beginning of this community program, brought to the public without charge. Area 1 is bounded on the north by Dempster, on the east by Skokie boulevard, and on the west and south by Skokie's natural boundaries. Testing in the other areas will be made known at a later time.

Many technicians and volunteer workers will be needed to aid this effort. Please call Mrs. Hack, OR 3-0500 and offer your services.

Auto-bargain section introduced by LIFE

A NEW SERVICE offered by The LIFE, beginning Jan. 8, will be our Super-Auto Mart section, which will feature a choice of automobile bargains, both new and used.

Dealers serving the entire LIFE-land areas, from Skokie, Morton Grove, Niles, Lincolnwood, Glenview, Des Plaines, Highland Park, Highwood, Deerfield, Fort Sheridan, Northbrook and Lake county, will advertise in this regular two-page section.

Edward Berliant, general manager of White and Cronen Ford, 9401 Milwaukee, Niles, said "Since most of our customers are from this area, we want to take care of the people in our vicinity through this service, where it has a more personal touch."

Mel Waldorf, president of Public Pontiac, 7501 N. Lincoln, Skokie, said "I think it will be advantageous for local people particularly at this time of the year. Like any other business, after January we have heavy inventories, and this is a good time for people to buy."

Red Weiss, used car manager at Walton Motors, 5050 Dempster, Skokie, said "We feel it will be advantageous for local people to buy locally, for the best service."

Super-Auto Mart will be advertised on WLFD TV, Channel 32, on WEEF and WSDM am-fm radio and on bus cards in Skokie.

Figure 14–3. Nameplate moved to the side. [*Courtesy Lerner Newspapers, Chicago, Illinois.*]

First of two sewer
survey reports
given city Monday

The city council two months back voted $3500 for the survey; then later voted another $3500 for a storm sewer survey. The latter will be presented at a later date.

The Casler report is based on the idea of repairing the present system, adding relief or bypass sewers where necessary, the building of a new treatment plant to handle the western half of the city and the rehabilitation and additions to the present sewerage disposal plant east of the city.

The engineer's report gave the city several alternate plans but all are based on the idea of repairing the present system and treatment plant plus the new plant. The city sewer committee, Citizen's Sewer committee and mayor will meet in the next 60 days to study the report.

It is expected that the complete repair of the system and relief mains would not exceed $243,000 including all extra fees such as legal and engineering. The two treatment plants, old work and construction of a new one, would

cost approximately $410,000. The city could apply and probably receive a Federal grant of $120,000 for the latter work, leaving a balance of $290,000. The city would have to sell bonds to pay for the bulk of the cost with some work payable by reserve funds in the three city utility departments which presently total over $100,-000.

Presently the city is debt free, owning its own water, gas and sewerage departments.

The main part of the repair work of the present system would consist of a televised survey of the system which would tell exactly where all leaks and breaks were located. The breaks would have to be repaired by excavation and with new materials to the lines. Leaks would be filled with a plastic grout which would seal them. A machine, with the grout, is sent through the line and automatically fills the leaky spots. The work done by the tv method is guaranteed and it is estimated that repairs along this line would

last 20 or more years.

City workmen would be used to excavate and repair the major breaks in the line.

The new treatment plant would be constructed north of the city and would take some of the load off the present treatment plant which is not adequate for the number of residents presently served by it. New state laws also require some changes at the plant which would be incorporated with the repairs.

The new treatment plant would have pumping station and an influent sewer while the present plant would be repaired. The present plant would be repaired to meet state requirements and would provide for a tertiary treatment, flood protection and chlorination.

The report also shows that projecting the present population trends of the city that the present system and the treatment plant would not be able to handle the load. Auburn's population was 2441 in 1965 and is expected to be close to 2800 by 1970 with a projected population of 3500 by 1975.

The first of two sewer survey reports was presented to the city council Monday at its regular meeting. The report concerned the sanitary system and was compiled by city engineers, Casler and Associates of Jacksonville.

Figure 14–4. Headline at the left of the story. [*Courtesy the Cedar Falls, Iowa Record.*]

By Tillman Durdin

HONG KONG—China-watchers are inclined to believe the Mao Tse-Tung-inspired Great Proletarian Cultural Revolution on the Communist mainland is at long last becoming a spent force.

Recent developments represent a decided gain for right-wing forces and a sharp setback for the radical aims and the most ardent partisans of the revolution as it was originally conceived.

Directives from Peking in the last two months widen still further the authority and the latitude of the military of conservative, bureaucratic elements allied to the military in a common desire to bring order and stability out of the chaos generated by the revolution.

The Red Guards and other "rebel" revolutionaries have been the instrument and power base of the so-called Cultural Revolution group in Peking, a directorate headed by Chen Po-Tan, an intimate of Communist party Chairman Mao Tse-Tung, with Mao's wife, Chiang Ching, its deputy director.

In late 1966 and early 1967 the Red Guards and other radicals were on effective force.

They rampaged about the country spreading and mercilessly enforcing the tenets of the new Maoism, disrupting the

China-watchers see shift from Mao revolution

old power structure at all levels, 'dragging out" the old power-holders for denunciation and dismissal, staging massive demonstrations and fomenting a profound revolutionary climate.

Early in the game, however, these vanguard elements revealed what eventually became their greatest weakness and the cause of their downfall. They developed factions that began to fight each other in struggles and disputes over what was and who genuinely represented the Cultural Revolution and the Maoist philosophy.

In many cases officials threatened by the Cultural Revolution formed protective Red Guards of their own. These were set against guard groups seeking their ouster.

Since all groups, as well as the officials backing them, professed boundless

loyalty to the revolution and Mao, it became difficult, indeed, often impossible, for officials and army men not directly involved to tell if any one Red Guard group was more genuinely Maoist than another and which to favor.

The faction fighting added chaos to turmoil.

Last fall the Peking leadership, under pressure from the army and moderates, authorized the military to move in and restore order. There was relative stability over the winter, but the Cultural Revolution's left-wing reasserted itself again this summer and the predictable faction-fighting flared up again on a national scale.

The regime now has authorized another crackdown, once more presumably because of arguments from military lead-

ers and the Maoist right wing that to let the mounting strife go on would risk national disintegration.

This time the measures taken to subordinate the Red Guards and other revolutionaries of the left may mean the coup de grace for this sector of the Cultural Revolution.

Even Mao-Tse-Tung, whose concept of the revolution is "leftist and radical," has had to admit disillusionment with the Red Guards. Reliable Peking sources report here that he broke down and wept in a session with five Red Guard leaders in Peking in late July during which he bitterly condemned them for their disunity and failure to carry through effectively revolutionary objectives.

Mao has, reluctantly, it can be assumed, given his signature to directives which have authorized military units to suppress faction-fighting with arms, if necessary, normalize railway traffic, particularly along the Vietnam supply route through Kwangsi, and push through the formation of new power organs, or revolutionary committees, in provinces where they had not been organized at the end of July.

Closely related to these measures was a directive from Mao which proclaimed older workers and peasants, backed by the army, as the leading force in the Cultural Revolution. Student Red Guards along with older intellectuals have been told they must integrate with the workers and peasants in a subordinate status.

Figure 14–5. Headline in the center. [*Courtesy the Cedar Falls, Iowa, Record.*]

This arrangement requires the typesetter to plan his work carefully so that he can set type around the headline. Because such treatment takes extra time, it is used primarily for feature stories.

Finally, a headline may be placed at the bottom of a story when the story is clearly set off from the remainder of the page, such as in a large box. When the headline is at the bottom of the box, it will be apparent that it belongs to the story above. If not set inside a box, there is a possibility the readers may assume it belongs to some other story.

Lead paragraphs of most stories consist of placing the first paragraph at the top of a story, set in type sizes that are larger than body type and, sometimes, leaded. The widths of most lead

**Treatment
of Lead
Paragraphs**

Details of Contemporary Makeup and Design 303

View of Washington National Cathedral Monday during funeral for Gen. Eisenhower

After three days of military pomp and ceremony and a last trip together through the streets of the federal city, Mamie Doud Eisenhower is taking her husband's body back home to the plains of Kansas.

After the rigors of state funeral, the family left Washington Monday night aboard a special train winding through the heartlands of the nation toward Abilene where Gen. Dwight David Eisenhower will be buried.

An aged baggage car, flaked with rust and draped in black, holds the simple soldier's coffin of Gen. Eisenhower.

At the rear of the funeral train, like a riderless horse, trails the private railroad car of the former president, this time carrying his widow on the long trip westward from Washington.

Baggage car No. 314, freshly painted to hide its blotches of age, holds the plain black bier, flanked with the U.S. and presidential flags.

At 7:09 p.m. the train pulled out of the station on the long journey westward, black crepe drawn over the windows of the funeral car.

The funeral train is scheduled to arrive in Abilene, Kan., at midnight on Tuesday for the burial the next day at the Eisenhower Center within sight of the general's boyhood home.

Stops were planned at Charlottesville, Va.; White Sulphur Springs, W.Va.; Huntington, W.Va.; Cincinnati, Ohio; Washington, Ind., and St. Louis.

However, railroad officials said the doors to the baggage car would remain closed at each stop. The presidential coffin will be shrouded from public view by black crepe drawn across the baggage car windows the entire trip.

It will be peaceful in Abilene, half a nation away from the manicured green and chiseled marble where the leaders of scores of countries gathered Monday to attend services for the 34th president of the United States.

In the majestic Washington National Cathedral, the determined composure shown by the family over the past days slipped noticeably several times.

During the hymn, "Onward Christian Soldiers," Mrs. Eisenhower grabbed the arm of her son, John, and wept quietly. He reached down to console her, but intermittently throughout the services, Mrs. Eisenhower wiped her eyes.

Before it was over, most members of the family, including John, who had been everyone else's pillar of strength, wept.

John was unable to listen dry-eyed as Rev. Edward L.R. Elson, minister of the National Presbyterian Church, spoke of his father:

"...For the nobility of his manhood, the integrity of his person, the hospitality of his mind and magnanimity of spirit..."

John's wife, Barbara, and daughter, Mary Jane, broke down. David Eisenhower, the late president's grandson, wiped his eyes.

However, by the time the service ended, all members of the family had regained their composure and kept it during the trip south from the cathedral to Union Station where the train to Abilene waited.

Before the funeral services began, heads of state and world leaders called on Mrs. Eisenhower, including the Shah of Iran, Presiden Zelman Shazar of Israel, Prince Bernhard of The Netherlands, Lord Mountbatten of Great Britain, Grand Duke John of Austria, the Grand Duke of Luxembourg, King Constantine of Greece and President Ferdinand E. Marcos of the Philippines.

'It will be peaceful in Abilene...'

Figure 14–6. Headline at the bottom. [*Courtesy the Cedar Falls, Iowa, Record.*]

paragraphs are the same as body type, although occasionally they are set one or even two columns wider than the body type. Lead paragraphs are often made to stand out not only from the headlines above them, but from the body type below.

In contempoary newspaper design, however, lead paragraphs are often given more prominence than they would receive in traditional design. The feeling is that because lead paragraphs have replaced the old headline decks, they deserve more prominence. Decks were formerly used to summarize a story, with each deck featuring one outstanding aspect of that story. The lead paragraph, by employing more words set in smaller-sized type than decks, did a better job of summarizing the essential details. But as lead paragraphs came into common use, they were often accorded no better type treatment than body type. In contemporary design, they have been made more dramatic in appearance and placed in more obvious positions relative to the remainder of the story.

When headlines are moved to the sides, center or bottom of a story, the lead paragraphs may be placed underneath the headline. However, in such cases, they should be set in a typeface and size that clearly contrasts with the remainder of the body type. Because the goal is to give them display treatment, the difference between lead paragraph appearance and body type appearance should be marked (Figure 14–7). The typeface should be one or two points larger than body type, set in sans serif, or boldface or italic. Leading is necessary to make the lead stand out and yet be readable. One final treatment may be to set the lead paragraph flush left with ragged right, a distinctly contemporary appearance.

Professors Assess Viet War

SPECTRUM: Is American intervention selfishly motivated?

MacDOUGALL: We are there out of imperialism, plain and simple. For years after the French moved out we stayed on, calling ourselves nominal advisors. Today we have dropped that pretense, but we're still continuing the policies of John Foster Dulles.

All of us who voted for Lyndon Johnson thought he would bury these policies, but he has not. We still seem to be interested in maintaining economic influence in Southeast Asia, and the military is there only to protect economic interests.

PERRY: Trying to exercise moral influence is one thing; we are exercising military influence and that is something else. President Johnson is ill-advised. Either a vacuum developed in his staff during the transition from the Kennedy administration, or Johnson has made a poor choice of assistants. He is a far better exploiter of somebody else's programs than he is a formulator of his own.

THE BHIKKHU: American foreign aid is a good thing, but the question is "Does it reach the suffering masses?" Foreign aid in South Viet Nam is going for the war, not for the masses. If the money spent on the war was spent to help the people, you could make a paradise in South Viet Nam.

WESTFALL: The U.S. must stay in Viet Nam as long as it takes to make the country a free nation. It will take time, even if the Viet Cong were driven out tomorrow. But we must stay until a stabilized democracy exists, and no one is exerting outside influence on the country. At that point, we should get out.

SPECTRUM: Does the revolutionary movement in South Viet Nam spring from internal unrest or from Red Chinese and North Vietnamese imperialism?

MacDOUGALL: The movement is a home-grown one. It springs from nationalism, aimed at winning independence from American colonialism. The

U. S. policy in Viet Nam recently has drawn heated comment from college faculties around the nation. Spectrum here holds a reach-in for four Northwestern faculty members: Curtis MacDougall, professor of journalism; Edmund Perry, professor of religion; Bhikkhu Walpola Rahula, visiting theology professor from Ceylon; and Ralph Westfall, professor of marketing.

Viet Cong are the people of Viet Nam. They walk the streets unrecognized in the daytime and fight at night.

We talk about self-determination, but it is about time we practiced it. Any aid the Viet Cong has gotten from North Viet Nam and Red China is peanuts compared to the billions the U.S. has spent there. But I'm surprised there hasn't been more aid from China. We act like we're picking a fight with them.

THE BHIKKHU: Viet Nam, South and North, is one country. To the Vietnamese, Ho Chi Minh is not a Communist, he's a national hero. They hear in the South that the North is well organized and disciplined and is working for the welfare of the community. In the South there has been suffering and corruption.

It is not Communism, but national feeling. Nobody considers South Viet Nam independent. It is pseudo-independent. The people have nothing to say about who leads them. It is the United States that controls South Viet Nam and chooses its cabinet members and leaders.

WESTFALL: Outside influences definitely control the Viet Cong. Undoubtedly the movement has support among the peasants, but its meaning would be insignificant without support from North Viet Nam and Red China.

SPECTRUM: What is the reaction in the rest of Asia to American intervention in Viet Nam?

PERRY: In the eyes of all Asia our position is now one of advancing the national interests of the United States and not of protecting the free will of the South Vietnamese. We have a rec-

ord of tying our assistance to our efforts to contain Communist expansion, rather than helping countries for their own good. A positive policy of helping free nations without attaching strings is the only thing that would get us out of this negative image.

THE BHIKKHU: Asians have bad memories of white Europeans. It is not exactly enmity or antagonism. They just ask, "Why so much compassion for us now?" Outsiders have conquered, dominated, and exploited Asians for centuries, and now they're interfering again. There's just a little suspicion of this sudden compassion.

If the United States leaves Viet Nam, it may lose the support of the people of Thailand and the Philippines but it would gain the support of millions of other Asians.

SPECTRUM: What about the domino theory? If the Americans were to pull out, would Southeast Asia become a Communist bloc?

MacDOUGALL: To hell with the domino effect. The movement in Viet Nam is strictly nationalistic, and this nationalism would be directed at any country, including China, who tried to exert its power and influence.

THE BHIKKHU: China would be happy if the countries of Southeast Asia turned toward socialism. It doesn't have to be China's brand of Communism.

China has economic relations with Ceylon, but doesn't try to influence its affairs. The danger of world war would stop the Chinese from invading and conquering the countries of Southeast Asia.

WESTFALL: Southeast Asia would very definitely go Communist if the United States were to pull out now. We must stay. We have an obligation to the Philippines, even if to nobody else.

SPECTRUM: Can we win in Viet Nam?

MacDOUGALL: We could never conquer the Viet Cong, because they are most of the population. We have no friends there, and they don't want us. We should leave the question to the United Nations. That's what it was set up for.

WESTFALL: Yes, we can win. We have a chance to preserve South Viet Nam as a viable country, as part of the free world. We are involved in a battle between North and South Viet Nam—one side must give in. It will take time. The Viet Cong won't capitulate tomorrow, but we can drive them back.

SPECTRUM: What would you like to see done in Viet Nam?

MacDOUGALL: We have no business in Viet Nam, and we should get out as gracefully and as fast as possible. Getting out gracefully means running the boats up to shore and bringing the soldiers home.

PERRY: I'd like to see us withdraw completely. We're no longer there at the will of the Vietnamese people. The South Vietnamese ought to be able to do what they want. If they want to go Communist, that's their business.

THE BHIKKHU: I don't approve of any country interfering in the affairs of another. American intervention in Viet Nam is not exactly the same as colonialism. But if any country intrudes in the affairs of another, I don't approve. Whatever the people of South Viet Nam want to become. it's their business.

WESTFALL: I do not favor our pulling out. It would be a mistake, even though staying puts us in an unenviable position. I also feel we cannot fight an entirely defensive war. We must take some aggressive action.

Curtis MacDougall

Bhikkhu Walpola Rahula

Edmund Perry

Ralph Westfall

Figure 14–7. Lead paragraph in center. [*Courtesy the Medill School of Journalism, Northwestern University, Evanston, Ill.*]

The traditional way of identifying photographs is to place cutlines underneath them. Overlines and underlines may be used alone or with cutlines. If the photograph is less than three columns wide, the cutlines are set full width, but if the photograph is wider, the cutlines may be wrapped in two columns underneath. When overlines and underlines are used, they are usually centered.

New Approaches to Cutlines, Overlines and Underlines

Details of Contemporary Makeup and Design

In contemporary makeup, cutlines may be set flush left, with ragged right or flush right with ragged left (Figure 14–8). When it is necessary to wrap cutlines into two adjacent columns, the flush-left or flush-right approach does not look pleasing. If, however, two pictures of the same size are placed next to each other (because they are related), it may be possible to set the left cutlines flush left and the right cutlines flush right.

Boat delivery

in Britian

Policemen deliver a bottle of milk to Arthur Philpott. 70, by rubber raft yesterday in Yalding, England. Philpott has refused to leave his house since Sunday when torrential rains caused flooding throughout much of southeast England. Having submerged the basement of the Philpott's home, the raging flood waters began to seep into the upper story of the house, but Philpott refused to leave. See story page 16. (UPI Telephoto).

Figure 14–8. Cutlines set flush right, ragged left. [*Courtesy the Cedar Falls, Iowa, Record.*]

A particularly modern style of cutline treatment, borrowed from magazine makeup, is to place them at the lower side of photographs. In such positions, they may be set in very narrow measures (from 6 to 9 picas in width), flush on both sides. But they also may be given the flush left or flush right treatment. In the latter instance the cutlines are set differently, depending on which side of the photograph they are to be placed. When placed on the right side, they should be flush left, and when placed on the left side, they should be set flush right (Figures 14–9 and 14–10) because the type nearest the photograph is aligned and looks more attractive.

Overlines may be repositioned above cutlines placed at the sides of cuts. They, too, may receive the same flush left or flush

**Getting ready
for inaugural**

Although the next president has not yet been elected, work has already begun on erecting a presidential inaugural platform and a television tower on the east front of the Capitol. Here Ignatius A. Jones of Waldorf, Md. unloads lumber. (UPI Telephoto)

Figure 14–9. Cutlines at the left, flush both sides. [*Courtesy the Cedar Falls, Iowa, Record.*]

Lynda Bird

attends

State dinner

Mrs. Charles (Lynda Bird) Robb is escorted by Oliver Jackman, permanent secretary, Minister of External Affairs, Barbados, during a recent White House dinner in honor of visiting Barbados Prime Minister Errol Barrow. Mrs. Robb is expecting her first child. (UPI Telephoto)

Figure 14–10. Cutlines at the left, flush right, ragged left. [*Courtesy the Cedar Falls, Iowa, Record.*]

right treatment as the cutlines. When positioned that way, there probably will be a large amount of white space above the overline (or above the cutlines when there is no overline). But this white space will enhance the appearance of the treatment and should not be considered wasted space.

Freaks, Refers and Other Inserts and Their Effects on Page Design

In traditional makeup practices, editors often inserted freaks, refers or other material into the main body of a story. The ostensible purpose of breaking into a story was to provide information that would help the reader better understand the news. But, no matter what the purpose was, the effect of any break in the news was a break in the reader's continuity.

What are the most likely alternative actions a reader may take when he is confronted by an insert? He may notice the insert, ignore it temporarily and, upon finishing the article, return and read it. Another alternative is that the reader may ignore it entirely. Or, he may stop and read it and then try to pick up the thread of thought in the remainder. But no matter which he does, the insert must break the flow of reading, if only for an instant, and because it impedes readership, it is undesirable.

Inserts also may be undesirable because they interrupt the rhythm of reading. Even if the reader stops to read the insert, he may not read much more of the story.

Editors often tend to make inserts a continuing practice, perhaps at least one in every edition. Too many inserts on one day may make the page appear to be full of spots that are unattractive and uninviting. Even when one insert is used, it stands out as a spot on the page. The makeup editor interrupts the reader, with rules and even a small headline within the insert. That one spot, then, may hamper the efforts of the editor to design a pleasing page because inserts tend to call attention to themselves.

The question then arises about what to do with the material that may have been used in inserts? One answer might be to place that material at either the beginning or the end of the story, set in italics or boldface and indented. Perhaps it can be incorporated into the body of the story and not be obtrusive. Finally, by careful analysis of the news, the editor may treat additional editorial material as another story and place it adjacent to the story in question. If there is reference to a picture, then this may be incorporated into the story, set in lightface italics.

Boxed Stories

The use of boxed stories in contemporary makeup is radically different from that in traditional makeup. In traditional makeup, a short, human interest story or an insert might have been placed in a box. Rarely was a long story boxed.

In contemporary makeup, there is a need to dramatize a story or there is a need to dramatize the makeup on a given page, and a large boxed story is used. There is, of course, a danger in using too many such stories on a page. If only one is used per page, it may liven that page considerably.

When boxing a story, the editor assumes it is significant. Perhaps it is not as significant as the top two stories on the page, but it is still of major importance. The procedure, then, is to place the entire story in a hairline box. The story must, of course, be squared off so that it fits neatly into the box. A photograph may accompany the story. But the keys to making this box look attractive are the use of hairline rules and more than an ordinary amount of white space inside the box. The only function of the hairline rule is to set the story apart from all other stories on the page. It will not look well if any heavier-weight rules are used, even a 2-point rule. If a fancy border of any kind is used it will call attention to itself and not to the contents of the box. The white spaces, especially between the rules and the body type, are the framing devices that, with the hairline rules, make the story stand out and easy to read. Headlines within a box also may be set smaller and in lighter-faced types than those normally used because the rules and white space framing the box make a large-sized type unnecessary. There is little competition from headlines outside the box.

Boxes, therefore, should be no less than two columns wide, and preferably larger so that they may have dramatic impact. Some editors place at least one such box on every page where possible as a means of adding dramatic impact to the pages. The position of such boxes on a page depends on the sizes and weights of other elements. When other headlines on the page are large and bold, a boxed story should be placed at the opposite side to bring about page balance. Often, they look well at the bottom of the page. In some cases, they might well be used in place of the number-one story (upper-right-hand side).

Policy for Design of Jump Heads

There is enough evidence available through research studies to prove that stories that have been jumped or continued to other pages lose a great deal of readership (see Chapter 2). Nevertheless, the practice of jumping stories sometimes cannot be avoided. Consequently, there should be a policy regarding the design of such heads.

There are two related problems that arise in the design of jump heads: (1) how to make them easy to find on a page; and (2) how to keep their design consistent with both the page and overall newspaper design. The first problem may seem to be easily resolved by setting the headlines in larger and bolder typefaces than other headlines. But if the type is too large or too bold, then it will call attention to itself and tend to make the page look unattractive. If it is too light, readers may not be able to find the heads. Both problems may be resolved if the following guidelines are observed:

1. The type faces and style of arrangement should be consistent with the headline schedule used for other headlines.

2. The number of lines and sizes of type used for jump heads should be the same as if the jumped portion were a separate story. In such a case, the story length and importance would be considered.

3. A contrasting type face may be used to help the head stand out. If Tempo has been used for most other headlines, a Bodoni Bold italic may provide the necessary contrast.

4. Stars, bullets or asterisks, if they are not too obtrusive, may precede the first letter of the jump head to serve as attention-getting devices.

5. Ben Day screens may be used in the background for such heads. This is done easily for newspaper printed by the offset technique. Where letterpress is being used, perhaps the page number from which the story originally started may be placed in a screened background. If a number of such page numbers could be screened and kept in logo form on the stone, they could be inserted easily under jump heads.

Tombstoning in Contemporary Design

Almost every editor, be he from the largest metropolitan newspaper or the smallest high school paper, knows that tombstoning should be avoided. But tombstoning was considered a poor makeup practice in an age where only 6-point hairline rules were used between columns. Because some newspapers have used hairline rules of even less than 6 points (2- or 3-point rules), there is more of a danger that a reader might read across the column into the adjacent headline and be confused (Figure 14–11).

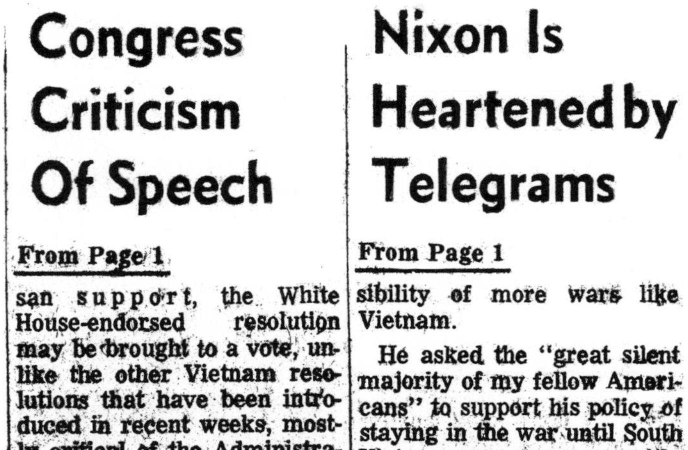

Congress Criticism Of Speech

From Page 1

san support, the White House-endorsed resolution may be brought to a vote, unlike the other Vietnam resolutions that have been introduced in recent weeks, mostly critical of the Administration.

House Speaker John W. McCormack, who will have much to say about what is done with the resolution, made clear that he supported the President's position and said he is "confident the American people will overwhelmingly support this effort to bring peace with justice."

Nixon Is Heartened by Telegrams

From Page 1

sibility of more wars like Vietnam.

He asked the "great silent majority of my fellow Americans" to support his policy of staying in the war until South Vietnam can carry on without U.S. troops.

The main theme of the telegrams of support, Mr. Nixon told reporters yesterday, was "we are silent Americans who are behind you."

Obviously pleased that he had coined a phrase, Mr. Nixon said, "about 50 per cent used the term silent

Figure 14–11. Tombstoned jump heads.

But in contemporary design, where the space between columns is at least 9 points and as much as 2 picas, tombstoning may not be objectionable. There may be so much white space between the columns that the reader can't be confused into reading a headline in the adjacent column. Then the only objection to tombstoning may be that there is not enough variety shown when two headlines of the same size, weight and number of lines are placed next to each other. This is a design consideration and one of the heads may be changed to provide more type variety on the page.

Banner Headlines and Readout Problems

The use of daily across-the-page banners has been abandoned by many modern newspapers and often replaced by spread heads without readouts. But when a story is assigned a banner headline, it is assumed that the body copy will be placed in the extreme right-hand column. Even though the first, or left-hand, column is the most important position on the page, the right-hand column is the one which enables the reader to continue reading the story without returning to the left-hand side of the page (Figure 14–12). In contemporary design, a number of questions arise affecting the reader's ability to continue reading the story smoothly. The answers to these questions lead to principles of handling banner headlines and readouts.

Can the story be continued in any other column? The reason for wanting to place the story elsewhere is to provide a change of pace and variety in makeup. The answer to the question is that there are few occasions when the story can be continued elsewhere. Least effective is to continue the story to an inside column. The reason it should not be placed anywhere but in the extreme right-hand column (with exceptions that will be noted) is that the reader will have to search for it if placed elsewhere (Figures 14–13 and 14–14). Although one may argue that the reader will not have to search very long, any time—even a fraction of a second—is too long. That fraction of a second may be just the timing that is necessary for the reader to search for some other interesting story. After all, he already knows the material in the banner headline and perhaps he isn't interested enough to continue when there are any impediments to his reading. This is the problem of all makeup devices. None should slow the reader more than a fraction of a second. If they are considered individually, each makeup device may seem to be effective. But when there are many such devices on a page, the even rhythm of reading may be broken and reading becomes a troublesome rather than a pleasant experience.

When stories are continued from a banner headline to any column other than the extreme right, a cutoff rule is used to separate the banner from nonrelated stories. The assumption is that because the only column not carrying a cutoff rule must be the one where the story is continued, it will be obvious at a glance. Indeed, it is obvious at the right-hand side, less obvious

NIXON TALK ON VIET TODAY

7 Killed as Bus Overturns

Vehicle Skids, Snaps Pole, and Falls Downhill

New Israeli Government Tells Goals

[By the Associated Press]

Israel's new government published its program of action today, pledging to pursue peace with its Arab neighbors but warning it would build up its army "to deter and repulse aggression."

The program also declared that Jerusalem's Jewish and Arab sectors would remain united as Israel's capital.

It made clear that Israel intends to establish permanent

GOES ON TV AT 5 TO TELL TROOP PLAN

More Reduction Considered

BY GLEN ELSASSER
[Chicago Tribune Press Service]

Washington, Dec. 14 — The White House announced today that President Nixon will go

NATURE NOTES

THE KANGAROOS MAY BE FACING EXTERMINATION IN THE WILD. PROFESSIONAL HUNTERS SLAUGHTER HUNDREDS OF THOUSANDS EACH YEAR FOR PET FOOD —

THE BOWFIN FREQUENTLY SURFACES TO GULP AIR —

THE 315 MEMBERS OF THE PARROT ORDER INCLUDE PARAKEETS, COCKATOOS, COCKATIELS, LORIES, MACAWS, LORIKEETS, LOVEBIRDS, BUDGERIGARS, ET AL—

PARROTS RANGE IN SIZE FROM

Figure 14–12. Readout into right-hand column. [*Courtesy the Chicago Tribune.*]

FIRE HITS W. SIDE HOSPITAL

FORAN TELLS PROBE PLANS OF SLAYINGS

U.S. Grand Jury Inquiry Set

60 Patients Carried from Their Rooms

BY DAVID GILBERT

Fire and smoke spread thru the Franklin Boulevard Community hospital last night, forcing 60 of the 104 patients in the hospital to be evacuated from their rooms.

The fire started shortly before

Tax Reform Bill Is Approved by Committee Vote

BY PHILIP WARDEN
[Chicago Tribune Press Service]

Washington, Dec. 19—Agreement was reached on a tax bill today which raises the personal exemption to $750 by 1973, boosts social security checks

Figure 14–13. Readout into inside column. [*Courtesy the Chicago Tribune.*]

SLAY 2 HIJACKERS IN SKY

Security Guards Kill Pair After Spain Take-off

ATHENS, Dec. 13 [Saturday] [Reuters] — Three security guards shot and killed two hijackers in a battle aboard a

U.S. Opens Probe of Raid

U. N. RESOLUTION

The United Nations has adopted a resolution calling for all nations to take action to punish hijackers

SHOWING OFF TO HIS GIRL FRIEND

WATCH ME GET THIS ROLLING!

Coroner to Pick Jury in Deaths of Panthers

Figure 14–14. Readout into left-hand column. [*Courtesy the Chicago Tribune.*]

when placed at the left-hand side (first column) and almost obscure when placed inside. Cutoff rules help, but not much. It is hard to find the column where the story is continued.

Another question arises when using a banner headline. Can more than one story relating to the banner headline be arranged so that the banner reads into each story successfully? Such an occasion might be when an election story breaks and one political party wins both gubernatorial and mayoral races. The banner headline may therefore refer to both stories. When the readout headlines are only one column wide, they are often hard to find. But when they are two or more columns wide, they are relatively easy to find.

A final question concerns whether a banner headline should lead into a multiple- or single-column headline? One of the older makeup rules was that when a large-sized type was used in a top headline, the reader's eyes would have difficulty in adjusting to smaller types in the decks or lead paragraphs. Therefore, the reduction in size was supposed to be at least 50 per cent. If a 120-point headline was used for the banner, then it should read into a headline of no less than 60-point type. The 60-point type would then read into a 30-point deck, which in turn might read into an 18-point deck and from there into a 10-point lead paragraph. There was never any valid evidence that readers had difficulty in adjusting their eyes to the changes in type sizes. Therefore, the only reason for reading from a banner into a multiple-column headline is simply to provide more details in the headline than could have been included in the banner. The only trouble with multiple-column headlines is that they usually lead into a single-column story, leaving the space underneath to be filled in the best way possible. If a headline for a nonrelated story is placed underneath a multiple-column headline, the effect might be to confuse the reader. At times a picture is placed underneath. But neither of these solutions looks attractive.

In contemporary makeup, banner headlines often lead into a single-column headline, a simple device. Or, if a banner is used, it may lead into a three-column headline and a story may be wrapped for three columns underneath, through the process of squaring off the bottom. A final alternative is to limit the use of banner headlines to rare occasions. When it is used with a multiple-column readout it won't look awkward because the news is so sensational. Too many multiple-column headlines on a page, however, make the page spotty because these headlines appear dark (being set in bold typefaces and relatively large-sized types). They become centers of interest because of their weight and may be difficult to balance.

Other Contemporary Treatments

Other practices differentiate the traditional from the contemporary made-up newspaper. Some practices are the result of major editorial policy and can be changed only by those in top authority, such as a publisher or an editor. Others, however, are within the province of the makeup editor, who daily has the option of using traditional or contemporary treatments of editorial material.

Elimination of Column Rules

One of the distinguishing features of contemporary design is the elimination of column rules from the newspaper. The purpose is to bring more light (or white space) into the page and to bring about a cleaner looking page. When column rules are used, they simply add blackness to the page even though they separate the columns. But the additional white space not only separates the columns, but makes the page more inviting to the reader because it is less black-appearing.

In eliminating column rules, editors did not simply replace a 6-point hairline rule with 6 points of white space. They added more white space so that the columns were more clearly separated. The minimum amount of white space between columns seems to be 9 points, but more is preferred. The better-designed newspapers use no less than 12 points of white space and many use more.

Reduction in the Number of Columns to a Page

To gain more white space on a page, editors who use contemporary makeup have reduced the number of columns to a page from eight to as few as five (Figure 14–15), which releases more space to be used between columns than was formerly possible. In contemporary makeup it is not unusual to find some pages with as much as 24 points of space between columns.

Another benefit of reducing the number of columns to the page is that the body type is made more readable because the line widths are increased. From a standard 11-pica width, some newspapers have increased the column widths to more than 14 picas. (The *National Observer* uses a 15½-pica width.)

On inside pages, the reduction in number of columns has proved to be harder to work with because advertising often is sold on a basis of a narrower column width. Some newspapers use the wider column widths for news and narrower column widths for advertisements. Makeup of such pages may be difficult because of the differences in measures.

Limited Use of Cutoff Rules

The cutoff rule is used sparingly in contemporary makeup. Wherever white space can be substituted for a cutoff rule, it should be used. When white space is substituted, a bit more space is used so that the reader will clearly understand that two stories near each other are not related in any way. But there are certain times, especially when the page is crowded, that a cutoff rule is necessary. In such a case, the makeup editor should not hesitate to use it.

Headline Styles in Contemporary Makeup

The flush left headline style is used almost exclusively in contemporary makeup. Droplines, inverted pyramids and hanging indentions are styles of the past. Flush left is preferred because it is free-form in appearance, a style that is distinctly modern, and because it is so easy to set on the linotype machine, especially on machines with automatic quadding devices. On the

The Art of Editing

TELEVISION, RADIO, SPORTS, COMICS, AND LOCAL NEWS

The Courier-Journal

MONDAY, DECEMBER 8, 1969
SECTION B

n Long Haul to Kentucky

Truck Stops: Highway Haven For Lonely Men of the Road

By PAUL M. BRANZBURG
Courier-Journal Staff Writer

›b Bierd is a solitary man in one of ›rica's most solitary trades.
›erd, who wears a brown cowboy hat a green cowboy shirt, travels 140,000 s a year.
one.
›ery week he leaves his home in ›er for a round-trip drive to Louis-, California, Texas or Chicago.
›erd is a long-haul truck driver on ›-driver truck.
›hen these lonely travelers come to ass through the Louisville area, they are likely to seek out men who ply the same trade. And the places they frequent most are the Indiana truck stops along Interstate 65, just a few miles north of Louisville.

On a foggy Monday midnight, Bierd walked into Cliff's Truck Stop, Cementville, Ind., and sat down at a counter. He pushed his cowboy hat back on his graying head, and began to talk about truck stops and truck driving.

"I left Denver Saturday night at 4 o'clock and I got here this morning at 11:30," he said matter-of-factly. "It's about 25 hours from here to Denver, so I had time for eight hours' sleep. I fuel at Salina, Kans., and I fuel at Effingham, Ill.

"I stop at places where there is good food and you see guys that you know. Also, truck stops have enough room for us to park our trucks. There's not enough room in most other places."

Bierd, who brings various products to Kentucky and takes whisky back to Denver, stops at the same places each trip, "so they get to know you and let you cash a check."

In addition to good food, companionship, parking space for trucks and check-cashing services, truck stops also offer a surprising variety of other services.

Cliff's has showers, rooms, a barber, an ice house for drivers who are hauling perishable food, a 65-foot grease pit, an overhead crane for washing trucks, a repair service, and a potpourri of products for truck drivers.

Everything from electric cattle prods to laundry bags to underwear to "windshield wiper snuggies" to "overdimensional load banners" to workclothes to truck tags reading: "No Riders Except Brunettes, Blondes & Redheads."

There even is a Western Union service so that drivers can receive messages from their employers.

Clearly, truck drivers visit truck stops for a great number of reasons. It might be as simple as a meal. Or as extensive as repairs, fuel, ice, and a room for a week while waiting for a new load.

While they are at truck stops, they talk of many things, often of their families.

At the Mobil truck stop near Cementville, Marion Boewe, 42, of West Salem, Ill., ate a big steak and talked about his wife.

"She just don't like it when I'm away too long," he said. "You can't blame her.

"I'm usually home a couple of days a week, sometimes three days, but sometimes you lose a day—you break down, or you have a bad connection—and that's what causes trouble. You've told her you'll be home, and you don't make it."

Boewe hauls textiles between Chicago and Knoxville.

Some local truck drivers like to go to the truck stops to listen to the long-haul drivers talk.

John Huddle of Jeffersonville, Ind., a driver for Royal Crown, said:

"I like to come to this stop and listen to the fellows. They talk about road conditions. I like to hear which way they are heading, north or south. And where they've been. I'd say that the long-haul drivers have more problems than I do. A big vehicle is harder to maneuver quickly than a smaller vehicle."

Truck drivers are not a complaining lot, but they do have a few pet peeves.

A driver in a gray shirt and a black bow tie said: "You've got to be careful of people who are impatient—who want to whiz past trucks. Trucks only have a small area of visibility in the rear view mirror. And you can't hear cars coming up to pass."

Some drivers avoid stops frequented by "tourists."

Mrs. Dolores Nicholson of New Albany, Ind., a clerk at Cliff's, said: "We have some who complain about tourists. They say that if tourists come in a place, the drivers don't get waited on as quickly."

Drivers were asked about the food at truck stops. Is it really that good?

It's "basic," but you get a lot for your money, they said.

Drivers like to talk about their equipment. And when some trucks cost more than $35,000, that's a lot to talk about. A man who wants to buy a truck on time may have to pay about $600 a month.

"I once tried going independent," said one driver. "I bought a used truck, and I couldn't hold it together. It kept breaking down."

If there is anything truck drivers particularly resent, it is the way some people regard them as roughnecks. Many make over $200 a week, often work decade after decade for the same employer and are proud of their behavior on the highways.

"Truck drivers are the most courteous people on the road," says Bierd. "If you're in trouble, they'll stop and help you. My wife has been cross-country four or five times, and she never worries because she knows a truck driver will stop and help."

There also is tragedy in the truck-driving fraternity. The day that all remember sadly is Jan. 17, 1968, when five people were killed and more were injured in a spectacular series of crashes near Sellersburg, Ind.

"Some of them were our customers," said an employe of one of the truck stops.

His expression revealed that they were more than just "customers."

Staff Photos by Michael Coers

THE CLASSIC Western look comes naturally to Bob Bierd, of Denver, Colo., who makes the long haul frequently between Colorado and Kentucky, bringing a wide variety of products, and taking back a cargo of whisky. He's taking a break near Cementville, Ind.

LATE ON A FOGGY NIGHT, Everett Prather, of Washington County, Ind., cleans the window of a truck at Cliff's Truck Stop.

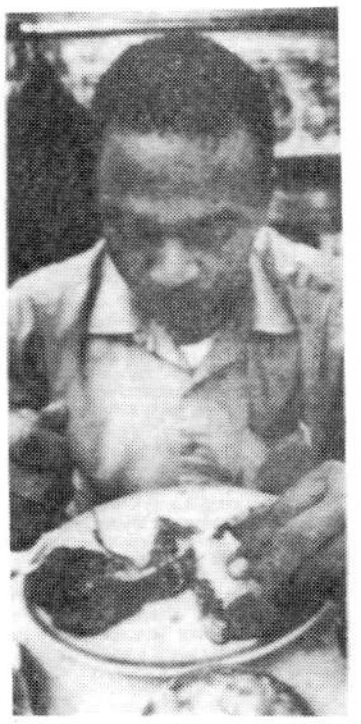

GOOD FOOD and plenty of it is the main attraction for drivers at the nation's truck stops, where drivers get to know each other.

Louisville Army Reserve Commander Doubts GIs Massacred Vietnamese

By JAMES NOLAN
Courier-Journal Staff Writer

Maj. Gen. Benjamin J. Butler is the image of his rank. He's also a booming speaker.

He talked so loudly about remembering Pearl Harbor yesterday that many of the 300 officers and men in the Bowman Field Armory may have had a hard time understanding what the commander of their division — the 100th Army Reserve — was saying.

The message of the blunt, outspoken military and business leader came across later in an interview in his self-decorated office at the Armory.

At 52, Butler looks somewhat like actor Lloyd Nolan. When he speaks about patriotism and love of country, his right hand reaches forward as if he's trying to grab something. His voice is firm — sometimes loud again — and his face contorts slightly to convey the intensity of his emotion. His eyes pierce the listener, who can be made to squirm slightly.

The subject was the public image of the Army since the alleged killing of hundreds of South Vietnamese civilians by U.S. troops.

The general took a deep breath, as if preparing to get something off his decorated chest, and stated flatly: "I'll never believe it until someone proves to me that it actually happened. I'm not convinced it did."

If it were true, Butler said he would be "chagrined and embarrassed." The general, who has not been to Vietnam, compared it to finding out that "my own son had committed murder."

Butler, a native of Trimble County, conceded the Army's image is under attack, but he blames the whole "movement to degrade the military" on "our permissive society."

"I mean that sincerely," the decorated World War II hero said quietly. And then more emphatically, "And the Army fighting man is not the villian the press would make him out to be."

"I have a speech I give," Butler said, reaching from his black leather armchair to pull back a copy of it from his desk.

Butler went on to say that "the ideals and principles" on which this country was founded are being ignored.

For this, he blamed "apathy toward rightful responsibility," a "defiance of proper authority," the "decaying moral standards, the leniency of our courts, and our growing acceptance of mediocrity."

Butler, who in civilian life is manager of the Louisville Space Center, an industrial park on the National Turnpike, said his cure for "this apathetic, permissive society of ours" is more personal involvement. "Get involved, get involved," he said with the intensity of a preacher, "you've got to put more of yourself into what you do."

Butler's career has included a stint as Fayette County extension agent, a rapid military career that included being the youngest man named general of an Army ground force, a period as state agriculture commissioner under A. B. Chandler, and an unsuccessful try for the Democratic nomination for lieutenant governor in 1960.

During the Pearl Harbor commemoration ceremonies at Bowman field yesterday, Gen. Butler announced the appointment of Col. Owsley C. Costlow as his new chief of staff, raplacing the late Col. Ralph Duncan. Costlow was also presented the Army Commendation Medal for his service with the 100th Division.

Col. Frank Stone spoke to members of the division prior to Butler, recalling his experience on the day the Japanese attacked Pearl Harbor 28 years ago.

Humor Not On Strike At GE Appliance Park

By JOHN LONG
Courier-Journal Staff Writer

A strike is deadly serious business, ›ecially when it directly involves about 500 workers and their families. But ›ny things happen anyway in the strike Louisville's General Electric Appliance ›rk, which entered its seventh week ›ay.

For instance:

In the past, the Kentucky Skilled ›aft Guild and Local 761 of the Inter›tional Union of Electrical Workers ›UE) have had their differences.

But on the picket line in this strike, › guild members are sharing Local ›1's shelters and propane gas heaters ›d Local 761 members are sharing the ›ild's portable toilets.

Explained William Waggoner, guild ›e president: "They furnish the heat ›d we furnish the seat."

✔✔✔

A striker was applying for employment the state employment office, as a pre›quisite to applying for food stamps.

"What was your job at Appliance ›rk?" he was asked by a state inter›ewer.

"I'm an accumulator," the striker re›ied.

"But just what did you do?" asked the ›terviewer.

"That's my job title—accumulator," ›sisted the striker.

"But what exactly does an accumulator ›?" the interviewer patiently inquired.

"I accumulate parts," explained the ›riker.

"Okay," said the interviewer, with a ›nile of resignation, and he jotted some›ing on the striker's application.

✔✔✔

IUE Local 761's ladies' auxiliary has ›een distributing leaflets that ask shop›ers not to buy GE products until the ›rike's over. One such leaflet was ›anded to an Appliance Park executive ›ho was out shopping.

As the executive accepted the leaflet, the woman hastily added that she hoped ›e'd hold out for a GE product until ›fter the strike and not switch to another ›rand. "We make the best appliances ›n the world," she said.

✔✔✔

Don Rock, president of IUE Local 761, was interrupted by a phone call during › press interview in his office at the ›nion hall. After hanging up, Rock ›urned to the reporters and said, "That was my most important product," his 17-year-old son, Steven.

Steven hadn't called just to pass the time of day.

"I told him 'This is no damn time to buy a motorcycle. I'm on strike—I can't afford it,' " Rock said.

✔✔✔

Six pickets were trying to stop the rush-hour flow of salaried workers' home-bound cars at Appliance Park's main gate. One of the pickets noticed that a well-dressed GE official was attempting to direct the cars through gaps in the picket line and was rubbing his cold hands together.

The picket reached into his pocket, pulled out a pair of green, woolen Army gloves, and offered them to the surprised official. The official smiled, but declined, shoving his hands into the deep pockets of his topcoat.

Staff Photo by James N. Keen

Sleigh Sans Santa

THESE FOUR BOYS thought they had Santa yesterday when they spotted his sleigh at the Children's Zoo in Louisville. But their hopes of meeting the jolly giver soon faded when they found Santa wasn't due to take up his annual residence at the zoo until next Sunday. Trying out the sleigh are Mark and Peter Andresen, of Lexington, Ky. and Robby and Eric Theller of Richmond, Ky.

'Sounds Like a Band'

Orchestra Pulls Stops For Central Audience

By HELEN McCLOY
Courier-Journal Staff Writer

Cymbals crashed and the piccolo tremolos hit a feverish pitch. Nine-year-old Jessie Swift covered her ears and exclaimed, "It sounds like a band!"

Jessie, who lives on 27th Street, had never heard a concert until yesterday's free Louisville Orchestra performance at Central High School, 1130 W. Chestnut.

She liked what she heard, especially the drums—"which kept me awake"—and the way director Jorge Mester "looked like he was going crazy," conducting the orchestra through a series of flamboyant scores.

Mester was also pleased with the 5 p.m. concert, even though only 100 people turned out for it. The audience was fully integrated and that fact, Mester said, "is a winner."

"We shouldn't have a separation (of races)" at cultural events, Mester told a reporter."

This is the way our audiences should be—only fuller."

Yesterday's concert was the first in a hoped-for series to be sponsored by the Chestnut Street Branch of the YMCA and underwritten by the City of Louisville. The idea behind the concerts is to help narrow the cultural gap between rich and poor, Negro and white, in Louisville.

Though yesterday's crowd was small, it was enthusiastic. Mester himself, sweat pouring from his brow, was greeted after the program by several small girls, one of whom told him, "That last number was terrific! I couldn't take no more."

"I couldn't either," said Mester, who had decided that the piece, Ravel's "La Valse," was so rip-roaring, even " 'The Stars and Stripes Forever' would be an anti-climax."

His audience's enthusiasm wasn't confined to the music, but extended to the efforts made to bring that music to Louisville's Negroes. Apprentice cellist Bob Bardston, 19, and a Negro noted that there were no free concerts of this sort when he was growing up in Louisville's Cotter Homes housing project. And 14-year-old Karen Lowry, a Highland Junior High School pupil, said the concerts are a good idea because people who live far from the orchestra's home at Fourth and Broadway, "usually can't get to where they're (playing)."

The next free concert is planned for March 15 and, like the one yesterday, will cost the city some $1,500. To get a larger crowd, YMCA executive director Walter Barnes said the spring concert probably will be held in the Buechel-Newburg area, which is more highly residential than the area surrounding Central High. Bus transportation and free soft drinks at intermission also will be provided by the Chestnut Street Y, Barnes predicted.

Collegians Forming Lobby Coalition

By MARTIN K. PEDIGO
Courier-Journal Staff Writer

GENERAL BUTLER STATE PARK, Ky.—Student government leaders from 13 colleges and universities decided here yesterday to form a lobbying group to represent all higher-education students in Kentucky at the 1970 General Assembly.

Some 30 student-council leaders met here over the weekend to discuss the need for such an organization and the issues that might be of interest to college students. The organization will be known as the Kentucky College Student Coalition.

The coalition will include at least two representatives from every college and university in the state, including two-year schools. Schools with enrollments of more than 2,000 will have an additional representative for each 3,000 students over 2,000.

Lacey T. Smith, a Louisville attorney who heads the sponsoring Kentucky Youth Conference, said the student government leaders who met here will begin to organize the coalition.

They will visit schools that did not send representatives and will consult at their own schools to get student council approval of the coalition.

Smith said the coalition will probably send members to lobby on such issues as votes for student members on college boards of trustees, and possibly public support of non-public schools. On the latter issue, he added, the coalition has not decided which side it will take.

Another issue on which the coalition is likely to do some lobbying is the merger proposal for the University of Kentucky and the University of Louisville.

Smith said the students leaders were decided to let a 12-member steering committee guide the coalition, but added that the entire membership will meet twice yearly to decide major policy and issues.

This was the first time the Kentucky Youth Conference had sponsored a meeting for college students, Smith said.

Many of the participants had worked with the conference as high-school students, he said, and saw it as a vehicle for opening lines of communication among students all over the state.

Figure 14–15. Six-column page. [*Courtesy The Louisville, Kentucky, Courier-Journal.*]

LAGOS, Nigeria (AP)—**Radio Biafra declared Tuesday "no force on earth can conquer Biafra's will to survive."** The broadcast expressed defiance even as the stage apparently was set for a last stand by secessionists in the 14-month-old civil war.

Following up the federal government's announcement Monday that its troops had captured the city of Owerri, the radio said the Biafrans plan to continue to fight.

The seccessionists have only one major town left to run to. This is Umuahia, the headquarters of their, Lt. Col. C. Odumegwu Ojukwu. And this is where the Biafrans will perhaps make their final stand.

LISBON (AP)—**Prime Minister Antonio de Oliveira Salazar clung** precariously to life last night and Portugal's Council of State met in emergency session.

The 15-member body, from which President Americo Thomaz must draw advise to name a successor should Salazar die or become incapacitated, conferred for two hours, then adjourned. There was no communique after the meeting.

Figure 14–16. Flush left, ragged right column. [*Courtesy the Cedar Falls, Iowa, Record.*]

Use of Body Copy Set Flush Left, Ragged Right

Subheads in Makeup

other hand, each of the other three styles of headlines mentioned are difficult to set, and they call attention to themselves because of their unusual shapes.

Three other headlines styles are sometimes considered contemporary. Each may serve a special purpose, so they are rarely used extensively. They are kickers, hammerheads and wickets.

In using a kicker, hammerhead or wicket, the disadvantages may outweigh the advantages. The danger is that these devices may call too much attention to themselves, primarily because they are attention-getting devices. If more than one of these are used on a page, the effect may be a series of white spaces that tend to destroy the harmony of page unity. As an alternative to these headline treatments, makeup men could use a boxed story or have headlines set to the right or in the center of a story. The latter are contemporary treatments that accomplish the same task but do not call too much attention to themselves.

One of the most dramatic design treatments is a column of body type set flush left, ragged right (Figure 14–16). Like the flush left headline, its free form gives a page a contemporary appearance, found in modern furniture, swimming pools and architecture. The use of one such column to a page also provides pleasant contrast to the remainder of the type, which is justified on both sides. Finally, such type allows more white space into the page than the flush left and flush right columns, and this results in a cleaner looking page. In planning pages, care should be taken not to overdo the use of the flush left, ragged right style of column. When the entire page is set this way, the charm and elegance of the style is lost because there is too much of it. Another suggestion for its use is that more leading may be required to make the lines easier to read. When they are set solid, they seem to be crowded. With the addition of even a 1-point lead per line, they appear to be easier to read.

In traditional forms of makeup, long gray columns were often broken by the use of boldface paragraphs. Perhaps every fourth or fifth paragraph might be set boldface and indented one en on each side to minimize the effect of the boldness. It is true that pages never became masses of dull grayness through the use of intermittent boldface paragraphs. On the other hand, the page did become full of spots that distracted the reader somewhat and also made the page look too bold.

The practice of using subheads, however, in place of boldface paragraphs is contemporary in style. The best way to use subheads is to set them flush left, keeping them consistent with the main headline styles. Then, too, they should be set in boldface italic, boldface sans serif or any distinctly contrasting typeface. Because these lines will be so short and infrequent, they will not glare at the reader as the boldface does. In some newspapers, editors have tried subheads set flush right rather than flush left with apparent success. Centered subheads tend to look old-fashioned, however.

Some editors have tried using various-sized dots or bullets at the beginning of a paragraph as a means of breaking up large gray masses of type. Instead of allowing the usual one-em paragraph indention, the dot is placed in the indented space. The effect, however, is to call attention to the dot. In fact, dots are sometimes used to help the reader find paragraphs that are more significant than others. So the makeup editor might place a dot before key paragraphs. But neither technique is as adequate as the use of subheads.

A further consideration in the proper use of subheads is the amount of space above and below them. Generally, the best technique is to use about 4 points above and 2 points below as a means of clearly breaking up the mass of grayness and as a means of nullifying a bit the effect of a contrasting typeface (Figure 14–17).

In the discussion of nameplates, it was suggested that the ears be eliminated by moving the nameplate either to the left or right side of the page and bringing a column of news up to the top. But when the newspaper's policy is to keep the nameplate in the center, then there is the likelihood that ears will be used to fill the gaps of white space on either side.

What To Do with Ears

In contemporary design, ears have been eliminated because they have become distracting devices that call attention to themselves rather than to the news columns. Most often ears are set within a boxed rule of some kind and no matter how light these rules, they set the ears off from everything else on the page. They not only distract from the news but they distract from the nameplate itself. Therefore, white space is preferable to ears. Only when the rules have been eliminated and the typeface used is unobtrusive (small and lightface types) should ears be used. In such cases, the ears will not tend to distract.

Dets. Joseph McSorley, Bernard Joseph and Howard Baynard.

The three teachers were arraigned before Municipal Judge Ralph Dennis.

Police said they presented a search and seizure warrant to Miss Pincus at 6:30 P. M. Monday at her second floor apartment. They said they found a package wrapped in foil allegedly containing hashish lying on a table.

WAITED FOR SECOND

Miss Pincus attended the University of Wisconsin.

The officers said they then spent several hours in Stelzer's third floor apartment w   ;
his ret 1. :

It was estimated that as much as 20 acres might be needed for such facilities.

OPPOSITION VOICED

Any use of park land for school purposes, however, would have to be approved by the park commission, which has demonstrated strong opposition to the plan.

The only site among the four suggested which the Board of Education could purchase through condemnation is the Five Points tract.

Tate opposes use of this land, however, because its private use could mean attractive ratables for the city.

The Board of Education is

Figure 14–17. Improper and proper line spacing of subheads.

In the scheme of contemporary makeup, pictures are given dramatic treatment. They are sized larger, but that is not the main consideration. Now they are sized to be strongly vertical or strongly horizontal. The effect of such boldly shaped pictures is a dramatic change in page appearance, a change that makes a page look exciting. The reader can't help but look at the main picture, nor can he help notice the difference in the entire page. Not every picture lends itself to such treatment, but when one is available and is significant, it should be handled in a contemporary manner. The makeup editor must have the imagination to look at a smaller-sized picture and be able to visualize it in a larger size (Figures 14–18 and 14–19).

When such boldly shaped pictures are used, an increase in the amount of white space in the total page design should be made. Otherwise the picture alone may be too strong for all other material on the page and readers may have difficulty reading the news. White space should be increased between columns, headlines and stories as compensatory devices.

At times, questions arise about the use of pictures in outside columns and the directions in which individuals are facing. In the former situation, pictures may be used anywhere, even in outside columns if the page is designed with adequate white space between columns. When the page appearance is tight because of 2- or 3-point column rules used throughout the paper, a picture in an outside column may not look attractive. In the latter situation, it has been the traditional practice to have individuals looking into the paper rather than out of it. The assumption is that when a person shown in the picture is looking away from the page, the reader, too, will tend to look in the same direction and perhaps turn to some other page. Research is not available to prove the truth of this assumption, and it is doubtful that it is true. But occasionally a reader may find it distracting, and for that reason, pictures ought to be faced inwardly. Most readers have been brought up on pages designed with pictures facing into a page.

Finally, there is a question about the traditional makeup practice of not placing pictures on the folds. Contemporary makeup ignores this practice because it started in the days when newspapers were sold folded, primarily from newsstands. Readers might make a decision to buy or not buy a newspaper on the basis of which newspaper looked best. Because only the top half of the paper was visible on the stand, it was prepared in such a way as to make it attractive. Any picture printed across the fold could not be seen in its entirety. Perhaps a sale might have been lost if only half a picture were seen. Therefore pictures were never positioned across the folds. Now the practice seems unreasonable and the rule is outmoded. Although papers are still delivered folded, they are read unfolded and the entire picture is thereby visible.

The Art of Editing

MINNEAPOLIS TEMPERATURES

Midnight ..37	5 a.m. 36	10 a.m. ...40
1 a.m. 37	6 a.m. 35	11 a.m. ...42
2 a.m. 36	7 a.m. 34	*Noon 44
3 a.m. 36	8 a.m. 34	*Unofficial.
4 a.m. 36	9 a.m. 38	

TOMORROW: MILD.

THE MINNEAPOLIS STAR

Tuesday, Nov. 4, 1969 XCI—No. 295 Four Sections ★ Single Copy Price 10c Lower Price for Carrier Delivery

Minneapolis Star Photo by Richard Olsenius

Homeward bound Against the gray November sky, a cow stands alone on a barren hill and looks toward the barn, a shelter from the chilling breeze. The scene is not as bleak as it looks. Otto and Tom Arens, father and son, find farming the good life one mile north of Loretto. (Details, other photos, Page 1C.)

"Our answer will be half a million people in Washington demanding immediate and total withdrawal"—Antiwar organizer Rennie Davis, commenting on the planned protest next week in light of Mr. Nixon's address.

Nixon 'dismays' protest heads

WASHINGTON, D.C. (UPI)—Leaders of antiwar demonstrations scheduled later this month ridiculed President Nixon's war policy speech as disappointing and insulting, predicting that his comments will only drive more protesters into the streets.

"I think in a sense the speech is a clear impetus to our efforts to bring large numbers of people to Washington," said Ed Johnson, a leader of the New Mobilization Committee to End The War in Vietnam (New Mobe). That group is sponsoring a Nov. 13-15 march on Washington.

"People perhaps who were uncertain they would come here are now convinced that the only way they can have any effect is to come here," Johnson said.

Dave Hawk, one of the coordinators of the Oct. 15 Vietnam moratorium, said "I anticipate that the reaction will be one of dismay and the people who were active in Oct. 15 will see the need to continue and intensify their efforts."

Hawk's group is sponsoring another moratorium Nov. 13-15. He said moratorium leaders were hoping Mr. Nixon would make public a new peace initiative."

"The American people want the war to end. It's apparent that the President has not gotten that message and we shall have to continue."

Nixon 'shares youth concern'

WASHINGTON, D.C. (AP)—Assuring them he has a "plan for peace," President Nixon aimed a brief portion of his Monday night speech at youth:

"I would like to address a word to the young people of this nation who are concerned about the war.

"I respect your idealism.

"I share your concern for peace.

"I want peace as much as you do.

"There are powerful personal reasons I want to end this war. This week I will have to sign 83 letters to mothers, fathers, wives and loved ones of men who have given their lives for America in Vietnam. It is very little satisfaction to me that this was only one-third as many as I signed during my first week in office. There is nothing I want more than to see the day come when I no longer must write any of these letters.

"I want to end the war to save the lives of those brave young men in Vietnam.

"I want to end it in a way which will increase the chance that their younger brothers and their sons will not have to fight in another Vietnam someplace in the world.

"I want to end the war so that the energy and dedication of our young people, now too often directed into bitter hatred against those they think are responsible for the war, can be turned to the great challenges of peace, a better life for all Americans and for people throughout the world.

"I have chosen a plan for peace. I believe it will succeed."

Hanoi and Cong condemn talk, see prolonged war

PARIS, France (UPI)—North Vietnam and the Viet Cong officially condemned today President Nixon's peace program as a maneuver allegedly designed to prolong the war in South Vietnam.

The delegations of both Hanoi and the Viet Cong at the Paris peace talks issued statements denouncing the chief executive's policies as set forth in his speech.

The Viet Cong said Mr. Nixon displayed in his speech a desire "to prolong and intensify the American war of aggression in South Vietnam."

Soon afterward, the North Vietnamese issued a statement saying Mr. Nixon's speech "clearly shows that his administration follows and always prolongs more obstinately the war of aggression, and reveals the warlike and perfidious nature of his administration."

An American delegation spokesman said Henry Cabot Lodge's peace negotiating team was "disappointed they have made this snap characterization. We hope they'll take the time to study the text of the President's speech more carefully because there's a lot in it for them."

The Viet Cong, while condemning Mr. Nixon's policies and upholding unchanged their own negotiating stand, announced they will go on striving for a settlement here. This remark ruled out any Communist walkout from the parley, observers said.

The Viet Cong accused Mr. Nixon of having repeated in his Vietnam policy statement his already-stated policies.

Although the Communist negative answer to Mr. Nixon's speech was largely expected, its harshness and virulent tone nevertheless surprised observers.

'The silent majority' 'overwhelms' Nixon

By LOUIS CASSELS

WASHINGTON, D.C. (UPI) — President Nixon said today he was overwhelmed by an outpouring of public support for his plan to extricate the United States from the Vietnam War.

On the morning after his broadcast saying he had worked out with Saigon a plan for complete withdrawal of all American forces from Vietnam, Mr. Nixon met briefly with reporters, sitting behind stacks of telegrams on his desk.

"It's very important in our quest for peace to realize the country is behind you," he said some 13 hours after appealing for public support for his course to wind down the war.

He added: "I would put it this way very flatly — this demonstration of support can have more effect on ending the war sooner than the most skilled diplomacy, military tactics or training of South Vietnamese forces."

In the speech to the nation — and the world — Monday night from the same desk where he displayed the wires, Mr. Nixon had asked the "silent majority" of Americans to support him in his plan to get out of Vietnam.

"For the future of peace, precipitate withdrawal would be a disaster of immense magnitude"—President Nixon, in his Vietnam address to the nation.

He did not fix a timetable for pulling out all troops, saying it would be a gradual process which could be accelerated as South Vietnam was able to take over more and more of its own defenses.

Press Secretary Ronald L. Ziegler said the outpouring of wires of support — he said the uncounted number was in "the high thousands" — appeared to be a direct, quick response from the "great silent majority" supporting the President's course.

Ziegler said a White House assistant whose tenure dated back to the Truman era reported he had never seen the like of the flow of messages.

Mr. Nixon, displaying the wires with arms sweeping out wide, told reporters: "This can be most effective in bringing the war to an end."

In obvious good spirits, he opened a few of the wires while reporters and photographers gathered around. He said the major theme of all was "We are silent Americans who are behind you."

"About 50 percent used the term silent Americans," he said.

He also held up a long yellow roll of paper he described as "the longest wire in history." He said it came from "some fellow in Colorado" who got 20,066 signatures on it pledging support to Mr. Nixon.

In his speech, Mr. Nixon seemed to abandon hopes of a peace breakthrough at the Paris talks, but he told reporters today "the diplomatic track" is still open. He added that "The train would move on that track on a much faster pace in direct relation of the support of the people of the United States.

In his speech, he said "no progress whatever has been made except agreement on the shape of the bargaining tables," despite the Paris talks and a series of "secret initiatives," including a summer exchange of letters between Mr. Nixon and the late Ho Chi Minh.

The other side, he said, has not shown "the least willingness to join in seeking a just peace."

The Nixon approach was sharply criticized by most of his previous critics and praised by his supporters. Sen. J. William Fulbright, D-Ark., said today he would schedule new Vietnam hearings soon by his Senate Foreign Relations Committee. **(Details: Page 3A.)**

Mr. Nixon was asked if any of the messages opposed his stand. He held up a three - inch stack of wires and said: "These think we ought to get out now." But he put a hand on a three-foot pile of telegrams and said, "At least these think we are on the right track."

In the speech, Mr. Nixon rejected demands for a total immediate American pullout as a course that would lead to "massacres" in South Vietnam and lead to Communist aggression in other areas. He specifically mentioned Berlin, the Middle East and "eventually even in the Western Hemisphere."

"For the future of peace, precipitate withdrawal would be a disaster of immense magnitude," he said in a broadcast from the White House. The speech had aroused great public expectations because it was announced three weeks in advance.

United Press International
PRESIDENT RICHARD NIXON

Thieu 'completely agrees' with Nixon

U.S. soldiers' reactions to President Nixon's speech are split: Page 2A

SAIGON, South Vietnam (AP)—President Nguyen Van Thieu expressed total agreement today with President Nixon's speech on the Vietnam war.

Thieu in a statement said:

"The people of Vietnam want nothing more than to gradually take the responsibility to preserve their own independence and freedom with the efficient assistance of the allied countries, especially that of the people of the United States, with a view to achieving the self-sufficiency and self development which I have affirmed many times."

Thieu termed the speech "one of the most important and greatest addresses of a president of the United States."

"I believe that the policy to end the war and restore a genuine peace to Vietnam, which President Nixon has recalled in his address today, is the right policy which conforms with our just position," the official English translation of Thieu's statement said.

"This policy is one which President Nixon and I have completely agreed upon," Thieu said.

N. Viets launch heavy attacks

SAIGON, South Vietnam — North Vietnamese troops launched their heaviest ground attacks in two months Tuesday, some 12 hours before President Nixon said that a "significant" increase in enemy activity might force him to stretch out his timetable for withdrawal of U.S. troops.

However, an official U.S. source said the current upsurge in enemy attacks, which began last weekend in the central highlands, didn't appear to be sufficient to slow the withdrawal program.

U.S. and South Vietnamese headquarters reported at least 45 enemy rocket and mortar attacks during the night, and infantry assaults on four American bases north of Saigon, an American night bivouac in the central highlands, and two South Vietnamese positions in the southern central highlands.

The enemy lost heavily in the ground attacks, with the allied commands claiming 180 killed, while allied casualties were four Americans and five South Vietnamese killed, 61 Americans and 12 South Vietnamese wounded, plus 23 Americans wounded in the shellings. The Americans captured seven North Vietnamese in the fighting north of Saigon.

"I think what the President is talking about is whether or not they launch something that would be relatively large scale," said the U.S. source. "We've said all along we anticipated that in the immediate future they would continue the campaign idea, a low level of action with periodic peaks, as opposed to a sustained offensive. I think President Nixon is thinking in those terms.

"The latest action isn't significantly different from what has been going on. Periodically there are days in which attacks pick up."

The attacks were the heaviest since the night of Sept. 5-6, when the enemy shelled more than 100 bases and towns and launched several ground attacks. This was during the final "high point" of the enemy's fall campaign.

The Saigon government reported 47 Vietnamese civilians were killed, 107 were wounded and 47 were kidnapped by Viet Cong terrorists in the week ending Oct. 29.

New York spurns U.S. gift of $10-million fair building

By WALTER R. MEARS

WASHINGTON, D.C. (AP)— The government claims it's a marvelous building, despite a sagging, leaking roof, but they won't give away the $10-million U.S. pavilion at the New York World's Fair.

So an appropriations bill is before the Senate to provide $350,000 to tear it down and clear the site where little more than four years ago fairgoers stood in line to ride a miniature train through scenes from American history.

Vacant since the spring of 1966, the pavilion now has been officially spurned by the city in which it stands, and Mayor John V. Lindsay wants it cleared away.

When Larry A. Jobe, an assistant secretary of commerce, brought the word to the Senate Appropriations Committee, Sen. John L. McClellan, D-Ark., was incredulous.

"It is a structure of permanent nature," he said. "It seems to me they could find some use for it. And they are demanding now that it be removed, they have no use for it?"

"Yes, sir," said Jobe. "When the World's Fair closed we entered into negotiations with the city saying it is a marvelous building, can't you use it? We drew up an agreement handing it over to the city free. No deal."

While the pavilion was made of concrete, Jobe said, the roof wasn't so durable. "It was not made for permanent use and it has begun to leak and sag."

The pavilion is on city-owned land, the World's Fair Corp. is out of business and the Commerce Department says demolition is now a federal responsibility.

"It is the old story, the government is always liable," complained Sen. Margaret Chase Smith, R-Maine. "We are always expected to pick up the tab."

Pakistan troops again fire on battling mobs

DACCA, East Pakistan (UPI) — Pakistani soldiers fired for the second successive day Monday at battling mobs of Bengals and Indian refugees.

The fighting has killed at least nine by official count but unofficial reports placed the dead at 25 or more. Soldiers patrolled the streets to enforce a curfew that has closed all schools and public places.

The violence erupted in a dispute over the use of the Urdu and Bengali languages on electoral forms.

'70s will be a time for femininity

Roy Swan's photos: Page 6C

Editorials, Page 6A	Weather, B Section
Business, B Section	Books & Arts, B Section
Comics, Pages 4, 5C	Theaters, Page 5D
TV, Radio, B Section	Women's, Pages 6-7C

Sports, Pages 1-3D

3

STAR TELEPHONES		
	News, General	372-4141
	Circulation	372-4343
	Want Ads	372-4242

Dow Jones Averages

(Noon N.Y.)	Avg.	Chg.
30 Industrials	849.13	−5.41
20 Rails	199.83	− .58
15 Utilities	118.39	− .48
65 Stocks	285.27	−1.41

Noon sales, 6,240,000 shares.

Nixon, Ho Chi Minh letters: Page 4A
Text of Nixon speech: Page 6D

Figure 14–18. Bold horizontal picture. [*Courtesy the Minneapolis Star.*]

Nation's Jobless Highest Since 1963

WASHINGTON (AP) – Unemployment rose to 5.8 per cent of the nation's work force last month, the highest level in 7½ years, the government reported today.

At the same time, average weekly earnings of some 45 million rank and file workers dropped 66 cents to $121.07 per week because of shorter working hours, said the Bureau of Labor Statistics.

Although the average pay-check was more than 5 per cent larger than a year ago, the nation's continuing worst inflation in more than 20 years cut purchasing power 2 per cent below a year ago, the bureau said.

Total employment dropped 165,000 during the month to 78.7 million compared with a normally expected rise in November. The report blamed in part the recent General Motors strike and declines in transportation and other industries.

The rise of unemployment was two-tenths of one per cent, from 5.6 to 5.8 per cent, highest since May of 1963, the bureau said.

The number of jobless Americans rose 350,000 during the month to 4.6 million, it said.

The jobless rate for men edged up from 4.1 to 4.2 per cent to a total of 1,815,000. The rate for women rose from 5.1 to 5.5 per cent to a total of 1,557,000. The rate for teen agers went up from 17.1 to 17.5 per cent to a total of 1,235,000.

In the past year, the total number of unemployed has climbed nearly two million including 905,000 men, 565,000 women and 430,000 teenagers, the bureau said.

The national jobless rate over the year was up from 3.5 to 5.8 per cent of the labor force.

BELOIT DAILY NEWS
Dedicated to Community Service

Established 1848, Vol. 123, No. 141 BELOIT DAILY NEWS, FRIDAY, DEC. 4, 1970 PRICE 10¢

Beloit's budget is more than dollars and cents. It is a massive document. It weighs just under a pound and contains some 154 pages of facts and figures on past and future needs for the various departments. Pictured with the readout sheets are Richard Calland (left), city finance director, and City Manager Robert Quinlan. The City Council is expected to approve the budget and set the tax rate Monday night. (Daily News Photo by Bob Borich)

Tax Under $32 Seen Unlikely

By Maureen Martin

Barring unforseen developments, the city tax rate will be about $32, City Council President Everett C. Haskell said today.

Haskell said the school board has said any cuts are "impossible" below the present 1971 spending of about $7.76 million, dashing his hopes of setting the tax rate at $30.

The budget hearing scheduld for Monday at 7:30 p.m., will be held in the Municipal Center Council Chambers. Although the council wanted it held at the larger Memorial High School Auditorium, the city clerk's office said today the meeting must by ordinance be held in the Council Chambers.

The council president said he requested the school budget be slashed an additional $533,000, to bring the rate to $300.

Reactions from School Supt. Dr. Eugene Tornow and several school board members confirmed Haskell's remarks. Tornow said any further budget cuts could reduce school aids by an additional $1.5 million.

"I'm just overwhelmed," said Ovid Smedstead, a member of the school board. "We just can't do it."

"Anything is possible," said another board member, Gim Wong. "But you can't do it and still maintain a decent school system."

As the rate stands now, Beloiters will pay $33.56 per $1,000 of their property's assessed value.

This amount includes $18.56 for schools, $8.37 for city services, $6.04 for county services, and $1.04 for the Vocational School.

Haskell said the council would still attempt to cut $1.39 from the city tax rate, the equivalent of slashing the budget by about $340,000.

These cuts would include dismissing the assessor's secretary, the administrative intern, leaving three vacancies unfilled and dismissing three men from the Fire Department, and leaving unfilled two Police Department vacancies, Haskell said.

The cuts also would reduce maintenance, snow removal, and equipment expenditures in the Department of Public Works, he said.

Asked if these cuts could reduce the tax rate to the hoped-for $30 level, Haskell said, "Not unless we come up with some brainstorms and the school board comes up with some brainstorms between now and Monday night."

Dr. Tornow said he "agreed 100 per cent" with previous statements by school board members that "any further cuts would significantly harm the present program of instruction.

"Not to maintain the present program could cause the state to withhold aids which would roughly amount to $1.5 million," Tornow said.

E. J. Justus, president of the school board, said the board had not examined the budget

Turn to BUDGET, Page 4

Manager Hunt On — Or Is It?

Two men whose names have been mentioned as possible interim or permanent successors to City Manager Robert W. Quinlan said today that such speculation is premature.

Quinlan has not resigned, although he told the City Council at a recent unofficial meeting that he was looking for a new position and would resign when he finds one.

No Candidates Sought

City Personnel Director James Main said he has received no instructions to advertise for either an interim or permanent manager, pointing out that thus far there is nothing formal about Quinlan's plans to leave the office.

City Public Works Director Roger Plumb and Donald P. Goiffon, Beloit district manager for the Wisconsin Power & Light Co., were quoted publicly Thursday as saying they haven't been asked about taking the city manager position. They were less specific in their reply to a question about whether they would take the job if it were offered, but both made it clear that they haven't entertained such thoughts as yet.

"I would want to help in any way that I could," said Plumb. "If there were no other way for Beloit to get temporary administrative service I would do my best to be cooperative."

Flattered at Suggestion

But Plumb said, he has not discussed the possibility of either interim or permanent service as city manager with any city official, and prefers to make no further comment on it now.

"I'm flatt... at such a suggestion," said Goiffon, "because any ... nd of a challenge fascinates me, and being city manager of Beloit surely is a challenge."

However, Goiffon added, "I have a vested interest in the Wisconsin Power & Light Co. I like my job. It has many challenges, in the areas of the environ-

Turn to MANAGER, Page 4

Cross Free; 7 Banished

MONTREAL (AP) – British envoy James Richard Cross was freed today after spending 60 days in a windowless room watched over around the clock by Quebec separationists armed with submachine guns.

Despite his long ordeal, a doctor's report said Cross was "in excellent" condition, except for the loss of 22 pounds due to the poor quality of food he was fed.

Cuban intermediaries handed Cross over after the Canadian government flew his captors to political asylum in Cuba. Cross was driven to the Jewish General Hospital for a checkup.

In a taped interview on television, Cross declared: "It's almost like being out of hell— perhaps purgatory would be a better expression."

He referred to all the days since his abduction Oct. 5 when he never saw the sun.

Pleas Flight to Europe

"It's a small thing and suddenly you come out of a house and its a bright day like today and you suddenly realize how much a little thing like that, that costs you nothing, means in one's day to day life," he said.

The British trade commissioner in Montreal described his captivity as "a state of suspended animation."

He spent a great deal of time watching television with his captors and estimated he had seen more than 160 films on television.

The exchange for Cross took place at the site of the Expo 67 world's fair.

Premier Robert Bourassa,

James Cross

who talked with Cross, said the British diplomat would fly to Europe today or Saturday.

Cross has high blood pressure, but the doctors said this condition was not affected by his ordeal.

'Wife is Deliriously Happy'

His wife, waiting in Bern, Switzerland, for news of her husband, said she hoped to be reunited with him Saturday in London.

"I am deliriously happy after these long weeks of tension," she said. "But I never gave up hope."

Cross telephoned her Thursday night after he was delivered to the Cubans. He told her "he had seen 162 French films on television," and this improved his understanding of the language. But he said he

Turn to MONTREAL, Page 4

Hockey Watched

Canada Hunts UW Suspects

OTTAWA (AP) – Four young Americans, on the FBI's most wanted list may be in Canada, where two were seen Sept. 3, the Royal Canadian Mounted Police report.

An RCMP statement Thursday said one of the four, David Sullivan Fine, 18, sought in connection with the dynamiting of a University of Wisconsin building Aug. 24, is an "avid hockey fan who may be tempted to attend hockey games."

Fine and Leo Frederick Burt, 22, were seen in Peterborough, Ont., Sept. 3. The other two, brothers Dwight Allen Armstrong, 19, and Carleton Louis Armstrong, 23, were seen on that day near Albany, N.Y. The RCMP said they were in a stolen car.

All four are charged with sabotage and destruction of government property in the Wisconsin explosion that killed a graduate student at work in the school's mathematics center.

The Armstrongs were picked up by police in Little Falls, N.Y., about 65 miles northwest of Albany, on a minor traffic infraction. They were released before it was learned the car they were using was stolen and that they were wanted.

Farmer to Quit As Nixon Aide

WASHINGTON (AP) – President Nixon is expected to announce Monday the resignation of administration aide James Farmer, the noted civil rights figure.

Government sources disclosed today that Farmer—an assistant secretary of the Department of Health, Education and Welfare and former national director of the Congress on Racial Equality—has informed employes of his resignation.

His successor is reportedly Rodney H. Brady, former vice president for management of Hughes Tool Co., Culver City, Calif.

Farmer had no comment on the report. But employes have scheduled a farewell party for him Dec. 16.

Farmer has wanted for several months to leave his post as assistant secretary for administration.

The 50-year-old black Texan helped found CORE in 1942 and was its national director from 1961 to 1966. He left the CORE post to head a national literacy program.

Irish Invoke Intern Powers

DUBLIN (AP) – The Irish government tonight assumed sweeping powers to intern any citizen because of what it called "a secret armed conspiracy" against the state.

Prime Minister Jack Lynch said in a statement that Ireland's police forces had uncovered a plot to kidnap prominent personalities, carry out raids on banks and even attempt murder of leading officials.

He said he was taking Ireland out of the European Human Rights Convention in order to intern suspected citizens without trial.

Sun Bathers Study

Believe it or not? That's a bare foot sticking out. And why not? Beloit temperatures Thursday reached a record high of 65 degrees. Ann Pace and Joel Gordon, two Beloit College students from Washington, D.C., took advantage of the weather offering to study at the Riverside Lagoon. Wisconsin's previous December high was a 64 set in 1962. (Daily News Photo by Dave Greenlee)

Check Cashing Policies Toughened

By Bob Borich

If you're like most persons in the habit of writing your check for a few dollars above the purchase price for extra pocket cash – forget it!

Unless you're a familiar face, or bearing one of the new bank guaranteed checking account cards, or registered with the store, chances are your check can cover purcase amount only.

Area businesses that normally handle a heavy flow of personal checks have been tightening up on their check cashing policies in recent months. And those that haven't are beginning to think about it.

Stuck for $600

Businessmen report increasing problems with worthless checks – mainly the "insufficient funds," or "no account" variety.

One drug store manager reports getting stuck with $600 in unrecoverable bad checks in a recent three-week period. He has now changed his policy. No more checks over the purchase amount.

"We had to do something," he said "the district attorney's office is swamped. They really can't help us.

Beloit Police Capt. James Mattison, who is in charge of investigations, reports a steady rise in the increase of fraudulent checks – so much so that the Department has assigned in the past year a sergeant to work full-time on the problem.

"The rise in incidents reflects the whole range of check abuses," said Mattison. "We have had a rash of forgeries resulting from lost or stolen checkbooks. Also, we have had a problem with stolen welfare checks which were passed in the community."

Hard-Line Policy

Other businesses also are responding to the condition with a hard line toward check cashing. Another large drug store manager who got "burned with three big ones lately" will cash a check over the purchase amount only if he knows the customer.

Grocers and discount stores have long had a card registration system for check cashers. That is, if a customer wishes to cash checks on a regular basis in the store she must have her identification listed with the store. Once registered, a customer usually has no trouble cashing a check – even for above the purchase amount.

A grocery store manager who admitted previous "laxity" in enforcement of his store's registration policy, is now ardently applying the policy. He will, however, authorize the cashing of registered customers' checks for a

Turn to CHECKS, Page 4

Figure 14–19. Bold, vertical picture. [*Courtesy, Beloit Daily News.*]

Another objection to placing pictures on the fold was that because the picture was a piece of art, it should not be ruined by the fold. Here, the reasoning is rather poor. Readers ordinarily do not perceive pictures as art forms and are not upset because it appears on the fold. If the details of a picture should be obliterated because of a fold, then there might be some objection to the practice. But this rarely, if ever, happens. The main and only consideration about picture placement is to find the position where it best harmonizes with every other element on the page.

Elimination of Type Rules

Contemporary design is recognized easily because it is so simple. One of the ways that makeup editors have used to simplify pages was to remove as many type rules from the page as possible. For that reason, column rules were the first to be eliminated, and the effect was attractive. Once these rules were eliminated, more white space appeared on the page, and it began to be easier to read than when rules had been used.

Next to go were jim dashes and finish dashes. Jim dashes were used to separate decks of a headline or to separate headlines from body type. But they were not needed. Finish or 30 dashes are still used in some newspapers, but they too have been eliminated by many other editors. The white space at the end of a story did not confuse the reader as it was feared. In fact, the white space made the page easy to read because it eliminated one more black line that cluttered the page.

Now two more rules should be eliminated if possible. The first is the cutoff rule, which should be used sparingly. White space, too, should be substituted wherever possible. Finally, the dateline rules at the top of page 1 and inside pages should be removed. These also add to the clutter.

Features of Contemporary Makeup

The preceding discussion concerned major elements of contemporary makeup practices. If all were used, and with discretion, the results would be a newspaper that looked as follows:

It would be simply designed. It would be functional. It would be dramatic and exciting. It would be clean-looking. It would be slower-paced than traditionally designed papers. Older designs often looked hectic and bewildering. Newer designs would show the effect of planning and sophistication. Thus a modern newspaper would be inviting and easy to read.

Contemporary Makeup Checklist

The checklist shown on the next page is a convenient means of evaluating the design and makeup of any given page, according to the principles of contemporary makeup. The values given for each criterion are those used by many editors who use contemporary makeup and design. But it should be noted that there are sometimes exceptions to each criterion. In such cases, allowances can be made as explained. A perfect score is 125.

CONTEMPORARY MAKEUP AND DESIGN CHECKLIST

Evaluate your page on a scale from 0 to 10 points on each criterion. If your page fulfills the criterion perfectly, give it 10. If less than perfect, give it any number from 0 to 10. Note: there are occasionally some exceptions to each criterion. If your page qualifies for an exception to any criterion, then give the criterion any number between 0 and 10 that you think is applicable.

Score: 0 – 10

1. Page should be balanced from top to bottom and side to side. If page is top heavy it is not balanced. Deduct points for formal balance. ....

2. Avoid extreme vertical or horizontal makeup. Each used to an extreme is unsightly. Good design uses both horizontal and vertical—but in unequal amounts without becoming extreme. ....

3. Is there enough openness, cleanliness or white space on the page? White space should be fairly well distributed, not concentrated on one part of the page. ....

4. Is there enough white space between columns? Usually 12 points are the minimum, but 18 points or 24 points are better. On the other hand, more than 24 points between columns may be unsightly. ....

5. Is there good contrast in the size of pictures? Poor design consists of small sized pictures, or pictures whose dimensions are almost square. The larger and more dramatic the picture, the more likely the page will be attractive. Large pictures should be strongly vertical or horizontal. ....

6. Is the nameplate modern and contemporary? Old-fashioned nameplates detract from the appearance of the entire page. ....

7. Is the pattern of the entire page simple and uncluttered? Generally simple patterns are uncluttered. To get a feeling about the totality of design half close your eyes in order to make the type and words less obvious. ....

8. Is the page exciting and/or dramatic in totality (aside from the news)? ....

9. Have you avoided large masses of gray type matter (that tends to be boring)? ......

10. Are headline sizes and weights appropriate for the body type? Many times headlines are either too large or too bold, or both, and tend to spot the page. ....

| The following are worth only five points totally (or 0 to 5) |

Score: 0 – 5

11. Have you avoided too many different sizes and kinds of type faces? ....

12. Are there few type rules on the page? (Avoid as many rules as possible) ....

13. Are there no more than one "inverted L-shaped story" on the page? ....

14. Is there at least one dominating story on the page (but not much more)? ....

15. Have you avoided anything that might call attention to itself and not the news?

TOTAL SCORE

15

Makeup of Special Pages

Older textbooks on the subject of makeup usually included a section on front page design patterns. These patterns were recognizable styles of arranging news articles on the front page and were given descriptive names that helped identify them: brace, focused, symmetrical, quadrant, vertical or circus makeup. In this text, however, a discussion of older front page patterns has been omitted because they are not relevant to contemporary makeup practices. These patterns were old-fashioned, artificial, unattractive and inflexible and were not necessarily based on the best principles of artistic design.

Contemporary makeup, on the other hand, is modern, functional, attractive and very flexible. It is also based on the principles of artistic design. Contemporary makeup patterns, especially those of front pages, may be continually changing, just as the design of objects outside the newspaper changes. Therefore, any pattern that is contemporary today may not be after a period of time. Designer Gyorgy Kepes noted that:

> The laws of visual perception are conditioned by the visual habits of time. Visual communication can be efficient only if it adapts itself to the new landscape and the new psychology of contemporary man. . . . design, to be efficient must make significant adaptations to the contemporary scene.[1]

[1] Gyorgy Kepes, "Function in Modern Design," in *Graphic Forms* (Cambridge Mass.; Harvard University Press, 1949), p. 10.

The Front Page

Kepes argued that communication is optimized when it is placed in the framework of the world as contemporary man perceives it. It is the front page, more than any other, that can and should reflect changing formats to keep up with changing man. Contemporary design is never static. Its beauty is based on the excitement of design that surrounds each individual reader.

Also to be found in some older makeup textbooks was the admonition that makeup must be used to design newspapers that looked like newspapers. This was necessary because readers might be disturbed if newspapers should take on new and unfamiliar designs. Contemporary man, however, often likes and appreciates new and unfamiliar designs—not at first, perhaps, but in the long run. New designs eventually will be appreciated the most. Makeup of newspapers, therefore, should not be limited to techniques and practices editors always have used. Editors should borrow from whatever graphic communication has been shown to be successful, such as magazines, books and possibly even advertisements.

It should be noted again, however, that newsroom personnel are not allowed to change the design of the entire paper. This is not their prerogative; it is the management's. They do have many opportunities from day to day, working within the overall design framework, of creating attractive and readable new page designs. They have more such opportunities on special pages than they do anywhere else within the newspaper.

Concept of Front Page Makeup

One carryover from the older makup textbooks, however, still makes sense, namely that the front page ought to be a showcase of the newspaper. Because the front page does not carry advertising, its makeup is free from restrictions, so that it may reflect whatever the editor wishes it to reflect. Editors, however, although agreeing on the showcase concept, have not agreed on what should be displayed in the showcase. If one looks at the makeup of most front pages in this country, he will not find anything particularly exciting unless it happens to be the news. If the news is not exciting, then the front page showcase may have little to show.

There is an urgent need for editors to use the front page showcase to reflect a more sincere interest in the legibility of the page. It is suggested, therefore, that of all possible alternatives that might be featured in the showcase the most significant one is that the editor of the newspaper show that he cares a great deal about individuals' reading problems. The front pages of many newspapers do not reflect this interest. Front pages are not always easy to read, especially when they are compared with other printed communication such as books or magazines. They are designed, instead, on the basis of a traditional format that represents the easiest and quickest way to get the newspaper on the street in order to meet its deadlines.

Underlying the showcase concept, therefore, should be the following bases for front page makeup:

1. The makeup should reflect the editor's concern for the reader so that the page is not only easy to read but attractive and inviting. The front page should be easier to read than any other page in the newspaper. Any device that impedes reading should be eliminated or replaced, no matter how important it may be for editorial purposes. The use of freaks, refers, inserts and kickers have worthwhile editorial purposes, but they often mar the appearance of the page design.

2. The front page should also reflect the contemporary scene more than any other page in the newspaper. There is more opportunity on the front page than any other page to achieve this goal. It is not reasonable to place news in an old-fashioned setting, and the front page should not look like front pages of bygone days.

3. The front page should be orderly. But the order need not be graded from the most important stories placed at the top of the page to less important stories at the bottom. Other kinds of order can accomplish the same goal.

4. In addition to reflecting contemporary design, the front page should be distinctive, with a personality of its own. Although it should serve to set the tone of the entire paper, the front page personality should be one that readers like and respect because the news on that page is the most significant in the paper.

5. Readers should be offered alternative designs rather than one that is used every day with little change. Although it is true that readers may learn to like a format with no differences from day to day, such formats are not reasonable because the news changes, and designs should reflect these changes. The design itself, therefore, as well as the words, helps to communicate.

Structure of Page 1

One of the most important ways of achieving a well-designed page 1 is to use the principle of artistic dominance. Front pages are often busy and cluttered because there are too many stories competing for the reader's attention. As a result, the reader often doesn't know where to look. He may direct his attention somewhere at the top because the largest and blackest headlines are located there. Even when a few strong headlines are located elsewhere on the page, the reader can't focus his attention easily without some distraction from other headlines. In other words, the competition for attention is often too great. Another problem with front page structure is that the shape of the main story, aside from its headline, is often not dominant. A single- or double-column story, no matter how long, does not necessarily dominate a page. As a result, many front pages lack unity. Graphic designer Maitland Graves stated the problem as follows: "Equality of opposing forces produces incoherence.... Without dominance, a design disintegrates."[2]

[2] Maitland Graves, *The Art of Color and Design*, (New York: McGraw-Hill, 1941), p. 53, 54.

To overcome the pull of competing headlines and stories lacking any visual power at all, the structure of the front page should employ the principle of dominance.

The makeup man can employ this principle by first selecting one element to dominate the page. This element will undoubtedly be the story with the greatest news significance. Then, by careful placement, arrangement in columns, spacing and headline treatment, he can achieve his goal of page dominance. The one element, however, need not be a story alone. It may consist of a story and a related picture, a number of related stories, or a large picture alone (Figure 15–1a, b). A hairline box around the element, including generous amounts of white space, may help achieve dominance. But the traditional banner headline, with accompanying multiple-column deck, reading into a single-column story is not an example of page dominance.

When one element dominates a page, all other elements will clearly be subordinate. But this relationship is very subtle. An element may overdominate a page to such an extent that the reader has trouble reading shorter stories. On the other hand, the dominant element may not be dominating enough to keep it from competing with secondary elements. Here, the makeup man simply has to develop a sense of good design. The situation demands a sensitivity that tells the editor when an element is either too strong or too weak, neither of which may be correct.

Furthermore, a major factor in creating a pleasing page structure involves shaping the main element so that it is pleasing as well as dominating. The makeup man will have to use his sense of pleasing proportions to determine the shapes that add the most to page structure. Rectangular shapes are best. Odd shapes such as the inverted L are poorest.

Finally, the placement of the dominating element is related to its size. When a story with a bold headline is crammed into a small corner of the page, the remainder of the page may be hard to make up in a pleasing arrangement. The dominating element, therefore, should be relatively large and placed in positions close to the optical center of the page. To have stories long enough to be a center of dominant interest, the editor may have to create a policy that makes longer stories possible. Many newspapers have no such policy, and as a result it is hard to create front page dominance with relatively short stories.

New Ordering on Front Page

The order of traditional makeup on page 1 was always to place the most important story in the upper-right-hand corner. Other important stories may have been placed in the upper left, and less important stories were placed underneath. This is a logical way of ordering the placement of stories but it isn't the only way. In fact, it isn't suited to contemporary design because it tends to produce top-heavy pages and pages that never seem to vary in appearance.

A new ordering is based on the rotation of reading from the largest story to the smallest one, where the largest story is the

In The News This Week

Civil Strife Rips Viet

South Viet Nam is threatened by a war within a war, as troops loyal to Premier Nguyen Cao Ky's government battle rebel Buddhist forces in Northern Da Nang.
The Buddhists, seeking to overturn Ky factions in the constitutional elections now scheduled for September, have vowed to die for their cause. Ky has said he will use any means to crush the rebels.
Washington, anxious to retain military gains despite the political strife, has announced a major military buildup in Viet Nam between now and the elections.
Viet Cong forces have offered to support the Buddhist rebels.

Gemini 9 Scrubbed

An unmanned Agena target rocket failed to orbit Tuesday, spoiling a near-perfect countdown and scrapping the Gemini 9 space mission until May 31. A locked engine on the Agena's booster rocket caused the target to fall into the ocean off Florida. The mission would have sent Astronauts Thomas Stafford and Eugene Cernan on a three-day orbital trip. A rendezvous with the Agena and a space walk by Cernan were scheduled for the mission.

Strikes Hit UK, France

Strikes in England and France threatened crises for the two countries' economies this week. Prices rose, and the value of the pound declined in England after the 62,500-member National Union of Seamen struck shipowners Sunday night. The strikers, who have idled over 350 ships, are asking for a 40-hour instead of a 56-hour work week with no pay reduction. The union has warned Prime Minister Harold Wilson that Royal Navy attempts to clear the ship-clogged British ports could result in a general strike.
Meanwhile, 7 million Frenchmen joined a general strike protesting a government imposed 4.85 per cent ceiling on wage increases.

Artificial Heart Works

An artificial heart was removed in Houston Wednesday from the chest of Walter L. McCans, after it had successfully allowed his heart enough time to heal itself. The operation was similar to the one performed by Dr. Michael DeBakey last month at the same hospital on Marcel DeRudder, who died from respiratory complications without regaining consciousness.

Kidnapped Girl Freed

Peggy Ann Bradnick, chained by her neck for a week by her crazed kidnapper, was rescued Wednesday night after a farmyard gun battle near Shade Gap, Pa. The 17-year-old girl was freed when her abductor, William Hollenbaugh, was slain, reportedly by a 15-year-old boy. Hollenbaugh, known as "Bicycle Pete," had shot an FBI agent Tuesday during the state-wide manhunt.

Draft Sit-In Ends

Nearly 400 University of Chicago students called off their week-long sit-in Tuesday. The demonstrators were protesting the University's policy of giving class rank information to the Selective Service. They had barred administration workers from their officers, causing them to use other campus buildings.

Pickets Compete

Three groups demonstrated Thursday at Wayne State University in Detroit. One group, protesting the administration of draft deferment examinations by the University drew 41 pickets and 150 onlookers. A second group, demonstrating against the protestors, attracted 15 pickets and 50 viewers.
However, nearly 2,000 students observed an auction by a third group to raise money for the Children's Leukemia Fund of Michigan. Most onlookers were draft-age males.
The auctioneers were three Playboy Club bunnies.

Medill Spectrum

News and Analysis

A Weekly Published by the Medill School of Journalism

VOL. III, No. 1 FRIDAY, MAY 20, 1966 111 EVANSTON, ILL.

Planners Envision 'Office City'

South Tower of the State Bank and Trust Co.'s proposed Fountain Square project exemplifies the movement to make downtown Evanston an "Office City."

New Zoning To Revitalize Evanston Business District

Evanston once served commuters in the near north suburbs of Chicago as a retail shopping center. But as urbanization of the North Shore progresses, the commuter market for retail sales is moving into northwest suburbs. The city has proposed zoning amendments designed to transform Evanston into an "Office City."

By Elizabeth Rogers

Evanston has been squeezed by the intensive urbanization of the North Shore. To relieve the squeeze, and to open up commercial activity, the city has prepared a new set of zoning regulations designed to transform Evanston into an "Office City."

Business and population expansion, characteristic of suburban areas of the nation's larger cities, has bypassed Evanston in favor of suburbs with more favorable provisions for growth and expansion.

The "Office City" plan is an attempt to check the progressive movement of businesses away from Evanston and provide needed office space. The proposal is part of the Evanston Plan Commission's long-range goal to accelerate the city's trend toward becoming a center for national and regional headquarters.

Evanston, already the location of more than 30 national headquarters, is an ideal site for business offices, according to Gordon Campbell, vice-president and cashier of the State Bank and Trust Co. "The lake, the university and transportation," he said, "make Evanston a better location than the Loop for many companies."

Space Urgently Needed

According to Campbell, who also is director of operations for the bank's Fountain Square development, the demand for office space in Evanston greatly exceeds supply. He said the bank itself is expanding, displacing tenants who must then move out of Evanston because office space is so scarce.

Other business headquarters also have moved from Evanston because present zoning ordinances prohibited their expansion, according to City Planning Director Robert Wheeler. A. C. Nielsen moved to larger facilities in Chicago, and Standard Rate and Data moved to Skokie.

Some organizations, unable to expand old facilities in Evanston, have moved to new developments within the city. The National Merit Corporation, for example, has moved to the 990 Grove building in Evanston.

New Building Full

Myron Holmgren, developer of 990 Grove, said space in the building was 100 per cent committed before construction was completed, indicating the need for additional Evanston office space. Only 18 months old, the building already is expanding to house the offices of Educational Testing Service, presently located at 611 Church St.

Momentum for Evanston's transformation into an "Office City" started as workers began to live farther away from their jobs. White collar workers moved north to create Evanston's now well-established residential districts. Office workers and executives who now live here, Campbell said, would welcome the reduced transportation time necessary to reach offices in Evanston rather than in the Loop.

Because Evanston is an old city, its

(Continued on page 6)

Campus Shops Cost More

By Lois Chase

Convenience is expensive in Evanston, partially because people would rather pay more for a Camel than walk a mile — or even two blocks.

While prices are higher than normal in some of Evanston's downtown stores, they are more consistently high in the shops adjacent to the Northwestern University campus. Some merchants contend that Northwestern students are "too rich to care" if they spend 10 to 25 per cent more to avoid going a few blocks out of their way.

By keeping an open eye, the bargain hunter can find many instances of the "high price syndrome" near the NU campus. For example, a family-sized tube of Crest toothpaste costs 95 cents at Hoos Drug Store, 75 cents at Kresge's, and 59 cents at the Kroger Food Store.

The regular size box of Kleenex tissues sells for 33 cents at Hoos, Huerbinger's Drug Store, and the Co-op, but 25 cents at Woolworth's. The 12-oz. bottle of Micrin mouthwash costs 98 cents at the Co-op, Hoos, and Huerbinger's, but 81 cents at Walgreen's.

Students could go to alternate stores, such as the chain stores, but most do not. Local branches of these chain stores can raise or lower prices on specific products to meet neighborhood competition, but "there is little competition in Evanston for low prices," according to a manager of Walgreen's.

One explanation for this was offered by the owner of a small discount store on Davis Street: "The kids at Northwestern are so rich they don't mind paying more for the convenience of buying from the stores closest to campus."

Merchants in these stores have found that fringe benefits, such as check cashing, are more important to students than economy.

Their higher charges are partially due to high rents in the downtown area and a gradual decline in the number of customers in downtown Evanston. But the willingness of people to pay more is the basic factor.

"I just don't think the students care that much," said Byron Gregory, head of the NU Senate committee which studied prices two years ago. The 2,500 booklets printed by the committee and distributed free to students brought no substantial change in prices, or in students' buying habits.

According to the manager of one of the dime stores, if there were more selective purchasing, Evanston merchants would be forced to lower prices.

Johnson Backs McNamara's Draft Proposal

WASHINGTON, (UPI)—The White House gave President Johnson's approval yesterday to Defense Secretary Robert S. McNamara's proposal that all young men and women put in two years of military or civilian service for their country.

The White House support was voiced by Press Secretary Bill D. Moyers. He said, "Secretary McNamara was talking about a concept of public service — a concept which the President has had for some time."

McNamara, in his speech Wednesday before the American Society of Newspaper Editors in Montreal, said the program would overcome the present "inequity" of the military draft system which calls upon a minority of eligible young men. McNamara proposed that all young people be required to spend two years in the service of their country. But, they would be allowed to choose between military service, the Peace Corps, Vista and so forth.

The suggestion came under bipartisan fire in Congress where House members contended there were better ways to remedy the unfairness of the draft than by adopting what amounts to universal conscription.

Rep. William Bray, R-Ind., called the program "utterly preposterous." He said Congress had long ago buried the notion of universal military service training and would not permit young people to be drafted for other forms of service.

Authorities noted that each year about 2 million young men reach draft age. Training all of them, either for the army or Peace Corps, would cost billions.

Charles Liesenfeld, Selective Service advisor at the University of Minnesota, expressed doubts that a sufficient number of young people would volunteer for military service when given the chance to substitute civilian programs.

Liesenfeld said, "We'd probably get 99 per cent of the students in the Peace Corps and one per cent in the army."

Researcher Confirms Old Wives' Tales About Moon

NU Scientist Tests Man's Dependence on Biological Clocks

By Bonnie Croft

The Chinese believe the moon will blight anything it shines upon. Peruvian peasants fear bright moonlight, thinking it will bring them bad luck. In the United States some mountain people believe crops planted by the new moon will flourish, but if the moon is full, lunacy and murder will run rampant.

For centuries people have believed old wives' tales about the power of the moon, despite the efforts of scientists to disprove its influence.

Some experiments, conducted by Frank A. Brown Jr., professor of biology at Northwestern University, now indicate there may be some scientific basis for many beliefs that "grandma" has held all along. For more than 30 years he has been working on biological clocks, those mysterious rhythmic changes present in every organism.

For example, Dr. Brown took flatworms, started them crawling north and observed their tendency to veer to the right or left. Their paths clearly changed with the phase of moon and time of day. Switching the magnetic field from north to south with a simple magnet, Dr. Brown reversed the turning pattern from right to left.

Brown's theory is that external forces—unseen, unheard and unfelt —affect the rhythmic cycles of organisms. These forces are electromagnetic radiations, as well as electrostatic and magnetic fields. In humans, they influence daily rhythms in sleep, cell metabolism and hormonal output.

The idea of the biological clock is not new and resistance to it is old. Deep-seated rhythmic changes were observed in the early 18th century, when a French astronomer noted that leaves drooped nightly even when light changes were absent.

Dr. Brown with chart showing potato metabolism.

What is relatively new on the subject is Dr. Brown's explanation of the clock's timer. The conventional theory was first proposed near the turn of the century by Wilhelm Pfeffer, a German plant physiologist. Pfeffer claimed a clock ran steadily throughout the plant's life. Independent of outside forces, this clock presumably measured time accurately. Dr. Brown, on the other hand, argues the timer is external and that the regularity of the rhythms depend upon delicate, penetrating forces in the earth's atmosphere.

"Until about five years ago, my theory of essential subtle, external influences was not taken seriously," Brown says. "I had to first convince the other scientists that they actually had no real proof there was an internal timer such as nearly everyone assumed."

When Dr. Brown first introduced his theory in the 1950s, he was criticized by biologists who thought the problem had already been solved.

"All we have proved is that we still do not know where the timer is," Brown said slyly. "Five years ago every scientist in the country knew exactly where it was.

"I had to demonstrate to them that all living things are incredibly sensitive, sensitive enough to be getting their information from the outside, and that probably the primary things they are sensing are the earth's magnetic and electric fields. Some considered this possibility so ridiculous they would not even look at my data."

The Office of Naval Research first supported Brown's work, although he admits that several years ago "they seemed briefly to have their credulity stretched to the breaking point by my findings."

Dr. Brown has demonstrated that the rhythms can be altered by slight modifications of the atmosphere's electric, magnetic, and radiation fields. The 57-year-old professor currently has "a whole laboratory full" of experiments underway.

Some of his research has been with the potato, which grows underground away from the influence of sun and tides. His experiments showed it was no longer necessary to assume the organisms required an internal timer to measure the lengths of the day or year. Sealing the potatoes against light, temperature and humidity, Dr. Brown showed a link between metabolic rates and external changes.

"Living things might conceivably possess inherited, regular rhythms, but it is quite inconceivable that they are born with an inherited plan of all erratic temperature and barometric pressure fluctuations which are to occur during their lifetimes," Brown stated.

As startling as these results are, Dr. Brown cautioned that they do not prove living things have no internal timers. Until an organism can be completely removed from its environment, no final test of the timer's existence can take place. "We must find out how to stop the clock in order to find out how it runs," Brown said.

Dr. Brown studies biological responses of mice.

Photos by Ray Foster

Will the clocks run outside the earth's environment?

This question assumes special importance for the space age. If an organism cannot undergo prolonged absence from the atmosphere without biological damage, the hopes for manned interplanetary travel have hit a considerable snag.

The National Aeronautics and Space Administration has already talked to Dr. Brown and other biologists about the possibility of placing a potato aboard a Pioneer rocket in a solar orbit. The potato's metabolism would be monitored, with information sent back to earth hourly.

"This would demonstrate whether a living thing still had any rhythms and whether it could survive when removed from the earth's environment," said Dr. Brown.

If the clocks are indispensable to an organism as many believe and if Brown's theory that they are externally regulated is correct, the change in atmospheric conditions in space could be disastrous.

"I can't imagine what would happen if all the clocks stopped," he said. "I presume it might be death."

Figure 15–1a. Dominant stories on front pages. [*Courtesy the Medill School of Journalism, Northwestern University, Evanston, Illinois.*]

Clare Luce Vs. Keating and Kennedy
N.Y. Conservative Party Says She's Willing to Run. Page 2.

The Sunday
Herald Tribune

ESTABLISHED 124 YEARS AGO. A EUROPEAN EDITION IS PUBLISHED DAILY IN PARIS

AUGUST 23, 1964

1

CITY EDITION

Vol. CXXIV No. 42,845 © 1964 NEW YORK HERALD TRIBUNE, INC. • 230 WEST 41st STREET, NEW YORK, 10036 N.Y. TEL. PENNSYLVANIA 6-4000   35c IN AREAS 50 MILES FROM NEW YORK CITY EXCEPT ON LONG ISLAND   *THIRTY CENTS*

IN THE NEWS THIS MORNING

3 Congo Yanks Safe: The Colonel's Story

Two American Army colonels and a U.S. diplomat emerged safe from the eastern Congo bush after three days of terror that included being machine-gunned by Congolese rebels and threatened with death by hostile villagers. From the United Nations, Herald Tribune correspondent Darius Jhabvala notes a surprising change of pace: the Russians are being rather agreeable over the Congo, an issue on which they used to break records for vituperation. The reports are on Page 3.

Tense Cease-Fire in Cyprus

The United Nations peace force on Cyprus was acting boldly yesterday in defense of a tense cease-fire, especially when it came to getting food to beleaguered Turkish Cypriots. In Athens, however, the Greek government has had trouble making up its mind just how bold to be in dealing with Greek Cypriot President Makarios—and its indecision threatens to push the nation's politics leftward, reports Seymour Freidin. Page 23.

Castro: The Tough Questions

What question is Fidel Castro most reluctant to answer about his regime? And what question makes him *see* Red in more ways than one? Barnard L. Collier asked them both during his seven-day running interview with the Cuban dictator. Page 26.

Coming Red Victory in Chile

Within two weeks Chile will hold a Presidential election in which the Communists cannot lose even if they are beaten; both the other candidates have been driven far to the Left by the Reds' appeal to the voters. Henry Lee reports. Page 7.

Old Nazis in the New Germany

West Germany's 20-year statute of limitations on Nazi war crimes expires next May, but hundreds of ex-Nazis are still at large and many are back in government. Werner H. Guttmann, who saw the Nazi movement's rise before he left Germany in 1935, analyzes the problem in an article on Page 20.

Reapportionment Nears Vote

The Supreme Court's sweeping reapportionment edict—designed to give urban and rural dwellers equal voice in public affairs—will be put to another crucial battle in Congress early next month. That's when Senate Minority Leader Everett Dirksen hopes to force a vote on a bill to thwart the court's decision. Ironically, however, reporter Andrew Glass finds that politicians are far more perturbed than voters over the reapportionment matter. See Page 11.

Howard Hughes' $1 Billion Empire

The bankroll behind Howard Hughes is a Southwestern tool company whose penchant for anonymity makes circus Garbo appear to be a headline-hunter. But from this corporate headwater has come the millions of dollars that the brilliant and eccentric Hughes has used to spawn a billion-dollar empire. Dennis Duggan reports some little-known facts about the cornerstone of the Hughes complex on Page 1, Section 3.

Beauty & New York—By Bob Bird

National Correspondent Robert S. Bird take a penetrating look at places of beauty around New York. He begins at the Central Park Zoo, ends at Lincoln Center for the Performing Arts, and in between details New York's progress in making a fuller, richer life for us all. On Page 18.

—Index on Page 3—

Late TV-Radio listings—Page 33

Atlantic City: Democratic Sunshine and Shadows

- *People and Places and Problems in Boardwalk City. Page 8.*
- *Johnson's Choices for Vice-President. Page 8.*
- *White House 'to Run' Convention Electronically. Page 14.*
- *Platform Contrast — Justifiably Extreme. Page 14.*
- *Credentials Fight on Alabama, Mississippi. Page 14.*
- *Point by Point in Democratic Platform. Page 35.*

Boardwalk Bandwagon

It's Johnson's Convention

By David Wise
Washington Bureau Chief

ATLANTIC CITY.

This is, all the way, Lyndon B. Johnson's convention.

It was supposed to have been John F. Kennedy's.

That simple, delicate fact is everywhere, like the tang of the salt in the air. And the sea, that rolls in timelessly, is a reminder that all things human are fragile, even the "portraits of LBJ in indestructible metal" on sale in the lobby of the convention hall.

The truth is, President Johnson never wanted the convention here, in this land of salt-water taffy, frozen custard and pre-Cambrian plumbing.

Back in January, President Johnson explored the possibility of moving the 1964 national convention to Chicago, which he would have preferred. But he was told it could not be done.

President Kennedy had approved the Atlantic City convention site, and here it will take place.

Had it been as planned by the Democratic National Committee, this convention would have been a gay celebration of President Kennedy's renomination for a second term. The choice of a pleasure resort would have been in keeping with the occasion. But the occasion has changed.

Perhaps that is why Mr. Johnson tried to switch the convention to Chicago, although the reasons given for the White House discontent with Atlantic City had more to do with the alleged lack of hotel rooms and baths.

Delegates, alternates and the press are occupying 11,000 rooms. The Atlantic City Public Relations Bureau insists only 100 rooms are bathless. Because the convention is taking

It's a Johnson Convention with Kennedy in background...

... and Barry Goldwater on the Atlantic City boardwalk.

Herald Tribune—UPI telephoto

place nine months after the assassination of the President of the United States, Atlantic City seems even more tawdry than it might. Aged vacationers sit in the gloomy lobbies of cavernous Victorian hotels. They stare at the sea and at the aimless stream of people seeking carnival thrills along the boardwalk.

One reason that President Kennedy

approved Atlantic City as his renomination site was the $625,000 the city offered the national committee, along with free use of the Convention Hall. Miami Beach had offered more money. But in view of the civil rights issue and Miami's large Cuban exile population, it was thought wiser to come here.

On Thursday night, after the nomination of President Johnson, there will be a tribute to President Kennedy in the the form of a film called "A Thousand Days." White House officials said yesterday that Mrs. John F. Kennedy had talked with Mrs. Johnson yesterday by phone and "felt she could not watch" the movie about her husband's life and the scenes showing him with their two children.

Mrs. Kennedy has told convention officials she would rather enter the hall after the film, about fifteen minutes before President Johnson arrives to accept the cheers of the 17,000 persons in Convention Hall.

Earlier that day, Mrs. Kennedy will receive all 5,260 delegates and alternates at a tea at the Deauville Hotel given by Under Secretary of State W. Averell Harriman "to thank the delegates who supported" John F. Kennedy at the 1960 convention in Los Angeles.

But none of this can take away the fact that this is LBJ's convention. Mounted behind the speaker's platform in the great, empty hall yesterday there were three small photographs—of Franklin D. Roosevelt, John F. Kennedy and Harry S. Truman. Beneath them and dwarfing them in size were two Orwellian photographs of President Johnson, each 60 feet high. And there are also the new President's words:

"Let us continue . . . "

A View Within CIA: Can't Win in Viet

By Lawrence Barrett
Of The Herald Tribune Staff

WASHINGTON

A ranking Central Intelligence Agency official believes there is "serious doubt" that the Communist rebellion in South Viet Nam can be quelled and says a "prolonged stalemate" might be all the West can hope for.

This conclusion, reached in a scholarly paper called "Trends in the World Situation," promises to set off a political explosion because of Sen. Barry Goldwater's determination to make the Vietnamese war a major campaign issue. The Republican Presidential candidate accuses the Administration of being timid and feckless in dealing with Communists.

Although the CIA was prepared to allow publication of the entire paper in a scholarly journal, the Administration became concerned when it learned that one newspaper—the *Chicago Tribune*—had acquired a copy. The newspaper was understood to be planning a story on the document today.

The State Department took the unusual step of

attempting to reduce the impact of the story by making the paper available to a small group of State Department reporters Friday night. At the same time, Secretary of State Dean Rusk reportedly said the document did not represent the Administration's viewpoint.

Mr. Rusk was said to have emphasized that the paper was the work of one man only—the author, Willard Matthias—and that it had no official status. Other sources said the paper was not an official appraisal by CIA's Board of National Estimates, even though Mr. Matthias is a member of that important body and even though other board members saw the report and approved it in general terms.

The 45-page paper, dated June 9, 1964, touched on virtually every aspect of the cold war. Its controversial section on South Viet Nam consisted of these lines:

"The guerrilla war in South Viet Nam is in its fifth year and no end appears in sight. The Viet Cong in the South, dependably largely on their own resources but under direction and control of the

Communist regime in the North, are pressing their offensive more vigorously than ever. The political mistakes of the Diem regime inhibited the effective prosecution of the war, which 'a nearly more of a political contest than a military operation, and led to the regime's destruction.

"The counter-guerrilla effort continues to flounder, partly because of the inherent difficulty of the problem and partly because Diem's successors have not yet demonstrated the leadership and inspiration necessary.

"There remains serious doubt that victory can be won, and the situation remains very fragile. If large-scale United States support continues, and if further political deterioration within South Viet Nam is prevented, at least a prolonged stalemate can be attained. There is also a chance that political evolution within the country and developments upon the world scene could lead to some kind of negotiated settlement based on neutralization."

For other developments in Viet Nam, see Page 21.

Figure 15–1b. See caption for Figure 15–1a.

most dominant one. But now the most dominant story may be placed anywhere on the page, and because it is so dominant, it will be read first (assuming that the reader is interested in the news content). The reader easily sees where the most dominant story is located and proceeds from there to less dominant stories until he has finished reading the page. Because the dominant story may be moved from day to day, there should be no fixed pattern of front page makeup that becomes prosaic. Each day should bring about an exciting design showing that the makeup editor is attuned to placing the news of the day in a format unique for that day.

When reading a particular story, the reader's order is from the top down. When the story is continued to adjacent columns, however, the order is back up again to the top of the next column in which the story is continued. The best way to inform the reader where the story is continued is to wrap it at the top of the next column, underneath a headline. The squared-off design should immediately tell the reader the order of procedure without the loss of even a second.

Listed below are some recurring problems contributing to poor makeup and design on the front page. If the reader's best interest serves as the underlying basis for makup, these problems will not occur. But because they have occurred so often, they are mentioned here:

Problems To Avoid in Front Page Makeup

1. Use of a daily banner headline—Readers either resent newspapers that use a large banner headline daily or they learn to discount the effect of large type used in such headlines. They assume that what is printed is not necessarily most important. In some newspaper offices, banners are used each day because it has become traditional since the days when newspapers were sold on newsstands. Editorial policy should be changed so that banners are used only when the news warrants them. If not, then the entire page structure is forced into a page makeup where the readout almost always occurs at the top right, or, perhaps, somewhere at the top. It is difficult to create a contemporary design when a banner headline is used each day.

2. Breaking a page into two distinct sections—When the makeup editor attempts to use contemporary design through the use of page domination, there is the possibility he may divide the page into two distinct parts. This has the effect of asking the reader to read either one or the other part but not both. One part does not naturally lead into the other. Therefore, attempts should be made to prevent such a dichotomy from occurring. The makeup editor will have to be alert to the division of space into two parts. When he finds a line of white space that extends for eight columns across the page, he is apt to be dividing the page horizontally. When he uses a rule eight columns wide to separate elements on the page, the same thing may occur (Figure 15–2). In other words, the makeup man isn't deliberately dividing the

Carnivals Highlight Chicago Summers

Photos by June Hielscher

By Darlene Napady

As soon as the ferris wheel creaks into motion and the calliope notes sound, Chicagoans abandon their front stoops and television sets to crowd the summer fairs and carnivals.

The biggest is the widely-promoted Free Fair, which annually nets $75,000 to $100,000 for the Back of the Yards Council, a group of West Side community organizations. Sprawling over an athletic field at 4700 S. Damen Ave., the fair opens July 6 for a 28-day run. Free parking is a lure that partially makes up for the honky-tonk booths and rides.

The carnival at St. Benedict's Church, 2215 W. Irving Park Road, is more compact, more friendly, and adds the bonus of a good fireworks display. This year it will be held June 15 to June 19.

For some unusual and good food during the same week, there is the carnival at Our Lady of Vilna Church, 2327 W. 23rd Place. The featured items are bundukis (a Lithuanian sandwich of chopped ham in a bun) and kugelis (potatoes in sour cream). The dates are June 13 to June 17.

Food is also more important than games at the August 21st picnic at St. Andrews Greek Orthodox Church, 5649 N. Sheridan Road. Visitors can join in the Greek folk dancing,

have a reasonably priced shishkebab dinner and finish it off with loukoumadis, the traditional fried pastry dipped in honey.

Back to the south side for one of the more intimate and pleasant fairs, St. Michael's Church, 2325 W. 24th Place, puts on its annual Music and Pizza Fair July 16 through July 26. Somebody is always performing, and clams, Italian sausage and watermelon are available.

An Italian atmosphere also infuses the two festivals that mark the July 16 feast day of St. Mary of Mt. Carmel.

An evening candlelight procession through the street highlights the miniature county fair at St. Mary of Mt. Carmel Church, 6722 S. Hermitage. Ave.

The bigger event on this feast day is in suburban Melrose Park. Up to 20,000 people pack the streets for the festivities at Our Lady of Mt. Carmel Church. The celebration is climaxed by a procession in which a statue of the Virgin Mary, brought from Italy around the turn of the century, is carried through the streets. A full panoply of concessions, rides, and gaiety surrounds the procession

The fairs are promoted for money, and they make it. But the lure is not charity; it is fun for young and old alike.

Street Gospel Swings

By Dave Sullivan

If the sun's out and the weather's warm, Jim Brewer hauls his electric guitar and amplifier to the corner of Maxwell and Peoria streets Sunday morning.

Against the background of a flaking, red brick wall Jim and five other "Brothers and Sisters" sing, play, shout, dance and pray hard-driving gospel music. The guitar and the gospels he spins out of it are Jim Brewer's life. He had little choice, as he explained.

"I lost my eyes after I was born. My mother took me to a white doctor in Noo Orleans, Loosiana. An' by me bein' a kid, he put some medicine that wuz too strong in my eyes."

Jim's parents knew that he wouldn't ever be able to work regularly since his sight was almost totally destroyed. So his father went into Brookhaven, Miss., where the family lived, and bought a gujtar from a lady named Miss Lindsay.

"And he brought the guitar there one night. He made him a fire in the fireplace,

it wuz kinda de fall of de year. He took de guitar outa de case. I begin to hear him playin'. That's the first I know a guitar big enough to remember.

"I wanted to learn because I believed some day it might benefit me somethin'!" From his father, his grandfather, his friends Jim began to pick up knowledge of music, even though he couldn't tune the guitar right when he first got it.

"I had it tuned in the open chords, and I was just chordin' here and there, here and there."

He learned not only from friends and relatives, but also from wandering singers who came through Brookhaven. "There was this blind fellow named Johnny Williams. Whenever he come to town I could tell. I wouldn't make nothin'.

"But I didn't git angry with him. I found this out—if you git angry with a person 'cause he knows more'n you, you never will learn nothin'. That's the way it goes."

Today, others learn from Jim Brewer.

To Keep His Creativity Intact
J. D. Salinger Seeks Seclusion

By Jill Kasle

To his neighbors in tiny Cornish, N.H., J. D. Salinger is a name on a mailbox. To the New Hampshire Bell Telephone Company, J. D. Salinger is an unlisted number.

To his mailman, Salinger is a nuisance. The mailman was forced to equip his car with special brakes to get over the unpaved country road leading to Salinger's remote home.

Along the cocktail circuit in Connecticut, where he lived before fleeing to New Hampshire, Salinger was known as an amusing fellow with an enthusiasm for Zen Buddhism and yoga. As one cocktailer remarked: "There was a time when he would go home and stand on his head."

To Ernest Hemingway, he was Staff Sergeant Salinger during World War II when the two men served together in Europe. Whenever their area was under attack, Salinger would dive into a foxhole to peck out casually-worded stories. Upon reading them, Hemingway commented succinctly: "Jesus, he has a helluva talent."

And to millions of people — the ones who were 16 years old in 1951 or the ones who will be 16 tomorrow or the ones who are always endlessly 16 — Salinger is a demigod. His book, The Catcher in the Rye, is Bible to countless 16-year-olds, and Holden Caulfield, the book's math character, is part of many teenagers' alter egos.

Salinger's ability to speak to young people more effectively than any of his contemporaries is a natural talent for a man who has an unconcealed affection for children. "Some—in fact, all—of my best friends are children," he once remarked.

Salinger's appeal to college students equals Ernest Hemingway's popularity during the 1920's, although their styles differ. Hemingway was the author of cold detachment, whereas Salinger insists on bringing himself frankly, obtrusively, and lovingly into the picture.

An interesting paradox exists between Salinger the author and Salinger the man. The author Salinger has refined the technique of encounter instead of escape as an

answer to the futility of life. The other Salinger seems to be running away from the world, seeking privacy the way other men seek pleasure.

Salinger's home is set far back from the road in Cornish. It is a typical New England cabin surrounded by a typical six-foot-high redwood fence. Salinger lives the life of a recluse because he feels isolation keeps his creativity intact. He seems to have hung up a sign addressed to the world: "Do not disturb during working years."

Undisturbed, the man of isolation becomes the author of encounter. Because he is so much a part of his characters, he has to be explained through their eyes. Some

J. D. Salinger

of his characters—skillful combinations of imagination and autobiography—are more plausible than Salinger.

There are fascinating glimpses of the author in his classic character, Holden Caulfield. Holden yearns to do the unconventional; so does Salinger. Holden, a modern-day Huckleberry Finn, wants to retreat to an innocent nature; Salinger fled the horrors of suburbia for rustic New Hampshire. And for both Holden and his creator, the ultimate condemnation is the word "phony."

This sensitive, intense man is the product of a middle-class Jewish-Irish family. Jerome David Salinger was born in New York City in 1919. A solemn, polite child, he

liked to take long walks by himself. At 15, because of poor grades, his parents banished him to Valley Forge Military Academy, the model for Percy Prep. Holden Caulfield's alma mater.

Salinger, following the classic story of the aspiring young writer, spent his days struggling with mathematics and his nights writing feverishly, his blankets over his head to hide the beam of his flashlight from the duty officer.

After military school, Salinger drifted among universities, attending three but being graduated from none. After a two-year hitch with the army in Europe, he holed up in Greenwich Village to write.

His best work during this period was a group of short stories published in various magazines about the Gladwaller and Caulfield families. Holden, the younger son of the Caulfield clan, became Salinger's main interest in 1948. In 1951 The Catcher in the Rye appeared. It is Holden Caulfield's—and possibly J. D. Salinger's—autobiography.

Holden Caulfield, who became saint and savior for millions of teenagers, stumbled into the literary world through the back door. He wore a dirty trench coat and a red hunting cap placed backwards on his head, its peak pulled down snugly over the base of his skull. He was defiant and rebellious, refusing to accept conventional society and yet aching to find his place in it.

In the mid-1950s, Salinger created the gaudy and eccentric Glass saga. His whole life has since become wrapped up in Sid and Bessie Glass and their seven weird children. The youngest child, Franny, is the heroine of the first half of Franny and Zooey. Like Holden Caulfield, she suffers intensely from overexposure to all that is phony.

Salinger's intimate, almost self-conscious style and the small volumes of work which he has produced have caused critics to conclude that writing is difficult for him. Yet writing is the only way of life for this complex, highly introverted man, who encounters public life vicariously through his characters while remaining in his own private world of creativity and genius.

Figure 15–2. Horizontal division of the page into two sections. [*Courtesy the Medill School of Journalism, Northwestern University, Evanston, Illinois.*]

page horizontally. Instead, he is probably trying to separate two large elements. But although accomplishing one goal, he inadvertently is destroying another (unity). Sometimes the white space runs vertically, dividing the page from left to right rather than from top to bottom. Either way is undesirable.

3. Alignment of elements—Makeup editors sometimes have trouble noticing the effect of too many different alignments occurring on a contemporary front page. Alignment means placing elements on a page so that they form an imaginary straight line. In traditional makeup, alignment was easy because every story had to fit into a column structure, and columns were straight. In contemporary makeup, stories and pictures may have different widths and be positioned differently. If they do not align, at least to some extent, the reader is faced with a ragged, unattractive appearance. Too many things seem to be vying for attention because there are too many different starting places. The goal, therefore, is to deliberately bring about more alignment without having all elements align. A little off-center placement adds a dash of interest and excitement to the page. A lot of the same thing becomes unattractive. Most alignment should take place on the left side so that the reader's eyes always return to the same position when reading. For example, it is not as easy to read a column of type set flush left, ragged right as it is one set flush on both sides. The perfect alignment on the type set flush both sides brings about an orderly arrangement of lines, and readers know from experience where to find the next line. But flush left, ragged right is much easier to read than having both sides set ragged, as is sometimes done in advertisements. The design of type set with varying alignments presents an obstacle to reading. Lack of alignment on a page is something to be avoided.

Inside Page Makeup

Almost any page on which advertisements have been placed presents makeup problems. The only space for news is whatever remains after the advertisements have been dummied. Often the person who dummies advertisements does not consider the problems of the news makeup man. Other times, the advertising man simply cannot find enough pages on which to place advertising without increasing the total number of pages in the newspaper. So he may cram the advertisements into most of the available space, leaving the news makeup man with design problems. Modern techniques of contemporary makeup, therefore, are hard to apply on inside pages.

Some tabloid newspaper editors partially solve the problem by keeping the first few inside pages free of advertising. This practice gives the makeup man more opportunities to create attractive and readable inside pages. But larger-sized newspapers may not have the space to free such pages for news alone. To do so might result in other pages filled with so much advertising that neither the advertisements nor the news can be read easily. If the management, however, feels that it can spare the space, then a policy can be made that keeps advertising from the first few pages.

The following suggestions discuss ways in which the makeup man can improve the situation somewhat.

One way to help modernize inside pages is to eliminate datelines, folios and accompanying rules that traditionally have appeared at the top of inside pages. They not only waste space, but they look old-fashioned. If the space occupied by the dateline (including the rule and some white space underneath) is 2 picas, as it often is, then multiplying that by 8 (for the eight-column page) equals 16 picas of space a page that is wasted. If that same issue has 84 pages in it, then it wastes 1344 picas (16×84) or 226 inches (almost a full page and a half each day.) Datelines cannot be eliminated entirely from pages where advertisements appear because they must be included in the tearsheets sent to the advertisers as proof of publication.

But datelines can be shortened into one- or two-column widths and condensed into not more than three lines. The top line may carry the page number; the second line, the newspaper's name; and the last line, the date. These three lines may be placed in the first column on left-hand pages and in the last column on right-hand pages. If there is no first or last column either because this is a full page advertisement or because an eight-column banner headline is used, then the three lines may be placed at the bottom of the page or run sideways, but both set in the margin. In some newspapers, the datelines are buried anywhere near the top of the newspaper in the most convenient place possible. After all, they can be circled when they appear on tearsheets. If the newspaper has an index, then the page number may be of considerable importance in helping readers find a page. In such cases, plans can be made to position the page numbers as close to the outside columns as possible.

Newspapers of the future probably will have more compartmentalization of news than ever before. Compartmentalization is not new, but only recently has there been a determined effort to segment the news into smaller compartments as a convenience to the reader. The use of compartmentalization is well known in news magazines, where it is one of the strongest features of such makeup. In newspapers, the makeup editor usually does not have the prerogative of deciding whether or not compartmentalization should be used. It is decided by the managing editor, most likely. But the makeup editor should strongly recommend its use as a means of keeping the design consistent with contemporary makeup.

In contemporary newspapers, compartmentalization requires the use of standing headlines that a reader is supposed to recognize immediately as an aid in finding a story. There is one exception to the use of compartmental heads. They need not be used for pages whose characteristics are so obvious that the reader does not need a headline to tell him he is reading that page. The editorial page and perhaps the sports pages are sometimes that obvious.

But to keep the newspaper makeup policy consistent, standing headlines may be developed for these and other sections. No matter how many such headlines are used, they should be designed in a consistent and contemporary manner. Consistency is needed to prevent the newspaper from becoming a hodgepodge of design. This does not mean that different typefaces cannot be used in the design for heads. A more feminine-appearing typeface may be appropriate for the women's page but not for a sports page. But there should be some common element in the shape and design of standing heads that gives the reader the feeling he is reading the same newspaper, only a different section. Often this consistency can be achieved through the use of a common size of type, a hairline border around each head or a Ben Day background for each.

In terms of contemporary styles, the standing heads should not be set in old-fashioned typefaces. Other than the type selection, the design of such headlines should be entrusted to commercial artists or graphic designers—not the makeup man—to find the best possible design for the headline. At times, someone in the back shop, or perhaps the makeup editor himself, may try his hand at design. It probably would make more sense to intrust this kind of responsibility to a professional artist.

Picture Placement

There is a tendency to place pictures in the left-hand corner of inside pages. This was traditional makeup practice in bygone years, but it is unsatisfactory today. The upper-left-hand corners of both left- and right-hand pages are much too important to be used for pictures. Formerly, pictures were placed in such positions to anchor the page. Anchoring was a means of providing stability to the makeup design. But a more reasonable approach, and one that will not affect page stability, is to place these pictures as low as possible on any given page. They will get high readership no matter where they are placed. Therefore, the most important positions (corners) should not be wasted on material that automatically receives high readership. Some kind of headline belongs in the corners: presumably, a headline and story of significance if possible. The objective is to get the story read. If the story is buried underneath the picture it may not be read because it is in a less attractive position. By giving a story an outstanding position, the editor may help the reader learn something significant. Meanwhile, the buried picture will brighten any position on the page (Figure 15–3). The bottom of pages, particularly, where there is a combination of advertisements and editorial material, needs considerable brightening. Any effort to make this position more attractive not only benefits the reader, who finds the page better balanced, but the advertiser as well, who gets the reader to look at the bottom as well as the top of inside pages.

Racism sessions to start

Registrations are still being accepted for a series of six discussions on racism, sponsored by the UNI campus ministry.

The first session of "Color me Black, Poor and Angry," will be held at 8 p.m. tonight at the catholic chapel of St. Stephen the Witness, 2304 College St.

All persons of post-high school age are welcome. A $2 registration fee will be collected at the first meeting.

Tonight's meeting will center on the topic "Black Waterloo: The Shape of the Ghetto." According to the Rev. Walter Fishbaugh, "The who, what, when where, how and why of the present life situation of blacks in the community will be discussed."

The second half of the evening will feature a discussion on efforts of the church and other groups to find "handles" and to make approaches to the urban problems posed by such living patterns, Mr. Fishbaugh says.

Other sessions will include: Black burden: The mythology of race; Black history: The problem of roots; Black power: The strategy of pride; Black poverty: The economics of racism; Race and sex: The acid test.

State board seeks to keep drops-outs in school longer

A suggestion by the State Board of Public Instruction that students be required to stay in school until 17 years old, would not greatly affect the Cedar Falls school system. Principal C. C. Stanard says the CF drop-out rate is about three per cent—considerly lower than the state average of 20 per cent.

The State Department of Public Instruction has proposed a change in the compulsory education law that would keep most high school drop-outs in the classroom until age 17.

Department officials say some 20 per cent of Iowa's high school pupils drop out of school under the present law, which allows students to leave school at age 16 or at age 14 if they are employed.

C. C. Stanard, principal of the Cedar Falls high school, said the number of drop-outs there is much smaller. He said studies "a few years ago" showed only 3 per cent of high school students in Cedar Falls drop out of school.

The mandatory education law was one of several massive changes suggested to upgrade the quality of education in Iowa.

Other proposays provide for nursery school education and for merged county school districts.

The department also wants rewording of the law spelling out the state's equalization formula, establishment of a school district reorganization commission and extension of the "one-man, one-vote" principle to all school boards.

Dr. Richard Smith, associate superintendent for administrative services, said the department also wants to change its name to the State Department of Education, have the salary of its superintendent set by the State Board of Public Instruction and not the legislature, and increase vacation and fringe benefits for its employes.

He outlined the proposals—which are now being considered by the Board of Public Instruction—to the Advisor Council and the Coordinating Committee for the Improvement of Education in Iowa.

The group, representing public school officials and university officials, held its monthly meeting here.

"The compulsory education law needs to be updated," Smith said, calling for legislation that would require children age 5 through 17 to remain in school.

Exceptions could be made for immature 5-year-olds and for youths over 16 who were regularly employed, Smith said.

The present law, which Smith said was passed around the turn of the century when only about 10 per cent of Iowa's youngsters finished high school, allows pupils to drop out of school at age 16 or at 14 if they are employed.

Compulsory startage age under the present law is 7, Smith said.

Some school officials at the meeting objected to the proposed change on grounds that they would not always be able to determine if a youngster was employed.

"Everything points to the need to make available to some youngsters education before age 5 or kindergarten," Smith continued.

He said school districts should be able to provide nursery education when requested by 25 or more parents in the district.

"We also recommend a law mandating all counties to be formed into merged county school systems by July 1, 1970," Smith said.

Presently there are five such systems, providing special education classes, and psychological, library, audio-visual, and consultative services.

Today's weath

Cedar Falls Forecast — Skies should remain mostly cloudy through the morning with a chance of occasional showers. Skies should become partly cloudy this afternoon or tonight and continue through Friday. We had an overnight expected low of 52 degrees. Our high today should reach near 68 degrees. Tonight's low will be near 48 degrees with temperatures warming up on Friday.

Probability of measurable precipitation is 30 percent today and 10 percent tonight and Friday.

Sunset today 7:13 p.m.

Sunrise tomorrow 6:54 a.m.

Yesterday's high 63, low (at 10 p.m. Wednesday) 55.

Relative Humidity 100 percent.

Rainfall .07 and traces throughout afternoon and night.

Winds Southerly at 16 mph.

Precipitation since first of m since Jan. 1, 39.9 since Jan. 1, 25

Iowa Forecast dy skies with w tures are in stor the western part day, but eastern to experience cl occasional rain a tem gradually m out of the state.

The Weather B temperatures tod highs in the 70s i 60s in the east.

Evening tempe last night were upper 50s in the er 60s west.

Skies should cloudy through warmer temper forecast.

Rain and showers are forecast for the South the eastern coast and also in the Northwest. Clear cloudy skies elsewhere. Warmer readings are expe the upper Lakes through the central and southern into the southern plateaus. Cooler weather is through much of the west and in the Tennessee v.

	High	Low	Pr.
Albany, clear	82	49	—
Albuquerque, clear	80	43	—
Atlanta, cloudy	74	62	.67
Bismarck, clear	75	40	—
Boise, cloudy	85	60	—
Boston, clear	65	59	—
Buffalo, clear	81	62	—
Chicago, cloudy	67	61	.62
Cincinnati, clear	65	60	.44
Cleveland, rain	78	60	.05
Denver, clear	80	44	—
Des Moines, rain	61	52	.01
Detroit, rain	79	65	.22
Fairbanks, cloudy	45	37	—
Fort Worth, clear	89	50	—
Helena, rain	80	48	10
Honolulu, cloudy	91	76	—
Indianapolis, clear	68	60	.36
Jacksonville, cloudy	86	75	.13
Juneau, cloudy	53	42	—
Kansas City, cloudy	75	51	.02
Los Angeles, cloudy	75	62	—

Memphis, clear
Miami, cloudy
Milwaukee, clear
Mpls. St. P., clo
New Orleans, clea
New York, clear
Okla. City, clear
Omaha, rain
Philadelphia, clea
Phoenix, clear
Pittsburgh, cloudy
Ptlnd., Me., clea
Ptlnd., Ore., rain
Rapid City, cloud
Richmond, cloudy
St. Louis, cloudy
Salt Lk. City, clea
San Diego, clear
San Fran., cloudy
Seattle, rain
Tampa, cloudy
Washington, cloudy
Winnipeg, clear

Metropolitan deaths

Herndon infant

Funeral arrangements are pending at Kearns Dykeman Chapel, Waterloo, for Matthew Christian Herndon, infant son of the Rev. Daniel and Virginia Johnson Herndon, 601 Nevada St., Waterloo. The Rev. Mr. Herndon is pastor of the Linden United Methodist Church.

The infant was stillborn at 11:05 p.m. Monday at Allen Memorial Hospital.

He is survived by his parents, one sister, Sarah Walden at home, the maternal grandparents, Mr. and Mrs. Claud Johnson of Fort Thompson, Ky.; and the paternal grandparents, Mr. and Mrs. C. E. Herndon of Centerville.

Mrs. Zingg

Funeral services for Mrs. Newton Zingg, 72, Rt. 2, Waterloo, will be at 1:30 p.m. Saturday in the Chapel of Memories West, Waterloo. Burial will be in the Garden of Memories. The Rev. Richard Pfaltzgraff, Calvary United Methodist Church will officiate.

Mrs. Zingg died of a heart attack at the Kansas City, Kan., airport while enroute home from a vacation at Phoenix, Ariz.

Surviving are her husband, seven sons, five daughters, two sisters, one brother, 32 grandchildren and six great grandchildren.

ICH awards 63 contract

The Iowa Highway Commission on Wednesday awarded a contract to the J. F. Brennan Co., LaCrosse, Wisc., for construction of a reinforced concrete box culvert extension on U.S. 63 in Black Hawk County.

The commission accepted the low bid, totaling $10,717, during their monthly meeting.

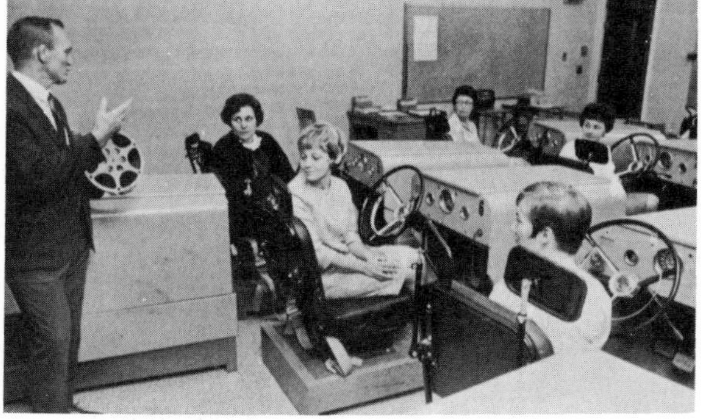

Preparing for the road...

Driver's training instructor Keith Young, explains the use of auto simulators during the first session of the adult course held Tuesday. Among the students enrolled are (from back to front) at left, Mrs. Clarence Covert, 284 Clark Dr., Mrs. Don Drumm, 1115 West 4th, Mrs. Chester Allen, 816 Melrose Dr.; at right, Mrs. Russell Hansen, 1626 Picturesque Dr., and Mrs. Ed Burns, Waterloo. (Record Photo).

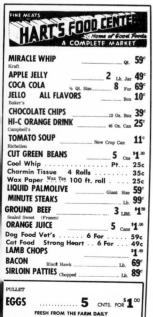

Ashley Montague to open UNI speakers program

Anthropologist Ashley Montegue will speak at the University of Northern Iowa Oct. 18, as the first of several persons scheduled in the Controversial Speakers Program.

Jan Seeland, co-chairman of the speakers committee with Sue Elde, said Montegue will speak on civil disorders. Montegue is the author of "Man's Most Dangerous Myth," "On Being a Woman," and "The Natural Superiority of Woman."

He will speak at 10 a.m. Oct. 18 in the UNI Auditorium.

The speakers committee has accepted an offer from the Waterloo Elks Club who said they would make arrangements for a refugee from an Iron Curtain country to speak at UNI.

The program, scheduled for Nov. 8, will be sponsored by the Controversial Speakers Committee.

David Schoenbrum, a news correspondent in Vietnam, is tentatively scheduled to appear Nov. 22.

Saul Alinski, a sociologist with a radical approach for urban renewal community development, will speak Feb. 21. Alinski advocates a new design for communities to replace city ghettos, Miss Seeland says.

The committee is completing arrangements for a spring program with Sen. Julian Bond and is "working on" plans to invite Sen. Eugene McCarthy to the campus.

Bond is the first Negro ever elected to the U. S. Senate and was nominated as vice-president at the Democratic National Convention.

See guard costs at $50,000

Iowa National Guard officials have indicated that the cost of keeping troops in Waterloo through September 29 may run up to nearly $50,000.

More than 300 troops have been on hand since Saturday, when they were called up at the request of Waterloo mayor, Lloyd Turner.

Turner said Tuesday that they would remain in the city until September 29 — the closing day of the National Dairy Cattle Congress.

The cost of mobilizing troops the first day was expected to be from $8,000 to $10,000 guard officials say.

Daily costs are estimated to run from $2,000 to $2,500 for the 16-day period.

Police reported continued calm Wednesday night as a dusk to dawn curfew was modified for minors.

The cost of keeping troops will be born from the Iowa general fund. Guard officials have indicated that some men who are on duty would be moved in and out, so that all will not be away from their homes and jobs too long.

DEEDS

Sale of the following Cedar Falls property has been filed in the office of Joan Glaza, Black Hawk county recorder.

Norman D. Folker to Paul Scott Cameron, part of lot 45 and 46, Pacific addition, revenue $3.85.

10 named semi finalists

Ten area youths were among 15,000 semifinalists in the National Merit Scholarship examinations.

Christine H. Anderson of Cedar Falls High School was one of 244 Iowans to receive the honor.

Others from this area to qualify to compete for about 3,000 merit scholarships to be awarded next spring include Steve Conyers and Dennis Guernsey of Orange High, Waterloo, and Fredrick Bahls, Carol Crosswaite, Henry Edsill, Ann Guetzlaff, William Marvell, Thomas Turnbull, and David Winegarden, all of West High, Waterloo.

News of reco

ACCIDENTS

A motorist's curiosity about a truck fire resulted in a three-car accident at the corner of 20th and College St. about 6:48 p.m. last night.

Jack L. Mutschler, 20, of Geneva, Ia., was charged with failure to stop with assured clear distance, when he hit the rear of a car driven by Debbie Adams, 17, of 815 West 26th St., which was stopped for a red light.

The impact of the collision caused the Adams car to slide into the rear end of another vehicle driven by Stephen T. King, 20, of 3320 Logan Ave., Waterloo, who was also stopped for the red light.

Damage to the King car was listed at $20 and $100 each to the Adams and Mutschler cars.

Police said the Adams and King cars were stopped for a red light at 20th and College when the Mutschler car hit from behind as Mutschler was looking back at a pizza delivery truck on fire in the parking lot of Fred's Super Value, College Hill.

An accident shortly before 11 p.m. Tuesday involving a car driven by Herbert D. Nadsen, 39, of McGregor, Minn., and one driven by Richard W. Brown, 54, 2227 W. 3rd, Waterloo, resulted in approximately $100 damages to each of the cars.

Police reported that the Brown car collided with the rear end of the Nadsen vehicle as it made a left turn off Hwy. 218 onto Terrace drive. No charges were filed.

A 19 year-old Cedar Falls youth, John J. Cook of 1622 W. 7th, received a cut over his eye that required treatment as the result of an accident shortly after noon yesterday.

Police said that a car driven by Cook collided at the corner of Walnut and W. 6th with one driven by Susan M. Jannette, 18, 2508 Franklin. Police charged Miss Jannette with faiure to stop for a stop sign.

Cook was taken by Cedar Falls fire department emergency unit to Sartori Hospital, where he was treated for the cut and a sore chest and then released. Damages to the front end of the Cook vehicle were estimated at $400.

FIRE CALLS

Cedar Falls firem a call at 6:41 p.m when a pizza de caught on fire acr Pizza House, 2024 Dave Lorenson, manager, received hands. Only slight done to the truck.

Hospital

SARTORI HOSP

Births

Mr. and Mrs. Thom Aplington, boy

Mr. and Mrs. Mich 119 Sunset Village, bo

Admissions

Linda Feldhacker medical

Kourt Miller, 2809 medical

John Brunskill, Rt.

Sheryl Corwin, 350 Dr., medical

Mrs. George McCh Carleton Dr., medical

Dismissals

Carl Rhode, 1409 C

Linda Feldhacker,

Mrs. Jack Myers, Waterloo

Glenn Sickle, 2503 Waterloo

Mrs. Emma Miller, St.

Mrs. Phillip Dorfr Grand Blvd.

Mrs. Gordon Horst son

Mrs. William Thro Francis St.

Mrs. Jack Pritchard, 2nd St.

WATERLOO HOSP

Births

Mr. and Mrs. John 919½ Janney Ave., girl

Mr. and Mrs. Fred Dayle St., Evansdale,

Mr. and Mrs. John R 913 Washington St., boy

Mr. and Mrs. Dougla 829 Huntington Blvd., girl

Figure 15–3. Buried picture on an inside page. [*Courtesy the Cedar Falls, Iowa, Record.*]

The makeup editor has little control over the placement of advertisements. But it may be wise to consult with the advertising department about the possibility of placing advertisements in positions that enhance the design of inside pages for the benefit of both readers and advertisers. Traditionally, ads have been pyramided diagonally from the lower left of a page to the upper right. The left side of the newspaper therefore received most of the editorial material. This is a reasonable approach to advertising placement in relation to editorial matter because it always freed the left side of the page for news. Because reading took place from left to right, it was assumed that all news material should align on the left as a means of making the page easy to read. Left- and right-hand pages were dummied in the same manner so that the pyramid faced the same direction on all pages (Figure 15–4).

It is also just as reasonable, however, to believe that the present system of dummying advertisements is not always correct. Most readers do not look at only one page at a time. Instead, they open the paper so that both the left- and right-hand sides of the paper are visible at once. Obviously a person cannot read two pages at one time, but he may see the total design of two facing pages in his peripheral vision. Therefore, the makeup of a single page carrying advertisements should never be considered alone. The opposite page is also part of the total page design. Makeup editors traditionally have not conceived of two facing pages as a single entity because they dummy only one page at a time. But it is reasonable to consider the combined effect of the two facing pages. In such a situation, the left-hand side of the paper ought to be dummied so that the advertisements are placed in the position opposite of their placement on right-hand pages (Figures 15–5 and 15–6). This means that the advertisements on the left side of the page are dummied with the diagonal running from the top left to the lower right. The right-hand page is dummied oppositely. As a result of this makeup procedure, all the news is concentrated in the center between the two facing pages in a concave shape.

When pages are tightly dummied so that there is little room for news on the page, the arrangement described above will not work very well. In the latter situation, perhaps both pages should be dummied the traditional way; the makeup editor will have to live with a situation where there is little he can do to design an attractive page.

If he has at least one-quarter page of space available on each of two facing pages, he should then ask the personnel responsible for advertising dummying whether he can reverse the pyramid on the left-hand page. It is that simple. Where one page has about one quarter of the space for news and the other has much more or much less, he should ask that an advertisement be shifted to another page so that he can make up as many two facing page units as possible in an attractive design.

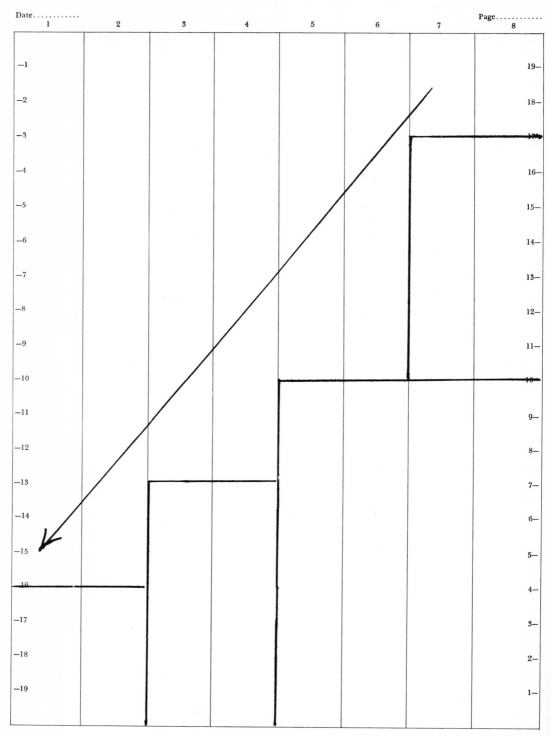

Figure 15–4. Pyramid style used for placing advertisements on both left- and right-hand pages.

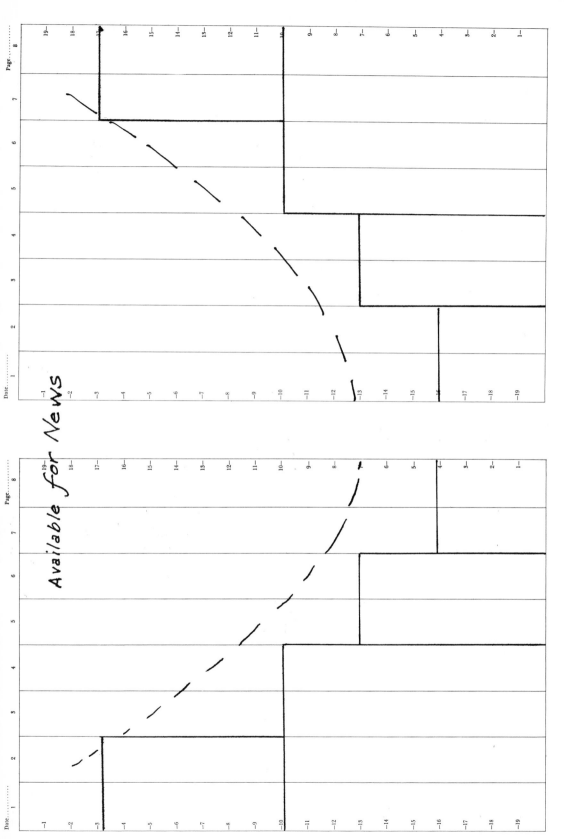

Figure 15–5. Two facing pages dummied with advertisements pyramided toward the center.

Housing

(Continued from page 1)

groups in the area whose members view proliferation of the buildings as a threat to neighborhood stability.

OUTLOOK for the Uptown Model Cities program is bleak. The program, which was heralded by former President Lyndon Johnson as the solution to the nation's urban ills, has failed to live up to its promise, especially in Chicago.

It is top-heavy in administration, uncreative in programming and incapable of involving the poor in the decision-making process. The program will roll on in Uptown and the city's three other Model Cities areas this year, but offers little hope of relief for the city's ills.

Some promise exists in the election of 20 members of the new 40-member model cities councils, but at present it appears that the cards are still stacked against community participation. Under the proposed rules for the election, the mayor makes his 20 selections either before or after—probably after—the elections are held.

LAKE VIEW may get some relief this year from the proliferation of four-plus-one buildings in its family residential areas. Ald. William Singer (44th), chief political spokesman for the community in its fight, said a few weeks ago that the city fathers are responding and may provide some changes to restrict development of the buildings.

Organizations in the Lake View area charge that the four-plus-one buildings are driving families from the community. Apartments in the buildings, which begin the first of five floors just below ground level, are primarily of the efficiency and one-bedroom types.

A few months ago, it appeared that Lake View would have an urban renewal program underway during 1970. However, the proposal may have to wait because of an impasse between community leaders and the Department of Urban Renewal over the naming of a Conservation Community Council.

The community has picked its own slate of 15 per-

HENRY Hindin, 2616 Farwell, whose hobbies include playing first violin in the Evanston Symphony Orchestra, was named second vice-president of Exchange National Bank.

sons to pass on renewal plans for an area bounded by Broadway, Racine, Belmont and Diversey and demanded the city accept the slate before the area is tabbed for urban renewal. Thus far, the DUR has refused to accede to the demand.

West Lake View might see the erection of some portable college classrooms on the site of the old Riverview amusement park at Western and Belmont by September, 1970. The Chicago City College board has instituted condemnation proceedings for the land, which is owned by the Arvey Corp.

However, a prolonged court battle could put the ax to college plans for 1970.

And the Lincoln Park Conservation Community council, whose meetings through most of 1969 were like search and destroy missions, may see relative calm in 1970. The decreasing supply of low-income housing units, which provided the rallying cry of protest in the last year, will diminish even more in 1970, due mainly to private housing rehabilitation in west Lincoln Park.

However, with the optimism that a new year and a new decade brings, we see more planning and less protest in the effort to get decent housing for the poor.

● Four generations celebrated Thanksgiving dinner in the Court of the Lions restaurant, 6935 N. Sheridan. Hostess was Mrs. Sophie Cohen, widow of the late Harry B. Cohen. Mrs. Cohen lives at Hollywood Towers, 5701 N. Sheridan Rd. Present were daughter, Aileen, and her husband, Harold D. Baum, 3900 Lyons, Skokie, and children

David and Debbie. Third generation was represented by Mr. and Mrs. Lawrence Charles Silton. Fourth generation consists of Steven, 17 months.

● Irwin W. Iroff, of Rogers Park, has been named midwest regional sales manager for business equipment by Toshiba America, Inc.

Schools picture resembles play

(Continued from page 1)

Daley put the responsibility of school financial support on the state—where it legally rests.

So where last year the city's revenue from the state income tax bailed the school's out—in 1970 there is no hope of the city arriving on a white horse and "saving the schools."

Waiting for the state legislature has proven to be the same as waiting for Godot. The state has never responded to the crisis. The legislature has only reacted with token aid.

To relieve the crisis, the governor would have to call a special session of the state legislature. This seems highly unlikely since the legislature met in early fall and froze all possibilities of additional aid to Chicago schools.

WHAT DOES appear certain in 1970 is that the Board of Education members will have, at least, learned from the experience of 1969. They will not sign a contract they cannot fulfill as they did last year.

They will either cutback in areas which will not directly hurt the teachers or they will bring on a strike. And it is very possible that the board will provoke a strike—in the hopes that the state legislature will respond.

This brings us back to 1969. The teachers union is again crying that the board is using the teachers to bring about a response from the state legislature. "The board has never met its responsibility to lobby for state aid," a union official recently told the Lerner Newspapers.

THE ABSURDITY is that even with the $20 million the children of Chicago will still be the victims of a school system that denies them quality education.

Dr. Redmond recently highlighted the school's

unmet needs for 1970. These totaled $139,456,767 plus the $20 million.

What they add up to is deficiencies in every area of the educational and building program of the Chicago schools.

THE YEAR 1970 may see a bond issue to relieve the crisis in the building fund. This would help a school system top heavy with deteriorated buildings and antiquated teaching facilities.

But in areas of special education, reading improvement, bi-lingual programs, vocational training, and pupil personnel services—areas which are crucial to the present crop of students in Chicago—their will be no improvement. Some relief may come but only at the sacrifice of teachers and the creation of over-crowded classrooms.

It will be a year with more problems than solutions. School buildings will deteriorate more, mobiles will increase to relieve overcrowded facilities, many retarded children will find no classes for them, Spanish-speaking children will move farther behind because they don't speak English, high school students will continue to drop out, and children who cannot read will fall deeper behind.

THE NEW YEAR will undoubtedly be another year of student riots and racial trouble. A human relations program costing upwards of $6 million will be buried in the 1970 budget.

Undoubtedly, in 1970 there will be more community organization over school problems. This is especially true of the Spanish-speaking community which only began organizing last year.

In the light of past experience, it seems unlikely that the community groups will be able to bring the Chicago school system closer to the schools. Again they will meet with powerless district and area superintendents, and again they will discover a bureaucracy unable to cope with the needs of individual schools.

Ideally, 1970 should bring the state legislature to the point of commitment to fulfilling the unmet needs of Chicago schools. And ideally, the Board of Education would create an atmosphere where community participation in school decision making would be more than words.

Realistically, however, waiting for the state and the board to take such action could only duplicate the characters of an absurd play who sit around waiting for Godot.

Police

(Continued from page 1)

ence. If there's any major crime, it'll probably be in or around the bars of the deteriorating Lawrence-Kedzie business strip.

TOWN HALL (19TH) DISTRICT: Cmdr. John Fahey shares the problems of the Young Lords with the 18th district. Fahey runs a tolerably tight ship, although a lot of the old-line policemen sometimes cause him public relations problems.

Major problems in the district will come from the poor Latins and from the drug scene. Policemen will continue to be the target of the largely class-orientated resentments, and this is the other North Side district with a good potential for violence.

Much will depend on whether or not Fahey manages to face his challenge in such a way that he satisfies the law and order demands of the older faction without provoking the anti-police groups into some sort of armed confrontation.

The Latins behind martyr images easily here, and, given a martyr and the excuse for confrontation, they could be explosive.

Crimes against persons will be on the upswing, despite aggressive patrol. This is one of the districts considered hazardous by those who are against oneman cars, and Fahey will probably be faced with a choice between the demands of the war on crime and the demands of some of his own policemen.

Police in general throughout the city will probably organize more and more into unions ("associations") to represent their views in discussion on everything from salaries to sin. Supt. James B. Conlisk will deplore the actions of the associations but won't risk his already shaky prestige in a direct confrontation.

For want ads that pull call BR 4-7100 and ask for a friendly Lerner ad-taker.

● Karen Hope Johnson, 2654 Ainslie, is enrolled as a student at Wheaton college for the 1969-70 academic year. The daughter of Rev. and Mrs. Ernest Johnson, she transferred to Wheaton from Moody Bible Institute.

● Steven A. Slor, 930 Agatite, has joined the All-state Insurance as a casualty claim supervisor.

Figure 15–6. Two facing pages printed with advertisements pyramided toward the center. [*Courtesy Lerner Newspapers, Chicago, Illinois.*]

Hope for state park on golf land may be fulfilled for NS in 1970

By LILY VENSON
Lerner Newspapers
Staff Writers

FOR THOSE who have long hoped for a public park on the beautiful Edgewater golf land, 1970 may be the year in which that dream could be fulfilled.

Gov. Richard B. Ogilvie has committed himself to every effort to save the land for the people. He has joined a community cause and taken it all the way to the White House.

BUT THERE is much work ahead before the gateway to an innovative state park on the North Side opens.

It will be a time for lacing everyone together to create unanimity of purpose.

State Rep. Edward J. Copeland (R-10th), who introduced the bi-partisan state park legislation, is on the side of the people in their fight against "concrete canyons" and for precious open green spaces in the city.

Philip Krone, conservationist, has been the quiet

Forecast 1970

voice working behind the scenes to make the park a reality.

NO ONE NEEDS to be reminded of the role of Allied North Side Community Organizations (ANSCO), headed by Dr. James Barry and later by Laurence Warren.

ANSCO never gave up the public park goal at one moment, not even when prospects were so dismal, a weaker group would have disbanded at the brink of failure.

Ald. Jack I. Sperling (50th) has been saying the same thing over and over again for almost four years —"there are federal funds under the open spaces program to save the land for public park use."

THERE ARE MANY, many more people and organizations, too numerous to mention here, working unceasingly toward the park goal.

But those who must now be drawn into this crusade with sincere commitment are representatives of the various levels of local governmental agencies.

The year 1970 must be the time of cohesive, realistic working together.

The mayor, the City Council, the Chicago Park district headed by Dan Shannon (who some people believe has started a new era in park planning) must work with the community, the governor and the state Conservation department headed by William Rutherford.

IF THIS JOINT effort does not begin early in 1970, the whole park acquisition process could be slowed down.

Lastly, the private developers should remember that 1970 could be the year when all their patient waiting will mean a return of a very fair market value on their land. They will, no doubt, be disappointed that they could not erect their Edgewater Village on the golf land.

But when that day should come, when a pioneering state park in the city of Chicago is a reality, the private developers can rightly feel they have their thumb print on it if they negotiated amicably for the sale of the land.

We hope they will have the vision to do so in 1970. The people will remember them for it.

Urban Line

Resident points out dead elm

A NORTH Side resident recently complained to URBAN LINE about "a huge dead elm tree" at 2006 Arthur.

The complainant said that many calls have been made in an effort to get the tree removed and that large branches hanging over the

sidewalk present a serious hazard to passers by. Some branches, he claimed, have fallen already.

URBAN LINE contacted Public Works Deputy Comr. Francis Patrick Kane, who promised that an inspector would be sent to investigate the situation during the first part of next week. Kane said that if the tree was found to be a hazard it would be removed immediately.

* * *

URBAN LINE received an acknowledgement from Mrs. Pearl Goldstone, 6253 N. Troy.

Mrs. Goldstone said that for the past three months the Forestry Bureau had failed to remove tree branches and other debris "that make the parkway in front of my home a danger to persons passing this area, and very unsightly to look at."

URBAN LINE contacted the Forestry department and the debris has been removed. Mrs. Goldstone sent in her vote of thanks.

Pollution hearings January 5

THE ILLINOIS House Air Pollution Study Committee will hold the second in a series of public hearings throughout the state at 10 a.m. Monday, Jan. 5, at the Illinois Commerce Commission, State of Illinois Building, 160 N. LaSalle.

State Reps. J. Theodore Meyer (R-28th), Chicago, chairman of the committee, and Harry Yourell (D-6th), Oak Lawn, chairman of the Metropolitan Chicago subcommittee, invite all civic and citizens organizations to offer their views with regard to the control of air pollution in the Metropolitan Chicago area.

Future hearings will be held in Chicago at which business, labor and the public will be invited to testify.

Those organizations planning to testify are urged to bring a written statement to submit to the Committee.

THERE IS ICE skating at Sam Leone Park, Touhy and Sheridan, and youngsters are taking advantage of this fact to become more proficient at figure skating. In the picture one ten year old girl has fallen, Kathleen Monahan, and her companion, Bridgid Donohue, also 10, tries to pick her up. The leg at left belongs to an unidentified adult, and our photographer got it in the picture for artistic effect.

(Photo by Charles Allen)

Open Inside Page Makeup

There are times when it is impossible to change the pyramid direction of advertisements, either because of the advertising department's policy or because there is little time left. Yet there is another approach to improving inside page design provided space is available for news. Perhaps there may be as much as one third or more of the space on a page for news. When that much space is available, the page may be considered to be "open." At that time a makeup procedure may be used whereby the space immediately adjacent to advertisements is filled completely so that the top of the news aligns across the page with the top of the highest-positioned advertisement. What remains then, is a rectangle of white space that is also available for news (Figure 15-7). A rectangular space is relatively easy to use for creating an attractive page design. If the page were filled in the traditional manner, then the odd-shaped space may or may not provide the means of creating an attractive page. The rectangular approach may be used only when the pyramided advertisements do not extend much above the fold.

Tight Page Makeup

Many times the makeup editor is faced with so many advertisements on a page, or a few large advertisements, that there is little space for news. Either constitutes a *tight* page. In this situation, it is best to dummy a single long story in the remaining space than to use a number of short stories on the page (Figure 15-8). The long story may be wrapped from column to column until the space is filled. The reader should have no difficulty determining which story he is reading because there is only one story on the page. On the other hand, where many short stories are dummied on a tight page, wraps are necessary and may be confusing to the reader because a headline may not cover each of them. There may not be enough time to reset a one-column headline in a two-column width, or there may not be enough multiple-column heads to cover all raw wraps. Furthermore, when many short stories are used on a tight page it may be difficult to avoid tombstones. If there are no long stories available and shorter ones must be used on tight pages, there is the possibility that more than one headline will be positioned across the top of the page, usually an unsightly makeup procedure. If the placement of headlines in such positions cannot be avoided, then they should be alternated at the top to avoid tombstones. Perhaps a two-column headline can be alternated with a single-column head, or perhaps a headline set in a roman type can be alternated with one set in italics (Figure 15-9). Least effective from a makeup point of view is the use of headlines positioned next to each other at the top where two-line heads are alternated with three-line heads, especially when both are set in the same size and typeface. Alternation should be more contrasting.

Boxed Stories Brighten Inside Pages

Pictures invariably brighten inside pages, but they may not be available or they may be too large for the space. Another means of brightening inside pages is boxing one story on a page. (Figure 15-10). Only those stories whose contents are significant should

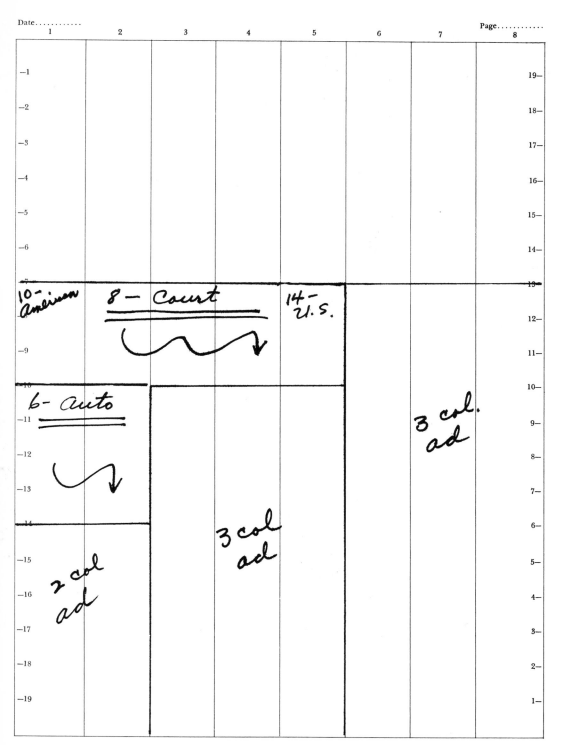

Figure 15–7. Rectangle of space remaining at top after the lower part of the page has been dummied to align with the top of the advertisements.

Cuts in Heart Aid Aired in Senate

Figure 15–8. Single story on a tight page.

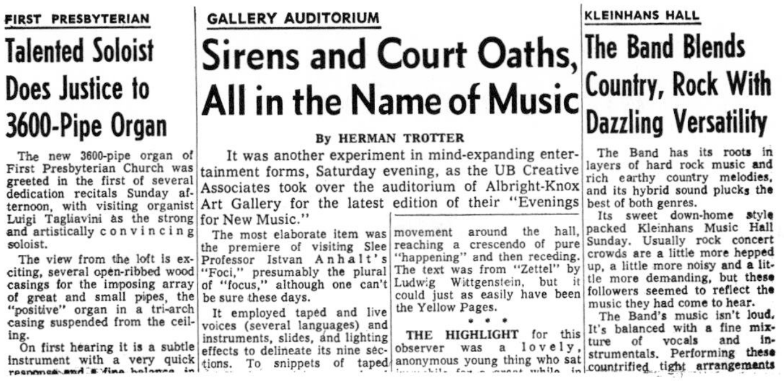

FIRST PRESBYTERIAN

Talented Soloist Does Justice to 3600-Pipe Organ

The new 3600-pipe organ of First Presbyterian Church was greeted in the first of several dedication recitals Sunday afternoon, with visiting organist Luigi Tagliavini as the strong and artistically c o n v i n c i n g soloist.

The view from the loft is exciting, several open-ribbed wood casings for the imposing array of great and small pipes, the "positive" organ in a tri-arch casing suspended from the ceiling.

On first hearing it is a subtle instrument with a very quick

GALLERY AUDITORIUM

Sirens and Court Oaths, All in the Name of Music

By HERMAN TROTTER

It was another experiment in mind-expanding entertainment forms, Saturday evening, as the UB Creative Associates took over the auditorium of Albright-Knox Art Gallery for the latest edition of their "Evenings for New Music."

The most elaborate item was the premiere of visiting Slee Professor Istvan A n h a l t ' s "Foci," presumably the plural of "focus," although one can't be sure these days.

It employed taped and live voices (several languages) and instruments, slides, and lighting effects to delineate its nine sections. To snippets of taped

movement around the hall, reaching a crescendo of pure "happening" and then receding. The text was from "Zettel" by Ludwig Wittgenstein, but it could just as easily have been the Yellow Pages.

* * *

THE HIGHLIGHT for this observer was a l o v e l y, anonymous young thing who sat

KLEINHANS HALL

The Band Blends Country, Rock With Dazzling Versatility

The Band has its roots in layers of hard rock music and rich earthy country melodies, and its hybrid sound plucks the best of both genres.

Its sweet down-home style packed Kleinhans Music Hall Sunday. Usually rock concert crowds are a little more hepped up, a little more noisy and a little more demanding, but these followers seemed to reflect the music they had come to hear.

The Band's music isn't loud. It's balanced with a fine mixture of vocals and instrumentals. Performing these countrified, tight arrangements

Figure 15–9. Alternated heads.

be boxed. Assuming that there usually will be at least one such story a page, it should be boxed with a hairline rule. The size of the box should be at least two columns but preferably three columns wide. The reason is that only a box of sufficient size to be noticed can bring about dominant appearance. The effect of boxing a story is to enhance the appearance of the news portion of the page.

If there is any objection to the boxing process, it usually is that too much production time is taken. The type to be boxed may have to be reset to a narrower measure or a column of news may have to be eliminated to provide the space taken by the box, which is larger than regular column width. When a column of news is eliminated as described previously, the remaining columns will have to be respaced to odd-column measures, a procedure that usually is not appreciated in the back shop because it takes so much time. Yet, the makeup man will have to determine whether he really wants to improve the appearance of inside pages at the cost of extra production time or whether his role is one of forcing news to fit into inside pages regardless of the appearance. Inside pages of most newspapers seem to have been made up with the latter idea in mind.

A final problem relating to boxed stories and improving the appearance of inside pages concerns the practice of not dummying any more than a few large stories on such pages and allowing the makeup to be done by the printer. When this happens the page may show the lack of planning. The printer, plagued by the necessity of speeding up production, usually takes the most traditional route toward finishing the makeup process. In fact, he is discouraged from even attempting new makeup procedures. Therefore, the remainder of such makeup is often less than the best. Even when the makeup editor stands next to the printer and directs him in filling undummied inside pages, the result is apt to look poor. The best technique is to tightly dummy the remaining space in the editorial office and take enough time to make the pages as attractive as possible.

'That kills my faith in pill': father of four

OTTAWA (AP)— Mrs. Victor Millar, 30, gave birth Friday to quadruplets— three boys and a girl.

"That kills my faith in the pill," said her 33-year-old husband when he got the news.

"I think I'll picket the company," he added.

Mrs. Millar was delivered of the babies in seven minutes, starting at 6:38 a.m. All babies and mother are "just fine," the hospital reported. The children will be kept in the hospital, most of the time in incubators, for at least a month because they are two months premature.

The Millars have known since last month that Mrs. Millar would give birth to three and possibly four babies.

Dr. Sydney Kronick, the mother's obstetrician, diagnosed the multiple pregnancy with X-rays Aug. 19, notifying the hospital of the probability of quadruplets.

The Millars have two other children, a girl 6, and a boy, 12.

"They took it very well," said the father while waiting a summons to his wife's bedside.

But when they told him in August of the prospects, "it was a shock, mainly because we had just bought a house and will have to buy a bigger one now."

Millar, a photographer employed by the Post Office Department, said his wife had been taking birth control pills for about a year, when she found she was pregnant but "the doctor said when she started you can't guarantee them."

He said the boys weighed three pounds 10 ounces, three pounds 14 and three pounds nine and the girl two pounds 10.

They were given excellent chances of survival.

Mrs. Millar is one of 12 children and her mother, Mrs. Roger Dubue of Ottawa, said all 12 came along "one at a time."

"I'm in a state of shock," she said when asked how she felt about her daughters' giving birth to quadruplets.

Police chief backs policy

DES MOINES (AP) — Des Moines Police Chief Wendell Nichols said Friday he sympathizes with a Spencer teacher who claimed to be "humiliated" by his police, but he defended the policy under which the police acted.

Nichols said Miss Carol Coburn was processed under a policy for persons who live outside an eight-county central Iowa area.

Those persons, when arrested for moving traffic violations in Des Moines, must post bond or plead guilty and pay a fine before being released, Nichols said.

Miss Coburn, officials said, was charged with failure to yield the right of way after a traffic accident here last Saturday while she and five students were in town to see presidential candidate Richard Nixon.

The high school dramatics coach complained that she was taken to police headquarters, fingerprinted, frisked by a matron for weapons, and lodged in a jail cell with a woman charged with shoplifting.

Miss Coburn, who was subsequently released when her students posted $35 bond, also complained that her glasses were taken away.

"I sympathize with Miss Coburn for being caught in this type of situation and I don't know how to make it any easier," Nichols said.

"It probably was embarrassing. Jails and arrests shock people who normally are just good citizens."

Nichols said he checked into Miss Coburn's situation and found that she was not fully fingerprinted, although police took an imprint of her right index finger.

He said she was in jail only 40 minutes, from 2:45 to 3:25 p.m.

The chief also said he was pretty well satisfied with the way his officers had handled the situation, although he said "greater efforts" might have been made in allowing her to complete a telephone call.

Miss Coburn said she attempted one call to a friend in Des Moines but got no answer. She said she was not allowed to make a second call.

Nichols said it is standard procedure to take prisoners' glasses for "safety reasons."

Schirra won't train

SPACE CENTER, Houston, Tex. (AP)— Veteran astronaut Wally Schirra said Friday he'll not train for another flight after the 10.8-day Apollo 7 million scheduled for October.

"It's appropriate that I move on," after the flight, Schirra, who flew in both the Mercury and the Gemini programs, told The Associated Press Friday.

Schirra, 45, was one of the original seven astronauts selected by the National Aeronautics and Space Administration. Only he and astronaut Gordon Cooper remain on flight status.

The veteran spaceman said in an interview after a general Apollo 7 crew press conference that he and his wife "are getting kind of tired of this business."

Schirra will be command pilot on the Apollo 7 mission, which is planned as a check out flight of the Apollo command and service module systems. His crew will be Donn Eisele and Walter Cunningham, both space rookies.

He said he would remain in the program "as long as I'm useful," probably through the moon landing, planned late next year.

After that, he said, he hopes to get a job offer from industry or elsewhere.

Schirra flew six orbits in Mercury spacecraft "Sigma 7" in 1962. He was command pilot on the two-man Gemini 6 flight in December 1965 which rendezvoused in space with the Gemini 7 spacecraft launched a few days before. It was the first rendezvous of two manned spacecrafts in space.

Kidnapped 7-year-old home

OAK BROOK, Ill. (AP)— The kidnaped 7-year-old grandson of a millionaire hosiery magnate came home to an impromptu party Friday hours after he was recovered, unharmed and unransomed, by FBI agents.

Hillard Willis Marks, who celebrated his seventh birthday Thursday in the hands of the kidnapers, was seized Wednesday as he got off a school bus.

The kidnapers had demanded $125,000 ransom from his father, William E. Marks, owner of a Chicago manufacturing firm. Federal agents said the ransom was not paid.

Arrested and charged with aggravated kidnaping were Daniel C. Pieler, 30, unemployed Chicagoan; Robert S. Marin, 24, a machinist, who lives on Chicago's South Side, and his wife, Ethel Marie, 26.

Pieler and the Marks were acquaintances.

The three were held without bond after a brief appearance in Circuit Court.

Mr. and Mrs. Marks first held a joyful reunion with their son in the Chicago office of the FBI, where the youngster described his delivery as "wonderful."

Later, on the patio of the Marks home, Hillard was reunited— along with a large birthday cake— with his mother, father, sister, Judy, 15, and brother, Barry, 4. Also present were Hillard's grandmother, Mrs. Margaret Marks, of Wilmette, a Chicago suburb, the boys' aunt and Uncle, Mr. and Mrs. Don Keith, of Elk Grove Village, another suburb, and their three young children, David, Douglas and Deborah.

Also on hand was Charley, a crow that hangs around the yard and is a special friend of Hillard's.

At the impromptu party, Marks told newsmen:

"I would like to thank each and every one of you personally for holding up information on the case until Hillard was recovered by the FBI. I don't believe a voluntary embargo like this ever has been effective before."

The three appeared in Cook County Circuit Court, rather than Du Page County Court, the FBI said, because the boy's imprisonment took place in Cook County. The abduction occurred in Du Page.

At the interview in the FBI office, young Hillard was asked if he had taken his experience in stride.

"Yes," he replied.

Glad to be back?

"Yeah. It's wonderful."

Were they nice to you?

"Yeah."

What did he think about being on TV and radio?

"I've been on TV before."

Marks reported that a man made the telephoned demand for ransom. He said he talked with the man four times on the phone.

"He indicated the boy's life might be in jeopardy," Marks related.

The victim's sister, Judy, and their grandmother, Mrs. Marks, related that the FBI had three extra telephone lines installed in the home. They said three FBI agents stayed overnight, but "sometimes there were as many as eight on the case."

Marks said he never was told by the kidnapers not to inform the police of his son's disappearance. Nor, he added, was he ever given any instructions for delivery of the $125,000.

"The only thing," he said, "they asked for the money in tens and twenties. Wednesday, they said to call the police and tell them it was a false alarm, which was rather strange since they apparently didn't know we had called the police."

The father said that during each conversation he urged the kidnapers: "Give it up, it's a bad deal. It won't work."

The FBI theorized that Hillard had been held in the Marin home since his abduction. The home on the far South Side is near a house where the Marks formerly lived until they moved to Oak Brook. The Marks knew Pieler.

Marks was asked for his reaction when the FBI told him Pieler was arrested as the alleged kidnaper of his son.

"I was shocked," Marks said. "I didn't believe it." He added that he didn't know the Marins and never heard Pieler mention the name.

The kidnaping was known in newsrooms in the Chicago area since Wednesday night. But news was withheld at the request of the parents.

The boy's uncle, Keith, who furnished the birthday cake, told newsmen:

"We are extremely thankful to the press for the way they used discretion. In fact, we are extremely proud of the press."

The boy was abducted about 4:05 p.m. Wednesday. About 10 that night Chief Robert Siudzinski of the Oak Brook police confirmed rumors of a kidnaping. Newspapers and broadcasters cooperated to aid investigators and to safeguard the kidnaped boy from harm.

Young Marks said the a[…] tors had been nice to him. […] the namesake and grands[…] Hillard Marks, president […] Perfect Plus Hosiery Co.

The boy's mother, who […] newsmen she and her hu[…] had but little sleep […] Wednesday, said "I couldn[…] happier. But, I don't know […] the kidnapers happened to […] on us."

The FBI reported that th[…] was recovered unharmed […] Marin Home on the South […] The boy's father was prese[…] court when the three defen[…] appeared for a hearing.

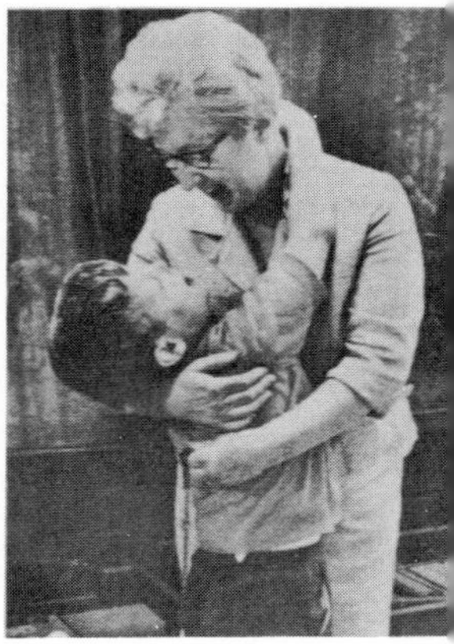

Hillard Marks, 7, who was kidnapped Wednesday and held for $125,000 ransom embraces his grandmother, Mrs. Margaret Marks, as he arrived safely at his suburban Oak Brook home near Chicago yesterday. (UPI Telephoto).

Death toll mounts in fiery English crash

FARNBOROUGH, England (AP) — A 40-ton French experimental plane crashed in flames Friday on the roof of a social club at the Farnborough Air Show while 16,000 spectators watched in horror.

At least 6 and possibly 12 persons died.

A greater tragedy was missed by minutes and yards. The plane erupted in a ball of fire on a building that had been packed with Royal Air Force men minutes before the crash. It blew up yards from a main fuel dump.

Police said the known victims were five air crewmen and one civilian. But some ambulance men spoke of carrying 12 bodies from the wreckage.

The crewmen were believed to be French air force officers.

A British air force official who was in his office about 40 yards from the scene, said: "I heard a whoosh and looked across and saw smoke and flame . . . ambulances and fire engines were on the scene within seconds."

The plane, a twin-engine turboprop aircraft built to the specifications of the North Atlantic Treaty Organization by the industry of six nations, was giving a display of flying on one engine.

It was circling slowly to the right before starting the second engine when it appeared to sideslip on to an air force social club on the field.

"There was not a big bang," a witness said. "It just seemed to disintegrate and then there was a huge ball of fire."

Firemen with five fire trucks poured foam on the blaze for more than 90 minutes before rescue workers could get near.

It was the first major air crash at the air show since 1952 when 30 persons were killed and 63 injured by a jet engine plummeting into the crowd.

The Farnborough show is sponsored by the Society of British Aerospace Companies and is the annual show window for British military craft.

The Breguet 115[…] built to designs […] NATO in 1958. […] volved in the co[…] the Dutch Fokke[…] man Dornier and […] gium. The electro[…] from the United […] Rolls-Royce of B[…] the engines. Final […] done by Breguet i[…]

The plane is i[…] the French and […] navies.

Detain passengers on hijacked

MIAMI, Fla. AP — An Eastern Air Lines jet hijacked over the Bahamas earlier in the day and diverted to Havana landed in Miami Friday night with only its crew aboard.

The aircraft's 43 passengers were detained in Havana as Cuban authorities, for the third consecutive time, refused to allow big commericial jets that had been hijacked to take off from Jose Marti Airport under full load.

On previous occasions, the passengers were flown to the United States later aboard other aircraft.

The plane left Havana at 10:02 p.m. about 12 hours after it was diverted from its scheduled San Juan-to-Miami route. It landed in Miami at 10:44 p.m.

Informants in Havana quoted airport witnesses as saying the plane landed during a rainstorm and the hijacker was a lone gunman who appeared to be a Latin, probably in his 20s.

They said he emerged from the plane alone, with a pistol in his hand.

"We won't know exactly how it happened until they return," said Paul Boatman, area administrator for the Federal Aviation Administration in Miami.

U.S. State Department officials, working through the Swiss embassy in Havana, attempted to negotiate release of the 46 passengers and seven crew members.

On the two most recent hijackings, passengers were forced to remain behind temporarily as the crews returned the planes to Miami. Cuban officials said the Jose Marti runway was too short for big jets. Passengers, minus the hijackers, were returned later on daily Çuban airlift flights.

Flying at 30,000 feet, Eastern Flight 950 had skirted Cuba to the east on the "Yankee Route" and was 40 miles southwest of Nassau, the Bahamas, at 9:12 a.m., EDT, when the plane suddenly veered to the left and headed southwest, toward Havana.

Boatman said the plane touched down in Havana at 9:45 a.m.

"There was no advance warning from the pilot, W. T. "Slim" Babbitt," said Boatman. "All communication between the tower and the plane ceased when Flight 950 changed its course."

The crew and all the passengers but seven were listed as Miami residents, the airline said.

In previous hijackings pilots have radioed Miami they were being forced to go to Havana, and asked landing clearance in Havana.

Of the eight pla[…] Cuba earlier this […] returned within 24[…]

So-called sky-[…] tween Miami and […] in 1959 when Fid[…] power in Cuba. T[…] such incidents sa[…] Cuba taken to Mi[…] agents of ousted […] dent Fulgencio […] were fleeing Castr[…]

Only one, an […] was detained for […] time. In July 1961, […] man Quendo, a f[…] secret policeman[…] supporters, forc[…] plane from Florid[…] Castro held the […] days. He finally s[…] a Cuban patrol […] three defectors t[…] West.

Since then, accu[…] have included a […] fugitive running fr[…] charge, a man wh[…] a Castro agent o[…] and a youth who s[…] grenade that later […] a bottle of shaving […]

Numerous sm[…] planes have been f[…] Cuba since 1959, […] who took along the[…]

Figure 15–10. Boxed story on inside pages. [*Courtesy the Cedar Falls, Iowa, Record.*]

The editorial page is usually better designed than most other pages in a newspaper. The typefaces used for editorials are often set in larger sizes and in wider column widths. Sometimes, column rules have been eliminated from this page even though they are used on all other pages. The effect of these makeup practices would seem to result in an attractively designed editorial page. Such is not always the case, however.

One reason that such pages are not attractive is that the type lines are not leaded. When larger typefaces (than used for body type) are set solid, they may not be as easy to read, and they certainly do not look as attractive as they might be if leaded. The appearance of these editorials is like a mass of letters crammed into paragraphs. The value of setting larger-sized type in wider column widths may be lost because of lack of white space between the lines of type. Research on the amount of leading needed for maximum legibility of type is indeterminate, but common sense should tell the makeup editor that when there is more white space between the lines the mass effect becomes easier to look at and it may be easier to read. Therefore, type lines used in editorials should be leaded anywhere from a minimum of 2 to 4 points a line, depending on the amount of white space within the individual letters. Paragraphs, too, should receive more white space through the addition of a bit more leading than between lines. This gives the reader a fraction of a second to pause before proceeding. Presumably this will aid reading and certainly will enhance the appearance of the editorials.

Some editors use the same size of body type and column widths for editorials as they do for regular news. The effect is to make the page appear to be simply another news page. It is not as inviting as pages where larger type and wider column widths are used. If the policy of the newspaper is such that editorials cannot be set in different sizes and widths, then the least that the makeup editor can do is to urge that more leading be placed between the lines of type. Although the result is not as dramatic as the above-mentioned procedure, it is better than treating editorials in the same typographical manner as news.

Page Structure

Although much attention has been given to the makeup of editorials themselves, less has been given to the structure of the editorial page. Because editorial pages carry such diverse items as cartoons, guest columnists, letters to the editor, news and sometimes advertisements, the remainder of the page often tends to become a catchall for material not included on news pages.

But the concept of editorial page makeup should be based on the desirability of utilizing full makeup control, coupled with a desire to personalize the page better than any other page. Editors have complete control over the contents of the editorial page, something they do not have in the makeup of front pages. Front page makeup is often affected by the nature of the news, which results in designs that are a compromise between what is desired and what is most practical. But the editor does not have this problem on the editorial page. Furthermore, the nature of editorial material is personal. Editorials are personal messages from the editor to readers whereby opinions of the newspaper are expressed. Guest columnists tend to be personal in their approach to opinion or interpretation, and letters to the editor also reflect readers' personal opinions. The concept of editorial page makeup, therefore, should be based on a more personalized design than used for any other page in the newspaper. A personalized style of makeup is warm, appealing and simple (Figure 15–11). The effect of such design is to make the page inviting. A complex and cold-looking page tends to make readers hesitate to read it. Because research has shown that readership traffic of editorial pages is often 50 per cent less than on front pages, there is an urgent need to make the page more readable and increase traffic there. Presumably the editors have something important to say and readers need help to read what has been written. Some newspapers have done remarkably well in executing this concept; many have not.

Other Makeup Techniques for Editorial Pages

The masthead (often incorrectly called the nameplate) is a small body of type in which the name of the newspaper, the top editorial and business officers and, sometimes, the philosophy of the paper are given. The masthead is often placed at the top of editorial columns, apparently to relate the name of the newspaper and its staff with the opinions shown below. Sometimes when the editorial page is placed within the first five pages of an issue, it serves as the source of necessary postal information for second-class matter. There is, however, a good reason for not placing the masthead at the top of editorial columns.

Editorial pages usually are found near the front of the newspaper, in the left-hand column of a left-hand page. The upper-left-hand corner of this page, therefore, is the most important position on the page, perhaps the most important position in the entire issue. It should be devoted to the most significant piece of information on the page, which is not the masthead. Editorials are much more significant and demand top position. There is little justification for wasting a key position. If the masthead is attractively designed, as many are, it will not matter where it is placed on the page. The best placement therefore, is in the lower-right-hand corner because in that position it can achieve readership without distracting from any other feature on the page.

Another editorial page feature that could well be buried is the editorial cartoon. As research has indicated, a cartoon will achieve readership no matter where it is located on a page. That being the case, why take one of the most crucial positions (top center) and place the cartoon there? If the position of the cartoon is fixed because of tradition, there is little that can be done. But attempts should be made to move it to the bottom, where it will

The Art of Editing

Editorials

Making divorce an adult decision

CALIFORNIA RECENTLY moved into the 20th century by adopting a revolutionary divorce law.

As of Jan. 1, a couple will be able to obtain a divorce without pleading grounds. Instead of the word divorce, the petitions will be entitled "dissolution of a marriage."

What this means is that when the two parties decide that their marriage is irreconcilable, either one can make the charge in court. Gone are the days when one party is blamed for the dissolution of the marriage, or when proof of grounds is necessary to obtain the divorce.

A strong advocate of divorce law reform for Illinois is State Rep. Bernard Wolfe (D-15th). Wolfe's Family Study commission last year recommended that a law similar to California's be adopted in Illinois. The commission made the recommendation based on studies conducted around the country and of English law.

Wolfe believes that the concept of punishment and guilt should be removed from our divorce laws.

"It is difficult to establish where the fault lies," Wolfe told the Lerner Newspapers. "We should eliminate a procedure that produces acrimony and trauma."

Too many divorced persons are forced to go into court and commit perjury in order to obtain a divorce. When people have to lie in a courtroom, the law becomes a mockery.

While Wolfe has not introduced a bill calling for such liberal reform in Illinois, he has introduced legislation that will codify our divorce laws and make them more realistic.

Rep. Wolfe: t avoid acrimony and trauma.

"Unfortunately, you can't jump to a completely new concept in Illinois," says Wolfe.

We hope Wolfe's legislation will pass in 1970, but only as a first step toward a "dissolution of marriage" law.

According to Wolfe, liberalizing divorce law does not increase the number of divorces. Instead, it makes divorce the decision of two adults and enables them to lessen the agony of an unfortunate situation.

How to win votes and influence young militants

By JANET YENCH

WITH LESS THAN 12 calendar months of his mayoral term spent, Maywood's Leonard Chabala has already proven himself a Champion of the People.

Or at least, some of the people.

Mr. Chabala swept up a smashing victory over Edgar Elbert (who was under two indictments at the time for mishandling funds in his Maywood bank) in the April, 1969 election.

Having secured the confidence of liberals and blacks in a grandiose manner strongly reminiscent of John Lindsay's original siege of New York City, and of conservatives who believed he might end the violence, destruction, barricades and curfews that Elbert could not, Chabala took his oath and stepped into the top seat of a town that was losing business, residents, prestige, respect and money, and losing it fast.

EVERYTHING was quiet for a long while. Proviso East, apparent source of Maywood's bleeding ulcer, won the State Basketball Championship in Urbana.

The whole town turned out for the "We're Number 1" parade and everything was great.

It seemed that the championship might turn the tide, that the good will and togetherness spurred by the victory would heal all wounds.

However, Chabala's liberal policies of satisfying demands of all minorities, but in particular the blacks,' was not truly tested until early in December.

WHEN PROVISO EAST graduate Fred Hampton, chairman of the Illinois Black Panther Party, was shot to death on Dec. 4, Chabala was among four village officials who signed a statement calling the state's attorney's police raid on Hampton's apartment "legitimatized murder."

A few days later, repercussions of Hampton's death erupted in disturbances at Proviso.

Black Power militants marched in front of the school while leaders inside organized a memorial service for Hampton to be held during school hours.

Hundreds of white students gathered too, to protest the memorial. To point out how absurd they felt a memorial service for Hampton would be, they demanded equal time in order to hold one for Al Capone.

THEN CAME Dec. 11 when a few more Maywood businessmen and several passing motorists suffered property loss and personal injury at the hands of militant blacks who became "inflamed" (as Mr. Chabala would put it) because riot-equipped sheriff's police pulled down their face masks and were ready to make arrests after the youths grouped and prepared for destruction.

Opinion

Enter Mayor Chabala, who brings forth to a public meeting a few hours later two leaders of the Black Youth Council who dutifully apologized for creating disorder on 5th Avenue that afternoon.

They even accepted a bill to replace Cushman's music store window, shattered in the melee, which is supposed to make everything alright.

AND THAT'S IT. A slap on the hand (they're too old for spankings), a reprimand (those are bad boys who break store windows and kick pregnant women in the head) and everyone cheers the youths (for accepting the guilt of their antics) and the mayor (hurrah) because he accomplished the impossible.

He made plain to the young militants the difference between right and wrong.

He forced upon them the responsibility of accepting the consequences of their action.

He elicited from them a public apology.

Unbelievable.

No wonder Acting Police Chief Wilbur Samuels resigned.

The irony of the entire second week of December and Mr. Chabala's teaching methods manifested last week, as far as this writer is concerned when a 20-year-old named Thomas Blair along with two of his comrades (Charles Flowers and Tyrone Jelkes) were arrested in the fatal shooting of a 55-year-old electrician in a Berwyn restaurant.

AFTER HIS ARREST, Blair reportedly requested permission to call Leonard Chabala. The mayor said he didn't know Blair (who was fingered as the trigger man in the slaying) and couldn't imagine why the youth would want to call him.

The answer is simple. Frighteningly simple. Blair, you see, is a member of the Black Youth Council that so graciously accepted the blame for tearing up 5th Avenue four weeks ago.

Chabala, their champion, was teaching them that as long as they knew they'd get a hand slap and a lecture for their actions, they could get away with anything.

Even murder.

Copyright (c) 1969 Stan Mack

Here's hoping – some New Year wishes, awards

By SHELDON HOFFENBERG
Lerner Newspapers
Political Bureau

HERE'S HOPING the new year brings to:

State's Atty. Edward Hanrahan—A can of tear gas, with instructions on how to use it.

Racing Board Secretary Timothy Sheehan—My address, in case he gets a hot tip.

Lar "America First" Daly—Presentation of the "If At First You Don't Succeed . . ." award.

The Chicago Daily News—The "Con Con Hypocrite" award, for trying to prove that although State Rep. Paul Elward is a partisan Democrat, Thomas Lyons—a committeeman—and Richard M. Daley—son of the mayor—aren't.

The Chicago Tribune—The "Make Believe" award, for trying to prove that William Rentschler's heart is really with the liberal Democrats.

Sen. Ralph Smith—A new set of windshield wipers to replace the set he symbolically wore out as he flopped back and forth on the Haynsworth issue.

Mayor Daley—The "Barbershop" award, for criticizing Ald. Seymour Simon's long locks two years ago, then telling a TV audience last week to be tolerant of those with long hair.

Gov. Ogilvie—A copy of the book "How to Be a Good Citizen," for announcing he would not vote in the Republican 13th district congressional primary.

State Rep. Edward Warman—The "Optimist of the Year" award, for giving up his seat in the legislature to run for Congress again.

Prof. Curtis MacDougall—The "You Gotta Be Kidding" award, for trying to convince the conservative Republican voters controlling the 13th district that Warman is too hawkish on Viet Nam.

Secretary of State Paul Powell—The Gov. Wallace award, for announcing he will defy the courts and list his political friends first on the ballot.

Comment

Supt. of Public Instruction Ray Page—A billion free pictures of himself, so that he will never again have to pay for such photos with school lunch funds.

Richard Daley—The "I Just Couldn't Wait" award, for jolting Con Con's harmonious spirit by springing to his feet at the very first session to make a partisan attack on Gov. Ogilvie.

Senatorial candidate Adlai Stevenson—The "Who Needs Notes?" award, for glancing around a roomful of Democrats, mentioning some names, and completely forgetting the powerful committeeman and No. 2 Democrat on the County board, Jerome Huppert.

Chief Judge William Campbell—A towel to wipe the egg off his face after he ridiculed a charge by Sherman Skolnick against a court clerk (within a week the clerk was indicted on the charge).

County Clerk Edward Barrett—The "Better Late Than Never" award, for admitting that the "porcupine" and other comments his organization made against Ald. William Singer's backers were too strong.

Cong. Roman Pucinski—The bill for the Safeguard anti-ballistic missile system.

Ald. Edwin Fifielski—A quick course in opera, ballet, great music and the fine arts, so he can lead us to the finer things of life as chairman of the Chicago City Council's committee on culture.

State Rep. Bernard Wolfe—The " 'E' for Effort" award, for trying to continue the work of his Family Study commission even though the state legislature couldn't find, in a yearly budget of more than $4 billion, a single penny for the commission.

State Rep. Edward Wolbank—A key to every executive bathroom in town, because his retirement from politics apparently ends his crusade against pay toilets.

State Rep. Robert Juckett—A bullet-proof vest and coat of armor, to protect him from the wrath of his colleagues after he asked for a roll-call vote on the state income tax bill.

Ald. Jack Sperling—An explanation of why the Chicago Sun-Times keeps referring to Ald. Leon Despres as leader of the City Council opposition bloc.

Ald. Claude Holman—The "Bad Taste of the Year" award, for referring to Sperling's family planning views as "genocide."

Sheriff Joseph Woods—The "I Knew I Forgot Something" award, for letting a whole year go by without forming a single posse.

• • •

NATIONALLY and internationally, let's hope that 1970 brings to:

President Nixon—A book about economics, so he can explain why spending billions on the anti-ballistic missile, the supersonic airliner, etc., is not inflationary, but spending some money for the poor and the poorly educated is.

Vice-President Agnew—A copy of Mr. Nixon's speeches about lowering our voices and bringing the country together, and a duncecap.

Atty. Gen. Mitchell—A map to remind him that there is more to the United States than just Dixie.

Sen. Edward Kennedy—Some credible answers to fill the gaps in his story about Chappaquiddick.

Dean Rusk—A set of binoculars to help him find "the light at the end of the (Viet) tunnel."

Editor's note

The third planet from the sun

By T. P. GORMAN

THE SPACESHIP hovered several hundred miles above the planet's surface, a tiny glistening piece of metal against a black sky.

"We're in orbit now, Capt. Joles," the helmsman reported. "Should I lock in or should we descend?"

"Lock in, helmsman. Let's have a good look before we go down."

The captain ordered the viewscreen into full intensity and zeroed in on the planet's fourth quadrant.

"SEE THOSE brown areas. That used to be heavy vegetation. Now it's all dead region — all scorched."

He turned to his science chief:

"Give me a reading on the atmosphere, Mr. Kliss."

"Mostly carbon derivatives — monoxide and dioxide, with traces of argon, ammonia and oxygen."

"What about the watery regions? Do our readings confirm those of our space probe?"

"Almost, captain, with few variations. The watery regions once covered 70 per cent of the planet and ran quite deep. They are now mostly swampland, however, and cannot be consumed without extensive chemical additives."

"PROBE FOR LIFE signs, Mr. Kliss. Let's make sure there's no life before we descend."

The computer-driven life detection system switched in, and a scan was made of the planet's surface.

"Nothing, captain. Life detectors indicate no positive vibrations—not even plant life."

"Let's go down then and have a look. Descend, helmsman."

The gleaming ship left orbit and began a steady glide toward the surface, its heat shields protecting it against the friction of the planet's dense, highly toxic atmosphere.

"HEIGHT 150 MILES and dropping. Height 100 miles and dropping. Height 75 miles and dropping."

"Hold at 25 miles, helmsman."

"Yes, captain. Fifty miles and dropping. Forty . . . thirty . . . holding at 25."

"Switch in viewscreen."

"Look, in the third quadrant. A structure of some kind. It's in fairly good condition, as well, captain."

"Yes, that confirms the photographs of our space probe. Those shadowy regions on the pictures are structures of some kind. It seems of an advanced nature, too."

"BUT, CAPTAIN, we know that no planet of the G-type can support life intelligent enough for this type of construction. The atmosphere is much too toxic even for lower forms, and the watery sections are hopelessly toxic as well.

"What could have possibly happened, captain. A nuclear holocaust?"

"No. I doubt it. Our readings show only a small trace of radioactive residue — nothing abnormal for a highly advanced society such as this. And a nuclear holocaust would have left unmistakable signs. I doubt also that structures such as those could remain standing after a war of such magnitude."

"What, then, captain?"

"PERHAPS THEY were overwhelmed by their own technology, helmsman. For every advance a society makes, it must take precautions to ensure its very existence. A society that is careless eventually will choke on its own waste."

"Shall we descend further, captain?"

"Not now. We shall leave that to the follow-up ship.

"Break back to high orbit, helmsman. Then prepare for inspection of inner planets in this system.

"So much for the third planet from the sun."

'Stop spending money to fight rezoning and abide by the courts': reader

OPEN LETTER to Joseph Vandlik, zoning chairman, Dunham Community council:

We read with much interest your letter directed to the residents of the Village of Harwood Heights, regarding the recent court decision pertaining to the proposed National Tea Store to be located at the corner of Gunnison and Nable.

As residents of Harwood Heights since its inception, we thought we could straighten you out on the selfish objections which you presented.

When we built our home, it was the open fields and dirt roads that attracted us to this location. It was like being in the country, but still close to the city. We were not even a village, we were an unincorporated area, and we liked it.

Time passed, and progress began. Soon, houses were being built, streets were being paved and all the appearances of another city were taking shape.

We did not particularly like this new development, but one can't stop progress, can they?

Next, we realized that we needed the protection and assistance of our neighbors, Harwood Heights, so we proceeded with annexation. We didn't particularly like the idea, we rather enjoyed being unincorporated, but for the future of our home and property, it was inevitable. One can't stop progress, can they?

Then came the multiple buildings, of which we are blessed with many. We didn't like these either and we all knew for sure our dream of living in a country-like atmosphere was over.

We objected and disapproved, but in the end, we realized it was best for the community. We didn't like it, but one can't stop progress, can they?

Now we have a hi-rise, factories and apartment buildings, all of which were objected to by some . . . but they were all for the betterment of our village. The proposed National Tea is also objected to, by some . . . but the overall picture shows betterment for our village. Sure a few people get hurt.

Each and every person cannot be considered. Each time any of the above mentioned changes took place, a few people were directly hurt, but in ruling a village, one must think of an over-all picture.

In our opinion, the National Tea will be an asset in many ways, certainly out-weighing the disadvantages to a few. This has been proven by other developments over the years.

I don't believe the village is too concerned with the National Tea making a slum area out of Nagle Manor . . . that is up to the people who live there. Many beautiful homes here and elsewhere are close to commercial buildings and remain quite desirable.

Editor's mail

In closing, we wish to state that we would be opposed to the village spending any more of our money to fight this rezoning. They have been fair with those who object and should now abide by the decision of the courts.

When there exists a grocery store on one corner and commercial property on the north side of Gunnison, just east of Nagle, how can one expect to disallow commercial building on the other corner?

If you good people of Chicago were so worried about commercial property, why didn't you object to the commercial building on Gunnison?

The area surrounding Nagle Manor, as you call it, is just tasting its first rezoning and they don't particularly like it. Others in Harwood Heights have been through this many times.

But, our village will do what is best for the majority of Harwood Heights and not disapproving residents of Chicago.

If your Community Council is so concerned about Harwood Heights, why don't you move into our village, we could use your tax dollars much more than we need your dissent.

By the way, where have you been for the past 15 years?

Name withheld
Upon request.

Figure 15–11. Contemporary design of editorial page. [*Courtesy Lerner Newspapers, Chicago, Illinois.*]

still achieve readership and yet free the top position for more significant editorial material.

Although larger type, wider columns, more white space between the columns and a cleaner page are the result, the editorial page often lacks drama because there is too much type on the page and relatively few illustrations. Occasionally a small portrait of a columnist may appear somewhere on the page, but that plus the cartoon is the extent of decorative material. One key editorial or an important column may be boxed each day as a means of dominating the page. Sometimes editorials, although important, are not long enough to receive dramatic treatment. But often a columnist's material is. Even then, the same individual may not have an exciting column each day. But some other columnist may have material worthy of being boxed. The makeup editor might select some story, editorial or column to be given a dramatic treatment each day.

Finally, large initial letters are sometimes used for the first letter of each editorial as a means of making the page look more attractive. Their use is debatable. On the one hand, they sometimes look attractive if not too many of them are placed on the page. They are decorative devices. But they pose problems for the composing room. Sometimes they break off in stereotyping. Other times they take too long to be cut in by printers. Perhaps the most significant factor in their use should be whether they enhance or detract from the editorials. When they are too bold or too large, they may detract. If there is not enough space around them, they may not look attractive. Therefore, the use of large initial letters as a desirable makeup device must be considered of indefinite value.

Women's Pages

The proper concept of women's pages makeup generally has not been clear. The basic idea was to present news and features of interest to women in a distinctly feminine makeup style. To implement that idea, a style of makeup adopted the form of lighter typefaces for headlines and body copy and perhaps a bit more space between the columns. Column rules were sometimes eliminated on these pages to help lighten the page. This concept, however, was really inadequate to fulfill the need for feminine design because the result was nothing more than lighter-appearing pages. The only change from the makeup of other pages in the same issue was the lightness of the pages. But lightness is hardly the most significant dimension needed for communicating with women who are often sensitive to good design. Women's facial makeup, hair, clothes, homes and gardens all express sensitivity to some or large proportions of contemporary design. In other words, there is still a need to change women's pages makeup radically to be more in line with the contemporary frame of reference in which women tend to think.

The use of lightface types for headlines often can result in rather ugly pages. Simply because a typeface is lightface rather than boldface does not make it feminine. Furthermore, the wide-spread use of italic, script or cursive typefaces on women's pages is intended to bring about a feminine appearance. But some of these typefaces are so grotesque they defeat the goal. For example, Lydian Cursive, Brush Script, Coronet or Mandate are types that, although different from roman faces, are not necessarily attractive on women's pages. They are too ornate and more suited for advertising. Ultra Bodoni Italic, Bodoni Book Italic, Cheltenham Light or Medium Italic and Century Italic also are not feminine. Garamond or Caslon Italic are feminine, but they lack charm in bolder versions, and neither are contemporary type styles. Contemporary styles are noted for their extended appearance and their use of ultrafine serifs coupled with contrasting heavier elements (Figure 15–12). Although headline types can help achieve some femininity, more than typeface selection is needed.

Old

HEADLINE GOTHIC

ABCDEFGHIJK | 12345

GARAMOND BOLD

ABCDEFGHIJKLMNOPQRSTUVWS
abcdefghijklmnopqrstuvwxyz | 123456

BODONI BOLD

ABCDEFGHIJKLMNOPQRSTUVW
abcdefghijklmnopqrstuvwxy | 12345

FUTURA BOLD

ABCDEFGHIJKLMNOPQRSTUVWXJ
abcdefghijklmnopqrstuvw | 12345

GOUDY EXTRA BOLD

ABCDEFGHIJKLMNOPQRS
abcdefghijklmnopqrstu | 12345

CHELTENHAM BOLD CONDENSED

ABCDEFGHIJKLMNOPQRSTUVWXYZ
abcdefghijklmnopqrstuvwxyz | 123456789

STYMIE BOLD

ABCDEFGHIJKLMNOPQRST
abcdefghijklmnopqrstu | 12345

CENTURY BOLD

ABCDEFGHIJKLMNOPQRSTU
abcdefghijklmnopqrstuvw | 12345

New

CLARENDON BOOK (CRAW)

ABCDEFGHIJKLMNOPQR
abcdefghijklmnopqr | 12345

CHISEL (Reduction)

ABCDEFGHIJKLMNOPQRS
abcdefghijklmnopvr | 123456

FORTUNE LIGHT

ABCDEFGHIJKLMNOPQRS
abcdefghijklmnopqrstuv | 12345

FOLIO MEDIUM EXTENDED ITALIC

ABCDEFGHIJKLMNOPQRSTUV
abcdefghijklmnopqrstuv | 12345

MODERN ROMAN NO. 20

ABCDEFGHIJKLMNOPQRSTU
abcdefghijklmnopqrstuvwxy | 12345

WEISS ROMAN

ABCDEFGHIJKLMNOPQRSTUVWXY
abcdefghijklmnopqrstuvwxyz | 12345678

TORINO ROMAN

ABCDEFGHIJKLMNOPQRSTUVWX
abcdefghijklmnopqrstuvwxyz | 12345

HELLENIC WIDE

ABCDEFGHIJKLMNI
abcdefghijklm | 12345

Figure 15–12. Traditional versus contemporary type samples.

A number of newspapers, mostly the larger ones, have understood the need for change and have designed women's pages that make them radically different from what they were before. They have adopted a newer concept, which is to make the page appear not only feminine but chic, charming and dramatic as well (Figures 15–13a, b). A page may appear feminine and yet may be in poor taste or lack charm. The newer concept has been implemented with bold and imaginative planning.

The most important means of implementing this new concept is to design, rather than make up, pages. In other words, pages are not dummied as pages have been traditionally—they are designed with the total page concept in mind. Because much of the material appearing on women's pages is advance or time copy that can be set before the current news is set, there is usually time to design a page rather than build it piece by piece. But the task of designing is of such major importance that sometimes newspapers hire persons with strong commercial art backgrounds to create the lead women's page. Unless the makeup editor is capable of creating a dramatic, imaginative design, it should be left to experts. Young persons who are now becoming makeup editors may have the kind of sensitivity and ability to design such pages.

Other than use a total page design concept of dramatic appearance, some papers use four-color printing to further enhance the page. But color added to unimaginative design does not achieve the goal of the newer concept. In fact, it calls the inadequacy of design to the attention of readers.

Conclusions on Special Page Makeup

The principles of makeup discussed apply to other special pages within the newspaper, even though there are some differences between these sections. The differences, for makeup purposes, however, are not that important. To a great extent the makeup of these pages is affected by the dummying of advertisements. Rarely are they free of advertisements. The goal of makeup editors should be to salvage a page whose design may have been distorted by the shape and positioning of the ads. Every attempt should be made to simplify these pages to the extent possible. It is virtually impossible to create the same kind of dramatic format required on the front, editorial and women's pages. Therefore, the following check points are offered with the goal of helping the makeup editor work within the built-in limitations of advertising to achieve the maximum amount of readability and aesthetic appearance.

Burying Standing Heads

The question is often raised about whether standing headlines such as **Sports, Financial** or **Feature Section** should be buried somewhere in the middle of the page, thereby freeing top space for news. The answer is, if such headlines can be buried, why use them at all? Will it not be obvious to an individual that he is reading the sports page or the financial page (Figure 15–14)? It would take only a little while to learn from either the headlines or the pictures on a page. Therefore, the function of standing headlines is to keep readers from having to study other headlines or pictures to learn which section they are reading. Furthermore, if an index appears on page 1 and it refers to a special page, then the standing headline serves as an advertisement to tell readers they have arrived at the correct section. Such labels, therefore, should not be buried.

Because the bottoms of inside pages lack news space, the makeup editor tends to allow that space to disintegrate. To whatever extent the bottoms of pages can be brightened, they should be. Pictures, horizontally made-up stories and boxes can help accomplish the job if the space is there. Even when the only editorial space available is a "well" between two ads, the makeup editor can use a one-column picture at the bottom to help brighten the page.

Bottoms of Special Pages Need Brightening

Smaller newspapers often will allow odd-shaped advertisements to be used on inside pages. A flexform is one with an unusual shape. Less obtrusive are L-shaped advertisements. If the management allows such advertisements within its pages, the makeup editor will have a struggle to make them appear attractive. The best procedure is to keep makeup display to a minimum on such pages and keep significant news for other pages. Any attempts to add display on a page with a flexform advertisement may simply make the page confusing.

Flexforms and Other Odd-Shaped Advertisements

Occasionally, to offer the reader a change of pace in design, the editor will round off the corner of pictures or boxes (Figure 15–15). The effect is novel and interesting, if not overdone. When used occasionally, it tends to brighten the page. When overused, it loses whatever novelty it has and may be ignored by readers.

Boxes or Pictures with Rounded Corners

Traditionally, columnists' articles are positioned in the same section of the newspaper every day so that readers will know where they may be found. But they need not be placed in or near major sections. If the columnist has a loyal following, chances are that readers will search for the column no matter where it appears. The main sports column is often placed in the most favorable position. It robs the more exciting sports stories because they must be placed in less conspicuous positions. The main columnist should be given a less favorable position to prevent this from happening. Readers will not avoid reading the column.

Positioning of Columnists' Articles

For the three fireplaces
in the two-story townhouse
of Roy Succa, designer John

Applegate used festive decoration to bring a holiday spirit and blend in with the decor. Old as well as new items are put together with natural materials. These old and new contrasts are so expertly utilized that one isn't immediately aware of separate components.

The wreath of bread on *feminique's* cover shows how Applegate has returned to one of man's staples for contrast with the sophisticated shimmer of silver, mirror, and glass in Succa's "upstairs parlor." Centering the mantle is a mercury sphere—adjacent to a mercury vase that holds frosted branches. Soft snowflakes on the mirror seem to float against the reflected walls.

The pale-lime and bright-blue color scheme for this upstairs living room was inspired by the unusual Turkish rug which has an intricate border design surrounding a solid color center. Highlights in an Oriental corner are pillows made from antique East Indian fabrics, which have tiny pieces of mirror in their pattern. A fireside chair with cane sides and black leather upholstery shares a lamp table with a Recamier sofa covered in a leopard print.

A YELLOW MING vase holds a pleated yellow paper shade. For another tactile sense in this joyous combination of textures and cultures, a small ball of velvet pieces sits on the lamp table like a Victorian toy. Above the sofa is a portrait that adds still more vivid combinations of red and yellow with exotic patterns. [An Oriental corner used to be considered a basic of every artist's studio in the gay '90s.]

Succa has the talent to combine many cultures into his home, for he is in touch with the trends of today's interior design. He is the manager of Decorators Walk, a showroom in the Merchandise Mart which carries fabrics, furniture, and accessories for interior designers.

Further proof of his talent is seen in a fireside chair, upholstered in a gold and white pattern, accompanied by an antique bootjack's bench. Occupying a minimum amount of space, the bench serves as a coffee table.

THE FLAMES OF the fireplace look like more thru the wire screen that fits within the arched fireplace opening. A simulated marble finish has been handpainted over a fireplace which replaced one that was in poor condition when Succa moved in.

In the front parlor, fireplace decoration is simple and classic. Elegant gold velvet ribbon cascades gently around an angel in flight in front of a fine French mirror.

Above the fireplace, the ribbons are curved gently to two crystal candle sconces, each encircled with small wreaths of greens. Seating includes a highback chair covered in gold damask—one of the main colors here.

A tiny pattern of gold squares on black provides a contemporary carpet for the collector's furniture, such as a round table which holds an old tole tray that can be lifted off for serving. A French bergere chair upholstered in brown velvet introduces a dark shade to this room of off-white walls. And a crouching gnome holding a shell becomes a fireside stool. This little fellow came from London, where Succa went antiquing in Portobello road.

The hearth front is a cast-iron French antique, complete with a fire basket and lift-off top. These are designed ingeniously to bring more of the fire warmth and glow into a room where deep fireplaces are not possible. This hearth front still retains its original deep green finish trimmed with brass ormolu.

An elaborate carving attributed to Grinling Gibbons, a 17th century English carver, is elegant trim on the mantleless hearth front. A winter landscape by Michigan artist Edna Anderson introduces the blues and browns of nature into the room.

ON THE MANTLE of the third fireplace in the dining room, polished fruit and vegetables, ranging from affluent artichokes to the common cucumber, have been arranged by John Applegate. This is in contrast with the wallpaper which transforms this room into a bower of blossoms. The thin, trim container for the arrangement is really a French antique dish drainer.

Sheaves of wheat continue the harvest mood of the fruit and vegetables, and twisted greens become an arching garland within an old Victorian mirror, complimenting the fireplace of pink granite.

This fireplace, like the others, has been restored to the approximate original appearance, and all are now in working order. Tall Spanish candlesticks hold fat candles twisted with ribbon.

THE ANTIQUE Dufour and Zuber wallpaper was manufactured from 1815 until 1914 in Europe. Out of print ever since, it is unlikely ever to be reprinted because it uses 37 colors and 52 wood blocks to create the intricate design.

An old gas chandelier from a former hotel holds candles in glass cups over a round Biedermeier fruitwood table. Here, in a large bowl, glossy artificial apples and pine cones contrast for interest. Thru French doors is the inclosed garden, a summer haven for the big plants stored indoors during the winter.

Antique serving and storage pieces in this dining room continue the elegant mood established by the lush design of the wallpaper.

IN A TINY FOYER, walls are papered in a dramatic pineapple design. [Since the days of Williamsburg and the clipper ships, the pineapple has been known in America as a symbol of hospitality. Their rarity at that time made them a compliment when served to guests.] Succa often uses real pineapples as a centerpiece, each one wearing a candle on its top.

The front room and the dining room, plus a connecting hall and kitchen, compose the first floor of Succa's town house. When entertaining, he greets guests in front of the fireplace in the front parlor, serving pre-dinner drinks here. Guests are served dinner, buffet style, in front of the fireplace in the dining room. And coffee and cordials are enjoyed in front of that fireplace on the second floor.

Holiday warmth abounds at the dining room hearthside in Roy Succa's townhouse. Rare wallpaper contrasts pleasantly with the mantel's vegetable arrangement and garland of greens.

Above the hearth in Succa's parlor, simple holiday trim consists of ribbon, greens, and an angel on the mirror.

In Manhattan's Celebrity Christmas Tree exhibit, Cardinal Cooke's 13-foot tree is trimmed with small gold-framed pictures of children around the world.

Christmas
trees trimmed
by celebrities, an

annual event at New York City's Hallmark galleries, this year have taken a different turn. Expensive opulence has given way to familiar objects, sometimes from the household, sometimes from private collections.

Ernest Trova, artist-sculptor, sprayed his tree black and trimmed it with cut-out comic strips of 1930 and 1940. Popeye and Little Orphan Annie come alive on his tree; also sparkling on its mark branches is his collection of cereal box premiums. Souvenirs of the artist's childhood are watches immortalizing Superman, Mickey Mouse, and Dick Tracy, and the rings that recall The Green Hornet radio serial and the Lone Ranger.

NEW YORK'S ARCHBISHOP Terence Cardinal Cooke's tree—13 feet high—is hung with children's pictures in tiny gold frames.

Not all the celebrities trim their own trees. In fact, few did. But all wrote detailed letters of instruction and sent either photos or sketches from which the Hallmark display department executed all 18 trees.

Football's Joe Namath trimmed his tabletop tree with open lipsticks that look—in a way—like candles. In lieu of an angel at the tree's top, there is a delicate lady's hand mirror.

Dress designer Halston by-passed the traditional tree; he chose, instead, one of his dressmaker dummies, decorated it with an assortment of barnyard feathers.

James Beard, the gourmet and food writer, considered his Christmas breakfast table an important rendezvous point. His vignette in a provincial setting consists of a buffet table with a 2-foot-tall tree decorated with seven varieties of sausage.

POETESS MARIANNE Moore didn't do a tree; she did, instead, a houseplant, a Norfolk pine which she hung with tiny wooden animals—deer, giraffes, dogs, and elephants.

The tree of John Lindsay is naked except for little white lights and a city pigeon and squirrel [stuffed, of course] perched in its branches.

Actress Ali McGraw cooked up a batch of gingerbread men, boiled and painted eggs, and trimmed her tree with these and tiny bows of ribbon from her dresses. . . . it was an echo of the tree trimming of pioneer days, when ornaments were made of lace, ribbon, or feathers from clothes.

The exhibit plays to throngs in the Hallmark galleries at 56th street and Fifth avenue; the doors are open from 9:30 a.m. until 9:30 p.m. [except Sunday] until Jan. 3.

Bill Cunningham

She

DAY PUBLICATIONS
Monday, January 5, 1970

If snow is your thing, you're not alone. You're probably destined to become one of the one million snowmobile owners in the North American snow belt.

There's no need to give up fashion for warmth. Ski-Doo Sports, Ltd. has designed a wardrobe especially for snowmobilers. From head to toe you'll find warm accessories for everyone, even in après snowmobiling attire.

A new fabric, Vistram, is used in this flattering one-piece snowmobile suit with fur-trimmed hood. Vistram looks like leather but doesn't become brittle in cold temperature. It's air permeable allowing it to breathe and maintain a suppliness at any temperature.

His and her one-piece nylon snowmobile suits with orlon fleece are the warmest thing on the snowmobile trail.

These boots are definitely made for snow. T'NT snowmobile boots are ankle-padded and come in black with yellow racing stripes and a removable felt liner.

Colorful hip hugger sweaters, 100 per cent wool, are great before and after snowmobiling.

There's still more—fiber glass helmets; goggles; wool tuques; finger mitts; socks; thermal underwear; seal skin boots; mukluks; shearling boots; snow shoes; kidney belts; saddlebags and a duffle bag to put it all in.

Snow safariers can be found where the action is—and they're very warm and fashionable.

— marilyn helfers, editor

Fashions available at Sports Chalet
Rolling Meadows
Photos from Ski-Doo Sports, Ltd.

Figure 15–13a, b. Samples of contemporary design on women's pages.

LIFE NEWSPAPER, THURSDAY, JANUARY 8, 1970 — Section Three—Page One

The key to a basketball championship isn't always a good big man, just usually. And the Central Suburban laegue has quite a few big men, especially 6-10 Mark Cartwright of Niles West (left) and 6-5 Mike Sachs of Niles North (right). With Cartwright leading the way, the Indians have won their first three CSL games. Without an injured Sachs, the Vikings dropped two of their first three. Sachs is back now.

KAZAK on sports

Revolt in sport?

By DON KAZAK
Lerner Newspapers Staff Writers

NOT ONLY is this a new year, it is also a new decade. And, by all indications, the new decade may be quite a bit different from the old one, or any old one.

One of the so-called "movements" that seems to be clutching at the vitals of this country is a plea for recognition of human rights, as opposed to legal rights, of all people at all levels of life.

The sports world, believe or not, may have to undergo some pretty drastic changes as a result of this human rights movement.

EVERYONE IS WELL AWARE of the troubles that colleges have been having with athletes. Racism is often charged. But more often disgruntled athletes simply complain that they are tired of being treated as hired hands, or bodies, for the glories of the old alma mater.

Ivy league schools have a policy that treats young men as: 1, people; 2, students, and 3, athletes. In that order. And that order is, roughly, the inverse of the order that most universities seem to follow.

Colleges have two choices. First, they can recognize their athletes as human beings who have certain dignities that should be protected by human rights. This is the Ivy league approach, and it is an admirable one.

SECONDLY, AS AN ALTERNATIVE, they can recognize their athletes as true hired hands — professionals — who have entered into an employer - worker contract relationship with them.

Since sports is at such a hallowed level in the Midwest and the South, this alternative is the likely one to be followed there. The difference from the present situation is that these schools would stop pretending that their hired hands are students who nappen also to be athletes. The schools would admit that their hired hands are really hired hands.

The 1970s will probably see this revolution, if you want to call it that, spread both upward and downward — to the professional level and the high school level.

INDEED, THE SPREAD has already started. For example, look at the trouble Argo high school had with its basketball team, which revolted against a coach they thought was repressive. The coach kicked the whole team off the team, giving himself a lighter work load and giving chagrined school officials a big headache.

And on the professional level, Curt Flood has started an interesting legal action against professional baseball. He is claiming that the Cardinals had no right to trade him to the Phillies without his consent.

In effect, he is questioning the whole concept of the player reserve clause, which makes athletes into "properties" that are "owned" by teams.

IF FLOOD'S LAWSUIT should win—and it would probably take a long time, with appeals, to get a final verdict — the moneyed palace of professional sports owners would suddenly be invaded by the athletes off of whom the owners make their millions.

Comes the revolution, the players will control their sports. "Sport for the players" might be their battle cry.

But don't hold your breath. The powers that be have more than just money in their corner.

Cagers resume league play

SPORTS In LIFE-Land

NOW THAT EVERYBODY'S celebrated the holidays, area basketball conferences are ready to resume league play in earnest.

Thus far, Notre Dame and Niles West are racing along undefeated in conference play in their roles of defending champs of the Suburban Catholic and Central Suburban leagues, respectively.

But the other four LIFE-land prep teams have been having problems. Niles North is 1-2 in the CSL; Glenbrook South is 0-3 in the CSL; Maine East is 1-3 in the West Suburban, and Niles East is 0-3 in the Suburban.

THIS FRIDAY NIGHT, Niles West travels to Maine South, The Titans of Glenbrook travel to Maine West, Niles North hosts Deerfield, Niles East goes to New Trier East, Maine East hosts York and Notre Dame hosts Immaculate Conception.

On Saturday night, ND's Dons travel to Joliet Catholic.

The Indians of Niles West, fresh off their victory in the Niles North tourney, have their hardest game of the young season waiting for them at Maine South.

The Hawks received statewide prominence when they upset East Aurora in a holiday tournament. Like the Indians, they're 3-0 in CSL play (as is Maine West), and they won last year's Indian-Hawk contest on the South floor.

LAST YEAR'S LOSS to Maine South was the Indians' only conference defeat, which might be added incentive for Coach Billy Schnurr's team.

The Indians have been flying along with their assorted bag of defenses and their potent offense. Everyone has long known what 6-10 center Mark Cartwright can do, but folks are beginning to learn that "the other Marc," (guard Marc Mirsky) can do quite a few things himself.

Mirsky has developed into a high-scoring outside threat, floor general, and solid defender. And behind the Mirsky-Cartwright combo, the Indians have a deep and able back-up crew.

BUT THE HAWKS are big, tough and balanced.

The Dons won their own holiday tourney and have four regulars scoring in double figures (the fifth is a point off).

Notre Dame coach Ralph Hinger knows that there can be problems when your team is 10-0 (4-0 in conference) and has already easily beaten two of the top three contenders.

But Joliet Catholic lost one game in league play last year — to Notre Dame. The defeat meant that they shared the SCC cage crown with the Dons, and they're likely to remember that Saturday, especially on their home court.

HINGER SAID HE is trying to make his team concentrate on the games "one at a time," but the more they win, the tougher it will be to do so.

Niles North, playing without playmaker Steve Huscher, lost the opener in their own tourney then recovered to edge Glenbrook South and bomb Niles East.

The Vikings may be without Huscher for as much as another three weeks or a month. "The doctor isn't optimistic," Florence noted sadly.

But North has found a willing replacement in sophomore Keith Schirmer, who has started finding his varsity feet and sparkle a bit.

MIKE SACHS, THE Vikings' high-powered inside threat, is still not 100 per cent either, according to Florence.

Maine East's coach, Bruce Brothers, is "fairly satisfied" with his team's record of 4-6, but is hoping for some more improvements, especially on defense.

"If we can get our defense squared away, we'll win some games," Brothers noted. The Demons beat Rock Falls in the DeKalb holiday tourney but then fell to a fast Evanston squad.

Bob Reiman, the only returning starter on the squad, has been providing some outside punch for the Demons, while the Bondeson brothers have been having some success inside.

BROTHERS HAS BEEN especially pleased with the progress of Mark, the younger Bondeson, a 6-5 center who is starting to rebound aggressively.

Ironically, the Demons haven't lost a game this year at home, or while wearing their home (white) uniforms. In their road blue, however, they haven't been too successful.

Brothers jokingly warns that the Demons might play their next road game with their white trunks and blue jerseys. Or maybe he isn't joking.

Niles East's Sheldon Bassett is "pleased" with the improvements made by the Trojans, even if their 0-9 record doesn't show it.

"IF WE CAN LOOK respectable against New Trier East," Bassett said; "we'll be ready for Morton East in a week."

Bassett noted that the Trojans will probably try a sagging man-to-man on the big New Trier East center.

Glenbrook South's coach, John Wilhelm, has been having some problems with his Titans. His team has lost its last six defeats by a total of 22 points.

"We were run out of the place by these same teams last year," said Wilhelm, "but we shouldn't be satisfied with being close.

"Our mental attitude is beating us. The team is content with being close."

WILHELM, WHO IS hoping his Titans can get mad enough to win a few, is juggling the lineup this week and is starting all juniors.

And if he didn't have enough problems, the team's big offensive threat, Roland Smith, had to transfer to Massachusetts, where his father was transferred.

Viking gymnasts topple Trojans

NILES NORTH'S gymnasts defeated Niles East last weekend, but the outcome was closer than Viking coach John Cress anticipated.

"I hope we don't score this low again all year," Cress said.

At the varsity level, the Vikings stopped the Trojans, 108.46 to 103.31. North also won the freshman and sophomore competitions.

For the Vikings, Bob Salstone won the floor exercise and was 3rd on the trampoline; David Frumm won the side horse; Bruce Waldman was 1st on the horizontal bar and in the all-around and 3rd on the horse and rings; Dean Scheck was 2nd on the trampoline and Loren Freidman was 2nd on the horizontal bar.

For the Trojans, Al Weiner won the trampoline and was 2nd in floor exercise; Gallai and Krause tied for top spot on the rings; Weinberg was 2nd on the horse and Cech, Shiffman and Epstein was 1-2-3 on the parallel bars.

The Vikings travel to York Saturday, Jan. 10, at 2 p.m.

• • •

SPORTS CAPSULES

THE LEANING TOWER YMCA, 6300 Touhy, Niles, has winter skill school classes scheduled to begin the week of Jan. 12.

Information, class schedules, and fees, may be obtained by calling the Leaning Tower YMCA, 647-8222, ext. 556.

• • •

SKOKIE PARK DISTRICT is accepting teams for the adult basketball league.

The games will be played at the Niles West gymnasium every Wednesday night beginning Jan. 14.

For further information, please call Devonshire Center, 4400 Grove, OR 4-1500.

• • •

THE McNALLY PARK Baseball League and the Skokie Pony League will have a registration Jan. 13, beginning at 6:30 p.m. at the Middleton School gym, 8300 St. Louis, Skokie.

All boys from 8 to 16 years of age are invited. 1969 World Series films will be shown and general registrations will be accepted. Additional information may be obtained from Charles Newman, 677-5721.

Jack Armstrong wasn't Irish

By DON KAZAK
Lerner Newspapers Staff Writers

"NOTRE DAME is the only team that never plays a road game," an opposing coach once grumbled about the Irish.

Never did it seem as true as during last week's Cotton Bowl game, when the visiting Irish had many fans in their Texas game. (The Cotton Bowl is in Dallas, and Dallas is in Texas, for those who don't know.)

The Irish, as everyone does know, were celebrating the 100th year of football by playing their first bowl game in 45 years—and laying all their years of Rockne-Grange-Four Horsemen-Leahy lore and glory on the line against no less an opponent than the No. 1 Longhorns. And in Texas, no less.

The Irish have guts.

AND THEY HAVE luck, too. Not enough luck to win against the Longhorns, but enough skill, luck and savy to look like winners when they were losers.

They played so well that all their gloried past still stands respectfully intact and untarnished. Notre Dame fans (and everyone knows there is an international conspiracy of Irish fandom) may even, in years to come, improve on the story of Notre Dame's Great Return to Football Bowl-Playing after Forty-Five Years.

Who knows, in 20 or 30 years, the football history books may even somehow record the fact that the Irish really defeated the Texans.

BUT, AT LEAST FOR NOW, Notre Dame didn't win that game. Almost, but not quite.

Joe Theismann made the best play of the game in the 4th quarter when he dropped back to pass from the Texas 24. His receivers covered, Theismann was buried under a rush of Texas linemen, except that he somehow scrambled out of the red avalanche, just like Jack Armstrong, dodged several diving tacklers, and unloaded a touchdown pass that won the game.

Except, however, for the fact that James Street, the Texas quarterback, soured the All-American story by changing the plot (or maybe Street was Jack Armstrong?) and one-upping Theismann with the very best play of the game a little later—a 4th down pass to Trusty Cotton Speyrer that set up the winning touchdown that really won the game.

THE LONGHORNS couldn't really lose, after all. With names like Cotton Speyrer and Slick Street and Ted Koy, it just sounds like you have to win. And don't forget the coach with the regal-sounding name of a winner, Darrell Royal.

Maybe Ara's name is too long.

Figure 15–14. Is the standing headline (Sports in Life-Land) necessary on this attractive page?

Subscription drive begins today at German Valley

GERMAN VALLEY – Students of the German Valley community officially opened the annual subscription drive today. The contest is open to all first through eighth graders of the area.

The youth may solicit the community for subscriptions to SCOPE and in turn receive commission for each subscription collected.

A bonus is available to the four top salesmen of the drive. Canvassing of the village will be Oct. 2 through Friday, Oct. 23. Subscription blanks may be picked up after school Friday at the home of German Valley Correspondent Mrs. Theresa Koehn.

Money for the subscriptions may be turned in at any time, but the receipt slips must ac-company the money. Commission will be paid upon receipt of the subscription money.

RULES

1. Students in the German Valley grade school and seventh and eighth grades are eligible to sell subscriptions to SCOPE from Oct. 2-23.

2. SCOPE sells for $5 per year for subscribers in Stephenson, Ogle and Winnebago counties and $7 per year for subscribers outside these three counties, unless they receive their mail from either of these three county post offices.

A special student subscription is offered for those away at college. This nine-month subscription is $4.

3. Each subscription sold will bring the salesman a 50 cent commission. This commission will be paid when the student turns in the subscription to Mrs. Koehn.

Prize money of $10; $7.50; $5; and $2.50 will be paid the top four salesmen of the drive.

4. Each subscription turned in must be marked either new or renewal. The cmplete name of the subscriber should be printed clearly on the stub. If a current SCOPE subscriber's renewal date is not until Jan. 1971, another subscription will extend the date to Jan. 1972.

5. The drive will close Friday, Oct. 23. Subscriptions will be accepted through Friday even-ing, but after this time any money turned in will not be eligible for a commission.

6. Each student selling a subscription has cards they will leave with the residents indicating they have solicited that particular house. This will avoid the confusion of having more than one student at anyone's home during the drive.

7. Students are asked to be sure to write their name on the stubs which are turned into Mrs. Koehn on the blank line which calls for the solicitor's name.

8. More blanks may be secured at any time at the home of Mrs. Koehn. There is no limit as to how many subscriptions a student may sell.

Figure 15–15. Boxes showing rounded corners. [*Courtesy Scope Newspaper, Van Sickle's Associated Publishers, Inc., Durand, Illinois.*]

Magazine Editing

The Sunday Special

For six days a week the staff of a metropolitan daily writes, edits, assembles and produces the daily paper. Then on the seventh day the giant emerges, the marvel of American journalism. This mighty tome is crammed with news and news summaries, interpretives and features, sports, business and finance, real estate, comics, classified and display advertising, advertising supplements and magazines.

Advertising probably claims 50 to 60 per cent of the Sunday paper's space. News and editorials, including interpretives and columns, may take roughly one fourth of the remaining space and magazine supplements nearly one half.

Unlike its daily counterpart, the Sunday edition has been days or weeks in the making. A closing deadline of four weeks before publication date is not unusual for a four-color rotogravure magazine page. Letterpress supplements may have a closing deadline of about a week.

Supplement sections have to be printed before the final run of the spot news, sports and markets. At one time some metropolitan dailies predated the Sunday edition. That is, they printed the entire Sunday paper in the middle of the week for delivery to outlying areas on Saturday or Sunday. Today, most run-of-press supplements have a one-week deadline. They are printed on the Friday before delivery.

Even with automation and high-speed presses, the production of the big Sunday edition is a week-long process involving the early closing of as many pages as possible. Copy for the Sunday paper bears the Sunday stamp and gets edited along with the regular daily copy. Copy for the supplements bears the name of the supplement and the date.

One of the gems of the Sunday paper is the locally edited magazine, especially those printed by rotogravure. These magazines differ from the oldtime Sunday supplement, started shortly after the Civil War, in that they no longer aim to startle and titillate or to concern themselves with the famous and the infamous. Instead, today's magazine seeks to educate as well as to entertain and to portray real people close to the readers.

Although this weekly supplement is an integral part of the newspaper, it is distinctly a magazine. As described by Derick Daniels, executive editor of the Detroit Free Press, in *The Bulletin of the American Society of Newspaper Editors* (June 1, 1968), "It is built like a magazine, printed like a magazine and lies around the house like a magazine." It may be identified with its parent newspaper but it has a style and personality of its own.

The Sunday magazine is more carefully designed and edited than the hastily prepared news sections. And because readers tend to judge it as a magazine and not as just another section of the newspaper, the magazine editor is compelled to follow exacting standards of magazine presentation.

Although some newspaper magazines exhibit provincialism in both content and presentation, more are demonstrating that readers in all regions have common interests in topics such as medicine, science, psychiatry, economics, ecology and religion. Almost any topic may be associated in some manner with a particular area.

For example, why would the Denver *Post's Empire Magazine,* which bills itself as the voice of the Rocky Mountain empire, feature a story on the great Alaskan oil rush? Because the oil rush in Alaska has some elements in common with the gold rush, a part of the heritage of the mountain states. Also, many of these states are engaged in the exploration and production of oil, especially Colorado, Wyoming and Utah with their oil shale deposits. Anyway, this particular story happened by chance. A free-lance photographer had brought in striking photos he had taken on a trip to the frozen North Slope of Alaska. But without an accompanying story the editor could not use the pictures. Then a professional writer offered a story based on material he had collected in the same area. The result was a well-written and well-illustrated piece for *Empire* readers.

Writing that goes beyond the reach of the routine feature writer and pictures that surpass those shot by a harried news photographer have made the newspaper magazine a favorite with readers. One survey has shown that 59 per cent of the women and 48 per cent of the men read the average inside page of a local magazine section, even topping the readership for a nationally syndicated supplement distributed with the same papers.

The Editing Process

A magazine format does not necessarily make a magazine. Some newspapermen who have taken over the job of editing a Sunday magazine or an independent magazine fail to produce a good magazine because newspaper techniques differ from magazine techniques, especially in focus and style, headlines, use of white space, color and typography. Even display advertising may not be the same in newspapers as it is in magazines.

Unless an editor is also an artist he cannot hope to produce a superior publication. Magazine editing is essentially a joint endeavor, with the editor providing editorial excellence and the artist creating the visual image.

Front pages of daily newspapers look distressingly alike. But the magazine comes in a distinctive wrapper or cover that reflects the nature of the publication, stresses a seasonal activity or merely directs readers to the "goodies" inside the magazine.

News, as we have seen, may be presented in many styles, but usually the traditional format of the summarized lead with details in descending order of significance prevails in the news department. In a magazine the space is likewise limited, but the writing style is more relaxed, more narrative and more personal. The pace of the magazine piece may be slower but certainly not less dramatic than the news story. Following is the beginning of a magazine feature (Paul Friggens, "The Great Alaska Oil Rush," Denver *Post Empire* Magazine, June 8, 1969, p. 12):

> The north coast of Alaska, that 1,000-mile-wide, 150-mile-deep plain that slopes from the Brooks Range into the Arctic Ocean, has long repelled even the hardiest of men.
>
> In winter, its killing cold plunges to 65 degrees below zero, and the whole land is locked in ice. In summer, thaws turn the flat, featureless tundra into a spongy, mosquito-infested quagmire of shallow lakes and streams.
>
> Yet, today, men are rushing into this "desert of the North" just as they rushed into the gold fields of the Klondike in 1896.

Not until later in the story does the angle that normally would be in the lead of a news story appear:

> For here in this deadly land lies what may be the biggest, most exciting oil field ever discovered in North America—a find of far-reaching significance not only to the United States but to the entire world.

So rigid are the style requirements of some magazine editors that they lean heavily on staff writers, use staff writers to re-shape free-lance material or buy only from free-lancers who demonstrate they are acquainted with the magazine's requirements. Still, Sunday magazines may get more than half their material from free-lancers, a greater volume than is procured by the news sections.

Free-lance photographers likewise seek out the Sunday magazine market. One magazine editor remarked, "An exciting roto works like a magnet, drawing in talented free-lance contributors you never realized existed."

Article Headings

A newspaper uses illustrations to focus the reader's attention to a page. It relies on the headline to lure him into the story. But in a magazine the whole page—headline, pictures, placement—is designed to stop the reader in his tracks. He may get part of the story from a big dramatic picture before he ever sees the head. It is the combination of elements that must make the reader say to himself, "I wonder what this is all about."

The magazine editor is not confined to a few standardized typefaces for headings. He may select, instead, a face that will help depict the mood of the story. Nor is he required to put the heading over the story. He may place it in the middle, at the bottom or on one side of the page.

The heading may occupy the whole page or only part of a page. It may be accented in a reverse plate or in some other manner. It may be overprinted on the illustration. More often it will be below the illustration rather than above it. Almost invariably it is short, not more than one line. Frequently it is a mere tag or teaser. A subtitle then gives the details:

Oil from the Heart Tree
**An exotic plant from Old China produces
a cash crop for the South**

I Can HEAR Again!
**This was the moment of joy, the rediscovering
of sound: Whispers . . . rustle of a sheet . . .
ticking of a clock**

The Pleasure of Milking a Cow
**Coming to grips with the task at hand
can be a rewarding experience,
especially on cold mornings**

Industry is finding
that it pays to rely on
Models of Efficiency

Magazine Layouts

Type and illustrations, or gray and black blocks, are basic elements in newspaper page layout. In magazine layout a third block—white—is used. To the magazine art editor, white space is not waste space but rather a means of emphasizing other elements.

He may use space generously around headings, between text and illustrations and around illustrations. He deliberately plans

---

Magazine Editing

to get white space on the outside of the pages. To gain extra space, he may bleed the illustrations.

Some stories are told effectively in text alone; others are told dramatically in pictures. The ideal is a combination of text and pictures, with the emphasis depending on the quality of the illustrations or the significance of the text. A picture's value, says one editor, is best exploited when it sweeps the reader rhythmically into the text. Too often, the story is adequate but good art is lacking, thus robbing the story of its dramatic appeal and producing a dull page of straight text.

A magazine page usually has these elements: (1) at least one dominant picture; (2) a title, preferably with a subtitle; and (3) a block of text, usually beginning with a typographical device that will compel the reader's attention to the opening of the story. The device may be a dingbat such as a black square followed by a few words in all-capital letters. Or it may be an initial capital letter, either an inset initial (its top lined up with the top of the indented small letter) or an upright or stick-up initial (the bottom of the initial lined up with the bottom of the other letters in the line).

Simplicity is the keynote in effective page layout. An easy, modular arrangement is more likely to attract readers than a tricky makeup with odd-shaped art and a variety of typefaces. Illustrations need not be in the same dimensions, but they should be in pleasing geometric proportions. Margins should be uniform or at least give the effect of being uniform. Usually the widest margin is at the bottom of the page, the next widest at the side, the third at the top and the narrowest at the inside or gutter. The content of the page is thus shoved slightly upward, emphasizing the eye level or optical center of a rectangle. The outside margin is larger than the gutter because the latter, in effect, is a double margin.

Kenneth B. Butler, author of a series of practical handbooks (published by Butler Typo-Design Research Center in Mendota, Ill.) treating the creative phases of magazine typography and layout, advises layout editors to touch each margin at least once, regardless of whether illustrations are used. He contends that the eye is so accustomed to the regular margin that even where the margin is touched only once, an imaginary margin is immediately formed by this treatment. If the illustration bleeds off the page, the margin on the bleed side may be widened to give more impact to the bleed device.

The art director must know the position of the page—whether left, right or double spread—and whether the page contains advertising. It would also help him if he knew the content and appearance of the advertising on the page to avoid embarrassing juxtaposition. If he is working on a one-page layout he should know the content and appearance of the facing page.

He tries to visualize what the page is supposed to say. From experience he has developed a feel for the magazine page, knowing in his mind's eye how it will look. The beginner may have to use trial and error to find an appropriate design. He may, for example, cut out pieces from construction paper to represent the black blocks, then juggle these blocks until he gets a usable design.

Layout is a means rather than an end in itself. If the reader becomes aware of the layout the chances are the layout is bad.

One danger most art directors seek to avoid is cluttering. This occurs when too many illustrations are attempted on the same page, when the pages are crowded because of lack of spacing or uneven spacing or when too many elements—dingbats, subtitles, boldface type—make the page appear busy. The primary goals of layout are to catch and direct the reader's attention and to make the pages easy to read.

Copy Fitting

Widths of magazine columns may vary with the number, shape and size of the ads or the size and shape of the illustrations. It is not unusual for a magazine story to be strung over four pages in four different widths. The editor must be able to estimate whether the story will fill despite these type changes.

The most accurate method of determining copy length is by counting characters in the manuscript. The following steps are used:

Count the number of typewritten characters, including spaces between words and for indentions, in an average line of the manuscript. An average line can be determined visually or it can be measured by placing a ruler over most of the line endings and drawing a line down these endings.

Multiply the number of lines of copy by the number of characters to the average typewritten line. A line extending half the width of the line is counted as a full line.

Consult a type book to determine the characters per pica in a given body size and typeface. For example, Bodoni Book in Linotype in 10-point size gives 2.75 characters per pica. If the type line is to be 20 picas wide, then 55 typewritten characters will fill one line of type.

Divide the number of lines of type by the number of type lines per column inch. If the type is set in 10 point with 2-point spacing, the number of type lines per column inch is determined by dividing 72 by 12. This will show the number of column inches the manuscript will occupy.

The same figure can be obtained by multiplying the number of type lines by the point size (including leading) of the typeface, then dividing the total points by 72 to find column inches. To convert into pica depth, the point total is divided by 12 (points per pica) rather than by 72.

For fitting copy into a specified space, the method can be used in reverse. Suppose the space to be filled is 6 inches deep and 24 picas wide. The type is to be 12 point. The type chart shows 2.45 characters per pica or 59 characters to the 24-pica line.

Twelve-point type set 6 inches deep requires 36 type lines. Multiplying 59 by 36 gives 2,124 characters. If the manuscript lines average 65 characters, then 32 lines of the manuscript will be needed.

A simpler method can be used. Set the typewriter stops at 59 characters and retype 36 lines of the manuscript. Some editors used ruled sheets so that for a given typeface, size and measure the copy can be sent to the printer typed with the proper number of characters to the line. The proof will run practically line for line with the copy.

Placement of Advertising

The usual newspaper practice is to pyramid the ads on the right of the page. In a magazine the ads generally go on the outside of the pages or may appear on both outside and inside, leaving the *well* for editorial copy. The ads need not restrict editorial display, especially if the well is on a double spread.

On magazines where the advertising manager makes up the dummy of ad placement, there is a give and take between ad manager and editor. The editor may want to start a story in a certain part of the magazine, but there is a two-column ad on the most likely page. The editor then asks the ad manager if the ad can be moved to another page where perhaps another story can end.

Scheduling and Dummying

No story, heading or picture will leave the editor's desk until it has been properly slugged and scheduled. Sluglines relay information such as name of publication, the date the story is to be used, story identification and the number of the page on which the story is to appear. Other instructions placed on the copy may include the set (width of type line in picas), body type size and typographic indicators such as initial capitals or italics.

The headline copy likewise carries all the information needed for the desired style, size and set and a line to match the headline with the story.

Illustrations contain special instructions for the roto cameraman for effects such as cropping and mortising. Usually the photos are numbered consecutively through a story and also carry the number of the page on which the photo is to appear.

The schedule is simply a record to remind the editor of the copy that has been edited and sent on for processing. An important item in the schedule is a line showing the date and time the material was delivered to roto (Figure 16–1).

As he starts to plan for an edition, the editor first obtains a schedule for the issue, showing the pages on which ads have been dummied and whether the ads are in monotone, duotone or full-color. This schedule then tells the editor how much space he has available and the likely color positions. If the editor has control of the ad dummy he simply receives a schedule of the ads or he may receive ad proofs.

EMPIRE MAGAZINE   ISSUE <u>JULY 27</u>   PAGES _____

FORM	PAGE	SLUG	TO ROTO	TIME
	1	COVER	7-3	
	2	POST TIME-LETTERS		
	3	FRITO PG 4/C		
	4	CAROUSEL	7-7	3⁰⁰
	5	MAY CO.		
	6	TOSHI	7-7	2⁰⁰
	7	"	7-7	2⁰⁰
	8	GHOST	7-8	9⁰⁰
	9		7-8	9⁰⁰
	10	MAGEE PG 4/C		
	11	MAGEE PG 4/C		
	12	GHOST	7-8	9⁰⁰
	13	SLEEP PG 4/C		
	14	LOMBARDI "	7-7	2⁰⁰
	15	HOMESTEAD PG 4/C		
32	16	DIGEST	7-7	3⁰⁰
33	17		7-7	3⁰⁰
34	18		7-7	3⁰⁰
35	19		7-7	3⁰⁰
36	20	DENVER DRY 20-32		
37	21			
38	22		7-8	8⁰⁰
39	23		7-8	8⁰⁰
40	24	HOUSE DOC	7-3	2³⁰
41	25	"	7-7	2⁰⁰
42	26	LIBRARY	7-7	2⁰⁰
43	27	"	7-7	2⁰⁰
44	28	FOOD	7-3	2⁰⁰
45	29	FOOD	7-3	2⁰⁰
46	30	JOHN	7-11	9⁰⁰
47	31			
48	32			
49	33	DIGEST	7-8	2⁰⁰
50	34	MOUSE	7-8	2⁰⁰
51	35	"	7-8	2⁰⁰
52	36	MAY CO PG 4/C		
53	37	MAY CO PG 4/C		
54	38	DANCERS	7-8	2⁰⁰
55	39	"	7-8	2⁰⁰
56	40			
57	41			
58	42			
59	43			
60	44			
61	45			
62	46			
63	47			
64	48			

Figure 16–1. A Sunday magazine schedule.

Closing deadlines regulate the priority of editing. A story may start toward the end of a run of monotone but spill over to a four-color page. This means the story will have to make the earlier deadline of the four-color pages rather than the later deadline of the monotone pages (Figure 16–2).

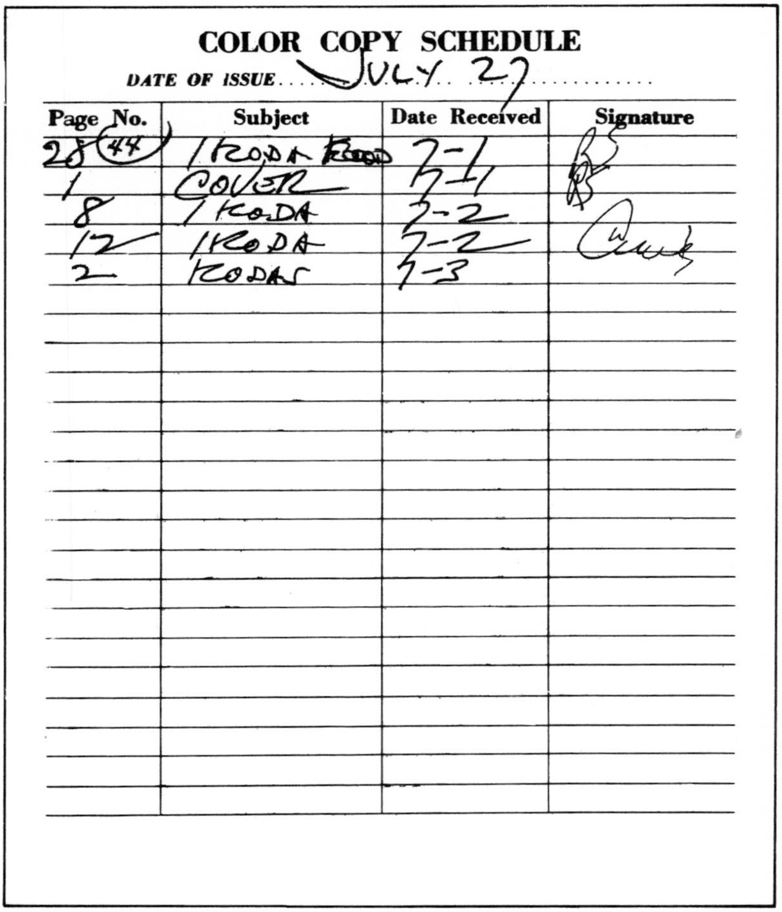

Figure 16–2. A color schedule for a Sunday magazine.

This would suggest that the editor should know something about imposition, or the arrangement of pages for binding. This means the way the pages are positioned on the imposing stone or on the reproduction proof and not the way they will appear on the printed sheet. The printer can give the editor the imposition pattern or the editor can diagram the imposition himself provided he knows whether pages in the form are upright or oblong.

For a 16-page form, upright and printed work and turn, the editor makes three right-angle folds and numbers the pages. This will show page 1 opposite page 8, 16 opposite 9, 13 opposite 12, 4 opposite 5. The remaining eight pages will be in this order—7 and 2, 10 and 15, 11 and 14, 6 and 3. For an oblong form, printed work and turn, the pattern is 1 and 16, 4 and 13, 5 and and 12, 8 and 9, 15 and 2, 14 and 3, 11 and 6, 10 and 7. Again, the editor may make his own pattern by making three parallel or accordion folds and one right-angle fold. Or he may use the following formula: the size of the book, plus one page. Thus, in a 16-page section, page 4 is opposite 13 (17 minus 4) (Figure 16–3).

If the editor has a spread story, he tries to get the pages on the fewest forms possible to avoid tying up too many forms with one story. Knowing imposition also can help guide him in using color. An ad in one color on one form invites the editor to use color also if he desires.

Page layout usually starts with the preparation of a thumbnail or miniature dummy. The rough sketch shows pages blocked off in rectangles of facing pages (Figure 16–4).

The thumbnail dummy serves as the artist's working plan. It gives him the first image of the total publication. Using the thumbnail as a guide, the artist is ready to sketch the layout on full-sized sheets (Figure 16–5a, b, c).

First he receives proofs on newsprint for copy checking and correction. These are returned to the composing room for changes. Then the art director receives corrected proofs on slick paper, which he uses for the paste-up. All the elements in the paste-up are arranged precisely as they will appear in print. In a sense, the art director assumes the function of makeup editor and in arranging the proved material on the page makes sure flaws in magazine makeup are avoided. Among such flaws are leaving a widow or lone word at the top of the column, placing subheads near the feet of the columns or in parallel positions in columns or having the last line on the right-hand page of a continued story end with a period.

When the paste-up is completed it goes to the makeup department where a layout man strips in negatives of the page materials. Generally the art director insists on inspecting page proofs to be sure his makeup pattern has been followed.

On some magazines the editors receive duplicate sets of corrected proofs. One set is used to check further for errors; the other is used in a paste-up. Galley proofs used for this paste-up bear numbers on each paragraph corresponding with the galley number. This helps the makeup man in the printing department locate the proper galley.

Magazine Production

A magazine editor relies on an artist to help him attain editorial excellence. By the same token, he relies on a production expert, usually a printer, to help him produce the best possible publication within his budget.

The editor is responsible for providing the printer with complete specifications of the magazine, not only the size of the publication, the number of pages and the press run but the use and placement of color, the number and size of the illustrations,

Figure 16–3. Imposition pattern for a 32-page section in 4-page forms. The pattern is obtained by gathering four quarter-sheets and making two right-angle folds. The facing pages total 33 (pages in the section plus one).

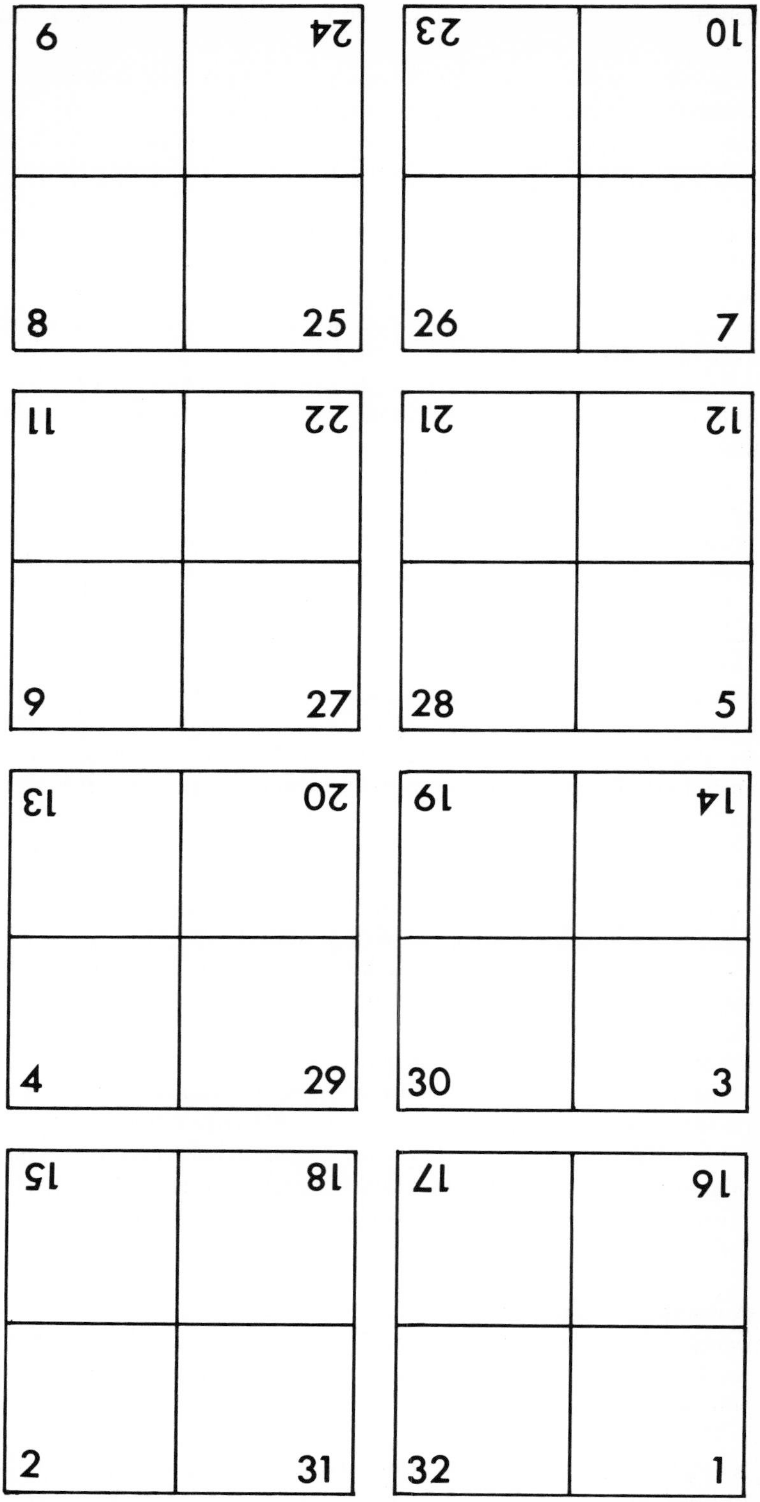

6	24	23	10
8	25	26	7

11	22	21	12
9	27	28	5

13	20	19	14
4	29	30	3

15	18	17	16
2	31	32	1

Figure 16–4 [*opposite*]. A sample of the thumbnail dummy roughing out the first pages of a 48-page magazine.

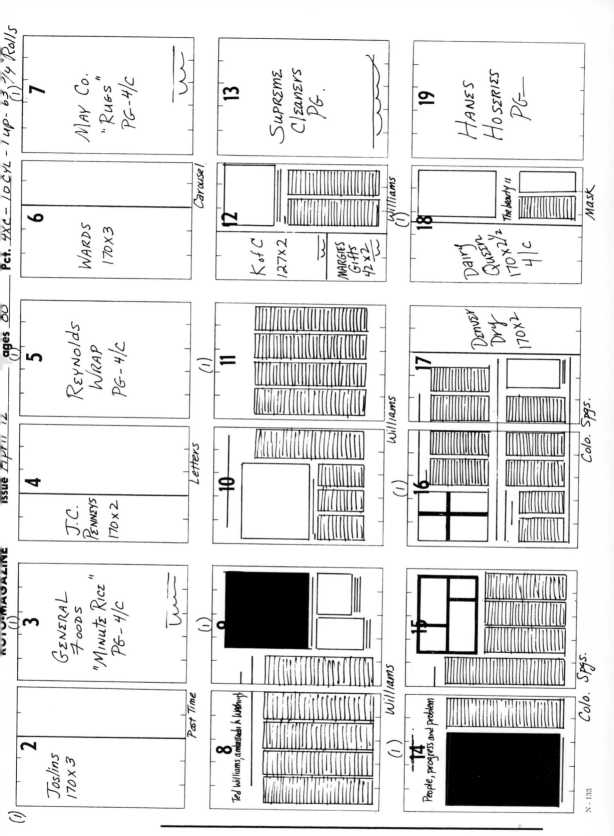

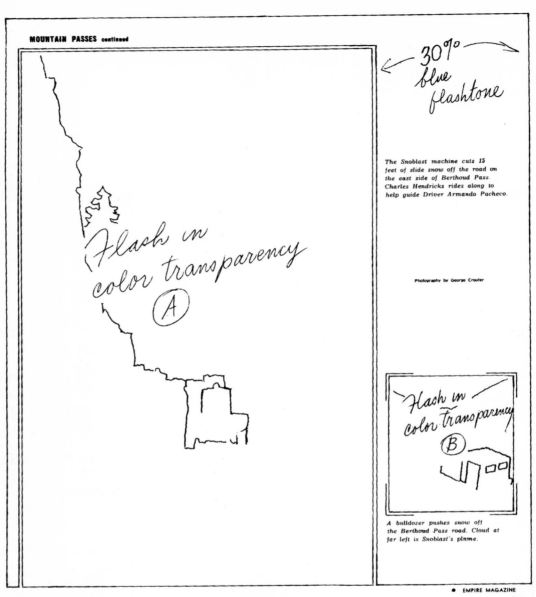

Figure 16–5a. Completed paste-up is ready for the roto cameraman. Note the instructions for flashing-in unattached photographs and for flash-tones (Figure 16–5b). "Flashing-in" involves a combination of line and tone work, created for double-exposing the negative or positive.

the type area, size of type and any items that will require special handling.

The editor can save money, and make his printer happy, by giving clear and adequate instructions, presenting clean copy, editing the copy thoroughly rather than making changes in proofs, reading and returning promptly all proofs, meeting copy deadlines and giving the printer time to do good-quality work.

The Art of Editing

SOLID

65%

50%

30%

20%

FLASH TONES

Figure 16–5b.

The editor on a tight budget would do well to consult the printer before he attempts special effects. He may assume that bleed pages entail no extra expense. They do. For a booklet 8½ × 11 inches, the recommended sheet size stock is 35 × 45 inches. This size will provide 32 pages to each sheet or 16,000 pages to the ream. This size of sheet, however, leaves only 1 inch on each side for trimming and therefore cannot be used for bleed pages. Stock in size 25 × 38 inches allows 3 inches of trim on one side and 4 inches on the other. But each sheet of this size produces only 16 pages of 8½ × 11, or 8,000 pages to a ream. One thousand copies of a 32-page booklet cut from 35 × 45 stock require two reams. If 100-pound paper is used, the weight of the two reams is 332 pounds. One thousand copies of the same booklet cut from 25 × 38 stock require four reams or 400 pounds. Because of the extra stock weight and other factors in making bleed pages, the printer will have to increase the cost. His printing catalog advises him to add $5 per bleed page.

Or an editor may take a fancy to "inconsequentials" such as lines of small capitals, numbered lines, various indentions and initial capitals. Fine. But he should know that such fancies are realized at double the regular composition cost.

Items in printing costs vary with the printing process, but among the basic ones are stock, composition, plate and camera work, imposition, lockup, makeready, press run, ink, folding, gathering, stapling and trimming.

Stock

Paper comes in various sizes, weights and textures. Use of the stock and its appearance determine the class of paper used. One grade may be used for the cover, another for inside pages. One grade may be preferred for color, another if the pages are in black and white. Almost any grade of paper can be used in letter-

---

Magazine Editing

PAGE 9 (29) Roto-Mag Issue AVIATION Paste-up ______ Form No. ______ Due at Plant ______

SLUG ______ Monotone ______ 4-Color ______ 2-Color ______

world

pleasure of it when I'm on the ground. And there is a cute little farm set, complete with the farmhouse, barn and outbuildings, a mirror for a pond and a nice assortment of animals. There's the farmer's truck and tractor, and look, he drives a school bus, too. He has plowed his fields, and the pasture land is starting to green up. The ground shows through in spots, like a carpet that is wearing out.

Here comes a train winding through the hills of a toy display in a department store. Will that little car on the road around the bend stop in time? Yes, the crossing gate is going down. At a little country airport a wee plane, like ours, is landing, and there's another one approaching in back of him—much too close. That second plane should have waited just a little longer, but it's all right now; they've both landed safely.

There's so much to oversee from up here. I just can't do everything at once. Now look at that factory belching reddish-brown smoke into the air. The sky ahead is completely filled with this ominous cloud. We'll have to do something about that. That has no place in this sparkling world of mine.

A lovely lake is nestled in the hills with some sailboats skimming over it, their wakes trailing through the water like knives cutting through the frosting on a cake. And back in that sheltered inlet is a fisherman, perhaps with a load of microscopic fish. Where have I seen that campground before, with the tents scattered through the woods where the little creek tumbles into the lake? Why, I know, that's the model Indian village we made for a display in grade school.

This miniature world of mine has everything you could possibly want. Wouldn't it be a delight to go down there and live? Back on earth again, the vantage point will be lower, but may I keep these pictures in my mind, and may I keep this joy in my heart.

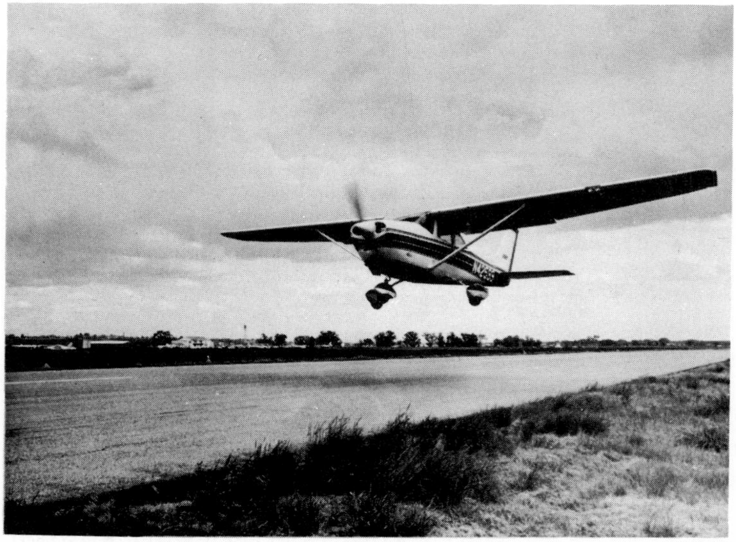

Orin A. Sealy

There's really no place in my personal kingdom for an ominous cloud. But that'll change soon.

(a)
RODA

Les Southern

There's a cute little farm set, complete with farmhouse and barn, and a mirror for a pond.

The Denver Post •

9

Figure 16–5c. Full-sized page layout.

press if halftones are not required. In offset printing the grade must be designed to accommodate moisture and other problems peculiar to offset printing. In roto printing the selection is determined by the paper's ability to absorb the large amount of ink required in that process.

The magazine editor is concerned with only three of the many classifications of stock—newsprint, book and cover. Newsprint does not necessarily mean cheap paper. A good grade of newsprint takes halftones up to 85-line screen and in roto up to 150-screen. It is adequate for run-of-press color and ideal for full-color roto work.

The surface smoothness of book paper is determined by the degree of calendering or smoothing during the paper-making process. Antique or eggshell has a minimum of calendering—hence its resemblance to paper used in the early days of printing. More extensive calendering is used on machine finish, giving a smoother surface. English finish, next in the degree of calendering, is used primarily in letterpress. Supercalendered paper has the slickest surface of the uncoated book stocks.

Coating is a supplementary process giving the paper a surface suitable for fine-screened halftones. Coated finishes range from dull-coated, which is smooth but not glossy, to grades of glossy-coated, usually called enamel finish.

Book paper ranges in sizes from $8\frac{1}{2} \times 11$ to 52×76 inches and in weights from 30 to 150 pounds. Weight of paper is calculated on the basis size. Book paper basis is 25×38 inches. This means that if a ream (500 sheets) of 25×38 inches weighs 100 pounds, the paper is 100-pound weight. The basis size of cover stock is 20×26 inches and for newsprint, 24×36. Most newsprint is 32 pounds basic weight. The different weights of basic sheet sizes may cause confusion. The basic sheet size for bond paper, for instance, is 17×22 inches. But 20-pound bond is not the equivalent of 20-pound book. Each sheet of 20-pound bond would be the equivalent of approximately 50-pound book because of the differences in the basic sheet sizes.

Paper may be ordered in any of several packing units, but not all papers are sold in the same units. Common units are package, ream, carton or box of one or several reams, case (approximately 500 pounds) and, when handled by skids, ton. These units are for sheet stock. For web presses, paper is ordered by the roll. The editor can effect a substantial saving in paper costs if he can anticipate his needs and have the printer order the stock in carload lots, usually 35,000 to 45,000 pounds.

The editor should remember that he will pay a premium for broken lots of paper. If his publication requires $24\frac{1}{2}$ reams he will be charged for 25 reams.

Cost of stock is based on the total pounds required for the job at so much a pound depending on the grade required. An arbitrary figure is 25 cents a pound in sheet sizes, but it varies with the quantity required.

Composition   The cost of setting type can be the most illusive of all printing costs. To a printer, ordinary straight matter means rapid, uniform composition without special attention to spacing. To an editor it might mean merely uniform type margins and the absence of tabular matter. Type areas are not easily converted from inches to picas because the scales are not compatible. A type line 2⅛ inches is slightly less than 13 picas.

The most common way of measuring type is by the em. Ems may be determined by several methods. One is to multiply the width of the type area in picas by the length of the type area in picas. This gives the number of picas in 12-point type (because a pica is 12 points). To determine the ems in a size other than 12 point, a factor must be used. For 10-point type the factor is 1.44. The ems in 10 point are found by multiplying the ems in 12 point by 1.44. This will produce an extended decimal, which is taken to the next full em.

Another way is to multiply the width of the type line in picas by 12 and divide by the size of type. This gives the ems for each line of type.

Still another method is to measure the width of the type line in points and divide by the size of type. This also gives the ems for each line of type.

Example: The type area is 24 picas wide and 42 picas deep and is to be in 10-point type. Here are three ways to find the number of ems:

24 times 42 equals 1008 times 1.44 equals 1451.52 or 1452 ems.

24 times 12 equals 288 divided by 10 equals 28.8.
7 inches (42 picas) times 7.2 (10-point lines per inch) equals 50.4. 50.4 times 28.8 equals 1451.52 or 1452 ems.

4 inches (24 picas) times 72 (points per inch) equals 288 divided by 10 equals 28.8. 28.8 times 50.4 equals 1451.52 or 1452 ems.

Another method is ems per square inch. In the preceding example, inches would be used instead of picas or points. The type area, therefore, would be 4 times 7 or 28 square inches. The number of ems in 10 point would be 51.84 per square inch or 1452 (1451.52) ems in 28 square inches.

The ems measurement is used primarily in hot metal composition. It is based on the number of ems an average typesetter can set in an hour. Much of the hot metal composition is being replaced by cold type or type produced photographically.

Although cold-type composition is faster and more economical than hot metal typesetting, both processes require a unit system to determine costs.

Some printers gauge composition on three scales, the equivalents of 10 point, 8 point and 6 point. The lower the point size, the greater the number of ems per line. Ordinary straight matter and medium display lines are evaluated as 10-point composition. Lines requiring more attention to spacing and heavier display lines are valued the same as 8-point composition. The 6-point value is used for the most intricate composition. Composition in sizes larger than 10 point is counted as 10-point composition.

Imposition, Lockup and Makeready

Cost of imposition varies with the page content. If the page contains but one illustration and a cutline, the imposition or makeup is negligible. If the page contains elements such as wrap-around type, tilted illustrations, boxes, borders, bleeds, mortises and the like, the imposition is considerable. Imposition costs are based on the time required for each form. In offset makeup the artist pastes up the form with reproduction proofs. When the page is completed, a negative is made and the plate is ready for the press.

Letterpress requires two additional steps, lockup and makeready. The form must be positioned in the chase, then secured so that nothing drops out or slips out of place when the forms are moved. By pulling a form proof, the lockup man can note the light and dark areas on the pages. He builds up the lighter areas by using makeready paper and thus assures uniform impression. Press makeready has to do with getting the presses ready.

Other Cost Items

Press-run costs reflect the time required to print the job. Here the printing process can determine the speed of the press run. Rotogravure is the fastest, then offset and finally letterpress. But gravure printing is limited to plants with roto presses and generally is more expensive than the other processes. Letterpress and offset costs differ primarily according to the number of illustrations used, with offset the cheaper when the ratio of illustrations to type is high and when the press run is higher.

The cost of ink depends on the total amount needed and this varies with the grade of paper, the printing process and other things. Tint blocks and zinc etchings, for example, require extra ink. Cost of color ink includes, in addition to the ink itself, the cost of washing up rollers and fountains. If color is applied by sizing or by metallic powders, printers may charge the equivalent of two extra colors.

Printing in color entails the separation of the colors as well as plates or negatives for each color and an additional expense in makeup and press work. In letterpress each color requires a separate form and this results in four times the cost of each lockup and makeready.

Final items in the production process are folding, gathering, stitching (the conventional saddle stitch for medium publications; the side stitch for bulkier ones) and trimming.

A printer can use the items listed to estimate production costs or he may refer to his bible, the printing catalog, which incorporates the basic items into unit rates depending on the number of copies required. The unit rate lists page prices in dollars and then shows adjustments in prices the printer must make for extra-heavy composition and the like.

The rate book guides the printer in arriving at a reasonable and profitable cost figure. It does not insure a uniform charge. Five printers can use the same printing catalog and quote the customer five different estimates. Or one printer may quote one price during a slack period and another during a rush period. Any job that requires overtime will be priced accordingly. The customer's choice will not always be the printer who quotes the lowest price but rather the printer who can turn out high-quality work and who will deliver the printed product on schedule.

17

Broadcast News Editing

Most of the techniques suggested for the presentation of news in newspapers apply as well to news by radio and television. Those responsible for news copy for any medium must have good news judgment, a feeling for an audience and the ability to handle the language.

Broadcast news differs from other news types in two major respects. Broadcasting must aim at the majority audience and cannot, as newspapers can, serve the interests of the minority. And because enough items must be packed into the newscast to give listeners and viewers the feeling they are getting a summary of the big and significant news of the moment, condensation is required.

A newspaper offers its readers a 1,000-word story, then lets the readers decide how much of the story, if any, they want to read. The broadcast audience has no such choice. If too much time is given to items in which listeners and viewers have only a mild interest, they can turn the dial.

Following are wire service accounts of the same story, one intended for the newspaper members, the other for radio and television stations:

MASSENA, N.Y. (AP)—Unarmed Canadian police scuffled with some 100 Mohawk Indians today and broke an Indian blockade of the international bridge that goes through Mohawk territory in linking the United States and Canada.

The Indians put up the human and automobile blockade after Canadian government officials refused to stop levying customs duties on Indians—duties the Indians say are illegal under the Jay Treaty of 1794.

The Indians had brought 25 automobiles into line at the center of the bridge linking the United States and Canada, and Indian women had thrown themselves in front of police tow trucks to hinder the clearing of the roadway.

There were no reports of serious injury. Forty-eight Indians were arrested—including most leaders of the protest—and taken into Canadian custody by police on Cornwall Island.

A spokesman for the Indians called for the other five nations of the Iroquois Confederacy to join the protest Thursday.

The Indians went on the blockade warpath after the Canadian government refused Tuesday to stop customs duties on Indians who live on the St. Regis Reservation, that includes parts of the United States and Canada.

Scattered fighting and shoving broke out among the Mohawks and police when officers tried to move in to clear away the automobile blockade. One automobile and two school buses were allowed over the international span around noon.

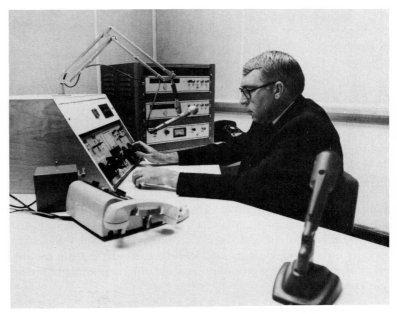

Figure 17–1. From this position the newscaster plays back his own cartridge tapes and can make use of telephone or two way radio reports. [*Photograph courtesy of KLZ-TV, Denver, Colorado.*]

At least 50 words of this story might be trimmed by a copyeditor to make the story tighter and to eliminate the repetition. The story was pared to about 70 words for the radio wire roundup item:

(MASSENA, NEW YORK)—UNARMED CANADIAN POLICE HAVE ARRESTED 48 MOHAWK INDIANS. THE INDIANS HAD FORMED A HUMAN WALL AND BLOCKED THE INTERNATIONAL BRIDGE LINKING CANADA AND THE UNITED STATES NEAR MASSENA, NEW YORK, TODAY.

The Art of Editing

THE MOHAWKS ARE UP IN ARMS ABOUT CANADA'S INSIS-
TENCE ON COLLECTING CUSTOMS DUTIES FROM INDIANS
TRAVELING TO AND FROM THEIR RESERVATION ON THE
BRIDGE. THEY SAY IT'S A VIOLATION OF THE 1794 JAY TREATY.

As an item in the news summary, it was cut even more:

FORTY-EIGHT INDIANS HAVE BEEN ARRESTED BY CANADIAN
POLICE NEAR THE NEW YORK STATE BORDER. THE INDIANS
BLOCKED THE BRIDGE, WHICH LINKS THE U-S AND CANADA.
THEY CLAIM VIOLATION OF A 1794 TREATY. THE MOHAWKS SAY
THEY PLAN NO BLOCKADE TOMORROW.

News is written and edited so that readers will have no trouble
reading and understanding the item. Broadcast news has to be
written so it can be read fluently by a reporter and so that it
sounds right to the listeners. Broadcast news style must be so
simple that listeners can grasp its meaning immediately. The
language must be such that even casual listeners will feel
compelled to give the story their full attention.

A reader's eyes may on occasion deceive him but not to the
extent that the listener's ears deceive him. If the reader misses
a point while reading he can go over the material again. If he
loses a point in listening to news, he has lost it completely.
All radio-television news manuals caution against clauses,
especially those at the beginning of a sentence and those that
separate subject and predicate. The AP Radio-Television News
Stylebook uses this example: "American Legion Commander
John Smith, son of Senator Tom Smith, died today." Many
listeners will be left with the impression that Senator Tom Smith
died.

The broadcast message is warm and intimate, yet not flip-
pant or crude. The tone is more personal than that of the newspaper story. It suggests, "Here, Mr. Doe, is an item that should
interest you."

The refreshing, conversational style of broadcast news writing
has many virtues that might be studied by all news writers. The
old International News Service was so adept at this style of presentation that a single wire served both newspaper and radio
clients. Radio writing emphasizes plain talk. The newspaper
reporter may want to echo a speaker's words, even in an indirect
quote: "The city manager said his plan will effect a cost reduction at the local government level." Broadcast style calls for
nickel words: "The city manager said his plan will save money
for the city."

The newspaper headline is intended to capture the attention
and interest of news readers. The lead on the broadcast news
story has the same function. First, then, a capsule of the news
item, then the details:

THE F-B-I SAYS THERE WAS AN OVER-ALL 19 PER CENT CRIME
RATE INCREASE THE FIRST MONTHS OF THIS YEAR. AND THE

CRIME WHICH INCREASED THE MOST WAS PURSE-SNATCHING
—UP 42 PER CENT. . . .

THE NEW YORK STOCK MARKET TOOK A SHARP LOSS AFTER
BACKING AWAY FROM AN EARLY RISE. TRADING WAS ACTIVE.
VOLUME WAS 15 (M) MILLION 950-THOUSAND SHARES COM-
PARED WITH 16 (M) MILLION 740-THOUSAND FRIDAY. . . .

The newscast is arranged so that the items fall into a unified
pattern. This may be accomplished by placing related items together or by using transitions that help listeners shift gears.
Such transitions are made with ideas and skillful organization of facts and not with crutch words or phrases. Said UPI,
"Perhaps the most overworked words in radio copy are MEAN-
WHILE, MEANTIME and INCIDENTALLY. Forget them,
especially 'incidentally.' If something is only 'incidental' it has
no place in a tight newscast."

Figure 17–2. In the foreground is the radio news editor's desk, which has
reel-to-reel and cartridge tape recorders available. With this equipment
he can record five telephone lines and two-way radio reports from field
reporters. The two desks facing the television monitors are for the
assignment editor and the producer-director of television news broad-
casts. The four desks in the background are for reporters. Through the
doorway in the far background is the radio recording studio. In the center
of the room is the cutting table and distribution boxes for wire copy.
Teletypes and a facsimile picture machine are at the left. [*Photograph
courtesy of KLZ-TV, Denver, Colorado.*]

Broadcast copy talks. It uses contractions and, if necessary,
fragmentary sentences. It avoids harsh, shrill or hissing sounds
such as those produced in combinations like "Sing a song of

sixpence." It dodges rhyming words that produce a singsong effect when spoken: "The boat passed the light on its way to Wight."

The present tense, when appropriate, or the present perfect tense is used in the broadcast message to create immediacy and freshness and to eliminate repetition of "today." Example:

AN AWESOME WINTER STORM HAS BLANKETED THE ATLANTIC SEABOARD—FROM VIRGINIA TO MAINE—WITH UP TO 20 INCHES OF SNOW. GALE FORCE WINDS HAVE PILED UP SIX-FOOT DRIFTS IN VIRGINIA, BRINGING TRAFFIC THERE AND IN WEST VIRGINIA TO A VIRTUAL HALT. SCHOOLS IN SIX STATES HAVE BEEN CLOSED.

TRAINS AND BUSES ARE RUNNING HOURS LATE. PENNSYLVANIA AND MASSACHUSETTS HAVE CALLED OUT HUGE SNOW-CLEARING FORCES.

Copy Sources

Copy for the broadcast newsroom comes from the wires of a news-gathering association and from local reporters. The news agencies deliver the news package in these forms:

1. Spot summary, a one-sentence item:

(NEW YORK)—NEW YORKERS FACE A HEALTH CRISIS BECAUSE OF COLD WEATHER, A FLU EPIDEMIC AND A STRIKE OF FUEL OIL DRIVERS.

2. Five-minute summary:

(NEW YORK)—HIGHER INTEREST RATES FOR LOANS ARE BEGINNING TO FILTER DOWNWARD. THE FEDERAL RESERVE BOARD RAISED ITS RATE TO MEMBER BANKS BY ONE-QUARTER OF ONE PER CENT YESTERDAY. TODAY, MAJOR BANKS REACTED WITH A SIMILAR INCREASE IN THEIR INTEREST RATES TO PRIME BORROWERS LIKE LARGE CORPORATIONS.

THE PRIME INTEREST RATE OF THE BANKS NOW STANDS AT SIX AND THREE-QUARTERS PER CENT—THE HIGHEST EVER.

3. News roundup or expanded summary—This is more detailed than the five-minute summary and is preceded by headlines:

THE U-S SUPREME COURT SAYS DRAFT BOARDS MAY NOT USE SO-CALLED "DELINQUENCY" REGULATIONS TO TAKE AWAY EXEMPTIONS OF YOUNG MEN SHIELDED FROM THE DRAFT BY CONGRESS (SCOTUS-DRAFT).

THE U-S SUPREME COURT SAYS DRAFT BOARDS MAY NOT USE "DELINQUENCY" REGULATIONS TO TAKE AWAY EXEMPTIONS OF DIVINITY STUDENTS AND OTHER YOUNG MEN SHIELDED FROM THE DRAFT BY CONGRESS. THE VOTE WAS SIX TO THREE.

AT THE SAME TIME, THE COURT HELD THAT DRAFT RESISTERS WHO DO NOT HAVE A CONGRESSIONAL EXEMPTION MUST —IN ORDER TO TEST THEIR ONE-A CLASSIFICATION—RISK PROSECUTION ON CHARGES OF DRAFT EVASION.

THE DELINQUENCY RULING WAS GIVEN IN THE CASE OF A MINISTERIAL STUDENT.–DASH–

(HE IS JAMES O—, A STUDENT AT ANDOVER-NEWTON THEOLOGICAL SCHOOL IN NEWTON CENTER, MASSACHUSETTS. O—, IS FROM CHEYENNE, WYOMING. HE IS ONE OF 357 PEOPLE WHO RETURNED THEIR DRAFT CARDS TO THE JUSTICE DEPARTMENT IN A PROTEST IN 1967 AGAINST U-S WAR ACTION IN VIETNAM. THREE WEEKS LATER HE WAS DECLARED A DELINQUENT.)

4. Takeout—This is a detailed, datelined dispatch concerning one subject or event.

5. Spotlights and vignettes—Both are detailed accounts, the latter usually in the form of a feature.

6. Flash—This is seldom used and is restricted to news of the utmost urgency. A flash has no dateline or logotype and is limited to one or two lines. It is intended to alert the editor and is not intended to be broadcast. The flash is followed immediately by a bulletin intended for airing.

7. Bulletin—This is preceded by a five-bell signal. Like the flash, it contains only one or two lines. A one-line bulletin is followed immediately by a standard bulletin giving details.

8. Double-spacers—This indicates a high-priority story but not as urgent as a bulletin. The double-spacing makes the item stand out on the wire and calls the item to the attention of news editors:

URGENT

(WASHINGTON)—THE SUPREME COURT RULED TODAY THAT

DRAFT BOARDS MAY NOT USE SO-CALLED "DELINQUENCY"

REGULATIONS TO TAKE AWAY THE EXEMPTIONS OF DIVINITY

STUDENTS AND GROUPS OF OTHER YOUNG MEN SHIELDED

FROM THE DRAFT BY CONGRESS.

9. Special slugs—These include **AVAILABLE IMMEDIATELY** (corresponds to the budget on the news wire), **NEW TOP, WITH** (or side bar), **SPORTS, WOMEN, FARM, WEATHER, BUSINESS, CHANGE OF PACE, PRONUNCIATION GUIDE, EDITORS NOTE, ADVANCE, KILL, CORRECTION, SUBS** (or subs previous).

On some local stations the news is broadcast in the form it is received from the news agency. This may suggest that an announcer dashes into the newsroom, rips the latest summary off the machine and goes on the air with it. This may have been true in the early days and on the smaller stations. The practice is becoming increasingly rare because news has commercial as well as public service value. Furthermore, the many typographical errors in wire copy forces the reporter to preread and edit for errors. Here is a fairly typical example: A U-S DEPART-

MENT OF AGRICULTURE OFFICIAL SAYS IN DENVER HE FEELS INSPECTION REPORTS OF COLORADO MEAT-PLANTING PACKS HAVE BEEN ACCURATE. How about "packing plants"?

Most broadcast news today is handled by trained newsmen who know how to tailor the news for a specific audience. This is done by "tacking up" items from several roundups and double-spacers to create the desired format. Increasingly, nearly all wire copy is rewritten before it is assembled for broadcast, giving the listener some variety in items that may be repeated several times during the broadcast period.

Some radio and television stations subscribe to the national newswire of a wire service as well as to the radio newswire. This gives an editor an opportunity to decide for himself what details to include. It also provides a greater number and variety of stories.

Preparation of Copy

All copy should be written double-spaced, preferably triple-spaced. Copy should be easier to read in capital and lower case than in all caps but because reporters are used to reading all cap wire copy, some prefer the all cap style. If a letter correction is to be made in a word, the word should be scratched out and the correct word substituted in printed letters. If word changes are made within sentences, the editor should read aloud the edited version to make sure the revised form sounds right. If the copy requires excessive editing it should be retyped before it is submitted to a narrator.

The type line in news copy averages 10 words a line. This makes it easy for the news editor to gauge the reading time of the item. A reporter's normal reading rate is 150 to 175 words a minute.

All editing of broadcast copy is done with the newscaster in mind. If a sentence breaks over from one page to another, the reporter will stumble. No hyphens should be used to break words from one line to the next.

Some news editors prefer to put each story on a separate sheet. This enables them to rearrange the items or to delete an item entirely if time runs short. A few briefs tacked near the end of the newscast help the reporter fill his allotted time.

Most reporters need pronunciation aids. A reporter can distinguish between *desert* and *dessert* but before the microphone he could easily falter over the phrase "his just deserts." The copyeditor can help him by adding phonetic spelling after the word ("dih-zurt'") or the reporter himself may underline the word or indicate the pronunciation.

Supplying the proper pronunciation, especially of regional place names, is part of the editing job. Words pronounced one way in one region may be pronounced differently in another. The Florida river in Colorado, for example, is pronounced "floor-ee'-duh." The Arkansas ("ar-kan-saw") river in Colorado is transformed into "Ar-kan'-sas" by the mere fact of flowing over the state line. Many Spanish place names have acquired a corrupted regional pronunciation: mawn-tuh-vihs'-tuh. The editors' and announcers' key is a state pronunciation guide.

The wire services provide a pronunciation list of foreign words and names appearing in the day's report. The guide is given in phonetic spelling (Gabon—Ga-boon') or by indicating the rhyme (Blough—rhymes with how; Likelike Highway—rhymes with leaky-leaky).

Broadcast Style

Phonetic Spelling System Used by Wire Services

A—like the "a" in cat
AH—like the "a" in arm
AW—like the "a" in talk
AY—like the "a" in ace
EE—like the "ee" in feel
EH—like the "ai" in air
EW—like the "ew" in few
IGH—like the "i" in time
IH—like the "i" in tin
OH—like the "o" in go
OO—like the "oo" in pool

OW—like the "ow" in cow
U—like the "u" in put
UH—like the "u" in but
K—like the "c" in cat
KH—gutteral
S—like the "c" in cease
Z—like the "s" in disease
ZH—like the "g" in rouge
J—like the "g" in George
SH—like the "ch" in machine
CH—like the "ch" in catch

Abbreviations

No abbreviations should be used in radio-television news copy with these exceptions:

1. Common usage: Dr. Smith, Mrs. Jones, St. Paul.
2. Names of organizations widely known by their initials: U-N, F-B-I, G-O-P (but AFL-CIO).
3. Acronyms: NATO.
4. Time designations: A-M, P-M.
5. Academic degrees: P-H-D.

Punctuation

To indicate a pause where the newscaster can catch his breath, the dash or a series of dots are preferable to commas: The House plans to give the 11-billion-500-million dollar measure a final vote Tuesday . . . and the Senate is expected to follow suit—possibly on the same day.

The hyphen is used instead of the period in initials: F-B-I. The period is retained in initials in a name: J. D. Smith. All combined words should have the hyphen: co-ed, semi-annual, de-segregation. (Spelling likewise should use the form easiest to pronounce: employee.)

Contractions are more widely used in broadcast copy than in other news copy to provide a conversational tone. Common contractions—isn't, doesn't, it's, they're—may be used in both direct and indirect quotes:

SENATOR GEORGE SMATHERS OF FLORIDA SAYS IT'S TIME THE UNITED STATES GOT TOUGH AND REMINDED ITS ALLIES TRADING WITH CUBA THEY STILL OWE AMERICA ABOUT 20-BILLION DOLLARS.

"WHAT MADE HIM SUDDENLY LOSE ALTITUDE?" HE ASKED, REFERRING TO THE ILL-FATED AIRLINER'S CAPTAIN. "WE DON'T KNOW. IT MUST HAVE BEEN ONE OF THOSE SMALL MOMENTS OF HUMAN ERROR."

A contraction should not be used if the stress is on the negative: "I do not choose to run." Or for emphasis: A U-S Air Force spokesman reported that several of the refugee islanders said they will never return to their homes.

Even in broadcast copy, contractions should not be overworked. Nor should the awkwardly contrived ones be attempted: they'd, he's, here's, they'll, that'll. The result would be something like this:

It's possible there's been a major air disaster in Europe.
A British airliner with 83 persons aboard disappeared during the day and is considered certain to've crashed in the Austrian Alps.
Apparently no search'll be launched tonight. There's no indication of where the aircraft might've gone down.

Quotation Marks

The listener cannot see quotation marks. If the reporter tries to read them into the script—"quote" and "end of quote"—the sentence sounds trite and stilted. It is easier and more natural to indicate the speaker's words by phrases such as "and these are his words," "what he called," "he put it in these words," "the speaker said." Direct quotes are used sparingly in the newscast. If quotes are necessary, they should be introduced casually:

SOVIET SPACEMAN YURI GAGARIN TOLD NEWSMEN IN STOCKHOLM TODAY THERE WOULD BE ANOTHER MANNED RUSSIAN SPACE FLIGHT THIS YEAR.
AS TO EXACTLY WHEN, GAGARIN SAID HE COULDN'T SAY.
ASKED WHO WOULD BE FIRST ON THE MOON, GAGARIN REPLIED: "AN ANIMAL."
HE ALSO ISSUED A FLAT DENIAL OF A REPORT THAT THERE HAD BEEN A SOVIET SPACE DISASTER RECENTLY. HE SAID—
"THIS IS REALLY A FAIRY TALE. THE SAME RUMORS OCCURRED DURING THE FIRST SPACE SHOTS BUT NO SOVIET COSMONAUTS HAVE EVER BEEN KILLED."

The source should always precede the quotation.
Quotation marks are placed around some names that would otherwise confuse the reporter.

IN ANSWER TO AN S-O-S, THE U-S COAST GUARD CUTTER "COOS BAY" ALONG WITH OTHER VESSELS STEAMED TO THE AID OF THE STRICKEN FREIGHTER. THE NORWEGIAN VESSEL "FRUEN" PICKED UP NINE SEAMEN FROM THE "AMBASSADOR" IN A TRICKY TRANSFER OPERATION IN THE TEMPEST TOSSED SEAS.

In this illustration the reporter is more likely to fumble "tempest tossed seas" than the names of the vessels.

Figures   Numbers are tricky in broadcast copy. "A million" may sound like "eight million." No confusion results if "one million" is used.

In most copy, round numbers or approximations mean as much as specific figures. "Nearly a mile" rather than "5,200 feet," "nearly a half" rather than "48.2 per cent," "just under two per cent" rather than "1.7 per cent."

An exception is vote results, especially where the margin is close. It should be "100-to-95 vote" rather than "100–95 vote." The writer or editor can help the listener follow statistics or vote tallies by inserting phrases such as "in the closest race" and "in a landslide victory."

Fractions and decimals should be spelled out: one and seven-eighths (not 1⅞), five-tenths (not 0.5).

Numbers under 10 and over 999 are spelled out and hyphenated: one, two, two-thousand, 11-billion-500-million, 15-hundred (rather than one-thousand-500), one-and-a-half million dollars (never $1.5 million). Despite the rules, some writers prefer to use figures whenever possible.

When two numbers occur together in a sentence the smaller number should be spelled out: twelve 20-ton trucks.

Any figure beginning a sentence should be spelled out.

Figures are used for time of day (4:30 p-m), in all market stories and in sports scores and statistics (65-to-59, 2:9.3). If results of horse races or track meets appear in the body of the story, the winning times should be spelled out: two minutes, nine and three-tenths seconds (rather than 2:9.3).

In dates and addresses the *-st*, *-rd*, *-th*, and *-nd* are included. June 22nd, West 83rd street. Figures are used for years: 1910.

On approximate figures, writers sometimes say, "Police are looking for a man 50 to 60 years of age." This sounds like "52" to the listener. It should read, "Police are looking for a man between 50 and 60 years of age."

Titles   The identification prepares the ear for the name. Therefore, the identification usually precedes the name: Secretary of State Rogers. If the title is long, break it with a comma: the President of the Marble Shooters' Union, John Kelley. Some titles are impossible to place before the name: The vice president of the Society for the Preservation and Encouragement of Barbershop Quartet Singing, Joe Doe. Use "Vice president Joe Doe of the Society for the Preservation and Encouragement of Barbershop Quartet Singing." Use "Police Chief Don Vendel" rather than "Chief of Police Don Vendel."

Some radio and television newsrooms insist that the President should never be referred to by his last name alone. It would be President Nixon, the President, Mr. Nixon.

Broadcast copy does not have the fetish of using middle initials and ages with all persons in the news. Some initials are well-known parts of names: John L. Lewis. Some persons prefer to use their middle name rather than their first name.

Ages may be omitted unless the age is significant to the story: "A 12-year-old boy—Mitchell Smith—was crowned winner," and so on. Ages usually appear in local copy to aid in identification. Place the age close to the name. It should not say, "A 24-year-old university student died in a two-car collision today. He was John Doe." Use "A university student died. . . . He was 24-year-old John Doe."

Obscure names need not be used unless warranted by the story. In many cases the name of the office or title suffices: "Peoria's police chief said," and so on. The same applies to little-known place names or to obscure foreign place names. If the location is important it may be identified by placing it in relation to a well-known place—"approximately one hundred miles south of Chicago." In local copy most names and places are important to listeners and viewers.

Where several proper names appear in the same story, it is better to repeat the name than to rely on pronouns unless the antecedent is obvious. Also, repeat the names rather than using *the former, the latter* or *respectively*.

Datelines

The site of the action should be included in broadcast copy. The dateline may be used as an introduction or a transition: "In Miami." Or the location may be noted elsewhere in the lead: "The Green Bay Packers and the Chicago Bears meet in Chicago tonight in the annual charity football game."

In the newspaper wire *here* refers to the place named in the dateline. In broadcast copy *here* refers to the place where the listener is. Because radio and television may cover a wide geographical area, the word *here* should be avoided. Said a UPI radio news editor, "If the listener is sitting in a friendly poker game in Ludowici, Georgia, and hears a radio report of mass gambling raids 'here,' he may leap from the window before realizing the announcer is broadcasting from Picayune, Mississippi."

Time Angle

In the newspaper wire story nearly everything happens "today." Radio copy breaks up the day into its component parts: "this morning," "early tonight," "just a few hours ago," "at noon today." The technique gives the listener a feeling of urgency in the news. Specific time should be translated for the time zone of the station's location: "That will be 2:30 Mountain Time."

Radio's use of the present and present perfect tenses helps to eliminate the time angle:

SEARCHERS HAVE FOUND THE WRECKAGE OF A TWIN-ENGINE AIR FORCE PLANE IN PUERTO RICO AND LOCATED THE BODIES OF SIX OF THE AIRCRAFT'S EIGHT CREWMEN. THE PLANE, MISSING SINCE SATURDAY, HAD GONE DOWN ON A PEAK 23 MILES SOUTHEAST OF SAN JUAN.

Taste

Broadcast news editors should be aware of all members of their captive audience—the young and the aged, the sensitive and the hardened. Accident stories can be reported without the sordid details of gore and horror. Borderline words that may appear innocent to the reader carry their full impact when given over the more intimate instruments of radio and television. If spicy items of divorce and suicide are tolerated by the station, at least they can be saved until the late-hour news show when the young and the infirm are abed.

The wire services protect the editor by prefacing the morbid or "gutsy" items with discretionary slugs:

(FOR USE AT YOUR DISCRETION)

(RAPE)

MIAMI, FLORIDA—POLICE IN MIAMI REPORT THEY SUSPECT JOHN DOE IN THE CRIMINAL ASSAULT (RAPE) OF AN 18-YEAR-OLD GIRL. DOE—27 YEARS OLD—WAS ARRESTED IN THE CITY MUSEUM AND CHARGED WITH STATUTORY ASSAULT (RAPE).

(END DISCRETIONARY MATTER)

References to physical handicaps or deformities are avoided unless they are essential to the story. Never say "Blind as a bat," "slow as a cripple" and the like. Similarly, unless they are essential, references to color, creed or race should not be used.

Wire services handle items involving pertinent profanity by bracketing the profanity:

"GODFREY SAID—IT HURTS (LIKE HELL)."

The practice of including a humorous item, usually near the end, in a newscast has produced some unfunny stories such as the one about a man breaking his neck by tripping over a book of safety hints. A truly humorous item leavens the heavy news report. Invariably it needs no embellishment by the editor or reporter.

On many stations someone other than the news reporter gives the commercials. One reason, among others, for this practice is to disassociate the newsman from the commercial plugger. Even so, the director or reporter should know the content of commercials sandwiched in news. If a news story concerns a car crash in which several are killed, the item would not be placed ahead of a commercial of an automobile dealer. Airlines generally insist that their commercials be canceled for twenty-four hours if the newscast contains a story of an airliner crash, a policy that is likewise applied to many metropolitan newspapers.

The sponsor does not control or censor the news. The story of a bank scandal might be omitted on a news program sponsored by a bank but it would be used on another newscast and would be heard on every newscast if it were of major importance. Similarly, a newspaper would be judicious enough not to place a bank scandal story next to a bank ad.

Attributions

Attribution is an important aspect of radio news writing. If an error is discovered, the station has an "out" if the item has official attribution. Example: "The state patrol said Smith was killed when his car overturned in a ditch" rather than "Smith was killed when his car overturned in a ditch." Attribution can also be vital in the event of any court action over a story written and aired by the news staff.

Should identification of accident victims be made before relatives have been notified? Some stations insist on getting the coroner's approval before releasing names of victims. If the release is not available, the tag would be, "The name of the victim is being withheld until relatives have been notified."

In stories containing condition reports on persons in hospitals, the report should not carry the same condition over from one newscast to another without a check with the hospital to find out whether there has been a change.

Tapes and Beepers

All news copy for radio and television should show the date, the time block, the story slug, the writer's name or initials, the story source and whether the story has a companion tape cartridge or a film segment. If there is more than one tape accompanying a story, the slug would indicate the number of tapes. A tape cartridge is simply a tape recording or audio tape from a news source.

If a tape is used, a cue line is inserted for each tape. Many stations use a red ribbon to type the out-cues or place red quotation marks around the cue line. At the end of the tape, the newscaster should again identify the voice used on the tape.

If several tapes are used in one newscast, the tapes should be spaced so that the same voices, or series of voices, are not concentrated in one part. The control room needs time to get the tapes ready for broadcast.

The out-cues of the tape should be made in the *exact* words of the person interviewed. This will insure that the engineer will not cut off the tape until the message is concluded. The newsman should provide the engineer or boardman with a list of news cartridges to be used and the order in which the newsman intends to use them.

The same would hold true of telephone "beeper" interviews, either taped or live. A beeper produces beep sounds, indicating the telephone message is being recorded.

The broadcast newsman also may have access to audio news services provided by networks, group-owned facilities and the wire services. These feeds, provided to the station on audio tapes, may be voiced reports or actuality situations. See Figure 17–4 for a wire service audio tape feed.

Broadcast News Editing

Figure 17–3. Editing room for news film preparation. The projection is through the window. [*Photograph courtesy KLZ-TV, Denver, Colorado.*]

Listeners with news tips frequently call the station newsroom. Such tips often lead to scoops. Those in the newsroom receiving such calls should try to get as much information as possible, including the caller's name and telephone number. If a telephoned message is to be used on the air, the newsman should get the caller's permission to use his voiced interview.

If something big arises, the newsman checks it out by telephone with the police department or sheriff's office before using it on the air. It is illegal to use information obtained from radio monitors. This prohibition, however, is flagrantly violated in times of emergency. During such times, police dispatchers are too busy to take calls from fifteen or twenty broadcasting stations. A newsman would be derelict in not warning the listeners of an oncoming flood or tornado merely because he couldn't reach a dispatcher to confirm what he was hearing on the police radio.

Television News Newspapers communicate by sight, radio by sound and television by sight, sound and motion. Editing a television news or special event show involves all three levels. As described by Chet Huntley, former National Broadcasting Company news commentator, television news editing is the marriage of words to pictures, words to sound, pictures to sound and ideas to ideas.

Reuvan Frank, president of NBC News, contended that the highest power of television is to produce an experience. Television cannot disseminate as much information as newspapers, magazines or even radio. But in many instances it causes viewers to undergo an experience similar to what would happen if they were at the scene. One can read about napalmed civilians or the drowning of a child at a swimming pool and think, "Isn't that a shame." But watching the same thing on a television newscast is a wrenching, personal experience that gets people

The Art of Editing

worked up and angry. Television is an instrument of power, not because of the facts it relates but because it conveys an experience to viewers.

Words speak for themselves to the newspaper reader. In radio, a newscaster voices the words for the listener. In television, the reporter is there, talking to the viewer about the news. He is the key actor and many a station has fallen behind in ratings for its news shows, not because the station did not have good newsmen and cameramen or lacked a well-paced news format, but because competing stations had better newsroom talent.

In the early days of television, stations hired journalists to report and write the news, then handed the polished manuscript over to a good-looking announcer with pearl-shaped tones. Today more and more newscasters are men and women with journalistic background who may or may not sound like movie stars but who know what they are talking about.

Television news editing, the sorting or processing of the news for television, requires more time than for radio. Producers and writers must spend hours reviewing, sifting and editing all the material available for a single, fifteen-minute newscast.

They use these criteria in selecting items—the significance of the item, whether it is interesting, either factually or visually, and (sometimes) whether the item will bring a chuckle.

All local newsfilm must be examined before it is edited to determine which of the films will be used and how much each should be cut. Sometimes a film may have relatively little news value but is included because of its visual quality. A barn fire might not rate mention on a radio newscast but the film could be spectacular.

Network films also are examined. Late afternoon network news commentaries are reviewed to determine what can be lifted for the late evening local news show. The networks provide their affiliates with an afternoon news feed for their use as they see fit. This closed-circuit feed from New York consists of overset material not used on the network news. These feeds are recorded on video tape and usually include a half-dozen or more one- or two-minute films and perhaps standup reports on national and world events. These have to be monitored so the editor can decide which ones can be used.

Chain-owned stations maintain a Washington or New York bureau that sends member stations daily film reports. These, too, must be reviewed.

In addition to editing this considerable amount of film reports, the editor must also go over the vast amount of wire agency news and facsimile pictures, not to mention stories filed by station reporters. Having selected what to use, the editor's next job is to determine how and where it can be used within the few minutes allotted the news show.

In film-editing the editor looks over the images on the film and directs a technician to delete (by cutting and splicing the film) the images the editor does not want to use. Before he orders the cutting of a video tape the editor must put the tape in a recorder where the tape can be stopped for cutting. An audio tape is edited by running the tape through a playback, cutting out the sounds not wanted or recording revised messages. Or, a tape may be edited by using duplicate recorders or a recorder and a tape cartridge. The original tape is placed in one recorder and fed into another. At points where material is to be deleted, the receiving recorder is stopped while the portions of the tape to be deleted are rolled through the playback recorder (see Figure 17–3).

```
T
(SIXTH AUDIO ROUNDUP)
73 :12 A GREAT NECK, N.Y. (PATRICIA MEARNS, WIFE OF AIRMAN MISSING IN
      NORTH VIETNAM, WHO JUST RETURNED FROM PARIS TO PLEAD FOR NEWS OF
      HUSBAND) RESPONDS TO NORTH VIETNAMESE SUGGESTION THAT POW WIVES JOIN
      PEACE GROUPS TO WORK FOR END OF WAR (IN PEACE)
74 :26 A GREAT NECK (PAT MEARNS) DOESN'T BLAME U-S FOR HER PREDICAMENT
      (SITUATION)
75 :40 A GREAT NECK (PAT MEARNS) REFLECTS ON REASONS FOR TRIP TO PARIS
      (LOTS OF US)
76 :42 V WASHINGTON (GENE GIBBONS, FOR VACATIONING UPI FARM EDITOR
      BERNARD BRENNER) HOUSE INVESTIGATION OF MEAT PRICES OPENS WITH
      TESTIMONY FROM ANGRY HOUSEWIFE
77 :22 A SAN FRANCISCO (CHARLES O'BRIEN, CHIEF DEPT ATT GENERAL FOR
      CALIF) SAYS CALIFORNIA CONSIDERING SUEING CAR MAKERS FOR SMOG
      DAMAGE (CALIFORNIA)
78 :42 A WASHINGTON (SEN ALAN CRANSTON, D-CALIF) CONDEMNS RISING
      UNEMPLOYMENT AND NIXON ADMINISTRATION INFLATION FIGHT (UNACEPTABLE)
79 :33 V UNITED NATIONS (MORRISON KRUS) ARGREEMENTS NOT BE BE
      RENEWED FOR U-S BASES IN LYBYA
                                    UPI/ AUDIO/NEW YORK
                                              BA953PED..
```

Figure 17–4. A United Press International audio tape feed roundup. The roundup, called a billboard, shows the news editor the number of the cut or selection and the length of the taped message. The first figure represents the number of the selection; the second shows the length of the tape in seconds. The letter A following the time indicates an actuality or a taped voice of a news source such as a governor. The letter V indicates a voicer or the voice of a wire service correspondent. V/A would indicate both an actuality and the correspondent's voice—an interview type. The words in the message itself provide an introduction to the tape by the newsman. The words in parentheses at the end of the selection are the out-cue words, showing the conclusion of the voice on tape. Out-cue words are not needed on voicers because the correspondents follow a standard out-cue, such as "This is Morrison Krus reporting for United Press International." Normally, six audio roundups are delivered daily.

Filmed pictures are similar to those produced by movie cameras. They may be films with sound (sound-on-film or SOF), sound under (audible background sounds) or silent film (SIL, sometimes called "voice over" or VO film). A taped film or video tape (VTR for video-tape recording) is one that has been recorded electronically.

Still pictures may be the standard two by two transparencies, either in black and white or in color, which are projected. Or they may be photos or printed material that are placed before the studio camera. The still pictures used most commonly on a television newscast are wire service news pictures—or facsimile pictures printed on tissue-thin paper. These are first mounted on heavy cardboard, then placed in a horizontal raster, or a pattern of scanning lines covering the area upon which the image is projected in the cathode-ray tube, to fit the television screen. At some stations these facsimile pictures are colored in the newsroom by using felt-tip color pens.

In a two-camera operation the still pictures must be aired either singly or in odd-numbered sequences. One camera is on the newscaster (usually referred to as a *standup* in this situation) and the other lingers on the sideline to shoot closeups of the still pictures. At the appropriate moment the director punches from camera 1 to camera 2. This frees camera 1 to pivot and focus on the second picture. If the scene were to shift back to the newscaster, camera 2 could be used but it is out of position. If camera 2 could focus on a third picture, camera 1 could get back to the newscaster. The problem does not arise when a third camera is used.

Figure 17–5 is a condensed script used on a typical day by KLZ-TV, Denver. This is from a 5:30 p.m. newscast devoted to local news. The underscored lines help alert the director and the newscaster to the impending use of film or video tape.

In the first item the reporter deleted the sentence referring to rape because the information adds little to the story and is in poor taste. In the second item the repórter added a thought and took out a needless phrase. In the item on picketing, the reporter had expected a complete story to go with the film. As newscast time neared he grabbed the story (first paragraph) then padded the account (second paragraph) to utilize all the film.

In the final item, Ch-7 is the reporter's abbreviation for Channel 7. CART means tape cartridge. In the video directions "cut to VO film & cart" tells the director to use voice over film with the tape cartridge. The film runs fifty-three seconds and has an obvious closing such as, "This has been Ken Nelson—Channel 7 —reporting."

Editing the television script conforms, in general, with the suggestions given for editing radio news copy. Because of the numerous cutbacks to pictures, the television news script contains more cue tips than the radio script and invites more mechanical problems. For instance, the newscaster would like to start off with two top stories. However, both are on video tape and only one video tape machine is available and the tapes have to be changed between something else. That means the news-

---

Figure 17-5.

PALMER ON CAMERA.....

Good Afternoon.

Denver Detectives are busy this afternoon trying to gather facts in the murder of a 23-year-old secretary whose

FILM CUE:
CUT TO FILM:

<u>body was found in her Capitol Hill</u> Apartment. The victim was Miss Lucille Martinez, of Trinidad, who came to Denver May 1st, to work ~~for~~ *with* the War-on-Poverty.

The body was found in the living room of her apartment at 1330 Race Street this morning by a niece and two other women.

(pls set) → Police said evidence indicated she'd been raped and stabbed to death with a paring knife.

The women went to the apartment after Miss Martinez failed to show up for work in a week. She was last seen alive June 23rd

FILM ROLLING...

by the apartment manager--Mrs. C.M. Bostock. Mrs. Bostock said she'd heard no unusual noises in the apartment.... and other occupants of the building had

END FILM:

observed nothing suspicious. Police are trying to trace the girl's activities on June 23rd...the day it's assumed she was murdered.

-0-

Meanwhile....all days off have been cancelled for uniformed policemen through July 5th. Chief George Seaton says thousands of young people---including many hippies, and others---are still in Denver after attending a Summer Pop-Music Festival and are expected to

Figure 17–5. Continued.

	remain here through the 4th-of-July
	weekend. He wants all police officers
FILM CUE:	available in case of further trouble.
CUT TO FILM...	City crews began trying to clean up
	Mile High Stadium this morning, where
FILM ROLLING ..	last night, 5 policemen and one TV
	reporter suffered minor injuries at the
	final night of the festival. Some thirty
	young people were arrested as police
	tangled with gate crashers. The cleanup
	job~~ as you can see ~~ done at no expense to the city-- is going to take
BACK TO PALMER:	awhile. In the meantime...the city is
	still offering a campground near 6th and
	Federal...and providing bus transportation
commercial cue:	there after the city parks close at 11 p.m.
SPOT #1	COMMERCIAL
PALMER ON CAMERA ..	Mayor Bill McNichols is said to be resting
	comfortably at Rose Memorial Hospital...
	where he was admitted yesterday. A
	spokesman said the 59-year-old Denver
	Mayor suffered a return of the heart
	pains ~~following~~ he experienced during a mild heart attack
	~~he~~ suffered last month. Doctors say
	he'll probably be in the hospital for
	2 weeks while undergoing various tests
	and treatment.
	–O–
PALMER ON CAMERA ...	Also in the hospital today is Gene
	Cervi, publisher of Cervi's Rocky
	Mountain Journal. The bombastic Denver
	editor was admitted to St. Joe's Saturday
	after what appears to have been a minor
	heart attack. His condition today is
FILM CUE:	listed as "fair."
	–O–
CUT TO FILM:	A group of between 50 and 75 people
	picketed the State Capitol in Denver this

Figure 17-5. Continued.

afternoon. They were demanding increased

welfare benefits. Governor Love met with

spokesmen from the group...but the pickets

asked that newsmen be kept out of the

meeting.

There is no report from the Governor's

meeting with the spokesmen---who claim

current Aid to Dependent Children

funds are not enough to support children

properly.

PALMER ON CAMERA . . .

Two more persons have been killed

so-far today in Colorado traffic accidents.

19-year-old Gary Roberts of Pagosa Springs

died this morning when his car ran off the

FILM CUE:

highway just north of Colorado Springs.

CUT TO FILM . . .

The second fatality was that of

a 9-year-old Sunnyside, Washington, girl--

Glenda Hall--who died on Interstate 70

near Denver, when her mother's car ran

off the road and overturned. The girl's

mother and 4 brothers and sisters were

also injured. A 13-year-old girl is

critical and the mother--Patricia Hall,

36--is in serious condition. The State

Patrol said Mrs. Hall simply lost control

of the vehicle, which travelled 240 feet

down the median, before it came back on

the highway in a broadside skid and went

off the other side of the road, where

it turned over several times.

FILM ROLLING . . .

The little girl who was killed was thrown

out and crushed by the car.

-O-

BACK TO PALMER:

The Stock Market got off to a better

comm cue:

start this week. The numbers in a minute:

SPOT #2

COMMERCIAL

PALMER ON CAMERA. . .

Investors showed renewed confidence

Figure 17–5. Continued.

```
                    on the New York Stock Market today,

                    although the volume was only 8,640,000.

                    Industrials climbed nearly 3½ points to

                    873.19.  An average share of common stock

                    gained 20 cents.
                                -0-

                        And finally....Black Leather Jackets

                    are still optional...but helmets have

                    become a must.  Here's a report with
        (cue cart)
        FILM        Ch-7 newsman, Ken Nelson:

CUT TO VO FILM & CART:
        Time:  :53              (FILM & CART)
        Outcue:  (Standard)
BACK TO PALMER:         Warren is next with the weather.  I'll

                    see you tonight, I hope, at 10 o'clock.
                                -0-
```

caster can start with one of the video tapes, then shift to a story of lesser importance while the tape machine is being changed.

Again, if only one tape machine is available, the script cannot call for a video tape story immediately preceding a taped commercial. The engineer has to have time to recue the machine.

Similar problems arise with news film. Commercial films may be spliced between the news stories, requiring a few seconds of padding following a news film before introducing a commercial.

The script prepares the viewer for what he is about to see but avoids repeating what the viewer can see for himself. If the mayor has criticized the city's water supply and his statement has been recorded, the script merely sets up the statement with a brief introduction. The script may contain a description of what the picture omitted or may direct the viewer's attention to a significant detail but it should avoid phrases such as "we're now looking at" or "this picture shows."

Because most television newsrooms function with only a fraction of the staff found on a metropolitan daily, each reporter must be a jack of all trades—a writer and editor, an engineer, a public speaker and a movie producer. The ideal newsman can report adequately on any assignment, from the arrival of the President to a water controversy between the states. He should be able to film the story with 16-millimeter silent or sound equipment, write and edit the script, record background sound on an audio tape machine, edit the film to fit, then voice the story on the air.

Both broadcast and newspaper news editors must have knowledge and talent if they are to perform the art of editing adequately.

Newspaper Style[1]

	Capitalize	*Lower case*
Capitalization	Titles preceding a name—Secretary of State William P. Rogers.	When standing alone or following a name—William P. Rogers, secretary of state. Occupational or false titles—the deputy defense attorney John Jones.
	The incumbent president—the President said. . . .	The general term *president*—the president may seize. . . .
	Government officials when used with name as title—Queen Elizabeth.	When standing alone or following a name—Jones, ambassador to Finland; the ambassador; the queen.
	Pope and Dalai Lama and foreign religious leaders.	The general religious terms—the pontiff, the patriarch.
	Union, Republic, Colonies referring to the United States—Republic of Korea, Fifth French Republic.	Long titles following a name—John Jones, executive director of the department.
	Legislative units—U.S. Congress, Senate, House, Cabinet. Legislature when preceded by the name of the state. City Council. Security Council. Titles of acts, bills, laws, historical documents—Social Se-	When standing alone—the legislature passed . . . ; he will run for council. When *congress* is used as a synonym for a convention—The congress of educators.

[1] Adapted, with permission, from *United Press International Stylebook,* 2nd ed. (1967) and *The Associated Press Stylebook,* rev. ed., (1968).

curity Act, the Constitution, the Declaration of Independence.

The legislative building—the Capitol.

The city. The capital is Denver.

Full names of committees—Senate Judiciary Committee.

When standing alone—the committee; the subcommittee. Shortened versions of long committees —the rackets committee.

Full titles of commissions—Interstate Commerce Commission.

When standing alone—the commission.

Courts—Supreme Court, Juvenile Court, 6th U.S. Circuit Court.

When standing alone—the court.

Governmental systems—Social Security.

General use—he was an advocate of security for old age.

U.S. armed forces—Army (USA), Air Force (USAF), Navy (USN), Marines or Leathernecks (USMC), Coast Guard, National Guard. Foreign armed forces—Royal Air Force (RAF), Royal Canadian Air Force (RCAF), French Foreign Legion, Swiss Guard, Bengal Lancers, Irish Republican Army.

General terms—soldier, sailor, airman, the army, the navy, the air force, the guards. But—the Marine.

Joint Chiefs of Staff

General—the chiefs of staff; the staff.

Holidays, historic events, ecclesiastical feasts, special events, fast days, hurricanes, typhoons— Mothers Day, Labor Day, Battle of the Bulge, Good Friday, Easter, Passover, Christmas, Halloween, New Year's Day.

General terms—the holidays, the feast, the hurricane, the typhoon, the new year, the battle, the armistice, the cease-fire.

Regions or areas, political or ideological—Antarctica, Arctic Circle, Middle East, Midwest, Upper Peninsula, Panhandle, Orient, Chicago's Loop, East-West, East Germany.

General—antarctic, arctic. Directions—western North Dakota, toward the east, traveled west, westerly winds.

Seasons of the year—spring, summer, fall, winter.

Political parties and members— Democrat, Democratic, Republican, Socialist, Independent, Communist.

Systems or ideologies—democratic form of government, republican system, socialism, communism.

Names of fraternal organizations —B'nai B'rith, Ancient Free & Accepted Masons (AF&AM), Knights of Columbus (K. of C.), Order of the Eastern Star (O.E.S.), the Elks.

All forms of the Deity—He, His, Him. Religious works—the Bible, Talmud, Koran, and books of the Bible and all confessions of faith

Devil, hell. Religious philosophies —he is catholic in his views.

and their adherents, and such terms as Satan and Hades.

Wars—Civil War, Korean War, World War I, World War II.

General—The war in the Pacific; nations at war, the war to end all wars.

Species of livestock, animals and fowls—Airedale, Percheron, Hereford, Angus.

Common nouns—terrier, horse, whiteface, bantam.

Names of races and nationalities —Caucasian, Chinese, Negro, Indian, Afrikaans, Afrikander, Israeli, Filipino.

General—black, white, red, yellow. Do not use *colored* for Negro except in National Association for the Advancement of Colored People.

Names of flowers, including Latin generic names—Peace rose, Thea.

General—camellia, japonica, rose, hollyhock.

Proper names that have acquired independent common meaning— paris green, dutch oven, brussel sprouts, german measles.

Common noun as part of formal name—Hoover Dam, Missouri River, Barr County Courthouse, Empire State Building, Blue Room, Carlton House (hotel), Wall Street, Hollywood Boulevard.

General—dam, river, courthouse, Carlton house (home). Plurals— Broad and Main streets.

Titles of books, plays, hymns, poems, songs (and place in quotation marks)—"The Courtship of Miles Standish." Words such as *a, in, of,* etc., are capitalized only at the beginning or end of a title—"Of Thee I Sing," "All Returns Are In."

Titles of newspapers and magazines should follow the style used by the publication. The titles are not inclosed in quotes. Greensboro *Daily News, The Christian Science Monitor, Harper's, Time* magazine.

Names of planets, expositions, organizations—Boy Scouts, World's Fair, Venus.

Sun, moon and earth unless they are used in a series with capitalized planets.

Names as their owners do— Charles de Gaulle, Gen. de Gaulle, De Gaulle, E.I. du Pont de Nemours, Du Pont, Irenee du Pont, Samuel F. Du Pont, Justice Van Devanter, Tertius van Dyke.

Names of firms and organizations (follow style of individual firm if possible)—Armour & Co.; Jones Co.; Reynolds Metal Assn.; Casey, Ltd.; Johns Hopkins University.

Fanciful appellations—Buckeye State, Leatherneck, Operation Deep Freeze.

Decorations, awards and degrees —Medal of Honor, Nobel Peace Prize, A.B. degree, Ph.D.

College degrees when spelled out —bachelor of arts, doctor of philosophy.

**Abbreviations
and
Contractions**

Abbreviate	Do Not Abbreviate
Agencies that are recognized by their initials—AFL-CIO, VISTA, YMCA, TVA.	First mention of organizations, firms, agencies, groups; thereafter the abbreviations may be used—Distant Early Warning line (DEW line), Organization of American States (OAS).
Time zones, airplane designations, ships, distress calls, military terms —EDT, CST, MIG17, SOS, USS Iowa.	First mention of some military terms—Absent without leave (AWOL); he is not a deserter until absent 90 days.
Addresses—St., Ave., Blvd., Ter.: 16 E. 72nd St., 16 Gregory Ave. NW.	Point, Port, Circle, Plaza, Place, Oval, Road, Lane, or where there is no address—Main Street, Fifth Avenue.
Business firms—Warner Bros.; Brown Implement Co.; Amalgamated Leather, Ltd.	
Lower case abbreviations usually take periods; also if the letters without periods spell out words, use periods—c.o.d., f.o.b., m.p.h., a.m., p.m. Periods are not needed in 35 mm (film), 105 mm (armament).	First mention of speed should be miles an hour (or miles per hour); thereafter—m.p.h., r.p.m.
Versus as vs. (with period). In court citations—v.	
Most states and provinces that follow cities, towns, airbases, Indian agencies, national parks—Ala., Ariz., Ark., Calif., Colo., Conn., Del., Fla., Ga., Ill., Ind., Kan., Ky., La., Md., Mass., Mich., Minn., Miss., Mo., Mont., Neb., Nev., N.C., N.D., N.H., N.J., N.M., N.Y., Okla., Ore., Pa., R.I., S.C., S.D., Tenn., Tex., Vt., Va., Wash., Wis., W. Va., Wyo., C.Z., Que., P.R., Ont., V.I., Sask., Alta., Nfld., N.B., Man., B.W.I., N.S.	All states standing alone—he went to Minnesota. Spell out—Alaska, Hawaii, Idaho, Iowa, Ohio, Maine, Utah.
B.C. as abbreviation of Canadian province must be preceded by town name; B.C., the era, must be preceded by a date.	
U.S.S.R. (Union of Soviet Socialist Republics) and U.A.R. (United Arab Republic).	
United States and United Nations in titles and when used as nouns in texts or in direct quotations—U.S. Junior Chamber of Commerce, U.N. Educational, Scientific, and Cultural Organization (UNESCO).	When used as nouns.

UN and US may be used without periods in headlines, except in an all-capital headline.

Religious, fraternal, scholastic or honorary degrees—A.B. degree, Ph.D.

Titles before names but not after names—Mr., Mrs., M., Mlle., Dr., Prof., Sen., Rep., Asst., Lt. Gov., Gov., Gen., Atty. Gen., Dist. Atty. Do not abbreviate attorney in "The statement by defense attorney John Jones," etc.

When standing alone or after a name or as a descriptive term— he is a doctor; John Jones, governor of Ohio; the statement by defense attorney John Jones (false title). Avoid Mesdames at the head of a list in social items.

Most military titles preceding a name—Gen. Pershing, Lt. Jones.

Commandant, commodore, field marshal, fleet admiral, general of the armies.

Port, association, joint, detective, department, deputy, general manager, secretary-general, secretary, treasurer.

Months when used with dates— Oct. 12. Abbreviate months as follows: Jan., Feb., Aug., Sept., Oct., Nov., Dec.

October 1492. March, April, May, June, July and days of the week except in tabular or financial listings.

St. and Ste.—St. Louis, Sault Ste. Marie.

Saint in Saint John, N.B.

Names of mountains and forts— Mt. Everest, Ft. Sill.

Mountain, mount or fort when used as part of a city—Mount Vernon, Mountainview, Fort Collins.

Proper first names unless the person himself does so.

Military Abbreviations

Army

General	Gen.	First Sergeant	1st. Sgt.
Lieutenant General	Lt. Gen.	Specialist Eight	Spec. 8
Major General	Maj. Gen.	Platoon Sergeant	Platoon Sgt.
Brigadier General	Brig. Gen.	Sergeant First Class	Sgt. 1.C.
Colonel	Col.	Specialist Seven	Spec. 7
Lieutenant Colonel	Lt. Col.	Staff Sergeant	Staff Sgt.
Major	Maj.	Specialist Six	Spec. 6
Captain	Capt.	Sergeant	Sgt.
Lieutenant	Lt.	Specialist Five	Spec. 5
Chief Warrant Officer	CWO	Corporal	Cpl.
Warrant Officer	WO	Specialist Four	Spec. 4
Sergeant Major	Sgt. Maj.	Private First Class	Pfc.
Specialist Nine	Spec. 9	Private	Pvt.
Master Sergeant	M. Sgt.	Recruit	Rct.

Navy, Coast Guard

Admiral	Adm.	Commodore	Commodore
Vice Admiral	Vice Adm.	Captain	Capt.
Rear Admiral	Rear Adm.	Commander	Cmdr.

The Art of Editing

Lieutenant Commander	Lt. Cmdr.	Chief Petty Officer	M.CPO
Lieutenant	Lt.	Senior Chief Petty Officer	S.CPO
Lieutenant Junior Grade	Lt. (j.g.)	Chief Petty Officer	CPO
Ensign	Ens.	Petty Officer 1st Class	PO 1.C.
Commissioned Warrant Officer	CWO	Petty Officer Second Class	PO 2.C.
		Petty Officer Third Class	PO 3.C.
Warrant Officer	WO	Seaman	Seaman
Master		Seaman Apprentice	Seaman Appren.
		Seaman Recruit	Seaman Rct.

Marine Corps

Commissioned officers are abbreviated the same as Army, warrant officers the same as Navy. Noncommissioned designations are the same as Army except specialist and

Master Gunnery Sergeant	Mgy. Sgt.	Gunnery Sergeant	Gunnery Sgt.
		Lance Corporal	Lance Cpl.

Air Force

Air Force commissioned officers are abbreviated the same as Army. Noncommissioned designations include:

Chief Master Sergeant	CM. Sgt.	Airman 1st Class	Airman 1.C.
Senior Master Sergeant	SM. Sgt.	Airman 2nd Class	Airman 2.C.
Master Sergeant	M. Sgt.	Airman 3rd Class	Airman 3.C.
Technical Sergeant	T. Sgt.	Airman Basic	Airman
Staff Sergeant	S. Sgt.		

The Air Force also may designate certain other descriptions as radarman, navigator, etc., but such designations are not abbreviated.

The Navy has numerous ratings such as machinist, torpedoman, etc., and they are not abbreviated.

The Army, Coast Guard and Marine Corps also may describe personnel by specific duty in addition to rank.

Note: The period is used in several abbreviations, such as Spec. 1.C., in Teletypesetter in the absence of the diagonal or slash mark.

Readers easily recognize common abbreviations such as U.N., FBI, AP, UPI, CBS, NATO and VISTA. Frequently, readers are more familiar with acronyms (names for words formed by combining initial letters or syllables of a series of words) than with the original combination of words. Examples: Alcoa (Aluminum Corporation of America), laser (light amplification through simulated emission of radiation), radar (radio detection and ranging), smog (smoke and fog), Socony (Standard Oil Company of New York).

A problem arises when the writer tries to force the reader to recognize unfamiliar abbreviations. The second paragraph in a story refers to the Naval Enlisted Scientific Education Program (NESEP). Eight paragraphs later, the organization is referred to by initials only. Will the reader remember what NESEP stood for? If he can't, will he go back to the second paragraph to find out?

Another problem is the tendency of headline writers to resort to abbreviations that puzzle readers: **HEP major killer next to CHD and stroke.**

Copy should be free from contractions except in direct quotations: "Walt Disney's hired four of them." This is supposed to mean Disney has hired four of them. It does not.

Some contractions are confusing: "Daddy's in Vietnam"; "Uncle Sam's Seeking Postal Clerks"; "a former college buddy of Darwin's."

Some contractions are ungrammatical: **Home sales tax; / here's the rules**

Some contractions should always be avoided: *It'll, who're,* "'d" for *would;* **Mother'd rather / fight than switch.**

Some reporters mistake *it's* for the possessive of *it.* By that reasoning, the possessive of *her* would be *her's* and of *their* would be *their's.*

Numerals

In general, spell below 10, and use numerals for 10 and above. Spell any number that starts a sentence.

Use Numerals	*Spell Out Numerals*
In all tabular and statistical matter, records, election returns, times (3 o'clock or 3 p.m.), time sequences (2:30:21.6—hours, minutes, seconds, tenths), speeds, latitude and longitude, temperatures, highways (U.S. 301, Interstate 6), distances, dimensions, heights (the flag hung from a 10-foot pole), ages of men and animals (3-year-old girl), ratios, proportions, military units (6th Fleet, 1st Army), political divisions (8th Ward), orchestral instruments, court districts or divisions (3rd district), handicaps, betting odds, dates, numbers (No. 1 boy), calibers (.38-caliber pistol).	Fourth of July, July Fourth (or July 4).
	Casual numbers—a thousand times no, Gay Nineties, mixed foursome, tenfold.
	Generalized—wouldn't touch it with a ten-foot pole.
	Under 10 for inanimates—four-mile trip, four miles from center.
	Fifth Avenue, Fifth Republic of France, Big Ten, Dartmouth eleven.
	Plurals—twos, threes.
Money—$4 million (the $ is the equivalent of the second numeral).	Cents in amounts less than $1—seven-cent stamp.
In a series—there are four 10-room houses, one 14-room house, 25 five-room houses, and 40 four-room houses.	
In amounts of more than 1 million, round numbers take the dollar sign and *million*—$4 million. Decimal-	Pounds rather than the English pound symbol and convert into dollars.

ization is carried to two places—$4.35 million. Exact amounts would be $4,351,242. In less than 1 million—$500, $6,000, $650,000.

In ranges—$12 million to $14 million, not $12 to $14 million.

Fractions in Teletypesetter are confined to matrices of eighths: 1/8, 1/4, 3/8, 1/2. Other fractions require the hyphen—3-16.

Fractions used alone—three fourths of a mile.

Serial numbers are printed solid—A1234567.

Sample Conversions

Nautical mile = approx. 6,076 feet
League = 3 miles
Furlong = 1/8 mile
Fathom = 6 feet

Peck = 8 quarts
Bushel = 4 pecks
Gross or long ton = 2,240 pounds

Centimeter = .3937 inches
Meter = 1.094 yards (39.37 inches)
Kilometer = 3,280 feet or approx. 5/8 mile; 10 kilometers = $6\frac{1}{4}$ miles
Millimeter = .03937 inches
Centimeter = 10 millimeters
Decimeter = 10 centimeters
Meter = 10 decimeters
Dekameter = 10 meters
Hectometer = 10 dekameters
Kilometer = 10 hectometers

Square centimeter = .155 square inches
Square meter = 10,764 square feet
Square kilometer = .386 square miles (247 acres)

Cubic centimeter = .061 cubic inches
Cubic meter = 1.308 cubic yards

Liter = 1.057 liquid quarts
British Imperial gallon = 1.201 U.S. gallons

For current rates of foreign exchange or price of metals, consult a bank or a recent paper of record such as the *Wall Street Journal.*

Spelling

The first preference in spelling is the short version in *Webster's New International Dictionary* with exceptions as given in this section; the U.S. Postal Guide; the U.S. Board of Geographic Names and the National Geographic Society with exceptions as given in this section. The news services have agreed on some spellings where authorities do not agree. The following list includes agreed spellings:

Algiers	Cologne	Kingstown	Romania
Antioch	Copenhagen	Kurile	Rome

Antwerp	Corfu	Leghorn	Saint John, N.B.
Archangel	Corinth	Lisbon	St. John's, Nfld.
Athens	Dunkerque	Macao	Salonika
Baghdad	Florence	Madagascar	Sofia
Bangkok	Formosa Strait	Marseille	Taipei
Basel	Frankfurt	Mt. Sinai	Tehran
Bayreuth	Genoa	Mukden	Thailand
Beirut	Goteberg	Munich	Tiflis
Belgrade	Gulf of Riga	Naples	Turin
Bern	The Hague	North Cape	Valetta
Brunswick	Hamelin	Nuernberg	Mt. Vesuvius
Bucharest	Hannover	Peking	Vietnam
Cameroon	Hong Kong	Pescadores I.	Warsaw
Cape Town	Jakarta	Prague	Wiesbaden
Coblenz	Katmandu	Rhodes	Zuider Zee

Where old and new names are used, or where quoted material uses a different form, one is bracketed: Formosa [Taiwan], Gdansk [Danzig] and so on. Use Toronto, Ont., rather than Toronto, Canada.

Words Frequently Misspelled

admissible	consul	hemorrhage
advertise	copter	hitchhiker
adviser*	council	
accommodate	counsel	impostor
accordion		impresario
accumulate	desiccate	incredible
all right	dietitian	indestructible
allotted, allotment	diphtheria	indispensable
anyone	disc	innocuous
appall	drought	inoculate
Asian flu	drunkenness	ionosphere
asinine	dumfounded	isotope
ax		
	embarrass	judgment*
baritone	employe*	jukebox
benefiting		
bettor	fallout	kidnaped*
blond (male)	firefighter	kimono
blonde (female, hue)	fulfill	
Borse		liaison
(German exchange)	gaiety	likable
Bourse	gaily	liquefy
(French exchange)	gauge	
buses (vehicle)	goodby*	mantel (shelf)
busses (kisses)	grammar	mantle (covering)
	Gray Lady	marshal
caliber	greyhound	medieval
candelabra	guerrilla	missile
cave-in		mold
chaperon	hangar	
cigarette	(aircraft shelter)	naphtha
clue	hanger	nerve-racking
coconut	(a hanging device)	
consensus	harass	occurred

* Preferred spelling.

old-timer

panicked
pantomime
parallel
paraphernalia
pastime
penicillin
per cent
percentage
permissible
personnel
phony
picnicking
pinscher
playwright
politicking
preceding
princesse (dress)
principal (main)
principle (concept)
privilege
procedure
propeller

Queensberry
    (Marquis of)

questionnaire
queue

rarefy
recommend
restaurant
restaurateur
Rigsdag
    (Danish parliament)
Riksdag
    (Swedish parliament)
rock 'n' roll

sacrilegious
schoolteacher
seize
separate
siege
sizable
skillful
specter
stanch (verb)
staunch (adj.)
strait jacket
strait-laced
strong-arm
subpoena

supersede
swastika
syrup*

teen-age (adj.)
teenager (noun)
theatre*
thrash (punish)
thresh (grain)
trampolin (general)
Trampoline
    (trade name)

vacuum
Veterans Day
veterinarian
vice versa
vilify
violoncello

weird
whisky*
wield

X ray (noun)
X-ray (adj.)

Place Names

Albuquerque
Allegany (county in New York and Maryland)
Alleghany (county in Virginia)
Allegheny Mountains
Arapaho (Indians, National Forest, peak)
Arapahoe (city, county, street, basin)
Arctic
Argentina (Argentines—people; Argentine—adj.)
Aroostook
Ascension (island)
Asuncion, Paraguay

Banff
Berkeley
Bosphorus (omit Strait; likewise with Dardanelles—but, Strait of Gibraltar, Straits of Florida)

Canon City, Colo.
Canyon, Tex.
Charleston, S.C., W. Va.
Charlestown, Mass. (navy yard)
Cheboygan, Mich.
Coeur D'Alene

Edinburg, Tex.
Edinburgh, Scotland

Guadalupe Hidalgo, Mex.
Guadeloupe, W.I.
Guiana
Guinea

* Preferred spelling.

Harpers Ferry
Hudson Bay (Hudson's Bay Co.)
Huntingdon—Pennsylvania and Tennessee
Huntington—West Virginia, Indiana, Missouri, Oregon, Arkansas, Utah

Kearney, Neb.
Kearny—New Jersey and Kansas
Kootenai River (U.S.)
Kootenay River (B.C.)

Lorain, Ohio
Loraine, Fr.

Macalester (College)
Mackenzie River
Manila
Matamores, Tex.
Matamoros, Mex.
Meriden, Conn.
Meridian, Miss.
Middle East (not Near East)
Monterey, Calif.
Monterrey, Mex.
Murfreesboro
Muscogee, Ga.
Muskogee, Okla.

New Castle, Pa.
Newcastle, Eng.

Oahu
Ogallala, Neb.
Oglala (Indians)
Okeechobee

Paterson, N.J.
Philippines (Filipino—male, Filipina—female)
Pittsburg, Kan.
Pittsburgh, Pa.
Poughkeepsie
Puebla, Mex.
Pueblo, Colo.

Rio, Ho and Kiang mean river—Rio Grande, Hwang Ho (or Hwang
   River), Yangtze Kiang (or Yangtze River)

Saguache, Colo.
Saint John, N.B.
St. John's, Nfld.
St. Johns, Que.
Santa Ana
Saranac
Schenectady
Scotts Bluff (county)
Scottsbluff, Neb.
Sequoia
Shansi, Sensi (Chinese provinces)
Sheboygan, Wis.

Taos

The Art of Editing

Uncompahgre River

Westminster

Yugoslavia (Yugoslav—person and adj.)

Proper Names

Jane Addams
Mark Antony
Jane Austen
Jakob Ludwig Felix Mendelssohn-Bartholdy
Ludwig van Beethoven
Sarah Bernhardt
Anthony J. Celebrezze
Lady Chatterley
Katharine Cornell
Fitzsimons (General Hospital)
Mohandas K. (or Mahatma) Gandhi
Hapsburg or Habsburg
Court of St. James's; St. James Palace
Ben Jonson

Kublai Khan
Nikita Khrushchev
Lillie Langtry
Nikolay Lenin (Vladimir Ilich Ulianov)
Charles Lindbergh
Walter Lippmann
Lloyd's (insurance)
Lloyds (bankers)
Clare Boothe Luce
Macmillan (book publisher)
Ignace Jan Padrewski
August Piccard
Richard Rodgers (American composer)
George Santayana
Arthur Schopenhauer
Franz Schubert
Ernestine Schumann-Heink
Herbert Spencer (philosopher)
Edmund Spenser (poet)
Oscar Straus (Austrian composer)
Johann Strauss (Austrian composer)
Richard Strauss (German composer)
Tutankhamen
Stephen Van Rensselaer
Josiah Wedgwood (potter)

Punctuation

Many authorities insist that the comma is the most troublesome of all punctuation marks. The use of commas cannot be learned by rule. Sir Ernest Gowers, a foremost British authority on style, wrote, in *The Complete Plain Words* (London: Her Majesty's Stationery Office, 1954), "The correct use of the comma—if there is such a thing as 'correct' use—can only be acquired by commonsense, observation and taste."

The Comma

Most news stylebooks are hostile to the comma and dictate that commas should be used sparingly. Roy H. Copperud, on the other hand, said, in the Editorial Workshop column in *Editor & Publisher* (May 5, 1956), "An examination of current newswriting shows that commas are more often omitted when required than used when necessary." Both Copperud, an arbiter of newspaper style, and stylebook compilers would agree that commas are required if they help make the passage clear. They should be omitted when they interrupt or slow down thought. H. W. Fowler's *A Dictionary of Modern English Usage* (New York: Oxford University Press, 1965) insists, "It may almost be said that what reads wrongly if the stops are removed is radically bad."

Note the role of the comma in the following examples:

"Erhard said the chancellor lacks the political sagacity required for the top government post." The sentence is absurd. It was the chancellor who said that Erhard lacked the political sagacity required for the top government post, a meaning made clear by inserting commas after *Erhard* and *chancellor*.

"No woman, whose attire makes her conspicuous, is well dressed." Again absurd. This says that no woman is well dressed. Both commas should be removed.

"We would walk out to the area where the animals roam free and talk for hours." This could mean that the animals talked for hours. Commas after *free* and before *where* make it clear who did the talking.

"I am going to Dublin perhaps with Murphy." This sentence needs a comma, but where? If placed after *Dublin,* the passage has one meaning. If placed after *perhaps,* it has another meaning.

The comma should not be used to perform the duty of a heavier stop such as a semicolon, a colon or a period. "I put my hand in the jar, this was a silly thing to do."

Commas generally are needed in the following:

To inclose words in apposition unless they are restrictive—"John Love, governor of Colorado, seconded the nomination." But, "The Cunard liner Queen Mary has been sold."

To set off parenthetical elements—"The letter, however, was never delivered."

To set off adjectives when they equally modify the same noun —"She wore an old, faded dress." The dress was both old and faded. Commas are superfluous if the adjectives apply cumulatively to their nouns. "Ned was a balky old mule."

To set off nonrestrictive phrases or clauses—"Committee members, who had feared White House suppression of the report, were jubilant." This means that all the committee members were jubilant. Without the commas, only those who had feared White House suppression of the report were jubilant.

In places and dates—"Their first son, John, was born in Charleston, Ill., on July 2, 1910, and their second son, Robert, on Feb. 2, 1915." But, "The dam was completed in June 1970."

To set off a noun of address—"Here's to you, sir."

In attributions—"'While ditching the plane,' Hamphill said, 'the craft flipped over.'"

To indicate stress or nuance—"Ancient Ostia is near, but not on, the sea." "The president, finally, signed the measure." There is an implication that the president should have signed the measure long before he did. Such an implication is absent in "The president finally signed the bill."

Commas generally are not needed in the following:

Before Roman numerals, jr., sr., the ampersand and the dash; in street addresses, telephone numbers and serial numbers— Louis XIV; John Jones jr.; Smith & Co.; 443-1808; 12345 Oak St.; A1234567.

Before *of*—"Brown of Arkadelphia."

Before *and* and *or*—"The flag is red, white and blue." A comma is needed in this sentence: "Fish abounded in the lake, and the shore was lined with deer."

After adverbs and adverbial phrases at the beginning of sentences—"Sometimes I rode but usually I walked."

As a substitute for *and*—"The house was old, dilapidated yet brought a good price." The house was old and dilapidated yet brought a good price.

To introduce *that* clauses—"The Air Cav unit (,) that took such a battering Tuesday (,) made a helicopter landing in a jungle clearing."

The comma is optional in some sentences. If the stop does not clutter it should be retained. "When the man filed suit (,) the court held that he too was entitled to a television set." "Three miles to the east (,) 12 U.S. B52s dropped 360 tons of bombs on enemy base camps and supply depots."

ONE-LEGGED COMMA. The term "one-legged comma" was used by Copperud to describe construction that should have two commas or none at all. He gives these examples:

"Severe storms accompanied by hailstones up to three-quarters of an inch in diameter, pounded western Texas." Either two commas (one after *storms*) or none.

"All New Orleans schools were closed as a precaution but the storm, bringing winds of 64 miles an hour passed the city without causing much damage." A comma is needed after *hour* to bracket the clause.

Commas that clutter usually indicate that the sentence is too long, too jerky or in poor order. "A corporation, which is unique in the rubber industry, has been formed." One remedy is to recast the sentence—"A corporation unique in the rubber industry has been formed."

The Period The period is used in some abbreviations—U.S., U.N., c.o.d. It is not used in abbreviations such as KMOX (radio station), FTC, YMCA, USS Iowa, NW, mm, SOS.

The period is used after a question intended as a suggestion: "Tell how it was done."

The period is used for ellipsis: "The combine . . . was secure."

The period is sometimes dropped in headlines: **OK, UN, US, OSU.**

The Semicolon The semicolon separates phrases containing commas to avoid confusion and separates statements of contrast and statements too closely related:

The draperies, which were ornate, displeased me; the walls, light blue, were pleasing.

The party consisted of B. M. Jordan; R. J. Kelly, his secretary; Mr. Jordan; Martha Brown, her nurse; and three servants.

The Apostrophe The apostrophe indicates the possessive case of nouns, the omission of figures, and contractions.

Usually the possessive of a singular noun not ending in "s" is formed by adding the apostrophe and "s"; the possessive of a plural noun is formed by adding the "s" and then the apostrophe: boys' wear.

The apostrophe also is used in the plural possessive "es"; Joneses' house.

The "s" is dropped and only the apostrophe is used in "for conscience' sake" or in a sibilant double or triple "s" such as Moses' tablet.

It is used in single letters: A's. But it is GIs for persons, and GIs' for the possessive.

The apostrophe is used in contractions—isn't—and in the omission of figures—'90s.

The apostrophe is omitted in words that form part of a noun: Johns Hopkins University, State Teachers College, Actors Equity Association.

The Colon The colon precedes the final clause summarizing prior matter; introduces listings, statements and texts; marks discontinuity; and takes the place of an implied "for instance":

The question came up: What does he want to do?

States and funds allotted were: Alabama $6,000, Arizona $4,000, etc.

The colon is used in Biblical and legal citations—Matt. 2:14; Missouri Statutes 3:245–260.

The Exclamation Point The exclamation point is used to indicate surprise, appeal, incredulity or other strong emotion. It may also replace the question mark in rhetorical questions:

How wonderful! He yelled, "Come here!"

Was there ever a day like this!

The mark should not be used after ordinary statements such as "I didn't say that." Nor should two exclamation points ever be used.

The question mark follows a direct question and marks a gap or uncertainty. In the latter use, it is enclosed in parentheses:

What happened to Jones?

It was April 13 (?) that I saw him.

Parentheses set off material or an element of a sentence: "It is not the custom (at least in the areas mentioned) to stand at attention."

When the parenthetical material ends a sentence, the period goes outside the final parenthesis. When the parenthetical material is a sentence in itself, the period goes inside the final parenthesis.

He habitually uses two words incorrectly (practical and practicable).

(The foregoing was taken from an essay.)

Several paragraphs of parenthetical matter start with the opening mark on each paragraph, and the final paragraph is ended with a closing parenthesis with the punctuation inside.

Parentheses are used where location identification is needed but is not part of the official name: "The Springfield (Ohio) Historical Society edition." It is not necessary to bracket "The Springfield, Ohio, area population."

Quotation marks enclose direct quotations; phrases in ironical uses; slang expressions; misnomers; titles of books, plays, poems, songs, lectures or speeches when the full title is used; hymns; movies; television programs, and so on.

The comma and period are placed inside the quotation marks. Other punctuation is placed according to construction:

Why call it a "gentlemen's agreement"?

In multiple quotations, the sequence is as follows: "The question is 'Does his position violate the "gentlemen's 'post-haste' agreement" so eloquently described by my colleague as 'tommy-rot'?"

The dash indicates a sudden change and can be used instead of parentheses in many cases:

He claimed—no one denied it—that he had priority.

The monarch—shall we call him a knave or a fool?—approved it.

The general rule for hyphens is that "like" characters take the hyphen, and "unlike" characters do not: A-bomb, 20-20 vision, 3D, B60, MIG17, north-central (Exception: 4-H Club.)

Adjectival use must be clear: "The 6-foot man eating shark was killed" (the man was). "The 6-foot man-eating shark was killed" (the shark was).

Suspensive hyphenation: "The A- and H-bombs were exploded."

Ordinarily in prefixes ending in vowels and followed by the same vowel, the hyphen is used: pre-empt, re-elect. (Check a dictionary for exceptions such as cooperate, coed and coordinates.)

Hyphens should not be used with an adverb ending in *ly* or with the adverb *almost:* badly damaged, almost insuperable obstacle.

The hyphen serves to distinguish the meanings of similarly spelled words: recover, re-cover; resent, re-sent.

The hyphen separates a prefix from a proper noun: pre-Raphaelite, un-American.

The hyphen has been abandoned in newspaper usage in *weekend, worldwide, nationwide* and the like.

Compounds Few agree as to the correct use of compound words—whether compounds are one word, two words or hyphenated words. A safe rule is to use the form that will not confuse the reader, even if the usage is not logical or consistent. The following list demonstrates some of these variations.[2] Copyeditors should adhere to the newspaper's stylebook. If one is lacking, editors can refer to a dictionary or a manual of style, such as the *Government Printing Office Style Manual.*

Able—able-bodied.
Above—above-mentioned.
Absent—absent-minded.
After—afterbeat, afterdeck, after-dinner.
Aide—aide-de-camp (aides-de-camp).
Air—airborne, air-condition, air conditioning, airdrop, airfield, air base, air mail, air raid (n.), airman, airlines, airplane, Alitalia Airlines, Bonanza Air Lines, Japan Air Lines.
All—all-star, all-America.
Ante, anti—antebellum, antislavery, anti-American, antichrist, anti-Christian, antifreeze, antilabor, antipoverty, antisocial, antitrust, anti-imperialistic.
Arch—archbishop, archduke, archenemy, arch-Protestant.

Baby—baby-sit, baby sitter, baby-sitting.
Back—back room (n.), back-room (adj.), backseat, back stairs (n.), backstairs (adj.), back yard, backstroke, backfire, comeback (n.).
Ball—ballplayer, ball park.
Bath—bathhouse, bath mat, bathroom, bath towel.
Battle—battle-ax, battlefield, battle front, battle cry, battleground, battleship.
Best—best-dressed, best seller, best selling, best man, best-known.

[2] Adj. = Adjective, n. = noun, v. = verb.

Bi—bicameral, bicentennial, bifocal, bistate, biweekly, bipartisan.

Black—blackjack, black list (n.), blackmail, blackout, black race.

Boat—boathouse, boat race.

Book—bookcase, bookstore.

Bound—eastbound, snowbound, Africa-bound, vacation-bound.

Box—box office (n.), box-office (adj.).

Brand—brand-new.

Business—businesswoman, small-business man.

By—byline, by-election, bylaw, bypass (n. and v.), bypath, byplay, by-product, bystander, byword.

Center—centerboard, center field.

Church—churchgoer.

City—city council, city-born, citywide.

Class—classmate, class day, classroom.

Clean—clean-cut, cleanup (n.).

Club—clubhouse.

Co—coop, cooperate, copilot, coauthor, codefendant, coequal, coexist, coordinate, copartner, cooperative (n. and adj.), costar, co-worker.

Coast—Coast Guard, Coast Guardman (if member of U.S. Coast Guard).

Commander—commander in chief.

Counter—counterargument, counterfoil, counterattack.

Court—court-martial (courts-martial), courtroom, courthouse.

Crack—crackup.

Cross—crosscurrent, crossroad, cross reference, cross-examine.

Cut—cut back (v.), cutback (n.).

Death—deathbed, death's-head, death knell, death rate.

Down—downcast, downstroke, touchdown.

Drive—drive-in.

Drop—dropouts.

Electro—electrolysis.

En—en route.

Ex, extra—ex-champion, ex post facto, extracurricular, extra-fine, extraterritorial, ex officio, ex-Waldorf waiter, ex-serviceman.

Far—far-fetched.

Farm—farmhouse.

Father—father-in-law, father love.

Feather—featherweight.

Fire—fire-escape, firetrap.

First—first-rate.

Fist—fistful, fistfight.

Fold—twofold, threefold, manifold.
Frame—frameup (n.).
Full—full-scale (adj.), full-time (adj.), full time (n.). [Also with part time (n.) and part-time (adj.), but pastime.]

Give—giveaway.
Go—go-between, go-getter.
Good—good-natured, good will (n.), goodwill (adj.).
Great—great-uncle.
Gun—gunfire, gun-shy.

Hair—hairdresser, hair shirt, red-haired, hair-do, hair-dos.
Half—half-staff, half-mast, halfback, halfway, half dollar.
Hold—hold up.
Home—homerun, homecoming, homemade, homeowner, home rule (n.), home-rule (adj.), homework, home town (n.).
Horse—horseplay, horse race.

In—insufferable, stand-in, inbound, in-law.
Infra—infrared.
Inter, intra—interstate, intrastate, intramural.

Law—law-abiding, lawbreaker, lawmaker, lawsuit.
Long—longshot, longtime.

Mid—mid-American, midday, mid-ocean, midwife, midship, midstream, midsummer, midtown.
Middle—middle-aged, middle-of-the-road (adj.), Middle Ages.
Multi—multimillion, multifaced, multicolored, multilateral.

Night—night club, nighttime.
No—no-hitter, no-trump.
Non—nonfarm, nonpartisan, non sequitur, nonprofit.

Open—open house, openhanded.
Out—out-box, out-talk, out-and-out, outboard, outdoor, out-of-doors (adj.).
Over—overabundant, overcome, pushover.

Place—place name, place kick.
Post—postwar, post-mortem, postnuptial, postmaster, post office, post card (postal card indicates the card is already stamped), post-Civil War, postgraduate.
Pre—predetermined, predawned, pre-empt, prejudge, prewar, preadolescent, pre-Roman.
Pro—pro-Arab, proclassical, pro-slavery.
Push—pushover.

Quarter—quarter-deck, Quarter Horse.
Quasi—quasi comfort, quasi-judicial.

Rain—raincoat, rainfall, rain-soaked, rainstorm.

Re—reappear, re-elect, re-enter, reopen, reinstated. Punctuation distinguishes between recover and re-cover, re-creation and recreation, re-treat and retreat.

Right—right wing, right-wing (adj.), right-hander, right field, right fielder, right-of-way, right-to-work, birthright, birth rate.

Round—round trip (n.), round-trip (adj.).

Run—runoff (n.), run-off (adj.).

Safe—safe-conduct, safe-cracker, safeguard.

Self—self-respect, selfsame, self-service, self-defense, self-control.

Semi—semiannual, semi-invalid, semiofficial, semiyearly.

Sit—sit-down.

Store—storehouse, storekeeper, cigar store, drugstore.

Sub—subzero.

Super—superabundant, super-Republican, superman, superbomb, supermarket.

Take—take-off.

Trade—trademark, trade name.

Trans—transcontinental, transatlantic, trans-Canada, transpacific, transoceanic, trans-American, trans-Siberian.

Tri—tricolor, trifocal.

Ultra—ultraviolet.

Un—un-American (Un-American Activities Committee), unshaven, unnecessary.

Under—underdog, underground, undersecretary, undersold, under way.

Uni—unicolor.

Up—up-to-date.

Vice—vice chairman, vice president.

War—warlike, warpath, warship.

Water—waterway, water-color.

Weight—weightlifting.

Wheel—wheel chair.

Wide—worldwide, nationwide, wide-awake, wide-brimmed, wide-eyed.

Wire—wiretapping.

Work—workaday, workhouse, workout (n.), workshop.

Proofreading

Proofs have several uses other than that of indicating typographical errors.

The copydesk, as we have seen in Chapters 3 and 9, uses a galley proof as a marker to show where insertions and new leads go.

The copydesk also may be assigned the task of updating overset matter and stories that made the later editions but not the earlier ones. On some papers such stories are called *pork*. Before the forms are torn up at the end of the press run, a makeup editor or his equivalent goes over the paper, circling items that should be retained for future use. Proofs of the circled stories go to the desk for updating. Proofs of overset material likewise go to the desk for updating.

On larger papers a dozen or so proofs may be pulled from each galley of type. A set goes to each department head, including the slotman, and to the wire service of which the paper is a member or client.

Duplicate sets of revised proofs go to the makeup editor on offset papers and to editors of out-of-office publications for paste-up dummies. When the dummies are returned, type is assembled in pages and page proofs go to the respective editors.

In nearly all publications a page proof is taken as soon as the form has been justified. A makeup editor scans the page quickly, yet carefully enough to note the following:

Whether the date, the issue number and the page number in the folio are correct.

Whether the headlines have been placed over the right stories.

Whether the pictures are right side up.
Whether the sluglines have been removed.
Whether the jump-line information is accurate.
Whether a makeup change is properly noted in the index.

The Proofreader

Thorough editing should be done on the story before the copy ever reaches the typesetter or the tapecutter. A proof is no place to make editing judgments. Printing departments charge the customer for all changes except typographical ones, basing the charge on time unit composition costs.

Misspelled words and names, factual errors, grammatical errors and libelous statements have to be changed even though the errors should have been caught in the editing. But minor or "nit-picking" errors usually are allowed to remain. The reason is a matter of cost. One change in a line of type may result in the resetting of a paragraph of type. Some estimates put the cost of replacing one line of type at $4. Sometimes, where a word replacement is desired, a word of similar character length can be used, thus averting the resetting of more than one line.

If the proofreader suspects a number of broken letters or uneven margins, he may ask for a set of cleaner proofs. The proofreader may or may not mark uneven spacing between words— but at least he might call the uneven spacing to the attention of the composing room foreman. Similarly, if wrong fonts, improperly aligned letters or lines that are indistinct in the upper or lower half of the line occur, the foreman should be notified. These errors would indicate that typesetting machines need attention.

One of the irritating flaws, and one that may or may not be corrected on proofs, is improper division of words at the end of the type line. Here are a few taken at random from several galleys of type: "reci-pient" for *recip-ient,* "opera-te" for *oper-ate,*" "pal-aver" for *pa-laver,* "ne-bula" for *neb-ula,* "reven-ue" for *reve-nue,* "obes-ity" for *obesi-ty,* "implac-able" for *implaca-ble,* "child-ren" for *chil-dren.*

Even in computerized typesetting, where rules, rule exceptions and tables can be applied, word division accuracy can never be reliable because of ambiguities, dual meanings, different hyphenations for identically spelled words and different hyphenations in different usages.

In newspaper composition one hyphenization occurs in every seven lines of text, depending on the type size and line length. Roughly 15 per cent of these hyphenations will be in error. Some newspapers manually reset the incorrect broken lines after the type has been set. Some do not, as already indicated in the examples given of words incorrectly divided.

When 8-point type is set in 12-pica measure, line-ending breaks average one for every five lines. When 8-point type is used on 15-pica lines, hyphenation drops to one for every 12 lines.

The same is true for unjustified line composition. To speed composition, the Denver *Post* began using unjustified lines. The editors expected reaction from readers who were used to reading justified lines but got none. In the 11-pica columns the ragged lines (sometimes lacking 12 points of filling the line) occur about once every four lines. In 14-pica columns the ragged line endings virtually disappear.

Broken lines can be eliminated by adding space between words to justify lines. This is being done increasingly by newspapers using automated typesetters. In one experiment, a group of newspaper executives were handed a printed sheet containing no hyphens. No one seemed to miss the hyphens. Too much word spacing, of course, wastes page space and causes rivers of space in the text column, making it relatively difficult for the eye to read. But the time may come, in newspapers at least, when readers will be spared all word breaks.

Typesetters are expected to follow copy. Some hew to this rule so closely that they faithfully reproduce misspelled words. Others take it upon themselves to make corrections. If the copyeditor suspects that a compositor will try to second-guess him, he indicates that the spelling as written is correct no matter what the typesetter thinks. If the name is Billi, the copyeditor or reporter marks *cq* after the spelling so that it will not come out as Billie.

Typesetters, like other humans, look at one word but see another. Errors that spell a word are harder to catch than misspelling. So, costumer comes out as customer, miliary as military, eclectic as electric, exorcise as exercise, diary as dairy, collage as college, calvary as cavalry, model as motel, farce as force, defective as detective, morality as mortality, bottle as battle, conservation as conversation, winch as wench.

Few typesetters can compose type without errors. A glance at first-edition stories that have been railroaded, that is, not proofread, will confirm this.

The proofreader, therefore, catches errors made in composition as well as the errors that should have been caught on the copydesk. It was a proofreader, not a copyeditor, who wondered why a bomber should be christened "Shadow Theory." (It was supposed to be Chateau-Thierry.) A proofreader wondered why a ship that had escaped many misfortunes should be renamed "Lucy." (It turned out to be "Lucky.")

Proofreading is an exacting task. Those who can do it well, in Dr. George P. Atwater's view, are real artists: "They must watch a dozen diverse things at once. They must look for errors of sense, uniformity of capitalization, punctuation, spelling, disarrangement of paragraphs, the use of wrong fonts of type, broken letters, letters upside down, incorrect page references, incorrect spacing, and many other difficulties." [Quoted in Rhoda A. Porte, *Proofreading* (Salt Lake City: The Porte Press, 1944), p. 11.]

Among other difficulties is lack of consistency. Are words, particularly names, spelled the same throughout the text? Are facts consistent, say, in compiled stories? Does the writer use one style in one paragraph and another in a later paragraph? In numbered series, are the numbers in order?

Even the best proofreaders in the trade will not catch all errors. In the larger publishing houses where proofs may be read by several persons, including the author, errors still occur— and this despite the fact that proofreaders have a chance to catch errors in galley proofs, again in revised proofs, in page proofs and perhaps in revised page proofs.

Ideally, two persons should read proofs. One, the copyholder, reads the copy aloud while the other follows the reading on the proof. Or, the process may be reversed with the proofreader reading the proof aloud to the copyholder. If only one person reads proof he would do well to place a ruler under the line of type, then concentrate on syllables rather than on words and sentences.

Copy should accompany proofs to the proof room. Even though the proofreader may not have to refer to the copy, he has the copy available in case he questions a construction. Also, by having copy available he does not have to mark on the proof "out—see copy."

Proofreading Methods

Two methods are used in marking proofs. One is the formal or book method in which two marks are used—one, within the line, to indicate the offender and the other, in the margin, to indicate the correction. If only one error appears in the line, the correction is noted in the left margin. If more than one error occurs, the corrections are in the right margin, each correction being separated by a slash mark (Figure II–1).

The second method is the guideline system, probably used in the majority of newspapers. Here a line is drawn from the error within a line to the nearest margin. If several errors appear within the same type line, the guidelines may be drawn to both margins. Care is taken not to obliterate the place in the type line where the error occurs. (Figure II–2).

In neither system is the correction made inside the type line or between lines of type.

If more than one error appears in the same word, the word should be circled and the correct word printed in the margin. Also, it is usually safer to rewrite a figure in the margin than to indicate changes in the figure by proof symbols.

If a line of type is upside down the proofreader not only makes this fact known in the margin notation but turns the proof around and reads the topsy-turvy line to be sure no typos occur in the reversed line. Similarly, typos should be sought out in transposed lines.

Arlette Schmitt, a brown-eyed blonde from Nice, France, speaks four languages and can tell a housewife how to use each item in the store.

Arlette and store manager Bal Raj ~~DKOGRA~~ [Dogra], OF New ~~De~~ [Delhi] India, agree on one point: The shoppers are mostly American — not foreign.

"A woman comes up to me and says, 'What's this stuff?' Dogra relates. "I tell her it's Egyptian jam. She says, 'okay, I'll try it,' and dumps it in her cart. Next week she may buy three jars."

Two years ago, Dogra says, items were new to most customers. But now he says they've become picky, even over brand names.

Although he is married Dogra, 29, came here seven years ago as a student. ~~Married~~ to an American girl, his food favorites still are Indian.

He's proud of an "instant curry dinner from Bombay. Just heat and serve it." There are packets of curry rice, herb rice and rice flamenco, too —

Add and water and boil.

Dogra says food is bought as soon as it's put on the shelves. "You can't believe how fast it goes. It's fantastic."

MORE MORE

Figure II–1. Formal method of marking proofs.

Using Proof Symbols

If an entire line of type appears to be missing, the proofreader should read farther down the proof for the missing line before rewriting the line. The line could be transposed rather than omitted.

If several lines have to be inserted, it is better to type the lines and show on the proof where they are to be inserted rather than to attempt to write the lines in longhand on the margin of the proof.

Proof symbols are used to indicate typographical changes (Figure II–3) and editorial changes (Figure II–4).

The Art of Editing

"I'm afraid the essence of this picture must challenge him — if it's done honestly."

He made one of his long pauses again. *I*

"All I can do is to say ʃ think this is a fair approximation of what Joyce intended. I think it would almost be fairer to call the film 'Homage to Joyce,' or 'Homage to Ulysses,' than to call it 'Ulysses.'

¶2 "I've gotten what I consider is the main line of the story. I want to give the audience a special thing that relates to Joyce's vision. If I can do that, then I'll be in great shape. We hope" — he emphasized the word — "to have the cooperation of the censor in Britain."

Strick must get "Ulysses" past the British censor, John Trevelyan. To get the $840,000 necessary to make the movie in Dublin — using Joyce's actual locations — he had to promise to get the censor's O.K.

"We don't have to cooperate with the censor in America," said the producer-director, who with associate producer Fred Haines, is filming in Ireland, "because the censor doesn't really exist in the United States."

No censorship in America?

"There are only two general territories in the United States, I believe, that require pre-censorship. They are Chicago and the state of Maryland.

"The only viable censorship in America rests in the hands of the police who are entitled to terminate the performance of *e* any show or screen exhibit. But they've got to say, 'This is deleterious to the public and *ℓc* we're going to end it.'

The more than 700-page book, first published in a limited edition in 1921, is about one day in the life of a Dublin Jew, Leopold Bloom. *K*

"It is, I believe," said Strick, "the central literary work of the century, concerning itself with the affirmation of life, the search of a father for a son, and of a son for a father.

f Strick looks on Bloom as the most fully developed character in fiction. He wanted an actor of stature to play such a part and he says he is sure he found him in the Dublin actor, Milo O'Shea. With the exception of the English actress, Barbara Jefford, who has the role of Molly, Scotland's Maurice Reeves, and Englishman Graham Lines, the cast is Irish.

Figure II–2. Informal or newspaper method of marking proofs.

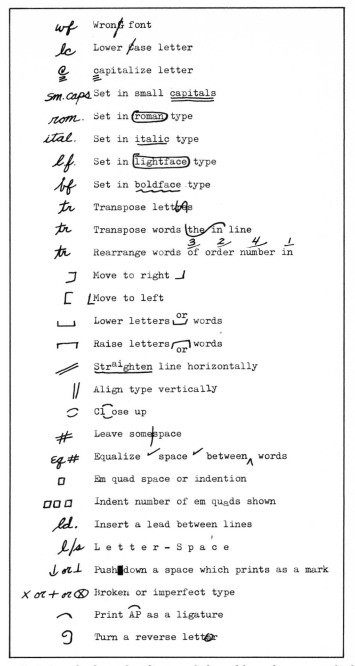

Figure II–3. Standard proofreading symbols and how they are applied.

e /	Common sense decres that every	*Add a letter*
cancel	A common gripe against ~~the~~ young	*Delete or take out*
close	N̶ever forget that the period	*Delete and close up*
stet	Don't strain to be ~~witty or~~ funny	*Let all matter above dots stand*
i /	Never stop trying to fi̶nd	*Correct the word marked*
⊙ or ⊗	Insert period⊗	
⌄ or , /	Insert comma⌄	
⌃ or : /	Insert colon⌃	
; /	Insert semicolon⌃	
⌄ or ' /	Put in apostrophe or ˅single ˅quote	
⌄ / ''	Insert quotation ˅marks ˅	
! /	Insert exclamation point !	
= / or - /	Insert hyphen —	
⟨SP⟩	Spell out	
⅟ₘ or ⊢⊣	Use one-em dash	
⌐2em⌐	Use two-em dash	
(/)	Insert (parentheses)	
[/]	Insert [brackets]	
¶	⌐Begin a paragraph	
no ¶	No paragraph.	
run in	Run in⌐ or run on	

ure II-4. Standard proofreading symbols.

Glossary

Accordion fold—parallel folds on sheet of paper to determine an imposition pattern.

Acetate—transparent sheet placed over art in mechanical color separation.

Ad—short for advertisement.

Ad alley—section in mechanical department where ads are assembled.

Add—material to be added to news story, usually with a number and slug: add 1 fire.

Ad lib—unscripted comment made before a microphone.

Ad-side—advertising department as distinguished from editorial department.

Advance—story sent out in advance of the scheduled publication date.

Agate—name of a type size, e.g., agate type, or type that is $5\frac{1}{2}$ points high. Advertising is also sold on the basis of agate lines, or 14 agate lines to an inch.

Align—to place adjacent to an even base line on a horizontal plane.

Alley—portion in composing room devoted to special sections, such as ad alley, Linotype alley.

All in hand—all available copy has been sent to composing department.

All up—all copy has been set into type.

A.M.—morning edition.

Angle—special aspect of a story; a slant.

Antique—rough-surfaced paper resembling old handmade papers.

AP—short for Associated Press, a major news agency.

Art—newspaper or magazine illustrations.

Astonisher—same as exclamation point.

Attribution—source of the material in a story.

Audio tape—tape on which sound has been transcribed.

A wire—usually the main wire of a news agency.

Back room—mechanical section as distinguished from front office. Also back shop.

Back timing—timing of a script so that it ends strong and clean.

Back up—printing the reverse side of a sheet.

Bad break—bad phrasing of a headline; bad wrapping of headline type; bad arrangement of type in columns, giving the reader the impression a paragraph ending is the end of the story.

Bank—cabinet or bench where type is kept; the lower portion of a headline (deck).

Banner—usually a headline stretching across all columns of a newspaper.

Barker—reversed kicker in which the kicker is in larger type than the lines below it.

Bastard type—type that varies from the standard point system.

Beeper—telephone interview recorded on audio tape.

Ben Day—a pattern of lines or dots to give a shaded effect as background for type or illustrations.

Binder—inside page streamer; head that binds together two or more related stories.

Black and white—reproduction in one color (black).

Black Letter—text or Old English style of type.

Blanket head—headline over several columns of type or over type and illustration.

Bleed—running an illustration off the page.

Blooper—any embarrassing error in print or broadcast.

Body—main story or text; body type is the size of type used for the contents.

Boil—to trim or reduce wordage of a story.

Boiler plate—syndicated material in mat or plate form.

Boldface—type that is blacker than normal typeface; also black face. Abbreviated bf.

Book—sheet of paper (usually half-sheet) on which a story is written. A basic category of printing paper.

Book number—number assigned to each item in a wire service report.

Box—unit of type inclosed by a border.

Brace—type of makeup, usually with a banner headline and the story in the right-hand column. A bracket.

Break—point at which a story turns from one column to another. An exclusive story.

Break over—story that jumps from one page to another.

Brightener—short, amusing item.

Broadside—large sheet printed only on one side.

Broken box—splitting the lines of a box to accommodate words or pictures. Also split box.

Broken heads—headlines with lines of different widths.

Broken rule—rule that has been broken or nipped so that it does not print. Also busted rule.

Bug—type ornament; a logotype; a star or other element that designates makeovers.

Bulldog—an early edition of a newspaper.

Bulletin—last-minute story of significance; a wire service designation of a story of major importance, usually followed by bulletin matter. Abbreviated bun.

Bullets—large periods used for decoration, usually at the beginning of paragraphs.

Bumper—two elements placed side by side or one immediately beneath the other. A bumped headline is also called a tombstone.

Butted slugs—composition that requires two or more slugs to make the desired width.

Byline—credit given to the author.

Canned copy—copy released by press agents or syndicates.

Canopy head—streamer headline from which two or more readout heads drop.

Caps—short for capital letters or upper-case letters.

Caption—display line over a picture or over the cutline. Also used as a synonym for a cutline. Also called an overline.

Cartridge—holder for audio tapes. Also a staccato lead.

Case—type cabinet.

Casting box—receptacle used to make or cast stereotype plates.

Catchline—same as guideline or slugline.

Centered—type placed in the middle of a line.

Center spread—two facing pages made up as one in the center of a newspaper section; also called double truck.

Chase—metal frame in which forms are locked before printing or stereotyping.

Chaser—fast, urgent replate.

Cheesecake—slang for photographs emphasizing women's legs. Also called leg art.

Circumlocution—wordy, roundabout expressions. Also redundancy.

Circus makeup—flamboyant makeup featuring a variety of typefaces and sizes.

City room—main newsroom of a newspaper. The city editor presides over the city desk.

Ck—short for *can kill* (usable but not important).

Clean copy—copy with a minimum of typographical or editing corrections. Clean proof is proof that requires few corrections.

Clips—short for clippings of newspaper stories.

Clipsheet—publicity material printed on a sheet so that each item may be cut out and used.

Closeup—photo showing head or head and shoulders or an object seen at close range.

Closing—time at which forms are closed. Also ending.

Cloze—method of testing readability. Respondents are asked to fill in words in blank spaces.

Col.—abbreviation for column.

Cold type—reproduction of characters composed photographically.

Color page—page on which color is used.

Color story—biased account or a feature story.

Column inch—unit of space measurement; one column wide and one inch deep.

Column rule—printing units that create vertical lines of separation on a page.

Combination cut—engraving that includes both halftone and line work.

Combo—short for combination, pictures of the same subject used as a single unit.

Compose—type is set or composed in a composing room by a compositor.

Composition—all typesetting.

Constant—element used regularly without change. Also called standing or stet material.

Copy—words typewritten by reporters or editors from which type is set. Printers set copy.

Copy cutter—composing room worker who distributes copy among compositors.

Copy fitting—editing copy to fit a required space.

Copyholder—person who reads manuscript while another person marks the proof.

Copyreader—same as copyeditor, one who edits copy and writes headlines.

Cq—symbol or word is correct; folo (follow) copy.

Credit line—same as byline.

Crop—to eliminate unwanted portions of a photograph. Marks used to show the elimination are called crop marks.

Crossbar—printing press attachment to guide or turn print paper.

Crossline—headline composed of a single line.

Cue—signal given to announcer; a line in a script indicating a change.

Cut—illustration or engraving. Or, a direction to trim or shorten a story.

Cut-in—may refer to an initial letter beginning a paragraph or to a side head that is set into the opening lines of a paragraph.

Cutline—explanatory material, usually placed beneath a picture. Also called underline, legend and caption.

Cutoff—hairline that marks the point where the story moves from one column to another or to separate boxes and cuts from text material or to separate a headline from other elements.

Cx—short for correction. Indicates that corrections are to be made in type. Also called fix.

Dangler—short for dangling participle or similar grammatical error.

Dash—short line separating parts of headlines or headline and story.

Dateline—opening phrase of story showing origin, source and sometimes date of story. Also the publication date at the top of each page.

Dead—newspaper copy or type that is no longer usable.

Deadline—the shutoff time for copy for an edition.

Deck—section of a headline.

Delete—take out. The proofreader uses a symbol for a delete mark.

Desk—standing alone, usually the copydesk. Also city desk, sports desk, etc.

Dingbat—typographic decoration.

Display—term given to a type of advertising that distinguishes it from classified advertising. Display lines are those set in larger sizes than regular body type.

Dissolve—in broadcasting, a smooth transition from one image to another.

Dog watch—late shift of an afternoon paper or early shift of a morning paper. Also lobster trick.

Double chain—film story on two reels going through two projectors simultaneously.

Double spacer—term used on radio news wire to designate a story of unusual significance. Extra space is used between copy lines to alert the editor to the story.

Double truck—two pages at the center of a section made up as a single unit.

Down style—style using a minimum of capital letters.

Drop line—headline in which each line is stepped. Also called step line.

Dub—transfer of film or tape.

Dummy—diagram outlining the makeup scheme. A rough dummy has little detail; a paste-up dummy is created by pasting page elements on a sheet of paper the actual size of the page.

Dupe—short for duplicate or carbon copy.

Dutch break—breaking body type from one column to another not covered by the display line. Also called dutch turn or raw wrap.

Ears—small box on one or both sides of the nameplate carrying brief announcements of weather, circulation, edition and the like.

Edition—one of several press runs such as city edition and late home edition.

Electrotype—engraving duplicate made by electroplating a waxed impression.

Em—measurement of type that is as wide as it is high. A pica em is 12 points wide. Some printers still refer to all picas as ems. Ems are sometimes referred to as mut or mutton.

En—one-half em. Mostly used to express space. If the type is in 10 points, an indention of an en would equal 5 points. Sometimes referred to as a nut.

Endmark—symbol (such as # or 30) to indicate the close of the story. An end dash (sometimes called a 30 dash) is used at the end of the story in type.

Etching—process of removing nonprinting areas from a relief plate by acid.

Etch proof—name given to a proof of type on a special paper on which the printing is photographed. Also called reproduction proof.

Extra—special edition published to carry an important news break.

Eyebrow—another name for a kicker head.

Face—style or cut of type; the printing surface of type or of a plate.

FAX—short for facsimile or transmission by wire of a picture.

Family—as applied to type, all the type in any one design. Usually designated by a trade name.

Fat head—headline too large for the space allowed for it.

Feature—to give special prominence to a story or illustration. A story that stresses the human interest angle.

Feed—story or program electronically transmitted to other stations or broadcast to the public.

Filler—short items, usually set in type in advance and used to fill out space in a column of type. Also called briefs or shorts.

Fingernails—parentheses.

Fix—to correct or a correction.

Flag—title of paper appearing on page 1.

Flash—brief announcement by a wire service of urgent news. Usually followed by a bulletin.

Flat—group of pictures engraved on a single unit. Also group of shots on one negative.

Flimsy—carbon copy.

Flip—to turn a story from last column of first page to first column of second page.

Float—ruled side bar that may go anywhere in a story. To center an element in space that is not large enough to fill.

Floorman—printer.

Flop—illustration reversed in engraving.

Floss—overwritten.

Flush—even with the column margin. Type aligned on one side. Alignment may be either on left or right side.

Folio—lines showing the newspaper name, date and page number. Generally, however, the page number only.

Follow—related matter that follows main story. Abbreviated folo.

Followup—second-day story.

Follow copy—set the story as sent, disregard seeming errors.

Font—complete set of type in one size and style.

Form—type and engraving assembled in a chase, ready for the press.

Format—physical form of a publication.

Foundry type—metal type cast in a type foundry and used for hand-set type.

Frame—top or cabinet or case rack upon which the compositor works.

Frame makeup—vertical makeup.

Frontispiece—illustrated leaf preceding a book's title page.

Fudge box—device, usually a clamp, inserted in a press plate allowing the paper to carry line scores and the like after the edition has gone to press.

Fullface—same as boldface.

Furniture—spacing material placed around type area to lock it into a chase.

Future book—record kept by the city desk of future events.

FYI—for your information.

Gain—sound level.

Galley—metal tray used to hold type.

Galley proof—print of the assembled type, used for proofreading purposes.

Gatekeeper—one who decides whether to pass a news story along. The account of an event goes through many gatekeepers before it reaches the reader.

Gathering—process of assembling all the signatures (or groups of pages) into a complete booklet.

Glossy—photograph with a hard, shiny finish.

Gobbledygook—editor's slang for material characterized by jargon and circumlocution. Also spelled gobbledegook.

Gothic—sans serif type. Also called block letter.

Graf—short for paragraph.

Gravure—process of photomechanical printing. Also rotogravure or intaglio (printing ink is transferred to paper from areas sunk below the surface) printing.

Grease pencil—type of pencil used to make crop marks on pictures.

Guideline—instructions on copy to direct a printer. Also called slug or slugline.

Gutter—vertical space that separates one page from another on two facing pages.

Hairline—finest line available in printing. Often used for rules between columns.

Hairspace—thin space.

Half stick—matter set in one half column measure. A depth one half of the column width.

Halftone—photoengraving. A dot pattern gives the illusion of tones.

Handout—release story from a public relations firm.

Hanger—headline that descends from a banner. Also called readout.

Hanging indention—headline style in which the top line is set full measure and succeeding lines are indented from the left.

Hard copy—original copy, distinguishing it from monitor copy or carbon copy. Also a glossy photographic print as contrasted to facsimile.

Hard news—spot news or news of record as contrasted to features and background material.

Head count—number of letters and spaces available for a headline.

Headlinese—overworked short words in a headline, such as *cop, nab, hit, set.*

Head shot—photo of person's head or head and shoulders. Also called face shots and mug shots.

Highlight—white or light portions of a photograph. Also the high point of a story.

Hold for release—copy that is not to be used until a specified time.

Holdout—portion held out of a story and placed in the overset.

Hood—border over the top and both sides of a headline.

Horseshoe—copydesk, once shaped like a horseshoe.

Hot metal—line-caster slugs as opposed to cold type or type set photographically.

HTK—headline to come. Also HTC.

Hugger mugger—newspaper lead crammed with details.

Imposition—process of placing type and illustrations in pages.

Impression—any printing of ink on paper. Also appearance of the printed page. Also the number of times a press has completed a printing cycle.

Index—newspaper's table of contents, usually found on page 1.

Initial (Initial cap)—first letter in a paragraph set in type larger than the body type.

Insert—addition to a story placed within the story.

Intertype—line-casting machine.

Intro—short for introduction. Opening copy to film or tape.

Inverted pyramid—news story structure in which the parts are placed in a descending order of their importance. Also a headline in inverted pyramid shape.

Issue—all copies produced by a newspaper in a day.

Italics—slanted letter form. Shortened form is itals.

Jargon—language of a profession, trade or group. Newspaper jargon.

Jim dash—short centered line between decks of a headline or between head and story. Also designated as 3-em or 4-em dashes.

Jump—to continue a story from one page to another.

Jump head—headline over the continued portion of a story.

Jump lines—continuation lines: continued on page X.

Justify—spacing out a line of type to fill the column; spacing elements in a form so form can be locked up.

Kicker—overline over a headline. Also eyebrow.

Kill—to discard copy, type, mats and so on.

Label head—dull, lifeless headline. Sometimes a standing head such as **News of the World.**

Layout—pattern of typographic arrangement. Similar to dummy.

Lead—beginning of a story or the most important story of the day (pronounced "leed").

Lead—piece of metal varying from 1 to 3 points placed between lines of type for spacing purposes (pronounced "led").

Leaders—line of dots.

Leading—process of placing leads (leds) between lines of type.

Lead out—to justify a line of type.

Legend—information under an illustration. Also cutline.

Letterpress—technique of printing from raised letters. Ink is applied to the letters, paper is placed over the type, and impression implied to the paper, resulting in printing on paper.

Library—newspaper's collection of books, files and so on. Also called morgue.

Ligature—two or more letters on a type character: fi, ffi.

Light pencil—device resembling a small flashlight used to edit copy displayed on a television screen. A light eraser is used in the same manner, but to delete unwanted portions.

Line-caster—any keyboarded machine that casts lines of type.

Line cut—engraving without tones. Used for maps, charts and so on.

Line gauge—pica rule or a ruler marked off in pica segments.

Linotype—line-casting machine.

Lock up—process of tightening a form.

Logotype—single matrix of type containing two or more letters commonly used together: AP, UPI. Also a combination of the nameplate and other matter to identify a section. Also an advertising signature. Commonly abbreviated logo.

Lower case—small letter as distinguished from a capital letter. Abbreviated lc.

Ludlow—machine to cast slugs from hand-set matrices.

Magazine—part of a typesetting machine that holds the matrices.

Makeready—process of aligning elements on the page to assure a uniform impression.

Makeover—to change page content or layout.

Makeup—design of a newspaper page. Assembling elements in a page.

Marker—proof or tearsheet used to show where inserts are to go after story has been sent to the composing room or other instructions for guidance of printers and makeup editors.

Masthead—informational material about a newspaper, usually placed on the editorial page.

Mat—short for matrix or mold for making a stereotype. The mat of a page is made of papier-mâché. In typesetting machines, the matrix is made of brass.

Measure—length of a line of type.

Monitor copy—tearsheet copy or copy produced electronically. A monitor is also a television or radio receiver. To monitor is to watch or time a radio or television program.

Monotype—line-casting machine that casts one letter at a time.

Montage—succession of pictures assembled to create an over-all effect. Usually a single photograph using several negatives.

Morgue—newspaper reference library or repository for clippings.

Mortise—cutaway section of an engraving into which type is inserted.

Mug shot—same as closeup or face shot.

Must—matter that someone in authority has ordered published.

Nameplate—name of newspaper displayed on page 1. Also called flag, title or line.

Newshole—space left for news and editorial matter after ads have been placed on pages.

Newsprint—low-quality paper used to print newspapers.

NH—slug on copy indicating new head.

NL—slug on copy and notation on a marker indicating new lead.

Obit—abbreviation for obituary.

Offset—method of printing differing from letterpress. A photograph is taken after the page has been assembled. The negatives are placed over a light-sensitive printing plate and light is exposed through the open spaces of the negative. The result is that the letters are hardened and the nonprinting surface is washed away. The method of printing involves inking the printed plate with water and then with ink. The water resides only on the nonprinting surface, whereas the ink resides on the printing surface. The inked letters are then printed on a rubber blanket, which in turn prints (or offsets) on paper.

Offsetter copy—Associated Press copy prepared for papers using offset printing.

Op. ed—page opposite the editorial page.

Optional—matter that may be used without regard to the time element. Also called time copy, grape and AOT (any old time).

Out-cue—cue telling a news director or engineer that a film or tape is near the end.

Outlined cut—halftone with background cut out. Also silhouette.

Overline—display head over a picture or over a cutline. Also called caption.

Overset—type in excess of amount needed.

Pad—to make a story longer with excess words.

Page proof—proof of an entire page.

Parameter—symbol in computer programming indicating a constant such as a figure.

Parens—short for parentheses.

Photocomposition—type composed photographically.

Photolithography—printing process such as offset where the impression is transferred from a plate to a rubber roller and to paper.

Pi—to jumble type hopelessly. Type is pied.

Pica—linear measure in 12 points. A pica em is a standard measure but only 12-point type can be a pica em.

Pickup—material in type that is to be used with new material such as a new lead.

Pix—short for pictures. The singular may be pic or pix.

Planer—block or mallet used to even a printing surface or to pound an impression on a page proof.

Plate—stereotyped page ready for the press.

Play—prominence given a story, its display. Also the principal story.

Plug—filler copy. Also time copy, grape, pork.

Point—unit of printing measurement, approximately $\frac{1}{72}$ inch. Actually .01384 inches. Also any punctuation mark.

Pork—matter saved from one edition and printed in another or matter taken from one day's final edition and used in the next day's early edition.

Pos.—positive film image.

Precede—material such as a bulletin or an editor's note appearing at the top of a story.

Predate—edition delivered before its announced date. Usually a Sunday edition delivered to outlying areas.

Printer—machine that produces copy by telegraphic impulses. A Teletype machine. Also a person who prepares composition for imprinting operations.

Printout—visual copy produced by a computer, usually for proofreading. Same as master copy or tear sheet.

Process color—method of printing that duplicates a full-color original copy.

Proof—print of type used for proofreading purposes.

Proofreader—one who corrects proofs.

Prop—an object used during a newscast to give credence to an item.

Puff—personal publicity story.

Pull-out—a special section within a paper but designed to be removed from the main portion.

Put to bed—to lock up forms for an edition.

Pyramid—arrangement of ads in half-pyramid form from top right to lower left.

Quad—short for quadrat, a blank printing unit for spacing.

Quadrant—layout pattern in which the page is divided into fourths.

Query—brief message outlining a story. Also a question put to a news source.

Quoins—metal wedges used to hold printing elements in a chase. The wedges are locked with a quoin key.

Quotes—short for quotation marks.

Race—classification of type, such as roman, text, script.

Rack—cabinet in which composition is kept.

Railroad—to rush copy to the printer before it is edited; to rush type to press without proofreading. Also a term for a headline type.

Reader—machine used with a computer to read copy or tape and record a justified tape.

Read in—to omit the rule.

Readout—secondary head accompanying a main head.

Rear projection—projection of a film, photo, map or graph placed on a screen behind the newscaster.

Regional split—interruption in the main radio wire to permit the transmission of regional news.

Register—alignment of plates to get true color reproduction.

Release copy—copy to be held until a specified release time. Same as advance copy.

Reperforator—machine that produces tape for automatic type-setting.

Replate—to make a page over after an edition has gone to press.

Reproduction—another name for an etch proof. Abbreviated as repro.

Retouch—to alter a photograph by painting or airbrushing.

Reverse plate—reversing the color values so that white letters are on a black background.

Revised proof—second proof after corrections have been made.

Ribbon—another name for a banner or streamer headline.

Rim—outer edge of a copydesk. Copyeditors are known as rimmen.

Ring—to draw a circle around a word or symbol to indicate a different form.

Ring bank—composing room stands where corrections are made in type. A ring man is an operator who makes corrections in type on a line-caster or ring machine.

Rip and read—derogatory expression applied to radio newsmen who simply read the latest summary from the radio wire without careful editing.

Rising initial—initial capital letter that aligns with the body type at the base line.

Rivers—streaks of white space caused by uneven typesetting.

ROP—run of the paper. Stories or art that do not demand up-front position. Ads that may appear anywhere in the paper. Color printed in a newspaper without the use of special presses.

Rotogravure—means of printing from recessed letters. One of the major printing techniques (along with letterpress and offset). Used mostly in catalogs, magazines and fine color work.

Rough—may be applied to a dummy that gives little or no detail or to an uncorrected, unjustified proof.

Roundup—compilation of stories.

Routing—removing nonessential parts from a plate.

Rules—any line that is printed. Lines are cast in type metal form. Hairline rules are often used in newspaper work. The underscore of the preceding is a type rule.

Run—reporter's beat.

Runaround—method of setting type around a picture.

Run-in—to incorporate sentences or lists into one paragraph.

Running story—story handled in takes or small segments. Each take is sent to the composing room as soon as it is edited.

Runover—portion of a story that continues from one page to the next. Also a jump story.

Sans serif—typeface without serifs.

Sc—proofreader's mark meaning "see copy."

Schedule—list of available stories and pictures; desk's record of stories edited.

Scoop—to get an exclusive story. Also a beat.

Screen—to view film or video tape.

Script—in broadcast news, the arrangement of news, together with an opening and closing and leads to commercials.

Second front page—first page of the second section. Also called a split page.

Section page—first page of a pull-out section.

Sectional story—same as running story where copy is handled in takes.

Serifs—the fine cross strokes at the top and bottom of most styles of letter.

Set solid—lines of type without extra spacing between lines.

Shirt tail—slang for a follow story.

Short—brief item of filler.

Side bar—brief story with a special angle that goes with the main story.

Signature—group of pages printed on one sheet. Also an advertiser's name displayed in an ad.

Silhouette—form of halftone with the background removed. Same as outline cut.

Skeletonize—copy sent by wire where unnecessary words are omitted. Same as cablese.

Skyline—headline across top of page over nameplate. Also called over-the-roof head.

Slant—angle of a story. A story written a certain way for policy reasons.

Slug—label identifying a story. Same as guideline or catchline. Also a piece of metal used for spacing. Also used to designate line-caster slugs.

Soc—short for society page material.

Sound-on-film—film carrying its own sound track. Abbreviated SOF.

Sound under—audio level where background sounds may be heard.

Space out—direction to the printer to add space between lines until the story fills the space allotted for it.

Split page—first page of the second section of a newspaper.

Split run—making a change in part of a press run of the same edition.

Spot news—news obtained firsthand; fresh news.

Spread—story prominently displayed, often over several columns and with art.

Squib—short news item or filler.

Standing box—type box kept on hand for repeated use. Likewise with standing head.

Standing type—similar to standing boxes and heads; type kept standing for future use.

Standupper—television report at the scene with the camera on the reporter.

Step lines—headline with successive lines indented; same as dropline.

Stereotype—process of casting a plate from a papier-mâché mold.

Stet—let it stand. Disregard correction.

Stick—typeholder. A story as long as a column width.

Sticker—refers to a page that will undergo no makeup changes from edition to edition.

Stinger—another term for kicker or eyebrow.

Stock—paper used for any printing job.

Stone—table on which type for the paper is assembled.

Straight matter—copy set in one size of type for the main reading matter of a page. Also called body type.

Streamer—another name for a banner or a ribbon headline.

String—clippings of stories, usually from a correspondent.

Stringer—correspondent paid on space rate. In television news, a free-lance cameraman.

Strip-in—to insert one illustrative element into another.

Sub—short for substitute. Sub bomber means a new story for a story slugged bomber.

Subhead—one- or two-line head used within the body of a story in type. Also called column break.

Summary—may be a news index or a news roundup. A summary lead gives the gist of the facts in the story.

Super card—in television, white lettering on a black card.

Supplemental service—syndicated service in addition to major wire service.

Swash cut—picture cut on the edges to give the effect of broken glass.

Tabloid—newspaper format, usually five columns wide and approximately 16 inches deep. Also refers to a sensational style of news presentation.

Take—small part of a running story. Also the part of a story given to a compositor.

Tape—perforated paper used in Teletype or Teletypesetter.

Tear sheet—sheet or part of a sheet used for corrections. Also copy produced by a computerized copy follower.

Tease—news announcement before the station break with details to follow the break.

Telephoto—UPI system of transmitting pictures by wire. UPI Unifax transmits facsimile pictures.

Teletype—automatic printer used to send and receive wire copy.

Teletypesetter—device attached to a line-caster so that the typesetting is controlled by perforated tape. Abbreviated TTS—copy (and tape) for papers with Teletypesetters.

Thirty dash—endmark.

Thumbnail—half-column portrait. Also a rough sketch or dummy.

Tie-back—part of a story providing background material.

Tight paper—paper containing so much advertising there is limited space for news.

Time copy—copy that may be used anytime. Also called grape, plug copy and so on.

Toenails—quotation mark or apostrophe. Also parentheses.

Tombstone—to place headlines of the same type side by side. Such adjacent heads are called bumped heads.

Tr—short for turn rule. A turned rule (upside-down slug) shows a printer where an insert is to be placed. Also refers to heavy rules used in an obituary of an outstanding person.

Turn story—same as jump story (continues from last column on one page to first column on the next page).

Trunk—main news wire of a news agency.

Typo—short for typographical error.

Undated—story without a dateline (but usually a credit line) summarizing related events from different origins.

Underline—same as cutline.

Unisetter—UPI service for papers using offset.

UPI—short for United Press International, a major news agency.

Up-date—to bring a story up to date or to give it a timely angle.

Up style—newspaper style using a maximum of capital letters.

Video tape—tape that projects pictures.

Vignette—halftone with a fading background. Also a feature story or sketch.

Visible—tape perforations arranged so that they spell words or symbols.

Visual—anything seen on a television screen.

Viz—short for vismo, a rear projection process.

VTR—short for video-tape recording.

Wf—short for wrong font or type of a different size or style from that used in the text.

Wicket—kicker-like element placed to one side of a headline.

Widow—one or two words appearing at the end of a paragraph and on the last line. It is unsightly because of the excessive white space appearing after the widow.

Wirephoto—AP system of transmitting pictures by wire. The AP facsimile system is called Fotofax.

Wooden head—one that is dull and lifeless.

Wrap around—ending the top line of a headline with a preposition, conjunction or the like, or splitting words that are properly a unit.

Wrap-up—complete story. Wire services use a wrap-up to contain in one story all elements of the same story sent previously.

Zinc—metal used for a photoengraving; zinc etching or a cut without a halftone screen.

Index

Headlines [cont.]
136; binder, 136; block buster, 142; building blocks, 142, 143, 144; clarity in, 150, 151; clues, 143; contractions, 162; counting, 140, 141, 142; crossline, 131; decks, *see* Headlines, banks; design, 135; designations, 137, 138; drop, 131, 135, 136; dropline, 316; editorializing, 158, 159, 164, 167; eyebrow, *see* Headlines, kicker; falsifying, 165; flush left, 316; functions, 137; future events, 161; grammar in, 162, 163; hammer (hammerhead), 137, 138, 142, 318; hanging indention, 131, 316; heady, 169; headlinese, 102, 165; hed to kum, 135; hood, 136; inverted pyramid, 316; jump, 138, 168; kicker, 135, 142, 318; label, 156, 157, 166; letter designation, 138, libel in, 165, 166; lifeless, 144; line, 134; main, 135; misleading, 145; muddled, 154; needled, 211; negating words, 167; neutrality, 158, 159, 160; news in, 146; number designation, 137; number and type family, 138, 139; phrasing, 147; placement, 301, 303; positive, 167; punchline, 160, 161; punctuation, 162; pyramid, 131; qualifications, 160; questions, 160, 167; quotations, 135, 138; ragged, 135; readout, 135, 138, 311, 312, 313, 314; refer, 138; repeating words, 164, 165; requirements, 148; reverse plate, 135, 136; ribbon, 134; rules, 148; runover, 168; say-nothing, 157, 158; schedule, 139; shaded box, 136; signposts, 145; size, 29, 30; skyline, 134; slang, 164; sports, 135, 164; standing, 142, 333, 350, 351; stepped, 131; stet, 135; streamer, 134; streamlining, 135; style changes, 131; subheads, 135, 138, 167, 168, 318, 319, 365; synonyms, 168; taste, 145, 146; tense, 161, 162; three-way box, 136; two-faced, 153, 154, 155, 156; type, 349; wicket, 136, 318; words, 145; word repetition, 164, 165; writing, 131 *ff*; zigzagged, 135
Hearst, 85

Herzberg, Joseph G., 89
Hits & Misses, 31
Hoaxes, 114, 115, 116
Hold bank, 35
Homestead (Fla.) South Dade *New Leader,* 59
Hometown Daily Newspapers of the West, 10
Horseshoe copydesk, 27
H-shaped desk, 28
Huntley, Chet, 388
Hyphens, 262, 381, 417; *see also* Compounds

I

Identification, 37, 387
Idiom, 41, 76, 77
Imposition, 364, 365, 366, 368, 373
Index, 417
Inheritance, 40
Initial letter, 348, 369
Injunction, 208
Insertions, 35, 173
International News Service, 377
International Typographical Union, 251
Interns, 7
Inverted pyramid structure, 13
It's Libel or Contempt if You Print It, 232

J

James, Howard, 232
Jargon, 43, 97, 98, 99, 100, 283, 287, 309, 310, 311, 329, 417; legal, 229
Johnson, Earl J., 64
Journalism Quarterly, 5
Joyce, James, 10
Judicial proceeding, 210
Jump stories, 13, 14, 283, 287, 309, 310, 311, 329, 417
Jury, 210, 227
Justification, 182, 283, 418
Juvenile delinquent, 230, 231

K

Kabel (type), 251
Karnak (type), 243
Kennerly (type), 253
Kepes, Gyorgy, 323
Kerner Commission, 222
Khayyam, Omar, 117
Klein, Lawrence R., 99
KLZ-TV (Denver), 376, 378, 388, 391

L

Labor, closed shop, 50; disputes, 50; longshoremen, 51; mediator, 50; stevedores, 51; strike breaker, 51; union leader, 51; union shop, 50

Lanham Trademark Act, 39

Lanston Monotype Company, 260, 261, 262

Late City Edition, 89

Law of Newspapers, The, 231 *ff*

Layout, magazine, 359, 360, 361, 365, 370; *see also* Makeup

Lead, 377; and headline, 89; cliché, 92; cluttered, 90, 91; conviction, 221, 222; delayed news, 89, 93; direct, 90; Dutch, 210; hard, 90; honing the, 88; hugger-mugger, 62; illogical, 92; inactive, 90; indirect, 90; inverted pyramid, 62; misleading, 89; needled, 89; opinion, 89; over-attribution, 93; over-long identification, 93; paragraphs, 303, 304, 305; say-nothing, 92; soft, 90; souped-up, 89; suspended interest, 89; statistics in, 93; under-attribution, 94, 143, 150, 173, 174, 175; undated, 172

Leading, 252, 290, 305, 345

Leckie, Robert, 69

Legal, Control of the Press, 232

Legal, jargon, 229; misused terms, 228; terminology, 226, 227, 228, 229, 230; threadbare phrases, 228; *see also* specific crimes

Legibility, 298

Lerner Newspapers (Chicago), 302, 338, 339, 347

Letters, aligning, 247; arrangement of, 249; capitals and lower case, 245, 249, 297, 298; descending, 246, 247; fat and thin, 140, 141; kern of, 245, 246; ligatures, 245, 246; transfer, 264, 265; widths of, 251; *see also* Type

Letterpress, 356, 369, 373

Libel, 208, 209, 210, 211, 212, 213, 214, 217, 219; corrections, 216, 217; criminal, 209, 213, 214; hazard, 209; insurance, 212; *It's Libel or Contempt if You Print It,* 211, 212, 232; reply and consent, 217, 218; trade, 213

Libel—Rights, Risks and Responsibilities, 232

Library Journal, The, 97

Life (magazine), 137

Light eraser, 2

Lightline Gothic (type), 242

Light pencil, 2

Lindstrom, Carl, 5

Linofilm, 263, 264

Linotype, 252, 253, 255, 258, 316, 361; Electronic Mixer, 256

Loaded terms. *See* Words, manipulators

Lockup, 369, 373

Logotype, 185

Los Angeles *Times,* 127, 148

Lotteries, 220

Louisville *Courier-Journal* and *The Louisville Times,* 25, 286, 317

Ludlow (slug-setting machine), 255, 259, 262, 263

Ludlow Typograph Company, 244, 262, 263

Lydian Cursive (type), 243, 349

M

McGill, Ralph, 88

Mach numbers, 41

Magazine, 271, 324, 357, 358, 359; artist, 358, 359, 360, 361; editing, 356

Mailing room, 28

Makeready, 369, 373

Makeup, 29, 62, 269, 278, 283, 285, 287, 289, 292, 300, 311, 323, 324, 326, 335, 345, 346, 348, 417; balance, 272, 273; contrast, 273; contemporary, 297, 308, 320, 322, 323, 324, 325, 329, 332, 348; dummy, 7, 173, *see also* Dummy; editor, 269, 270, 271, 275, 288, 297, 308, 316, 318, 326, 329, 331, 332, 335, 343, 348, 350, 351, 416; editorial pages, 345, 346, 347, 348; rules, 297, 298; sports pages, 354; tabloid, 331; women's pages, 348, 349, 350, 352, 353; *see also* Design

Malice, 211, 212, 216, 217, 218

Managing editor, 185

Mandate (type), 349

Margins, 360

Marion (Ind.), *Chronicle-Tribune,* 267, 268

Type [cont.]
249; lightface, 244; line width, 250; magazine, 255; matrices, 255; measurements, 246, 247; medium bold, 244; modern, 234, 235, 237, 238, 239, 240, 248; old-style, 235, 236, 238, 240, 248; production methods, 244; race, 240; regular, 244; roman, 240, 252, 340, 349; script, 242; selection, 247, 251; setting, 255, 293, 305, 309, 311, 345, 359, 360, 362, 373; shoulder, 246, 247; simplicity, 238; size, 234, 235; slab serif, 243; spacing, 254; square serif, 243, *see also* Sans serif; text, 241; transitional, 240; ultrabold, 244, 245; weights, 237, 244, 245; widths, 244; *see also* Automation, Computers

Typographic Quest, 235

Typography, 7, 248; errors in, 28, *see also* Proofs

U

Uncle Tom's Cabin, 117

United Press and United Press International, 15, 36, 63, 64, 103, 111, 113, 115, 117, 170, 171, 172, 178, 180, 186, 189, 378, 390; *Reporter,* 63; *Stylebook,* 396; Unisetter, 180

United States Board of Geographic Names, 403

United States Bureau of the Census, 10, 11

United States Postal Guide, 403

Universal desk, 27

V

Van Anda, Carr, 6

Vanderbilt, Cornelius, 117

Vanderbilt, William H., 117

Verdict, 227

Vignette, 20, 23, 24, 380

Voltaire, 116

W

Walker, Stanley, 1

Wall Street Journal, 403

Warner, Charles Dudley, 116

Warren Report, 171

Wars of America, The, 69

Washington *Post,* 151, 197

Weather clichés, 48, 49; National Weather Service, 47, 48, 49; records, 40; wind table, 49

Webster's New International Dictionary, 403

Wedding, stories, 59, 60, 61; headlines, 61; leads, 59, 60

Weiss Roman (type), 245, 349

Westin, Alan F., 232

Wiggins, James Russell, 197, 199

Wilmington (Del.) *News,* 31

Winners & Sinners, 16

Wire, A-wire, 180, 186; B-wire, 180, 186; book number, 177; bureau, 186; copy, 26, 186; circuits, 172; corrections, 173; errors, 185, 186; D-wire, 186; editor, 7, 26; foreign news, 189; gatekeepers, 187; glossary, 171, 172; pickup, 172; radio, 186; roundup, 172; sectional copy, 173; split, 172; state, 173, 186; stringer, 186; tape, 177; trunk line, 186; wirephoto, 174

Wittenberg, Philip, 232

Women, as copyeditors, 7; women's pages, 333, 349, 352, 353, 359; *see also* society; possessives of, 38

Wood, Alden S., 100, 101, 103

Words, abuse of, 103; circumlocutions, *see* Words, economy; close up, 4, 69, 145; division, 417; economy, 69, 70, 71, 72, 73; faraway, 4, 145; foreign, 102; headline, 102; into type, 76; little, 75; manipulators, 109; precision with, 79, 80, 81, 82, 83, 84, 125; superfluous, 75; word order, 74; wrong, 74

Wraps, 287, 288, 289, 290, 291, 340

Writing, clarity in, 73, 74, 75; colored, 109; deferred subject, 106; double-takes, 127; exactness, 76; interpretative, 64; narrative, 63; precision in, 62; poor, 65; styles, 63; tight, 67; wrap-up, 20, 23

Y

Yankwich, Leon R., Judge, 211, 212, 232

Years with Ross, The, 4, 6

Z

Zavin, Theodore S., 232

Zinc etching, 373